Part 1
Introduction and Key Principles

Discusses the economic way of thinking — the mindset that guides economists as they explain how the world works and explore ways to solve real-world problems.

Chapter 1
Introduction: What Is Economics

Explores the five key principles of economics, the five self-evident truths that provide the foundation for economic analysis.

Chapter 2
Key Principles of Economics

Explains why each of us is not self-sufficient, producing everything we want for ourselves, but instead uses markets to earn income and buy goods from others.

Chapter 3
Exchange and Markets

Uses the model of supply and demand to explain how prices are determined, and how various changes, such as bad weather, technological innovation, and population growth, affect prices.

Chapter 4
Supply, Demand, and Market Equilibrium

Part 2
A Closer Look at Supply and Demand

Uses the concept of elasticity to quantify the laws of supply and demand.

Chapter 5
Elasticity: A Measure of Responsiveness

Takes a closer look at the consumer's decision-making process, exploring the rational response to a change in price and the implications for market demand.

Chapter 6
Consumer Choice

Explores the benefits experienced by producers and consumers and shows how various public policies (price controls, import restrictions, licensing, and taxes) affect people on both sides of the market.

Chapter 7
Market Efficiency and Government Intervention

Part 3
Information and Externalities

Explores what happens when one side of the market—firms or consumers—has inferior information. For example, the seller of a used car knows more than a potential buyer about the car's durability; an insurance buyer knows more than an insurance company about risky behavior.

Chapter 8
Imperfect Information: Adverse Selection and Moral Hazard

Shows that the best response to market failure from pollution is not to abandon markets, but instead to use prices and markets to reduce pollution in the most efficient manner.

Chapter 9
Environmental Policy

Discusses the rationale for collective decision-making—also known as government—when the benefits of public goods like national defense, law enforcement, and space exploration are shared by a large number of people.

Chapter 10
Public Goods and Public Choice

Part 4
Market Structures and Pricing

Discusses the link between production technology and costs. Explores the cost of information goods, with large first-copy costs and low reproduction cost.

Chapter 11
Production Technology and Cost

Chapter 12
Perfect Competition

Explores the decisions of a perfectly competitive firm, defined as one of hundreds of firms in a market.

Explores the decisions of a monopolist, and explains why movie theaters have senior discounts for admission, but not for popcorn.

Chapter 13
Monopoly and Price Discrimination

Chapter 14
Market Entry and Monopolistic Competition

Examines the decision of a firm to enter a market and shows how entry squeezes a firm's profit by reducing the price, increasing cost, and decreasing the quantity produced.

Explores three types of strategic behavior among firms: price fixing (agreeing on a common price), entry deterrence (keeping other firms out of the market), and advertising.

Chapter 15
Oligopoly and Strategic Behavior

Chapter 16
Market Structure and Public Policy

Discusses public policies dealing with markets that are dominated by a small number of firms: price regulation, breaking up monopolies, and blocking mergers. Explores the effects of the recent deregulation of air travel, trucking, and electricity.

Part 5
The Labor Market and Income Distribution

Uses the model of supply and demand to show why some occupations pay more than others and why college graduates are paid more than high-school graduates. Shows how income is distributed among different households and explains recent changes in the distribution of income.

Chapter 17
The Labor Market and the Distribution of Income

Chapter 18
Beyond Perfect Competition: Unions, Monopsony, and Imperfect Information

Looks beyond the simple world of perfect competition in the labor market to see what happens when either side of the labor market has the power to influence wages, or one side of the market has inferior information.

Part 6
The International Economy

Discusses the key role that international trade plays in the economy in an increasingly global world, and what policies work best in the international arena.

Chapter 19
International Trade and Public Policy

Fourth Edition

MICROECONOMICS

Principles and Tools

Arthur O'Sullivan
LEWIS AND CLARK COLLEGE

Steven M. Sheffrin
UNIVERSITY OF CALIFORNIA, DAVIS

PEARSON
Prentice
Hall

Upper Saddle River, NJ 07458

Library of Congress Cataloging-in-Publication Data

O'Sullivan, Arthur

Microeconomics : principles and tools / Arthur O'Sullivan, Steven M. Sheffrin.—4th ed.
 p. cm.

Includes bibliographical references and index.

ISBN 0-13-153606-0

1. Microeconomics.   I. Sheffrin, Steven M.   II. Title.

HB172.08 2005

338.5—dc22   2004058663

AVP/Executive Editor: *David Alexander*
Acquisitions Editor: *Jon Axelrod*
VP/Editorial Director: *Jeff Shelstad*
Assistant Editor: *Marie McHale*
Editorial Assistant: *Katy Rank*
VP/Director of Development: *Steve Deitmer*
Developmental Editor: *Amy Ray*
Media Project Manager: *Peter Snell*
AVP/Executive Marketing Manager:
Sharon Koch
Marketing Assistant: *Tina Panagiotou*
Managing Editor (Production): *Cynthia Regan*
Production Editor: *Carol Samet*
Permissions Supervisor: *Charles Morris*
Manufacturing Buyer: *Arnold Vila*
Design Manager: *Maria Lange*
Art Director: *Kevin Kall*
Interior Design: *QT Design*

Cover Design: *Kevin Kall*
Cover Illustration/Photo: *Fotosearch.com*
Director, Image Resource Center:
Melinda Reo
Manager, Rights and Permissions:
Zina Arabia
Manager: Visual Research: *Beth Brenzel*
Manager, Cover Visual Research &
Permissions: *Karen Sanatar*
Image Permission Coordinator:
Cynthia Vincenti
Photo Researcher: *Teri Stratford*
Manager, Print Production: *Christy Mahon*
Composition/Full-Service Project
Management: *GGS Book Services,*
Atlantic Highlands
Printer/Binder: *Courier-Kendallville*
Typeface: 10.5/13 Minion

Credits and acknowledgments borrowed from other sources and reproduced, with permission, in this textbook on page iv.

Pearson Education LTD.
Pearson Education Singapore, Pte. Ltd.
Pearson Education, Canada, Ltd.
Pearson Education–Japan

Pearson Education Australia PTY, Limited
Pearson Education North Asia Ltd
Pearson Educación de Mexico, S.A. de C.V.
Pearson Education Malaysia, Pte. Ltd

10 9 8 7 6 5 4 3 2 1
ISBN 0-13-153606-0

To Our Children: Conor, Maura, Meera, and Kiran

Photo Credits

About the Authors

Arthur O'Sullivan

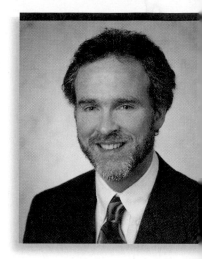

Arthur O'Sullivan is a professor of economics at Lewis and Clark College in Portland, Oregon. After receiving his B.S. degree in economics at the University of Oregon, he spent two years in the Peace Corps, working with city planners in the Philippines. He received his Ph.D. degree in economics from Princeton University in 1981 and has taught at the University of California, Davis, and Oregon State University, winning several teaching awards at both schools. He recently accepted an endowed professorship at Lewis and Clark College, where he teaches microeconomics and urban economics. He is the author of the best-selling textbook *Urban Economics*, currently in its fifth edition.

Professor O'Sullivan's research explores economic issues concerning urban land use, environmental protection, and public policy. His articles appear in many economics journals, including the *Journal of Urban Economics, Journal of Environmental Economics and Management, National Tax Journal, Journal of Public Economics,* and *Journal of Law and Economics.*

Professor O'Sullivan lives with his family in Lake Oswego, Oregon. He enjoys outdoor activities, including tennis, hiking, and paragliding. Indoors, he plays chess and Ping-Pong with his two kids.

Steven M. Sheffrin

Steven M. Sheffrin is dean of the division of social sciences and professor of economics at the University of California, Davis. He has been a visiting professor at Princeton University, Oxford University, and the London School of Economics and served as a financial economist with the Office of Tax Analysis of the United States Department of the Treasury. He has been on the faculty at Davis since 1976 and served as the chairman of the department of economics. He received his B.A. from Wesleyan University and his Ph.D. in economics from the Massachusetts Institute of Technology.

Professor Sheffrin is the author of 10 other books and monographs and over 100 articles in the fields of macroeconomics, public finance, and international economics. His most recent books include *Rational Expectations* (second edition) and *Property Taxes and Tax Revolts: The Legacy of Proposition 13* (with Arthur O'Sullivan and Terri Sexton), both from Cambridge University Press.

Professor Sheffrin has taught macroeconomics at all levels, from large introduction to principles classes (enrollments of 400) to graduate classes for doctoral students. He is the recipient of the Thomas Mayer Distinguished Teaching Award in economics.

He lives with his wife Anjali (also an economist) and his two daughters in Davis, California. In addition to a passion for current affairs and travel, he plays a tough game of tennis.

Brief Contents

PART 1   Introduction and Key Principles   1

Chapter 1   Introduction: What Is Economics?   2
Chapter 2   The Key Principles of Economics   26
Chapter 3   Exchange and Markets   44
Chapter 4   Supply, Demand, and Market
             Equilibrium   60

**PART 2   A Closer Look at Supply
            and Demand   93**

Chapter 5   Elasticity: A Measure
             of Responsiveness   94
Chapter 6   Consumer Choice   120
Chapter 7   Market Efficiency and Government
             Intervention   138

PART 3   Information and Externalities   169

Chapter 8   Imperfect Information: Adverse Selection
             and Moral Hazard   170
Chapter 9   Environmental Policy   194
Chapter 10   Public Goods and Public Choice   218

PART 4   Market Structures and Pricing   233

Chapter 11   Production Technology and Cost   234
Chapter 12   Perfect Competition   260
Chapter 13   Monopoly and Price Discrimination   288
Chapter 14   Market Entry and Monopolistic
             Competition   312
Chapter 15   Oligopoly and Strategic Behavior   326
Chapter 16   Market Structure and Public Policy   356

**PART 5   The Labor Market and Income
            Distribution   377**

Chapter 17   The Labor Market and the Distribution
             of Income   378
Chapter 18   Beyond Perfect Competition: Unions,
             Monopsony, and Imperfect Information   404

PART 6   The International Economy   419

Chapter 19   International Trade and Public Policy   420

Contents

PART 1   Introduction and Key Principles   1

Chapter 1   Introduction: What Is Economics?   2

What Is Economics?   3
   Positive Versus Normative Analysis   4
   *Decisions in a Modern Economy: The Invisible
      Hand?   5*
   **A CLOSER LOOK: When Do Economists
      Agree?   6**

Economic Analysis and Modern Problems   6
   Example 1: Traffic Congestion   6
   Example 2: Poverty in Africa   7
   Example 3: Japan's Economic Problems   8

The Economic Way of Thinking   8
   Rational People Respond to Incentives   10
   Application: Thinking About Congestion   11

Preview of Coming Attractions:
Microeconomics   12
   **A CLOSER LOOK: Even Kids Respond
      to Incentives   12**
   To Understand Markets and Predict Changes   13
   To Make Personal and Managerial Decisions   13
   To Evaluate Public Policies   13

Preview of Coming Attractions:
Macroeconomics   14
   To Understand Why Economies Grow   14
   To Understand Economic Fluctuations   14
   To Make Informed Business Decisions   15
   **A CLOSER LOOK: "Dismal" Depends On
      Your Point of View   15**

   Appendix: Using Graphs and Formulas 17

Using Graphs to Show Relationships   17

Chapter 2   The Key Principles of Economics   26

The Principle of Opportunity Cost   27
   *Opportunity Cost and the Production Possibilities
      Curve   28*
   *Using the Principle: Military Spending,
      Collectibles   29*
   Using the Principle: The Cost of College   30
   A CLOSER LOOK: Swords vs. Ecotels?   31

The Marginal Principle   32
   Example: How Many Movie Sequels?   32
   *Using the Marginal Principle: Renting College
      Facilities, Emissions Standards   34*

**ECONOMIC PUZZLE: Marginal Airlines Lives Up
to Its Name   35**

The Principle of Voluntary Exchange   35
   Exchange and Markets   36

The Principle of Diminishing Returns   37

The Real–Nominal Principle   38
**ECONOMIC EXPERIMENT: Producing
Fold-Its   39**
   *Using the Principle: Government Programs,
      Statistics, and Repaying College Loans   39*
USING THE TOOLS   40

Chapter 3   Exchange and Markets   44

Comparative Advantage and Exchange   45
   Specialization and the Gains from Trade   45
   Production and Consumption Possibilities   47
   *Comparative Advantage Versus Absolute
      Advantage   48*
   The Division of Labor and Exchange   48
   *Comparative Advantage and International
      Trade   49*
   **A CLOSER LOOK: Buzz Lightyear
      of China   51**

Markets   51
   Virtues of Markets   52
   *Example: Exchange in a Prisoner
      of War Camp   54*
   Shortcomings of Markets   54
   **A CLOSER LOOK: EverQuest and Fantasy
      Exchanges   55**

The Role of Government in a Market Economy   55
   Government Enforces the Rules of Exchange   56
   *Government Can Reduce Economic
      Uncertainty   56*

**Chapter 4   Supply, Demand, and Market
Equilibrium   60**

The Demand Curve   61
   *The Individual Demand Curve and the Law
      of Demand   62*
   *From Individual Demand to Market
      Demand   64*

**ECONOMIC PUZZLE: Saving Money Wherever
You Shop?   65**

The Supply Curve   65
   *The Individual Supply Curve and the Law
      of Supply   66*
   *Why Is the Individual Supply Curve Positively
      Sloped?   67*
   From Individual Supply to Market Supply   68

Market Equilibrium   69
   Excess Demand Causes the Price to Rise   69
   Excess Supply Causes the Price to Drop   70

Market Effects of Changes in Demand   71
   *Change in Quantity Demanded Versus Change
      in Demand   71*

Increases in Demand   72
Decreases in Demand   74

Market Effects of Changes in Supply   76
*Change in Quantity Supplied Versus Change
      in Supply   76*
Increases in Supply   77
A CLOSER LOOK: Increasing the Supply
      of Wind Power   79
Decreases in Supply   79

Market Effects of Simultaneous Changes in
Demand and Supply   80

Using the Model to Predict Changes in Price
and Quantity   82
Population Growth and Apartment Prices   82
Product Safety and Apples   83
Technological Innovation and Computers   83
Weather and Coffee   84

Explaining Changes in Price or Quantity   84
An Increase in Poultry Consumption   85
A Decrease in Drug Prices   86
A CLOSER LOOK: Higher Platinum Prices   87

ECONOMIC EXPERIMENT: Market
Equilibrium   87

USING THE TOOLS   88

PART 2   A Closer Look at Supply and Demand   93

Chapter 5   Elasticity: A Measure of Responsiveness   94

The Price Elasticity of Demand   95
Price Elasticity and the Demand Curve   96
*What Determines the Price Elasticity
      of Demand?   98*
*Computing Price Elasticity: Initial Value Versus
      Midpoint   99*
A CLOSER LOOK: How to Cut Teen Smoking
      by 60%   100

Elasticity Along a Linear Demand Curve   101

Using the Price Elasticity of Demand to Make
Predictions   103
Predicting Changes in Quantity Demanded   103
*Applications: College Education, Highway Deaths,
      and Medical Care   103*
Predicting Changes in Total Revenue   104
A CLOSER LOOK: Pricing Medical Care in
      Developing Countries   104
Applications: Transit Deficits, Property Crime   106

ECONOMIC PUZZLE: DVD Elasticity   107
Other Elasticities of Demand   108

The Price Elasticity of Supply   110
Predicting Changes in Quantity Supplied   111
*Extreme Cases: Perfectly Inelastic Supply and
      Perfectly Elastic Supply   111*

Predicting Changes in Price Using Supply
and Demand Elasticities   112
The Price Effects of a Change in Demand   112
The Price Effects of a Change in Supply   114
USING THE TOOLS   116

Chapter 6   Consumer Choice   120

Consumer Constraints and Preferences   121
Consumer Constraints: The Budget Line   122
Consumer Preferences: Indifference Curves   123

Maximizing Utility   125
The Tangency Condition   125
*The Utility-Maximizing Rule: MRS =
      Price Ratio   126*
Drawing the Demand Curve   127
Do Consumers Actually Do This?   128

Applications of the Consumer Choice Model   129
Music Piracy and Online Music Stores   129
A CLOSER LOOK: Modern Consumer Theory
      Versus Old Utility Theory   130
*Inflation, the Real–Nominal Principle,
      and Consumer Choice   131*
The Equimarginal Rule   133
A CLOSER LOOK: The Bang per Buck of
      Light Spirits   134
USING THE TOOLS   135

**Chapter 7   Market Efficiency and Government
Intervention   138**

Consumer Surplus and Producer Surplus   140
*The Demand Curve and Consumer
      Surplus   140*
The Supply Curve and Producer Surplus   141

Market Equilibrium and Efficiency   142
*Total Surplus Is Lower with a Price Below
      the Equilibrium Price   143*
*Total Surplus Is Lower with a Price Above
      the Equilibrium Price   145*
Efficiency and the Invisible Hand   145

Government Intervention in Markets   146

Controlling the Price   148
Setting Maximum Prices   148
Application: Rent Control   148
Setting Minimum Prices   150
A CLOSER LOOK: Milk Mountains   151

Controlling the Quantity—Licensing and Import
Restrictions   151
Application: Taxi Medallions   152
Licensing and Market Efficiency   153
ECONOMIC PUZZLE: Shortfall from Medallion
Sale   154
Winners and Losers from Licensing   154
Restricting Imports   154

A CLOSER LOOK: A Market For Used Human
Organs?   156

Who Really Pays Taxes?   157
Tax Shifting: Forward and Backward   157
*Predicting the Amount Shifted Forward
and Backward   159*
Applications: Cigarette and Luxury Taxes   160
Tax Burden and Deadweight Loss   161
A CLOSER LOOK: Taxes and December
Babies   163

ECONOMIC EXPERIMENT: Government
Intervention   163

USING THE TOOLS   163

PART 3   Information and Externalities   169

**Chapter 8   Imperfect Information: Adverse Selection
and Moral Hazard   170**

The Lemons Problem   171
*Uninformed Buyers and Knowledgeable
Sellers   172*
Equilibrium with All Low-Quality Goods   172
*A Thin Market: Equilibrium with Some High-
Quality Goods   174*

Responding to the Lemons Problem   176
Buyers Invest in Information   177
Sellers Provide Guarantees   177
Lemons Laws   177
A CLOSER LOOK: Consumer Satisfaction
Scores from ValueStar and eBay   178

Evidence of the Lemons Effect   179
The Price of a Week-Old Car   179
Used Pickup Trucks   179
California Kiwifruit   179
Used Baseball Pitchers   180

Uninformed Sellers and Knowledgeable Buyers:
Insurance   181
Health Insurance   182
Equilibrium with All High-Cost Consumers   183
*Responding to Adverse Selection in Insurance:
Group Insurance   184*
The Uninsured   185
Other Types of Insurance   185
A CLOSER LOOK: Genetic Testing, Thrill
Seekers, and Insurance   186

Moral Hazard   186

ECONOMIC PUZZLE: Bicycle Theft
Insurance   188

ECONOMIC EXPERIMENT: Rolling for
Lemons   189

ECONOMIC EXPERIMENT: Bike Insurance   189

USING THE TOOLS   190

Chapter 9   Environmental Policy   194

The Optimal Level of Pollution and Pollution
Taxes   194
*Application: Finding the Optimal Level of Sulfur
Dioxide Emissions   197*
A Firm's Response to a Pollution Tax   198
The Market Effects of a Pollution Tax   199

Traditional Regulation: Uniform Abatement
and Command-and-Control Policies   201
Uniform Abatement with Permits   201
Command and Control   202
Market Effects of Pollution Regulations   202
A CLOSER LOOK: Dear Abby and
Environmental Policy   203

Marketable Pollution Permits   204
*Voluntary Exchange and Marketable
Permits   204*
*Supply, Demand, and the Price of Marketable
Permits   205*
*Application: Marketable Permits for Sulfur
Dioxide   206*

ECONOMIC PUZZLE: Why Did the Price
of Permits Drop?   206

Global Warming and Public Policy   207
The Consequences of Global Warming   207
*The Kyoto Agreement and Developing
Nations   208*
The Effects of a Carbon Tax   209
Marketable Permits and Offsets for Carbon?   209
A CLOSER LOOK: Giving the Gift
of CO_2 210

Ozone Pollution and the Automobile   211

ECONOMIC EXPERIMENT: Pollution
Permits   213

USING THE TOOLS   214

Chapter 10   Public Goods and Public Choice   218

An Overview of Government Spending
and Taxes   219

External Benefits and Inefficiency   220
Public Goods and External Benefits   221
Private Goods with External Benefits   221
Public Goods and the Free-Rider Problem   222

ECONOMIC PUZZLE: Why Build a Three-Faced
Clock Tower?   223
Overcoming the Free-Rider Problem   223

Applications: Asteroids and Wildlife   224
Asteroid Diversion   224
Preservation of Wolves   224

Public Choice   225
Voting and the Median-Voter Rule   225
A CLOSER LOOK: Are Politicians Like Ice-
Cream Vendors?   227

Alternative Models of Government: Self-Interests and Special Interests 228
Which Theory or Viewpoint Is Correct? 229
ECONOMIC EXPERIMENT: Voluntary Contributions 230
USING THE TOOLS 230

PART 4   Market Structures and Pricing   233

Chapter 11   Production Technology and Cost   234
Introduction 235
Economic Cost Is Opportunity Cost 236
Short-Run Versus Long-Run Costs 236
The Fixed Production Facility: Short-Run Costs 237
Production and Marginal Product 237
Short-Run Total Cost 239
Short-Run Average Costs 240
Short-Run Marginal Cost 242
The Relationship Between Marginal Cost and Average Cost 243
ECONOMIC PUZZLE: Same Average Cost at Two or Three Quantities? 244
Production and Cost in the Long Run 246
Expansion and Replication 246
Scaling Down and Indivisible Inputs 248
A CLOSER LOOK: Indivisible Inputs and the Cost of Fake Killer Whales 249
Scaling Down and Labor Specialization 250
Economies of Scale 250
A CLOSER LOOK: Scale Economies in Wind Power 251
Diseconomies of Scale 252
Actual Long-Run Average-Cost Curves 252
Short-Run Versus Long-Run Average Cost 253
Information Goods and First-Copy Cost 254
USING THE TOOLS 255

Chapter 12   Perfect Competition   260
Preview: Alternative Market Structures 262
The Firm's Short-Run Output Decision 263
The Total Approach: Computing Total Revenue and Total Cost 264
The Marginal Approach 265
Economic Profit and the Break-Even Price 267
ECONOMIC PUZZLE: Fewer Deliveries and More Profit? 268
The Firm's Shut-Down Decision 268
Total Revenue, Variable Cost, and the Shut-Down Decision 269
The Shut-Down Price 270
Fixed Costs and Sunk Costs 271
Application: Break-Even and Shut-Down Prices for Corn Farmer 271

Short-Run Supply Curves 272
The Firm's Short-Run Supply Curve 272
The Short-Run Market Supply Curve 273
Market Equilibrium 274
A CLOSER LOOK: Wireless Women 275
The Long-Run Supply Curve for an Increasing-Cost Industry 276
Production Cost and Industry Size 276
Drawing the Long-Run Market Supply Curve 277
Application: Increasing-Cost Industries—Wolfram, Sugar, Rental Housing 278
Short-Run and Long-Run Effects of Changes in Demand 279
The Short-Run Response to an Increase in Demand 279
The Long-Run Response to an Increase in Demand 280
Long-Run Supply for a Constant-Cost Industry 281
Long-Run Supply Curve for a Constant-Cost Industry 281
Application: Hurricane Andrew and the Price of Ice 282
ECONOMIC EXPERIMENT: Butter Prices 283
USING THE TOOLS 284

Chapter 13   Monopoly and Price Discrimination   288
The Monopolist's Output Decision 290
Total Revenue and Marginal Revenue 290
The Marginal Principle and the Output Decision 292
Using the Marginal Principle to Pick the Profit-Maximizing Quantity and Price 294
The Social Cost of Monopoly 296
Deadweight Loss from Monopoly 296
Application: Ending the Monopoly on Internet Registration 298
Rent Seeking: Using Resources to Get Monopoly Power 299
Monopoly and Public Policy 300
Patents and Monopoly Power 300
Incentives for Innovation 300
Trade-Offs from Patents 301
A CLOSER LOOK: Barriers to Generic Drugs 302
Price Discrimination 302
Application: Senior Discounts in Restaurants 304
Price Discrimination and the Elasticity of Demand 304
A CLOSER LOOK: Interacting with a Soda Vending Machine on a Hot Day 305
Application: Movie Admission and Popcorn 306

ECONOMIC PUZZLE: Why Are Hardback Books So Expensive? 306
ECONOMIC EXPERIMENT: Price Discrimination 307
USING THE TOOLS 308

Chapter 14 Market Entry and Monopolistic Competition 312

The Effects of Market Entry 314
  Entry Squeezes Profits from Three Sides 315
  Application: Woofer, Tweeter, and the Stereo Business 316
  Entry Effects in the Real World 316
  A CLOSER LOOK: Restricting Entry of On-Line Wine Merchants 317

Monopolistic Competition 318
  When Entry Stops: Long-Run Equilibrium 319
  Trade-Offs Between Average Cost and Variety 319
  Application: Location and Consumer Travel Costs 320

ECONOMIC PUZZLE: Lower Profit per Unit Sold? 321
ECONOMIC EXPERIMENT: Fixed Costs and Entry 322
USING THE TOOLS 322

Chapter 15 Oligopoly and Strategic Behavior 326

What Is an Oligopoly? 327

Cartel Pricing and the Duopolists' Dilemma 329
  Price Fixing and the Game Tree 331
  Predicting the Outcome of the Price-Fixing Game 332
  A CLOSER LOOK: Vitamin, Inc. Gets Busted 333
  Representing a Game with a Payoff Matrix 334
  The Prisoners' Dilemma 334

Overcoming the Duopolists' Dilemma 336
  Guaranteed Price Matching 336
  Repeated Pricing Games with Retaliation for Underpricing 337
  Application: Different Airline Ticket Prices 338

Price Fixing and the Law 339

Alternative Models of Oligopoly Pricing 340
  Price Leadership 340
  The Kinked Demand-Curve Model 341

The Insecure Monopolist and Entry Deterrence 342
  The Passive Approach: Do Nothing to Deter Entry 342
  The Entry Deterrence Approach: Use Limit Pricing to Deter Entry 343
  Limit Pricing 344
  When Is the Passive Approach Better? 345

A CLOSER LOOK: Crafty—and Illegal—Entry Deterrence in Europe 345
  Applications: Aluminum, Plane Tickets, and Campus Bookstores 346
  Entry Deterrence and Contestable Markets 347

ECONOMIC PUZZLE: Ballpoint Pens from R.I.P. 347

The Advertisers' Dilemma 348

Game Theory and Nash Equilibrium 350

ECONOMIC EXPERIMENT: A Price-Fixing Game 352
USING THE TOOLS 352

Chapter 16 Market Structure and Public Policy 356

Natural Monopoly 357
  Picking an Output Level 357
  Will a Second Firm Enter? 358
  Price Controls for a Natural Monopoly 359

ECONOMIC PUZZLE: A Decrease in Demand Decreases the Price? 361
  A CLOSER LOOK: Will Satellite Radio Become a Natural Monopoly? 361

Antiturst Policy 362
  Breaking Up Monopolies 362
  Blocking Mergers 363
  Application: Merger Remedies for Xidex and Wonder Bread 365
  A CLOSER LOOK: Is Tripoly Better Than Duopoly? 365

ECONOMIC PUZZLE: Check the Yellow Pages? 367
  Regulating Business Practices: Price Fixing, Tying, and Cooperative Agreements 367
  Application: The Microsoft Case 368
  A Brief History of U.S. Antitrust Policy 368

Deregulation of Airlines and Telecommunications 369
  Deregulation of Airlines 370
  Deregulation of Telecommunications Services 370

Deregulation of Electricity 371
  Electricity Deregulation in California 372
  Electricity Deregulation in Other U.S. States 373
USING THE TOOLS 374

PART 5 The Labor Market and Income Distribution 377

Chapter 17 The Labor Market and the Distribution of Income 378

The Demand for Labor 379
  Labor Demand by an Individual Firm in the Short Run 379

Market Demand for Labor in the Short Run 382
What About Labor Demand in the Long Run? 383
Short-Run versus Long-Run Demand 383

The Supply of Labor 384
The Individual Labor-Supply Decisions: How Many Hours to Work? 384
The Market Supply Curve for Labor 385
A CLOSER LOOK: The Economics of Not Working 387
ECONOMIC PUZZLE: Response to a Wage Cut? 387

Labor Market Equilibrium 387
Changes in Demand and Supply for Labor 388
The Market Effects of the Minimum Wage Laws 389
A CLOSER LOOK: Foreign Sweatshops and Industry Codes of Conduct 390
The Trade-Offs from Immigration 390

Explaining Differences in Wages and Income 391
Why Do Wages Differ Across Occupations? 391
The Gender Pay Gap 393
Racial Discrimination 393
A CLOSER LOOK: Racial Discrimination in Hiring 394
Why Do College Graduates Earn Higher Wages? 395

The Distribution of Income 396
Income Distribution Facts 396
Recent Changes in the Distribution of Income 397
Changes in the Top End of Income Distribution: 1920–1998 398
USING THE TOOLS 400

Chapter 18 Beyond Perfect Competition: Unions, Monopsony, and Imperfect Information 404

Labor Unions 405
A Brief History of Labor Unions in the United States 406
Labor Unions and Wages 406
A CLOSER LOOK: Working Conditions and Unions 407
Effects of Unions on Worker Productivity and Turnover 408

Monopsony Power 409
Picking a Workforce and a Wage 409
Monopsony versus Perfect Competition 411
Monopsony and a Minimum Wage 412
Monopsony and the Real World 413

A CLOSER LOOK: Pubs and Labor-Supply Curve 414
Imperfect Information and Efficiency Wages 414
ECONOMIC PUZZLE: Higher Wages at Ford Motor Company 415
USING THE TOOLS 416

PART 6   The International Economy 419

Chapter 19 International Trade and Public Policy 420

Benefits from Specialization and Trade 421
Production Possibilities Curve 422
Comparative Advantage and the Terms of Trade 423
The Consumption Possibilities Curve 424
The Employment Effects of Free Trade 425

Protectionist Policies 426
Import Ban 426
Quotas and Voluntary Export Restraints 427
Tariffs 429
Responses to Protectionist Policies 429

Rationales for Protectionist Policies 430
To Shield Workers from Foreign Competition 431
To Nurture Infant Industries 431
A CLOSER LOOK: The Cost of Protecting Jobs 431
A CLOSER LOOK: Protection for Candle Makers 432
To Help Domestic Firms Establish Monopolies in World Markets 432

A Brief History of International Tariff and Trade Agreements 433

Recent Policy Debates and Trade Agreements 434
Are Foreign Producers Dumping Their Products? 435
Do Trade Laws Inhibit Environmental Protection? 436
Does Trade Cause Inequality? 438
Why Do People Protest Against Free Trade? 438
ECONOMIC EXPERIMENT: Protectionist Policies 440
USING THE TOOLS 440

Glossary 444

Answers to Odd-Numbered Problems and Discussion Questions 450

Index 457

Alternate Course Sequence

Flexibility Chart: Microeconomics

Chapter Number	Title	Core	Policy	Optional
1	Introduction	x		
2	The Key Principles of Economics	x		
3	Exchange and Markets			x
4	Supply, Demand, and Market Equilibrium	x		
5	Elasticity: A Measure of Responsiveness	x		
6	Consumer Choice			x
7	Market Efficiency and Government Intervention	x		
8	Imperfect Information: Adverse Selection and Moral Hazard		x	
9	Environmental Policy		x	
10	Public Goods and Public Choice		x	
11	Production Technology and Cost	x		
12	Perfect Competition	x		
13	Monopoly and Price Discrimination	x		
14	Market Entry and Monopolistic Competition	x		
15	Oligopoly and Strategic Behavior	x		
16	Market Structure and Public Policy		x	
17	The Labor Market and the Distribution of Income	x		
18	Beyond Perfect Competition: Unions, Monopsony, and Imperfect Information			x
19	International Trade and Public Policy		x	x

Alternative Microeconomics Sequences

Chapter Number	Title	Mix of Theory and Policy	Supply, Demand, and Policy	Supply, Demand, and Market Structure	Challenging Theory	Short Policy Course
1	Introduction	x	x	x	x	x
2	The Key Principles of Economics	x	x	x	x	x
3	Exchange and Markets	x	x	x	x	
4	Supply, Demand, and Market Equilibrium	x	x	x	x	x
5	Elasticity: A Measure of Responsiveness	x	x	x	x	x
6	Consumer Choice				x	
7	Market Efficiency and Government Intervention	x	x	x	x	x
8	Imperfect Information: Adverse Selection and Moral Hazard	x	x		x	x
9	Environmental Policy		x			x
10	Public Goods and Public Choice		x			x
11	Production Technology and Cost	x	x	x	x	
12	Perfect Competition	x	x	x	x	
13	Monopoly and Price Discrimination	x		x	x	
14	Market Entry and Monopolistic Competition	x		x	x	
15	Oligopoly and Strategic Behavior	x		x	x	
16	Market Structure and Public Policy	x		x	x	
17	The Labor Market and the Distribution of Income	x	x		x	x
18	Beyond Perfect Competition: Unions, Monopsony, and Imperfect Information			x	x	
19	International Trade and Public Policy	x	x		x	

Preface

When we set out to write an economics text, we were driven by the vision of the sleeping student. A few years prior to writing this book, one of the authors was in the middle of a fascinating lecture on monopoly pricing when he heard snoring. It wasn't the first time a student had fallen asleep in one of his classes, but this was the loudest snoring he had ever heard—it sounded like a sputtering chain saw. The instructor turned to "Bill," who was sitting next to the sleeping student, and asked, "Could you wake him up?" Bill looked at the sleeping student and then gazed theatrically around the room at the other students. He finally looked back at the instructor and said, "Well, professor, I think you should wake him up. After all, you put him to sleep." That experience changed the way we taught economics. It highlighted for us a basic truth—for many students, economics isn't exactly exciting. We took this as a challenge—to get first-time economics students to see the relevance of economics to their lives, their careers, and their futures.

In order to get students to see the relevance of economics, we knew that we had to engage them. With the first three editions of the book, we helped professors to do that by emphasizing an active learning approach. We engaged students by teaching them how to do something—economic analysis. We kept the book brief, lively, and to the point and used the five key principles of economics as an organizing theme. The result was that our first three editions were a success in classrooms across the country, and we strove in this edition to do even better.

Teaching Philosophy

We began with the idea that an introductory economics course should be taught as if it were the last economics class a student would ever take. Because this is true for most students, we have just one opportunity to teach them how to use economics. The best way to teach economics is to focus on a few key concepts and ideas and apply them repeatedly in different circumstances.

We start the book with the five key principles of economics and then apply them throughout the book. This approach gives students the big picture—the framework of economic reasoning. We make the key concepts unforgettable by using them repeatedly, illustrating them with intriguing examples, and giving students many opportunities to practice what they've learned.

Our book is designed to be accessible to students. We have kept the writing lean, the examples lively and topical, and the visuals exciting.

Principles and Tools

In keeping with the themes of relevance and student accessibility, we have once again organized our text around the five key principles of economics. Throughout the text, every point of theory is connected to the five key principles and is indicated by the key symbol (see margin).

1. **The Principle of Opportunity Cost.** The opportunity cost of something is what you sacrifice to get it.
2. **The Marginal Principle.** Pick the level of an activity at which the marginal benefit equals the marginal cost.
3. **The Principle of Diminishing Returns.** If we increase one input while holding the other inputs fixed, output will increase, but at a decreasing rate.
4. **The Principle of Voluntary Exchange.** A voluntary exchange between two people makes both people better off.
5. **The Real–Nominal Principle.** What matters to people is the real value of money or income—its purchasing power—not the face value of money or income.

We use these principles to explain the logic underpinning the most important tools of economics. By using these five principles repeatedly, we reveal the logic of economic reasoning and demystify the tools of economics. Students see the big picture and also learn how to use the tools of economics properly.

"What I Do, I Understand"—Confucius

Our book is based on active learning, a teaching approach based on the idea that students learn best by doing. Our book engages students by letting them do activities as they read. We implement active learning with the following features:

▶ **Economic Puzzle** exercises provide a few clues and then ask the student to solve the economic puzzle.
▶ **Using the Tools** questions at the end of each chapter give students opportunities to do their own economic analysis.
▶ **Economic Experiments** actively involve the student in role-playing as consumers, producers, and policymakers. All these activities are designed to be fun for students and easy for professors, who decide when and how to use them.
▶ **Test Your Understanding** questions help students determine whether they understand the preceding material before continuing. These are straightforward questions that ask students to review and synthesize what they have read. Complete answers appear at the end of each chapter.
▶ **Chapter-Opening Stories** open each chapter and provide motivation for the chapter's subject matter. Each chapter starts with a list of **practical questions** that are answered in the chapter.

▶ **Lively Examples** are integrated throughout the text and help bring economic concepts to life. We have hundreds of fresh, new examples in this edition.

▶ **A Closer Look** boxes are featured throughout the text and provide brief, interesting examples of the tools and concepts discussed in the text.

Part of active learning is feedback on exercises completed by the student. At the end of each chapter, we list the answers to the Test Your Understanding exercises and the chapter-opening questions. At the end of the book, we list the answers to odd-numbered end-of-chapter exercises. At the request of instructors who used the third edition, we have removed the answers to the Using the Tools exercises and instead provide them in the Instructor's Manual. This approach allows instructors to assign these exercises as homework.

Book Organization

A course in microeconomics starts with the first four chapters of the book, which provide a foundation for more detailed study of individual decision-making and markets. Part 2 provides a closer look at supply and demand, including elasticity, market efficiency, and consumer choice. Part 3 discusses the circumstances under which markets break down, including imperfect information, public goods, and environmental degradation. In Part 4 we start with a discussion of production and costs, setting the stage for an examination of alternative market structures, including the extremes of perfect competition and monopoly, as well as the middle ground of monopolistic competition and oligopoly. The last chapter in Part 4 discusses antitrust policy and deregulation. The final part explores the labor market and the distribution of income.

Key Changes

We knew that our text's brevity and student accessibility were key strengths, and we worked to enhance and preserve them in the fourth edition. We also found that professors and students truly appreciated our concerted effort to use economic principles to explain current and topical events. For the fourth edition, we made a systematic attempt to refine this feature of the book. We made a special effort to enhance our chapter-opening stories, Closer Look boxes, and Economic Puzzles (formerly known as the Economic Detective exercises). The result is a text that applies economic reasoning to current economic issues and debates.

We restructured the introductory chapters to focus more on the key ideas of economics. The first chapter uses three current policy issues—traffic congestion, poverty in Africa, and Japan's prolonged recession—to explain the economic way of thinking. Chapter 3 is devoted entirely to exchange and trade. We discuss the fundamental rationale for exchange and introduce some of the institutions developed in modern societies to facilitate trade.

There are some other important changes in the book. We moved the chapters on market failure forward in the book to immediately follow the discussion of supply and demand and market efficiency. The first of these chapters deals with imperfect information, an exciting new area in economics that garnered a Nobel Prize for economists George Akerlof, Michael Spence, and Joseph Stiglitz in 2001. In the chapter on environmental policy, we use a recent study of sulfur dioxide emissions to discuss the appropriate level of pollution and evaluate alternative policy options to achieve that level. We wrote a new chapter on consumer choice, using modern consumer theory rather than the outdated and awkward theory of utility. In the chapter on strategic behavior, we added a discussion of advertising strategy.

We incorporated new material on emerging policy issues and developed fresh applications of basic economic concepts. For example, in the microeconomics area, we added new sections on the distribution of income, strategic advertising, health insurance, sulfur dioxide pollution, traffic congestion, and music piracy. Among the fresh applications are cartoon imports from China, EverQuest (the online role-playing game), marketable permits for greenhouse gases, soda vending machines that charge more on hot days, price fixing by vitamin sellers, and evidence for racial discrimination in hiring,

The Active Learning Package

A fully-integrated teaching and learning package is necessary for today's classroom. A total package of supplements is available for this edition with an emphasis on making the classroom an "active" one.

Print Supplements

Test Banks

Our team of instructors have thoroughly checked, modified, and enhanced the near 5,000 questions available in the two test banks that accompany this textbook. All new questions comprise 25 percent of each test bank. To ensure the highest level of quality, a team of checkers carefully examined the content for accuracy, consistency with the text, a balance of difficulty level and question type, and overall functionality for the purpose of testing student knowledge of the material.

Each test bank offers multiple-choice, true/false, and short-answer questions. The questions are referenced by topic and are presented in sequential order. Each question is keyed by degree of difficulty as *easy, moderate,* or *difficult.* Easy questions involve straightforward recall of information in the text. Moderate questions require some analysis on the student's part. Difficult questions usually entail more complex analysis and may require the student to go one step further than the material presented in the text. Questions are also classified as *fact, definition, conceptual,* or *analytical.* A question labeled Fact tests student's knowledge of factual information presented in the text. A Definition question asks the student to define an economic concept. Conceptual questions test a student's understanding of a concept. Analytical questions require the student to apply an analytical procedure to answer the question.

The test banks include tables and series of questions asking students to solve for numerical values, such as profit or equilibrium output. They also contain numerous questions based on graphs. The test banks include examples of all of the graphs that students have seen in the textbook. The questions ask the students to interpret the information that is presented in the graph. There are also many questions in the test banks that do not refer to a graph, but which require students to sketch out a graph on their own to be able to answer the question.

Testbank #1 prepared by Sang Lee of Southeastern Louisiana University, offers approximately 3,000 multiple-choice, true/false, short-answer, and graphing questions. Many new, more applied questions have been added.

Testbank #2 prepared by Nora Underwood of University of Central Florida, contains over 2,000 multiple-choice, true/false, and short-answer questions.

Instructor's Manual

The Instructor's Manual, revised by Daniel Condon of Dominican University, follows the textbook's organization, incorporating useful exercises, extra questions, and Internet links. The manual also provides detailed outlines (suitable for use as lecture notes) and solutions to all questions in the textbook.

The Instructor's Manual contains by chapter: a summary, objectives, extended examples and class exercises, solutions to all of the problems in the text, and an outline incorporating key terminology, teaching tips, and topics for class discussion. The Instructor's Manual is also available for download from the Instructor's Resource Center.

Study Guide

The Study Guide for *Microeconomics: Principles and Tools*, created by Janice Boucher Breuer of University of South Carolina, emphasizes the practical application of theory. It is a practicum designed to promote comprehension of economic principles and develop each student's ability to apply them to different problems. Integrated throughout the Study Guide are Performance-Enhancing Tips (PETs), which are designed to help students understand economics by applying the principles and promoting analytical thinking.

Two practice exams, featuring both multiple-choice and essay questions, are included at the end of each chapter. Both exams require students to apply one or more economic principles to arrive at each correct answer. Full solutions to the multiple-choice questions are included, not only listing each correct answer but also explaining in detail why one answer is correct and the others are not. Detailed answers to the essay questions are also provided.

The Study Guide contains by chapter: an overview of the corresponding chapter in the textbook, a checklist to provide a quick review of material covered in the textbook and lectures, a list of key terms and their definitions, practice exams, and the detailed answer keys.

Color Transparencies

All figures and tables from the text are reproduced as full-page, four-color acetates.

Technology Supplements

Companion Website: http://www.prenhall.com/osullivan

The Website contains Internet exercises, activities, and resources related specifically to the fourth edition

For Students

Link to **EconUpdates** site, where you will find updated **In the News** articles and **Internet Exercises**. Nearly every chapter of the textbook will be updated with economics-based articles from current news publications as well as Web-destination exercises that will direct students to an appropriate Website to gather data and analyze a specific economic problem.

The **Online Study Guide**, prepared by Fernando Quijana of Dickinson State University, offers students another opportunity to sharpen their problem-solving skills and to assess their understanding of the text material. The Online Study Guide grades each question submitted by the student, provides immediate feedback for correct and incorrect answers, and allows students to e-mail results up to four e-mail addresses.

Printable version of the **PowerPoint Lecture Presentation**.

For Instructors

The Syllabus Manager allows instructors to create a syllabus that they may publish for their students to access. Instructors may add exams or assignments of their own, edit any of the student resources available on the companion Website, post discussion topics, and more.

Instructors may also find **downloadable resources** from the link for the Instructor's Resource Center described below.

Instructor's Resource Center

This password-protected site is accessible from **www.prenhall.com/osullivan** and hosts all of the resources listed next. Instructors may click on the *Help downloading Instructor Resources* link for easy-to-follow instructions on getting access or may contact their sales representative for further information.

Classroom Response Systems (CRS)

CRS is an exciting new wireless polling technology that makes large and small classrooms even more interactive because it enables instructors to pose questions to their students, record results, and display those results instantly. Students can easily answer questions using compact remote control style transmitters. Prentice Hall has partnerships with leading classroom response systems providers, and can show you everything you need to know about setting up and using a CRS system. We'll provide the classroom hardware, text-specific PowerPoint slides, software and support, and show you how your sutdents can benefit:

Instructor's Manual

Solutions to questions included on the student side of the EconUpdates site

The PowerPoint Lecture Presentation: This lecture presentation tool offers the following features and benefits:

▶ Follows the exact layout of the textbook, by title and subtitle and provides an identical reproduction of textbook graphics, content sequence, and color consistency.
▶ Includes all the graphs, tables, and equations in the textbook.
▶ Displays figures in step-by-step, automated mode, using a single click per slide.
▶ Makes efficient use of space and crisp graphics designed to look the best in the space available.
▶ Contains end-of-chapter key terms with hyperlinks to relevant slides.
▶ The package will allow for instructors to make full-color, professional-looking presentations.
▶ A separate set of slides for students to easily print out for the purpose of note taking is also available.

TestGen-EQ software: The printed test banks are designed for use with the TestGen-EQ test-generating software. This computerized package allows instructors to custom-design, save, and generate classroom tests. The test program permits instructors to edit, add, or delete questions from the test banks; edit existing graphics and create new graphics; analyze test results; and organize a database of tests and student results. This software allows for greater flexibility and ease of use. It provides many options for organizing and displaying tests, along with a search-and-sort feature. The software as well as the test banks are available for download here.

Instructor's Resource Center on CD-ROM

All of the resources mentioned under the Instructor Resource Center are also available on this CD-ROM. With this new, **highly accessible menu,** faculty can easily customize presentations or build their own online courses. By simply clicking on a chapter or searching for a keyword, they can access an interactive library of resources. Faculty can pick and choose from the various supplements and export them to their hard drive.

OneKey

Available by using one of the access codes shrink-wrapped with the book, OneKey is Prentice Hall's exclusive new resource for instructors and students. OneKey gives you access to the best online teaching and learning tools—all available 24 hours a day, 7 days a week. OneKey means all your resources are in one place for maximum convenience, simplicity, and success. **Instructors** have access online, in the course management system of their choosing, to all available course supplements. Instructors can create and assign tests, quizzes, or graded homework assignments. OneKey saves instructors time by grading all questions and tracking results in the online course grade book. **Students** have access to interactive exercises, quizzes, useful links, and much more. The following resources are available:

▶ **Active Graphs.** Two levels of interactive graphs help students to understand economic concepts. Active Graphs Level One support key graphs in the text. These JAVA applications invite students to change the value of variables and curves and see the effects in the movement of the graph. Active Graphs Level Two include exercises that ask students to modify graphs based on an economic scenario and questions. Students receive an instant response detailing how they should have changed the graph.

▶ **Egraph and Graphing Questions.** This electronic tool allows students to create precise, colorful graphs using Flash technology. Students can e-mail these graphs to their professor or print and save them. To apply this technology, we have included *Graphing Questions* that require students to analyze information gathered on the Web and then create graphs using the Graphing Tool. Complete answers, with graphs, are included.

▶ **EconUpdates.**

▶ **Practice Quizzes.**

▶ **PowerPoint Lecture Presentation.**

▶ **Learning Objectives.**

▶ **Chapter Summaries.**

▶ **Research Navigator.** Your OneKey course gives you direct access to Prentice Hall's powerful online research tool, Research Navigator™. Research Navigator is an online academic research service that helps students learn and master the skills needed to write effective papers and complete research assignments. Research Navigator includes three databases of credible and reliable source material.

▶ **EBSCO's ContentSelect**™ Academic Journal database gives you instant access to thousands of academic journals and periodicals. You can search these online journals by keyword, topic, or multiple topics. It also guides students step-by-step through the writing of a research paper.

▶ **The *New York Times* Search-by-Subject**™ Archive allows you to search by subject and by keyword

▶ **Link Library** It is a collection of links to Websites, organized by academic subject and key terms. The links are monitored and updated each week.

▶ *OneKey for CourseCompass* allows instructors to communicate with students, distribute course material, and access student progress online. For access to this material, see **http://www.prenhall.com/coursecompass**.

▶ *OneKey for WebCT* provides content and enhanced features to help instructors create a complete online course. See **http://www.prenhall.com/webct** for more information.

▶ *OneKey for Blackboard* allows instructors to create online courses using the Blackboard tools, which include design, communications, testing, and course management tools. See **http://www.prenhall.com/blackboard** for more information.

Subscriptions

Analyzing current events is an important skill for economic students to develop. To sharpen this skill Prentice Hall offers you and your students three news subscription offers:

The Wall Street Journal Print and Interactive Editions Subscription

Prentice Hall has formed a strategic alliance with the *Wall Street Journal,* the most respected and trusted daily source for information on business and economics. For a small additional charge, Prentice Hall offers your students a 10- or 15-week subscription to the *Wall Street Journal* print edition and the *Wall Street Journal* interactive edition. Upon adoption of a special package containing the book and the subscription booklet, professors will receive a free one-year subscription of the print and interactive versions as well as weekly subject-specific *Wall Street Journal* educators' lesson plans. Please contact your Prentice Hall representative for details and ordering information.

The Financial Times

We are pleased to announce a special partnership with *The Financial Times.* For a small additional charge, Prentice Hall offers your students a 15-week subscription to *The Financial Times.* Upon adoption of a special package containing the book and the subscription booklet, professors will receive a free one-year subscription. Please contact your Prentice Hall representative for details and ordering information.

Economist.com

Through a special arrangement with Economist.com, Prentice Hall offers your students a 12-week subscription to Economist.com for a small additional charge. Upon adoption of a special package containing the book and the subscription booklet, professors will receive a free six-month subscription. Please contact your Prentice Hall representative for further details and ordering information.

A World of Thanks

A long road exists between the initial vision of an innovative principles text and the final product. Along our journey we participated in a structured process to reach our goal.

We wish to acknowledge the assistance of the many people who participated in this process. First we want to thank the participants who took part in the focus groups for the first and second editions; they helped us see the manuscript from a fresh perspective:

Carlos Aquilar, El Paso Community College
Jim Bradley, University of South Carolina
Thomas Collum, Northeastern Illinois University
David Craig, Westark College
Jeff Holt, Tulsa Junior College
Thomas Jeitschko, Texas A & M University
Gary Langer, Roosevelt University
Mark McCleod, Virginia Polytechnic Institute and State University
Tom McKinnon, University of Arkansas
Amy Meyers, Parkland Community College
Hassan Mohammadi, Illinois State University

John Morgan, College of Charleston
Norm Paul, San Jancinto Community College
Nampeang Pingkaratwat, Chicago State University
Scanlan Romer, Delta Community College
Barbara Ross-Pfeiffer, Kapiolani Community College
Virginia Shingleton, Valparaiso University
Zahra Saderion, Houston Community College
Jim Swofford, University of South Alabama
Linda Wilson, University of Texas–Arlington
Janet West, University of Nebraska–Omaha
Michael Youngblood, Rock Valley Community College

A special acknowledgment goes to the instructors who were willing to class-test drafts in different stages of development. They provided us with instant feedback on parts that worked and parts that needed changes:

Sheryl Ball, Virginia Polytechnic Institute and State University
John Constantine, University of California, Davis
James Hartley, Mt. Holyoke College
John Farrell, Oregon State University
Kailash Khandke, Furman College

Peter Lindert, University of California, Davis
Louis Makowski, University of California, Davis
Stephen Perez, California State University, Sacramento
Barbara Ross-Pfeiffer, Kapiolani Community College

Many people read all or parts of the manuscript at various stages. For their helpful criticisms, we thank:

Christine Amsler, Michigan State University
Karijit K. Arora, Le Moyne College
Alex Azarchs, Pace University
Kevin A. Baird, Montgomery County Community College
Donald Balch, University of South Carolina
Collette Barr, Santa Barbara Community College
Mahamudu Bawumia, Baylor University
Charles Scott Benson, Jr., Idaho State University
Jay Bhattacharya, Oklahoma-Walton Community College
John Payne Bigelow, Louisiana State University
Scott Bloom, North Dakota State University
Janice Boucher Breuer, University of South Carolina
Kathleen K. Bromley, Monroe Community College
Cindy Cannon, North Harris College
Katie Canty, Cape Fear Community College
David L. Coberly, Southwest Texas State University

John L. Conant, Indiana State University
Ana-Maria Conley, DeVry Institute of Technology
Ed Coulson, Penn State University
Lee Craig, North Carolina State University
Peggy Crane, San Diego State University
Albert B. Culver, California State University, Chico
Norman Cure, Macomb Community College
Irma de Alonso, Florida International University
Sel Dibooglu, Southern Illinois University
Martine Duchatelet, Barry University
Mousumi Duttaray, Indiana University
Ghazi Duwaji, University of Texas, Arlington
David Eaton, Murray State University
Duane Eberhardt, Missouri Southern State College
Carl Enomoto, New Mexico State University
David Figlio, University of Oregon
Dan Georgianna, University of Massachusetts–Dartmouth

Linda Ghent, East Illinois University

Hossein Gholami, Fayetteville Tech Community College

Susan Glanz, St. John's University

Randy R. Grant, Linfield College

Paul C. Harris, Jr., Camden County College

James E. Hartley, Mount Holyoke College

Rowland Harvey, DeVry Institute of Technology

John Henry, California State University, Sacramento

Robert Herman, Nassau Community College

Charles W. Haase, San Francisco State University

Charlotte Denise Hixson, Midlands Technical College

Jeff Holt, Tulsa Community College

Brad Hoppes, Southwest Missouri State University

Calvin Hoy, County College of Morris

Jonathan O. Ikoba, Scott Community College

John A. Jascot, Capital Community Technical College

Thomas Jeitschko, Texas A & M University

George Jensen, California State University, Los Angeles

Taghi T. Kermani, Youngstown State University

Rose Kilburn, Modesto Junior College

Philip King, San Francisco State University

Steven F. Koch, Georgia Southern University

James T. Kyle, Indiana Sate University

Gary Langer, Roosevelt University

Susan Linz, Michigan State University

Marianne Lowery, Erie Community College

Melanie Marks, Longwood College

Jessica McCraw, University of Texas, Arlington

Bret McMurran, Chaffey College

Thomas J. Meeks, Virginia State University

Jeannette Mitchell, Rochester Institute of Technology

Rahmat Mozayan, Heald College

William Neilson, Texas A & M University

Alex Obiya, San Diego City College

Paul Okello, University of Texas, Arlington

Charles M. Oldham, Jr., Fayetteville Technical Community College

Jack W. Osman, San Francisco State University

Carl Parker, Fort Hays State University

Randall Parker, East Carolina University

Stephen Perez, California State University, Sacramento

Stan Peters, Southeast Community College

Chirinjev Peterson, Greenville Technical College

Nampeang Pingkarawat, Chicago State University

L. Wayne Plumly, Jr., Valdosta State University

Fatma Abdel-Raouf, Cleveland State University

Dan Rickman, Oklahoma State University

John Robertson, University of Kentucky

Barbara Ross-Pfeiffer, Kapiolani Community College

George Schatz, Maine Maritime Academy

Kurt Schwabe, Ohio University

Mark Siegler, Williams College

Terri Sexton, California State University, Sacramento

Dennis Shannon, Belleville Area College

Virginia Shingleton, Valparaiso University

Garin Smith, Daytona Beach Community College

Noel Smith, Palm Beach Community College

Xiaochuan Song, San Diego Mesa College

Ed Sorensen, San Francisco State University

Abdulwahab Sraiheen, Kutztown University

Rodney Swanson, University of California-Los Angeles

James Swofford, University of South Alabama

Evan Tanner, Thunderbird, The American Graduate School of International Management

Robert Tansky, St. Clair County Community College

Denise Turnage, Midlands Technical College

Tracy M. Turner, Kansas State University

Fred Tyler, Fordham University

James R. VanBeek, Blinn College

Daniel Villegas, Cal Polytechnic State University

Chester Waters, Durham Technical Community College, Shaw University

Irvin Weintraub, Towson State University

Donald Wells, University of Arizona

James Wheeler, North Carolina State University

Gilbert Wolfe, Middlesex Community College

Virginia York, Gulf Coast Community College

Our greatest appreciation goes out to Carlos Aguilar and his economics students from El Paso Community College, who gave us their feedback and evaluations with comparable textbooks. The students provided us with positive feedback and constructive criticism that helped us prepare the third edition:

Erik Acona

Erica Avila

Jaime Bermudez

Israel Castillo

Maribell Castillo	Eugene Jordan
Sarah Davis	Vanessa Lara
Rebekah Dennis	Harmony Lopez
Michele Donohoe	Stacey Lucas
Emmanuel Eck	Maria Lynch
Patrick Espinoza	Sindy McElvany
Edward Estrada	Roger Mitchell
Kim Gardner	Benny Ontiveros
Aleisa Garza	Louie Ortega
Daniel Heitz	Karen Seitz
Laura Herebia	Ana Smith
Hilda Howard	Beverly Stephens
Melanie Johnson	Adrian Terrazas
Brenda Jordan	Chris Wright

For the fourth edition, we enlisted a large group of reviewers; their comments and suggestions helped us improve the coverage and presentation of the book.

Rashid Al-Hmoud, Texas Technical University	Martin Markovich, Florida A & M University
Jay Bhattacharya, Oklahoma Walton Community College	Pete Mavrokordatos, Tarrant County College/University of Phoenix
Charles Benson, Jr., Idaho State University	Thomas McCaleb, Florida State University
Edward Bierhanzl, Florida A&M University	Stephen Miller, University of Nevada, Las Vegas
Calvin Blackwell, College of Charlestown	Ted Muzio, St. John's University, Jamaica, NY
Matthew Brown, Santa Clara University	Jon J Nadenichek, California State University, Northridge
Bruce Brunton, James Madison University	
Tom Carroll, Central Oregon Community College	Tahany Naggar, West Chester University
	Michael Nelson, Texas A & M University
Peggy Crane, Southwestern College	Stan Peters, Southeast Community College
John Farrell, Oregon State University	James Ragan, Kansas State University
Harry Ellis, University of North Texas	Taghi Ramin, William Patterson University
David Gillette, Truman State University	Joseph Santos, South Dakota State University
Lowell Glenn, Utah Valley State College	Richard Stahl, Louisiana State University
John Graham, Rutgers University	Tesa Stegner, Idaho State University
Miren Ivankovic, Southern Wesleyan University	Lawrence Stelmach, Delaware Valley College
Paul Johnson, University of Alaska, Anchorage	Rodney Swanson, University of California, Los Angeles
Janis Kea, West Valley College	
Youn Kim, Monash University	James Swofford, University of South Alabama
Sang Lee, Southeastern Louisiana University	Greg Trandel, University of Georgia
Anthony Lima, California State University, Hayward	Chad Turner, Clemson University
	Brock Williams, Metropolitan Community College
Marty Ludlum, Oklahoma City Community College	Virginia York, Gulf Coast Community College

We would also like to acknowledge the team of dedicated authors who contributed to the various ancillaries that accompany this book: Janice Boucher Breuer of University of South Carolina, Daniel Condon of Dominican University, Tori H. Knight of Carson-Newman College, Sang Lee of Southeastern Louisiana University, Cathleen Leue of University of Oregon, Fernando Quijano of Dickinson State University, and Nora Underwood of University of Central Florida.

We also owe a special thanks to Stephen J. Perez of California State University, Sacramento. He acted as the supplement coordinator and advisor. He provided valuable advice, guidance, and in-depth feedback on the entire supplement package.

From the start, Prentice Hall provided us with first-class support and advice. Over the first four editions, many people contributed to the project, including Leah Jewell, Rod Banister, P. J. Boardman, Marie McHale, Gladys Soto, Lisa Amato, Victoria Anderson, Cynthia Regan, Kathleen McLellan, Sharon Koch, David Theisen, Steve Deitmer, and Christopher Bath. We want to single out two people for special mention. Our development editor, Amy Ray, did an outstanding job identifying parts of the book that could be improved for the fourth edition and had many suggestions on how to improve it. Finally, we are indebted to David Alexander, executive editor at Prentice Hall, who guided the project from start to finish.

Last but not least, we must thank our families, who have seen us disappear, sometimes physically and other times mentally, to spend hours wrapped up in our own world of principles of economics. A project of this magnitude is very absorbing, and our families have been particularly supportive in this endeavor.

Arthur O'Sullivan
Steven Sheffrin

Features List

Chapter 1 Introduction: What Is Economics?   2

A Closer Look: When Do Economists Agree? 6
A Closer Look: Even Kids Respond to Incentives 12
A Closer Look: "Dismal" Depends On Your Point of View 15

Chapter 2 The Key Principles of Economics   26

A Closer Look: Swords vs. Ecotels? 31
Economic Puzzle 35
Economic Experiment: Producing Fold-Its 39

Chapter 3 Exchange and Markets   44

A Closer Look: Buzz Lightyear of China 51
A Closer Look: EverQuest and Fantasy Exchanges 55

Chapter 4 Supply, Demand, and Market Equilibrium   60

Economic Puzzle: Saving Money Wherever You Shop? 65
A Closer Look: Increasing the Supply of Wind Power 79
A Closer Look: Higher Platinum Prices 87
Economic Experiment: Market Equilibrium 87

Chapter 5 Elasticity: A Measure of Responsiveness   94

A Closer Look: How to Cut Teen Smoking by 60% 100
A Closer Look: Pricing Medical Care in Developing Countries 104
Economic Puzzle: DVD Elasticity 107

Chapter 6 Consumer Choice   120

A Closer Look: Modern Consumer Theory Versus Old Utility Theory 130
A Closer Look: The Bang per Buck of Light Spirits 134

Chapter 7 Market Efficiency and Government Intervention   138

A Closer Look: Milk Mountains 151
Economic Puzzle: Shortfall from Medallion Sale 154
A Closer Look: A Market For Used Human Organs? 156
A Closer Look: Taxes and December Babies 163
Economic Experiment: Government Intervention 163

Chapter 8 Imperfect Information: Adverse Selection and Moral Hazard   170

A Closer Look: Consumer Satisfaction Scores from ValueStar and eBay 178
A Closer Look: Genetic Testing, Thrill Seekers, and Insurance 186
Economic Puzzle: Bicycle Theft Insurance 188

Economic Experiment: Rolling for Lemons 189
Economic Experiment: Bike Insurance 189

Chapter 9 Environmental Policy   194

A Closer Look: Dear Abby and Environmental Policy 203
Economic Puzzle: Why Did the Price of Permits Drop? 206
A Closer Look: Giving the Gift of CO_2 210
Economic Experiment: Pollution Permits 213

Chapter 10 Public Goods and Public Choice   218

Economic Puzzle: Why Build a Three-Faced Clock Tower? 223
A Closer Look: Are Politicians Like Ice-Cream Vendors? 227
Economic Experiment: Voluntary Contributions 230

Chapter 11 Production Technology and Cost   234

Economic Puzzle: Same Average Cost at Two or Three Quantities? 244
A Closer Look: Indivisible Inputs and the Cost of Fake Killer Whales 249
A Closer Look: Scale Economies in Wind Power 251

Chapter 12 Perfect Competition   260

Economic Puzzle: Fewer Deliveries and More Profit? 268
A Closer Look: Wireless Women 275
Economic Experiment: Butter Prices 283

Chapter 13 Monopoly and Price Discrimination   288

A Closer Look: Barriers to Generic Drugs 302
A Closer Look: Interacting with a Soda Vending Machine on a Hot Day 305
Economic Puzzle: Why Are Hardback Books So Expensive? 306
Economic Experiment: Price Discrimination 307

Chapter 14 Market Entry and Monopolistic Competition   312

A Closer Look: Restricting Entry of On-Line Wine Merchants 317
Economic Puzzle: Lower Profit per Unit Sold? 321
Economic Experiment: Fixed Costs and Entry 322

Chapter 15 Oligopoly and Strategic Behavior   326

A Closer Look: Vitamin, Inc. Gets Busted 333
A Closer Look: Crafty—and Illegal—Entry Deterrence in Europe 345
Economic Puzzle: Ballpoint Pens from R.I.P. 347
Economic Experiment: A Price-Fixing Game 352

**Chapter 16 Market Structure
and Public Policy**   **356**

Economic Puzzle: A Decrease in Demand Decrease the Price? 361
A Closer Look: Will Satellite Radio Become a Natural
    Monopoly? 361
A Closer Look: Is Tripoly Better Than Duopoly? 365
Economic Puzzle: Check the Yellow Pages? 367

**Chapter 17 The Labor Market
and the Distribution of Income**   **378**

A Closer Look: The Economics of Not Working 387
Economic Puzzle: Response to a Wage Cut? 387
A Closer Look: Foreign Sweatshops and Industry Codes of
    Conduct 390

A Closer Look: Racial Discrimination in Hiring 394

**Chapter 18 Beyond Perfect Competition:
Unions, Monopsony, and Imperfect Information**   **404**

A Closer Look: Working Conditions and Unions 407
A Closer Look: Pubs and Labor-Supply Curve 414
Economic Puzzle: Higher Wages at Ford Motor Company 415

**Chapter 19 International Trade
and Public Policy**   **420**

A Closer Look: The Cost of Protecting Jobs 431
A Closer Look: Protection for Candle Makers 432
Economic Experiment: Protectionist Policies 440

Part 1

Introduction and Key Principles

Chapter 1

Introduction: What Is Economics?

Chapter 2

The Key Principles of Economics

Chapter 3

Exchange and Markets

Chapter 4

Supply, Demand, and Market Equilibrium

What Is Economics?

Positive Versus Normative Analysis
Decisions in a Modern Economy:
    The Invisible Hand?

Economic Analysis and Modern Problems

Example 1: Traffic Congestion
Example 2: Poverty in Africa
Example 3: Japan's Economic Problems

The Economic Way of Thinking

Rational People Respond to Incentives
Application: Thinking About Congestion

Preview of Coming Attractions: Microeconomics

To Understand Markets and Predict
    Changes
To Make Personal and Managerial
    Decisions
To Evaluate Public Policies

Preview of Coming Attractions: Macroeconomics

To Understand Why Economies Grow
To Understand Economic Fluctuations
To Make Informed Business Decisions
Appendix: Using Graphs and Formulas
To Make Informed Business Decisions

Introduction: What Is Economics?

conomics is the science of choice, exploring the choices made by individual people and organizations. In the last few centuries, these choices have led to substantial gains in the standard of living around the globe. The typical American household today has roughly seven times the income and purchasing power of a household 100 years ago. Our prosperity is the result of choices made by all sorts of people, including inventors, workers, entrepreneurs, and the people who saved money and loaned it to others to invest in machines and other tools of production. One reason we have prospered is greater efficiency: We have discovered better ways to use our resources—raw materials, time, energy—to produce the goods and services we value.

Although prosperity and efficiency are widespread, they are not universal. In some parts of the world, many people live in poverty. For example, in sub-Saharan Africa, 290 million people—almost half the population—live on less than $1 per day. And in all nations of the world, there are still inefficiencies, with valuable resources being wasted. For example, each year the typical urban commuter in the United States wastes more than 60 hours and $150 in gasoline while trapped in rush hour traffic.

conomics provides a framework to diagnose all sorts of problems faced by society and then evaluate various proposals to solve them. Economics can help us develop strategies to replace poverty with prosperity, to replace waste with efficiency. In this chapter, we explain what economics is and how it can be used to think about practical problems.

What Is Economics?

Economics

The study of choice when there is scarcity, that is, a situation in which resources are limited and can be used in different ways.

Scarcity

A situation in which resources are limited in quantity and can be used in different ways.

Economics studies the choices that can be made when there is scarcity. **Scarcity** is a situation in which resources—the things we use to produce goods and services—are limited in quantity and can be used in different ways. Because our resources are limited, or finite, we must sacrifice one thing for another. Here are some examples of scarcity:

▶ Like everyone else, you have a limited amount of time. If you take a part-time job, each hour on the job means one less hour for study or play.
▶ A city has a limited amount of land, so if the city uses an acre for a park, it has one less acre for housing, retailers, or industry.
▶ You have limited income this year, so every dollar you spend on music means one less dollar spent on other products, or one less dollar saved.

We make our choices in a variety of ways. Sometimes we make our decisions as individuals, and other times we participate in collective decision-making, allowing the government and other organizations to choose for us. Many of our choices happen within markets, where we buy and sell things. For example, most of us participate in the labor market, exchanging our time for money, and we all participate in consumer markets. On the other hand, we make other choices outside markets—from our personal decisions about everyday life to our political choices about matters that concern society as a whole. What unites all these decisions is the notion of scarcity: We can't have it all; there are trade-offs.

Economists are always reminding us that there is scarcity—that there are trade-offs in everything we do. Suppose that in a conversation with an economist, you share your enthusiasm about an upcoming launch of the space shuttle. The economist is likely to remind you that the resources used for the shuttle could be used instead for an unmanned mission to Mars. By introducing the notion of scarcity into your conversation, the economist is simply reminding you that there are trade-offs, that one thing (a shuttle mission) is sacrificed for another (a Mars mission). Talking about alternatives is the first step in a process that can help us make better choices about how to use our resources. For example, we could compare the scientific benefits of a shuttle mission to the benefits of a Mars mission, and choose the mission with the largest benefit.

The resources used for the Space Shuttle could be used instead to launch a mission to Mars. This is an example of the tradeoffs our society faces.

Positive Versus Normative Analysis

It's important to note that economics doesn't tell us what to choose—shuttle mission or Mars mission—but simply helps us understand the trade-offs. President Harry Truman once remarked,

> All my economists say, "On the one hand, . . . ; On the other hand, . . . " Give me a one-handed economist!

An economist might say, "On the one hand, we could use a shuttle mission to do more experiments in the gravity-free environment in earth orbit; on the other hand, we could use a Mars mission to explore the possibility of life on other planets." In using both hands, the economist is not being evasive, but simply doing economics, discussing the alternative uses of our resources. The ultimate decision about how to use our resources—shuttle mission or Mars exploration—is the responsibility of citizens or their elected officials.

Most modern economic analysis is based on positive analysis. **Positive economics** predicts the consequences of alternative actions, answering the questions "What *is*?" or "What *will be*?" Here are some questions answered by positive economics:

Positive economics

Analysis that answers the questions, "What is?" or "What will be?"

▶ If the minimum wage increases, how many workers will lose their jobs?
▶ If two office-supply firms merge, will the price of office supplies increase?
▶ If income taxes are cut, what fraction of the tax cut will be spent on consumer goods?
▶ If a nation restricts shoe imports, who benefits, and who bears the cost?

A second type of economic reasoning is normative in nature. **Normative economics** answers the question "What *ought to be*?" Here are some normative questions:

Normative economics

Analysis that answers the question "What ought to be?"

▶ Should the government increase the minimum wage?
▶ Should the government provide $1 billion in foreign aid to an African country?
▶ Should the government subsidize a college education?
▶ Should the government cut taxes to stimulate the economy?
▶ Should a nation reduce the size of its government?

Normative questions lie at the heart of policy debates. Economists contribute to policy debates by doing positive analysis about the consequences of alternative actions. For example, an economist could predict the effects of a minimum wage on the number of people employed, the income of families with minimum-wage workers, and consumer prices. Armed with the conclusions of the economist's positive analysis, citizens and policymakers could then make a normative decision about whether to increase the minimum wage. Similarly, an economist could study the projects that could be funded with $1 billion in foreign aid, predicting the effects of each project on the per capita income in an African country. Armed with this positive analysis, policymakers could then decide which projects to support.

It's important to note that economists don't always reach the same conclusions in their positive analyses. The disagreements often concern the magnitude of a particular effect. For example, most economists agree that an increase in the minimum wage will decrease employment, but there is disagreement about just how many people will lose their jobs. Similarly, economists agree that spending $1 billion to improve education in Africa will increase productivity and income, but there may be disagreement about just how much income will increase. There are ongoing efforts by economists to quantify these sorts of economic phenomena, but many factual questions remain unanswered. For a discussion of some of the points of agreement and disagreement among economists, read "A Closer Look: When Do Economists Agree?"

Decisions in a Modern Economy: The Invisible Hand?

Economic decisions are made at every level in society. Individuals decide what products to buy, what occupations to pursue, and how much money to save. Firms decide what products to produce and how to produce them. Governments decide what projects and programs to complete and how to pay for them. The choices made by individuals, firms, and governments answer three questions.

1 What products do we produce? There are trade-offs: If a hospital uses its resources to perform more heart transplants, it has fewer resources to care for premature infants.
2 How do we produce the products? There are alternative means of production: Power companies can produce electricity with coal, natural gas, or wind power; professors can teach in large lecture halls or small classrooms.
3 Who consumes the products? We must decide how the products of society are distributed among people. If some people earn more money than others, should they consume more goods? How much money should be taken from the rich and given to the poor?

When Do Economists Agree?

Although economists often disagree about policy matters, there is widespread agreement about many of today's most important issues. A recent survey asked economists to indicate whether they agreed or disagreed with a number of propositions.[1] Here are some of the statements for which there was widespread agreement, with the percentages of economists who agreed shown in parentheses.

1. The U.S. trade deficit is *not* primarily due to trade barriers erected by other nations (95%).
2. The best way to control pollution is to tax polluters—or to issue a limited number of pollution permits and allow firms to buy and sell the permits (93%).
3. Import restrictions and import taxes usually reduce the general welfare of society (93%).
4. The federal government can use its tax and spending policies to stimulate a sluggish economy and encourage investment (84%).
5. A large federal budget deficit has an adverse effect on the economy (80%).
6. Minimum wages increase unemployment among young and unskilled workers (74%).
7. Antitrust laws should be enforced vigorously to reduce monopoly power from its current level (71%).

On other issues, economists have not reached a consensus. For example, economists disagree about whether an economy would naturally correct the problem of widespread unemployment without intervention by the government. They also disagree about whether cutting taxes on investment income will promote economic growth and general prosperity. On the issue of why men earn more than women, some economists believe the wage gap is caused largely by differences in productivity and career choices, whereas others believe that sex discrimination plays an important role in the wage gap. The fact that economists disagree on these issues reflects our imperfect knowledge about various facets of the economy. There is still much work to be done to improve our knowledge and design policies to eliminate waste and promote prosperity.

As we'll see later in the book, most of these decisions are made in markets, with prices playing a key role in determining what products we produce, how we produce them, and who gets the products. In Chapter 3, we'll examine the role of markets in modern economies, exploring the virtues as well as the shortcomings of markets.

Economic Analysis and Modern Problems

Economic analysis provides important insights into real-world problems. To explain how economic analysis can be used in problem solving, we provide three examples, each of which will be explained here and in more detail later in the book.

Example 1: Traffic Congestion

Consider first the problem of traffic congestion. According to the Texas Transportation Institute, the typical U.S. commuter wastes about 62 hours per year because of traffic congestion.[2] In some cities, the time wasted by the typical commuter is much higher:

136 hours in Los Angeles, 92 hours in San Francisco, and 75 hours in Houston. In addition to time lost, we also waste $9 billion worth of gasoline and diesel fuel each year.

To an economist, the diagnosis of the congestion problem is straightforward. When you drive onto a busy highway during rush hour, your car takes up space and decreases the distance between the vehicles on the highway. The normal reaction to a shorter distance between moving cars is to slow down. So when you enter the highway, you are essentially forcing other commuters to spend more time on the highway. If each of your 900 fellow commuters spends just two extra seconds on the highway, you have increased the total travel time of the group by 30 minutes. But since you don't lose the 30 minutes all yourself, it's likely that you ignore this effect when deciding whether or not to enter. Similarly, your fellow commuters ignore the cost they impose on you and others when they enter the highway. Since no single commuter pays the full cost, too many people use the highway, and everyone wastes time.

One possible solution to the congestion problem is to force people to pay for using the road, just as they pay for gasoline and tires. A congestion tax of $8 per trip could be imposed on rush hour commuters. We could use a debit card system to collect the tax: Every time a car passes a checkpoint, a transponder would charge the commuter's card. Traffic volume during rush hours would then decrease as travelers (a) shift their travel to off-peak times, (b) switch to ride sharing and mass transit, and (c) shift their travel to other routes. The job for the economist is to compute the appropriate congestion tax and predict the consequences of imposing the tax.

Example 2: Poverty in Africa

Consider next the issue of poverty in Africa. In the last two decades of the twentieth century, the world economy grew rapidly, and the average per capita income (income per person) increased by about 35%. By contrast, the economies of poverty-stricken sub-Saharan Africa shrank, and per capita income decreased by about 6%. Economists have found that as a nation's economy grows, its poorest households share in the general prosperity.[3] Therefore, one way to reduce poverty in sub-Saharan Africa would be to increase economic growth. Economic growth occurs when a country expands its production facilities (machinery and factories), improves its public infrastructure (highways and water systems), widens educational opportunities, and adopts new technology.

The recent experience of sub-Saharan Africa is somewhat puzzling because in the last few decades, the region has expanded educational opportunities and received large amounts of foreign aid. Some recent work by economists on the sources of growth suggests that institutions such as the legal system and the regulatory environment play key roles in economic growth.[4] In sub-Saharan Africa, a simple legal dispute about a small debt takes about 30 months to resolve, compared to five months in the United States. In Mozambique, it takes 174 days to complete the procedures required to set up a business, compared to just two days in Canada.[5] In many cases, institutions impede rather than encourage the sort of investment and risk taking that causes economic growth and reduces poverty. As a consequence, economists and policymakers are exploring ways to reform the region's institutions. They are also challenged with choosing among development projects that will generate the biggest economic boost per dollar spent— that is, the biggest bang per buck.

Example 3: Japan's Economic Problems

Consider next the economic problems experienced by Japan in the last decade. Following World War II, Japan grew rapidly, with per capita income increasing by about 4% per year between 1950 and 1992. But in 1992, the economy came to a screeching halt. For the next 10 years, per capita income, or income per person, either decreased or increased slightly. In 1995, the prices of all sorts of goods—including consumer goods and housing—actually started to decrease, and the downward slide continued for years. In an economy with declining prices, consumers expect lower prices tomorrow, so they are reluctant to buy things today. Business managers are reluctant to borrow money to invest in production facilities because if prices for their products drop, they might not have enough money to repay the loans.

The challenge for economists was to develop a set of policies to get the Japanese economy moving again. Economists responded by designing policies to stimulate spending by consumers and businesses and to make needed changes to their financial system. The Japanese political system was slow to adopt these difficult reforms, but recent political developments in Japan have increased the likelihood that the necessary reforms will be made in the future.

TEST Your Understanding

1. List the three basic questions asked about an economy.
2. Why is economics labeled the "dismal science?"
3. Explain the difference between positive and normative analysis.

The Economic Way of Thinking

How do economists think about problems and decision-making? The economic way of thinking is best summarized by British economist John Maynard Keynes (1883–1946), who is responsible for a branch of economics bearing his name:

> The theory of economics does not furnish a body of settled conclusions immediately applicable to policy. It is a method rather than a doctrine, an apparatus of the mind, a technique of thinking which helps its possessor draw correct conclusions.

Let's look at the three elements of the economic way of thinking.

1. Use Assumptions to Simplify

Economists use assumptions to make things simpler and focus attention on what really matters. If you use a road map to plan a car trip from Seattle to San Francisco, you make two unrealistic assumptions to simplify your planning:

▶ The earth is flat: The flat road map doesn't show the curvature of the earth.
▶ The roads are flat: The standard road map doesn't show hills and valleys.

Instead of a map, you could use a globe that shows all the topographical features between Seattle and San Francisco, but you don't need those details to plan your trip. A map, with its unrealistic assumptions, will suffice because the curvature of the earth and the topography of the highways are irrelevant to your trip. Although your analysis of your road trip is based on two unrealistic assumptions, that does not mean your analysis is invalid. Similarly, if economic analysis is based on unrealistic assumptions, that doesn't mean the analysis is faulty.

What if you decide to travel by bike instead of by automobile? Now the assumption of flat roads really matters, unless of course you are eager to pedal up and down mountains. If you use a standard map and thus assume there are no mountains between the two cities, you may inadvertently pick a mountainous route instead of a flat one. In this case, the simplifying assumption makes a difference. The lesson is that we must think carefully about whether a simplifying assumption is truly harmless.

2. Isolate Variables—*Ceteris Paribus*

Economic analysis often involves variables and how they affect one another. A **variable** is a measure of something that can take on different values. Economists are interested in exploring relationships between two variables; for example, the relationship between the price of apples and the quantity of apples purchased. Of course, the quantity of apples purchased depends on many other variables, including the consumer's income. To explore the relationship between the quantity and price of apples, we must assume that the consumer's income—and anything else that influences apple purchases—doesn't change.

Alfred Marshall (1842–1924), was a British economist who refined the economic model of supply and demand and provided a label for this process.[6] He picked one variable that affected apple purchases (price) and threw the other variable (income) into what he called the "pound" (in Marshall's time, the "pound," was an enclosure for holding stray cattle; nowadays, a pound is for stray dogs). The "other" variables waited in the pound

Variable
A measure of something that can take on different values.

To study a single variable, **Alfred Marshall** threw the other variables into a "pound" where they waited until he examined the influence of the first variable. This notion of isolating variables is called *ceteris paribus*.

Ceteris paribus

The Latin expression meaning other variables being held fixed.

while Marshall examined the influence of the first variable. Marshall labeled the pound ***ceteris paribus***, the Latin expression meaning that other variables are held fixed:

> . . . the existence of other tendencies is not denied, but their disturbing effect is neglected for a time. The more the issue is narrowed, the more exactly can it be handled.

This book contains many statements about the relationship between two variables. For example, the quantity of computers produced by a firm depends on the price of computers, the wage of computer workers, and the cost of microchips. When we say, "An increase in the price of computers increases the quantity of computers produced," we are implicitly assuming that the other two variables—the wage and the cost of microchips—do not change. Sometimes, we will make this assumption explicit by adding "*ceteris paribus.*"

3. Think at the Margin

Marginal change

A small, one-unit change in value.

Economists often consider how a small change in one variable affects another variable and what impact that has on people's decision-making. In other words, if circumstances change ever so slightly, how will people respond? A small, one-unit change in value is called a **marginal change**. The key feature is that the first variable changes by only one unit. For example, you might ask, If I study just one more hour, by how much will my exam score increase? Economists call this process "thinking at the margin." Thinking at the margin is sort of like thinking on the edge. You will encounter marginal thinking throughout this book. Here are some other marginal questions:

▶ If I stay in school and earn another degree, by how much will my lifetime earnings increase?
▶ If a car dealer hires one more sales associate, how many more cars will the dealer sell?
▶ If national income increases by $1 billion, by how much will spending on consumer goods increase?

As we'll see in the next chapter, economists use the answer to a marginal question as a first step in deciding whether to do more or less of something.

Rational People Respond to Incentives

A key assumption of most economic analysis is that people act rationally, meaning that they act in their own self-interest. British philosopher Adam Smith (1723–1790), who is also considered the founder of economics, wrote that he discovered within mankind:[7]

> a desire of bettering our condition, a desire which, though generally calm and dispassionate, comes with us from the womb, and never leaves us until we go to the grave.

Smith didn't say that people are motivated exclusively by self-interest, but instead that self-interest is more powerful than kindness or altruism. In this book, we will assume that people act in their own self-interest.

Rational people respond to incentives. When the payoff, or benefit, from doing something changes, people change their behavior to get the benefit. For an example of incentives and corresponding behavior, read "A Closer Look: Even Kids Respond to Incentives ."

Application: Thinking About Congestion

To illustrate the three elements of the economic way of thinking, let's consider again how an economist would approach the problem of traffic congestion. Recall that each driver on the highway slows down other drivers but ignores these costs when deciding whether or not to use the highway. If the government imposes a congestion tax to alleviate congestion during rush hour, the question for the economist is: How high should the tax be?

To determine the appropriate congestion tax, we, as economists, would use the three elements of the economic way of thinking.

▶ Make Assumptions. To simply the problem, we would assume that every car has the same effect on the travel time of other cars. Of course, this is unrealistic because people drive cars of different sizes in different ways. But the alternative—looking at the effects of each car on travel speeds—would needlessly complicate the analysis.

▶ Isolate Variables (*Ceteris Paribus*). To focus attention on the effects of a congestion tax on the number of cars using the highway, we would make the *ceteris paribus* assumption that everything else that affects travel behavior—the price of gasoline, bus fares, and consumer income—remains fixed.

▶ Think at the Margin. To think at the margin, we would estimate the effects of adding one more car to the highway. The marginal question is: If we add one more car to the highway, by how much does the total travel time for commuters increase?

Before London imposed an $8, rush-hour congestion tax, the city experienced some of the worst congestion in Europe.

Once we answer this question, we could determine the cost imposed by the marginal driver. If the marginal driver forces each of the 900 commuters to spend two extra seconds on the highway, total travel time increases by 30 minutes. If the value of time is $16 per hour, the appropriate congestion tax would be $8.

If the idea of charging people for using roads seems odd and dismal, consider the city of London, which for decades had experienced the worst congestion in Europe. In February of 2003, the city imposed an $8 tax per day for driving in the city between 7:00 A.M. and 6:30 P.M. The tax reduced traffic volume and cut travel times for cars and buses in half. This application of economics decreased the time and fuel wasted in traffic. Given the success of London's congestion tax, other cities are exploring similar policies.

TEST Your Understanding

4. List the three elements of the economic way of thinking.
5. Suppose your grade on an economics exam is affected by the number of lectures you attend. What is the relevant marginal question?

Preview of Coming Attractions: Microeconomics

Microeconomics

The study of the choices made by households, firms, and government and of how these choices affect the markets for goods and services.

There are two types of economic analysis: microeconomics and macroeconomics. **Microeconomics** is the study of the choices made by households, firms, and government and of how these choices affect the markets for goods and services. Let's look at three ways we can use microeconomic analysis.

A CLOSER LOOK   Even Kids Respond to Incentives

To illustrate the notion that people are rational and respond to incentives, consider an experiment conducted by researchers at St. Luke's Roosevelt Hospital in New York City.[8] The researchers addressed the following question: If a child must pedal a stationary bicycle to run a television set, will he watch less TV?

The researchers randomly assigned obese children, age 8 to 12, to two types of TVs. The first had a stationary bicycle in front of the TV, but the TV operated independently of the bicycle: No pedaling was required to operate the TV. In contrast, the second type of TV worked only if the child pedaled a bike facing the TV. The kids in the control group (no pedaling required) watched an average of 21 hours of TV per week, whereas the kids in the treatment group (pedaling required) watched just two hours per week. In other words, kids respond to incentives, watching less TV when the cost of watching is higher.

To Understand Markets and Predict Changes

One reason for studying microeconomics is to better understand how markets work. Once you know how markets operate, you can use economic analysis to predict how various events affect product prices and quantities. In this book, we answer dozens of practical questions about markets and how they operate. Let's look at one practical question that can be answered with some simple economic analysis.

How would a tax on beer affect the number of highway deaths among young adults? Research has shown that the number of highway fatalities among young adults is roughly proportional to the total beer consumed by that group. A tax on beer would make the product more expensive, and young adults, like other beer drinkers, would therefore consume less of it. Consequently, a tax that decreases beer consumption by 10% will decrease highway deaths among young adults by about 10% too.

To Make Personal and Managerial Decisions

On the personal level, we use economic analysis to decide how to spend our time, what career to pursue, and how to spend and save the money we earn. As workers, we use economic analysis to decide how to produce goods and services, how much to produce, and how much to charge for them. Let's use some economic analysis to look at a practical question confronting someone considering starting a business.

If the existing music stores in your city are profitable, and you have enough money to start your own music store, should you do it? If you enter this market, the competition among the stores for consumers will heat up, leading to lower prices for CDs. In addition, your costs may be higher than the costs of the stores that are already established. It would be sensible to enter the market only if you expect a small drop in price and a small difference in cost. Of course, there is the risk that the existing stores may try to protect their market shares by cutting prices and increasing their advertising. Indeed, entering what appears to be a lucrative market may turn out to be a financial disaster.

To Evaluate Public Policies

Although modern societies use markets to make most of the decisions concerning production and consumption, the government has several important roles in a market-based society. We can use economic analysis to determine how well the government performs its roles in the market economy. We can also explore the trade-offs associated with various public policies. Let's look at a practical question about public policy.

Like other innovations, prescription drugs are protected by patents, giving the developer the exclusive right to sell the drug for a fixed period of time. Once the patent expires, generic versions of a drug are marketed, causing prices to drop. Should drug patents be shorter? There are some trade-offs associated with shortening the patent. The good news is that a shorter patent means that generic versions of the drug will be available sooner, so prices will be lower. The bad news is that a shorter patent means the payoff from developing new drugs will be smaller, so drug companies won't develop as many new drugs. The question is whether the benefit of shorter patents (lower prices) exceeds the cost (fewer drugs developed).

Preview of Coming Attractions: Macroeconomics

Macroeconomics

The study of the nation's economy as a whole.

Macroeconomics is the study of the nation's economy as a whole. In macroeconomics we learn about important topics that are regularly discussed in newspapers and on television, including unemployment, inflation, the budget deficit, and the trade deficit. Macroeconomics explains why economies grow and change and why economic growth is sometimes interrupted. Let's look at three ways we can use macroeconomics:

To Understand Why Economies Grow

As we discussed earlier in the chapter, the world economy has been growing in recent decades, with per capita income increasing by about 1.5% per year. Increases in income translate into a higher standard of living for consumers—better cars, houses, and clothing, and more options for food, entertainment, and travel. People in a growing economy can consume more of all goods and services because the economy has more of the resources needed to produce these products. Macroeconomics explains why some of these resources increase over time and how an increase in these resources translates into a higher standard of living. Let's look at a practical question about economic growth:

Why do some countries grow much faster than others? In recent decades, the economic growth rate was 2.1% per year in the United States, compared to 2.4% in Mexico and 2.8% in France. But in some countries, the economy actually shrunk, and per capita income dropped. Among the countries with declining income were Romania, Sierra Leone, Haiti, and Zambia. In the fastest-growing countries, citizens save a large fraction of the money they earn. Firms can then borrow the funds saved to purchase machinery and equipment that make their workers more productive. The fastest-growing countries also have well-educated workforces, allowing firms to quickly adopt new technologies that increase worker productivity.

To Understand Economic Fluctuations

All economies, including ones that experience a general trend of growth, are subject to economic fluctuations, including periods when the economy shrinks. During an economic downturn, some of the economy's resources are idle. Many workers are unemployed, and many factories and stores are closed. By contrast, sometimes the economy grows too rapidly, causing inflation. Macroeconomics helps us understand why these fluctuations occur—why the economy sometimes cools and sometimes overheats—and what we can do to moderate the fluctuations. Let's look at a practical question about economic fluctuations.

Should Congress and the president do something to reduce the unemployment rate? If unemployment is very high, they may want to reduce it. However, it is important not to reduce the unemployment rate too much because, as we'll see later in the book, a low unemployment rate will cause inflation. Moreover, unemployment can't be reduced overnight. Therefore, it is sensible to take action only if we believe that inaction will cause persistent unemployment.

To Make Informed Business Decisions

A third reason for studying macroeconomics is to make informed business decisions. A manager who intends to borrow money for a new factory or store could use knowledge of macroeconomics to predict the effects of current public policies on interest rates and then decide whether to borrow the money now or later. Similarly, a manager must keep an eye on the inflation rate to help decide how much to charge for the firm's products and how much to pay workers. A manager who studies macroeconomics will be better equipped to understand the complexities of unemployment, interest rates, and inflation and how they affect the firm.

A CLOSER LOOK

"Dismal" Depends On Your Point of View

You may have heard economics called "the dismal science." Economic historian David Levy recently discovered that the label comes from the British essayist Thomas Carlyle,[9] who in 1849 wrote that economics was "dismal, dreary, and desolate" because it found "the secret of the universe in supply and demand." Just like economists today, economists in the nineteenth century argued that markets empower common people to make their own choices. In contrast, Carlyle believed that most people were incapable of making good choices for themselves and should rely on the advice of religious and civic leaders. Given Carlyle's discomfort with individual choice, it's not surprising that he was hostile to markets (supply and demand).

So what did Carlyle find so "dismal" about individual choice and markets? Carlyle wrote his essay "Occasional Discourse on the Negro Question" 16 years after the emancipation of black slaves in the West Indies. Emancipation extended market choices to former slaves, allowing them to voluntarily participate in markets and decide for themselves what to produce. They could continue to produce the export products they had produced as slaves—cinnamon, pepper, and other spices for British consumers—or they could instead produce food for themselves. They chose food over spices, much to the dismay of Carlyle. In Carlyle's mind, economics was dismal because the application of its fundamental ideas—individual choice and markets—didn't result in an outcome he preferred—cheap spices for British consumers.

SUMMARY

This chapter explains what economics is and why it is useful. Economics is about making choices when the options are limited. We can use economic analysis to understand the consequences of our choices, as individuals, organizations, and society as a whole. Here are the main points of the chapter.

1 Positive analysis answers the questions "What *is*?" or "What *will be*?"
2 Normative analysis answers the question "What *ought to be*?"

3 To think like an economist, we (a) use assumptions to simplify, (b) use the notion of *ceteris paribus* to focus on the relationship between two variables, and (c) think in marginal terms.
4 Rational people respond to incentives.
5 We use microeconomics to understand how markets work, make personal and managerial decisions, and evaluate the merits of public policies.
6 We use macroeconomics to understand why an economy grows, understand economic fluctuations, and make informed business decisions.

KEY TERMS

ceteris paribus, 10
economics, 3
macroeconomics, 14

marginal change, 10
microeconomics, 12
normative economics, 5

positive economics, 4
scarcity, 3
variable, 9

PROBLEMS AND DISCUSSION QUESTIONS

1 President Truman had a sign on his desk that read, "The Buck Stops Here." Is the philosophy behind this sign consistent with his complaint about two-handed economists?
2 "If I study one more hour for my economics exam, I expect my grade to increase by 3 points." List the variables that are assumed to be fixed in the statement.

3 It's your first day on your job in the advertising department of a baseball team. Your boss wants to know whether it is sensible to run one more television advertisement for an upcoming game. List the relevant marginal questions.

MODEL ANSWERS

Answers: Test Your Understanding

1 What products do we produce? How do we produce the products? Who consumes the products?
2 Economists discuss scarcity, alternatives, and trade-offs.
3 Positive analysis answers the questions "What *is*?" or "What *will be*?" Normative analysis answers the question "What *ought to be*?"

4 To think like an economist, we (a) use assumptions to simplify, (b) use the notion of *ceteris paribus* to focus on the relationship between two variables, and (c) think in marginal terms.
5 "If I attend one more lecture, by how much will my exam grade increase?"

NOTES

1. Dan Fuller, and Doris Geide-Stevenson, "Consensus Among Economists: Revisited," *Journal of Economic Education*, Fall 2003, pp. 369–387.
2. Texas Transportation Institute, *2002 Urban Mobility Study* (*http://mobility.tamu.edu/ums/*).
3. William Easterly, *The Elusive Quest for Growth* (Cambridge MA: MIT Press, 2001), Chapter 1.
4. William Easterly, *The Elusive Quest for Growth* (Cambridge MA: MIT Press, 2001).
5. World Bank, *World Development Report 2000/2001: Attacking Poverty* (New York: Oxford University Press, 2000).
6. Alfred Marshall, *Principles of Economics*, 9th ed., edited by C.W. Guillebaud (London: Macmillan, 1961 [first published in 1920]), p. 366.
7. Adam Smith, *An Inquiry into the Nature and Causes of the Wealth of Nations* (First published in 1776; New York, Random House, 1973), Book 2, Chapter 3.
8. Myles Faith et al., "Effects of Contingent Television on Physical Activity and Television Viewing in Obese Children," *Pediatrics* vol. 107, May 2001, pp. 1043–1048; *USA Today*, April 19, 1999, p. 1.
9. David Levy, *How the Dismal Science Got Its Name: Classical Economics and the Ur-Test of Racial Politics* (Ann Arbor, MI: University of Michigan Press, 2001); Thomas Carlyle, "Occasional Discourse on the Negro Question," *Fraser's Magazine for Town and Country*, 40 (1849), p. 672; Thomas Carlyle, *Past and Present*, edited by Richard D. Altick (Boston, MA: Houghton Mifflin, 1965), p. 211.

APPENDIX

Using Graphs and Formulas

In this appendix, we review the mechanics of graphing. You'll recognize most of the simple graphs and formulas in this appendix because they were covered in your high school mathematics. We'll review them here to prepare you to use them as you begin your own economic analysis.

Using Graphs to Show Relationships

A graph is a visual representation of the relationship between two variables. As we saw earlier in Chapter 1, a variable is a measure of something that can take on different values. For example, suppose that you have a part-time job and you are interested in the relationship between the number of hours you work and your weekly income. The relevant variables are the hours you work per week and your weekly income.

We can use a table of numbers such as Table 1A.1 to show the relationship between time worked and income. Let's assume that your weekly allowance from your parents is $40 and your part-time job pays $8 per hour. If you work 10 hours per week, for

TABLE 1A.1				
Hours worked per week	0	10	22	30
Income per week	$40	$120	$216	$280

TABLE 1A.1

Relationship Between
Work Time and Income

example, your weekly income is $120 ($40 from your parents and $80 from your job). The more you work, the higher your weekly income: If you work 22 hours, your weekly income is $216; if you work 30 hours, it is $280.

Drawing a Graph

A graph makes it easier to see the relationship between time worked and income. To draw a graph, we perform seven simple steps:

1 Draw a horizontal line to represent the first variable. In Figure 1A.1, we measure time worked along the horizontal axis (also known as the *x* axis). As we move to the right along the horizontal axis, the number of hours worked increases, from zero to 30 hours.
2 Draw a vertical line intersecting the first line to represent the second variable. In Figure 1A.1, we measure income along the vertical axis (also known as the *y* axis). As we move up along the vertical axis, income increases from zero to $280.
3 Pick a combination of time worked and income from the table of numbers. From the second column, for instance, time worked is 10 hours and income is $120.
4 Find the point on the horizontal axis with that number of hours worked—10 hours worked—and draw a dashed line vertically straight up from that point.
5 Find the point on the vertical axis with the income corresponding to those hours worked ($120) and draw a dashed line horizontally straight to the right from that point.
6 The intersection of the dashed lines shows the combination of those hours worked and the income for working those hours. Point *b* shows the combination of 10 hours worked and $120 income.
7 Repeat steps 3 through 6 for different combinations of work time and income from the table of numbers. Once you have a series of points on the graph (*b, c,* and *d*), you can connect them to draw a curve that shows the relationship between hours worked and income.

Positive relationship

A relationship in which an increase in the value of one variable increases the value of another variable.

Negative relationship

A relationship in which an increase in the value of one variable decreases the value of another variable.

There is a **positive relationship** between two variables if an increase in the value of one variable increases the value of the other variable. An increase in the time you work increases your income, so there is a positive relationship between the two variables. As you increase the time you work, you move upward along the curve shown in Figure 1A.1 to higher income levels.

There is a **negative relationship** between two variables if an increase in the value of one variable decreases the value of the other variable. For example, there is a negative relationship between the amount of time you work and your performance in

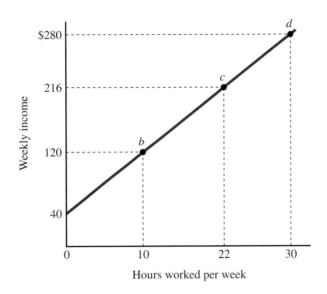

FIGURE 1A.1

Relationship Between Hours Worked and Total Income
There is a positive relationship between the amount of work time and income. The slope of the curve is $8: Each additional hour of work increases income by $8.

school. Some people refer to a positive relationship as a *direct* relationship and to a negative relationship as an *inverse* relationship.

Computing the Slope

How sensitive is one variable to changes in the other variable? We can use the slope of the curve to measure this sensitivity. The **slope of a curve** is the change in the variable on the vertical axis resulting from a one-unit increase in the variable on the horizontal axis. Once we pick two points on a curve, we can compute the slope as follows:

Slope of a curve

The change in the variable on the vertical axis resulting from a one-unit increase in the variable on the horizontal axis.

$$\text{slope} = \frac{\text{vertical difference between two points}}{\text{horizontal difference between two points}}$$

To compute the slope of a curve, we take four steps:

1 Pick two points on the curve: For example, points *b* and *c* in Figure 1A.1.
2 Compute the vertical distance between the two points (also known as the rise). For points *b* and *c*, the vertical distance between the points is $96 ($216 − $120).
3 Compute the horizontal distance between the same two points (also known as the run). For points *b* and *c*, the horizontal distance between the points is 12 hours (22 hours − 10 hours).
4 Divide the vertical distance by the horizontal distance to get the slope. The slope between points *b* and *c* is $8 per hour:

$$\text{slope} = \frac{\text{vertical difference}}{\text{horizontal difference}} = \frac{96}{12} = 8$$

In this case, a 12-hour increase in time worked increases income by $96, so the increase in income per hour of work is $8, which makes sense because this is the hourly wage.

Because the curve is a straight line, the slope is the same at all points along the curve. You can check this yourself by using the values between points *c* and *d* to calculate the slope.

Moving Along the Curve Versus Shifting the Curve

Up to this point, we've explored the effect of changes in variables that cause movement along a given curve. In Figure 1A.1, we see the relationship between a student's hours of work (on the horizontal axis) and her income (on the vertical axis). The student's income also depends on her allowance and her wage; so we can make two observations about the curve in Figure 1A.1:

1 To draw this curve, we must specify the weekly allowance ($40) and the hourly wage ($8).

2 The curve shows that an increase in time worked increases the student's income, *ceteris paribus.* In this case, we are assuming that her allowance and her wage are fixed.

A change in the student's weekly allowance will shift the curve showing the relationship between time worked and income. In Figure 1A.2, when the allowance increases from $40 to $70, the curve shifts upward by $30. For a given time worked, the student's income increases by $30. Now the income associated with 10 hours of work and the higher allowance is $150 (point *z*), compared to $120 with 10 hours of work and the original allowance (point *b*). In general, an increase in the allowance shifts the curve upward and leftward: For a given amount of time worked, the student will have more income (an upward shift as a result of the increased allowance). To reach a given amount of income, the student needs fewer hours of work (a leftward shift).

FIGURE 1A.2

Shifting the Curve
To draw a curve showing the relationship between hours worked and total income, we assume that the weekly allowance ($40) and the wage ($8) are fixed. An increase in the weekly allowance form $40 to $70 shifts the curve upward by $30: For each quantity of work hours, income is $30 higher.

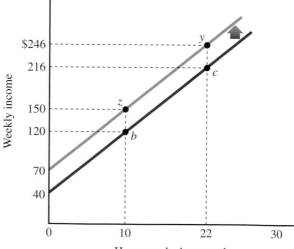

This book uses dozens of two-dimensional curves, each of which shows the relationship between only two variables. That is all a single curve can show. A common error is to forget that a single curve tells only part of the story. In Figure 1A.2, we needed two curves to show what happened when we looked at three variables (work time, allowance, and income). Here are some simple rules that will help us avoid this error:

▶ A change in one of the variables shown on the graph causes movement along the curve. In Figure 1A.2, an increase in work time causes movement along the curve from point *b* to point *c*.

▶ A change in one of the variables that is not shown on the graph (one of the variables held fixed in drawing the curve) shifts the entire curve. In Figure 1A.2, an increase in the allowance causes the entire curve to shift upward.

Negative and Nonlinear Relationships

We can use a graph to show a negative relationship between two variables. Consider a consumer who has a monthly budget of $300 to spend on CDs (at a price of $20 per CD) and cassette tapes (at a price of $10 per tape). Table 1A.2 shows the relationship between the number of CDs purchased and the number of tapes purchased. If the consumer buys 5 CDs in a certain month, he will spend a total of $100 on CDs, leaving $200 to spend on tapes. With the $200, he can buy 20 tapes at a price of $10 per tape. As the number of CDs increases, the number of tapes decreases, from 20 tapes and 5 CDs, to 10 tapes and 10 CDs, to zero tapes and 15 CDs.

Using the seven-step process outlined earlier, we can use the numbers in Table 1A.2 to draw a curve showing this negative relationship. In Figure 1A.3, the curve is negatively sloped: The more the consumer spends on CDs, the fewer tapes he can buy. We can use points *e* and *f* to compute the slope of the curve. The slope is −2 tapes per CD: A five-unit increase in CDs (the horizontal difference, or the run) decreases the number of tapes by 10 (the vertical difference, or the rise):

$$\text{slope} = \frac{\text{vertical difference}}{\text{horizontal difference}} = \frac{-10}{5} = -2$$

The curve is a straight line with a constant slope of −2 tapes per CD.

We can use a graph to show a nonlinear relationship between two variables. Panel A of Figure 1A.4 shows the relationship between study time and the exam grade that results from study time. Although the exam grade increases as study time increases, the grade increases at a decreasing rate; that means the increase in grade is smaller and

| Number of CDs purchased | 0 | 5 | 10 | 15 |
| Number of tapes purchased | 30 | 20 | 10 | 0 |

TABLE 1A.2

Relationship Between CDs and Tapes

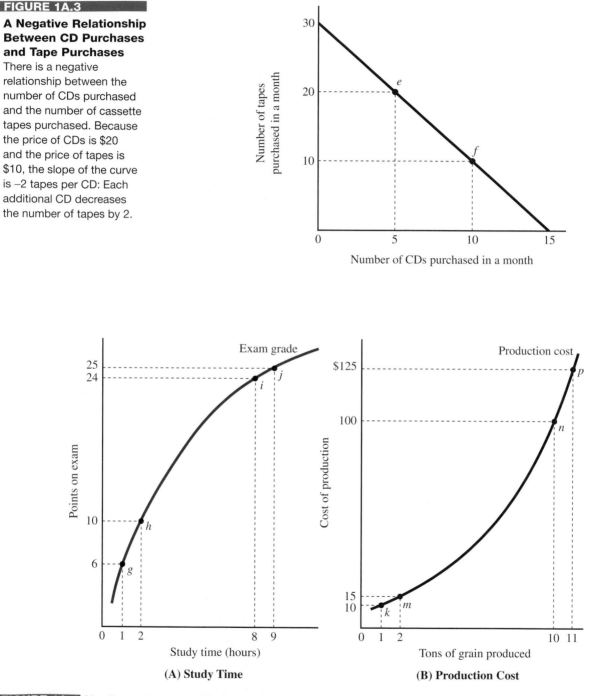

FIGURE 1A.3

A Negative Relationship Between CD Purchases and Tape Purchases
There is a negative relationship between the number of CDs purchased and the number of cassette tapes purchased. Because the price of CDs is $20 and the price of tapes is $10, the slope of the curve is –2 tapes per CD: Each additional CD decreases the number of tapes by 2.

(A) Study Time

(B) Production Cost

FIGURE 1A.4 **Nonlinear Relationships**

(A) Study time There is a positive and nonlinear relationship between study time and the grade on an exam. As study time increases, the exam grade increases at a decreasing rate. For example, the second hour of study increases the grade by 4 points (from 6 points to 10 points), but the ninth hour of study increases the grade by only 1 point (from 24 points to 25 points).

(B) Production cost There is a positive and nonlinear relationship between the quantity of grain produced and total production cost. As the quantity increases, total cost increases at an increasing rate. For example, to increase production from 1 ton to 2 tons, production cost increases by $5 (from $10 to $15), but to increase production from 10 to 11 tons, total cost increases by $25 (from $100 to $125).

smaller for each additional hour of study. For example, the second hour of study increases the grade by 4 points (from 6 points to 10 points), but the ninth hour of study increases the grade by only 1 point (from 24 points to 25 points). This is a non-linear relationship: The slope of the curve changes as we move along the curve. In Figure 1A.4, the slope decreases as we move to the right along the curve: The slope is 4 between points *g* and *h* but only 1 between points *i* and *j*.

Another possibility for a nonlinear curve is that the slope increases (the curve becomes steeper) as we move to the right along the curve. This is shown in Panel B of Figure 1A.4. The slope of the curve increases as the amount of grain increases, meaning that total production cost increases at an increasing rate. If the producer increases production from 2 tons to 3 tons, the total cost increases by $5 (from $10 to $15). On the upper portion of the curve, if the producer increases production from 10 to 11 tons, the total cost increases by $25 (from $100 to $125).

Using Formulas to Compute Values

Economists often use formulas to compute the values of the relevant variables. Here is a brief review of the mechanics of formulas.

Computing Percentage Changes

In many cases, the formulas that economists use involve percentage changes. In this book, we use the simple approach to computing percentage changes: We divide the change in the variable by the initial value of the variable and then multiply by 100. For example, if the price of pizzas increases from $20 to $22, the percentage change is 10%: The change ($2) divided by the initial value ($20) is 0.10; multiplying this number by 100 generates a percentage change of 10%:

$$\text{percentage change} = \frac{\text{absolute change}}{\text{initial value}} = \frac{2}{20} = 0.10 = 10\%$$

Going in the other direction, if the price decreases from $20 to $19, the percentage change is −5%: The change (−$1) divided by the initial value ($20) is −0.05, or −5%. The alternative to the simple approach is the midpoint approach, under which the percentage change equals the absolute change in the variable divided by the average value or the midpoint of the variable. For example, if the price of pizza increases from $20 to $22, the computed percentage change under the midpoint approach would be 9.52381%:

$$\text{percentage change} = \frac{\text{absolute change}}{\text{average value}} = \frac{2}{(20 + 22)/2}$$

$$= \frac{2}{21} = 0.0952381 = 9.52381\%$$

If the change in the variable is relatively small, the extra precision associated with the midpoint approach is usually not worth the extra effort. The simple approach allows us to spend less time doing tedious arithmetic and more time doing economic analysis. In this book, we use the simple approach to compute percentage changes: If the price increases from $20 to $22, the price has increased by 10%.

If we know a percentage change, we can translate it into an absolute change. For example, if a price has increased by 10% and the initial price is $20, then we add 10% of the initial price ($2 is 10% of $20) to the initial price ($20), for a new price of $22. If the price decreases by 5%, we subtract 5% of the initial price ($1 is 5% of $20) from the initial price ($20) for a new price of $19.

Using Formulas to Compute Missing Values

It will often be useful to compute the value of the numerator or the denominator of a formula. To do so, we use simple algebra to rearrange the formula to put the missing variable on the left side of the equation. For example, consider the relationship between time worked and income. The formula for the slope is

$$\text{slope} = \frac{\text{difference in income}}{\text{difference in work time}}$$

If we're interested in how much more income you'll earn from more work hours, we rearrange the formula by multiplying both sides of the equation by the difference in work time:

$$\text{slope} \times \text{difference in work} = \text{difference in income}$$

Then swapping sides, we get

$$\text{difference in income} = \text{slope} \times \text{difference in work time}$$

For example, if the slope is $8 and you work seven extra hours, your increase in income will be $56, computed as $8 per hour times seven hours.

We can use the same process to compute the difference in work time required to achieve a target change in income. In this case, we multiply both sides of the slope formula by the difference in work time and then divide both sides by the slope. The result is

$$\text{difference in work time} = \frac{\text{difference in income}}{\text{slope}}$$

For example, to achieve a target of $56 more income, you need to work seven hours, computed as $56/$8 per hour.

KEY TERMS

Negative relationship 18   Positive relationship 18   Slope of a curve 19

PROBLEMS AND DISCUSSION QUESTIONS

1 Suppose you belong to a tennis club that has a monthly fee of $100 and a charge of $5 per hour for court time to play tennis.

   a. Use a curve to show the relationship between the monthly bill from the club and the hours of tennis played.

   b. What is the slope of the curve?

   c. If you increase your monthly tennis time by three hours, by how much will your monthly bill increase?

2 Suppose that to make pizza, Terry uses three ingredients: tomato sauce, dough, and cheese. Terry initially uses 100 gallons of tomato sauce per day, and the cost of the other ingredients (dough, cheese) is $500 per day.

   a. Draw a curve to show the relationship between the price of tomato sauce and the daily cost of producing pizza (for prices between $1 and $5).

   b. To draw the curve, what variables are assumed to be fixed?

   c. What sort of changes would cause movement upward along the curve?

   d. What is the slope of the curve?

   e. What sort of changes would cause the entire curve to shift upward?

3 Compute the percentage changes for the following changes:

Initial Value	New Value	Percentage Change
10	11	_____
100	98	_____
50	53	_____

4 The price of jeans decreases by 15%. If the original price was $20, what is the new price?

5 Suppose the slope of a curve showing the relationship between the number of burglaries per month (on the vertical axis) and the number of police officers (on the horizontal axis) is −0.5 burglaries per police officer. Use the slope formula to compute the change in the number of burglaries resulting from hiring eight additional police officers.

6 Complete the statement: A change in one of the variables shown on a graph causes movement _____ a curve, while a change in one of the variables that is not shown on the graph _____ the curve.

The Principle of Opportunity Cost

Opportunity Cost and the Production
    Possibilities Curve
Using the Principle: Military Spending,
    Collectibles
Using the Principle: The Cost of College

The Marginal Principle

Example: How Many Movie Sequels?
Using the Marginal Principle: Renting
    College Facilities, Emissions Standards

The Principle of Voluntary Exchange

Exchange and Markets

The Principle of Diminishing Returns

The Real–Nominal Principle

Using the Principle: Government
    Programs, Statistics, and Repaying
    College Loans
Using the Tools

The Key Principles of Economics

our student film society is looking for an auditorium to use for an all-day Hitchcock film program and is willing to pay up to $200 for one. Your college has a new auditorium that would be perfect for your event. However, according to the campus facility manager, "The daily rent on the auditorium is $450, an amount that includes $300 to help pay for the cost of building the auditorium, $50 to help pay for insurance, and $100 to cover the extra costs of electricity and janitorial services for a one-day event."

How should you respond to the facility manager? As we'll see, if you could persuade the manager to use the marginal principle—one of the five key principles of economics—you should be able to get the facility for an amount between $100 and $200.

In this chapter, we introduce five key principles that provide a foundation for economic analysis. A principle is a self-evident truth that most people readily understand and accept. For example, most people readily accept the principle of gravity. As you read through the book, you will see the five key principles of economics again and again as you do your own economic analysis. Here are some practical questions we answer in this chapter using those principles:

1 What do military goods such as bombs and warships really cost in terms of what we sacrifice to pay for them?
2 When is it sensible to tighten the emissions standards on cars in order to reduce pollution? Does it ever make sense to loosen emissions standards?
3 After a market transaction is completed, both people—buyer and seller—usually say, "Thank you." Are they just being polite, or is there a reason to be thankful?
4 If a firm doubles its workforce, is the company's total output likely to double too?
5 If you graduate with $20,000 in student loans, which type of an economy would make it easier for you to repay them: one with steady prices, one with rising prices (inflation), or one with falling prices (deflation)?

The Principle of Opportunity Cost

Opportunity cost

What you sacrifice to get something.

The principle of **opportunity cost** incorporates the notion of scarcity: No matter what we do, there is always a trade-off. We must trade off one thing for another because resources are limited and can be used in different ways. By acquiring something, we use up resources that could have been used to acquire something else. The notion of opportunity cost allows us to measure this trade-off.

Principle OF OPPORTUNITY COST

The opportunity cost of something is what you sacrifice to get it.

Most decisions involve several alternatives. For example, if you spend an hour studying for an economics exam, you have one less hour to pursue other activities. To determine the opportunity cost of something, we look at what you consider the best of these "other" activities. For example, suppose the alternatives to studying economics are studying for a history exam and working in a job that pays $10 per hour. If you consider studying for history a better use of your time than working, then the opportunity cost of studying economics is what you sacrifice by not studying history. We ignore the work option because that is not the best alternative use of your time.

How can we measure the opportunity cost of an hour spent studying for an economics exam? Suppose an hour of studying history—instead of economics—would increase your grade on a history exam by four points. In this case the opportunity cost of an hour studying economics is four points lost on the history exam. On the other hand, if the best alternative to studying economics were working, then the opportunity cost would be the $10 your could earn in your job.

The principle of opportunity cost can also be applied to decisions about how to spend money on a fixed budget. For example, suppose that you have a fixed budget to spend on music. You can either buy your music at a local music store for $15 per CD or you can buy your music online for $1 per song. The opportunity cost of one CD is 15 one-dollar online songs. A hospital with a fixed salary budget can increase the number of doctors only at the expense of nurses or physician's assistants. If a doctor costs five times as much as a nurse, the opportunity cost of a doctor is five nurses.

In some cases, a product that appears to be free actually has a cost. That's why economists are fond of saying, "There's no such thing as a free lunch." Suppose someone offers to buy you lunch if you agree to listen to a sales pitch for a time-share condominium. Although you don't pay any money for the lunch, there is an opportunity cost because you could spend that time in another way. The lunch isn't free because you sacrifice an hour of your time to get it.

Opportunity Cost and the Production Possibilities Curve

Just as individual people face limits, so do entire economies. The production possibilities curve shown in Figure 2.1 illustrates the principle of opportunity cost for an entire economy. The ability of an economy to produce goods and services is determined by its **factors of production**, including labor, land, and capital (machines and buildings). Figure 2.1 shows a production possibilities graph for an economy that produces products on farms (wheat, barley, beef) and factory products (cars, computers, boats, steel, lamps,

FIGURE 2.1

Scarcity and the Production Possibilities Curve

The production possibilities curve illustrates the principle of opportunity cost for an entire economy. An economy has a fixed amount of resources. If they are fully employed, an increase in the production of farm goods comes at the expense of factory goods.

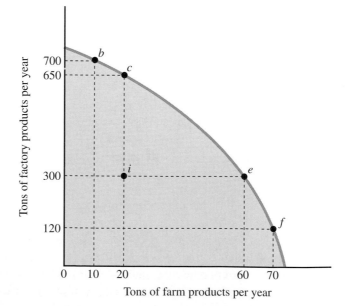

desks). The horizontal axis shows the quantity of farm products produced by the economy, and the vertical axis shows the quantity of factory products produced. The shaded area shows all the possible combinations of the two goods that can be produced. At point *b* for example, the economy can produce 700 tons of factory products and 10 tons of farm products. By contrast, at point *i*, the economy can produce 300 tons of factory goods and 20 tons of farm products. The set of points on the border between the shaded and unshaded area is called the **production possibilities curve** (or *production possibilities frontier*) because it separates the combinations that are attainable (the shaded area within the curve and the curve itself) from the combinations that are not attainable (the unshaded area outside the curve). The points on the curve show the combinations that are possible if the economy's resources are fully employed or "maxed" out.

The production possibilities curve illustrates the notion of opportunity cost. If an economy is fully utilizing its resources, it can produce more of one product only if it produces less of another product. So, to produce more farm goods, we must take resources away from factories. As we move resources out of factory production, the quantity of factory goods will decrease. For example, if we move from point *b* to point *c* along the production possibilities curve in Figure 2.1, we sacrifice 50 tons of factory goods (700 tons − 650 tons) to get 10 more tons of farm goods (20 tons – 10 tons). Further down the curve, if we move from point *e* to point *f*, we sacrifice 180 tons of factory goods to get the same 10-ton increase in farm goods.

Why is the production possibilities curve bowed outwards, with the opportunity cost farm goods increasing as we move down the curve? The reason is that resources are not perfectly adaptable for the production of both goods. Some resources are more suitable for factory production, whereas others are more suitable for farming. Starting at point *b*, the economy uses its most fertile land to produce farm goods. A 10-ton increase in farm goods reduces the quantity of factory goods by only 50 tons because plenty of fertile land is available for conversion to farming. As the economy moves downward along the production possibilities curve, farmers will be forced to use land that is progressively less fertile, so to increase farm output by 10 tons, more and more resources must be diverted from factory production. In the move from point *e* to point *f*, the land converted to farming is so poor that increasing farm output by 10 tons decreases factory output by 180 tons.

The production possibilities curve shows the production options for a given set of resources. As shown in Figure 2.2, an increase in the amount of resources available to the economy shifts the production possibilities outward. For example, if we start at point *d* and the economy's resources increase, we can produce more factory goods (point *g*), more farm goods (point *h*), or more of both goods (points between *g* and *h*). The curve will also shift outward as a result of technological innovations that allow us to produce more output with a given quantity of resources.

Using the Principle: Military Spending, Collectibles

We can also use the principle of opportunity cost to explore the cost of military spending. In 1992, Malaysia bought two warships. For the price of the warships, the country instead could have provided safe drinking water for five million citizens who lacked it.[1] In other words, the opportunity cost of the warships was safe drinking water for five million

Production possibilities curve

A curve that shows the possible combinations of products that an economy can produce, given that its productive resources are fully employed and efficiently used.

FIGURE 2.2

Shifting the Production Possibilities Curve

An increase in the quantity of resources in an economy shifts the production possibilities curve outward. Starting from point *d*, a nation could produce more agricultural goods (point *h*), more manufacturing goods (point *g*), or more of both goods (points between *g* and *h*).

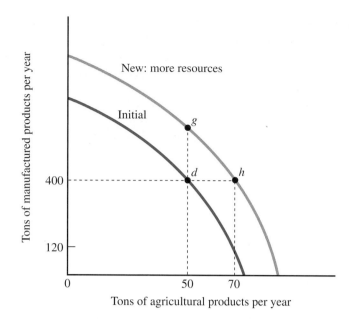

people. Likewise, in the United States, the opportunity cost of warships could be spent on housing programs for the homeless, or vice versa. For another interesting illustration of the trade-offs opportunity costs present, read "A Closer Look: Swords vs. Ecotels?"

What is the cost of buying a collectible good such as a baseball card, an antique Barbie doll, a Beanie Baby, or a work of art? Suppose you buy an antique Barbie doll for $1,000, intending to resell it for more money a year later. If the price doesn't change and you resell it for $1,000, does that mean that owning the doll for a year didn't cost you anything? Applying the principle of opportunity cost, you could have invested the $1,000 in a bank account earning 5% interest, so the cost of having the Barbie doll is the $50 you could have earned in a bank account during the year.

Using the Principle: The Cost of College

What is the opportunity cost of a college degree? Consider a student who spends a total of $40,000 for tuition and books. Instead of going to college, the student could have spent this money on a wide variety of goods, including housing, stereo equipment, and world

For Malaysia, the opportunity cost of a single battleship is safe drinking water for 2.5 million people.

travel. Part of the opportunity cost of college is the $40,000 worth of other goods the student sacrifices to pay for tuition and books. Also, instead of going to college, the student could have worked as a bank clerk for $20,000 per year and earned $80,000 over four years. That makes the total opportunity cost of this student's college degree $120,000:

Opportunity cost of money spent on tuition and books	$ 40,000
Opportunity cost of college time (four years at $20,000 per year)	80,000
Economic cost or total opportunity cost	$120,000

We haven't included the costs of food or housing in our computations of opportunity cost. That's because a student must eat and live somewhere even if he or she doesn't go to college. But if housing and food are more expensive in college, then we would include the extra costs of housing and food in our calculations.

There are other things to consider in a person's decision to attend college. As we'll see later, a college degree can increase a person's earning power, so there are benefits from a college degree. In addition, there is the thrill of learning and the pleasure of meeting new people. To make an informed decision about whether to attend college, we must compare the benefits to the opportunity costs.

A CLOSER LOOK   Swords vs. Ecotels?

The prophet Isaiah predicted, "They will beat their swords into plowshares, and their spears into pruning hooks." This quote illustrates the opportunity cost of military equipment: The opportunity cost of a sword is a plowshare; the opportunity cost of a spear is a pruning hook.

All over Central America, old military facilities are being transformed to give ecotourists a close look at the region's flora and fauna. In the middle of Panama's rain forest, a radar tower used earlier by the U.S. military has been transformed into a seven-room ecolodge, giving tourists from around the world the opportunity to watch king vultures soar above the forest and view howler monkeys swing from the trees.[2] *Audubon* magazine selected the tower, now called Canopy Tower, as one of the world's nine "ultimate outposts" for bird lovers.

On the Atlantic side of Panama, the infamous School of the Americas—where the U.S. military once educated Latin America military dictators in the arts of war—has been con-

The conversion of old military facilities into wildlife viewing sites like the Canopy Tower in Panama illustrates the notion of opportunity cost.

verted into a 310-room hotel. Its concrete amphitheater that once hosted military briefings is now being used as a vantage point for tourists viewing monkeys and tropical birds.

The Marginal Principle

The marginal principle provides a simple decision-making rule that helps individuals and organizations make decisions. Economists think in marginal terms, considering how a one-unit change in one variable affects the value of another variable and people's decisions. When we say *marginal*, we're looking at the effect of only a small, or incremental, change.

The marginal principle is based on a comparison of the marginal benefits and marginal costs of a particular activity. The **marginal benefit** of some activity is the extra benefit resulting from a small increase in the activity; for example, the extra revenue generated by keeping a barbershop open for one more hour. Similarly, the **marginal cost** is the additional cost resulting from a small increase in the activity; for example, the additional expense incurred by keeping the barbershop open for one more hour. Applying the marginal principle to the barber's problem, the barber should stay open for one more hour if the extra revenue from the additional hour is at least as large as the extra cost. In other words, people have an incentive to perform an activity if it provides them a marginal benefit over and above their marginal cost. When deciding whether to engage in an activity or how much to do, people should follow the marginal principle.

Marginal benefit

The extra benefit resulting from a small increase in some activity.

Marginal cost

The additional cost resulting from a small increase in some activity.

MARGINAL *Principle*

Increase the level of an activity if its marginal benefit exceeds its marginal cost; reduce the level of an activity if its marginal cost exceeds its marginal benefit. If possible, pick the level at which the activity's marginal benefit equals its marginal cost.

Thinking at the margin enables us to fine-tune our decisions. We can use the marginal principle to determine whether a one-unit increase in a variable would make us better off. Just as a barber could decide whether to keep the shop open for one more hour, you could decide whether to study one more hour for a psychology midterm. When we reach the level where the marginal benefit equals the marginal cost, the fine-tuning is done.

Example: How Many Movie Sequels?

To illustrate the marginal principle, let's consider movie sequels. When a movie is successful, its producer naturally thinks about doing another movie, continuing the story line with the same set of characters. If the first sequel is successful too, the producer thinks about producing a second sequel, then a third, and so on. We can use the marginal principle to explore the decision of how many movies to produce.

Table 2.1 shows the marginal benefits and marginal costs for movies. On the benefit side, a movie sequel typically generates about 30% less revenue than the original

Number of Movies	Marginal Benefit	Marginal Cost
1	$300 million	$125 million
2	$210 million	$150 million
3	$135 million	$175 million

TABLE 2.1
Marginal Benefits and Marginal Costs of Movie Sequels

movie, and revenue continues to drop for additional movies. In the second column of Table 2.1, the first movie generates $300 million in revenue (point *b*), the second generates $210 million, and the third generates $135 million. This is shown in Figure 2.3 as a negatively sloped marginal-benefit curve. In the United States, the typical movie costs about $50 million to produce and about $75 million to promote.[3] In the third column of Table 2.1, the cost of the first movie (the original) is $125 million. The marginal cost increases with the number of movies because film stars typically demand higher salaries to appear in sequels. For example, Angelina Jolie was paid more for *Tomb Raider 2* than for *Tomb Raider*, and the actors in *Charlie's Angels 2* received raises too. In Table 2.1, the marginal cost increases to $150 million for the second movie and to $175 for the third. This is shown in Figure 2.3 as a positively sloped marginal-cost curve.

In this example, the first two movies are profitable, but the third is not. For the original movie, the marginal benefit ($300 million) exceeds the marginal cost ($125 million), generating a profit of $175 million. Although the second movie has a higher cost and a lower benefit, it is profitable because the marginal benefit still exceeds the marginal cost, so the profit on the second movie is $60 million ($210 million − $150 million). In contrast, the marginal cost of the third movie of $175 million exceeds its marginal benefit of only $135 million, so the third movie is a losing proposition. In this example, the movie producer should stop after the second movie.

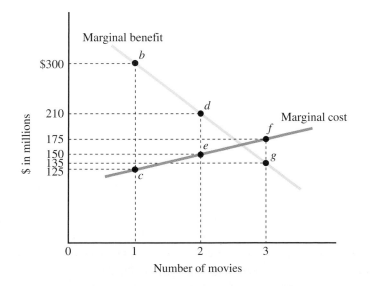

FIGURE 2.3
The Marginal Principle and Movie Sequels
The marginal benefit of movies in a series decreases because revenue falls off with each additional movie, whereas the marginal cost increases because actors demand higher salaries. The marginal benefit exceeds the marginal cost for the first two movies, so it is sensible to produce two, but not three, movies.

Although this example shows that only two movies are profitable, other outcomes are possible. If the revenue for the third movie were larger, making the marginal benefit greater than the marginal cost, it would be sensible to produce the third movie. Similarly, if the marginal cost of the third movie were lower—if the actors didn't demand such high salaries—the third movie could be profitable. Indeed, there are many examples of movies with multiple sequels. Conversely, there are many examples of profitable movies that didn't result in any sequels. In these cases, the expected drop off in revenues and the run-up in costs for the second movie were large enough to make a sequel unprofitable.

Using the Marginal Principle: Renting College Facilities, Emissions Standards

Recall the chapter opener about renting a college auditorium to your student film society. Suppose the society offers to pay $150 for using the auditorium? Should the college accept the offer? The college could use the marginal principle to make the decision.

To decide whether to accept the group's offer, the college should determine the marginal cost of renting out the auditorium. The marginal cost equals the extra costs the college incurs by allowing the student group to use an otherwise vacant auditorium. In our example, the extra cost is $100 for additional electricity and janitorial services. It would be sensible for the college to rent the auditorium because the marginal benefit ($150 offered by the student group) exceeds the marginal cost ($100). In fact, the college should be willing to rent the facility for any amount greater than $100. If the students and the college's facility manager split the difference between the $200 the students are willing to pay and the $100 marginal cost, they would agree on a price of $150, leaving both parties better off by $50.

Most colleges do not use this sort of logic. Instead, they use complex formulas to compute the perceived cost of renting out a facility. In most cases, the perceived cost includes some costs that are unaffected by renting out the facility for the day. In our example, the facility manager included $300 worth of construction costs and $50 worth of insurance, for a total cost of $450 instead of just $100. Because many colleges include costs that aren't affected by the use of a facility, they overestimate the actual cost of renting out their facilities, missing opportunities to serve student groups and make some money at the same time.

We can use the marginal principle to analyze emissions standards for automobiles. The U.S. government specifies how much carbon monoxide a new car is allowed to emit per mile. The marginal question is: "Should the standard be stricter, with fewer units of carbon monoxide allowed?" On the benefit side, a stricter standard reduces health care costs resulting from pollution: If the air is cleaner, people with respiratory ailments will make fewer visits to doctors and hospitals, have lower medication costs, and lose fewer work days. On the cost side, a stricter standard requires more expensive control equipment on cars and may also reduce fuel efficiency. Using the marginal principle, the government should make the emissions standard stricter as long as the marginal benefit (savings in health care costs and work time lost) exceeds the marginal cost (the cost of additional equipment and extra fuel used).

Marginal Airlines Lives Up to Its Name

Marginal Airlines runs 10 flights per day at a total cost of $40,000, or an average of $4,000 per flight. On the tenth flight, there are only 20 passengers on the 40-seat aircraft. Each passenger pays $150, so the revenue from the tenth flight is only $3,000. Although the tenth flight doesn't seem to generate enough revenue to cover its costs, the company continues to run the flight. The managers of the airline are neither stupid nor irrational. Solve this puzzle: Why does the airline continue to run the flight?

The key to solving the puzzle is in the airline's name: Marginal Airlines bases its decision about running the tenth flight on the marginal benefit and marginal cost of the flight. The marginal benefit is the $3,000 in revenue from passengers. Although the average cost is $4,000 per flight, what matters is the *marginal* cost of the tenth flight. If the marginal cost of the tenth flight is only $2,000, the marginal benefit exceeds the marginal cost, and the airline can make $1,000 (equal to $3,000 − $2,000) by running the flight.

This example is based on the actual experience of Continental Airlines, which in the 1960s used the marginal principle to increase its profits.[4] At the time, the average cost of a flight was about $4,000, half of which involved fixed costs such as airport fees and the cost of running the reservation system. The other half of the average cost involved costs that varied with the number of flights, including the cost of a flight crew, jet fuel, and that wonderful airline food. These other costs added up to $2,000 per flight. In other words, the marginal cost of a flight was only $2,000, so running a flight that generated $3,000 in revenue was sensible. Using the marginal principle, Continental ran flights with up to half the seats empty, making money in the process. ■

TEST Your Understanding

1. True or false: The cost of a master's degree in engineering equals tuition plus the cost of books.
2. Explain the logic behind the economist's quip, "There is no such thing as a free lunch."
3. If a bus company adds a third daily bus between two cities, the company's total costs will increase from $500 to $600 per day and its total revenue will increase by $150 per day. Should the company add the third bus?
4. If a company decides to replace a double-bladed razor with a triple-bladed razor, what does this mean about how much consumers are willing to pay for razors?

The Principle of Voluntary Exchange

The principle of voluntary exchange is based on the notion that people act in their own self-interest.

Principle OF VOLUNTARY EXCHANGE

A voluntary exchange between two people makes both people better off.

Self-interested people won't exchange one thing for another unless the trade makes them better off. Here are some examples.

▶ If you voluntarily exchange money for a college education, you must expect you'll be better off with a college education. The college voluntarily provides a college education in exchange for your money, so the college must be better off too.

▶ If you have a job, you voluntarily exchange your time for money, and your employer exchanges money for your labor services. Both you and your employer are better off as a result.

Exchange and Markets

Adam Smith stressed the importance of voluntary exchange as a distinctly human trait.[5] He noticed

> a propensity in human nature . . . to truck, barter, and exchange one thing for another. . . . It is common to all men, and to be found in no other . . . animals. . . . Nobody ever saw a dog make a fair and deliberate exchange of one bone for another with another dog.

Market

An arrangement that allows people to exchange things.

A **market** is an arrangement that allows people to exchange things. If participation in a market is voluntary, both buyer and seller must be better off as a result of a transaction. The next time you see a market transaction, listen to what people say after money changes hands. If both people say "Thank you," that's the principle of voluntary exchange in action: the double thank-you reveals that both people are better off.

The next chapter of the book explains the rationale for voluntary exchange. The alternative to exchange is self-sufficiency: Each of us could produce everything for ourselves. As we'll see in the next chapter, it is more sensible to specialize, doing what we do best and then buy products from other people, who in turn are doing what they do best. For example, if you are good with numbers but an awful carpenter, you could specialize in accounting and buy furniture from Woody, who could specialize in furniture and pay someone to do his bookkeeping. In general, exchange allows us to take advantage of differences in people's talents and skills.

The exchange principle tells us that both buyer and seller are made better off by an exchange. But under what circumstances can we infer that a market exchange makes society as a whole better off? If the exchange doesn't affect anyone else, then clearly the two market participants are better off and society as a whole is better off too. If, however, another person—a third party—is affected by the transaction, we can't be sure that the transaction makes society as a whole better off. Later in the book, we will explore what happens when a third party is either helped or harmed by a transaction. If these third parties are integrated into the exchange process as voluntary participants, the exchange principle will be relevant: A set of voluntary transactions will make all the participants better off.

The Principle of Diminishing Returns

Xena has a small copy shop, with one copying machine and one worker. When the backlog of orders piled up, she decided to hire a second worker, expecting that doubling her workforce would double the output of her copy shop from 500 pages per hour to 1,000. She was surprised when output increased to only 800 pages per hour. If she had known about the principle of diminishing returns, she would not have been surprised.

Principle OF DIMINISHING RETURNS

Suppose output is produced with two or more inputs and we increase one input while holding the other input or inputs fixed. Beyond some point—called the point of diminishing returns—output will increase at a decreasing rate.

Xena added a worker (one input) while holding the number of copying machines (the other input) fixed. Because the two workers shared a single copying machine, each worker spent some time waiting for the machine to be available. As a result, adding the second worker increased the number of copies, but did not double the output. With a single worker and a single copy machine, Xena has reached the point of diminishing returns: That is, as she increases the number of workers, output increases, but at a decreasing rate. The first worker increases output by 500 pages (from 0 to 500), but the second worker increases output by only 300 pages (from 500 to 800).

This principle of diminishing returns is relevant when we try to produce more output in an existing production facility (a factory, a store, an office, or a farm) by increasing the number of workers sharing the facility. When we add a worker to the facility, each worker becomes less productive because he or she works with a smaller piece of the facility: There are more workers to share the machinery, equipment, and factory space. As we pack more and more workers into the factory, total output increases, but at a decreasing rate.

It's important to emphasize that diminishing returns occurs because one of the inputs to the production process is fixed. When a firm can vary all of its inputs, including the size of the production facility, the principle of diminishing returns is not relevant. For example, if a firm doubled all of its inputs, building a second factory and hiring a second workforce, we would expect the total output of the firm to at least double. The principle of diminishing returns does not apply when a firm is flexible in choosing all its inputs.

TEST Your Understanding

5. True or false: When two people involved in a market exchange say "Thank you" afterwards, they are merely being polite.

(continued)

6. When a table producer hired its tenth worker, the output of its factory increased by five tables per month. Would you expect the same increase in output for the twentieth worker and the thirtieth worker?

7. True or false: According to the principle of diminishing returns, an additional worker decreases total output.

The Real–Nominal Principle

One of the key ideas in economics is that people are interested not just in the amount of money they have but also in how much their money will buy.

REAL–NOMINAL *Principle*

What matters to people is the real value of money or income— its purchasing power—not the "face" value of money or income.

To illustrate this principle, suppose you work in your college bookstore to earn extra money for movies and newspapers. If your take-home pay is $10 per hour, is this a high wage or a low wage? The answer depends on the prices of the goods you buy. If a movie costs $4 and a newspaper costs $1, with one hour of work you could afford to see two movies and buy two papers. The wage may seem high enough for you. But if a movie costs $8 and a newspaper costs $2, an hour of work would buy only one movie and one paper, and the same $10 wage doesn't seem so high. This is the real–nominal principle in action: What matters is not how many dollars you earn, but what those dollars will purchase.

The real–nominal principle can explain how people choose the amount of money to carry around with them. Suppose you typically withdraw $40 per week from an ATM to cover your normal expenses. If the prices of all the goods you purchase during the week double, you would have to withdraw $80 per week to make the same purchases. The amount of money people carry around depends on the prices of the goods and services they buy.

Economists use special terms to express the ideas behind the real–nominal principle:

Nominal value

The face value of an amount of money.

Real value

The value of an amount of money in terms of what it can buy.

▶ The **nominal value** of an amount of money is simply its face value. For example, the nominal wage paid by the bookstore is $10 per hour.

▶ The **real value** of an amount of money is measured in terms of the quantity of goods the money can buy. For example, the real value of your bookstore wage would fall as the prices of movies and newspapers increase, even though your nominal wage stayed the same.

Economic Experiment

Producing Fold-its

Here is a simple economic experiment that takes about 15 minutes to run. The instructor places a stapler and a stack of paper on a table. Students produce "fold-its" by folding a page of paper in thirds and stapling both ends of the folded page. One student is assigned to inspect each fold-it to be sure that it is produced correctly. The experiment starts with a single student, or worker, who has one minute to produce as many fold-its as possible. After the instructor records the number of fold-its produced, the process is repeated with two students, three students, four students, and so on. The question is, "How does the number of fold-its change as the number of workers increases?" ●

Using the Principle: Government Programs, Statistics, and Repaying College Loans

Government officials use the real–nominal principle when they design public programs. For example, Social Security payments are increased each year to ensure that the checks received by the elderly and other recipients will purchase the same amount of goods and services, even if prices have increased.

The government also uses this principle when it publishes statistics about the economy. For example, when the government issues reports about changes in "real wages" in the economy over time, these statistics take into account the prices of the goods purchased by workers. Therefore, the real wage is stated in terms of its buying power, rather than its face value or nominal value.

For another application of the principle, recall the chapter-opening question about repaying college loans. Suppose you finish college this year with $20,000 in student loans payable in 10 years and start a job that pays $40,000 in the first year. If all prices in the economy are stable—including the price of labor (yours, too)—the real cost of repaying your loans is the half-year of work you must do to earn the $20,000. However, if prices and wages increase over the 10-year period, doubling your nominal wage to $80,000, it will take you only a quarter of a year to earn the $20,000. A general increase in prices lowers the real cost of your loan. If on the other hand, prices and wages decrease, dropping your annual salary to $20,000, it will take you a full year to earn the money to repay the loan. In other words, a general decrease in prices increases the real cost of your loan.

TEST Your Understanding

8. Average hourly earnings in the United States increased between 1970 and 1993, but real hourly earnings fell. How could this occur?   (*continued*)

9. Suppose your wage doubles and so do the prices of all consumer goods. Are you better off, worse off, or just as well off?

10. Suppose your savings account pays 4% per year: Each $100 in the bank grows to $104 over a one-year period. If prices increase by 3% per year, how much do you really gain by keeping $100 in the bank for a year?

USING THE TOOLS

We've explained the five key principles of economics, which provide the foundation of economic analysis. Here are some opportunities to use the principles to do your own economic analysis.

1. The Cost of an Army

Your job is to estimate the economic cost of maintaining an army for one year. There are 50 soldiers, who are picked at random from the population and forced to serve. Each soldier is paid $1,000 per year. The cost of supplies and equipment is $10,000 per year, and the military occupies a base that could be rented to the private sector for $30,000 per year. According to an economist, "The economic cost of the army is $1,040,000." Explain the logic behind the economist's calculation.

2. How Many Police Officers?

As the mayor of a city where the only crime is burglary, you must decide how many police officers to hire. The cost of each police officer (for salary, benefits, and general support) is $40,000 per year. Each burglary involves the loss of $5,000 worth of possessions. The first officer hired will reduce crime by 40 burglaries, and each additional officer will reduce crime by half as much as the previous one. How many officers should the city hire? Illustrate your answer with a completely labeled graph.

3. Tiger Woods as Weed Whacker

The swinging skills that make Tiger Woods one of the world's best golfers also make him a skillful weed whacker. If he can knock down weeds faster than the best gardener in town, should he take care of his own weeds? Explain.

4. Cost of Living in Different Cities

Suppose you are currently living and working in Cleveland, Ohio, earning a salary of $60,000 per year. Your boss has decided to transfer you to a California city where the housing is 50% more expensive. If your annual housing cost is $10,000 in Cleveland, how much higher must your salary be in California to generate the same real income?

SUMMARY

This chapter covers five key principles of economics, the simple, self-evident truths that most people readily accept. If you understand these principles, you are ready to read the rest of the book, which will show you how to do your own economic analysis. In fact, if you've done the exercises in this chapter, you're already doing economic analysis.

1 Principle of opportunity cost. The opportunity cost of something is what you sacrifice to get it.

2 Marginal principle. Increase the level of an activity if its marginal benefit exceeds its marginal cost; reduce the level if its marginal cost exceeds its marginal benefit. If possible, pick the level at which the marginal benefit equals the marginal cost.

3 Principle of voluntary exchange: A voluntary exchange between two people makes both people better off.

4 Principle of diminishing returns. Suppose that output is produced with two or more inputs and that we increase one input while holding the other inputs fixed. Beyond some point—called the *point of diminishing returns*—output will increase at a decreasing rate.

5 Real–nominal principle. What matters to people is the real value of money or income—its purchasing power—not the face value of money or income.

KEY TERMS

factors of production, 28
marginal benefit, 32
marginal cost, 32

market, 36
nominal value, 38
opportunity cost, 27

production possibilities curve, 29
real value, 38

PROBLEMS AND DISCUSSION QUESTIONS

1 Consider the following statements about costs. Are they correct? If not, provide a correct statement about the relevant cost.
  a. One year ago, I loaned $100 to a friend, and she just paid me back the whole $100. The loan didn't cost me anything.
  b. Our sawmill bought five truckloads of logs a year ago for $20,000. Today, we'll use the logs to make picnic tables. The cost of using the logs is $20,000.
  c. Our new football stadium was built on land that a wealthy alum donated to our university. The university didn't have to buy the land, so the cost of the stadium equals the $50 million construction cost.

2 Opie is currently renting a house for $800 per month, with utilities included in the rent. He just inherited an identical house from his grandmother. The market value of the inherited house is $200,000 (not expected to change) and the monthly costs for maintenance, insurance, and utilities add up to $100. If Opie moves into the inherited house, by how much will his monthly housing cost increase or decrease? If you don't have enough information to answer the ques-

tion, make up some numbers for the missing information and answer with your assumed numbers.

3 Jack left a job that paid $50,000 per year to start his own business in a building he owns. Similar buildings rent for $10,000 per year. Over the course of the year, Jack paid his part-time employees $75,000 and paid $150,000 for supplies. What is the economic cost of Jack's business?

4 You are about to buy a personal computer and must decide how much random-access memory (RAM) to have in the computer. Suppose each 128-megabyte block of RAM costs $40. For example, a computer with two blocks of memory (256 MB) costs $40 more than a computer with one block (128 MB). The marginal benefit of memory is $320 for the first block and decreases by half for each additional block, to $160 for the second block, $80 for the third block, and so on. How many blocks of memory should you get in your computer? Illustrate your answer with a graph.

5 Consider a city that must decide how many mobile cardiac arrest units (specially equipped ambulances designed to treat people immediately after a heart attack) to deploy. Explain how you could use the marginal principle to help make the decision.

6 You are the manager of a firm that makes computers. If you had to decide how much output to produce in the next week, would you use the principle of diminishing returns? If you had to decide how much output to produce 10 years from now, would you use the principle of diminishing returns?

7 Your coffee shop has a single espresso machine. As the firm adds more and more workers, would you expect output (espressos per hour) to increase at a constant rate? Why or why not?

8 Explain this statement: In the last 10 years, the salaries of baseball players have increased in both real and nominal terms.

MODEL ANSWERS

Chapter-Opening Questions

1 To get a warship, we must sacrifice something else, such as safe drinking water for 2.5 million Malaysians.

2 According to the marginal principle, the standard should be made stricter if the marginal benefit (the savings in health care costs from a cleaner environment) exceeds the marginal cost (the cost of additional equipment and extra fuel).

3 According to the exchange principle, a voluntary exchange between two people makes both people better off.

4 If the firm experiences diminishing returns, output will increase but will not double.

5 A world with rising prices is best for a debtor because it causes higher wages. That means it will take less time to earn the $20,000 you owe. For example, if prices double, your wage will double too, so it will take you half as much time to earn money to pay back the loan.

Answers: Test Your Understanding

1 False. This statement ignores the opportunity cost of time spent in school.

2 One of the costs of a lunch is the time spent eating it. Even if someone else pays for your lunch, it is not truly free.

3 The marginal benefit is $150, and the marginal cost is only $100 (equal to $600 − $500), so it would be sensible to add the third bus.

4 The marginal benefit (the extra revenue from selling three-bladed razors) must be greater than the marginal cost (the extra cost associated with producing razors with three blades instead of two).

5 False. Both people involved in a voluntary transaction are better off, so each thank-you could be sincere.

6 No. If the factory experiences diminishing returns, the marginal product of the tenth worker will exceed that of the twentieth worker, which exceeds that of the thirtieth worker.

7 False. The principle says that output increases but at a decreasing rate. Its does not say that hiring another worker decreases output, although this is a possibility with a very crowded factory.

8 The price of consumer goods increased faster than wages.

9 Your real wage hasn't changed, so you are just as well off.

10 A set of goods that cost you $100 will cost you $103 today, so you must use $3 of your $4 interest earnings to cover the higher costs, leaving you with only $1 in actual interest earnings.

NOTES

1. United Nations Development Program, *Human Development Report 1994* (New York: Oxford University Press, 1994).
2. Jose de Cordoba, "Panama Has Plans for U.S. War Stuff: Turn It Into Hotels," *Wall Street Journal*, January 11, 2000, p. A1.
3. Colin Kennedy, "Lord of the Screens," *Economist: The World in 2003*, p. 29 (London, 2003).
4. "Airline Takes the Marginal Bone," *Business Week*, April 20, 1963, pp. 111–114.
5. Adam Smith, *An Inquiry into the Nature and Causes of the Wealth of Nations* (First published in 1776; New York: Random House, 1973), Book 1, Chapter 2.

Comparative Advantage and Exchange

Specialization and the Gains from Trade
Production and Consumption Possibilities
Comparative Advantage Versus Absolute
    Advantage
The Division of Labor and Exchange
Comparative Advantage and International
    Trade

Markets

Virtues of Markets
Example: Exchange in a Prisoner of War
    Camp
Shortcomings of Markets

The Role of Government in a Market Economy

Government Enforces the Rules
    of Exchange
Government Can Reduce Economic
    Uncertainty

Exchange and Markets

he Barbie doll, the most profitable doll in history, is sold in 140 countries around the world at a rate of two dolls per second. Annual sales are $1.7 billion.[1] Most people think the Barbie doll symbolizes American culture, but the truth is, Barbie is really an international product. The dolls are designed in the United States, but most of the production occurs elsewhere. Saudi Arabia provides the oil used in Taiwanese factories to produce the vinyl plastic pellets that become Barbie's body. Japan supplies Barbie's nylon hair, and China provides her cotton clothes. The machinery used in Barbie factories in China, Indonesia, and Malaysia comes from Japan, Europe, and the United States. The United States provides the molds used to form the dolls and the pigments and oils used to paint them. Barbie dolls come in a box labeled "Made in China," but only about $0.33 of the $10 retail price goes to the factories in China that assemble the dolls. The rest goes to input suppliers around the world and to Mattel, which collects a $1 profit on each Barbie sold.

In Chapter 1, we saw that a society makes three types of economic decisions: what products to produce, how to produce them, and who gets them. In modern economies, most of these decisions are made in markets. Most of us participate in the labor market and are paid for jobs in which we produce goods and services for others. All of us participate in consumer markets, spending our incomes on food, clothing, housing, and other products. In this chapter, we first explain why markets exist, and then we explore the virtues and the shortcomings of markets. We also examine the role of government in a market-based economy.

The material in this chapter will help you understand the reasons for exchange and markets. Here are some of the practical questions we answer:

1 Why aren't people self-sufficient, producing everything they need for themselves?
2 Why have the economies of the former Soviet Union and China moved away from central planning, relying to a greater extent on market dynamics?
3 Why are profits an important part of a market economy?
4 How does EverQuest, the online multiplayer adventure game, illustrate the benefits of exchange and markets?

Comparative Advantage and Exchange

Markets exist to facilitate exchange between people. The alternative to exchange is to be self-sufficient, with each of us producing everything we need for ourselves. Rather than going it alone, most of us specialize by producing one or two products for others and exchanging the money we earn for the products we want to consume.

Specialization and the Gains from Trade

We can explain how people can benefit by specialization and trade with a simple example of two people and two products: Paintings and pizza. As shown in the first row in Table 3.1, Abe can produce either 2 paintings or 6 pizzas per day, while Bea can produce either a painting or a pizza per day. We can use one of the key principles to explore the rationale for specialization.

Principle OF OPPORTUNITY COST
The opportunity cost of something is what you sacrifice to get it.

TABLE 3.1
Productivity and Opportunity Costs

	Abe		Bea	
	Paintings	**Pizzas**	**Paintings**	**Pizzas**
Output per day	2	6	1	1
Opportunity cost	3 pizzas	1/3 painting	1 pizza	1 painting

Comparative advantage
The ability of one person or nation to produce a good at a lower opportunity cost than another person or nation.

Abe's opportunity cost of a painting is 3 pizzas—that's how many pizzas he could produce in the time it takes him to produce 1 painting. Similarly, Abe's opportunity cost of a pizza is 1/3 of a painting, the number of paintings he could produce in the time it takes him to produce 1 pizza. For Bea, the opportunity cost of a painting is 1 pizza and the opportunity cost of a pizza is 1 painting.

To demonstrate the benefits of exchange, let's imagine that both people are initially self-sufficient, with each producing enough of both goods to satisfy their own desires. Suppose there are 6 workdays per week. As shown in the first row of Table 3.2, Abe initially devotes 2 days per week to painting (producing 4 paintings) and 4 days per week to pizzas (producing 24 pizzas). He then consumes everything he produces. In a week, Bea produces and consumes 1 painting and 5 pizzas. As shown in the last two columns of the table, the total output for the two people is 5 paintings and 29 pizzas.

Specialization will increase total output. It is sensible for each person to specialize in the good for which he or she has a lower opportunity cost. We say that a person has a **comparative advantage** in producing a particular product if he or she has a lower opportunity cost than another person.

TABLE 3.2 Specialization, Exchange, and Gains from Trade

	Abe		Bea		Total	
	Paintings per Week	**Pizzas per Week**	**Paintings per Week**	**Pizzas per Week**	**Paintings per Week**	**Pizzas per Week**
Abe and Bea are self-sufficient.	4	24	1	5	5	29
Abe and Bea specialize.	0	36	6	0	6	36
After specializing, Abe and Bea exchange 2 pizzas per painting.	0 + 5 = **5** (Abe gets 5 paintings)	36 − 10 = **26** (Abe gives up 10 pizzas)	6 − 5 = **1** (Bea gives up 5 paintings)	0 + 10= **10** (Bea gets 10 pizzas)	6	36
Gain from specialization and exchange.	1	2	0	5	1	7

▶ Abe has a comparative advantage producing pizzas because his opportunity cost of pizzas is 1/3 painting, compared to 1 painting per pizza for Bea.

▶ Bea has a comparative advantage in painting because her opportunity cost of paintings is 1 pizza, compared to 3 pizzas per painting for Abe.

As shown in the second row of Table 3.2, when the two people specialize, Abe produces 36 pizzas and Bea produces 6 paintings. The total output of both goods increases: The number of paintings increases by 1 (from 5 to 6), and the number of pizzas increases by 7 (from 29 to 36). Specialization increases the output of both goods because both people are focusing on what they do best.

If specialization is followed by exchange, both people can be made better off. Suppose Abe and Bea agree to exchange 2 pizzas per painting. Abe could give up 10 pizzas to get 5 paintings. As shown in the third row of Table 3.2, that leaves him with 5 paintings and 26 pizzas, so compared to the self-sufficient outcome, he has more of both goods—one more painting and two more pizzas. If Bea gives up 5 paintings to get 10 pizzas, that leaves her with 1 painting and 10 pizzas, which is better than her self-sufficient outcome of 1 painting and 5 pizzas. Specialization and exchange make both people better off, illustrating one of the key principles of economics:

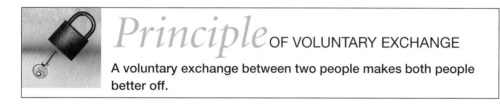

Principle OF VOLUNTARY EXCHANGE

A voluntary exchange between two people makes both people better off.

Production and Consumption Possibilities

Figure 3.1 provides a graphical representation of the numbers in Table 3.2. Let's start with the effects of specialization. The figure shows the production possibilities curves for the two people. In contrast with the possibilities curves drawn in Chapter 2, these curves are linear, reflecting the assumption that opportunity costs don't change as a person devotes more and more time to a particular product. In other words, there is a constant trade-off between the two activities. The self-sufficiency points are a_1 for Abe (4 paintings and 24 pizzas) and b_1 for Bea (1 painting and 5 pizzas). With specialization, each person produces only one of the products and thus moves to a point on either the horizontal or vertical axis.

▶ Abe produces only pizzas, so he moves to point a_2 on the vertical axis.

▶ Bea produces only paintings, so she moves to point b_2 on the horizontal axis.

The next step is to show the effects of exchange. In Figure 3.1, the **consumption possibilities curve** shows the possible combinations of the two goods when Abe and Bea specialize and exchange two pizzas per painting, For Abe, one option is to stay at point a_2, consuming all the pizzas he produces. Another option is to exchange 10 pizzas for 5 paintings, moving him to point a_3. Compared to the self-sufficient outcome (point a_1), he consumes more of both goods, so he is better off. Bea can move from her

Consumption possibilities curve

A curve showing the combinations of two goods that can be consumed when a nation specializes in the production of one good and trades with another nation.

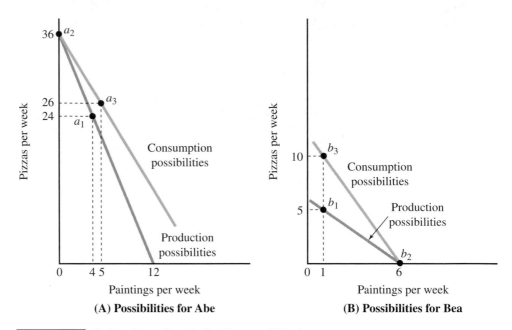

FIGURE 3.1 **Gains from Specialization and Exchange**

(A) Abe starts at the self-sufficient point a_1. Specialization moves him to point a_2, and exchange moves him down the consumption possibilities to point a_3. Compared to the self-sufficient point, he gets more of both goods.

(B) Bea starts at the self-sufficient point b_1. Specialization moves her to point b_2, and exchange moves her up the consumption possibilities curve to point b_3. Compared to the self-sufficient point, she gets more pizzas and the same number of paintings.

specialized point (b_2) to point b_3, exchanging 5 paintings for 10 pizzas. Compared to the self-sufficient outcome (point b_1), she consumes the same number of paintings and 5 more pizzas, so she is better off too.

Comparative Advantage Versus Absolute Advantage

We've seen that it is beneficial for each person to specialize in the product for which he or she has a comparative advantage, that is, a lower opportunity cost. You may have noticed that Abe is more productive than Bea in producing both goods. Economists say that Abe has an **absolute advantage** in producing both goods. Despite his absolute advantage, Abe gains from specialization and trade because he has a comparative advantage in pizza. Abe is twice as productive as Bea in producing paintings, but *six* times as productive in producing pizza. By relying on Bea to produce paintings, Abe frees up time to spend producing pizza, the good for which he has the largest productivity advantage over Bea. The lesson is that specialization and exchange result from comparative advantage, not absolute advantage.

The Division of Labor and Exchange

So far, we've seen that specialization and trade exploit differences in people's innate productivities. Adam Smith noted that specialization actually increased productivity through the division of labor. He used the example of the pin factory to illustrate how the division of labor increased output:[2]

Absolute advantage

The ability of one person or nation to produce a good at a lower absolute cost than another person or nation.

A workman . . . could scarce, perhaps with his utmost industry, make one pin a day, and certainly could not make twenty. But the way in which this business is now carried on . . . one man draws out the wire, another straightens it, a third cuts it, a fourth points it, a fifth grinds the top for receiving the head; to make the head requires two or three distinct operations. . . . The . . . making of a pin is, in this manner, divided into about eighteen distinct operations. . . . I have seen a small manufactory of this kind where ten men . . . make among them . . . upward of forty eight thousand pins in a day.

Smith listed three reasons for productivity to increase with specialization, with each worker performing a single production task.

1 Repetition. The more times a worker performs a particular task, the more proficient the worker becomes at that task.
2 Continuity. A specialized worker doesn't spend time switching from one task to another. This is especially important if switching tasks requires a change in tools or location.
3 Innovation. A specialized worker gains insights into a particular task that leads to better production methods. Smith believed that workers were innovators:[3]
   > A great part of the machines made use of in those manufactures in which labour is most subdivided, were originally the inventions of common workmen, who, being each of them employed in some simple operation, naturally turned their thoughts toward finding out easier and readier methods of performing *it*.

To summarize, specialization and exchange result from differences in productivity. Differences in productivity result from differences in innate skills and the benefits associated with the division of labor. Adam Smith wrote that "every man thus lives by exchanging, or becomes in some measure a merchant, and the society itself grows to be what is properly a commercial society."[4]

Comparative Advantage and International Trade

The lessons of comparative advantage and specialization apply to trade between nations. Each nation could be self-sufficient, producing all the goods it consumes, or it could instead specialize in products for which it has a comparative advantage. Even if one nation is more productive than a second nation in producing all goods, trade will be beneficial if the first nation has a bigger productivity advantage in one product—that is, if one nation has a comparative advantage in some product. For an example of comparative advantage giving rise to trade, read "A Closer Look: Buzz Lightyear of China."

National governments often intervene in international trade by erecting barriers to trade. One motivation for a trade barrier is to protect domestic industries from foreign competition. To illustrate the rationale for protectionist policies, let's extend our example of Abe and Bea to the international scale. Suppose Abeland is populated by people identical to Abe, while Bealand is full of people like Bea. Both nations are initially self-sufficient, with half the people in Abeland producing paintings and the other half producing pizzas. Similarly, the population in Bealand is split equally between painting and pizza making. Suppose that each occupation requires four years of schooling.

If both nations allowed international trade, Abeland would specialize in pizza and Bealand would specialize in painting. As in the earlier example with two individuals, specialization will increase total output of both products, generating net gains from trade. If you were a painter in Bealand, you would certainly be better off because your painting job would be secure and you would get more pizzas per painting. Instead of exchanging (within Bealand) one pizza per painting, you could get two pizzas per painting. But what about the former pizza makers, who would lose their jobs and be forced to switch to painting? If the two jobs required identical skills, the transition would be relatively easy. But because the two jobs require different skills (and education), former pizza workers will bear a cost from free trade. Similarly, there is a cost associated with switching painters in Abeland to pizza making.

The government can respond to this problem in two ways. One option is to cover the costs of switching occupations by paying the educational expenses of workers who must retrain for new careers. For example, the government could pay the educational expenses for former painters switching to pizza production. A second option is to erect barriers to trade such as an import tax or quota (a limit on the volume of goods imported). These trade barriers impose a cost on consumers, who miss the opportunity to pay lower prices for imported goods. For example, restrictions in the United States on textile imports protect 126,000 jobs at an annual cost of $10 billion, or $82,000 for each protected job.

Many people are skeptical about the idea that international trade can make everyone better off. President Abraham Lincoln expressed his discomfort with importing goods:[5]

> I know if I buy a coat in America, I have a coat and America has the money—If I buy a coat in England, I have the coat and England has the money.

What Lincoln didn't understand is that when he buys a coat in England, he sends dollars to England, and the dollars don't just sit there, but eventually are sent back to the United States to buy goods produced by American workers. In the words of economist Todd Buchholz, the author of *New Ideas from Dead Economists*:[6]

> Money may not make the world go round, but money certainly goes around the world. To stop it prevents goods from traveling from where they are produced most inexpensively to where they are desired most deeply.

TEST Your Understanding

1. In an hour, Abby can produce two financial statements or answer eight phone calls. What is the opportunity cost of a financial statement? What is the opportunity cost of a phone call?
2. Suppose Abby has an officemate, Slokum, who in an hour can either produce a financial statement or answer a phone call. How should the two tasks be allocated between the two workers?
3. Wally, the manager of a car wash, is more productive at washing cars than any of the potential workers he could hire. Should he wash all the cars himself?

Buzz Lightyear of China

Buzz Lightyear is a distinctly American cartoon character, but the 30,000 frames of *Buzz Lightyear of the Star Command* were actually drawn in China by the artists of Shenzhen Jade Animation Company.[7] The company employs 300 artists and produces cartoon frames for studios in the United States, Canada, France, and Japan. With a monthly salary of $845, veteran cartoon artists in China cost a fraction of their American counterparts. The Chinese have a comparative advantage in producing cartoon frames.

Markets

In a **market economy**, people exchange things, trading what they have for what they want. Most people specialize in one productive activity—that is, they have one occupation and use their incomes to buy most of the goods they consume. In addition to consumer markets, many of us also participate in the market for financial capital, lending money for interest income (earned on savings accounts, bonds, or stocks) or borrowing money and paying interest. Friedrich Hayek, a famous economist from the twentieth century, suggested that if the market system hadn't arisen naturally, it would have been proclaimed the greatest invention in human history.

Although it appears markets arose naturally, a number of social inventions have made them work better.

▶ Contracts specify the terms of exchange, facilitating exchange between strangers.

Market economy

An economy in which people exchange things, trading what they have for what they want.

▶ Insurance reduces the risk associated with commercial ventures, making new ventures more viable for entrepreneurs.

▶ Patents increase the profitability of inventions, encouraging people to develop new products and production processes.

▶ Accounting rules provide reliable information about commercial enterprises, encouraging other people to invest their time and money in them.

Virtues of Markets

Centrally planned economy

An economy in which a government bureaucracy decides how much of each good to produce, how to produce the goods, and who gets them.

To assess the virtues of the market system, imagine the alternative—a **centrally planned economy** in which a planning authority decides what products to produce, how to produce them, and who gets them. To make these decisions, a planner must first collect a huge amount of widely dispersed information about consumption desires (what products each individual wants), production techniques (what resources are required to produce each product), and the availability of productive resources (labor, raw materials, and machines). Then the planner must decide how to allocate the productive resources among the alternative products. Finally, the planner must divide the output among the economy's citizens. Clearly, the planner has a formidable task.

Under a market system, the people with dispersed information about consumers' desires, production technology, and resources make the decisions. Their decisions are guided by prices. To illustrate, suppose you buy a wool coat. The dozens of people who contributed to the production of the coat—including the farmers who manage the sheep, the workers who transform raw wool into cloth and the cloth into a coat, the truckers who transport the inputs and the actual coat, and the merchant who sold the coat—didn't know you wanted a coat. The farmer knew that the price of wool was high enough to justify raising and shearing sheep. The workers knew that wages were high enough to make their efforts worthwhile. The merchant knew that the price of the coat was high enough to make it worthwhile to acquire the coat in anticipation of selling it. In a market system, prices provide individuals the information they need to make decisions.

Prices provide signals about the relative scarcity of a product and help an economy respond to scarcity. For example, suppose wool becomes more scarce, either because a new use for wool is discovered or an old source of wool disappears. The greater scarcity will increase the price of wool, and consumers and producers will respond in ways that diminish scarcity. The higher price encourages fabric producers to use the available wool more efficiently and encourages farmers to produce more of it. The higher price also encourages consumers to switch to alternative fabrics. These two responses help the economy accommodate an increase in scarcity. Consumers and producers don't need to know why wool is more scarce for these mechanisms to kick in—only that the price is higher.

The decisions made in markets result from the interactions of millions of people, each motivated by their own interests. Adam Smith used the metaphor of the "invisible hand" to explain that people acting in self-interest may actually promote the interest of society as a whole:[8]

It is not from the benevolence of the butcher, the brewer, or the baker that we expect our dinner, but from their regard to their own interest. **We address ourselves, not to their**

humanity but to their self-love, and never talk to them of our own necessities but of their advantages. . . . [Man is] led by an invisible hand to promote an end which was no part of this intention. . . . By pursuing his own interest he frequently promotes that of the society more effectually than when he really intends to promote it. . . . Nobody but a beggar chooses to depend chiefly upon the benevolence of his fellow citizens.

The market system works by getting each person, motivated by self-interest, to produce products for other people.

Entrepreneurs play a key role in a market economy. Prices and profits provide signals to entrepreneurs about what to produce. If a product suddenly becomes popular, competition among consumers will increase its price and increase the profits earned by producers. Entrepreneurs will enter the market and increase production to meet the higher demand, converting resources that had been used to produce other products. As entrepreneurs enter the market, they compete for customers, driving the price back down to the level that generates just enough profit for them to remain in business. In contrast, if a product becomes less popular, the process is reversed. Producers will cut prices in order to sell the product to the smaller number of customers who want it. Entrepreneurs will leave the unprofitable market, finding other products to produce, and the price will eventually rise back to the level where profits are high enough for the remaining producers to justify staying in business.

One way to see the advantages of a market system is to see what happened in economies that were once centrally planned.[9] In the former Soviet Union, state-run auto repair shops, plagued by shortages of parts, were replaced by repair shops run by entrepreneurs with a profit incentive. In China, farmers moved away from the inefficient communal system and started selling their produce themselves.

Adam Smith, the founder of economics, stressed that markets guide people with an "invisible hand," promoting the general interest.

Prisoners of war used
cigarettes to facilitate
exchange of food, clothing,
and laundry services.

Example: Exchange in a Prisoner of War Camp

To illustrate the pervasiveness of exchange, consider the emergence of markets in prisoner of war (POW) camps in World War II, as documented by economist Roy Radner. During World War II, the Red Cross gave each Allied prisoner a weekly parcel, with the same mix of products—tinned milk, jam, butter, biscuits, corned beef, chocolate, sugar, and cigarettes. In addition, many prisoners received private parcels from family and friends. The prisoners used barter to exchange one good for another, and cigarettes emerged as the medium of exchange.[10] Prisoners wandered through the camp calling out their offers of goods. For example, "cheese for seven" meant that the prisoner was willing to sell a cheese ration for seven cigarettes. In addition to food, the prisoners bought and sold clothing (80 cigarettes per shirt) laundry services (2 cigarettes per garment), and hot cups of coffee (2 cigarettes per cup).

The prices of products reflected their scarcity. The tea-drinking British prisoners, who were confined to their compound, demanded little coffee. Consequently, packets of coffee beans sold for just a few cigarettes in that compound. Enterprising British prisoners subsequently bribed prison guards to permit them to travel to the French compound, where they could sell the cheap coffee for dozens of cigarettes. Similarly, the demand for beef among Sikhs was low. One prisoner who knew the Sikh language bought beef at a low price in the Sikh compound and sold it at a higher price in other compounds. Eventually, other people entered the Sikh beef trade, and beef prices across compounds became roughly equal. For another example of a market appearing unexpectedly, read "A Closer Look: EverQuest and Fantasy Exchanges."

Shortcomings of Markets

Although markets often operate efficiently, sometimes they do not. This phenomenon is known as "market failure," which is what happens when markets fail to produce the most efficient outcomes on their own. One example of market failure is pollution. For

A CLOSER LOOK

EverQuest and Fantasy Exchanges

As another illustration of the power of exchange, consider the virtual world of online games. EverQuest is a role-playing game that allows thousands of people to interact online, moving their characters through a landscape of survival challenges. Each player constructs a character—called an "avatar"—by choosing some initial traits for it. The player then navigates the avatar through the game's challenges, where it acquires skills and accumulates assets, including clothing, weapons, armor, and even magic spells. The currency in EverQuest is a "platinum piece" (PP). Avatars can earn PP by performing various tasks and use PP to buy and sell assets.

The curious part about EverQuest is that players use real-life auction sites, including eBay and Yahoo!Auction, to buy things normally purchased in the game with PP.[11] Byron, who wants a piece of armor for his avatar (say, a Rubicite girdle), can use eBay to buy one for $50 from Selma. The two players then enter the online game, and Selma's avatar transfers the armor to Byron's avatar. It is even possible to buy another player's avatar, with all of its skills and assets. Given the time required to acquire various objects like Rubicite girdles in the game versus the prices paid for them on eBay, the implicit wage earned by the typical online player auctioning them off is $3.42 per hour: That's how much the player could earn by first taking the time to acquire the assets in the game and then selling them in the "real world."

markets to work efficiently, the people making the decisions about production and consumption must bear the full costs and reap the full benefits related to their decisions. When they don't, market failure occurs. The role of government is to correct this problem. Market failure can also occur when buyers and sellers have imperfect information about the quality of goods and services they are exchanging. Later in the book, we'll explore several cases of market failure and what government can do to help.

TEST Your Understanding

4. List the social inventions that support markets.
5. Why would a POW who didn't smoke trade some of his rations for cigarettes?
6. How could you earn money playing the online adventure game EverQuest?

The Role of Government in a Market Economy

What is the role of government in a market-based economy? As mentioned earlier in the chapter, the government deals with the problems associated with market failure. In addition, the government enforces property rights, protecting property and possessions from theft. The protection of private property encourages production and exchange because people are assured that they can keep the fruits of their efforts. The government has two additional roles to play:

▶ Establishing rules for exchange in markets and using its police power to enforce the rules

▶ Reducing economic uncertainty and providing for people who are unlucky—because of job losses, poor health, bad luck, or other circumstances

Government Enforces the Rules of Exchange

The market system is based on exchanges between strangers, who may have trouble trusting each other. These exchanges are covered by implicit and explicit contracts that establish the terms of trade. For example, real-estate transactions are sealed with contracts that specify who pays what, and when. To facilitate exchange, the government helps to enforce contracts by maintaining a legal system that punishes people who violate contracts. This allows people to trade with the confidence that the terms of the contract will be met.

In the case of consumer goods, the implicit contract is that the product is safe to use. The government enforces this implicit contract through product liability or tort law. If a consumer is harmed by using a particular product, the consumer can file a lawsuit and seek compensation for the harm done. For example, some consumers who are injured in defective automobiles are awarded settlements to cover the cost of medical care, lost work time, and pain and suffering.

Another role in the realm of exchange is the dissemination of information on consumer products. Producers are required by the government to provide information to consumers about the features of their products, including warnings about potentially harmful uses of the product.

To ensure that innovators benefit from their inventions, the U.S. government enforces patent laws. The costs associated with inventing new products and production processes—research and development costs—can be substantial. A patent grants an inventor the exclusive right to sell the product for a specified time (currently 20 years), increasing the payoff from innovation and encouraging people to invest resources in the development of new products and processes. Later in the book, we'll take a closer look at patents and innovation.

As noted earlier in the chapter, one of the virtues of a market system is that competition among producers tends to keep prices low. Another set of government policies is designed to foster competition between firms. As we'll see later in the book, antitrust policy can be used to (a) break up a monopoly, (b) prevent firms from colluding to fix prices, and (c) prevent two competing firms from merging into a single firm. There are some markets in which a single firm—a monopolist—is inevitable. Governments regulate these firms, controlling the price of the products they produce.

Government Can Reduce Economic Uncertainty

A market economy provides plenty of opportunities to people, but there are risks. Your level of success in a market economy—how much income you earn and how much wealth you accumulate—will depend on your innate intelligence as well as your efforts. But there is also an element of luck: Your fate is affected by where you were born, what occupation you choose, and your genetic makeup and health. There are also chance events such as natural disasters and human accidents that can affect your prosperity. Finally, some people lose their jobs when the national economy is in a slump.

Given the uncertainty of the market economics, most governments have a "social safety net" that provides for citizens who fare poorly in markets. The safety net includes programs that redistribute income from rich to poor and other programs of support. The idea behind having a social safety net is to guarantee a minimum income to people who suffer from job losses, poor health, or bad luck.

Of course, there are private responses to economic uncertainty. For example, we can buy insurance to cover losses from fire and theft, to cover our medical expenses, and to provide death benefits to our survivors in the event of an accident or disaster. Private insurance works because only a fraction of the people who buy insurance file claims and receive reimbursements from insurance companies. In other words, the payments, or premiums, of many are used to pay the claims of a few. Private insurance works when enough low-risk people purchase insurance to cover the costs of reimbursing the high-risk people.

Some types of insurance are unavailable in the private insurance market. As a result, the government steps in to fill the void. For example, unemployment insurance (UI) is a government program that provides 26 weeks of compensation for people who lose their jobs. It is financed by contributions from employers. Because UI is mandatory, all employers, including those facing low risks and high risks of unemployment, contribute to the system, thereby keeping the cost of the insurance down.

USING THE TOOLS

1. Prices in a POW Camp

Recall the discussion of markets in the POW camps. Suppose the price of bread is initially 40 cigarettes. Predict the effects of the following events on the price of bread; will the price of bread increase, decrease, or remain unchanged?
a. Prisoners' cigarette rations double while their food rations remain the same.
b. All rations—for cigarettes as well as food—are cut in half.
c. Air raids near the camp increase prisoners' anxiety, increasing cigarette consumption as a coping mechanism.

2. Arbitrage: Exploiting Price Differences

Late in World War II, a German guard exchanged bread and chocolate at the rate of one loaf for one chocolate bar. Inside the Allied POW camp, the price of chocolate was 15 cigarettes per bar, and the price of bread was 40 cigarettes per loaf. Arbitrage refers to the process of buying and selling products in different places to exploit differences in prices.
a. Design an arbitrage scheme for a prisoner in the POW camp. For each exchange with the German guard, what is the prisoner's profit?
b. Predict the effects of arbitrage on the prices of bread and chocolate within the POW camp.

3. Comparative Advantage and the Gains from Trade

Robin and Terry are stranded on a deserted island and consume two products, coconuts and fish. In a day, Robin can catch two fish or gather eight coconuts, and Terry can catch one fish or gather one coconut.
a. Use these numbers to prepare a table like Table 3.1. Which person has a comparative advantage in fishing? Which person has a comparative advantage in gathering coconuts?
b. Suppose that each person is initially self-sufficient. In a six-day week, Robin produces and consumes 32 coconuts and four fish, and Terry produces and consumes four coconuts and two fish. Show that specialization and exchange (at a rate of three coconuts per fish) allows Robin to consume more coconuts and the same number of fish and allows Terry to consume more coconuts and the same number of fish. Use a graph like Figure 3.1 and a table like Table 3.2 to illustrate your answer.

SUMMARY

This chapter explored specialization and exchange and the virtues and shortcomings of markets. We also discussed the role of government in a market economy. Here are the main points of the chapter:

1 It is sensible for a person to produce the product for which he or she has a comparative advantage, that is, a lower opportunity cost than another person.

2 Specialization increases productivity through the division of labor, a result of the benefits of repetition, continuity, and innovation.

3 A system of international specialization and trade is sensible because nations have different opportunity costs of producing goods, giving rise to comparative advantages.

4 Under a market system, self-interested people, guided by prices, make the decisions about what products to produce, how to produce them, and who gets them.

5 Government roles in a market economy include establishing the rules for exchange, reducing economic uncertainty, and responding to market failures.

KEY TERMS

absolute advantage, 48

centrally planned economy, 52

comparative advantage, 46

consumption possibilities curve, 47

market economy, 51

PROBLEMS AND DISCUSSION QUESTIONS

1 Recall the example of Abe and Bea shown in Table 3.1. Suppose a technological innovation increases painting productivity of both people: Abe can now produce three paintings per day, while Bea can now produce two paintings per day. Their productivity for pizza has not changed. Suppose they agree to trade one painting for each pizza. Will both people gain from specialization and trade?

2 Consider two financial planners, Phil and Frances. In an hour Phil can either produce one financial statement or answer 10 phone calls, while Frances can either produce three financial statements or answer 12 phone calls. Does either person have an absolute advantage in producing both products? Should the two planners be self-sufficient (each producing statements and answering phones), or should they specialize?

3 Professor Lucy is a better teacher than Professor Buster for both an undergraduate course (U) and a graduate course (G). Teaching performance is measured by the average score on students' standardized tests:

	Professor Lucy	Professor Buster
Average Score in Undergraduate Course	48	24
Average Score in Graduate Course	60	20

a. If each professor teaches one course and the objective is to maximize the sum of the test scores, which course should each professor teach?

b. Is your answer to (a) consistent with Lucy teaching the course for which she has the largest productivity advantage over Buster?

4 Use the notion of comparative advantage to explain why two countries, one of which is less efficient in producing all products, will still find it advantageous to trade.

MODEL ANSWERS

Chapter-Opening Questions

1 Markets exist because most people are not self-sufficient but instead specialize in producing one or two products and then buy other products from other people.

2 Under a market system, self-interested people, guided by the prices of products and resources, make better decisions.

3 Profits provide incentives for entrepreneurs to enter markets and produce goods that consumers are willing to pay for.

4 EverQuest players use online auction sites like eBay to purchase assets (armor, weapons, spells) for their characters in the game, which are then transferred from one character to another within the game.

Test Your Understanding

1 The opportunity cost of a financial statement is four phone calls, and the opportunity cost of a phone call is one-fourth of a financial statement.

2 Abby has the lower opportunity cost for phone calls (one-fourth of a financial statement), and Slokum has the lower opportunity cost for financial statements (one phone call). Abby should answer the phone, and Slokum should prepare the financial statements.

3 No. If he has a comparative advantage at managerial tasks such as doing the books or marketing, he should hire some workers to wash the cars, allowing him to specialize in the tasks for which he has a comparative advantage.

4 Contracts, insurance, patents, and accounting rules.

5 Cigarettes served as a medium of exchange.

6 Acquire assets in the game and sell them on eBay.

NOTES

1. Rone Tempest, "Barbie and the World Economy," *Los Angeles Times*, September 22, 1996, p. A1. **http://www.surferess.com/CEO/html/jill_barad.html**
2. Adam Smith, *An Inquiry into the Nature and Causes of The Wealth of Nations* (First published in 1776; New York: Random House, 1973), Book 1, Chapter 1.
3. Adam Smith, *An Inquiry into the Nature and Causes of The Wealth of Nations* (First published in 1776; New York: Random House, 1973), Book 1, Chapter 1.
4. Adam Smith, *An Inquiry into the Nature and Causes of The Wealth of Nations* (First published in 1776; New York: Random House, 1973), Book 1, Chapter 4.
5. Todd G. Buchholz, *New Ideas from Dead Economists* (New York: Penguin, 1999), p. 75.
6. Todd G. Buchholz, *New Ideas from Dead Economists* (New York: Penguin, 1999), p. 76.
7. Associated Press Online, "China Targets Cartoons," October 4, 2000.
8. Adam Smith, *An Inquiry into the Nature and Causes of The Wealth of Nations* (First published in 1776; New York: Random House, 1973), Book 4, Chapter 2.
9. Steven Greenhouse, *"The Global March to Free Markets,"* New York Times, July 19, 1987, Sec. 3, p. 1.
10. R.A. Radford, "The Economic Organization of a P.O.W. Camp," *Economica*, November, 1945.
11. Robert Shapiro, *Fantasy Economics* (slate.msn.com, February 4, 2003); Edward Castronova, "Virtual Worlds: A First-Hand Account of Market and Society on the Cyberian Frontier," CESifo Working Paper No. 618, December 2001.

The Demand Curve

The Individual Demand Curve and the Law
    of Demand
From Individual Demand to Market
    Demand

The Supply Curve

The Individual Supply Curve and the Law
    of Supply
Why Is the Individual Supply Curve
    Positively Sloped?
From Individual Supply to Market Supply

Market Equilibrium

Excess Demand Causes the Price to Rise
Excess Supply Causes the Price to Drop

**Market Effects of Changes
in Demand**

Change in Quantity Demanded Versus
    Change in Demand
Increases in Demand
Decreases in Demand

**Market Effects of Changes
in Supply**

Change in Quantity Supplied Versus
    Change in Supply
Increases in Supply
Decreases in Supply

**Market Effects of Simultaneous
Changes in Demand and Supply**

**Using the Model to Predict Changes
in Price and Quantity**

Population Growth and Apartment Prices
Product Safety and Apples
Technological Innovation and Computers
Weather and Coffee

**Explaining Changes in Price
or Quantity**

An Increase in Poultry Consumption
A Decrease in Drug Prices

**Economic Experiment:
Market Equilibrium**

Using the Tools

Supply, Demand, and Market Equilibrium

etween 2000 and 2002, the price of vanilla beans quadrupled, from $50 to $200 per kilo. Was this good news for vanilla growers in Madagascar, the world's leading producer? The soaring price was actually bad news for the growers. The price hike was caused by tropical storms that reduced harvests, so the growers sold a smaller quantity at the higher price. The higher price unleashed the forces of supply and demand to the detriment of Madagascar growers. On the demand side of the market, consumers and food manufacturers switched to synthetic vanilla, which sells for as little as $15 per kilo. On the supply side, the high price encouraged people in other countries to enter the lucrative market. In India, 10,000 hectares are expected to be cultivated in the next few years. In East Timor, the world's newest nation, coffee growers switched to vanilla beans and harvested their first crop in 2002.

Our discussion of the virtues of exchange and markets in Chapter 3 has set the stage for this chapter, where we explore the mechanics of markets. We use the model of supply and demand—the most important tool of economic analysis—to see how markets work. We'll see how the prices of goods and services are affected by all sorts of changes in the economy, including bad weather, higher income, technological innovation, bad publicity, and changes in consumer preferences. This chapter will prepare you for the applications of supply and demand you'll see in the rest of the book.

The model of supply and demand explains how a perfectly competitive market operates. A **perfectly competitive market** has a very large number of firms, each of which produces the same standardized product in amounts so small that no individual firm can affect the market price. The classic example of a perfectly competitive firm is a wheat farmer, who produces a tiny fraction of the total supply of wheat. No matter how much wheat an individual farmer produces, the farmer can't change the market price of wheat.

This chapter includes many applications of supply and demand analysis. Here are some practical questions we answer:

1 The supply of electricity generated from wind power doubled in 2001. Why?
2 Ted Koppel, host of the ABC news program *Nightline*, once suggested that the price of cocaine had fallen because the supply of cocaine had increased. Was he correct?
3 Over the last few decades the consumption of chicken and turkey has increased. Why?
4 You shop for groceries at a different store each week. At each store, the clerk says, "You saved $12 by shopping here instead of at another store." Is it possible to "save money" wherever you go?

The Demand Curve

On the demand side of a product market, consumers buy products from firms. The main question concerning the demand side of the market is: How much of a particular product are consumers willing to buy during a particular period? A consumer who is "willing to buy" a particular product is willing to sacrifice enough money to purchase it. The consumer doesn't merely have a desire to buy the good but is willing to sacrifice something to get it. Notice that demand is defined for a particular period, for example, a day, a month, or a year.

We'll start our discussion of demand with the individual consumer. How much of a product is an individual willing to buy? It depends on a number of variables. Here is a list of the variables that affect an individual consumer's decision, using the pizza market as an example:

▶ The price of the product, for example, the price of a pizza
▶ The consumer's income
▶ The price of substitute goods such as tacos or sandwiches
▶ The price of complementary goods such as beer or lemonade
▶ The consumer's tastes and advertising that may influence tastes
▶ The consumer's expectations about future prices

Quantity demanded

The amount of a product consumers are willing to buy.

Together, these variables determine how much of a particular product an individual consumer is willing to buy, the **quantity demanded**. We'll start our discussion of demand with the relationship between the price and quantity demanded, a relationship that is represented graphically by the demand curve.

The Individual Demand Curve and the Law of Demand

Demand schedule

A table of numbers that shows the relationship between price and quantity demanded, *ceteris paribus*.

The starting point for a discussion of individual demand is a **demand schedule**, which is a table of numbers showing the relationship between the price of a particular product and the quantity that an individual consumer is willing to buy. The demand schedule shows how the quantity demanded by an individual changes with the price, *ceteris paribus* ("everything else held fixed"). The variables that are held fixed in the demand schedule are the consumer's income, the prices of substitutes and complements, the consumer's tastes, and the consumer's expectations about future prices.

Table 4.1 shows Al's demand schedule for pizza. At a price of $2, Al buys 13 pizzas per month. As the price rises, he buys fewer pizzas: 10 pizzas at a price of $4, 7 pizzas at a price of $6, and so on, down to only 1 pizza at a price of $10. It's important to remember that in a demand schedule, any change in quantity results from a change in price alone.

Individual demand curve

A curve that shows the relationship between price and quantity demanded by an individual consumer, *ceteris paribus*.

The **individual demand curve** is a graphical representation of the demand schedule. By plotting the numbers in Al's demand schedule—various combinations of price and quantity—we can draw his demand curve for pizza. The demand curve shows the relationship between the price and the quantity demanded by an individual consumer, *ceteris paribus*. To get the data for a single demand curve, we change only the price of pizza, and observe how a consumer responds to the price change. In Figure 4.1, Al's demand curve shows the quantity of pizzas he is willing to buy at each price.

TABLE 4.1

Al's Demand Schedule for Pizzas

Price	Quantity of pizzas per month
$ 2	13
4	10
6	7
8	4
10	1

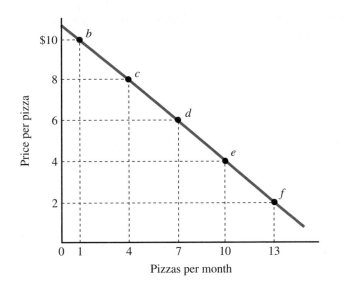

FIGURE 4.1

The Individual Demand Curve
According to the law of demand, the higher the price, the smaller the quantity demanded, everything else being equal. Therefore, the demand curve is negatively sloped: When the price increases from $6 to $8, the quantity demanded decreases from 7 pizzas per month (point *d*) to 4 pizzas per month (point *c*).

Notice that Al's demand curve is negatively sloped, reflecting the **law of demand**. This law applies to all consumers:

Law of demand
The higher the price, the smaller the quantity demanded, *ceteris paribus*.

■ Law of Demand

The higher the price, the smaller the quantity demanded, *ceteris paribus*.

The words *ceteris paribus* remind us that to isolate the relationship between price and quantity demanded, we *must* assume that income, other prices, and tastes are unchanged. As the price of pizza increases and nothing else changes, Al moves upward along his demand curve and buys a smaller quantity of pizza. For example, if the price increases from $8 to $10, Al moves upward along his demand curve from point *c* to point *b*, and he buys only 1 pizza per month, down from 4 pizzas at the lower price. A movement along a single demand curve is called a **change in quantity demanded**, a change in the quantity a consumer is willing to buy when the price changes.

To see why the law of demand is sensible, think about how Al might react to an increase in the price of pizza.

Change in quantity demanded
A change in the quantity consumers are willing to buy when the price changes; represented graphically by movement along the demand curve.

▶ **Substitution effect**. The more money Al spends on pizza, the less he has to spend on other products such as tacos, music, books, and travel. The price of pizza determines exactly how much of these other goods he sacrifices to get a pizza. If the price of pizza is $6 and the price of tacos is $1, Al will sacrifice 6 tacos for each pizza he buys. If the price of pizza increases to $8, he'll now sacrifice 8 tacos for each pizza. Given the larger sacrifice associated with buying pizza, he is likely to buy fewer pizzas, substituting tacos for pizza.

Substitution effect
The change in consumption resulting from a change in the price of one good relative to the price of another good.

▶ **Income effect**. Suppose Al has a food budget of $100 per month and buys 10 pizzas at a price of $6 each (for a total cost of $60) and spends $40 on other food. If, for example, the price of a pizza rises to $7, the cost of Al's original food choices will be

Income effect
The change in consumption resulting from a change in purchasing power caused by a price change.

$110—$70 for pizza and $40 for other items. This is well above his $100 total food budget. To avoid exceeding his budget, Al must cut back on something. That might end up being pizzas as well as other items. This is called the *income effect* because when the price of pizza increases, the purchasing power of Al's income (and budget) decreases.

From Individual Demand to Market Demand

Market demand curve

A curve showing the relationship between price and quantity demanded, *ceteris paribus*.

The **market demand curve** shows the relationship between the price of the good and the quantity that *all* consumers—you, me, Al, and everyone else—together are willing to buy, *ceteris paribus*. As in the case of the individual demand curve, when we draw the market demand curve, we assume that the other variables that affect individual demand (income, the prices of substitute and complementary goods, tastes, and price expectations) are fixed. In addition, we assume that the number of consumers is fixed. The market demand curve shows the relationship between price and the quantity demanded by all consumers, everything else being equal.

Figure 4.2 shows how to derive the market demand curve when there are only two consumers. Panel A shows Al's demand curve for pizza, and panel B shows Bea's demand curve for pizza. At a price of $8, Al will buy 4 pizzas (point *c*) and Bea will buy 2 pizzas (point *g*), so the total quantity demanded at this price is six pizzas (4 + 2). In panel C, point *j* shows the point on the market demand curve associated with a price of $8. At this price, the market quantity demanded is 6 pizzas. At a price of only $4, Al buys 10 pizzas and Bea buys 6 pizzas, for a total of 16 pizzas (shown by point *k* on the market demand curve).

The market demand is negatively sloped, reflecting the law of demand. This is sensible because if each consumer obeys the law of demand, consumers as a group will

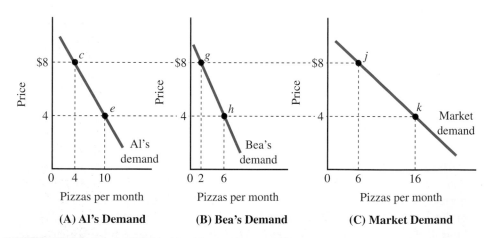

FIGURE 4.2 **From Individual to Market Demand**

The market demand equals the sum of the demands of all consumers. In this case there are only two consumers, so at each price, the market quantity demanded equals the quantity demanded by Al plus the quantity demanded by Bea. At a price of $8, Al's quantity is 4 pizzas (point c) and Bea's quantity is 2 pizzas (point g), so the market quantity demanded is 6 pizzas (point j). Each consumer obeys the law of demand, so the market demand curve is negatively sloped.

too. When the price increases from $4 to $8, there is a change in quantity demanded as we move along the demand curve from point *k* to *j*. The movement along the demand curve occurs if the price of pizza is the only determinant of demand that has changed.

Saving Money Wherever You Shop?

Grocery stores often boast that they have lower prices than their competitors. One boasting strategy happens at the checkout stand. After a clerk computes your bill, he or she uses data on a competitor's prices to compute how much you would have paid if you had purchased your basket of goods at the other store. Then the clerk says, "You saved $12 by shopping with us instead of with our competitor." It seems that wherever you shop, you get the same message: "You save by shopping with us." It appears that each store has lower prices than its competitors. Is this possible, or are the clerks dishonest?

It turns out that the clerks are being honest. To see how you would "save money" no matter where you shop, consider Frieda, who each week picks a store at random for her fruit shopping. She buys exactly six pounds of fruit per week but is flexible about the variety of fruit she buys. In week one, she shops at Alpha market, where the price of apples is $1 per pound and the price of bananas is $3 per pound. She buys six pounds of apples, spending $6. At Beta market across town, the prices are reversed, with apples at $3 per pound and bananas at $1 per pound. If Frieda had purchased six pounds of apples at Beta, she would have spent $18, so the clerk at Alpha correctly observes, "Frieda, you saved $12 by shopping at Alpha instead of Beta." In week two, Frieda shops at Beta market and buys the cheaper fruit (bananas) instead of apples, spending $6 on fruit that would have cost her $18 at the other market. In two successive weeks, she "saves money" at each store. This is possible because she obeys the law of demand, purchasing the less expensive product at each store. ■

The Supply Curve

On the supply side of a market, firms sell their products to consumers. Suppose you ask the manager of a firm, "How much of your product are you willing to produce and sell?" The answer is likely to be "it depends." The manager's decision about how much to produce depends on many variables, including the following (using pizza as an example):

▶ The price of the product—in this case, the price per pizza
▶ The cost of the inputs used to produce the product, for example, wages paid to workers, the cost of dough and cheese, and the cost of the pizza oven
▶ The state of production technology, such as the knowledge used in making pizza
▶ The number of producers—in this case, the number of pizzerias
▶ Producers' expectations about the future price of pizza
▶ Taxes paid to the government or subsidies received from the government

Together, these variables determine how much of a product will be produced and offered for sale, the **quantity supplied**. We'll start our discussion of market supply with the relationship between price of a good and quantity of that good supplied, a relationship that is represented graphically by the supply curve.

Quantity supplied
The amount of a product firms are willing to sell.

The Individual Supply Curve and the Law of Supply

Consider the decision of an individual producer. The starting point for a discussion of individual supply is a **supply schedule**, a table of numbers that shows the relationship between the price of a particular product and the quantity that an individual producer is willing to sell. The supply schedule shows how the quantity supplied by an individual producer changes with the price, *ceteris paribus*. The variables that are held fixed in the supply schedule are input costs, technology, expectations, and government taxes or subsidies.

Table 4.2 shows Nora's supply schedule for pizza. At a price of $4, she supplies 100 pizzas per month. As the price rises, she supplies more pizza: 200 pizzas at a price of $6, 300 pizzas at a price of $8, and so on, up to 500 pizzas at a price of $12. It's important to remember that in a supply schedule, a change in quantity results from a change in price alone.

The **individual supply curve** is a graphical representation of the supply schedule. By plotting the numbers in Nora's supply schedule—various combinations of price and quantity—we can draw her supply curve for pizza. The supply curve shows the relationship between the price of a product and the quantity supplied by a single firm, *ceteris paribus*. To get the data for a single supply curve, we change only the price of pizza and observe how a producer responds to the price change. In Figure 4.3, Nora's supply curve shows the quantity of pizzas she is willing to sell at each price.

Nora's supply curve is positively sloped, reflecting the law of supply, a pattern of behavior that we observe in producers.

Supply schedule

A table of numbers that shows the relationship between price and quantity supplied, *ceteris paribus*.

Individual supply curve

A curve showing the relationship between price and quantity supplied by a single firm, *ceteris paribus*.

■ Law of Supply

The higher the price, the larger the quantity supplied, *ceteris paribus*.

The words *ceteris paribus* remind us that to isolate the relationship between price and quantity supplied, we assume that the other factors that influence producers are unchanged. As the price of pizza increases and nothing else changes, Nora moves upward along her supply curve and produces a larger quantity of pizza. For example, if the price increases from $8 to $10, Nora moves upward along her supply curve from point *p* to point *q*, and she produces 400 pizzas per month, up from 300 pizzas at the lower price. A movement along a single supply curve is called a **change in quantity supplied**, a change in the quantity a producer is willing to sell when the price changes.

Change in quantity supplied

A change in the quantity firms are willing to sell when the price changes; represented graphically by movement along the supply curve.

TABLE 4.2

Nora's Supply Schedule for Pizza

Price	Quantity of pizzas per month
$ 4	100
6	200
8	300
10	400
12	500

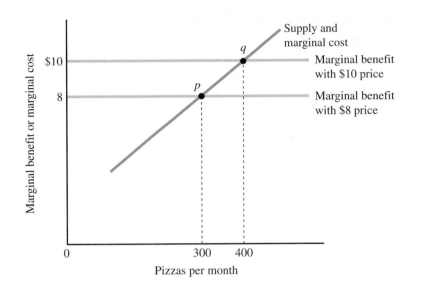

FIGURE 4.3

The Marginal Principle and the Output Decision

The marginal benefit curve is horizontal at the market price. To satisfy the marginal principle, the firm produces the quantity at which the marginal benefit equals the marginal cost. An increase in the price shifts the marginal-benefit curve upward and increases the quantity at which the marginal benefit equals the marginal cost.

Why Is the Individual Supply Curve Positively Sloped?

To see why the law of supply is sensible, think about how Nora might react to an increase in the price of pizza. Suppose the initial price of pizza is $8, and at this price Nora supplies 300 pizzas per month (point *p* on the supply curve). Like other business people, Nora doesn't choose a quantity arbitrarily, but instead picks the quantity that satisfies the marginal principle.

MARGINAL *Principle*

Increase the level of an activity if its marginal benefit exceeds its marginal cost; reduce the level of an activity if its marginal cost exceeds its marginal benefit. If possible, pick the level at which the activity's marginal benefit equals its marginal cost.

The marginal benefit of selling a pizza is the $8 price Nora gets when she sells it. The fact that Nora chose 300 pizzas at a price of $8 reveals that the marginal cost of producing each of the first 299 pizzas is less than the $8 marginal benefit and the marginal cost of the 300th pizza equals the $8 benefit. Nora stops at 300 pizzas because the marginal cost of one more pizza—the 301st—exceeds the $8 benefit from selling it. For example, if the marginal cost of the 301st pizza is $8.02, Nora would lose $0.02 by producing and selling it.

The supply curve shows that if the price rises above $8, Nora will produce more pizzas. As long as the new price is above the marginal cost of the 301st pizza ($8.02), it will be profitable to produce that pizza. For example, if the price rises to $10, Nora can make a profit of $1.98 on the 301st pizza ($10.00 − $8.02). At a price of $10, the supply curve indicates that she will actually produce 400 pizzas. An increase in price from $8 to $10 raises the marginal benefit above the marginal cost for the 301st through the 400th pizza, and she satisfies the marginal principle by selling 400 pizzas. At this new point, the best Nora can do is produce 400 pizzas because the marginal cost of the 400th pizza is $10 and the marginal cost of one more pizza ($10.02) exceeds the price she can get for it.

Why does the marginal cost of pizzas increase as the quantity produced increases? When Nora produces a relatively small quantity of pizzas, she will have just a few workers for every pizza oven, so workers won't face much competition for oven time. In this environment, Nora's costs will be relatively low. Imagine that Nora had to double her pizza output. To do so, she may be forced to pay overtime to her original workers and pay higher wages to attract more workers. In addition, there would be more workers sharing a fixed number of pizza ovens, and there may be a bottleneck as workers wait to use the oven. Because in the larger operation workers are less productive and more expensive, the cost of making pizzas will be higher. In general, the larger the quantity Nora produces, the higher her marginal cost of producing pizza.

To summarize, the individual supply curve is positively sloped because to get Nora to produce more pizza, the price must increase. To go from 300 pizzas to 400 pizzas, the price must increase from $8 to $10 to cover the higher marginal cost associated with producing more pizzas.

From Individual Supply to Market Supply

Market supply curve

A curve showing the relationship between price and quantity supplied, *ceteris paribus*.

The **market supply curve** for a particular good shows the relationship between the price of the good and the quantity that all producers together are willing to sell, *ceteris paribus*. To draw the market supply curve, we assume that the other variables that affect individual supply are fixed. In addition, we assume that the number of producers is fixed. Panel B of Figure 4.4 shows the market supply curve when there are 100 producers, each of which has the same individual supply curve as Nora. At a price of $8, Nora supplies 300 pizzas per month (point *p*), so the 100 firms together produce 30,000 pizzas (300 pizzas per firm times 100 firms), as shown by point *u*. If the price increases to $10, Nora supplies 400 pizzas (point *q*), so the quantity supplied by the market is 40,000 (point *v*).

The market supply curve is positively sloped, reflecting the law of supply. This is sensible because if each firm obeys the law of supply, firms as a group will too. When the price increases from $8 to $10, there is a change in quantity supplied as we move along the market supply curve from point *u* to point *v*. The movement along the supply curve occurs if the price of pizza is the only determinant of supply that has changed.

TEST Your Understanding

1. Complete the statement with "increase" or "decrease": When a price increases, the law of demand suggests that the quantity demanded will _____, while the law of supply suggests that the quantity supplied will _____.
2. List the variables that are held fixed in drawing a market demand curve.
3. List the variables that are held fixed in drawing a market supply curve.

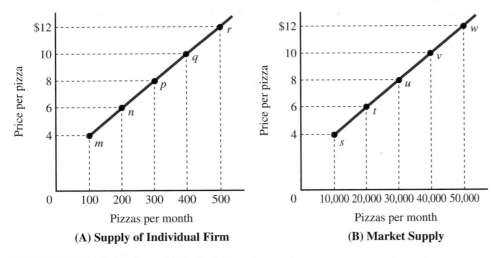

FIGURE 4.4 **Individual and Market Supply**

(A) Supply of an individual firm. Nora supplies 300 pizzas at a price of $8 (point *p*) but 400 pizzas at a price of $10 (point *q*).

(B) Market supply. There are 100 identical pizzerias, so the market quantity equals 100 times the quantity supplied by Nora's, the typical pizzeria. At a price of $8, Nora supplies 300 pizzas (point *p*), so the market quantity supplied is 30,000 pizzas (point *u*).

Market Equilibrium

When the quantity of a product demanded equals the quantity supplied, this is called a **market equilibrium**. When a market reaches an equilibrium, there is no pressure to change the price. For example, if pizza firms produce exactly the quantity of pizza consumers are willing to buy, there will be no pressure for the price of pizza to change. The equilibrium price is shown by the intersection of the supply and demand curves. In Figure 4.5 at a price of $8, the supply curve shows that firms will produce 30,000 pizzas, which is exactly the quantity that consumers are willing to buy at that price.

Market equilibrium
A situation in which the quantity of a product demanded equals the quantity supplied, so there is no pressure to change the price.

Excess Demand Causes the Price to Rise

If the price is below the equilibrium price, there will be excess demand for the product. **Excess demand** (sometimes called a shortage) occurs when consumers are willing to buy more than producers are willing to sell. In Figure 4.5 at a price of $6, there is an excess demand equal to 17,000 pizzas: Consumers are willing to buy 37,000 pizzas (point *d*), but producers are willing to sell only 20,000 pizzas (point *c*). This mismatch between supply and demand will cause the price of pizza to rise. Firms will increase the price they charge for their limited supply of pizza, and anxious consumers will pay the higher price to get one of the few pizzas that are available.

An increase in price eliminates excess demand by changing both the quantity demanded and quantity supplied. As the price increases, the excess demand shrinks for two reasons:

▶ The market moves upward along the demand curve (from point *d* toward point *e*), decreasing the quantity demanded.

Excess demand
A situation in which, at the prevailing price, consumers are willing to buy more than producers are willing to sell.

▶ The market moves upward along the supply curve (from point *c* toward point *e*), increasing the quantity supplied.

Because quantity demanded decreases while quantity supplied increases, the gap between the quantity demanded and the quantity supplied narrows. The price will continue to rise until excess demand is eliminated. In Figure 4.5, at a price of $8, the quantity supplied equals the quantity demanded.

In some cases, government creates an excess demand for a good by setting a maximum price (sometimes called a price ceiling). If the government sets a maximum price that is less than the equilibrium price, the result is a permanent excess demand for the good. We will explore the market effects of such policies in the next chapter.

Excess Supply Causes the Price to Drop

Excess supply

A situation in which, at the prevailing price, producers are willing to sell more than consumers are willing to buy.

What happens if the price is above the equilibrium price? **Excess supply** (sometimes called a surplus) occurs when producers are willing to sell more than consumers are willing to buy. This is shown by points *r* and *s* in Figure 4.5. At a price of $12, the excess supply is 35,000 pizzas: Producers are willing to sell 50,000 pizzas (point *s*), but consumers are willing to buy only 15,000 pizzas (point *r*). This mismatch will cause the price of pizzas to fall as firms cut the price to sell them. As the price drops, the excess supply will shrink for two reasons:

▶ The market moves downward along the demand curve, increasing the quantity demanded.
▶ The market moves downward along the supply curve, decreasing the quantity supplied.

Because the quantity demanded increases while the quantity supplied decreases, the gap between quantity supplied and demanded narrows. The price will continue to

FIGURE 4.5

Market Equilibrium
At the market equilibrium (point *e*, with price = $8 and quantity = 30,000), the quantity supplied equals the quantity demanded. At a price lower than the equilibrium price ($6), there is excess demand (the quantity demanded exceeds the quantity supplied). At a price above the equilibrium price ($12), there is excess supply (the quantity supplied exceeds the quantity demanded).

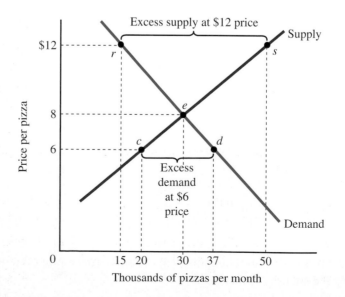

drop until excess supply is eliminated. In Figure 4.5, at price of $8, the quantity supplied equals the quantity demanded.

The government sometimes creates an excess supply of a good by setting a minimum price (sometimes called a price floor). If the government sets a minimum price that is greater than the equilibrium price, the result is a permanent excess supply. We'll discuss the market effects of minimum prices in the next chapter.

TEST Your Understanding

4. Complete the statement: The market equilibrium is shown by the intersection of the _____ curve and the _____ curve.
5. Complete the statement with "less" or "greater": Excess demand occurs when the price is _____ than the equilibrium price; excess supply occurs when the price is _____ than the equilibrium price.
6. Complete the statement with "supply" or "demand": A maximum price below the equilibrium price causes excess _____, while a minimum price above the equilibrium price causes excess _____.

Market Effects of Changes in Demand

We've seen that a market equilibrium occurs when the quantity supplied equals the quantity demanded, shown graphically by the intersection of the supply curve and the demand curve. In this part of the chapter, we'll see how changes on the demand side of the market affect the equilibrium price and equilibrium quantity.

Change in Quantity Demanded Versus Change in Demand

Earlier in the chapter, we listed the variables that determine how much of a particular product consumers are willing to buy. One of the variables is the price of the product, and the demand curve shows the negative relationship between price and quantity demanded, *ceteris paribus*. In Panel A of Figure 4.6, when the price increases from $8 to $12, we move along the demand curve from point *b* to point *c*, and the quantity demanded decreases. As noted earlier in the chapter, this is called a *change in quantity demanded*. Now, we're ready to take a closer look at the other variables that affect demand besides price—income, the prices of related goods, tastes, advertising, and the number of consumers—and see how changes in these variables affect the demand for the product and the market equilibrium.

If any of these other variables change, the relationship between the product's price and quantity—shown numerically in the demand schedule and graphically in the demand curve—will change. That means we will have an entirely different demand schedule and an entirely different demand curve. In Panel B of Figure 4.6, for example, this is shown as a *shift* of the entire demand curve from D_1 to D_2. A shift means that at

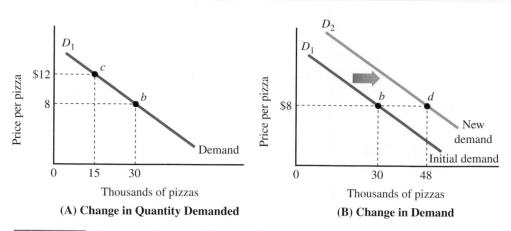

(A) Change in Quantity Demanded   **(B) Change in Demand**

FIGURE 4.6 **Change in Demand Versus Change in Quantity Demanded**
(A) A change in price causes a change in quantity demanded, a movement along a single demand curve. For example, an increase in price causes a move from point *b* to point *c*.
(B) A change in demand (caused by changes in something other than the price of the good) shifts the entire demand curve. For example, an increase in demand shifts the demand curve from D_1 to D_2. For any given price (for example, $8), a larger quantity is demanded (48,000 pizzas instead of $30,000).

Change in demand
A change in the amount of a good demanded resulting from a change in something other than the price of the good; represented graphically by a shift of the demand curve.

As income increases, consumers buy more of a "normal" good like restaurant meals and less of an "inferior" good like Spam.

any price, consumers are willing to buy a larger quantity of the product. For example, at a price of $8, consumers are willing to buy 48,000 pizzas, up from 30,000 with the original demand curve. To convey the idea that changes in these other variables change the demand schedule and the demand curve, we say that a change in any of these variables causes a **change in demand**.

Increases in Demand

We'll start with changes in the pizza market that increase the demand for pizza. An increase in demand means that at each price, consumers are willing to buy a larger quantity. In Figure 4.7, an increase in demand shifts the market demand curve from D_1

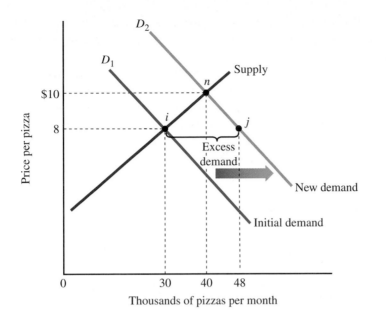

Thousands of pizzas per month

FIGURE 4.7

Market Effects of an Increase in Demand
An increase in demand shifts the demand curve to the right: At each price, the quantity demanded increases. At the initial price ($8), the shift of the demand curve causes excess demand, causing the price to rise. Equilibrium is restored at point *n*, with a higher equilibrium price ($10, up from $8) and a larger equilibrium quantity (40,000 pizzas, up from 30,000 pizzas).

to D_2. At the initial price of $8, the quantity demanded increases from 30,000 pizzas (point *i*) to 48,000 (point *j*). An increase in demand like the one represented in Figure 4.7 can occur for several reasons, which are listed in the first column of Table 4.3:

▶ Increase in income. Consumers use their income to buy products, and the more money they have, the more money they spend. For a normal good there is a positive relationship between consumer income and the quantity consumed. A **normal good** is a good that consumers buy more of when their income *increases*. Most goods fall into this category. New clothes, movies, and pizza are examples of normal goods.
▶ Decrease in income. An **inferior good** is the opposite of a normal good. Consumers buy more of inferior goods when their income *decreases*. For example, if you were laid off from your job, you might resort to buying more used clothing,

Normal good
A good for which an increase in income increases demand.

Inferior good
A good for which an increase in income decreases demand.

TABLE 4.3

Changes in Demand Shift the Demand Curve

An increase in demand shifts the demand curve to the right when:	A decrease in demand shifts the demand curve to the left when:
The good is normal and income increases	The good is normal and income decreases
The good is inferior and income decreases	The good is inferior and income increases
The price of a substitute good increases	The price of a substitute good decreases
The price of a complementary good decreases	The price of a complementary good increases
Population increases	Population decreases
Consumer tastes shift in favor of the product	Consumer tastes shift away from the product
Consumers expect a higher price in the future	Consumers expect a lower price in the future

renting DVDs instead of going to the theatre, and eating more macaroni and cheese. In this case, used clothing, DVDs, and macaroni and cheese are examples of inferior goods.

Substitutes

Two goods that are related in such a way that an increase in the price of one good increases the demand for the other good.

Complements

Two goods related in such a way that a decrease in the price of one good increases the demand for the other good.

▶ Increase in price of a substitute good. When two goods are **substitutes**, an increase in the price of the first good causes some consumers to switch to the second good. Tacos and pizzas are substitutes, so an increase in the price of tacos increases the demand for pizzas as some consumers substitute pizza for tacos, which are now more expensive relative to pizza.

▶ Decrease in price of a complementary good. When two goods are **complements**, they are consumed together as a package, and a decrease in the price of one good decreases the cost of the entire package. As a result, consumers buy more of both goods. Pizza and beer are complementary goods, so a decrease in the price of beer decreases the total cost of a beer-and-pizza meal, increasing the demand for pizza.

▶ Increase in population. An increase in the number of people means that there are more potential pizza consumers—more individual demand curves to add up to get the market demand curve—so market demand increases.

▶ Shift in consumer tastes. Consumers' preferences or tastes can change over time. If consumers' preferences shift in favor of pizza, the demand for pizza increases. The purpose of advertising is to shift consumers' preferences. Therefore, a successful pizza advertising campaign will increase the demand for pizza.

▶ Expectations of higher future prices. If consumers think next month's pizza price will be higher in the future than they had initially expected, they may buy a larger quantity today (and a smaller quantity next month). That means that the demand for pizza today will increase.

We can use Figure 4.7 to show how an increase in demand affects the equilibrium price and equilibrium quantity. An increase in the demand for pizza resulting from one or more of the factors listed in Table 4.3 shifts the demand curve to the right, from D_1 to D_2. At the initial price of $8, there will be excess demand, as indicated by points i and j: Consumers are willing to buy 48,000 pizzas (point j), but producers are willing to sell only 30,000 pizzas (point i). Consumers want to buy 18,000 more pizzas than producers are willing to supply, and the excess demand causes upward pressure on the price. As the price rises, the excess demand shrinks because the quantity demanded decreases while the quantity supplied increases. The supply curve intersects the new demand curve at point n, so the new equilibrium price is $10 (up from $8), and the new equilibrium quantity is 40,000 pizzas (up from 30,000).

Decreases in Demand

What sort of changes in the pizza market will decrease the demand for pizza? A decrease in demand means that at each price, consumers are willing to buy a smaller quantity. In Figure 4.8, a decrease in demand shifts the market demand curve from D_1 to D_0. At the initial price of $8, the quantity demanded decreases from 30,000 pizzas (point i) to 12,000 pizzas (point k). A decrease in demand like the one represented in Figure 4.8 can occur for several reasons, which are listed in the second column of Table 4.3.

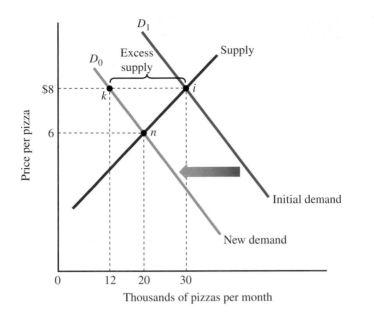

FIGURE 4.8

Market Effects of a Decrease in Demand
A decrease in demand shifts the demand curve to the left: At each price, the quantity demanded decreases. At the initial price ($8), the leftward shift of the demand curve causes excess supply, causing the price to fall. Equilibrium is restored at point *n*, with a lower equilibrium price ($6, down from $8) and a smaller equilibrium quantity (20,000 pizzas, down from 30,000 pizzas).

▶ Decrease in income. A decrease in income means that consumers have less to spend, so they buy a smaller quantity of each normal good.

▶ Decrease in price of a substitute good. A decrease in the price of a substitute good such as tacos makes pizza more expensive relative to tacos, causing consumers to demand less pizza.

▶ Increase in price of a complementary good. An increase in the price of a complementary good such as beer increases the cost of a beer-and-pizza meal, decreasing the demand for pizza.

▶ Decrease in population. A decrease in the number of people means that there are fewer pizza consumers, so the market demand for pizza decreases.

▶ Shift in consumer tastes. When consumers' preferences shift away from pizza in favor of other products, the demand for pizza decreases.

▶ Expectations of lower future prices. If consumers think next month's pizza price will be lower than they had initially expected, they may buy a smaller quantity today, meaning the demand for pizza today will decrease.

We can use Figure 4.8 to show how a decrease in demand affects the equilibrium price and equilibrium quantity. The decrease in the demand for pizza shifts the demand curve to the left, from D_1 to D_0. At the initial price of $8, there will be an excess supply, as indicated by points *i* and *k*: Producers are willing to sell 30,000 pizzas (point *i*), but given the lower demand, consumers are willing to buy only 12,000 pizzas (point *k*). Producers want to sell 18,000 more pizzas than consumers are willing to buy, and the excess supply causes downward pressure on the price. As the price falls, the excess supply shrinks because the quantity demanded increases while the quantity supplied decreases. The supply curve intersects the new demand curve at point *n*, so the new equilibrium price is $6 (down from $8), and the new equilibrium quantity is 20,000 pizzas (down from 30,000).

TEST Your Understanding

7. Which of the following go together?
   a. A change in demand
   b. A change in quantity demanded
   c. A change in price
   d. Movement along the demand curve
   e. A shift in the demand curve
   f. A change in income
8. What's wrong with the following statement? "Demand increased because the demand curve shifted."
9. Complete the statement with "right" or "left": An increase in the price of cassette tapes will shift the demand curve for CDs to the _____; an increase in the price of CD players will shift the demand curve for CDs to the _____.
10. Circle the following variables that change as we move along the demand curve for pencils, and cross out the ones that are assumed to be fixed:
    Quantity of pencils demanded
    Number of consumers
    Price of pencils
    Price of pens
    Consumer income

Market Effects of Changes in Supply

We've seen that changes in demand shift the demand curve and change the equilibrium price and quantity. In this part of the chapter, we'll see how changes on the supply side of the market affect the equilibrium price and equilibrium quantity.

Change in Quantity Supplied Versus Change in Supply

Earlier in the chapter, we listed the variables that determine how much of a particular product firms are willing to sell. Of course, one of the important variables is the price of the product. The supply curve shows the positive relationship between price and quantity, *ceteris paribus*. In Panel A of Figure 4.9, when the price increases from $6 to $8, we move along the supply curve from point *e* to point *f*, and the quantity of the product supplied increases. As noted earlier in the chapter, this is called a *change in quantity supplied*. Now we're ready to take a closer look at the other variables that affect supply—input costs, technology, the number of firms, and price expectations—and see how changes in these variables affect the supply of the product and the market equilibrium.

If any of these other variables changes, the relationship between price and quantity—shown numerically in the supply schedule and graphically in the supply curve—will change. That means that we will have an entirely different supply schedule and a different supply curve. In Panel B of Figure 4.9, this is shown as a shift of the entire

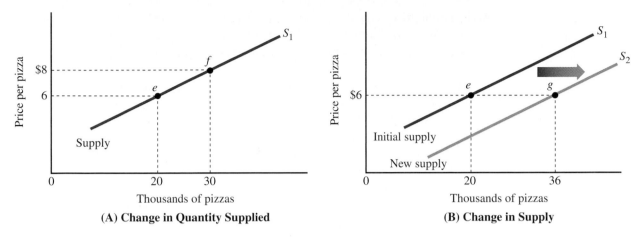

(A) **Change in Quantity Supplied**   (B) **Change in Supply**

FIGURE 4.9 **Change in Supply Versus Change in Quantity Supplied**

(A) A change in price causes a change in quantity supplied, a movement along a single supply curve. For example, an increase in price causes a move from point *e* to point *f*.
(B) A change in supply (caused by changes in something other than the price of the good) shifts the entire supply curve. For example, an increase in supply shifts the demand curve from S_1 to S_2. For any given price (for example, $6), a larger quantity is supplied (36,000 pizzas instead of 20,000).

supply curve from S_1 to S_2: at any price, producers are willing to sell a larger quantity. For example, at a price of $6, producers are willing to sell 36,000 pizzas, up from 20,000 with the initial supply curve. To convey the idea that changes in these other variables change the supply schedule and the supply curve, we say that a change in any of these variables causes a **change in supply**.

Increases in Supply

We'll start with changes in the pizza market that increase the supply of pizza. An increase in supply means that at each price, producers are willing to sell a larger quantity. In Figure 4.10, an increase in supply shifts the market supply curve from S_1 to S_2.

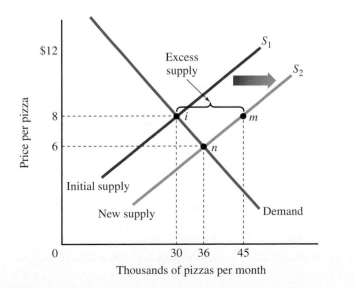

Change in supply
A change in the amount of a good supplied resulting from a change in something other than the price of the good; represented graphically by a shift of the supply curve.

FIGURE 4.10

Market Effects of an Increase in Supply
An increase in supply shifts the supply curve to the right: At each price, the quantity supplied increases. At the initial price ($8), the rightward shift of the supply curve causes excess supply, causing the price to drop. Equilibrium is restored at point *n*, with a lower equilibrium price ($6, down from $8) and a larger equilibrium quantity (36,000 pizzas, up from 30,000 pizzas).

At the initial price of $8, the quantity supplied increases from 30,000 pizzas (point *i*) to 45,000 (point *m*). An increase in supply like the one represented in Figure 4.10 can occur for several reasons, which are listed in the first column of Table 4.4.

▶ A decrease in input costs. A decrease in the cost of labor or some other input will make pizza production less costly and more profitable at a given price, so producers will supply more.

▶ An advance in technology. A technological advance that makes it possible to produce pizza at a lower cost will make pizza production more profitable, so producers will supply more of it.

▶ An increase in the number of producers. The market supply is the sum of the product supplied by all producers, so the larger the number of producers, the greater the supply.

▶ Expectations of lower future prices. If firms think next month's pizza price will be lower than they had initially expected, they may be willing to sell a larger quantity today (and a smaller quantity next month). That means that the supply of pizza today will increase.

▶ Subsidy. If the government subsidizes the production of the product (pays firms some amount for each unit produced), the subsidy will make the product more profitable, so firms will produce more.

We can use Figure 4.10 to show the effects of an increase in supply on the equilibrium price and equilibrium quantity. An increase in the supply of pizza shifts the supply curve to the right, from S_1 to S_2. At the initial price of $8 (the equilibrium price with the initial supply curve), there will be an excess supply, as indicated by points *i* and *m*: Producers are willing to sell 45,000 pizzas (point *m*), but consumers are willing to buy only 30,000 (point *i*). Producers want to sell 15,000 more pizzas than consumers are willing to buy, and the excess supply causes pressure to decrease the price. As the price decreases, the excess supply shrinks because the quantity supplied decreases while the quantity demanded increases. The new supply curve intersects the demand curve at point *n*, so the new equilibrium price is $6 (down from $8) and the new equilibrium quantity is 36,000 pizzas (up from 30,000).

How has technological change in electricity generation affected the supply of electricity from alternative sources, including wind power? To see the effects of technological innovation in the production of wind power, read "A Closer Look: Increasing the Supply of Wind Power."

TABLE 4.4

Changes in Supply Shift the Supply Curve

An increase in supply shifts the supply curve to the right when:	A decrease in supply shifts the supply curve to the left when:
The cost of an input decreases	The cost of an input increases
A technological advance decreases production cost	
The number of firms increases	The number of firms decreases
Producers expect a lower price in the future	Producers expect a higher price in the future
Product is subsidized	Product is taxed

A CLOSER LOOK   Increasing the Supply of Wind Power

In recent years, the supply of electricity generated from wind power has increased dramatically, doubling in 2001.[1] The rapid increase in wind-generated electricity resulted from technological innovations that decreased production costs. In the 1980s, the cost of wind electricity was about 50 cents per kilowatt hour. Several design innovations—including the replacement of small, rapid rotors with large, slow-moving blades and the development of monitoring systems that permit the turbines to change their direction and blade angle to more efficiently harness the wind—have decreased the cost of maintaining the turbines and increased the electricity output per hour. By 2001, the cost of wind power had dropped to about four cents per kilowatt hour, compared with 2.5 to three cents for electricity generated by conventional sources (natural gas and coal). Because the producers of wind power receive a federal tax credit of 1.5 cents per kilowatt hour, wind power is often competitive with conventional power sources.

In graphical terms, the technological innovations decreased production costs, shifting the supply curve for wind electricity to the right, increasing the equilibrium quantity and decreasing its price.

Decreases in Supply

What sort of changes in the pizza market will decrease the supply of pizza? A decrease in supply means that at each price, producers are willing to supply a smaller quantity. In Figure 4.11, a decrease in supply shifts the market supply curve from S_1 to S_0. At the initial price of $8, the quantity supplied decreases from 30,000 pizzas (point i) to 14,000 pizzas (point p). A decrease in supply like the one represented in Figure 4.11 can occur for several reasons, which are listed in the second column of Table 4.4.

▶ Increase in input costs. An increase in the cost of labor or some other input will make pizza production more costly and less profitable at a given price, so producers will supply less.

▶ A decrease in the number of producers. The market supply is the sum of the supplies of all producers, so a decrease in the number of producers decreases supply.

▶ Expectations of higher future prices. If firms think next month's pizza price will be higher than they had initially expected, they may be willing to sell a smaller quantity today (and a larger quantity next month). That means that the supply of pizza today will decrease.

▶ Taxes. If the government imposes a tax on each unit produced by the firm, the tax will make the product more costly and less profitable. Consequently, firms will supply less of it.

FIGURE 4.11

Market Effects of a Decrease in Supply
A decrease in supply shifts the supply curve to the left: At each price, the quantity supplied decreases. At the initial price ($8), the leftward shift of the supply curve causes excess demand, causing the price to rise. Equilibrium is restored at point *n*, with a higher equilibrium price ($10, up from $8) and a smaller equilibrium quantity (23,000 pizzas, down from 30,000 pizzas).

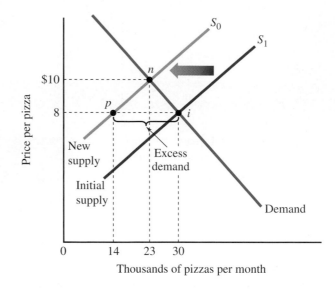

We can use Figure 4.11 to show the effects of a decrease in supply on the equilibrium price and equilibrium quantity. A decrease in the supply of pizza shifts the supply curve to the left, from S_1 to S_0. At the initial price of $8 (the equilibrium price with the initial supply curve), there will be an excess demand, as indicated by points *i* and *p*: Consumers are willing to buy 30,000 pizzas (point *i*), but producers are willing to sell only 14,000 pizzas (point *p*). Consumers want to buy 16,000 more pizzas than producers are willing to sell, and the excess demand causes upward pressure on the price. As the price increases, the excess demand shrinks because the quantity demanded decreases while the quantity supplied increases. The new supply curve intersects the demand curve at point *n*, so the new equilibrium price is $10 (up from $8), and the new equilibrium quantity is 23,000 pizzas (down from 30,000).

Market Effects of Simultaneous Changes in Demand and Supply

What happens to the equilibrium price and quantity when both supply and demand increase? It depends on which change is larger. In Panel A of Figure 4.12, the increase in demand is larger than the increase in supply, meaning the demand curve shifts by a larger amount than the supply curve. The market equilibrium moves from point *i* to point *d*, and the equilibrium price increases from $8 to $9. This is sensible because an increase in demand tends to pull the price up, while an increase in supply tends to push the price down. If demand increases by a larger amount, the upward pull will be stronger than the downward push, and the price will rise.

We can be certain that when supply and demand both increase, the equilibrium quantity will increase. That's because both changes tend to increase the equilibrium quantity. In Panel A of Figure 4.12, the equilibrium quantity increases from 30,000 to 44,000 pizzas.

Panel B of Figure 4.12 shows what happens when the increase in supply is larger than the increase in demand. The equilibrium moves from point *i* to *s*, meaning that

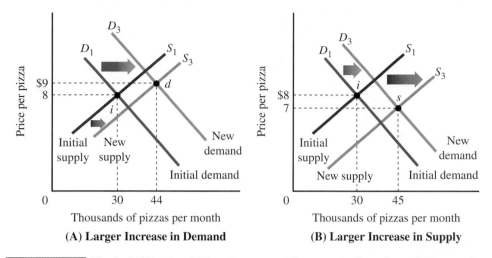

FIGURE 4.12 **Market Effects of Simultaneous Changes in Supply and Demand**
(A) Larger increase in demand. If the increase in demand is larger than the increase in supply (if the shift of the demand curve is larger than the shift of the supply curve), both the equilibrium price and the equilibrium quantity will increase.
(B) Larger increase in supply. If the increase in supply is larger than the increase in demand (if the shift of the supply curve is larger than the shift of the demand curve), the equilibrium price will decrease and the equilibrium quantity will increase.

the price falls from $8 to $7. This is sensible because the downward pull on the price resulting from the increase in supply is stronger than the upward pull from the increase in demand. As expected, the equilibrium quantity rises from 30,000 to 45,000 pizzas.

What about simultaneous decreases in supply and demand? In this case the equilibrium quantity will certainly fall because both changes tend to decrease the equilibrium quantity. The effect on the equilibrium price depends on which change is larger, the decrease in demand, which pushes the price downward, or the decrease in supply, which pulls the price upward. If the change in demand is larger, the price will fall because the force pushing the price down will be stronger than the force pulling it up. In contrast, if the decrease in supply is larger, the price will rise because the force pulling the price up will be stronger than the force pushing it down.

TEST Your Understanding

11. Which of the following items go together?
   a. A change in quantity supplied
   b. A change in an input cost
   c. A change in price
   d. A shift of the supply curve
   e. Movement along the supply curve
   f. A change in supply

(continued)

12. An increase in the wage of computer workers will shift the supply curve for computers to the left. True or false? Explain.
13. Circle the following variables that change as we move along the market supply curve for housing, and cross out the variables that are assumed to be fixed:
    a. Quantity of housing supplied
    b. Number of firms
    c. Price of wood
    d. Price of houses
    e. Technology

Using the Model to Predict Changes in Price and Quantity

We've used the model of supply and demand to show how equilibrium prices are determined and how changes in demand and supply affect equilibrium prices and quantities. Table 4.5 summarizes what we've learned about how changes in demand and supply affect equilibrium prices and quantities.

▶ When demand changes and the demand curve shifts, price and quantity change in the *same* direction: When demand increases, both price and quantity increase; when demand decreases, both price and quantity decrease.
▶ When supply changes and the supply curve shifts, price and quantity change in *opposite* directions: When supply increases, the price decreases but the quantity increases; when supply decreases, the price increases but the quantity decreases.

We can use these lessons about supply and demand to predict the effects of various events on the equilibrium price and equilibrium quantity of a product.

Population Growth and Apartment Prices

How will an increase in enrollment at a university affect the equilibrium price of apartments in a university town? An increase in university enrollment will increase the number of students seeking apartments thereby increasing the demand for apartments. As shown in the first row of Table 4.5, we would expect the increase in demand

TABLE 4.5

Market Effects of Changes in Demand or Supply

Change in Demand or Supply	Change in Price	Change in Quantity
Increase in demand	Increase	Increase
Decrease in demand	Decrease	Decrease
Increase in supply	Decrease	Increase
Decrease in supply	Increase	Decrease

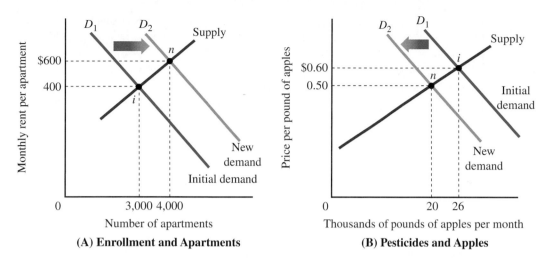

(A) Enrollment and Apartments   **(B) Pesticides and Apples**

FIGURE 4.13 **Predicting the Effects of Changes in Demand**

(A) An increase in university enrollment will increase the demand for apartments, shifting the demand curve to the right. The equilibrium price increases from $400 to $600, and the equilibrium quantity increases from 3,000 to 4,000.

(B) A report of pesticide residue on apples decreases the demand for apples, shifting the demand curve to the left. The equilibrium price decreases from $0.60 to $0.50, and the equilibrium quantity decreases from 26,000 to 20,000 pounds.

to increase both the price and quantity of apartments. In Panel A of Figure 4.13, the initial equilibrium in the apartment market is shown by point *i*, with a monthly rent of $400 per apartment. An increase in university enrollment shifts the demand for apartments to the right, leading to a new equilibrium at point *n*, with a higher price ($600) and a larger quantity.

Product Safety and Apples

How will public information about the safety of products affect equilibrium prices and quantities? In 1999, a controversial report suggested that pesticide residue on apples made them unsafe for infants and small children. Although many experts disputed the report, it nonetheless decreased the demand for apples. Essentially, the report had the opposite effect of advertising. As shown in the second row of Table 4.5, we would expect the decrease in demand to decrease both the price and quantity of apples. In Panel B of Figure 4.13, the initial equilibrium is shown by point *i*, with a price of $0.60 per pound and a quantity of 26,000 pounds per month. After the pesticide report is released, the demand curve shifts to the left, leading to a new equilibrium at point *n*, with a lower price ($0.50) and a smaller quantity (20,000 pounds).

Technological Innovation and Computers

How will technological innovations affect equilibrium prices? Let's look at the market for personal computers. Recent innovations in electronics have decreased the cost of producing personal computers, increasing the supply of computers. As shown in the

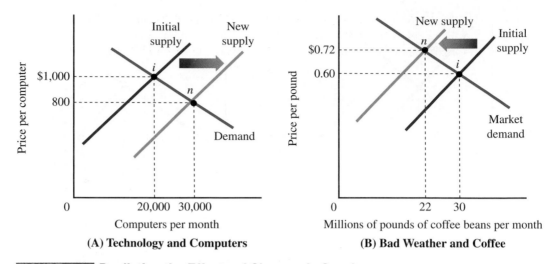

(A) Technological innovation decreases production costs, shifting the supply curve to the right. The equilibrium price decreases from $1,000 to $800, and the equilibrium quantity increases from 20,000 to 30,000. Bad weather decreases the supply of coffee beans, shifting the supply curve to the left. **(B)** The equilibrium price increases from $0.60 to $0.72, and the equilibrium quantity decreases from 30 million to 22 million pounds.

third row of Table 4.5, we would expect the increase in supply to decrease the price but increase the quantity of computers. In Panel A of Figure 4.14, the initial equilibrium is shown by point *i*, with a price of $1,000 and a quantity of 20,000 computers. The innovation that decreased production costs shifts the supply curve to the right, generating a new equilibrium at point *n*, with a lower price ($800) and a larger quantity (30,000).

Weather and Coffee

How will poor weather affect equilibrium prices? In 1992, several events combined to decrease the world supply of coffee. Poor weather and insect infestations in Brazil and Colombia decreased the coffee bean harvest by about 40%. Some farmers lost their entire crop, so the number of producers decreased. In addition, a slowdown by dockworkers at Santos, Brazil's main coffee bean port, decreased the amount supplied to the world market. As shown in the fourth row of Table 4.5, we would expect the decrease in supply to increase the price but decrease the quantity of coffee. In Panel B of Figure 4.14, the initial equilibrium is shown by point *i*, with a price of $0.60 and a quantity of 30 million pounds. The poor weather, insect infestations, and other supply disruptions shifted the supply curve to the left, generating a new equilibrium at point *n*, with a higher price ($0.72) and a smaller quantity (22 million pounds).

Explaining Changes in Price or Quantity

We can use the lessons listed in Table 4.5 to explain the reasons for changes in prices or quantities. Suppose we observe changes in the equilibrium price and quantity of a particular good, but we don't know what caused these changes. Perhaps it was a change in demand, or maybe it was a change in supply. We can use the information in Table 4.5 to work backwards, using what we've observed about changes in prices and quantities to determine which side of the market—supply or demand—caused the changes.

An Increase in Poultry Consumption

Why has the consumption of poultry (chicken and turkey) increased so much over the last several decades? One possibility is that consumers have become more health conscious and have switched from red meat to poultry in an effort to eat healthier. In other words, the demand curve for poultry may have shifted to the right, increasing the equilibrium quantity of poultry. Of course, an increase in demand will increase the price too, so if this explanation is correct, we should also observe higher prices for poultry.

According to the U.S. Department of Agriculture, this popular explanation is incorrect.[2] In fact, the increase in poultry consumption was caused by an increase in supply, not an increase in demand. This conclusion is based on the fact that poultry prices have been decreasing, not increasing. Between 1950 and 1990, the real price of poultry (adjusted for inflation) actually decreased by about 75%. As shown in Panel A of Figure 4.15, an increase in supply causes the market equilibrium to shift from point *i* (where price = $2 and quantity = 50 million pounds) to point *n* (price = $0.80 and quantity = 90 million pounds). In other words, the increase in supply decreased the equilibrium price. The supply of poultry increased because innovations in poultry processing decreased the cost of producing poultry products. The lesson here is that we shouldn't jump to conclusions based on limited information. A change in the equilibrium quantity could result from either a change in supply or a

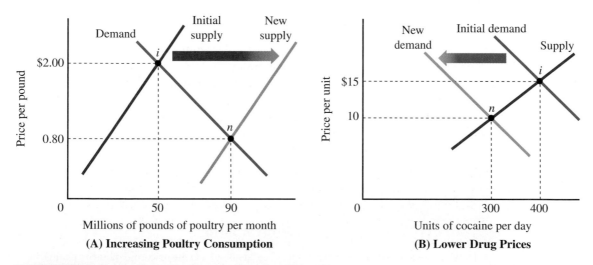

FIGURE 4.15 **Explaining Changes in Price or Quantity**
(A) At the same time the quantity of poultry increased (from 50 million pounds to 90 million), the price decreased (from $2.00 to $0.80). Therefore, the increase in consumption resulted from an increase in supply, not an increase in demand.
(B) At the same time the price of cocaine decreased (from $15 to $10), the quantity of cocaine consumed decreased (from 400 units to 300 units). Therefore, the decrease in price was caused by a decrease in demand, not an increase in supply.

change in demand. To draw any conclusions, we need information about both price and quantity.

Nonetheless, there may be a grain of truth in the popular explanation that poultry consumption increased because consumers were trying to eat healthier. It is indeed possible that the demand curve shifted to the right, meaning that both supply and demand increased. Because the price of poultry decreased, however, we know that the shift of the supply curve (which tends to decrease the price) overwhelmed any shift of the demand curve (which tends to increase the price). So although changes in consumer preferences might have contributed to the increase in poultry consumption, the changes in consumption were caused largely by changes on the supply side of the market.

A Decrease in Drug Prices

Ted Koppel, host of the ABC news program *Nightline*, once said, "Do you know what's happened to the price of drugs in the United States? The price of cocaine, way down, the price of marijuana, way down. You don't have to be an expert in economics to know that when the price goes down, it means more stuff is coming in. That's supply and demand."[3] According to Koppel, the price of drugs dropped because the government's efforts to control the supply of illegal drugs had failed. In other words, the lower price resulted from an increase in supply. According to the U.S. Department of Justice, the quantity of drugs consumed actually decreased during the period of dropping prices.[4] Is Koppel's economic detective work sound?

In this case, both the price and the quantity decreased. As shown in the second row of Table 4.5, when both the price and the quantity decrease, that means demand has decreased. For example, in Panel B of Figure 4.15, a decrease in demand shifts the demand curve to the left, and the market moves from point *i* (price = $15 and quantity = 400 units per day) to point *n* (price = $10 and quantity = 300 units per day). Koppel's explanation (an increase in supply) would be correct if the quantity of drugs increased at the same time that the price decreased. However, because the quantity of drugs consumed actually decreased during the period of dropping prices, Koppel's explanation is incorrect. Lower demand—not a failure of the government's drug policy and an increase in supply—was responsible for the decrease in drug prices.

TEST Your Understanding

14. Complete the statement with "supply" or "demand": If the price and quantity change in the same direction, _____ is changing; if the price and quantity change in opposite directions, _____ is changing.

15. Suppose a freeze in Florida wipes out 20% of the orange crop. How will this affect the equilibrium price of Florida oranges? Defend your answer with a graph.

A CLOSER LOOK

Higher Platinum Prices

In early 2003, the price of platinum reached its highest point in 23 years—$700 per ounce—up by 17% from just a year earlier.[5] The precious metal is used for jewelry and in catalytic converters that control air pollution from automobiles. The higher price was caused by changes on both sides of the platinum market. On the supply side, Russia cut its production to almost zero. It appears that the cut in Russian production was motivated by (1) a desire to stockpile platinum in anticipation of a miners' strike and (2) a desire to get automakers to switch from platinum to palladium, another Russian export. On the demand side, a new interest in fuel-cell technology for cars, which relies on platinum to generate cleaner electricity, increased the demand for the precious metal.

Economic Experiment

Market Equilibrium

This simple experiment takes about 20 minutes. We start by dividing the class into two equal groups: consumers and producers.

- The instructor provides each consumer with a number indicating the maximum amount he or she is willing to pay (WTP) for a bushel of apples: The WTP is a number between $1 and $100. Each consumer has the opportunity to buy 1 bushel of apples per trading period. The consumer's score for a single trading period equals the gap between the WTP and the price actually paid for apples. For example, if the consumer's WTP is $80 and he or she pays only $30 for apples, the consumer's score is $50. Each consumer has the option of not buying apples. This will be sensible if the best price the consumer can get exceeds the WTP. If the consumer does not buy apples, his or her score will be zero.
- The instructor provides each producer with a number indicating the cost of producing a bushel of apples (a number between $1 and $100). Each producer has the opportunity to sell 1 bushel per trading period. The producer's score for a single trading period equals the gap between the selling price and the cost of producing apples. So if a producer sells apples for $20, and the cost is only $15, the producer's score is $5. Producers have the option of not selling apples, which is sensible if the best price the producer can get is less than the cost. If the producer does not sell apples, his or her score is zero.

Once everyone understands the rules, consumers and producers meet in a trading area to arrange transactions. A consumer may announce how much he or she is willing to pay for apples and wait for a producer to agree to sell apples at that price. Alternatively, a producer may announce how much he or she is willing to accept for apples and wait for a consumer to agree to buy apples at that price. Once a transaction has been arranged, the consumer and producer inform the instructor of the trade, record the transaction, and leave the trading area.

(continued)

There are several trading periods, each of which lasts a few minutes. After the end of each trading period, the instructor lists the prices at which apples sold during that period. Then another trading period starts, providing consumers and producers another opportunity to buy or sell 1 bushel of apples. After all the trading periods have been completed, each participant computes his or her score by adding the scores from each trading period.

USING THE TOOLS

In this chapter you learned how to use two tools of economics—the supply curve and the demand curve—to find equilibrium prices to predict changes in prices and quantities. Here are some opportunities to use these tools to do your own economic analysis.

1. Using Data to Draw a Demand Curve

The following table shows data on gasoline prices and gasoline consumption in a particular city. Is it possible to use these data to draw a demand curve? If so, draw the demand curve. If not, why not?

Year	Gasoline Price (per gallon)	Quantity Consumed (millions of gallons)
2003	1.20	400
2004	1.40	300
2005	1.60	360

2. Foreign Farm Workers and the Price of Berries

Current law allows thousands of Mexican workers to work on farms in the United States during harvest season. Suppose a new law outlaws the use of foreign farm workers. Assume that the resulting excess demand for labor increases the wage paid to farm workers by 20%. Use a supply–demand graph to predict the effects of the higher wage on the price of berries.

3. Market Effects of an Import Ban on Shoes

Consider a nation that initially imports half the shoes it consumes. Use a supply–demand graph to predict the effect of a ban on shoe imports on the equilibrium price and quantity of shoes.

4. The Puzzle of Free Used Newspapers

In 1987 you could sell a ton of used newspapers for $60. Five years later, you could not sell them at any price. In other words, the price of used newspapers dropped from $60 to zero in just five years. Over this period, the quantity of used newspapers bought and sold increased. What caused the drop in price? Defend your answer with a supply–demand graph.

SUMMARY

In this chapter, we've seen how supply and demand determine prices. We also learned how to predict the effects of changes in demand or supply on prices and quantities. Here are the main points of the chapter.

1 To draw a demand curve, we must be certain that the other variables that affect demand (consumer income, the prices of related goods, tastes, con-

sumers' price expectations, and the number of consumers) are held fixed.

2 To draw a market supply curve, we must be certain the other variables that affect supply (such as input costs, technology, the number of producers, their price expectations, and taxes and subsidies) are held fixed.

3 Equilibrium in a market is shown by the intersection of the demand curve and the supply curve. When a market reaches equilibrium, there is no pressure to change the price.

4 A change in demand changes price and quantity in the same direction: An increase in demand increases the equilibrium price and quantity; a decrease in demand decreases the equilibrium price and quantity.

5 A change in supply changes price and quantity in opposite directions: An increase in supply decreases price and increases quantity; a decrease in supply increases price and decreases quantity.

KEY TERMS

change in demand, 72
change in quantity demanded, 63
change in quantity supplied, 66
change in supply, 77
complements, 74
demand schedule, 62
excess demand, 69
excess supply, 70

income effect, 63
individual demand curve, 62
individual supply curve, 66
inferior good, 73
law of demand, 63
market demand curve, 64
market equilibrium, 69
market supply curve, 68

normal good, 73
perfectly competitive market, 61
quantity demanded, 62
quantity supplied, 65
substitutes, 74
substitution effect, 63
supply schedule, 66

PROBLEMS AND DISCUSSION QUESTIONS

1 Figure 4.A shows the supply and demand curves for CD players. Complete the following statements.

a. At the market equilibrium (shown by point _____), the price of CD players is _____ and the quantity of CD players is _____.

b. At a price of $100, there would be excess _____, so we would expect the price to _____.

c. At a price exceeding the equilibrium price, there would be excess _____, so we would expect the price to _____.

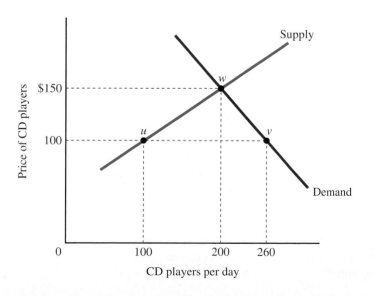

FIGURE 4.A

Supply and Demand for CD Players

2 The following table shows the quantities of corn supplied and demanded at different prices:

Price per Ton	Quantity Supplied	Quantity Demanded	Excess Demand or Excess Supply
$80	600	1,200	_____
$90	800	1,100	_____
$100	1,000	1,000	_____
$110	1,200	900	_____

    a. Complete the table.

    b. Draw the demand curve and the supply curve.

    c. What is the equilibrium price of corn?

3 Consider the market for personal computers. Suppose that the demand is stable: The demand curve doesn't change. Predict the effects of the following changes on the equilibrium price of computers. Illustrate your answer with a supply and demand diagram.

    a. The cost of memory chips (one component of a computer) decreases.

    b. The government imposes a $100 tax on personal computers.

4 Draw a supply–demand diagram to illustrate the effect of an increase in income on the market for restaurant meals.

5 Suppose that the tuition charged by public universities increases. Draw a supply-demand diagram to illustrate the effects of the tuition hike on the market for private college education.

6 Suppose that the government imposes a tax of $1 per pound of fish and collects the tax from fish producers. Draw a supply-demand diagram to illustrate the market effects of the tax.

7 As summer approaches, the equilibrium price of rental cabins increases and the equilibrium quantity of cabins rented increases. Draw a supply-demand diagram that explains these changes.

8 Suppose that the initial price of a mobile phone is $100 and that the initial quantity demanded is 500 phones per day. Depict graphically the effects of a technological innovation that decreases the cost of producing mobile phones. Label the starting point with "*i*" and the new equilibrium with "*n*."

9 The Multifiber Agreement sets import quotas for various apparel products—including shirts—coming into the United States. Use a supply-demand graph to show the effects of the shirt quota on the equilibrium price of shirts in the United States.

10 Suppose a freeze in Florida wipes out 20% of the orange crop. How will this affect the equilibrium price of California oranges? Defend your answer with a graph.

MODEL ANSWERS

Chapter-Opening Questions

1 As explained in "A Closer Look: Increasing the Supply of Wind Power," innovations in the design of wind turbines decreased the cost of generating electricity from wind power, increasing supply.

2 As explained in the last section of the chapter, the equilibrium quantity of drugs decreased at the same time that prices decreased, so the price drop was caused by a decrease in demand, not an increase in supply.

3 As explained in the last section of the chapter, the price decreased while the quantity increased, so the increase in quantity was caused by an increase in supply, not an increase in demand. Supply increased because innovations in poultry processing decreased the cost of producing poultry.

4 As explained in "Economic Puzzle: Saving Money Wherever You Shop," this is possible because you obey the law of demand, choosing low-price products at each store.

Test Your Understanding

1 decrease, increase

2 consumer income, the prices of substitute goods, the prices of complementary goods, consumer tastes, advertising, the number of consumers, and price expectations

3 input costs, technology, price expectations, number of producers, taxes and subsidies

4 supply, demand

5 less, greater

6 demand, supply

7 One group is a, e, and f; another group is b, c, and d.

8 The statement is incorrect because it confuses the direction of causality. The correct statement is: "The demand curve shifted because demand increased." When something other than the price of the product changes, the relationship between price and quantity changes, causing the demand curve to shift.

9 right, left

10 Circle quantity of pencils demanded and price of pencils. Cross out number of consumers, price of pens, and consumer income.

11 One group is a, c, and e; another group is b, d, and f.

12 True. An increase in the wage increases production cost, so fewer computers will be supplied at each price.

13 Circle quantity of housing supplied and price of houses. Cross out number of firms, price of wood, and technology.

14 demand, supply

15 The supply of oranges decreases, shifting the supply curve to the left. The equilibrium price will increase.

NOTES

1. *The News and Observer*, "Raleigh, N.C.-Based Companies Tap Growing Market for Wind Power," January 26, 2001; *Associated Press Online*, "Wind Farm to Power 70,000 Homes," January 10, 2001.

2. Mark R. Weimar and Richard Stillman, "Market Trends Driving Broiler Consumption," *Livestock and Poultry Situation and Outlook Report LPS-44* (Washington, DC: U.S. Department of Agriculture, Economic Research Service, November 1990).

3. Kenneth R. Clark, "Legalize Drugs. A Case for Koppel," *Chicago Tribune*, August 30, 1988, sec. 5, p. 8.

4. U.S. Department of Justice, "Drugs, Crime, and the Justice System" (Washington, DC: U.S. Government Printing Office, 1992), p. 30.

5. "Going Platinum," *The Economist*, February 8, 2003, p. 68.

Part 2

A Closer Look at Supply and Demand

Chapter 5

Elasticity: A Measure of Responsiveness

Chapter 6

Consumer Choice

Chapter 7

Market Efficiency and Government Intervention

The Price Elasticity of Demand

Price Elasticity and the Demand Curve
What Determines the Price Elasticity
    of Demand?
Computing Price Elasticity: Initial Value
    Versus Midpoint
Elasticity Along a Linear Demand Curve

**Using the Price Elasticity of
Demand to Make Predictions**

Predicting Changes in Quantity Demanded
Applications: College Education, Highway
    Deaths, and Medical Care
Predicting Changes in Total Revenue
Applications: Transit Deficits, Property
    Crime
Other Elasticities of Demand

The Price Elasticity of Supply

Predicting Changes in Quantity Supplied
Extreme Cases: Perfectly Inelastic Supply
    and Perfectly Elastic Supply

**Predicting Changes in Price Using
Supply and Demand Elasticities**

The Price Effects of a Change in Demand
The Price Effects of a Change in Supply
Using the Tools

Elasticity: A Measure of Responsiveness

I n every large city in the United States, the public bus system runs a deficit: Operating costs exceed revenues from passenger fares. Suppose your city wants to reduce its bus deficit and is trying to decide whether to increase fares by 10%. Consider the following exchange between two city officials:

Buster: A fare increase is a great idea. We'll collect more money from bus riders, so revenue will increase, and the deficit will shrink.

Bessie: Wait a minute, Buster. Haven't you heard about the law of demand? The increase in the bus fare will decrease the number of passengers taking buses, so we'll collect less money, not more, and the deficit will grow.

Who is right? As we'll see in this chapter, we can't predict how an increase in price will affect total revenue unless we know just how responsive consumers are to an increase in price. Like other consumers, bus riders obey the law of demand, but that doesn't necessarily mean that total fare revenue will fall.

In Chapter 4, we discussed the law of demand, the observation that an increase in price decreases the quantity demanded, *ceteris paribus*. The law of demand is useful, but sometimes we need to know the numbers behind the law of demand, that is, exactly how much less will be demanded at a higher price. In this chapter, we will quantify the law of demand, exploring the responsiveness of consumers to changes in price. Suppose your student group has decided to increase the price for its film series from $2 to $3. You know from the law of demand that you'll sell fewer tickets, but the question is: How many fewer tickets? As we'll see in this chapter, you can use the notion of elasticity to predict how many tickets you'll sell and how much money you'll collect in total. Similarly, in the case of hiking the bus fare, we can use the notion of elasticity to determine whether Buster or Bessie is correct.

Switching to the supply side of the market, the law of supply tells us that an increase in price increases the quantity supplied, *ceteris paribus*. Sometimes the question is: By how much? We'll quantify the law of supply, showing how to predict just how much more of a product will be supplied at a higher price. For example, if the world price of oil increases from $25 to $28 per barrel, we know from the law of supply that domestic producers will supply more oil, but the question is: How much more? We can use the notion of elasticity to predict how much more domestic oil will be supplied at the higher price.

This chapter contains many applications of the concept of elasticity. Here are some practical questions that we answer:

1. How would a tax on beer affect the number of highway deaths among young adults?
2. Why is a bumper crop bad news for farmers?
3. Why do policies that limit the supply of illegal drugs increase the number of burglaries and robberies?
4. If the population of a city increases by 9%, by how much will housing prices increase?

The Price Elasticity of Demand

Price elasticity of demand

A measure of the responsiveness of the quantity demanded to changes in price; computed by dividing the percentage change in quantity demanded by the percentage change in price.

The **price elasticity of demand** (E_d) measures the responsiveness of consumers to changes in price. We compute the price elasticity by dividing the percentage change in quantity demanded by the percentage change in price:

$$E_d = \frac{\text{percentage change in quantity demanded}}{\text{percentage change in price}}$$

For example, if the price of milk increases by 10% and the quantity demanded decreases by 15%, the price elasticity of demand is 1.5:

$$E_d = \frac{\text{percentage change in quantity demanded}}{\text{percentage change in price}} = \frac{15\%}{10\%} = 1.5$$

When we compute the price elasticity of demand, we ignore any minus signs, so the elasticity is always a positive number. The law of demand tells us that price and quantity demanded always move in opposite directions. This means that the percentage change in price will always have the opposite sign of the percentage change in quantity. In our example, a +10% change in price results in a −15% change in quantity. Although the price elasticity could be reported as a negative number, the conventional approach is to ignore the minus sign and always report the elasticity as a positive number: A large positive elasticity number indicates that the demand for the product is very elastic, or very responsive to changes in price; a small positive elasticity number indicates that the demand for a product is very inelastic. As long as we remember the law of demand, there is no harm in dropping minus signs and reporting all price elasticities of demand as positive numbers.

Price Elasticity and the Demand Curve

Figure 5.1 shows five different demand curves, each with a different elasticity. We can divide products into five types, depending on their price elasticities of demand.

Elastic demand

The price elasticity of demand is greater than 1.

> ▶ **Elastic Demand** (Panel A). In this case, a 20% increase in price (from $5 to $6) decreases the quantity demanded by 40% (from 20 to 12), so the price elasticity of demand is 2.0. When the price elasticity is greater than 1.0, we say that demand is "elastic," or highly responsive to changes in price. Some examples of goods with elastic demand are restaurant meals, air travel, and movies.

Inelastic demand

The price elasticity of demand is less than 1.

> ▶ **Inelastic Demand** (Panel B). The same 20% increase in price decreases the quantity demanded by only 10% (from 20 to 18), so the price elasticity of demand is 0.50. When the elasticity is less than 1.0, we say that demand is "inelastic," or not very responsive to changes in price. Some examples of goods with inelastic demand are eggs, coffee, cigarettes, and electricity.

Unitary elastic

The price elasticity of demand equals 1.

> ▶ **Unitary Elastic Demand** (Panel C). A 20% increase in price decreases the quantity demanded by exactly 20%, so the price elasticity of demand is 1.0. Some examples of goods with close to unitary elasticity are housing, gasoline, and recreation.

Perfectly inelastic demand

The price elasticity of demand equals 0.

> ▶ **Perfectly Inelastic Demand** (Panel D). When demand is perfectly inelastic, the quantity doesn't change as the price changes, so the demand curve is vertical at the fixed quantity. This extreme case is rare because for most products, consumers can either switch to a substitute good or do without. For example, although there are no direct substitutes for household water, as the price of water rises, people install low-flow showerheads, water their lawn less frequently, and drive dirty cars. The rare cases of perfectly inelastic demand are medicines that have no substitutes.

Perfectly elastic demand

The price elasticity of demand is infinite.

> ▶ **Perfectly Elastic Demand** (Panel E). In this case, the demand curve is horizontal, meaning that only one price is possible. At that price, the quantity demanded could

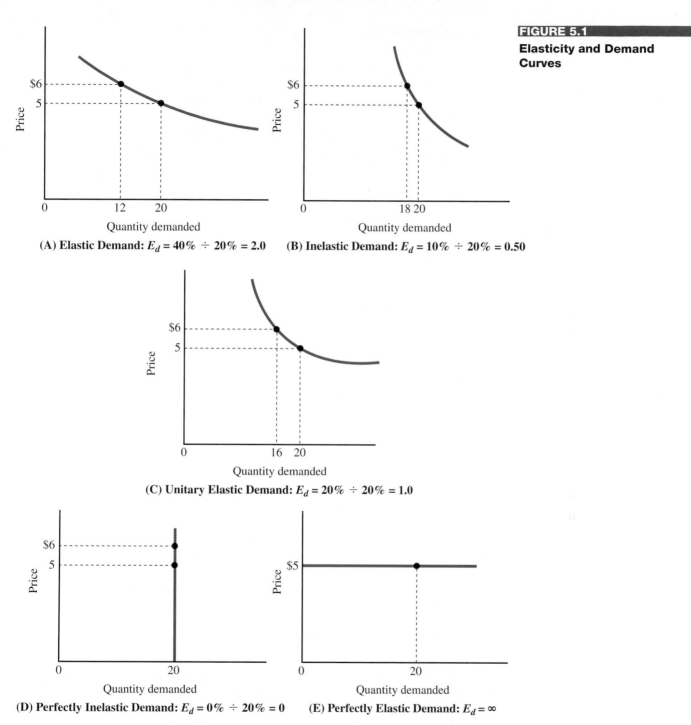

FIGURE 5.1

Elasticity and Demand Curves

(A) Elastic Demand: $E_d = 40\% \div 20\% = 2.0$ **(B) Inelastic Demand:** $E_d = 10\% \div 20\% = 0.50$

(C) Unitary Elastic Demand: $E_d = 20\% \div 20\% = 1.0$

(D) Perfectly Inelastic Demand: $E_d = 0\% \div 20\% = 0$ **(E) Perfectly Elastic Demand:** $E_d = \infty$

be any quantity, from one unit to millions of units. If the price were to increase even a penny, the quantity demanded would drop to zero. As we'll see in Chapter 9, firms in a perfectly competitive market face this sort of demand curve: Each firm can sell as much as it wants at the market price but would sell nothing at any price above the market price.

What Determines the Price Elasticity of Demand?

The price elasticity of demand for a particular product depends on the availability of substitutes. Consider the substitution possibilities for insulin (a medicine for diabetics) and cornflakes. There are no good substitutes for insulin, so consumers are not very responsive to changes in price. The demand for insulin is therefore inelastic. In contrast, there are many substitutes for cornflakes, including different types of corn cereals, as well as cereals made from wheat, rice, and oats. Faced with an increase in price of cornflakes, consumers can easily switch to substitute products, so the demand for cornflakes is relatively elastic.

Table 5.1 shows the price elasticities of demand for various products. The different elasticities illustrate the importance of substitutes in determining the price elasticity of demand. Because there are no good substitutes for water and salt, it is not surprising that the elasticities are small. For example, the price elasticity of demand for water is 0.20, meaning that a 10% increase in price decreases the quantity demanded by 2%. The demand for coffee is inelastic as well. Although there are alternative beverages and caffeine delivery systems (tea, infused soft drinks, and pills), coffee provides a unique combination of taste and caffeine, which explains the relatively low elasticity of 0.30. Although there is an artificial substitute for eggs (for people concerned about dietary cholesterol), there are no natural substitutes, so demand is relatively inelastic, 0.30.

The demand for a specific brand of a product is typically elastic. For example, the elasticity of demand for a specific brand of coffee is 5.6, compared to an overall elasticity for coffee of 0.30. This means that a 10% increase in the price of coffee in general (all brands) will decrease the quantity of coffee sold by 3%, but a 10% increase in the price

TABLE 5.1	
Price Elasticities of Demand for Selected Products	

Product	Price Elasticity of Demand
Salt	0.1
Water	0.2
Coffee	0.3
Eggs	0.3
Cigarettes	0.3
Shoes and footwear	0.7
Housing	1.0
Automobiles	1.2
Foreign travel	1.8
Restaurant meals	2.3
Air travel	2.4
Motion pictures	3.7
Specific brands of coffee	5.6

Sources: Frank Chaloupka, "Rational Addictive Behavior and Cigarette Smoking," Journal of Political Economy, August 1991, pp. 722–742; Gregory Chow, Demand for Automobiles in the United States (Amsterdam: North-Holland, 1957); David Ellwood and Mitchell Polinski, "An Empirical Reconciliation of Micro and Grouped Estimates of the Demand for Housing," Review of Economics and Statistics, vol. 61, 1979, pp. 199–205; H. F. Houthakker and Lester B. Taylor, Consumer Demand in the United States: Analysis and Projections, 2nd ed. (Cambridge, MA: Harvard University Press, 1970); John R. Nevin, "Laboratory Experiments for Estimating Consumer Demand: A Validation Study," Journal of Marketing Research, vol. 11, August 1974, pp. 261–268; Herbert Scarf and John Shoven, Applied General Equilibrium Analysis (New York: Cambridge University Press, 1984).

of a specific brand will decrease the quantity of that brand sold by 56%. This illustrates the importance of substitutability: Each brand is a substitute for the other brands, so consumers are very responsive to a change in the price of a specific brand. Similarly, the demand for specific brands of tires is more elastic than the demand for tires in general.

It often takes time for consumers to respond to price changes, so the short-run price elasticity of demand is typically smaller than the long-run elasticity. For example, when the price of gasoline increases, consumers can immediately drive fewer miles in their existing cars. The longer-term consumer responses to higher prices include buying more fuel-efficient cars and moving closer to workplaces. As time passes, consumers have more options to cut gasoline consumption, so demand becomes more elastic.

Elasticity is generally larger for goods that take a relatively large part of a consumer's budget. If a good represents a small part of the budget of the typical consumer, demand is relatively inelastic. For example, suppose the price of pencils is 20 cents and then increases by 10%, or 2 cents. Because the price change is tiny compared to the income of the typical consumer, we would expect a relatively small decrease in the quantity of pencils demanded. In contrast, if the price of a car is $20,000 and then increases 10% ($2,000), we would expect bigger response because the change in price is large relative to the income of the typical consumer.

International comparisons of the price elasticity of demand for food suggest that demand is more price elastic when the good represents a large part of the consumer's budget. In wealthy countries such as the United States, Canada, and Germany, the price elasticity of demand for food is around 0.15.[1] In poor countries such as India, Nigeria, and Bolivia, people spend a larger fraction of their budget on food, so they are more responsive to changes in food prices. In these countries the price elasticity of demand is around 0.34.

Let's summarize what we know about the determinants of the price elasticity of demand. The demand for a product will be relatively elastic if

▶ There are good substitutes for the product.
▶ Consumers have time to respond to the price change.
▶ The product represents a large fraction of the consumer's budget.

The price elasticity of demand for some products varies with the age of the consumer. For the general population, the demand for cigarettes is inelastic, with $E_d = 0.30$. For teenagers, the demand for cigarettes is elastic, with $E_d = 1.30$. The elasticity is larger for teenagers because cigarettes take up a bigger fraction of a teenager's budget and most teenagers are not yet addicted to them. For the implications for the effort to cut teenage smoking, read "A Closer Look: How to Cut Teen Smoking by 60%."

Computing Price Elasticity: Initial Value Versus Midpoint

To compute the price elasticity of demand from market data, we divide the percentage change in the quantity by the percentage change in price. As explained in the Appendix to Chapter 1, there are two ways to compute a percentage change. The simplest approach is to use the initial value of the variable. Suppose the price of milk increases from $2.00 to $2.20 and the quantity falls from 100 to 85 (shown in Table 5.2). The percentage change in price is the change ($0.20) divided by the initial value ($2.00), or

A CLOSER LOOK

How to Cut Teen Smoking by 60%

Under the 1997 tobacco settlement, if smoking by teenagers does not decline by 60% by the year 2007, cigarette makers will be fined $2 billion.[2] The settlement is expected to increase cigarette prices by about 62 cents per pack, a percentage increase of about 25%. Will that be enough to reduce teen smoking by the target percentage? The answer depends on the price elasticity of demand for cigarettes by teens.

The demand for cigarettes by teenagers is elastic: 1.3. This means that a 10% increase in the price of cigarettes will decrease teen cigarette consumption by 13%.[3] About half the reduction results from fewer teen smokers, and the other half results from fewer cigarettes for each teen smoker. Although the teen demand for cigarettes is relatively elastic, a 25% price hike will not be enough to cut teen smoking by the target amount. Given an elasticity of 1.3, cigarette prices would have to increase by about 46% to reach the 60% reduction required

by the settlement (60% divided by 1.3). Recognizing this, tobacco companies have taken other measures to reduce teen smoking, including antismoking campaigns aimed at teens.

10%. The percentage change in quantity is the change (15) divided by the initial value (100), or 15%. Using the initial values to compute the percentage changes, the price elasticity of demand is 1.50:

$$E_d = \frac{\text{percentage change in quantity}}{\text{percentage change in price}} = \frac{\dfrac{15}{100}}{\dfrac{\$0.20}{\$2.00}} = \frac{15\%}{10\%} = 1.5$$

Midpoint method

A method of computing a percentage change by dividing the change in the variable by the average value of the variable, or the midpoint between the old value and the new one.

The **midpoint method** provides a more precise way to compute a percentage change: We divide the change in the variable by the average value of the variable, or the midpoint between the old value and the new one. We can use the midpoint approach to compute the price elasticity associated with the changes listed in Table 5.2. The percentage change in price equals the change in price (0.20) divided by the average price ($2.10), for a percentage change of 9.52%:

$$\text{percentage change in price} = \frac{0.20}{(2.00 + 2.20)/2} = \frac{0.20}{2.10} = 9.52\%$$

TABLE 5.2 Computing Percentage Changes and Elasticity

	Old	New	Initial Value Method	Midpoint Value Method
Price	$2.00	$2.20	Percent change: 10% = $0.20 ÷ $2.00	Percent change: 9.52% = 0.20 ÷ 2.10
Quantity	100	85	Percent change: **15%** = 15 ÷ 100 Elasticity: 1.5 = 15% ÷ 10%	Percent change: 16.22% = **15** ÷ 92.5 Elasticity: 1.70 = 16.22% ÷ 9.52%

The percentage change in quantity equals the change in quantity (15) divided by the average quantity (92.5), for a percentage change of 16.22%:

$$\text{percentage change in quantity} = \frac{15}{(100 + 85)/2} = \frac{15}{92.5} = 16.22\%$$

If we plug these percentage changes into the formula for the price elasticity of demand, the computed price elasticity is 1.70:

$$E_d = \frac{\text{percentage change in quantity}}{\text{percentage change in price}} = \frac{16.22\%}{9.52\%} = 1.70$$

Why is this elasticity different from the elasticity computed with the initial values (1.50)? The midpoint approach measures the percentage changes more precisely, so we get a more precise measure of price elasticity. In this case, the percentage changes are relatively small, so the two elasticity numbers aren't too far apart. If the percentage changes were larger, however, the elasticity numbers generated by the two approaches would be quite different, and it would be wise to use the midpoint approach. In this book, we will use the simpler approach (initial value).

Elasticity Along a Linear Demand Curve

If a demand curve is linear—a straight line—does that mean that the elasticity of demand is the same at all points on the line? As shown in Figure 5.2, the price elasticity of demand decreases as we move downward along a linear demand curve.

▶ On the upper part of a linear demand curve, demand is elastic. Moving from point *r* to point *s*, the percentage change in quantity is 20%, equal to the change in quantity (2) divided by the initial quantity (10). The percentage change in price is 5%, equal to the change in price ($4) divided by the initial price ($80). Dividing the 20% change in quantity by the 5% change in price gives us an elasticity of 4.0 on the upper part of the demand curve.

▶ On the lower part of a linear demand curve, demand is inelastic. Moving from point *v* to point *w*, the percentage change in quantity is 5%, equal to the change in

Price Elasticity Along a Linear Demand Curve
The price elasticity of demand decreases as we move downward along a linear demand curve. Demand is elastic on the upper half of the demand curve and inelastic on the lower half.

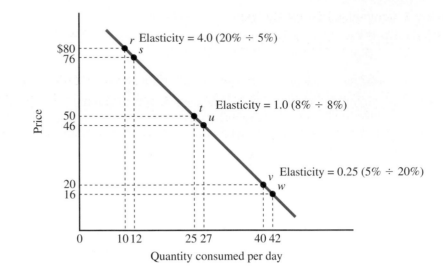

quantity (2) divided by the initial quantity (40). The percentage change in price is 20%, equal to the change in price ($4) divided by the initial price ($20). Dividing the 5% change in quantity by the 20% change in price gives us an elasticity of only 0.25 on the lower part of the demand curve.

Why does the price elasticity vary along a linear demand curve? It's tempting to think the elasticity is constant because a straight line has a constant slope. But that's incorrect, because elasticity is measured by percentage changes, not absolute changes. As we move downward along the demand curve, we're moving in the direction of larger quantities, so the same absolute change in quantity (2 units) becomes a smaller *percentage* change in quantity. Between points *r* and *s*, the percentage change in quantity is 20% (2/10), compared to only 5% (2/40) between points *v* and *w*. At the same time, the movement downward along the curve leads to a larger *percentage* change in price. As a result, the elasticity becomes smaller and smaller.

TEST Your Understanding

1. Complete the statement: To compute the price elasticity of demand, we divide the percentage change in _____ by the percentage change in _____.
2. Complete the statement: If a 10% increase in price decreases the quantity demanded by 12%, the price elasticity of demand is _____.
3. Explain why the demand for movies on DVDs is more elastic in the long run than in the short run.
4. If we are on the upper portion of a linear demand curve and the price increases by 10%, will the quantity demanded decrease by more than 10% or by less than 10%?

Using the Price Elasticity
of Demand to Make Predictions

The price elasticity of demand is a very useful tool for economic analysis. If we know the elasticity of demand for a particular good, we can quantify the law of demand, predicting exactly how much more of a product will be sold at a lower price or how much less will be sold at a higher price. We can also predict whether a change in price will increase or decrease total spending on the good.

Predicting Changes in Quantity Demanded

The formula for the elasticity has three variables: The price elasticity of demand (one variable) equals the percentage change in quantity (the second variable) divided by the percentage change in price (the third variable). If we know two of the three variables, we can compute the third. For example, suppose you run a campus film series and you've decided to increase your admission price by 15%. If you know the elasticity of demand for your movies, you could use the elasticity formula to predict how many fewer tickets you'll sell at the higher price. Suppose the elasticity of demand is 2.0, and you increase the price by 15%. Rearranging the elasticity formula, we would predict a 30% decrease in the quantity of tickets demanded:

$$\text{percentage change in quantity demanded} = E_d \cdot \text{percentage change in price}$$
$$= 2.0 \cdot 15\% = 30\%$$

Applications: College Education, Highway Deaths, and Medical Care

How could university officials use the price elasticity of demand? Suppose a university increases its tuition from $4,000 to $4,400 and wants to predict how the price hike will affect enrollment. Suppose the price elasticity of demand for an education at the university is 2.40. In this case, a 10% increase in tuition will decrease enrollment by 24%:

$$\text{percentage change in quantity demanded} = E_d \cdot \text{percentage change in price}$$
$$= 2.40 \cdot 10\% = 24\%$$

How would a tax on beer affect highway deaths among young adults? The price elasticity of demand for beer among young adults is about 1.30, and the number of highway deaths is roughly proportional to the group's beer consumption.[4] If a state imposes a beer tax that increases the price of beer by 20%, what will happen to the number of highway deaths among young adults? Using the elasticity formula, we predict that beer consumption will decrease by 26%:

$$\text{percentage change in quantity demanded} = E_d \cdot \text{percentage change in price}$$
$$= 1.30 \cdot 20\% = 26\%$$

If the number of highway deaths among young adults is proportional to their beer consumption, the number of deaths will also decrease by 26%. Of course, if young adults switch from beer to other alcoholic beverages, the number of highway deaths will decrease by a smaller amount.

If the price of medical care increases, how will consumers respond? The rising cost of medical care has forced many nations to take a closer look at programs that subsidize medical care for their citizens. If prices are increased to cover more of the costs of providing medical care, how will this affect poor and wealthy households? For an answer, read "A Closer Look: Pricing Medical Care in Developing Countries."

Predicting Changes in Total Revenue

If a firm increases the price of its product, will total sales revenue increase or decrease? The answer depends on the price elasticity of demand for the product. If we know the price elasticity, we can determine whether a price hike will increase or decrease the firm's total revenue.

Let's return to the example of the campus film series. Suppose you are thinking about increasing the price of tickets from $4.00 to $4.40. An increase in the ticket price brings good news and bad news:

▶ Good news. You get more money for each ticket sold.
▶ Bad news. You sell fewer tickets.

A Closer Look   Pricing Medical Care in Developing Countries

Many developing nations subsidize medical care, charging consumers a small fraction of the cost of providing the services. If a nation were to cut its subsidies and thus increase the price of medical care, how would the higher price affect its poor and wealthy households? In Côte d'Ivoire in Africa, the price elasticity of demand for hospital services is 0.47 for poor households and 0.29 for wealthy households.[5] This means that a 10% increase in the price of hospital services would cause poor households to cut back their hospital care by 4.7%, whereas wealthy households would cut back by only 2.9%. In Peru, the differences between poor and wealthy households are even larger: The price elasticity is 0.67 for poor households but only 0.03 for wealthy households. The same pattern occurs in the demand for the medical services provided in outpatient clinics. The poor are much more sensitive to price, so when prices increase, they suffer much larger reductions in medical care.

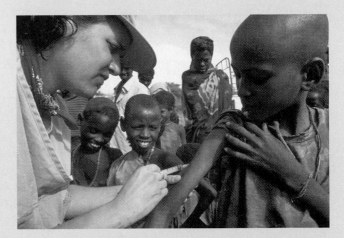

In developing nations, the poor are relatively sensitive to changes in the price of medical care.

TABLE 5.3

Price and Total Revenue with Elastic Demand

Price	Quantity of Tickets Sold	Total Revenue
4.00	100	$400
4.40	80	$352

Your total revenue will decrease if the bad news (fewer tickets sold) dominates the good news (more money per ticket). The elasticity of demand tells us how the good news compares to the bad news. If demand is elastic, consumers will respond to the higher price by purchasing many fewer tickets, so although you will collect more money per ticket, you'll sell so few tickets that your total revenue will decrease. For example, as Table 5.3 shows, if the price elasticity of demand is 2.0, a 10% increase in price will decrease the quantity demanded by 20%, from 100 to 80 tickets. Because the percentage decrease in quantity (the bad news) exceeds the percentage increase in price (the good news), total revenue decreases, from $400 to $352. In general, an elastic demand means that the percentage change in quantity (the bad news from a price hike) will exceed the percentage change in price (the good news), so an increase in price will decrease total revenue.

We get the opposite result if the demand for the good is inelastic: An increase in price increases total revenue. If demand is inelastic, consumers are not very responsive to an increase in price, so the good news (more money per unit sold) dominates the bad news (fewer units sold). For example, suppose that your campus bookstore starts with a textbook price of $50 and a quantity of 100 books. If the bookstore increases its price by 10% (from $50 to $55 per book) and the elasticity of demand for textbooks is 0.40, the quantity of textbooks sold will decrease by only 4% (from 100 to 96). Therefore, the store's total revenue will be $5,280 ($55 × 96), compared to only $5,000 at the lower price ($50 × 100). In general, an inelastic demand means that the percentage change in quantity will be smaller than the percentage change in price, so an increase in price will increase total revenue.

Table 5.4 summarizes the revenue effects of changes in prices for different types of goods:

▶ *Elastic demand.* There is a negative relationship between price and total revenue: An increase in price decreases total revenue; a decrease in price increases total revenue.

TABLE 5.4 Elasticity and Total Revenue

Type of Demand	Value of Price Elasticity of Demand	Change in Quantity Versus Change in Price	Effect of Higher Price on Total Revenue	Effect of Lower Price on Total Revenue
Elastic	Greater than 1.0	Larger percentage change in quantity	Decreases	Increases
Inelastic	Less than 1.0	Smaller percentage change in quantity	Increases	Decreases
Unitary elastic	1.0	Same percentage changes in quantity and price	Does not change	Does not change

▶ *Inelastic demand.* There is a positive relationship between price and total revenue: An increase in price increases total revenue; a decrease in price decreases total revenue.

▶ *Unitary elastic demand.* Total revenue does not vary with price.

The relationship between elasticity and total revenue provides a simple test of whether demand is elastic or inelastic. Suppose that when a music store increases the price of its CDs, its total revenue from CDs drops. The negative relationship between price and total revenue means that demand for the store's CDs is elastic: Total revenue decreases because consumers are very responsive to an increase in price, buying a much smaller quantity. In contrast, suppose that when a city increases the price it charges for water, the total revenue from water sales increases. The positive relationship between price and total revenue suggests that the demand for the city's water is inelastic: Total revenue increases because consumers are not very responsive to an increase in price.

We can use Figure 5.3 to reinforce what we've learned about price elasticity and total revenue. Panel A shows a linear demand curve (the same as the one in Figure 5.2), and Panel B shows the total-revenue curve associated with the demand curve. We know that demand is elastic along the upper half of a linear demand curve; that means that a decrease in price will increase the quantity sold by a larger percentage amount. As a result, total revenue will increase, as shown by the positively sloped total-revenue curve between points *b* and *c*. In contrast, demand is inelastic along the lower half of a linear demand curve; that means that a decrease in price will increase the quantity sold by a smaller percentage amount. As a result, total revenue will decrease, as shown by the negatively sloped total-revenue curve between points *c* and *d*. The total-revenue curve will reach its maximum at the midpoint of the linear demand curve, where demand is unitary elastic. In Figure 5.3, demand is unitary elastic at point *t* on the demand curve, so total revenue reaches its maximum at $1,250 at point *c* on the total-revenue curve.

Applications: Transit Deficits, Property Crime

At the beginning of the chapter, we considered the question of whether increasing the price of bus rides would reduce a city's transit deficit. The price elasticity in the typical city is 0.33, meaning that a 10% increase in fares will decrease ridership by only about 3.3%.[6] Because demand for bus travel is inelastic, the good news associated with a fare hike (10% more revenue per rider) will dominate the bad news (3.3% fewer riders), and total fare revenue will increase. In other words, an increase in fares will reduce the transit deficit.

What's the connection between antidrug policies and property crimes such as robbery, burglary, and auto theft? The government uses search-and-destroy tactics to restrict the supply of illegal drugs. If this approach succeeds, drugs become scarce, and the price of drugs increases. Because the demand for illegal drugs is inelastic, the increase in price will increase total spending on illegal drugs. Many drug addicts support their habits by stealing personal property—robbing people, stealing cars, and burglarizing homes. This means that drug addicts will commit more property crimes to support the higher total spending level associated with pricier drugs.[7] Given the inelas-

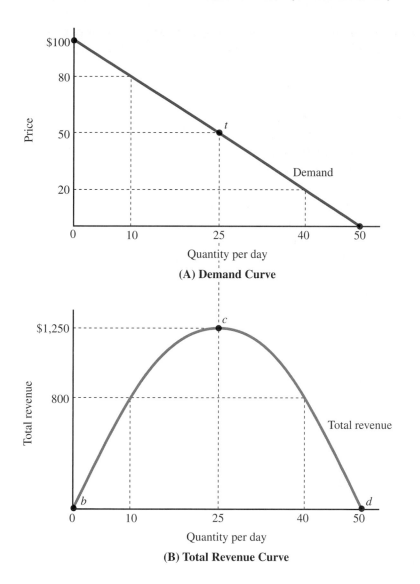

Elasticity and Total Revenue Along a Linear Demand Curve
Demand is elastic along the upper half of a linear demand curve, so an increase in quantity (from a decrease in price) increases total revenue, as shown between points *b* and *c*. Demand is inelastic along the lower half of a linear demand curve, so an increase in quantity (from a decrease in price) decreases total revenue, as shown between points *c* and *d*. Total revenue reaches its maximum at the midpoint of the demand curve (point *t*), where demand is unitary elastic.

tic demand for illegal drugs and the connection between drug consumption and property crime, there is a trade-off: A policy that increases drug prices will slightly reduce drug consumption and the number of drug addicts, but it will also increase property crime committed by addicts who continue to abuse drugs.

DVD Elasticity

The manager of a DVD rental store has asked you to solve a puzzle. According to national studies of the DVD rental market, the price elasticity of demand for DVD rentals is 0.80: A 10% increase in price decreases the quantity of DVDs demanded by about 8%. In other words, the demand for DVDs is inelastic. Based on this information, the manager of the DVD store increased her prices by 20%, expecting her total revenue to increase. She expected the good news (more money per rental) to dominate the bad news (fewer rentals). But in fact her total revenue decreased. Why?

The demand for DVDs at an individual rental store is more elastic than the overall demand for DVDs at all rental stores.

The key to solving this puzzle is to recognize that the manager can't use the results of a national study to predict the effects of increasing her own price. The national study suggests that if all DVD stores in the nation increased their prices by 10%, the nationwide quantity of DVDs demanded would drop by 8%. But when a single DVD store in a city increases its price, consumers can easily rent DVDs at other competing stores in the city. As a result, a 10% increase in the price of DVD rentals at one store will decrease the quantity sold by that store by much more than 8%. The demand facing an individual store is elastic, so an increase in price will decrease total revenue. ∎

TEST Your Understanding

5. Complete the statement: If the price elasticity of demand is 0.60, a 10% increase in price will _____ the quantity demanded by _____%. (Fill in the blanks with "increase" or "decrease".)

6. If an increase in the price of accordions does not change total revenue from accordion sales, what can we infer about the price elasticity of demand for accordions?

7. Suppose the price elasticity of demand for vanity license plates in the state of Ohio is 2.60. If the state's objective is to maximize its revenue from vanity plates, should it pick a higher price or a lower one?

Other Elasticities of Demand

We've seen that the price elasticity of demand measures the responsiveness of consumers to changes in the price of a particular good. Of course, the demand for a particular product also depends on other variables such as consumer income and the prices of related goods—substitutes and complements. We can use two other elasticities to measure the responsiveness of consumers to changes in these other variables that affect demand.

We saw in Chapter 4 that the demand for a particular product depends in part on the consumer's income. The **income elasticity of demand** measures the responsiveness of demand to changes in income, indicating how much more or less of a particular product is purchased as income changes. The income elasticity of demand is defined as the percentage change in quantity demanded divided by the percentage change in income:

$$E_i = \frac{\text{percentage change in quantity demanded}}{\text{percentage change in income}}$$

Income elasticity of demand

A measure of the responsiveness of the quantity demanded to changes in consumer income; computed by dividing the percentage change in the quantity demanded by the percentage change in income.

For example, if a 10% increase in income increases the quantity of books demanded by 15%, the income elasticity of demand for books is 1.50 (equal to 15% ÷ 10%).

We can use the income elasticities of demand for various products to categorize the products into different types. Recall from Chapter 4 that when a consumer's income increases, he or she buys more of a "normal" good. If the income elasticity is positive—indicating a positive relationship between income and demand—we say that the good is normal. New cars and new clothes are products that have positive income elasticities and are thus considered normal goods. On the other hand, the consumption of other products, called "inferior" goods, increases as income *decreases.* For these goods, the income elasticity is negative—revealing a negative relationship between income and demand. Some examples are intercity bus travel, used clothing, and used cars.

We saw in Chapter 4 that the demand for a particular product also depends in part on the prices of related goods—substitutes and complements. The **cross elasticity of demand** measures the responsiveness of demand to changes in the prices of other goods, indicating how much more or less of a particular product is purchased as other prices change. The cross elasticity is defined as the percentage change in quantity demanded of one good (X) divided by the percentage change in the price of a related good (Y):

$$E_{xy} = \frac{\text{percentage change in quantity of } X \text{ demanded}}{\text{percentage change in price of } Y}$$

Cross elasticity of demand

A measure of the responsiveness of the quantity demanded to changes in the price of a related good; computed by dividing the percentage change in the quantity demanded of one good (X) by the percentage change in the price of another good (Y).

As we saw in Chapter 4, two goods are considered substitutes if there is a positive relationship between the quantity demanded of one good and the price of the other good. For example, an increase in the price of bananas increases the demand for apples as consumers substitute apples for the now relatively expensive bananas. For substitute goods, the cross elasticity is positive. In contrast, two goods are considered complements if there is a negative relationship between the quantity demanded of one good and the price of the other. For example, an increase in the price of ice cream increases the cost of apple pie with ice cream, causing consumers to demand fewer apples. For complementary goods, the cross elasticity is negative.

Estimates of cross elasticity of demand are useful to retailers in their pricing decisions. For example, when a grocery store cuts the price of peanut butter by 10%, the store will sell more peanut butter but will also sell more complementary goods such as jelly and bread. If the cross elasticity of demand for jelly is 0.5, a 10% decrease in the price of peanut butter will increase the demand for jelly by 5%. Retailers use coupons for one product to promote the sales of that good as well as complementary goods. Armed with the relevant cross elasticities, retailers can predict just how much more of a complementary good consumers will buy.

The Price Elasticity of Supply

Price elasticity of supply
A measure of the responsiveness of the quantity supplied to changes in price; computed by dividing the percentage change in quantity supplied by the percentage change in price.

Let's look at elasticity on the supply side of the market. The **price elasticity of supply** measures the responsiveness of producers to changes in price. We compute this elasticity by dividing the percentage change in quantity supplied by the percentage change in price:

$$E_s = \frac{\text{percentage change in quantity supplied}}{\text{percentage change in price}}$$

In Figure 5.4, when the price of milk increases from $2.00 to $2.20, the quantity supplied increases from 100 million gallons to 120 million gallons. In other words, a 10% increase in price increased the quantity supplied by 20%, so using the initial-value formula for percentage change, the price elasticity of supply is 2.0:

$$E_s = \frac{\text{percentage change in quantity supplied}}{\text{percentage change in price}} = \frac{\dfrac{20}{100}}{\dfrac{\$0.20}{\$2.00}} = \frac{20\%}{10\%} = 2.0$$

Time is an important factor in determining the price elasticity of supply for a product. When the price of a particular product increases, the immediate response is that current producers produce more of the product in their existing production facil-

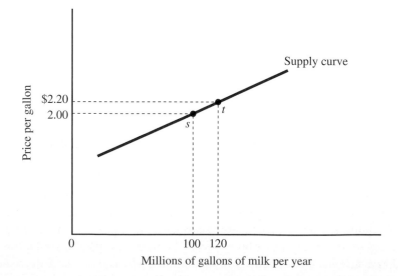

FIGURE 5.4

The Market Supply Curve and Price Elasticity of Supply
A 10% increase in the price of milk (from $2 to $2.20) increases the quantity supplied by 20% (from 100 million gallons to 120 million), so the price elasticity of supply is 2.0 = (20% ÷ 10%).

ities (for example, in their factories, stores, offices, or restaurants). Although a higher price will certainly induce firms to produce more, the response is limited by the limited capacity of the firms' production facilities. Over time, however, new firms can enter the market and old firms can build new production facilities, so there will be a larger response in the long run. As time passes, supply becomes more elastic because more and more firms have the time to build production facilities and produce more output.

The milk industry provides a good example of the difference between the elasticity over a short period of time and a longer period. The price elasticity of supply over a one-year period is 0.12: If the price of milk increases by 10% and stays there for a year, the quantity of milk supplied will rise by only 1.2%.[8] In the short run, dairy farmers can squeeze just a little more output from their existing production facilities. Over a 10-year period, however, the price elasticity is 2.5: The same 10% rise in price will increase the quantity supplied by 25%. In the long run, dairy farmers can expand existing facilities and build new ones, so in the long run, there is a larger response to a higher price.

Predicting Changes in Quantity Supplied

We can use the price elasticity of supply to predict the effect of price changes on the quantity supplied. For example, suppose that the elasticity of supply is 0.80 and the price increases by 5%. Rearranging the elasticity formula, we would predict a 4% increase in quantity supplied:

$$\text{percentage change in quantity supplied} = E_s \cdot \text{percentage change in price}$$
$$= 0.80 \cdot 5\% = 4\%$$

As we saw in Chapter 4, many governments establish minimum prices for agricultural products. The higher the minimum price, the larger the quantity supplied, consistent with the law of supply. If we know the price elasticity of supply, we can predict just how much more will be supplied at a higher minimum price. For example, if the minimum price of cheese increases by 10% and the price elasticity is 0.60, the quantity of cheese supplied will rise by 6%:

$$\text{percentage change in quantity supplied} = E_s \cdot \text{percentage change in price}$$
$$= 0.60 \cdot 10\% = 6\%$$

Extreme Cases: Perfectly Inelastic Supply and Perfectly Elastic Supply

Figure 5.5 shows two supply curves that show the extreme cases of supply elasticity. The supply curve in Panel A of Figure 5.5 is a vertical line, indicating that regardless of price, the quantity supplied is 50 units. This is the case of **perfectly inelastic supply**, with a price elasticity of supply equal to zero. The numerator in the elasticity expression (the percentage change in quantity supplied) is zero, regardless of the percentage change in the price of the good. Land is an example of a product that has a perfectly inelastic supply. In the words of Will Rogers, "The trouble with land is that they're not making it any more."

Perfectly inelastic supply
The price elasticity of supply equals 0.

Perfectly Inelastic Supply and Perfectly Elastic Supply

In Panel A, the quantity supplied is the same at every price, so the price elasticity of supply is zero. In Panel B, the quantity supplied is infinitely responsive to changes in price, so the price elasticity of supply is infinite.

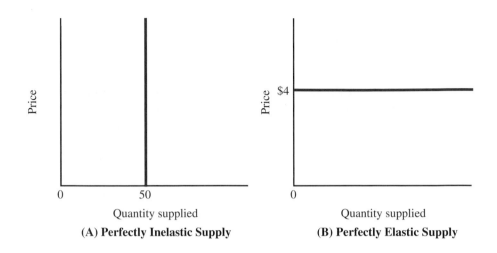

(A) Perfectly Inelastic Supply   (B) Perfectly Elastic Supply

Perfectly elastic supply

The price elasticity of supply is infinite.

The supply curve in Panel B of Figure 5.5 is a horizontal line, indicating that the quantity supplied is infinitely responsive to any change in price. This is the case of **perfectly elastic supply**, with a price elasticity of supply equal to infinity. The numerator in the elasticity expression (the percentage change in quantity supplied) is infinite, regardless of the percentage change in the price of the good. One implication of this supply curve is that if the price were to drop from $4 to any lower price, the quantity supplied would fall to zero. Later in the book we'll explain the economics behind a perfectly elastic supply.

Predicting Changes in Price Using Supply and Demand Elasticities

When supply or demand changes—that is, when the supply curve or demand curve shifts—we can draw a supply and demand diagram to predict whether the equilibrium price will increase or decrease. In many cases, the simple diagram will show all we need to know about the effects of a change in supply or demand. But what if we want to predict how much a price will increase or decrease? We can use a simple formula to predict the change in the equilibrium price resulting from a change in supply or a change in demand.

The Price Effects of a Change in Demand

In Figure 5.6, an increase in demand shifts the demand curve to the right and increases the equilibrium price. We explained in Chapter 4 that a demand curve shifts as a result of a change in something other than the price of the product—for example, a change in income, tastes, or the price of a related good. When demand increases, the immediate effect is excess demand: At the original price ($2.00), the quantity demanded exceeds the quantity supplied by 35 million gallons (135 million − 100 million). As the price increases, both consumers and producers help to eliminate the excess demand: Consumers buy less (the law of demand), and firms produce more (the law of supply).

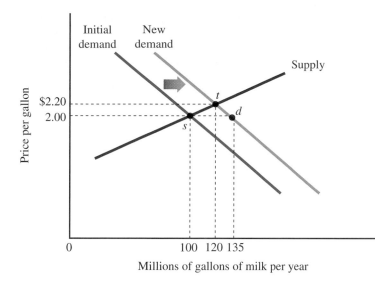

FIGURE 5.6

An Increase in Demand Increases the Equilibrium Price
An increase in demand shifts the demand curve to the right, increasing the equilibrium price. In this case, a 35% increase in demand increases the price by 10%. Using the price-change formula, 10% = 35% ÷ (2.0 + 1.5).

If both consumers and producers are very responsive to changes in price, it will take a small increase in price to eliminate the excess demand. In other words, an increase in demand will cause a small increase in price if both demand and supply are elastic.

We can use the following **price-change formula** to predict the change in the equilibrium price resulting from a change in demand. We divide the percentage change in demand by the sum of the price elasticities of supply and demand:

$$\text{percentage change in equilibrium price} = \frac{\text{percentage change in demand}}{E_s + E_d}$$

Price-change formula
A formula that shows the percentage change in equilibrium price resulting from a change in demand or supply, given values for the price elasticity of supply and the price elasticity of demand.

The numerator is the rightward shift of the demand curve in percentage terms. In Figure 5.6, the initial quantity demanded at a price of $2.00 is 100 million gallons (shown by the initial demand curve), and the new quantity demanded at the same price is 135 million gallons (shown by the new demand curve). The change in demand is 35% (35/100). The two price elasticities appear in the denominator. This is sensible because if consumers and producers are very responsive to changes in price (the elasticities are large numbers), excess demand will be eliminated with a relatively small increase in price.

We can use a simple example to see how to use the price-change formula. Suppose that demand increases by 35% (the demand curve shifts to the right by 35%). If the supply elasticity is 2.0 and the demand elasticity is 1.5, the predicted change in the equilibrium price is 10%:

$$\text{percentage change in equilibrium price} = \frac{35\%}{2.0 + 1.5} = 10\%$$

In Figure 5.6, the equilibrium price increases by 10%, from $2.00 to $2.20. If either demand or supply were less elastic (if either of the elasticity numbers were smaller), the predicted change in price would be larger. For example, if the supply elasticity were 0.25 instead of 2.0, we would predict a 20% increase in price (35% ÷ 1.75).

What about the direction of the price change? We know from Chapter 4 that an increase in demand increases the equilibrium price, and a decrease in demand decreases the equilibrium price. Therefore, the percentage change in price is positive when the change in demand is positive (when demand increases and the demand curve shifts to the right), and negative when the change in demand is negative (when demand decreases and the demand curve shifts to the left). For example, suppose the demand for a product decreases by 15% (the demand curve shifts to the left by 15%). If the supply elasticity is 1.0 and the demand elasticity is 0.50, the price-change formula shows that the equilibrium price will decrease by 10%:

$$\text{percentage change in equilibrium price} = \frac{-15\%}{1.0 + 1.5} = -10\%$$

We can use the price-change formula to predict the effects of changes in demand on equilibrium prices. Suppose a city is expected to grow by 9% in the next few years, and you want to predict the effects of population growth on the equilibrium price of housing. If the price elasticity of supply is 2.0 and the price elasticity of demand is 1.0, the population growth will increase the equilibrium price of housing by 3%:

$$\text{percentage change in equilibrium price} = \frac{9\%}{2.0 + 1.0} = 3\%$$

We could also use the price-change formula to predict the price effects of an increase in the demand for organic produce. Suppose the demand for organic food is expected to increase by 10% in the next two years. If the price elasticity of supply for organic food is 2.0 and the price elasticity of demand is 0.50, we would predict a 4% increase in price:

$$\text{percentage change in equilibrium price} = \frac{10\%}{2.0 + 0.50} = 4\%$$

The Price Effects of a Change in Supply

We can use a slightly different version of the price-change formula to predict the change in the equilibrium price resulting from a change in supply. As explained in Chapter 4, a change in supply results from changes in something other than the price of the product—for example, a change in the cost of labor or raw materials, a change in production technology, or a change in the number of firms. The immediate effect of an increase in supply is excess supply: At the original price, the quantity supplied exceeds the quantity demanded. As the price drops, consumers respond by purchasing more and producers respond by producing less, so the gap between quantity supplied and quantity demanded narrows. If both consumers and producers are very responsive to changes in price, it will take only a small decrease in price to eliminate the excess supply. In other words, an increase in supply will cause a small decrease in price if both demand and supply are elastic.

To predict the change in price resulting from a change in supply, we just substitute the percentage change in supply for the percentage change in demand in the numerator of the price-change formula and add a minus sign. The minus sign indicates that there is a negative relationship between the equilibrium price and supply: When supply increases—that is, when the supply curve shifts to the right—the price drops; when supply decreases, the price rises. For example, suppose the supply of milk increases by 10%. If the price elasticity of demand is 0.6 and the price elasticity of supply is 1.4, the equilibrium price will decrease by 5%:

$$\text{percentage change in equilibrium price} = -\frac{\text{percentage change in supply}}{E_s + E_d}$$

$$\text{percentage change in equilibrium price} = -\frac{10\%}{1.4 + 0.6} = -5\%$$

The price-change formula can be used by firms and government to predict the effects of changes in supply on equilibrium prices. Suppose a city decides to limit the amount of new housing by limiting the amount of land that can be developed and the policy decreases the supply of housing by 6%. If the price elasticity of supply is 2.0 and the price elasticity of demand is 1.0, the policy will increase the equilibrium price of housing by 2%:

$$\text{percentage change in equilibrium price} = -\frac{-6\%}{2.0 + 1.0} = 2\%$$

Similarly, we can use the formula to predict the effects of a war in the Middle East on the equilibrium price of oil. Suppose a war disrupts supply from a major oil exporter, decreasing the world supply of oil by 12.5%. If the price elasticity of supply is 0.50 and the price elasticity of demand is 0.75, the war will increase the equilibrium price of oil by 10%:

$$\text{percentage change in equilibrium price} = -\frac{-12.5\%}{0.50 + 0.75} = 10\%$$

TEST Your Understanding

8. Complete the statement: If a 10% increase in price increases the quantity supplied by 15%, the price elasticity of supply is _____.
9. Suppose the price elasticity of a supply of cheese is 0.80. If the price of cheese rises by 20%, by what percentage will the quantity supplied change?
10. Suppose that the elasticity of demand for chewing tobacco is 0.70 and the elasticity of supply is 2.30. If an antichewing campaign decreases the demand for chewing tobacco by 30%, in what direction and by what percentage will the price of chewing tobacco change?
11. Suppose that the elasticity of demand for motel rooms in a town near a ski area is 1.0 and the elasticity of supply is 0.50. If the population of the surrounding area increases by 30%, in what direction and by what percentage will the price of motel rooms change?

USING THE TOOLS

This chapter introduced several new tools of economics, including four different elasticities and a formula that can be used to predict the change in price resulting from a change in supply or demand. Here are some opportunities to use these tools to do your own economic analysis.

1. Projecting Transit Ridership

As a transit planner, you must predict how many people ride commuter trains and how much money is generated from train fares. According to a recent study,[9] the short-run price elasticity of demand for commuter rail is 0.62, and the long-run elasticity is 1.59. The current ridership is 100,000 people per day. Suppose fares increase by 10%.
a. Predict the changes in train ridership over a one-month period (short run) and a five-year period (long run).
b. Over the one-month period, will total revenue increase or decrease? What will happen in the five-year period?

2. Bumper Crops

Your job is to predict the total revenue generated by the nation's corn crop. Last year's crop was 100 million bushels, and the price was $4.00 per bushel. This year's weather was favorable throughout the country, and this year's crop will be 110 million bushels, or 10% larger than last year's. The price elasticity of demand for corn is 0.50.
a. Predict the effect of the bumper crop on the price of corn, assuming that the entire crop is sold this year.
b. Predict the total revenue from this year's corn crop.
c. Did the favorable weather increase or decrease the total revenue from corn? Why?

3. Price Controls for Medical Care

Suppose that in an attempt to control the rising costs of medical care, the national government imposes price controls on visits to physicians. The maximum price for a physician visit is 10% less than the equilibrium price. Assume that the price elasticity of demand for physician visits is 0.60 and the price elasticity of supply is 1.5.
a. By what percentage will the quantity of medical care supplied decrease?
b. By what percentage will the quantity of medical care demanded increase?
c. Illustrate your answer with a graph.
d. What sort of inefficiencies will occur as a result of the maximum price?
e. Would you expect patients and physicians to find ways around the maximum price?

4. Price Effects of Increased Enrollment

Consider a college town where the initial price of apartments is $400 and the initial quantity is 1,000 apartments. The price elasticity of demand for apartments is 1.0, and the price elasticity of supply of apartments is 0.50.
a. Use supply and demand curves to show the initial equilibrium, and label the equilibrium point *i*.
b. Suppose an increase in college enrollment is expected to increase the demand for apartments in a college town by 15%. Use your graph to show the effects of the increase in demand on the apartment market. Label the new equilibrium point *f*.
c. Predict the effect of the increase in demand on the equilibrium price of apartments.

SUMMARY

This chapter deals with the numbers behind the laws of demand and supply. The law of demand tells us that an increase in the price of a product will decrease the quan-

tity demanded, *ceteris paribus*. If we know the price elasticity of demand for that good, we can determine just how much less of it will be sold at the higher price.

Similarly, if we know the price elasticity of supply for a product, we can determine just how much more of it will be supplied at a higher price. Here are the main points of the chapter.

1 The price elasticity of demand—defined as the percentage change in quantity demanded divided by the percentage change in price—measures the responsiveness of consumers to changes in price.

2 Demand is relatively elastic if there are good substitutes.

3 If demand is elastic, there is a negative relationship between price and total revenue. If demand is inelastic, there is a positive relationship between price and total revenue.

4 The price elasticity of supply—defined as the percentage change in quantity supplied divided by the percentage change in price—measures the responsiveness of producers to changes in price.

5 If we know the elasticities of supply and demand, we can predict the percentage change in price resulting from a change in demand or supply.

KEY TERMS

cross elasticity of demand, 109
elastic demand, 96
income elasticity of demand, 109
inelastic demand, 96
midpoint method, 100

perfectly elastic demand, 96
perfectly elastic supply, 112
perfectly inelastic demand, 96
perfectly inelastic supply, 111
price elasticity of demand, 95

price elasticity of supply, 110
price-change formula, 113
unitary elastic, 96

PROBLEMS AND DISCUSSION QUESTIONS

1 When the price of compact discs (CDs) increased from $10 to $11, the quantity of CDs demanded decreased from 100 to 87. What is the price elasticity of demand for CDs? Is demand elastic or inelastic?

2 Explain why the demand for residential natural gas (gas used for heating, cooling, and cooking) is more elastic than the demand for residential electricity.

3 Would you expect the demand for a specific brand of running shoes to be more elastic or less elastic than the demand for running shoes in general? Why?

4 For each of the following goods, indicate whether you expect demand to be inelastic or elastic, and explain your reasoning: opera, foreign travel, local telephone service, DVD rentals, and eggs.

5 You observe a positive relationship between the price your store charges for CDs and the total revenue from CDs. Is the demand for your CDs elastic or inelastic?

6 Suppose that at the current price, the price elasticity of demand for a campus film series is 1.40. If the objective of the film society is to maximize its total revenue (price times the number of tickets sold), should it increase or decrease its price?

7 As the head of a state chapter of MADD (Mothers Against Drunk Driving), you are to speak in support of policies that discourage drunk driving. The number of highway deaths among young adults, which is roughly proportional to the group's beer consumption, is initially 100 deaths per year. You have scheduled a news conference to express your support for a beer tax that will increase the price of

beer by 10%. The price elasticity of demand for beer is 1.30. Complete the following statement: "The beer tax will decrease the number of highway deaths among young adults by about _____ per year."

8 When the price of paper increases from $100 to $104 per ton, the quantity supplied increases from 200 to 220 tons per day. What is the price elasticity of supply?

9 You are a tax analyst for Washington, D.C., and have been asked to predict how much revenue will be generated by the city's gasoline tax. The initial quantity of gasoline is 100 million gallons per month, and the price elasticity of demand for gasoline in the typical large city is 4.0. The tax, which is $0.10 per gallon, will increase the price of gasoline by 5%.
   a. How much revenue will the gasoline tax generate?
   b. In 1980, tax analysts in Washington, D.C., based their revenue predictions for a gasoline tax on

the elasticity of demand for gasoline in the United States as a whole, which is 1.0. Would you expect the national elasticity to be larger or smaller than the elasticity for the typical large city? Would you expect the analysts to overestimate or underestimate the revenue from the gasoline tax?

10 Suppose that the government restricts logging to protect an endangered species. The restrictions increase the price of wood products and shift the supply curve for new housing to the left by 4%. The initial price of new housing is $100,000, the elasticity of demand is 1.0, and the elasticity of supply is 3.0. Predict the effect of the logging restriction on the equilibrium price of new housing. Illustrate your answer with a graph that shows the initial point (*i*) and the new equilibrium (*f*).

MODEL ANSWERS

Chapter-Opening Questions

1 A beer tax will increase the price of beer, decreasing beer consumption. Highway deaths are roughly proportional to beer consumption, so the tax will also decrease highway deaths. The actual change in highway deaths depends on the price elasticity of demand for beer.

2 As shown in "Using the Tools: Bumper Crops," a bumper crop of corn decreases the equilibrium price of corn by a relatively large amount because the demand for corn is inelastic. Although corn farmers will sell more bushels, they will receive much less per bushel, so total revenue will drop.

3 The policies increase the price of the illegal drug, which increases total spending on the drug because demand is inelastic. If drug addicts support their habits with property crime, they commit more crime to support their more expensive habits.

4 As explained in the section "The Price Effects of a Change in Demand," if the elasticity of demand is 1.0 and the elasticity of supply is 2.0, a 9%

increase in demand will increase the equilibrium price by 3%.

Test Your Understanding

1 Quantity, price.

2 1.20.

3 A decrease in the price of DVDs will cause some consumers to buy DVD players and switch from videocassettes to DVDs, but this takes some time.

4 On the upper portion, demand is elastic, so quantity will decrease by more than 10%.

5 Decrease, 6.

6 The price elasticity is 1.0 (neither elastic nor inelastic).

7 Demand is elastic, so a decrease in price would increase total revenue.

8 1.50 = 15% ÷ 10%.

9 The quantity supplied will increase by 16%.

10 Using the price-change formula, the price will decrease by 10% = 30% ÷ 3.

11 Using the price-change formula, the price will increase by 20% = 30% ÷ 1.50.

NOTES

1. Chin-Fun Cling and James Peale, Jr., "Income and Price Elasticities," in *Advances in Econometrics Supplement*, edited by Henri Theil (Greenwich, CT: JAI Press, 1989).

2. Michael M. Phillips and Suein L. Hwang, "Why Tobacco Pact Won't Hurt Industry," *Wall Street Journal*, September 12, 1997, p. A2.

3. Frank J. Chaloupka and Michael Grossman, "Price, Tobacco Control Policies, and Smoking among Young Adults," *Journal of Health Economics*, vol. 16, 1997, pp. 359–373.

4. Henry Saffer and Michael Grossman, "Beer Taxes, the Legal Drinking Age, and Youth Motor Vehicle Fatalities," *Journal of Legal Studies*, vol. 16 , June 1987, pp. 351–374.

5. Paul Gertler and Jacques van der Gaag, *The Willingness to Pay for Medical Care: Evidence from Two Developing Countries* (Baltimore, MD: Johns Hopkins University Press, 1990.)

6. Kenneth A. Small, *Urban Transportation Economics* (Philadelphia, PA: Harwood Academic Publishers, 1992).

7. L. P. Silverman and N. L. Sprull, "Urban Crime and the Price of Heroin," *Journal of Urban Economics*, vol. 4, 1977, pp. 80–103.

8. Richard Klemme and Jean-Paul Chavas, "The Effects of Changing Milk Price on Milk Supply and National Dairy Herd Size," *Economic Issues*, No. 92 University of Wisconsin, June 1985.

9. Richard Voith, "The Long Run Elasticity of Demand for Commuter Rail Transportation," *Journal of Urban Economics*, vol. 30, 1991, pp. 360–372.

Consumer Constraints and Preferences

Consumer Constraints: The Budget Line
Consumer Preferences: Indifference
  Curves

Maximizing Utility

The Tangency Condition
The Utility-Maximizing Rule:
  MRS = Price Ratio
Drawing the Demand Curve
Do Consumers Actually Do This?

Applications of the Consumer Choice Model

Music Piracy and Online Music Stores
Inflation, the Real–Nominal Principle,
  and Consumer's Choices
The Equimarginal Rule
Using the Tools

Consumer Choice

n 2003, Apple Computer started selling music online, with a price of $0.99 per song. This was a dramatic departure from the traditional way of selling music on CDs, with each "bundle" of songs on a CD selling for between $15 and $20. In the first year, Apple sold 70 million songs through its online music service, and other firms entered the market with their own online music stores. One of the purposes of launching the service was to provide an alternative to Internet music piracy for people who wanted just a few songs, not an entire CD. In designing the online music store, the folks at Apple applied some of the basic concepts of consumer choice, although they might not have realized it.

Consumer choice theory is based on the notion that consumers do the best they can, given the limitations dictated by their incomes and consumer prices. The first step in consumer choice is to figure out your options: Given your income or budget, what are the alternative ways you can spend your budget? In other words, you can develop a sort of "menu" of options for spending your money. The menu reveals that there are trade-offs: If you spend more on music, you'll have less for books, movies, and other products. The second step in consumer choice is to pick the best item on your menu of affordable options, the one that generates the highest level of satisfaction.

Why study consumer choice? We are all consumers, and a discussion of consumer choice could help us spend our money in more fruitful ways. Consumer theory also provides insights into how consumers make decisions, and these insights are useful to firms and other organizations that sell products to consumers. Consumer theory also helps us understand why consumption patterns change. For example, the theory helps us understand the trend away from home cooking and toward restaurant meals, and the success of online music stores. Finally, consumer theory provides a decision-making framework that can be applied to a wide variety of decisions.

Consumer choice is really about doing the best with limited resources. Here are some of the practical questions we answer:

1 If you want to determine whether a consumer is doing the best she can, what single question can you ask?
2 Does inflation make the typical consumer better off, worse off, or just as well off?
3 In an attempt to curb teen drinking, New Zealand imposed a special tax on the favorite alcoholic beverage of teens. How did teens respond?

Consumer Constraints and Preferences

Let's consider the decisions of Maxine, a consumer who must decide how many movies and paperback books to buy each month. Maxine has a fixed income per month to spend on the two goods, so her options are limited by her budget. To decide how to spend her money, Maxine takes two steps:

1 She figures out her menu of options, the list of alternative combinations of books and movies her budget allows.
2 She picks the combination of movies that generates the highest level of satisfaction. To pick a combination from the menu, Maxine will carefully consider her own personal preferences and tastes.

We'll start with a discussion of Maxine's budget options, and then discuss her preferences.

Consumer Constraints: The Budget Line

Consider first the constraints faced by a consumer. Maxine's ability to purchase movies and other goods is limited by her income and the prices of movies and other products. Suppose Maxine has a fixed income of $30 per month, which she spends entirely on movies and used paperback books. The price of movies is $3 and the price of books is $1.

A consumer's **budget line** shows all the combinations of two goods that exhaust the consumer's budget. In Figure 6.1, if Maxine spends her entire $30 budget on books, she gets 30 books and no movies (point *y*). At the other extreme, she can spend her entire budget on movies, getting 10 of them (point *x*). The points between these two extremes are possible too. For example, she could reach point *b* (1 movie and 27 books) by spending $3 on movies and $27 on books, or point *c* (2 movies and 24 books) by spending $6 on movies and $24 on books. Although the budget line may look similar to a consumer's demand curve, they are very different graphical tools. The budget line shows the different combinations of two goods that a consumer can buy. The demand curve, on the other hand, shows the quantity of a single good that a consumer is willing to buy at different prices.

A consumer's **budget set** is the set of all the affordable combinations of two goods. The budget set includes the budget line (combinations that exhaust the budget) as well as combinations that leave the consumer with leftover money. In Figure 6.1, Maxine's budget set is shown as a shaded triangle. She can afford any combination below the budget line, but cannot afford combinations above it.

Budget line

The line connecting all the combinations of two goods that exhaust a consumer's budget.

Budget set

A set of points that includes all the combinations of goods that a consumer can afford, given the consumer's income and the prices of the goods.

FIGURE 6.1

Budget Set and Budget Line

The budget set (the shaded triangle) shows all the affordable combinations of books and movies, and the budget line (with endpoints *x* and *y*) shows the combinations that exhaust the budget.

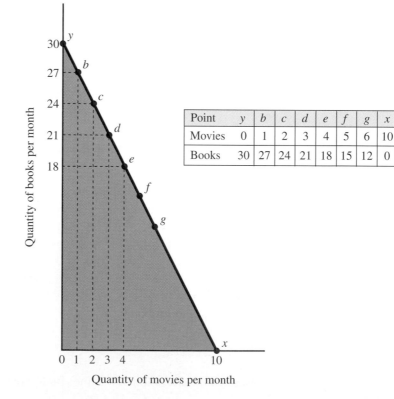

Point	*y*	*b*	*c*	*d*	*e*	*f*	*g*	*x*
Movies	0	1	2	3	4	5	6	10
Books	30	27	24	21	18	15	12	0

Quantity of books per month

Quantity of movies per month

The budget line shows the market trade-off between books and movies. Starting from any point on the budget line, if Maxine buys one more movie, she diverts $3 from book purchases, reducing the number of $1 books she can purchase by 3. The market trade-off equals the **price ratio**, the price of movies ($3) divided by the price of books ($1), or 3 books per movie. The market trade-off also equals the slope of the budget line, the "rise" (the change in books) divided by the "run" (the change in movies). Because all consumers pay the same price for the two goods, they all have the same market trade-off of 3 books per movie.

Price ratio

The ratio of the price of one good to the price of a second good; the market trade-off.

Consumer Preferences: Indifference Curves

We've seen the consumer's budget set, which shows what the consumer can afford. The next step in our discussion of consumer choice is to look at what the consumer wants, what makes the consumer happy. Once we have a means of representing consumer preferences, we can show how a consumer makes her choice, picking the best of the combinations shown by the budget set.

We can represent the consumer's preferences or tastes with **indifference curves**. An indifference curve represents the fundamental idea that there are different ways for a consumer to reach a particular level of satisfaction, or what economists call **utility**. An indifference curve shows the different combinations of two goods that generate the same level of utility or satisfaction. In Figure 6.2, the indifference curve passing through points *b, z, m,* and *n* separates the combinations of books and movies into three groups.

Indifference curve

A curve showing the different combinations of two goods that generate the same level of utility or satisfaction.

Utility

The satisfaction experienced from consuming a product.

▶ *Superior combinations.* All the combinations above the indifference curve generate higher utility than combinations on the curve. Maxine would prefer point *h* to point *z* because she gets more of both goods with point *h*.

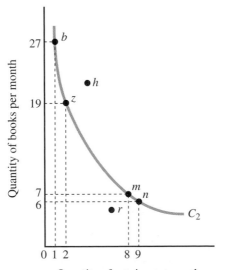

FIGURE 6.2

Indifference Curve and the Marginal Rate of Substitution

The indifference curve shows the different combinations of books and movies that generate the same utility level. The slope is the marginal rate of substitution (*MRS*) between the two goods. The *MRS* is eight books per movie between points *b* and *z*, but only one book per movie between points *m* and *n*.

▶ *Inferior combinations.* All the combinations below the indifference curve generate lower utility than combinations on the curve. Maxine would prefer point *m* to point *r* because she gets more of both goods with point *m*.

▶ *Equivalent combinations.* All combinations along the indifference curve generate the same utility as combination *u*. Maxine is therefore indifferent between combinations *b, z, m,* and *n*.

An indifference curve shows the preferences of an individual consumer, so indifference curves vary from one consumer to another. Nonetheless, the indifference curves of all consumers share two characteristics: They are negatively sloped, and they become flatter as we move downward along an individual curve.

Why is the indifference curve negatively sloped? If we increased Maxine's movie consumption by one unit without changing her book consumption, her utility would increase. To restore the original utility level, we must take away some books, and that's what happens along an indifference curve. To keep utility constant, there is a negative relationship between books and movies, so the indifference curve is negatively sloped. The slope of the curve is called the **marginal rate of substitution (*MRS*)** between the two goods; it is the rate at which a consumer is willing to substitute one good for another. The *MRS* is the consumer's trade-off between the two goods, the number of books we must take from Maxine to offset the effect of giving her 1 more movie. In Figure 6.3, if Maxine starts at point *b* and we give her 1 more movie, we take away 8 books to keep her on the same indifference curve. Therefore, starting from point *b*, her marginal rate of substitution is 8 books per movie. When she starts with many books and only 1 movie, she is willing to trade a lot of books to get 1 more movie.

The indifference curve becomes flatter as we move downward along the curve. This reflects the assumption that consumers prefer balanced consumption to extremes. As we move down Maxine's indifference curve, movie consumption increases while book consumption decreases. Starting from one extreme (few movies and many books), she is willing to sacrifice many books to get another movie: The *MRS* is large and the indifference curve is steep. For example, starting from point *b*, her *MRS* is 8

Marginal rate of substitution (*MRS*)

The rate at which a consumer is willing to trade or substitute one good for another.

FIGURE 6.3

Indifference Map
An indifference map shows a set of indifference curves, with utility increasing as we move northeasterly to higher indifference curves (from C_1 to C_2 to C_4).

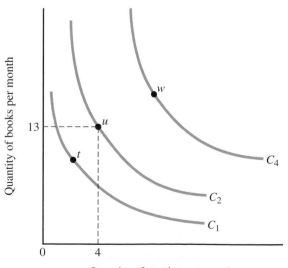

books per movie. But as she gets more and more movies (and fewer and fewer books), she isn't willing to sacrifice as many books to get more movies. As a result, her *MRS* decreases, and the indifference curve becomes flatter. For example, between points *m* and *n*, the *MRS* is 1 book per movie.

An **indifference map** is a set of indifference curves, each with a different level of utility. Figure 6.4 shows three indifference curves: C_1, C_2, and C_4. As Maxine moves from a point on indifference curve C_1 to any point on C_2, her utility increases. This is sensible because she can get more of both goods on C_2, so she will be better off. In general, Maxine's utility increases as she moves in the northeasterly direction to a higher indifference curve (from C_1 to C_2 to C_4, and so on).

> **Indifference map**
> A set of indifference curves, each with a different utility level.

TEST Your Understanding

1. Rob consumes muffins (shown on the horizontal axis) and bagels (shown on the vertical axis). He has a budget of $20; the price of bagels is $1 and the price of muffins is $2. Draw his budget line.
2. Draw a representative indifference curve for Rob. Provide enough numbers to show that when he consumes three muffins and 14 bagels, his *MRS* is six bagels per muffin.
3. Why does the marginal rate of substitution decrease as a consumer moves downward along an indifference curve?

Maximizing Utility

Maxine's objective is to maximize her utility, given her budget and the prices of movies and books. Maxine can pick from many affordable combinations of books and movies, and she should pick the one that generates the highest level of utility or satisfaction. In graphical terms, Maxine will reach the highest indifference curve possible, given her budget set.

The Tangency Condition

In Figure 6.4, Maxine maximizes her utility at point *e*, with 4 movies and 18 books. She achieves the utility level associated with indifference curve C_3. Why does she choose point *e* instead of other points such as *z, b,* or *w*?

► Point *z*. Maxine doesn't choose this point for two reasons. First, it is not on the budget line, so it does not exhaust her budget: She would have some money left over. Second, it is on a lower indifference curve—and thus generates less utility—than point *e*.
► Point *b*. Although point *b* exhausts Maxine's budget, it lies on a lower indifference curve than *e*, so it generates less utility than point *e*. Starting from point *b*, Maxine could reallocate her budget and buy more movies and fewer books. As she moves down her budget line, she moves to progressively higher indifference curves, ultimately reaching point *e* on indifference curve C_3.

FIGURE 6.4

Maximizing Utility
To maximize utility, the consumer finds the combination of books and movies where an indifference curve is tangent to the budget line. At the utility-maximizing combination, the marginal rate of substitution (the consumer's own trade-off) equals the price ratio (the market trade-off).

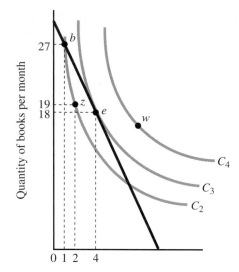

▶ Point w. Although point w is on a higher indifference curve and thus would generate a higher utility level than point e, it lies outside Maxine's budget set, so she cannot afford it.

At point e, Maxine reaches the highest indifference curve possible, given her budget set. Notice that at point e, the indifference curve touches—but does not pass through—the budget line. In other words, the indifference curve is tangent to the budget line.

Utility-maximizing rule

Pick the affordable combination that makes the marginal rate of substitution equal to the price ratio.

The Utility-Maximizing Rule: MRS = Price Ratio

What is the economic interpretation of the tangency condition? At the point of tangency, the slope of the indifference curve equals the slope of the budget line. The slope of the budget line equals the opportunity cost of movies, computed as the movie price ($3) divided by the book price ($1), or 3 books per movie. The slope of the indifference curve is the marginal rate of substitution (MRS), so if the two curves are tangent at point e, the MRS is also 3 books per movie. In other words, the consumer's trade-off between the two goods (the MRS) equals the market trade-off (the price ratio) between the two goods.

■ Utility Maximizing Rule

$$MRS = \frac{\text{price of movie}}{\text{price of book}}$$

To show why the tangency point is best, suppose Maxine tentatively chooses a point where the MRS is not equal to the price ratio. For example, starting at point b, the indifference curve is relatively steep, and the MRS is eight books per movie: She is willing to give up eight books to get a single movie. But given market trade-off, she can actually get that movie by sacrificing only three books, so she will move down her budget line and consume more movies. The same argument applies to any combination for which the *MRS* (the consumer's own trade-off) is not equal to the price ratio (the market trade-off). Anytime Maxine is willing to trade at a rate that is different from market trade-off, it will be in her best interest to do so. The benefits of trading will be exhausted only when the *MRS* equals the price ratio. In Figure 6.4, this happens at point *e*.

Drawing the Demand Curve

We can use the budget line and indifference curve for movies and books to draw Maxine's demand curve for just one of those products—say, movies. We've already derived one point on her demand curve. In Figure 6.5, the upper panel shows the consumer-choice model, with indifference curves and a budget line. When the price of movies is $3, she maximizes utility at point *e*, with 4 movies. The lower panel shows Maxine's demand curve for movies, with the number of movies shown on the horizontal axis and the price of movies on the vertical axis. When the price is $3, her utility-maximizing choice is shown as point *e* in the upper panel and point *E* in the lower panel. In other words, the demand curve shows her utility-maximizing choice.

With so many curves floating around, it is worth reviewing their roles in consumer decision-making.

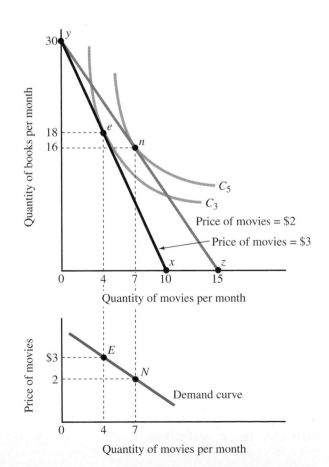

FIGURE 6.5

Drawing the Demand Curve

A decrease in the price of movies tilts the budget line outward. The indifference curve is tangent to the budget line at a larger quantity of movies (7 instead of 4). This is the law of demand: The higher the price, the smaller the quantity demanded.

1 The budget line shows the affordable combinations of two goods, representing the consumer's constraints.

2 An indifference curve shows the different combinations of two goods that generate the same utility level, and thus shows the consumer's preferences.

3 The demand curve shows how much of a *single* product a consumer is willing to buy at a particular price. To get the demand curve, we use both the budget line and indifference curves.

The upper panel Figure 6.5 shows what happens to the budget line when the price of movies decreases to $2. The decrease in price tilts the budget line outward. The original vertical intercept (point *y*) is still in the budget set because if the entire budget is spent on books, the price of movies is irrelevant. The horizontal intercept moves outward from *x* (10 movies) to *z* (15 movies) because with a lower movie price, a given budget will buy more movies. If Maxine buys both books and movies, she will choose a point on the new budget line between points *y* and *z*. In general, the decrease in the movie price makes more combinations affordable.

How will Maxine respond to the lower price of movies? Given the new budget line and the same set of indifference curves, Maxine picks point *n*, where one of her indifference curves is tangent to the new budget line. Maxine responds to the decrease in the movie price by consuming 7 movies instead of 4. With this combination, her *MRS* is equal to the new price ratio of 2 books per movie. The decrease in price means that the market trade-off is lower, and so to satisfy the utility-maximizing rule, Maxine picks a combination of movies and books with a lower *MRS*—2 books per movie, down from 3 books per movie.

The lower panel of Figure 6.5 shows the point on the demand curve associated with a movie price of $2 (point *N*). When the price is $2, Maxine consumes 7 movies. This is consistent with the law of demand: The lower the price, the larger the quantity demanded, *ceteris paribus*. Recall that when we draw a demand curve, we use the *ceteris paribus* assumption that everything except the *price* of the product is fixed. To draw Maxine's demand curve for movies, we change the price of movies, holding fixed the other variables that affect her consumption of movies. These other variables include her income (fixed at $30) and the price of related goods like books, with a fixed price of $1. We also hold fixed her personal preferences for the two goods, meaning that we use a single set of indifference curves.

We've used the consumer choice model to find two points on the individual demand curve. We could repeat the process for other prices to find other points on the demand curve. For each price, we find the quantity of movies that generates the highest possible utility level, given the consumer's budget and the price of the other good. Each point on the demand curve satisfies the utility-maximizing rule that the *MRS* (the consumer's own trade-off) equals the price ratio (the market trade-off).

Do Consumers Actually Do This?

We've used the consumer choice model to find a point on the demand curve of one consumer, given the consumer's budget and her personal preferences. A consumer with a different budget would have a different budget line and by following the utility-maximizing rule (*MRS* = price ratio) would choose a different point on his or her budget line. Similarly, a consumer with different personal preferences would have different indifference curves and would maximize utility with a different combination of movies and books.

Do consumers actually use the consumer choice model to make decisions? When you think about going to the movies, do you compute your *MRS*, and then go only if the *MRS* exceeds the price ratio? Although consumers don't actually base their decisions on *MRS* computations, most consumer choices are consistent with the consumer choice model.

To see how consumers act as if they are using consumer choice model, consider the billiard (pool) play of Minnesota Fats, a legendary player from the 1950s and 1960s. The movement of balls on a pool table obey various laws of physics, including the laws of inertia and friction. Although Minnesota Fats could not state the relevant laws of physics, he played pool as if he applied the laws to every shot. Similarly, although consumers may not compare their *MRS* to the price ratios, they act as if they are applying the utility-maximizing rule.

TEST Your Understanding

4. Recall Rob's situation from an earlier question. He has a $20 budget to spend on muffins (price = $2) and bagels (price = $1). At his current consumption bundle of 3 muffins and 14 bagels, Rob is willing to sacrifice 6 bagels to get 1 muffin. Is he maximizing utility? If not, should he buy more or fewer muffins?
5. What is the difference between the budget line and the demand curve?

Applications of the Consumer Choice Model

We can use the consumer choice model to explore two questions. First, how is the development of online music stores related to Internet music piracy? Second, how does inflation affect a consumer's buying habits and well-being? Third, how is the notion of utility maximization related to the commonsense notion that a person should choose the action with the largest bang per buck?

Music Piracy and Online Music Stores

The chapter opener described the new online music stores, which provide an alternative to the traditional method of buying bundles of songs on CDs. We can use the consumer choice model to explain the logic behind this new development in the music business.

Consider Sam, who has $30 to spend on music and arcade games. In an ideal world, he could buy music by the song, just as he buys arcade games individually.

A CLOSER LOOK

Modern Consumer Theory Versus Old Utility Theory

This chapter presents modern consumer theory, which is based on indifference curves and the marginal rate of substitution. This theory does not require a measure of the actual *utility* or satisfaction a consumer gets from a product. It simply requires a measure of the consumer's personal trade-off between two goods, the consumer's marginal rate of substitution. To decide if a consumer could do better, we simply compare the *MRS* to the price ratio.

In contrast, utility theory of the nineteenth century was based on the idea that we could actually measure the utility people get from consuming products. Some social scientists thought it would even be possible to hook people up to a "utility meter" and then see what happens when they consumed a product. The following figure shows the framework for utility theory. The horizontal axis measures the quantity of a product consumed, and the vertical axis measures the person's total utility, in "utils." The slope of the utility curve decreases as consumption increases, reflecting the assumption that the more of a product a person consumes, the lower the marginal utility of the product. Although this theory provides some insights into consumer choice, the assumption of "measurable" utility is troublesome to most economists. Instead, we use budget lines and indifference curves to model consumer choice.

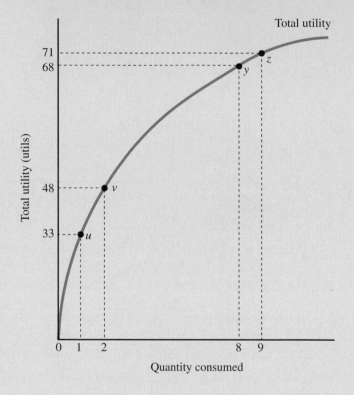

Suppose the price of music in this ideal world is $1 per song and the price of arcade games is $0.50 per game. In Figure 6.6, Sam's budget line is the line connecting points *y* and *x*. He can spend his entire budget on games, getting 60 games (point *y*), or spend it all on songs, getting 30 songs (point *x*). Alternatively, he could split his budget between the two goods. With a price ratio of 2 games per song, the market trade-off is 2 games per song. Suppose that in this ideal world, Sam's best point is *i*, where an indifference curve is tangent to his budget line, meaning that his *MRS* equals the price ratio. At point *i*, Sam would have 6 songs and 48 arcade games.

Suppose that music cannot be purchased by the song but instead must be purchased on CDs. Each CD carries 15 songs and has a price of $15. In this case, Sam has only three options: He can spend his entire budget on games (60 games, as shown by point *y*), or he can get one CD with 15 songs and also get 30 games (point *j*), or he can spend his entire budget on two CDs (30 songs, point *x*). All of these points are

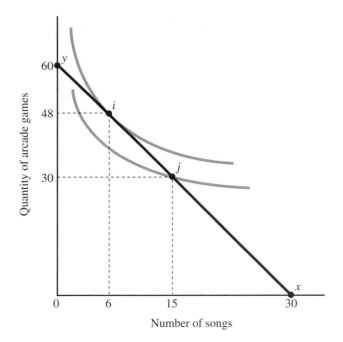

Internet Music Piracy and iTunes

When music is sold as 15-song bundles on CDs, the consumer has three budget points (*y*, *j*, and *x*) rather than an entire budget line. If songs are sold individually, the consumer has a full budget line and can legally reach his or her ideal combination of 6 songs and 48 arcade games (point *i*).

below the indifference curve associated with point *i*, so his utility is lower at any of these other points. He'd prefer point *i* (6 songs and 48 games) to any of these other points.

In the world of CDs and Internet file sharing, Sam actually has another option. He can use a swapping service to get songs for free. Of course, this is illegal, and Sam risks a penalty and may also feel bad about breaking the law. If the benefit (free songs) exceeds the cost (risk and bad feelings about law breaking), he will engage in piracy.

Consider next the effects of iTunes and other online music services that sell single songs. Now Sam has a third alternative to buying an entire CD or stealing songs. Sam can get his ideal combination of goods without any risk of criminal penalties, and he may prefer paying for his music to engaging in piracy. One motivation for online music stores is to reduce music piracy by people who want just a few songs off a particular CD. Of course, there are other motives for piracy, and it is expected to continue. But the early experience with online music stores suggest that many consumers prefer the flexibility of buying music by the song and are willing to pay for it.

Inflation, the Real–Nominal Principle, and Consumer Choice

We can use our model of consumer decision-making to address the issue of inflation, defined as a general increase in all prices, including the price of labor. Consider the effects of a doubling of all prices. Using our example, the prices of movies and books would double, along with wages and salaries paid to workers. If Maxine's income comes from a job, the doubling of wages would cause her income to double. How would she respond to inflation?

Online music services that sell single, downloadable songs help consumers achieve maximum utility and avoid music-piracy penalties.

Inflation will not affect Maxine's consumer decision. If consumer prices double, the price of movies doubles to $6 and the price of books doubles to $2, but Maxine's income doubles too, from $30 to $60. Consequently, she will continue to purchase 4 movies, just as she did before inflation. Inflation doesn't affect her consumer decision because it doesn't affect her budget set: Her new budget set, with doubled prices and income, is identical to the old one. To see this, think about the horizontal and vertical intercepts of the budget line—the point where Maxine's budget line crosses the x and y axes. The horizontal intercept shows how many movies Maxine can buy if she spends her entire income on movies. Before inflation, her $30 income could buy 10 movies at $3; after inflation, her $60 income can buy 10 movies at $6 each. Similarly, when the price of books and income both double, the vertical intercept doesn't change.

The implication of this analysis is that inflation doesn't harm or help Maxine. Inflation doesn't affect her budget set or her consumer choices, so she is just as well off as she was before inflation. This is an application of one of the five key principles.

THE REAL–NOMINAL *Principle*

What matters to people is the real value of money or income, not the nominal value.

In our example, what matters to Maxine is her real income, or the purchasing power of her income. Although inflation doubles her income, it also doubles prices, leaving her real income the same.

The Equimarginal Rule

The utility-maximizing rule tells consumers how to pick the best mix of two goods. The logic behind this rule can be used to find the best mix of other things, such as the best mix of skilled and unskilled labor or the best mix of radio and television advertising. For these types of decisions, we can use the **equimarginal rule**, which is a variation on the utility-maximizing rule.

Equimarginal rule

Pick the combination of two things that equalizes the marginal benefit per dollar spent.

■ Equimarginal Rule

If the marginal benefit per dollar spent on one thing exceeds the marginal benefit per dollar spent on a second, do more of the first and less of the second. To get the best possible combination of the two things, pick the mix that equalizes the marginal benefit per dollar spent.

Recall that Maxine picks the mix of movies and books where the *MRS* is 3 books per movie, the same as the price ratio. Maxine is willing to sacrifice 3 books to get 1 movie, meaning that her benefit from 1 movie equals her benefit from 3 books. In other words, the marginal benefit per movie is three times the marginal benefit per book. Compared to books, movies have three times the marginal benefit and *exactly* three times the price, so Maxine's mix of movies and books satisfies the equimarginal principle: She has equalized the marginal benefit per dollar spent on the two goods.

A firm can use the equimarginal principle to pick the best mix of skilled and unskilled workers. Skilled workers are expensive and highly productive, whereas unskilled workers are cheaper but produce less. The firm should pick the worker type with the largest marginal benefit (output produced) per dollar spent. If skilled workers produce $120 worth of output and receive a wage of $20, the benefit per dollar spent is $6 ($120 worth of output divided by the $20 wage). If an unskilled worker produces $30 worth of output and receives a wage of $10, the benefit per dollar spent is only $3 ($30 divided by the $10). Although skilled workers are twice as expensive, they are actually a better deal because they are *four* times as productive. In other words, skilled workers give the firm more bang (output) per buck.

A firm could also use the equimarginal principle to pick the best mix of radio and television advertising. The marginal benefit of advertising is the increase in sales from one more minute of airtime. If a minute of television advertising increases sales by $18,000 and costs $6,000, the marginal benefit per dollar is $3. If a minute of radio advertising increases sales by $2,000 and costs $1,000, the marginal benefit per dollar is only $2. In this case, television gives a bigger bang per buck, so television is a better choice.

Should our hypothetical firm allocate all of its advertising budget to television? We would expect the first television advertisement to be more effective in increasing sales than the second, and the second to be more effective than the third. In general, the marginal benefits of television advertising will decrease as the number of ads increases and so will the marginal bang per buck. Eventually, the marginal bang per buck from television may drop to the point where it is less than

The Bang per Buck of Light Spirits

To illustrate the relevance of the equimarginal rule, consider New Zealand's recent experiences with taxing alcoholic beverages. Policymakers who were concerned about teen drinking discovered that the favored beverages among teens were "light spirits"—beverages with alcohol content between 14% and 24%. These light spirits provided the biggest alcoholic bang per buck for teens. For example, cheap rum with an alcohol content of 23% sold for $8, generating a bang per buck of $23 \div 8 = 2.88$.

The government imposed a special tax on light spirits, nearly doubling the price of teens' favorite beverages, from $8 to $14. The bang per buck of light spirits therefore decreased to 1.64, and teens responded by cutting back on light spirits. Producers responded by changing their beverage recipes, cutting the alcohol content to 13.9% to avoid the tax. Moreover, they priced these new "super-light" beverages below the prices of the original light beverages. For example, super-light rum with an alcohol content of 13.9% was priced at $7, yielding a bang per buck of 2.25—bigger than the 1.64 bang per buck from light beverages subject to the tax. Given the equimarginal principle, we would expect many teens to switch to super-light beverages,

and that's exactly what happened. In addition, some teens went the other direction, switching to beverages that were too potent to be subject to the light-spirits tax.

The simple lesson is that consumers respond to price changes and taxes. A tax decreases the bang per buck of the taxed good, causing consumers to switch to products that now have a higher bang per buck than the taxed good. In this case, the tax increased the consumption of beverages with both lower and higher alcohol content.

the marginal bang per buck for the first radio advertisement. At that point, the firm will buy some radio time. For the best mix of radio and television, the marginal benefit per dollar spent on television will equal the marginal benefit per dollar spent on radio.

TEST Your Understanding

6. In the labor example, suppose the wage of skilled workers increases to $60. Which type of worker has a bigger bang per buck?
7. Explain how you would use the equimarginal rule to allocate a fixed amount of time to study for two exams, one in history and one in psychology.

In this chapter, we use some of the key principles of economics to explain the logic behind consumer choice and the law of demand. Here are some opportunities to do your own economic analysis.

1. Utility Maximization for Holiday Party

At your company's annual holiday party, people eat food (price per unit = $1) and drink punch (price per unit = $2), and the firm pays for everything. This year, the firm spent $20 per employee, with equal quantities of food and punch. Your job is to determine whether the company spent this year's party budget wisely, given its objective of maximizing the utility of the typical employee. To simplify matters, assume that all employees have identical tastes for food and punch, so data from a single person will apply to every employee. You can ask the typical employee a single question.
a. What's your question?
b. Provide an answer to your question that would suggest that the firm should have spent more on punch and less on food. Illustrate your answer with a completely labeled graph.

2. Product Design: Horsepower Versus Cubic Feet

Carla has a fixed budget for a new car and has tentatively decided to buy a car with 80 horsepower (hp) and 100 cubic feet (cf) of interior space. Given the current selection of cars and their prices, the price of horsepower is one-third the price of cubic

feet. After some prompting from the used-car salesperson, Carla said, "To get an additional unit of horsepower, I would be willing to sacrifice two cubic feet of interior space." Does her tentative choice (80 hp and 100 cf) maximize her utility subject to her auto budget? If not, should she choose an auto with more or less horsepower?

3. Allocating an Advertising Budget to Different Markets

You are responsible for allocating a fixed advertising budget for your firm in various markets. Your budget is $12 million. The benefits and costs of advertising in the markets are shown in the following table (in millions of dollars):

Market	B	C	D	E	F	G	H
Benefit of campaign	$3	$14	$6	$15	$40	$30	$48
Cost of campaign	$1	$2	$2	$3	$4	$5	$6

a. How would you allocate the budget?
b. How would the total benefits change if you spent the $12-million budget on the least expensive campaigns?

We've used modern consumer theory to explore the decision-making process of a rational consumer. The consumer's objective is to maximize utility, given her income and the prices of consumer goods. Here are the main points of the chapter.

1 To maximize utility, the consumer finds the point at which one of her indifference curves is tangent to her budget line.

2 At the utility-maximizing combination of two goods, the marginal rate of substitution (the consumer's own trade-off between the two goods) equals the price ratio (the market trade-off).

3 According to the equimarginal rule, you should pick the mix of two things at which the marginal benefit per dollar spent on the first equals the marginal benefit per dollar spent on the second.

KEY TERMS

budget line, 122
budget set, 122
equimarginal rule, 133
indifference curve, 123

indifference map, 125
marginal rate of substitution
  (*MRS*), 124
price ratio, 123

utility, 123
utility-maximizing rule, 123

PROBLEMS AND DISCUSSION QUESTIONS

1 Suppose the price of amusement rides is $2 and the price of a video arcade game is $1. The following table shows points on the budget line (given an income of $30) and the associated *MRS*:

	b	c	d	e
Quantity of rides	1	2	3	4
Quantity of video games	28	26	24	22
Marginal rate of substitution	5	3	2	1

   a. Explain why point b is not the best the consumer can do.
   b. What is the utility-maximizing combination of rides and games?

2 Suppose you have a fixed budget of $3,000 per year to spend on food and music. The price of food is $1 per pound, and the price of music is $10 per CD. You currently spend $2,400 on food and $600 on music.
   a. If you want to determine whether you are spending your money wisely, what question must you ask yourself?
   b. Provide an answer such that you should spend less on CDs and more on tapes.

3 Suppose you have a fixed monthly budget for audiotapes and CDs. The price of CDs is $15, and the price of tapes is $5. Given your current choice of CDs and tapes, your marginal rate of substitution is one tape per CD. Are you doing the best you can with your music budget? If not, should you buy more CDs (and fewer tapes) or more tapes (and fewer CDs)? Relate your answer to the utility-maximizing rule and illustrate with a completely labeled graph.

4 Consider a person who spends a total of $200 on hats and violets. The price of hats is $20, and the price of violets is $5. Draw a budget line with hats on the horizontal axis and violets on the vertical axis.
   a. What is the slope of the budget line?
   b. Draw a conventional indifference curve (negatively sloped and convex to the origin) that intersects the budget line. Explain why the consumer can reach a higher utility level than the level shown by this indifference curve.
   c. Draw a second indifference curve that shows the highest possible utility level.
   d. Complete the statement: To maximize utility, the consumer finds the combination of hats and violets such that _____ equals four.

5 Biff consumes two entertainment goods, arcade games and CDs. When you ask him in week one, "How many arcade games are you wiling to sacrifice for one more CD?" he says, "two." When you ask him the same question a week later (week two), he says, "five." Over this period, his underlying preferences for arcade games and CDs haven't changed.
   a. What could explain the change in his trade-off from week one to week two? Illustrate with a completely labeled graph, with CDs on the horizontal axis and arcade games on the vertical axis.
   b. Suppose Biff reached the same utility levels in weeks one and two. In week three, you offer to provide Biff his average consumption bundle from weeks one and two, that is, the average number of CDs and the average number of arcade games. Will he be better off, worse off, or equally well off compared to weeks one and two? Illustrate with a completely labeled graph.

6 Wolfgang has a fixed budget for a new car and has tentatively decided to buy a car that gets 20 miles per gallon (mpg) and has a performance level of 60 ms (the maximum speed at which a turntable can play Mozart's first symphony without skipping). A salesperson recently asked Wolfgang about his attitudes toward cars with different combinations of mpg and ms. Wolfgang would prefer a car with 19 mpg and 64 ms to his tentative choice but would prefer his tentative choice to a car with 19 mpg and 62 ms. Suppose that the cost of an additional mpg is six times the cost of an additional unit of ms.

a. Does Wolfgang's tentative choice (20 mpg and 60 ms) maximize his utility subject to his auto budget? If not, should he choose an auto with more or fewer mpg?

b. Illustrate your answer with a completely labeled graph. Label Wolfgang's tentative choice with a "*T*" and his utility-maximizing choice with a "*U*."

7 Consider the following statement: "My car can use either gasoline or gasohol (a mixture of methanol and gasoline). I use whatever fuel has a lower price per gallon." Is this a good rule for deciding what type of fuel to use in a car? If not, develop a rule that is consistent with the utility-maximizing rule.

MODEL ANSWERS TO QUESTIONS

Chapter-Opening Questions

1 What's your marginal rate of substitution between two goods? If her *MRS* equals the price ratio, she is maximizing her utility.

2 A doubling of prices and incomes does not affect the consumer's budget line, so the consumer is just as well off.

3 As explained in "A Closer Look: The Bang per Buck of Light Spirits," teens switched to super-light and heavy beverages.

Test Your Understanding

1 The vertical intercept is 20 bagels, and the horizontal intercept is 10 muffins. The slope (the market trade-off) is two bagels per muffin.

2 One point on the indifference curve is {three muffins, 14 bagels}. Given an *MRS* = 6, another point is {four muffins, eight bagels}. If Rob is like other consumers, who prefer balanced consumption to extremes, his *MRS* decreases as he consumes more muffins and fewer bagels.

3 Consumers prefer balanced consumption of two goods to extremes.

4 The price ratio (the market trade-off) is two bagels per muffin. His *MRS* exceeds the price ratio, so he should consume more muffins and fewer bagels.

5 The budget line shows the affordable combinations of *two* goods, and the demand curve shows how much of a *single* good a consumer is willing to buy at a particular price.

6 For skilled workers, the marginal benefit per dollar is now $2, which is less than the marginal benefit per dollar for unskilled workers ($3).

7 Allocate time to the exam that has the largest bang (increase in score) per minute of study time.

Consumer Surplus and Producer Surplus

The Demand Curve and Consumer Surplus
The Supply Curve and Producer Surplus

Market Equilibrium and Efficiency

Total Surplus Is Lower with a Price Below
    the Equilibrium Price
Total Surplus Is Lower with a Price Above
    the Equilibrium Price
Efficiency and the Invisible Hand

Government Intervention in Markets

Controlling the Price

Setting Maximum Prices
Application: Rent Control
Setting Minimum Prices

**Controlling the Quantity—Licensing
and Import Restrictions**

Application: Taxi Medallions
Licensing and Market Efficiency
Winners and Losers from Licensing
Restricting Imports

Who Really Pays Taxes?

Tax Shifting: Forward and Backward
Predicting the Amount Shifted Forward
    and Backward
Applications: Cigarette and Luxury Taxes
Tax Burden and Deadweight Loss
Using the Tools

Market Efficiency and Government Intervention

group of citizens in College Town recently proposed a rent-control law under which the monthly rent on apartments would decrease from $400 to $300. The mayor of College Town, who has the power to approve or disapprove the proposed law, recently made the following statement to the citizens of the city:

> I know that some of you would be harmed by rent control, and others would be helped. To help me decide whether to approve the proposed law, send me a note stating whether you favor or oppose rent control, along with a campaign contribution equal to just 1% of your cost or benefit from rent control. If the total contributions of citizens favoring rent control exceed the contributions of those who oppose it, I will approve the proposed law. Otherwise, I won't.

If everyone follows the mayor's directions, she will not approve rent control.

I n Chapter 3, we discussed the exchange principle, which conveys the simple idea that transactions make both buyer and seller better off:

THE *Principle* OF VOLUNTARY EXCHANGE

A voluntary exchange between two people makes both people better off.

In this chapter, we will take a closer look at the benefits of exchange, examining the experiences of both buyers and sellers. We will see how to compute the surplus or net benefit from a market and see why the market equilibrium—where the quantity demanded equals the quantity supplied—*may* generate the largest possible surplus. We'll explore the logic behind Adam Smith's metaphor of the invisible hand, the idea that individual buyers and sellers, each acting in his or her own self-interest, *may* promote the social interest.

You'll notice that we use the word "may" in noting the virtues of markets and the invisible hand. A market equilibrium will generate the largest possible surplus and thus be efficient when four conditions are met:

▶ *No external benefits:* The benefits of a product are confined to the person who pays for it.
▶ *No external costs:* The cost of producing a product is confined to the person who sells it.
▶ *Perfect information:* Buyers and sellers know enough about the product to make informed decisions about whether to buy or sell it.
▶ *Perfect competition:* Each firm produces such a small quantity that the firm cannot affect the price.

In this chapter, we discuss markets that meet these four conditions. As we'll see later in the book, when these conditions are not satisfied, free markets are not efficient.

Governments around the world intervene in markets, sometimes promoting efficiency and other times preventing it. In this chapter, we'll see that when the four efficiency conditions are met, government intervention is inefficient in the sense that it decreases the total surplus of the market. Here are some of the practical questions we answer:

1 If a college town uses a rent-control policy to cut the monthly rent on apartments, will some students be harmed by the policy?

2 If you want to operate a taxi in New York City, Toronto, or Boston, you must first buy a taxi medallion for over $100,000. Why does the medallion cost so much?

3 Why is there a shortage (excess demand) for human organs for transplanting?

4 Who bears the cost of restrictions on textile imports, and what is the cost per textile job saved?

5 How would a monthly apartment tax of $100 affect monthly rents?

Consumer Surplus and Producer Surplus

We'll begin our discussion of market efficiency by showing how to measure the benefits experienced by consumers and producers. We'll start with consumers, and then we'll look at producers.

The Demand Curve and Consumer Surplus

If you said "thank you" the last time you purchased a CD, did you mean it? If you were willing to pay more for the CD than the price you actually paid, you probably really *did* mean it when you said "thank you" because you got what you consider to be a good deal. Your **willingness to pay** for a product is the maximum amount you are willing to pay for the product. Your **consumer surplus** is the difference between your willingness to pay and the price you actually pay for it. For example, if you are willing to pay $21 for a CD that you buy for $10, your consumer surplus is $11.

The market demand curve shows consumers' willingness to pay for a product. Consider the demand for lawn cutting in a small town, with the market demand curve shown in Figure 7.1. The demand curve shows that at a price of $25, no one will pay to have the lawn cut (point *t*), but if the price drops to $22, the first consumer (Juan) will pay for a lawn cut. This suggests that Juan is willing to pay up to $22 to have his lawn cut, but no more. Moving down the demand curve, the second consumer (Tupak) will pay for a lawn cutting when the price drops to $19, meaning that his willingness to pay is $19. As we continue to move downward along the demand curve, the price drops below the willingness to pay for more and more consumers, so more people have their lawns cut.

We can use the demand curve to measure just how much of a net benefit or surplus consumers get. Suppose that the price of a lawn cut is $10, and everyone in town pays this price. Juan's consumer surplus is $12, equal to his willingness to pay ($22) minus the price. Similarly, Tupak's consumer surplus is $9, equal to the difference between his willingness to pay ($19) and the market price. To compute the total consumer surplus in the lawn-cutting market, we simply add up the surpluses for each of the five consumers who buy lawn cutting at a price of $10. In this example, the market consumer surplus is $30, equal to $12 (Juan) + $9 (Tupak) + $6 (Thurl) + $3 (Forest) + $0 (Fivola). The fifth consumer (Fivola) gets no consumer surplus because the price equals her willingness to pay. The sixth person (Siggy) doesn't have his lawn cut because the amount he is willing to pay is less than the price.

Willingness to pay

The maximum amount a consumer is willing to pay for a product.

Consumer surplus

The difference between a consumer's willingness to pay for a product and the price that he or she pays for the product.

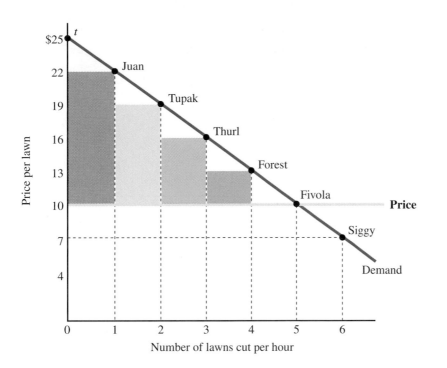

FIGURE 7.1

The Demand Curve and Consumer Surplus
Consumer surplus equals the maximum amount a consumer is willing to pay (shown by the demand curve) minus the price paid. Juan is willing to pay $22, so if the price is $10, his consumer surplus is $12. The market consumer surplus equals the sum of the surpluses earned by all consumers in the market. In this case, the market consumer surplus is $30 = $12 + $9 + $6 + $3 + $0.

The Supply Curve and Producer Surplus

Like consumers, the people who produce goods and services say "thank you" when they sell their products. This suggests that they too receive a net benefit or surplus from voluntary transactions. A seller's **willingness to accept** is the minimum amount he or she is willing to accept as payment for a product and is equal to the marginal cost of production. For example, if your marginal cost of cutting a lawn is $4, you will be willing to accept any amount greater than or equal to $4. Of course, you'd prefer $10 to $4, but you'll accept as little as $4 because the lower amount covers all your costs, including the opportunity cost of your time. **Producer surplus** is the difference between the price a producer receives for a product and the willingness to accept, or the difference between the price and marginal cost. For example, if your marginal cost for cutting a lawn is $4 and you do it for $10, your producer surplus is $6.

Figure 7.2 shows the market supply curve for lawn cutting in our small town. Let's imagine that six people are willing to cut lawns if the price is right, and each person can cut one lawn per hour. Each person incurs the same cost for renting a lawn mower but has a different opportunity costs for his or her time. The first producer (Abe) incurs a cost of $2, so he is willing to accept as little as $2 to cut a lawn. On the supply curve, if the price is $2, one person—Abe—will cut lawns. Bea has a higher opportunity cost of time, so her cost is $4, meaning that she won't cut a lawn unless she is paid at least $4. So if the price is $4, two people—Abe and Bea—will cut lawns. Moving upward along the supply curve, the other potential lawn cutters have even higher costs, so they don't start cutting until the price reaches their higher willingness to pay: $6 for Cecil, $8 for Dee, and so on. The higher the price, the larger the number of people willing to cut lawns.

Willingness to accept
The minimum amount a producer is willing to accept as payment for a product; equal to the marginal cost of production.

Producer surplus
The difference between the price a producer receives for a product and the producer's willingness to accept for the product.

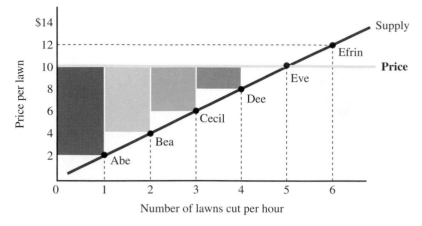

FIGURE 7.2 **The Supply Curve and Producer Surplus**

Producer surplus equals the market price minus the producer's willingness to accept or marginal cost (shown by the supply curve). Abe's marginal cost is $2, so if the price is $10, his producer surplus is $8. The market producer surplus equals the sum of the surpluses earned by all producers in the market. In this case, the market producer surplus is $20 = $8 + $6 + $4 + $2 + $0.

We can use the supply curve to measure just how much of a net benefit or surplus producers get. If the price of lawn cutting is $10, Abe's producer surplus for cutting the lawn is $8, the price he receives minus his cost ($2). Similarly, Bea's producer surplus is $6, equal to the difference between the price and her cost ($4). To compute the total producer surplus in the lawn-cutting market, we simply add up the surpluses for each of the five producers who cut lawns at a price of $10. In this example, the market producer surplus is $20, equal to $8 (Abe) + $6 (Bea) + $4 (Cecil) + $2 (Dee) + $0 (Eve). The fifth producer (Eve) gets no producer surplus because the price equals her cost, and the sixth potential producer (Efrin) doesn't cut any lawns because the price is less than his cost.

Market Equilibrium and Efficiency

Total surplus

The sum of consumer surplus and producer surplus.

Figure 7.3 puts the demand and supply curves together to show the equilibrium in the market for lawn cutting. The demand curve intersects the supply curve at a price of $10 per lawn. At this price, five lawns are cut, meaning that there are five buyers and five sellers. The **total surplus** of a market is the sum of consumer surplus and producer surplus. In Figure 7.3, the consumer surplus is $30 and the producer surplus is $20, so the total surplus of the market—shown by the shaded area—is $50. As we'll see in this part of the chapter, the market equilibrium generates the highest possible total surplus. That's why we say that the market equilibrium is efficient: We can't do any better in terms of the total surplus.

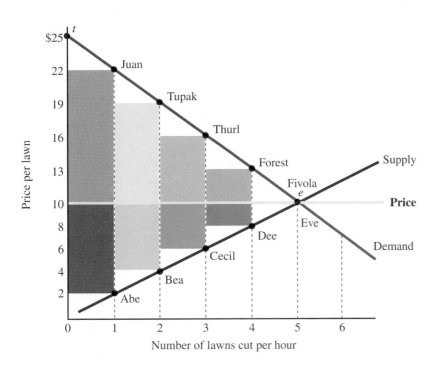

FIGURE 7.3

Market Equilibrium and the Total Market Surplus
The total surplus of the market equals consumer surplus (the lightly shaded areas) plus producer surplus (the darkly shaded areas). The market equilibrium generates the highest possible total market value, equal to $50 = $30 (consumer surplus) + $20 (producer surplus).

Total Surplus Is Lower with a Price Below the Equilibrium Price

To see why the market equilibrium maximizes the total surplus of the market, let's look at the total surplus of the market when the price is less than the equilibrium price. Suppose the government imposes a maximum price of $4 on lawn cutting. As shown in Panel A of Figure 7.4, at this price only two people cut lawns—Abe and Bea. Abe's producer surplus is shown by the darkly shaded area between the price line and the supply curve. For Bea, the price equals her willingness to accept, so she participates in the market but gets no producer surplus, receiving a price just high enough to keep her in the market. Consumers can buy only as much as producers are willing to sell, so the market consumer surplus equals the surpluses of just the first two consumers—Juan and Tupak. This is shown as the lightly shaded areas between the price line and the demand curve. By comparing Panel A in Figure 7.4 to Figure 7.3, we see that the maximum price reduces the total surplus of the market. For the first two lawns, consumers simply gain at the expense of producers. The maximum price also eliminates the surpluses from the third and fourth lawns because these transactions don't happen, so the total surplus decreases.

The maximum price reduces the total surplus of the market because it prevents some mutually beneficial transactions. For example, the third consumer, Thurl, is willing to pay $16 to have his lawn cut, and the third producer, Cecil, is willing to cut a lawn if he is paid at least $6. Thurl is willing to pay more than Cecil requires, so cutting Thurl's lawn would generate a net benefit of $10. If they split the difference, agreeing

FIGURE 7.4

**A Maximum Price
or a Minimum Price
Decreases the Total
Surplus of the Market**
(A) A maximum price of $4
reduces the total surplus of
the market. The first two
consumers gain at the
expense of the first two
producers. The consumer
and producer surpluses for
the third and fourth lawns
are lost entirely, so the
total value of the market
decreases.
(B) A minimum price of $19
reduces the total surplus of
the market. The first two
producers gain at the
expense of the first two
consumers. The consumer
and producer surpluses for
the third and fourth lawns
are lost entirely, so the total
value of the market
decreases.

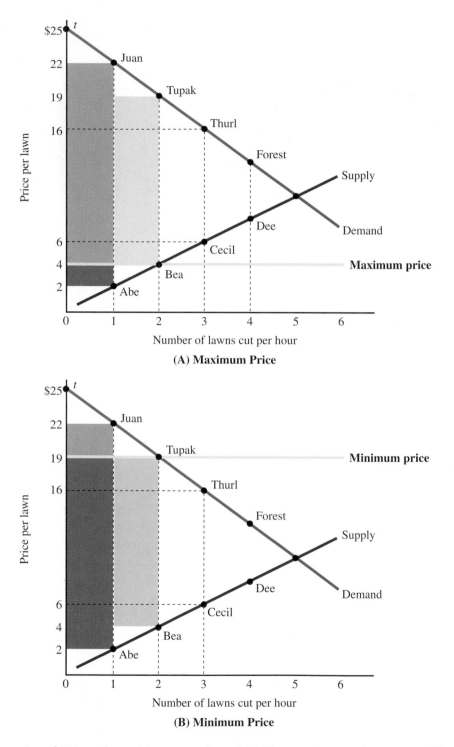

(A) Maximum Price

(B) Minimum Price

on a price of $11, each would get a surplus of $5. The maximum price prevents Thurl
and Cecil from executing their transaction. The same logic applies to the fourth lawn:
The maximum price prevents Forest and Dee from executing a transaction that would
generate a net benefit of $5, equal to Forest's willingness to pay ($13) minus Dee's marginal cost ($8).

Total Surplus Is Lower with a Price Above the Equilibrium Price

What happens when the government imposes a minimum price instead of a maximum price? If the minimum price is $19, as shown in Panel B of Figure 7.4, the demand curve indicates that only two consumers, Juan and Tupak, will have their lawns cut. The total surplus of the market is the sum of consumer and producer surplus for these first two lawns, the same as it was under the maximum price. Again, this is lower than the total surplus that could have been gained, as shown by Figure 7.3. The difference between the two pricing policies is that under a maximum price, the first two consumers gain at the expense of the first two producers, whereas under the minimum price, the first two producers gain at the expense of the first two consumers. Like the maximum price, the minimum price prevents mutually beneficial transactions for the third, fourth, and fifth lawns.

Efficiency and the Invisible Hand

The market equilibrium maximizes the total surplus that can be squeezed out of the market because it guarantees that all mutually beneficial transactions will happen. Once we reach the market equilibrium at point *e* in Figure 7.3, there are no more transactions that would benefit a buyer and a seller. The market demand curve tells us that the potential buyer of the sixth lawn cut (Siggy) is willing to pay only $7, and the supply curve tells us that the potential seller of the sixth lawn cut (Efrin) has a marginal cost of $12. This transaction doesn't happen because the potential buyer is not willing to pay the cost of producing the good.

Our little example of the market for lawn cutting illustrates a general lesson about markets. The typical market has thousands of buyers and thousands of sellers, each acting in his or her own self-interest. If the market has no externalities, the market reaches the quantity that maximizes the total surplus of the market and is therefore efficient. Instead of using a bureaucrat to coordinate the actions of everyone in the market, we can rely on the actions of individual consumers and individual producers, each guided only by self-interest. This is the invisible hand in action.

The experience of the former Soviet Union demonstrates the importance of prices and the power of Adam Smith's ideas as embodied in the metaphor of the invisible hand. The Soviet economy was a planned economy in the sense that bureaucrats—not individual producers—decided how much of each good to produce and at what prices to sell them. There were no market prices to guide the decisions of consumers and producers. When the Soviets discovered a persistent mismatch between what they were producing and what consumers wanted, they asked a team of experts to propose a solution to the problem. The experts told the bureaucrats to figure out the prices that would have occurred if the Soviet economy were a market economy instead of a planned one. Once the bureaucrats predicted the prices, they could then base their production decisions on them. In other words, the experts told the bureaucrats to base their decisions on the prices that would have emerged from a market economy.

The Soviet economy relied on bureaucrats—not markets—to decide how much of each product to produce, resulting in widespread shortages.

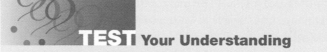

TEST Your Understanding

1. Complete the statement: Consumer surplus equals _____ minus _____, whereas producer surplus equals _____ minus _____.
2. You are willing to pay $2,000 to have your house painted, and Pablo's marginal cost of painting a house is $1,400. If you split the difference, what's your consumer surplus? What's Pablo's producer surplus?
3. Looking back at Figure 7.4, how much is Forest willing to pay for the fourth cut lawn? What is Dee's marginal cost for cutting the fourth lawn? Describe a mutually beneficial transaction that would be blocked by a maximum price of $4.

Government Intervention in Markets

In most modern economies, governments take an active role in the economy. Government action can be justified on efficiency grounds when one of the four efficiency conditions listed at the beginning of the chapter is not met.

▶ *External benefit.* When a person who doesn't pay for a product benefits from it, the government can intervene to ensure that all the people who benefit share in its cost. For example, the government could intervene to build a dam to provide flood protection for everyone in a valley and use taxes to pay for the dam. Later in the book, we explore government intervention in response to external benefits.

▶ *External cost.* When the cost of producing a product is incurred by people who don't sell the product, the government can intervene to "internalize the external cost," forcing sellers to bear the full cost of production. In a later chapter, we'll explore government intervention in response to the external costs associated with air and water pollution.

▶ *Imperfect information.* When one side of the market has better information than the other, the government can intervene to provide information. Later in the book, we look at the problems experienced in markets with imperfect information and explore government responses to these problems.

▶ *Imperfect competition.* When a market is dominated by few large firms, the government can intervene, directly controlling the prices monopolies can charge and promoting competition. Later in the book, we look at a wide range of policies to deal with imperfect competition.

These are cases of **market failure**, situations in which markets, if left on their own, will fail to generate socially efficient outcomes.

    In some markets, government intervention cannot be justified on efficiency grounds. For a market that meets the four efficiency conditions, the market equilibrium generates the largest possible total surplus, so government intervention can only decrease the surplus and cause inefficiency. A government motivated exclusively by efficiency would not intervene in such a market, but instead would permit the invisible hand to guide consumers and producers to the market equilibrium.

    So why would a government intervene in an efficient market? Sometimes the government's objective is not to promote efficiency—maximize the size of the pie—but instead to slice the pie in favor of one group or another. For example, a government that restricts shoe imports prevents some domestic workers from losing their shoe-making jobs. Of course, limiting imports will decrease the supply of shoes, and consumers will pay higher prices. As we'll see, when the government intervenes in a market to slice the pie in favor of one group, the pie shrinks, so there is a trade-off between efficiency (maximizing the size of the pie) and distributional concerns (slicing the pie).

    What is the role of economic analysis in exploring government intervention in efficient markets? We will focus our attention on the inefficiencies of government intervention, looking at how much the pie shrinks. We will briefly discuss some of the distributional consequences of intervention—how the slices change. The decision about whether intervention in an efficient market is worthwhile—whether the changes in the slices are worth losing part of the pie—is made in the political sphere. The economic analysis you learn in this book will help you understand the trade-offs associated with various public policies.

    There are circumstances under which groups of people who fare poorly in the market economy deserve special consideration. If a society decides that a particular group merits special treatment—for example, workers who lose their jobs because of imports—a more direct form of assistance is generally superior than intervention in efficient markets by the government. One alternative would be for the government to retrain workers for new jobs.

Market failure

A situation in which a market fails to be efficient because of external benefits, external costs, imperfect information, or imperfect competition.

Controlling the Price

We'll start with government policies that control product prices, setting either a maximum or a minimum price. In both cases, if the market meets the four efficiency conditions, government intervention reduces the total surplus of the market and causes inefficiency.

Setting Maximum Prices

We've already seen two different effects of a maximum price, sometimes known as a price ceiling. In Chapter 4, we saw that when the government sets a maximum price that is less than the equilibrium price, the result is permanent excess demand for the product. The decrease in price reduces the quantity supplied and increases the quantity demanded, so at the controlled price, consumers want to buy more than producers want to sell. In this chapter, we saw from Panel A in Figure 7.4 that a maximum price decreases the total surplus of the market: Some consumers gain at the expense of producers, and the total surplus decreases. Here are some examples of goods that have been subject to maximum prices or may be subject to maximum prices in the near future:

▶ Rental housing. During World War II, the federal government instituted a national system of rent controls. Although only New York City continued rent control after the war, during the 1970s, rent control spread to dozens of cities.
▶ Gasoline. In response to sharp increases in the price of gasoline in the 1970s, the national government set a maximum price on gasoline.
▶ Medical goods and services. Some proposals to control medical costs include price controls for prescription drugs.

In all three cases, a maximum price will cause excess demand and reduce the total surplus of the market.

Application: Rent Control

Figure 7.5 shows the effects of rent control on consumer and producer surplus. Panel A shows the market equilibrium, with a price (monthly rent) of $400 per apartment and a quantity of 1,000 apartments. The total surplus is the sum of the consumer surplus and producer surplus, shown as the area between the demand curve and the supply curve. Panel B shows the effect of a maximum price of $300 per apartment. The decrease in price causes movement downward along the supply curve to point s, and the quantity of apartments supplied decreases to 700. Because the policy decreases the number of apartments from 1,000 to 700, the total surplus of the market decreases. For the first 700 apartments, consumers gain at the expense of producers, paying $300 per apartment rather than $400. The 701st through the 1,000th apartments disappear from the market, so the surpluses associated with these apartments are lost entirely. The decrease in total surplus means that the market is inefficient.

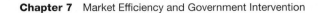

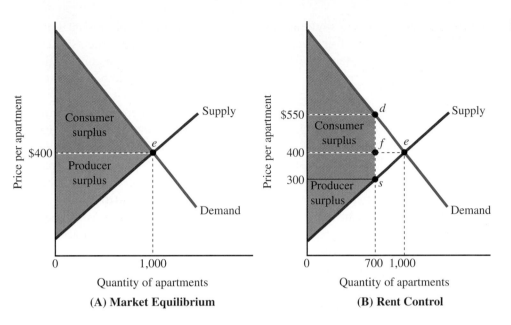

(A) **Market Equilibrium** (B) **Rent Control**

FIGURE 7.5

Rent Control Decreases Total Surplus
(A) In the market equilibrium, with a price of $400 and 1,000 apartments, the total surplus is the area between the demand curve and the supply curve.
(B) Rent control, with a maximum price of $300, reduces the quantity to 700 apartments and decreases the total surplus.

Because rent control decreases the total surplus of the market, the policy generates a **deadweight loss**. In Figure 7.5, the deadweight loss is shown by the triangle *des*, the decrease in the total surplus of the market. This is a deadweight loss in the sense that it is not offset by a gain to anyone else. The consumers and producers who are excluded from the market by rent control lose the surpluses they could have received in the market.

Let's return to the chapter opener about the mayor's curious strategy for deciding whether to approve a rent-control policy. Recall that the mayor announced that if the supporters of rent control contributed more money than the opponents, she would approve rent control. As a start, we know from Figure 7.5 that rent control decreases the total surplus of the rental market because the losses of the losers exceed the gains of the winners. Therefore, if everyone contributes 1% of his or her loss to the mayor, the contributions in opposition to rent control will be larger, and the mayor will not approve rent control.

Table 7.1 provides a detailed look at the winners and losers and their campaign contributions. For the 700 apartments that would remain in the market even after rent control, each consumer gets a $100 benefit, for a consumer benefit of $70,000 (700 consumers times $100). If each of these consumers contributes 1% of the potential

Deadweight loss

The decrease in the total surplus of the market.

TABLE 7.1 College Town's Campaign Contributions

	Benefit	Cost	Contribution
Consumers 1–700	$70,000 = $100 × 700		+$700 = 1% of $70,000
Producers 1–700		$70,000 = $100 × 700	–$700 = 1% of $70,000
Consumers 701–1,000		$22,500 = 1/2($150 × 300)	–$225 = 1% of $22,500
Producers 701–1,000		$15,000 = 1/2($100 × 300)	–$150 = 1% of $15,000
TOTAL	$70,000	$107,500	–$375

benefit, the consumer contributions in support of rent control will be $700. But these consumers would gain at the expense of the suppliers of the 700 apartments: Each supplier would lose $100, so their total losses would be $70,000, and their contributions in opposition to rent control will be $700. The two groups who would be excluded from the market under rent control—consumers and producers knocked out of the market when the transactions from apartments 701 through 1,000 disappear—will contribute in opposition. The loss of the excluded consumers is shown by triangle *def* in Panel B of Figure 7.5 and totals $22,500. These consumers will therefore contribute $225. The loss of the excluded producers is shown by triangle *fes* ($15,000); these producers will contribute $150. The contributions opposing rent control exceed the contributions favoring it by $375. Therefore, the mayor will not approve rent control.

Another way to see the inefficiency of rent control is to look at the consumers and producers who are excluded from the market. As shown by the points between *d* and *e* on the demand curve, 300 consumers are willing to pay between $400 and $550 for an apartment. As shown by the points between *s* and *e* on the supply curve, there are 300 producers who are willing to rent out an apartment for amounts between $300 and $400. Although the 300 excluded consumers are willing to pay more than these suppliers require to provide an apartment, the transactions are illegal under rent control. Because rent control outlaws transactions that would make both parties better off, it causes inefficiency.

There are three more subtle effects associated with rent control. First, at the artificially low maximum price, the number of people seeking apartments exceeds the number of apartments available. Consumers will spend more time searching for apartments, and an additional cost of rent control is the opportunity cost of the extra time spent searching for apartments. Second, because rent control outlaws mutually beneficial transactions, many people violate the spirit and the letter of the law by executing transactions of dubious legal merit. In some rent-control cities, consumers pay extra money to property owners to outbid other consumers. These extra payments are often disguised as "nonrefundable security deposits" or as "key money"—thousands of dollars to get the keys to an apartment. Third, given the lower payoff from providing apartments for rent, property owners will have less incentive to spend money on repair and maintenance, so the quality of apartments will decrease. In other words, lower rent is offset in part by lower housing quality.

Is rent control good for the poor? Rent control specifies a maximum rent for an apartment, regardless of who lives there. Rent-controlled apartments are occupied by the rich and the poor, so many wealthy people benefit from rent control. In other words, rent control is a very blunt instrument for helping the poor. As we explain later in the book, the government could use other policies to more effectively improve the economic circumstances of the poor.

Setting Minimum Prices

We've already seen two different effects of a minimum price. In Chapter 4, we saw that when the government sets a minimum price that exceeds the equilibrium price, the result is permanent excess supply. The increase in price encourages producers to produce more at the same time it encourages consumers to buy less. At the minimum price, producers want to sell more than consumers want to buy. In Chapter 4, we saw

A CLOSER LOOK — Milk Mountains

In the United States, the minimum price for powdered milk is $9.90 per hundredweight. To prevent the market price from falling below $9.90, the U.S. government purchases any resulting surpluses at this price. In recent years, the market demand for powdered milk has been relatively low, so the government has purchased millions of pounds of powdered milk each year. By 2003, the government's stockpile of powdered milk reached 1.28 billion pounds.[1] In fact, mountains of dried milk are stored in warehouses across the United States and even in caves near Kansas City. Why doesn't the government just give all of its powdered milk away? Why stockpile it? The problem is that giving it away would ultimately reduce the amount of powder that farmers could sell to consumers. The government would then be forced to buy more unsold powder from farmers.

that when the government sets a minimum price that is less than the equilibrium price, the result is permanent excess supply of the product. The increase in price increases the quantity supplied and decreases the quantity demanded, so at the controlled price, producers want to sell more than consumers want to buy. In this chapter, we saw from Panel A in Figure 7.4 that a minimum price decreases the total surplus of the market: Some producers gain at the expense of consumers, and the total surplus decreases.

Governments around the world establish minimum prices for agricultural goods. Under a price-support program, a government sets a minimum price for an agricultural product and then buys any resulting surpluses at that price. For an example of what can happen under agricultural price supports, read "A Closer Look: Milk Mountains."

Controlling the Quantity— Licensing and Import Restrictions

What happens when the government controls the quantity of a particular product instead of its price? We'll consider two policies that control quantities. In the domestic economy, many state and local governments limit the number of firms in particular markets by limiting the number of business licenses to operate in those markets. Many national governments restrict imports, using import bans or quotas on the quantity of a product—for example, shoes or cheese—that can be imported.

You may be surprised by the sheer number of state and local government business licensing programs. For example, many cities and states limit the number of taxicabs, dry cleaners, tobacco farms, liquor stores, bars, and even dog groomers. Some people defend licensing programs on the grounds that they protect consumers from low-quality products and poor service. But studies have shown that most licensing programs increase prices without improving the quality of products and service.[2] Another motive for cities to issue licenses is to limit the number of establishments that could be considered nuisances to some citizens, for example, bars, convenience stores, and gas stations.

Application: Taxi Medallions

We can use the licensing of taxis to explain how the practice affects the market for taxi service and other markets in which licenses are common. Panel A of Figure 7.6 shows the market equilibrium in the taxi market. The demand curve intersects the supply curve at point *e*. The industry provides 10,000 miles of taxi service per day at a price of $3.00 per mile. Each taxi is capable of producing a maximum of 100 miles of service per day, and there are 100 taxicabs in the market. The total surplus of the market equals the sum of consumer surplus and producer surplus, shown by the area between the demand curve and the supply curve.

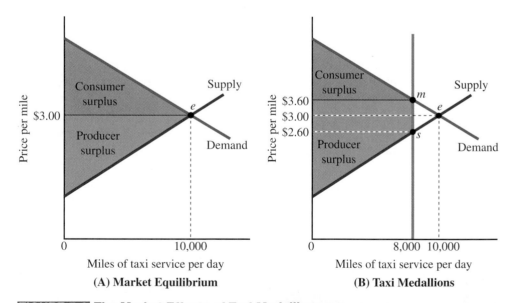

FIGURE 7.6 **The Market Effects of Taxi Medallions**

(A) The market equilibrium is shown by point *e*, with a price of $3.00 and a quantity of 10,000 miles of service per day. The total surplus is the area between the demand and supply curves.
(B) A medallion policy that fixes the number of taxis at 80 fixes the quantity of taxi service at 8,000 miles per day (100 miles per taxi) and increases the price to $3.60 (point *m*). The producers of the first 8,000 miles gain at the expense of consumers, but the surpluses that could have been gained between 8,000 and 10,000 miles are lost entirely, so the total surplus decreases.

Now suppose that the city passes a law requiring each taxicab to have a license—also known as a taxi "medallion"—and limits the number of medallions to 80. The city then gives taxi medallions to the first 80 people who show up at City Hall. In Panel B of Figure 7.6, the vertical line at 8,000 miles of service shows that this policy fixes the quantity of taxi service at 8,000 miles per day (80 taxis times 100 miles per taxi per day). The medallion policy creates an excess demand for taxi service: At the original price ($3.00), the quantity demanded is 10,000 miles, but the city's 80 taxicabs provide only 8,000 miles of service. As a result, the market moves upward along the demand curve to point m, where the price is $3.60 per mile of service. The medallion policy increases the price and decreases the quantity of taxi services.

Licensing and Market Efficiency

The medallion policy decreases the total surplus of the taxi market. In Figure 7.6, we see that the total surplus in Panel B is less than the total surplus in Panel A. The medallion policy decreases consumer surplus, a result of the higher price and the smaller quantity supplied. Producer surplus could increase or decrease, depending on the shapes of the market supply and market demand curves. In this example, the producer surplus of taxi drivers with medallions actually increases by a small amount. As in the cases of a maximum price or a minimum price, the medallion policy decreases the quantity of goods sold, decreasing the total surplus of the market. The producers of the first 8,000 miles of service gain at the expense of consumers, but the surpluses that could have been gained between 8,000 and 10,000 miles are lost entirely, so the total surplus of the market decreases. The deadweight loss is shown by the area of triangle *mes*.

Another way to see the inefficiency of taxi medallions is to look at just the consumers and producers who are excluded from the market and what they would lose. Some of the excluded consumers would gladly pay the cost of providing taxi service. As shown by the points between m and e on the demand curve, many consumers are willing to pay between $3.00 and $3.60 per mile for taxi service. Although there are plenty of drivers who would be willing to provide taxi service at these prices, they can't do so without a medallion. Because the medallion policy prevents these riders and drivers from executing mutually beneficial transactions, the policy causes inefficiency.

Our analysis of taxi medallions applies to any market subject to quantity controls. State and city governments use licensing to limit many types of small businesses. When an establishment such as a convenience store or dry cleaner would cause a nuisance to its neighbors, the inefficiency of the sort shown in Figure 7.6 may be at least partly offset by the benefit of controlling nuisances. Of course, the alternative policy is to control nuisance directly by restricting the location of the establishment rather than simply limiting the number of establishments. In general, a policy that limits entry into a market increases price, decreases quantity, and causes inefficiency in the market. In evaluating such a policy, we must compare the possible benefits from controlling nuisances to the losses of consumer and producer surplus.

Winners and Losers from Licensing

Who benefits and who loses from licensing programs like the city's medallion policy? The losers are consumers, who pay more for taxi rides. The winners are the people who receive a free medallion and the right to charge an artificially high price for taxi service. In some cities, people buy and sell taxi medallions. The market value of a medallion reflects the profits it can earn its owner. For example, the market price of a medallion is over $150,000 in New York City, $140,000 in Boston, and $100,000 in Toronto.[3] In cities such as Chicago, where medallions are more plentiful, the market price is much lower.

Why don't governments simply eliminate the taxi medallion system and allow free entry into the taxi market? Because doing so would drop the price of taxi service and reduce the market value of medallions to zero. Some city governments are reluctant to eliminate medallions because owners wield a lot of political power to keep the system (and the value of their medallions) in place.

Shortfall from Medallion Sale

Last month, a city decided to increase its number of taxi medallions from 500 to 600 and to auction off the new medallions to the highest bidders. Before the new medallions were issued, the market price of a medallion was $40,000, so the mayor figured that the medallion auction would generate about $4 million (100 medallions times $40,000 per medallion). The mayor was surprised when the auction raised only $3 million. What happened?

The key to solving this puzzle is that the market price of medallions is affected by the price of taxi service, which in turn is affected by the number of taxi medallions. An increase in the number of medallions—an increase in supply—will lead to lower prices for taxi rides. Restricting the number of taxis leads to higher prices, so loosening the restrictions will lead to lower prices. Lower prices means lower profits from operating taxis, so investors are willing to pay less for a taxi medallion. In this example, the market price drops from $40,000 to $30,000. ∎

Restricting Imports

We've seen that the government can control the quantity of a good produced by issuing a limited number of business licenses to producers. Another way to control quantity is to limit the imports of a particular good. Like a licensing policy, an import restriction increases the market price and decreases the total surplus of the market.

To show the market effects of import restrictions, let's start with an unrestricted market. Panel A of Figure 7.7 shows the market equilibrium in the sugar market when there is free trade. The domestic supply curve shows the quantity supplied by domestic (U.S.) firms at different prices. Looking at point *m*, we see that U.S. firms will not supply any sugar unless the price is at least $0.26 per pound. The total supply curve, which shows the quantity supplied by both domestic and foreign firms, lies to the right of the domestic curve. At each price, the total supply exceeds the domestic supply because foreign firms also supply sugar. Point *i* shows the free-trade equilibrium: The domestic demand curve (which shows the demand by U.S. consumers) intersects the total sup-

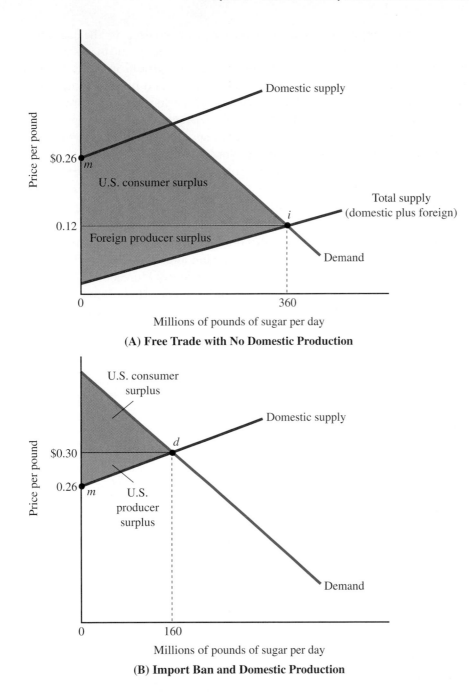

(A) Free Trade with No Domestic Production

(B) Import Ban and Domestic Production

FIGURE 7.7

The Effects of an Import Ban on U.S. Prices and Consumer and Producer Surplus
(A) With free trade, demand intersects the total supply curve at point *i*, with a price of $0.12 and a quantity of 360 million pounds. This price is below the minimum price of domestic suppliers ($0.26, as shown by point *m*), so domestic firms do not participate in the market. The total surplus is shown by the shaded areas (U.S. consumer and foreign producer surplus).
(B) If sugar imports are banned, the equilibrium is shown by the intersection of the demand curve and the domestic (U.S.) supply curve (point *d*). The price increases to $0.30. Although the ban generates a producer surplus for domestic producers, their gain is less than the loss of domestic consumers.

ply curve at a price of $0.12 per pound and a quantity of 360 million pounds per day. Because this price is below the minimum price for domestic firms, domestic firms do not supply any sugar to the U.S. markets.

What would happen if the United States banned sugar imports? Foreign suppliers would disappear from the market, so the total supply of sugar would consist of only the domestic supply. In Panel B of Figure 7.7, the new equilibrium would be shown by point *d*: The demand curve would intersect the domestic supply curve at a price of $0.30 per pound and a quantity of 160 million pounds. The decrease in supply resulting from the import ban would increase the price and decrease the quantity. As a result, domestic firms would produce all the sugar for the domestic market.

The import ban would ultimately decrease the total surplus in the sugar market. The shaded areas in the two graphs show the consumer and producer surpluses that would result with and without free trade. As you can see, the import ban would reduce U.S. consumer surplus, as shown by the two rust triangles in the two graphs. The ban would also eliminate the producer surplus of foreign suppliers (shown by the blue triangle in Panel A of Figure 7.7) and generate a producer surplus for domestic suppliers (shown by the blue triangle in Panel B of Figure 7.7). Therefore, the import ban would cause domestic producers to gain at the expense of domestic consumers. Since consumers would lose more than domestic producers would gain, the import ban would cause a net loss for people in the United States.

Import restrictions are often defended on the grounds that they increase employment in the "protected" industries, such as apparel and steel. But the protection of these jobs increases consumer prices, so there is a trade-off: More jobs in the protected industry, but higher prices for consumers. According to one study, import restrictions in 1993 protected 56,464 jobs in the U.S. textile and apparel industries at a cost to consumers of about $178,000 per job and protected 3,419 jobs in the motor vehicle industry at a cost of about $271,000 per job.[4] A recent study commissioned by the Swedish Ministry for Foreign Affairs concluded that import quotas imposed by the European Union increased the cost of clothing for the typical family in the European Union by about 270 euros (about $270) per year.[5] The quotas protected jobs in the domestic clothing industry, but the cost per job saved is about 41,000 euros per year.

We've just explored two types of policies that influence markets by controlling the quantity produced: license restrictions and import limits. Sometimes governments go beyond simply reducing the quantity produced and outlaw market transactions entirely. For an example, read "A Closer Look: A Market for Used Human Organs?"

A CLOSER LOOK

A Market For Used Human Organs?

Each year, thousands of Americans die waiting for replacement kidneys, hearts, livers, pancreases, and lungs. In the last decade, improvements in the effectiveness of organ transplants have increased the demand for used human organs. Because the supply hasn't increased along with demand, there are shortages of transplantable organs. In a normal market, the price would rise to eliminate the shortage, but because it is illegal to buy and sell human organs, there is no pricing mechanism to close the gap between the quantity supplied and the quantity demanded. The conventional approach to the organ shortage is to appeal to people's generosity, urging them to commit their organs to the transplant program. The failure of this approach led Nobel-winning economist Gary Becker to suggest monetary incentives for organ donors.[6] Under his proposal, the federal government would pay donors and their survivors for the organs they donate and would distribute the organs to hospitals for transplanting. This proposal raises all sorts of ethical questions and has not been embraced by many policymakers or health experts.

TEST Your Understanding

4. Why do tenants in cities with rent control voluntarily pay extra money for nonrefundable cleaning deposits and keys?
5. In Figure 7.6, consider a consumer who is represented by a point on the demand curve halfway between point *m* and point *e*. How much is the consumer willing to pay for a mile of taxi service? Consider a producer who is represented by a point on the supply curve halfway between point *s* and point *e*. What is the producer willing to accept for a mile of taxi service? Describe a mutually beneficial transaction between the consumer and the producer.
6. In Figure 7.7, how much sugar will domestic firms produce at a price of $0.15?
7. Complete the statement with "increases" or "decreases": An import ban _____ the price of sugar, _____ the quantity of sugar, and _____ the output of the domestic sugar industry.

Who Really Pays Taxes?

In this part of the chapter, we'll look at the market effects of taxes and answer two important questions. First, who really bears the burden of a tax? As we'll see, it is not necessarily the person who actually pays the tax to the government. Second, is the total burden of a tax equal to the revenue collected by the government? As we'll see, a tax changes people's behavior, so the total burden actually exceeds the revenue collected.

Figure 7.8 shows the revenue sources for local governments (including cities and counties), states, and the federal government. The major revenue source for local governments is the property tax, which is a fixed percentage of the value of residential, commercial, or industrial property. The sales tax is a fixed percentage of the purchase price of a consumer good. A person's state income tax liability is based on how much he or she earns, with tax rates that typically increase as income increases. The major revenue sources for the federal government are individual income taxes and "social insurance and retirement receipts," which are taxes collected to support Social Security, Medicare, and workers' compensation.

Tax Shifting: Forward and Backward

We can use supply and demand curves to look at the market effects of taxes. Suppose that your city imposes a tax of $100 per apartment and collects the tax from housing firms. You may think the burden of the tax falls exclusively on the housing firm, since that's who mails the check to the government. But some simple supply and demand analysis will show why this is incorrect. The housing firm will charge more for apartments and pay less for its inputs such as labor and land, so the tax will actually be paid by consumers and input suppliers.

FIGURE 7.8

Revenue Sources for Local, State, and Federal Governments

Source: *Statistical Abstract of the United States*, 2002.

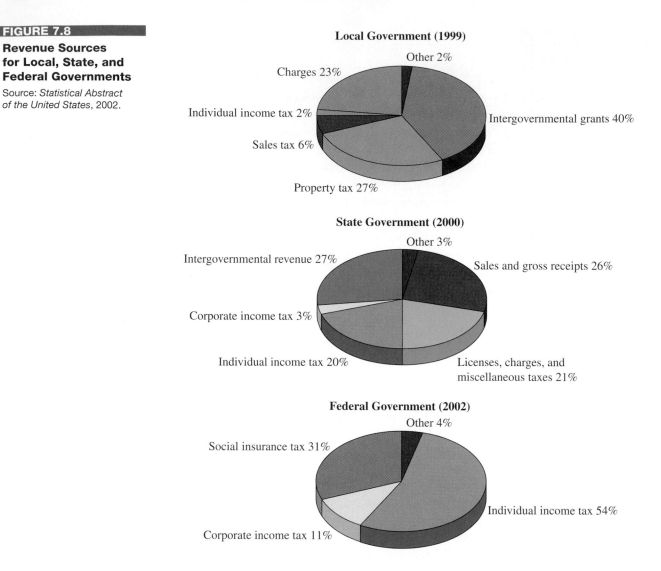

Local Government (1999)

Other 2%

Charges 23%

Individual income tax 2%

Sales tax 6%

Property tax 27%

Intergovernmental grants 40%

State Government (2000)

Other 3%

Intergovernmental revenue 27%

Corporate income tax 3%

Individual income tax 20%

Sales and gross receipts 26%

Licenses, charges, and miscellaneous taxes 21%

Federal Government (2002)

Other 4%

Social insurance tax 31%

Corporate income tax 11%

Individual income tax 54%

Figure 7.9 shows the market effects of a $100 tax on apartments As we saw earlier in the chapter, the market supply curve tells us how high the price must be to get producers to supply a particular quantity of output. The price must be high enough to cover all the costs of production. A unit tax increases the cost of production, so we need a higher price to get firms to produce any given quantity. In other words, the supply curve shifts upward by the amount of the tax. A unit tax of $100 per apartment increases a property owner's cost per apartment by $100, so the supply curve shifts up by $100.

The shift of the supply curve increases the equilibrium price of apartments. At the $300 price, there will be an excess demand for apartments, and the price will increase to eliminate the excess demand. In Figure 7.9 the market moves from point *i* to point *f*: The demand curve intersects the new supply curve at a price of $360, compared to $300 before the tax. In other words, housing firms shift part of the tax forward on to consumers, who pay $60 of the $100 tax. Although housing firms pay the entire $100

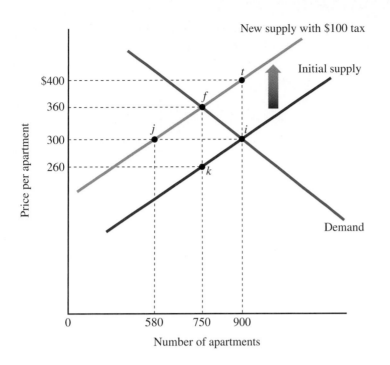

FIGURE 7.9

The Market Effects of an Apartment Tax
A tax of $100 per apartment shifts the supply curve up, moving the market equilibrium from point *i* to point *f*. The equilibrium price increases from $300 to $360, and the equilibrium quantity decreases from 900 to 750 apartments.

tax in a legal sense, they get some of the money to pay the tax by charging consumers $60 more for apartments.

The apartment tax also affects the people who supply inputs like land and labor to the housing industry. The tax decreases the output of the industry, so the industry needs smaller quantities of the inputs used to produce apartments. The resulting excess supply of inputs like labor and land will decrease land and labor prices, decreasing the cost of producing apartments. As a result, part of the $100 tax gets shifted backward on to input suppliers. Although housing firms pay the apartment tax in a legal sense, they get some of the money to pay the tax by paying less to workers and landowners.

Predicting the Amount Shifted Forward and Backward

The amount of the tax shifted forward to consumers depends on the price elasticity of demand for the taxed good. If the demand for a taxed good is inelastic—meaning that consumers are not very responsive to price changes—we need a large price hike to eliminate the excess demand caused by the tax. Therefore, consumers will be hit by a large increase in price, and so they will pay the bulk of the tax. This is shown in Panel A of Figure 7.10. Demand is inelastic—that is, the demand curve is steep—so a $5 tax increases the equilibrium price by $4 (from $10 to $14). In other words, consumers pay four-fifths of the tax. In Panel B of Figure 7.10, demand is elastic—that is, the demand curve is relatively flat—so consumers pay just a small part of the tax. A $5 tax increases the equilibrium price by only $1 (from $10 to $11). In this case, consumers pay only one-fifth of the tax.

FIGURE 7.10

Elasticities of Demand and Tax Effects
If demand is inelastic (Panel A), a tax will increase the market price by a large amount, so consumers will bear a large share of the tax. If demand is elastic (Panel B), the price will increase by a small amount and consumers will bear a small share of the tax.

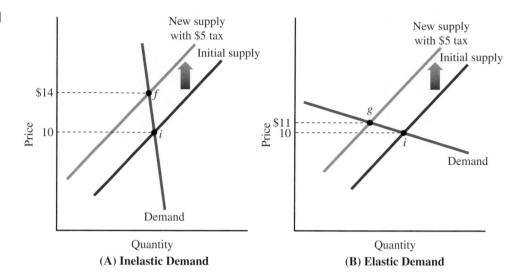

(A) Inelastic Demand   (B) Elastic Demand

Why should we care about tax shifting? We've seen that a tax increases consumer prices and decreases input prices, so to determine who actually pays a tax, we must look beyond the actual taxpayer. The subtleties of tax shifting are often missed by the people who design our tax policy and the media folks who report on it, as the following applications illustrate.

Applications: Cigarette and Luxury Taxes

We can use what we've learned about tax shifting to discuss some recent episodes in tax policy. In 1994, President Clinton proposed an immediate $0.75 per pack increase in the cigarette tax. The tax had two purposes: to generate revenue for Clinton's health care reform plan and to decrease medical costs by discouraging smoking. Based on our discussion of the market effects of a tax, we would predict that the tax would be shared by consumers, who would pay higher prices, and the owners of land where tobacco is grown. It appears tobacco farmers and landowners understand the economics of cigarette taxes. Led by a group of representatives and senators from tobacco-growing areas in North Carolina, Kentucky, and Virginia, the Congress scaled back Clinton's proposed tax hike from $0.75 to $0.05. Although the government would have collected the tax from cigarette manufacturers, savvy tobacco farmers realized the tax would decrease the price of their tobacco-growing land.

Another lesson on backward shifting occurred when Congress passed a steep luxury tax on boats and other expensive goods in 1990. Under the new luxury tax, a person buying a $300,000 boat had to pay an additional $20,000 in taxes. The burden of the tax was actually shared by consumers and input suppliers, including people who worked in boat factories and boatyards. Because the demand for luxury goods is elastic, the tax caused demand for the boats to fall sharply. The boat industry produced fewer boats, and the resulting decrease in the demand for boat workers led to layoffs and lower wages for those who managed to keep their jobs. Although the idea behind the luxury tax was to "soak the rich," the tax actually harmed low-income workers in the boat industry. It was repealed a few years later.

Tax Burden and Deadweight Loss

We've seen that people respond to a tax by changing their behavior. As a result, the total burden of a tax will exceed the total amount of money the government actually collects from the tax. To see why, suppose the government imposes a tax on No. 3 pencils, and the tax is large enough that everyone who initially used No. 3 pencils switches to other types of pencils or other writing implements. If no one purchases No. 3 pencils, the tax won't raise any revenue for the government, but the tax still generates a burden because some people who would prefer to use No. 3 pencils have switched to other writing implements.

We'll use the fish market to explore the total burden of a tax. To simplify matters, let's assume that the supply curve for fish is horizontal, as shown in Figure 7.11. As we'll see later in the book, a supply curve will be horizontal if the prices of the inputs used in the industry don't change as the total output of the industry changes. For the fish market, this means that wages and the cost of bait and fuel don't change as the total fish harvest changes. The demand curve intersects the initial supply curve at point *i*, so the price is $2 per pound and the quantity is 60,000 pounds of fish per day.

Suppose the government imposes a tax of $1 per pound of fish, and the tax is paid in legal terms by producers. As we saw earlier, a unit tax shifts the market supply upward by the amount of the tax. As shown in Figure 7.11, a $1 tax on fish producers shifts the supply curve up by $1: Each firm now needs $3, not $2, to cover all of its costs, including the tax.

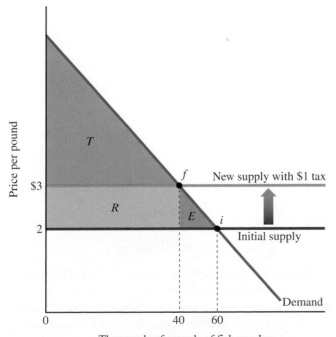

FIGURE 7.11

The Deadweight Loss or Excess Burden of a Tax

When the supply curve is horizontal, a tax increases the equilibrium price by the tax ($1 per pound in this example). Consumer surplus decreases by areas *R* and *E*. Total tax revenue collected is shown by rectangle *R*, so the total burden exceeds tax revenue by triangle *E*. Triangle *E* is sometimes known as the deadweight loss or excess burden of the tax

In Figure 7.11 the fish tax increases the equilibrium price of fish from $2 to $3. Why does the price increase by an amount equal to the tax? The supply curve is horizontal because input prices are fixed, regardless of how much output is produced. There is no opportunity to shift the tax backward onto input suppliers, so consumers bear the full cost of the tax.

We can use the concept of consumer surplus to determine just how much consumers lose as a result of the tax. Before the fish tax, the consumer surplus is shown by the area between the initial supply curve and the demand curve, or areas *T*, *R*, and *E*. When the price increases to $3, the consumer surplus shrinks to the area of triangle *T*, so the loss of consumer surplus (the total burden of the tax) is shown by rectangle *R* and triangle *E*. Let's take a closer look at these two areas.

▶ Rectangle *R* shows the extra money consumers must pay for the 40,000 pounds of fish they purchase. The tax increases the price by $1 per pound, so consumers pay an extra $40,000.
▶ Triangle *E* shows the loss of consumer surplus on the fish that are not consumed because of the tax. Consumers obey the law of demand, so when the price rises, they cut their purchases, buying 20,000 fewer pounds of fish. As a result, they give up the consumer surplus they would have received on these 20,000 pounds of fish.

How does the total burden of the tax compare to the tax revenue raised by the government? The total tax revenue is the tax per pound ($1) times the quantity consumed (40,000 pounds), or $40,000. This is shown by rectangle *R*: Part of the loss experienced by consumers is the revenue gain for government. But in addition to losing rectangle *R*, consumers also lose triangle *E*, so the consumer's total burden of the tax exceeds the tax revenue. Triangle *E* is sometimes known as the **deadweight loss** from taxation or the **excess burden** of a tax.

In the example shown in Figure 7.11, we used a horizontal supply curve to simplify matters and make the analysis of deadweight loss transparent. In a market with a positively sloped supply curve, a tax generates a deadweight loss, but the analysis is a bit more complex. For students interested in a challenge, one of the problems at the end of the chapter deals with deadweight loss for the apartment market, a market with a positively sloped supply curve.

The essential reason for excess burden is that taxes cause people to change their behavior, making choices to avoid taxes. For another example of changes in behavior in response to taxes, read "A Closer Look: Taxes and December Babies."

Deadweight loss from taxation

The difference between the total burden of a tax and the amount of revenue collected by the government.

Excess burden of a tax

Another name for deadweight loss.

TEST Your Understanding

8. Suppose a city proposes tax on hotel stays, equal to $20 per person per night. What sort of people would you expect to oppose the tax?
9. The demand for coffee is relatively inelastic. Therefore, we would expect _____ to pay a relatively large share of a tax on coffee.
10. Explain why a tax that generates zero tax revenue can be costly to society.

A CLOSER LOOK

Taxes and December Babies

The current tax law includes a tax credit for children: A child born on or before December 31 reduces the household's tax liability in that year and every subsequent year until the child reaches 18. A recent study shows that the higher the tax credit, the larger the percentage of children born in the last week of the year and the smaller the percentage of children born in the first week of the year.[7] It appears that couples time the births of their children to take advantage of the tax credit. The authors estimate that increasing the tax benefit of having a child by $500 raises the probability of having the child in the last week of December by about 27%.

Economic Experiment

Government Intervention

Recall the market equilibrium experiment from Chapter 4. We can modify that experiment to show the various forms of government intervention in the market. After several trading periods without any government intervention, you can change the rules as follows:

- The instructor sets a maximum price for apples.
- The instructor sets a minimum price for apples.
- The instructor issues licenses to a few lucky producers.
- The instructor divides producers into domestic producers and foreign producers, and some of the foreign producers are excluded from the market. ●

USING THE TOOLS

In this chapter, we used two of the tools of economics—the supply curve and the demand curve—to study the effect of government intervention in markets without externalities. Here are some opportunities to use these tools to do your own economic analysis.

1. Price Controls for Medical Care

Consider a town where the equilibrium price of a doctor's visit is $60 and the equilibrium quantity supplied is 90 patient visits per hour. For suppliers (doctors), each $1 increase in price increases the quantity supplied by two visits. For consumers, each $1 increase in price decreases the quantity demanded by one visit. Suppose that in an attempt to control the rising costs of medical care, the government imposes price controls, setting a maximum price of $50 per visit.

a. Use a completely labeled graph to show the effects of the maximum price on (i) the quantity of visits to doctors and (ii) the total surplus of the market.
b. What sort of inefficiencies does the price control cause?
c. Would you expect patients and doctors to find ways around the maximum price?

2. Barber Licensing

Consider the market for haircuts in a city. In the market equilibrium, the price per haircut is $6 and the quantity is 240 haircuts per day. For consumers, each $1 increase in price decreases the quantity demanded by 20 haircuts. For producers, each $1 increase in price increases the quantity supplied by 60 haircuts. In the market equilibrium, there are 24 barbers, each of whom produces 10 haircuts per day. Suppose the city passes a law requiring all barbers to have a license and then issues only 18 barber licenses. Each licensed barber continues to provide 10 haircuts per day. Use a completely labeled graph to show the effects of licensing on (i) the price of haircuts and (ii) the total surplus in the haircut market.

3. Bidding for a Boston Taxi Medallion

In 1997, there were 1,500 taxi medallions in the city of Boston, and each medallion generated a profit of about $14,000 per year. In 1998, the city announced that it would issue 300 new taxi medallions, auctioning the new medallions to the highest bidders.[7] Even with the new medallions, the number of taxis in the city would still be less than the number that would occur in an unregulated market. Your job is to predict the annual profit from a

medallion after the new medallions were issued. To predict the new annual profit, assume the following:
● The cost of providing taxi service is constant at $2.00 per mile of service.
● The initial price of taxi service (with 1,500 medallions issued) is $2.14 per mile.
● Each taxi (or medallion) provides 100,000 miles of service per year, so issuing the 300 new medallions increases the total quantity of taxi service from 150 million miles to 180 million miles.
● For consumers, each $0.01 decrease in the price of taxi service increases the quantity demanded by 10 million miles.

a. Compute the new price of taxi service.
b. Compute the new profit per medallion.

4. Shifting a Housecleaning Tax

Consider a city where poor people clean the houses of rich people. Initially, housecleaning firms charge their customers $10 per hour, keep $1 per hour for administrative costs, and pay their workers $9 per hour. Like many luxury goods, the demand for housecleaning service is very elastic. Housecleaning workers are not very responsive to changes in the wage.

a. Use supply and demand curves to show the initial equilibrium in the market for cleaning services (price = $10 per hour; quantity = 1,000 hours of cleaning per week), and label the equilibrium point with an *i*.
b. Suppose the city imposes a tax of $3 per hour of cleaning services, and one-third of the tax is shifted forward to consumers. Use your graph to show the effects of the tax on the housecleaning market. Label the new equilibrium point with an *f*. What is the new price?
c. Is it reasonable that only one-third of the tax is shifted forward? Explain.
d. Suppose that firms continue to keep $1 per hour for administrative costs. Predict the new wage.
e. Who bears the bulk of the housecleaning tax, wealthy households or poor ones?

SUMMARY

In this chapter, we discussed the efficiency of markets and the consequences of government intervention in perfectly competitive markets. Government intervention in a market without externalities prevents consumers and producers from executing beneficial transactions, meaning that intervention reduces the total surplus of the market and causes inefficiency. We also saw that taxes affect the prices of consumer goods and inputs and that we must look beyond the taxpayer to determine who actually bears the cost of a tax. Here are the main points of the chapter:

1 The total surplus of a market equals the sum of consumer surplus and producer surplus.

2 In a market that meets the four efficiency conditions (no external cost, no external benefits, perfect information, perfect competition), the market equilibrium maximizes the total surplus and is therefore efficient.

3 Price controls reduce the total surplus of a market because they prevent mutually beneficial transactions.

4 Quantity controls (like licensing and import restrictions) decrease consumer surplus and the total surplus of the market.

5 A tax on a good will be shifted forward onto consumers and backward onto input suppliers.

6 Because a tax causes people to change their behavior, the total burden of the tax exceeds the revenue generated by the tax.

KEY TERMS

consumer surplus, 140
deadweight loss, 149
deadweight loss from taxation, 162

excess burden of a tax, 162
market failure, 147
producer surplus, 141

total surplus, 142
willingness to accept, 141
willingness to pay, 140

PROBLEMS AND DISCUSSION QUESTIONS

1 List the four assumptions that ensure a market equilibrium is efficient. For each assumption, provide an example of a good for which the assumption is likely to be violated.

2 According to Ida, "I'm willing to buy a CD player for $50, but I can't find anyone willing to sell me one for that price." Does that mean that the market for CD players is inefficient?

3 Figure 7.A shows a supply curve and a demand curve and several areas between the curves. Identify the areas on the figure that represent the following:
   a. Consumer surplus in the market equilibrium
   b. Producer surplus in the market equilibrium
   c. Total surplus in the market equilibrium
   d. Consumer surplus under a maximum price of $10

   e. Producer surplus under a maximum price of $10
   f. Total surplus under a maximum price of $10
   g. Consumer surplus under a maximum quantity of 70
   h. Producer surplus under a maximum quantity of 70
   i. Total surplus under a maximum quantity of 70

4 In your city, the market equilibrium price of apartments is $500 per month, and the equilibrium quantity is 1,000 apartments. Under a new rent-control program, the maximum price for apartments will be $400 per month. For producers, each $1 increase in price increases the quantity supplied by two apartments.
   a. Use a supply–demand diagram to show the effects of the rent-control program on the rental

FIGURE 7.A
**Identifying the
Surpluses**

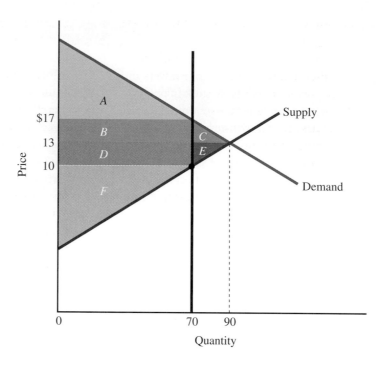

housing market. Label the initial equilibrium point with *i* and the point that shows the quantity supplied under rent control with *r*.

b. How many apartments are lost to rent control?

5 Why are rent controls in cities more common than maximum prices on food or clothing?

6 In the gasoline market, the equilibrium price is $2 and the equilibrium quantity is 100 million gallons per day. Suppose the government sets a maximum price of $1.90. For producers, each $0.01 increase in price increases the quantity supplied by three million gallons.

a. Use a supply–demand diagram to show the effects of the maximum price on the gasoline market. Label the initial equilibrium point with *i* and the point that shows the quantity supplied under the maximum price with *m*.

b. How does the maximum price affect the quantity of gasoline sold?

7 In the example in the text of taxi medallions (see Figure 7.6), suppose the city announces that it will issue 110 medallions instead of 80. Predict the market price of taxi service and the market price of medallions.

8 Using Figure 7.6 as a starting point, suppose the demand for taxi service decreases and the new

demand curve intersects the supply curve at a quantity of 7,000 miles per day. If the government doesn't change the number of medallions, what happens to the price of a medallion?

9 Predict the effect of each of the following policies on the price of the relevant good. Then draw a supply–demand diagram to defend your answer.

a. Licenses for dry cleaners

b. Limits on building permits for housing

c. Import restrictions on clothing

10 Suppose that initially there are no restrictions on importing kiwi fruit. The supply curves are the same as the supply curves for sugar shown in Figure 7.7. The initial price of kiwi fruit is 12 cents per piece. When imports are banned, the equilibrium price increases to 22 cents. Draw a market demand curve consistent with these numbers.

11 Under a special luxury tax passed by Congress, buyers of expensive cars pay a 10% tax on the portion of the purchase price above $30,000.

a. Will the luxury car tax be paid exclusively by the wealthy consumers who buy expensive cars?

b. What information do you need to determine the share of the taxes paid by wealthy consumers?

12 In the words of Will Rogers, "The trouble with land is that they're not making it any more." In other words, the supply of land is fixed and the supply curve is a vertical line.

   a. If the government imposes a tax on land, which side of the market—land consumers or landowners—will pay a larger part of the tax?

   b. Will the land tax generate a deadweight loss?

13 Consider the market effect of a tax on hotel rooms. The initial equilibrium price is $50 per night, and the initial equilibrium quantity is 100 rooms rented out per day. Draw a supply and demand graph so that a $10 tax per room increases the equilibrium price from $50 to $56 and decreases the equilibrium quantity from 100 rooms to 80 rooms. How is the tax divided between consumers and input suppliers?

14 Consider the analysis of the $100 apartment tax shown in Figure 7.9.

   a. Use the graph to show the following after the tax: Consumer surplus (the triangle between the demand curve and the new price), producer surplus (the triangle between the initial supply curve and the price received by an apartment firm after paying the $100 tax), and total tax revenue (the rectangle with height of $100 and width of the new equilibrium number of apartments).

   b. The new total value of the market is the sum of the consumer surplus, producer surplus, and tax revenue. How does it compare to the total value (consumer surplus plus producer surplus) before the tax?

   c. Use your graph to show the deadweight loss from taxation (a triangle).

15 After 20 years of dog haircuts, perms, and pedicures, Doug wants to sell his pet-grooming salon. Several months earlier, a similar pet salon sold for $50,000. But Doug hasn't found anyone willing to buy his salon for more than $20,000. He suspects that the city has quietly increased the number of pet-grooming licenses, and that's why the price of grooming services has dropped, pulling down the market price of pet salons like his. According to Doug's local pet-grooming association, the quantity of grooming services in the area (the number of pet haircuts, perms, pedicures, and so forth) has not changed in recent years. So why has the market price of a pet salon decreased so much? Has the city issued more licenses, or is there another explanation?

16 In the Economic Puzzle, when the city increased the number of medallions from 400 to 500, the market price of the medallions dropped from $40,000 to $30,000. Assume that the supply curve for taxi service is horizontal. What's the implied price elasticity of demand for taxi service?

MODEL ANSWERS TO QUESTIONS

Chapter-Opening Questions

1 The rent-control policy decreases the quantity of apartments supplied, forcing some students out of the market.

2 The city limits the number of taxi licenses or medallions, leading to higher taxi prices and large profits for people who own the medallions.

3 It is illegal to buy or sell human organs, so there is no pricing mechanism to close the gap between quantity demanded and quantity supplied.

4 Consumers pay higher prices, and the cost per job saved is about $178,000.

5 The housing firm will collect more money from consumers (the price of apartments will be higher) and pay less money to input suppliers (the prices of inputs will be lower), so consumers and input suppliers will indirectly pay the tax.

Test Your Understanding

1 The willingness to pay, price, price, marginal cost.

2 The price would be $1,700, giving you and Pablo each a surplus of $300.

3 Forest is willing to pay $13, and Dee's marginal cost is $8. If they split the difference, the price would be $10.50, and each would get a surplus of $2.50.

4 Many consumers are willing to pay more than the controlled price for an apartment, and deposits and key money allow them to do so and get an apartment they could otherwise not get.

5 The consumer is willing to pay $3.30, and the producer's willingness to accept is $2.80. If they split the difference, agreeing on a price of $3.05, each will get a surplus of $0.25.

6 Zero. This is below the minimum domestic price.

7 Increases, decreases, increases.

8 The tax will be shifted forward to consumers and backward to input suppliers such as landowners (less land will be needed for hotels), construction workers (fewer will be needed to build new hotels), and housekeeping workers (fewer will be needed to clean rooms).

9 The inelastic side of the market (coffee consumers) will pay a larger share of the tax.

10 If a tax changes people's behavior, it generates a deadweight loss or excess burden.

NOTES

1. Tom Webb, "As Powdered Milk Piles Up, U.S. Taxpayers pay $1 Billion," *Oregonian*, August 24, 2003, p. 1.

2. J. K. Smith, "An Analysis of State Regulations Governing Liquor Store Licensees," *Journal of Law and Economics,* October 1982, pp. 301–319; David Kirp and Eileen Soffer, "Taking Californians to the Cleaners," *Regulation,* September/October 1985, pp. 24–26

3. D. W. Taylor, "The Economic Effects of Direct Regulation of Taxicabs in Metropolitan Toronto," *Logistics and Transportation Review,* June 1989, pp. 169–182; Laura Brown, "Hub Cabbie Hopefuls Cry: The Russians Are Coming!" *Boston Herald,* December 16, 1998, p. 1.

4. *The Economic Effects of Significant U.S. Import Restraints* (Washington, DC: U.S. International Trade Commission, initial report in 1993; update in 1996).

5. Joseph F. François, Hans-Hinrich Glismann, Dean Spinanger, "The Cost of EU Trade Protection in Textiles and Clothing", March 2000, p. 49.

6. Gary S. Becker, "How Uncle Sam Could Ease the Organ Shortage," *Business Week,* January 20, 1997, p. 18.

7. Stacy Dickert-Conlin and Amitabh Chandra, "Taxes and the Timing of Births," *Journal of Political Economy*, vol. 107, February 1999, pp. 161–77.

Part

3

Information and Externalities

Chapter 8

Imperfect Information: Adverse Selection
and Moral Hazard

Chapter 9

Environmental Policy

Chapter 10

Public Goods and Public Choice

The Lemons Problem

Uninformed Buyers and Knowledgeable
    Sellers
Equilibrium with All Low-Quality Goods
A Thin Market: Equilibrium with Some
    High-Quality Goods

Responding to the Lemons Problem

Buyers Invest in Information
Sellers Provide Guarantees
Lemons Laws

Evidence of The Lemons Effect

The Price of a Week-Old Car
Used Pickup Trucks
California Kiwifruit
Used Baseball Pitchers

**Uninformed Sellers and
Knowledgeable Buyers: Insurance**

Health Insurance
Equilibrium with All High-Cost Consumers
Responding to Adverse Selection
    in Insurance: Group Insurance
The Uninsured
Other Types of Insurance

Moral Hazard

Using the Tools

Imperfect Information: Adverse Selection and Moral Hazard

"So, why are you selling this used car?"

he buyers of used cars ask this question frequently and then listen carefully to the answer.
Assuming the car seller is honest, the answer the buyer hopes for is, "Because I need a different car
for my new job," or "I buy a new car every three years." The buyer is trying to avoid sellers who are
trying to get rid of a "lemon"—a car that breaks down frequently and generates large repair bills.
People don't ask this sort of question in other markets. For example, no one ever asks, "So, why are
you selling this pizza?"

"Does my insurance policy cover accidental death from bungee jumping?"

Life is risky, and people buy insurance to diminish the monetary consequences of unfortunate
events such as theft, sickness, injury, and death. This question from the potential bungee jumper
reveals an important fact about insurance: It causes people to take greater risks, knowing that part
of the cost of an undesirable outcome will be covered by insurance.

This chapter explores the role of information in markets, looking at what happens when one side of the market has better information than the other. In the market for used cars, sellers know more about the quality of the product than buyers. In the market for life insurance, buyers know more about the risk they face than sellers do. As we saw earlier in the book, the model of supply and demand is based on several assumptions, one of which is that buyers and sellers have enough information to make informed choices. In a world of fully informed buyers and sellers, markets operate smoothly, generating an equilibrium price and an equilibrium quantity for each good. In a world with imperfect information, some goods will be sold in very small numbers, or not sold at all. In addition, buyers and sellers will use resources to acquire information to help make better decisions.

This chapter explores the effect of imperfect information on several types of markets. Here are some of the practical questions that we answer:

1 If you buy a new car for $20,000 today and then try to sell it a week later, you probably won't get more than $16,000 for it. Why does a new car lose so much of its value in the first week?

2 Why do professional baseball pitchers who switch teams spend so much time on the disabled list, nursing their injuries instead of playing?

3 Why did kiwi fruit growers in California support government regulations that established a minimum maturity level for harvested fruit?

4 What is the rationale for group health insurance, as opposed to health insurance purchased by individuals?

The Lemons Problem

Asymmetric information

A situation in which one side of the market—either buyers or sellers—has better information about the product than the other.

Mixed market

A market in which products of different qualities are sold for the same price.

The classic example of a market with imperfect information is the market for used cars.[1] Suppose prospective buyers cannot distinguish between "lemons" (cars with relatively high repair costs) and "plums" (high-quality cars). Although a buyer can get some information about a particular car by looking at the car and taking it for a test drive, the information gleaned from this kind of inspection is not enough to determine the quality of the car. By contrast, the seller (the current owner of a used car) knows from experience the quality of the car. We say that there is **asymmetric information** in a market if one side of the market—either buyers or sellers—has better information than the other side. Because buyers cannot distinguish between lemons and plums, there will be a single market for used automobiles: Both types of cars will be sold together in a **mixed market** for the same price.

Uninformed Buyers and Knowledgeable Sellers

How much is a consumer willing to pay for a used car that could be either a lemon or a plum? To determine a consumer's willingness to pay in a mixed market with both lemons and plums, we must answer three questions:

1 How much is the consumer willing to pay for a plum?
2 How much is the consumer willing to pay for a lemon?
3 What is the chance that a used car purchased in the mixed market will be of low quality?

Suppose the typical buyer is willing to pay $4,000 for a plum and $2,000 for a lemon. The buyer is willing to pay less for a lemon because it is less reliable and has higher repair costs. For someone who is willing to put up with the hassle and repair expense, a lemon is a reasonable car. That's why the typical buyer is willing to pay $2,000, not zero, for a low-quality car that we tag with the label "lemon." Someone who pays $2,000 and gets a lemon is just as happy as someone who pays $4,000 and gets a plum.

Consumer expectations play a key role in determining the market outcome when there is imperfect information. Suppose that half the used cars *on the road* are lemons, and consumers know this. A reasonable expectation for consumers is that half the cars *on the used-car market* will be lemons too. In other words, buyers initially expect a 50–50 split between the two types of cars. A reasonable assumption is that a buyer in the mixed market is willing to pay the average value of the two types of cars, or $3,000. In other words, a buyer is willing to pay $3,000 for a 50–50 chance of getting either a plum or a lemon.

The current owner of a used car knows from everyday experience whether the car is a lemon or a plum. For each owner, the question is, given the single market price for all used cars, lemons and plums alike, should I sell my car? The answers to this question are shown by the two supply curves in Figure 8.1, one for lemons and one for plums.

▶ Plum supply. As shown by the upper curve, the minimum supply price for plums is $2,500: At any price less than $2,500, no plums will be supplied. Consistent with the law of supply, the higher the price of used cars, the larger the number of plums supplied. For example, 20 plums will be supplied at a price of $3,000 (point *n*).

▶ Lemon supply. As shown by the lower curve, the minimum supply price for lemons is $500: At any price less than $500, no lemons will be supplied. Lemons have a lower minimum price because they are worth less to their current owners. The number of lemons supplied increases with price. For example, 80 cars will be supplied at a price of $3,000 (point *m*).

Equilibrium with All Low-Quality Goods

Table 8.1 shows two scenarios for our hypothetical used-car market, with numbers consistent with the supply curves shown in Figure 8.1. In the first column we assume that buyers have 50–50 expectations about the quality of used cars. As we saw earlier, if buyers expect a 50–50 split between lemons and plums, the typical buyer will be willing to

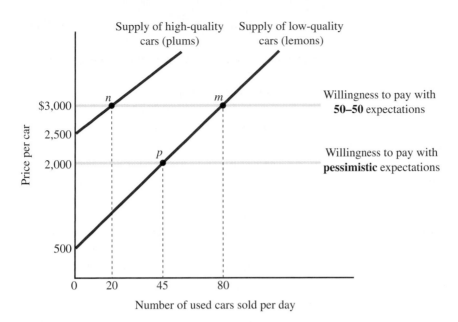

FIGURE 8.1 **All Used Cars on the Market Are Lemons**

If buyers assume that there is a 50–50 chance of getting a lemon or a plum, they are willing to pay $3,000 for a used car. At this price, the supply of plums is 20 (point *n*) and the supply of lemons is 80 (point *m*). This is not an equilibrium because consumers' expectation of a 50–50 split are not realized. If consumers are pessimistic and assume that all cars on the market are lemons, they are willing to pay $2,000 for a used car. At this price, only lemons will be supplied (45 lemons, as shown by point *p*), so pessimism is an equilibrium.

TABLE 8.1

**Equilibrium with All
Low-Quality Goods**

	Buyers Initially Have 50–50 Expectations	Equilibrium: Pessimistic Expectations
Demand Side of Market		
Amount buyer is willing to pay for lemon	$2,000	$2,000
Amount buyer is willing to pay for a plum	$4,000	$4,000
Assumed chance of getting a lemon	50%	100%
Assumed chance of getting a plum	50%	0%
Amount buyer is willing to pay for a used car in mixed market	$3,000	$2,000
Supply Side of Market		
Number of lemons supplied	80	45
Number of plums supplied	20	0
Total number of used cars supplied	100	45
Actual chance of getting a lemon	80%	100%

pay $3,000 for a used car. From the supply curves in Figure 8.1, we know that at this price, 20 plums and 80 lemons will be supplied, so 80% of the used cars (80 of 100) will be lemons. In this case, consumers are too optimistic and underestimate the chance of getting a lemon.

The experiences of these 100 consumers show that the actual chance of getting a lemon is 80%, not 50% as initially assumed. Once future buyers realize this, they will of course become more pessimistic about the used-car market. Suppose they assume that all the used cars on the market will be lemons. Under this assumption, the typical buyer will be willing to pay only $2,000 (the value of a lemon) for a used car. As shown in Figure 8.1, this price is less than the $2,500 minimum price for supplying plums, so plums will disappear from the used-car market. At a price of $2,000, the quantity of plums supplied is zero, but the quantity of lemons supplied is 45 (point *p*). In other words, all the used cars will be lemons, so consumers' pessimism is justified. Because consumers' expectations are consistent with their actual experiences in the market, the equilibrium price of used cars is $2,000. The equilibrium in the used-car market is shown in the second column of Table 8.1.

In this equilibrium, no plums are bought or sold, so every buyer will get a lemon. People get exactly what they pay for: They are willing to pay $2,000 for a lemon (a serviceable but low-quality car), and that's what each consumer gets. The domination of the used-car market by lemons is an example of the **adverse-selection problem**. The uninformed side of the market (buyers in this case) must choose from an undesirable or adverse selection of goods (used cars). The asymmetric information in the market generates a downward spiral of price and quantity in the market:

Adverse-selection problem
A situation in which the uninformed side of the market must choose from an undesirable or adverse selection of goods.

▶ The presence of low-quality goods on the market pulls down the price consumers are willing to pay.
▶ A decrease in price decreases the quantity of high-quality goods supplied.
▶ The decrease in the quantity of high-quality goods pulls down consumers' willingness to pay again.

In the extreme case, this downward spiral continues until all the cars on the market are lemons.

A Thin Market: Equilibrium with Some High-Quality Goods

Thin market
A market in which some high-quality goods are sold but fewer than would be sold in a market with perfect information.

The disappearance of plums from our hypothetical used-car market is an extreme case. The plums disappeared from the market because informed plum owners decided to keep their cars rather than selling them at a relatively low price in the used-car market. This outcome would change if the minimum supply price of lemons were lower, specifically if it is below $2,000. In this case, most but not all the used cars on the market will be lemons, and some lucky buyers will get plums. In this case, we say that asymmetric information generates a **thin market**: Some high-quality goods are sold, but fewer than would be sold with perfect information.

Figure 8.2 shows the situation that leads to a thin market. The minimum supply price for plums is $1,833, and the quantity of plums supplied increases with the price of used cars. Suppose that consumers are initially pessimistic, assuming that all cars for sale will be lemons. This means that consumers are willing to pay only $2,000 for a used car. Because the minimum supply price ($1,833) is now less than the willingness to pay for a lemon, some plums will be supplied at a price of $2,000. In Figure 8.2, five plums and 45 lemons are supplied at this price, so one out of every 10 buyers will get a plum. In this case, pessimism is not an equilibrium because some buyers will get plums when they expect lemons. This is also shown in the first column of Table 8.2.

In equilibrium, consumer expectations about the chances of getting the two types of cars are realized. Suppose that consumers expect one of every four cars to be a plum. Let's assume that each consumer is willing to pay $2,500 for a used car under these circumstances. Consumers are willing to pay a bit more than the value of a lemon because there is a small chance of getting a plum. In Figure 8.2, at this price, there are 20 plums supplied (point e) and 60 lemons supplied (point f), so in fact one in four consumers actually gets a plum. This is an equilibrium because 25% of the cars sold are plums and 75% are lemons, consistent with consumers' expectations. This is also shown in the second column of Table 8.2.

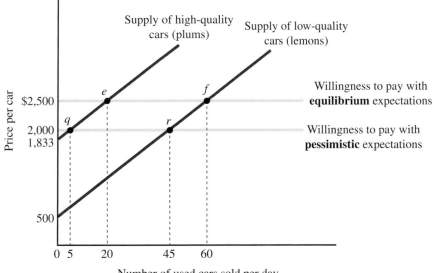

FIGURE 8.2 The Market for High-Quality Cars (Plums) Is Thin

If buyers are pessimistic (assume that only lemons will be sold), they are willing to pay $2,000 for a used car. At this price, the supply of plums is five (point q) and the supply of lemons is 45 (point r). This is not an equilibrium because one of 10 consumers gets a plum, contrary to the pessimistic expectations. If consumers assume that there is a 75% chance of getting a lemon, they are willing to pay $2,500 for a used car. At this price, the supply of plums is 20 (point e) and the supply of lemons is 60 (point f), so the actual chance of getting a lemon is 75% (60 of 80 cars). Consumer expectations are realized, so this is an equilibrium.

TABLE 8.2

A Thin Market for High-Quality Goods

	Buyers Initially Have Pessimistic Expectations	Equilibrium: 75–25 Expectations
Demand Side of Market		
Amount buyer is willing to pay for a lemon	$2,000	$2,000
Amount buyer is willing to pay for a plum	$4,000	$4,000
Assumed chance of getting a lemon	100%	75%
Assumed chance of getting a plum	0%	25%
Amount buyer is willing to pay for a used car in mixed market	$2,000	$2,500
Supply Side of Market		
Number of lemons supplied	45	60
Number of plums supplied	5	20
Total number of used cars supplied	50	80
Actual chance of getting a lemon	90%	75%

TEST Your Understanding

1. Complete the statement with "buyers" or "sellers": There is asymmetric information in the used-car market because _____ cannot distinguish between lemons and plums but _____ can.
2. Suppose the typical consumer is willing to pay $4,000 for a plum and $1,000 for a lemon. If there is a 50% chance of getting a lemon, how much is the consumer willing to pay for a used car?
3. Why do goods of different qualities (such as used cars) sell for the same price, but goods of different sizes (such as apples) sell for different prices?
4. Complete the statement: The fact that a buyer must pick a used car from an undesirable selection of cars is called the _____ problem.
5. When buyers assume that there is a 70% chance of getting a lemon, seven lemons and three plums are supplied. Is this an equilibrium? Explain.

Responding to the Lemons Problem

In a market with asymmetric information, there are strong incentives for buyers and sellers to do something to solve the lemons problem. In our example of a thin market, the price of a used car is $2,500, but consumers are willing to pay $4,000 for a plum. If the owner of a plum could persuade a buyer that the car was a true plum, they could split the difference, agreeing on a price of $3,250, making both the buyer and seller better off by $750. The buyer gets a car worth $4,000 to him for only $3,250. The seller gets $3,250 for a car that would otherwise sell in the mixed market for $2,500. Given the potential payoff from distinguishing between lemons and plums, both sides of the market take action.

Buyers Invest in Information

Recall that in our model of the thin market, one of four buyers gets a plum that is worth $4,000, paying only $2,500 for it. The more information a buyer has, the greater the chance of picking a plum from the available cars. A successful pick generates a payoff of $1,500 (the $4,000 willingness to pay minus the $2,500 price). A buyer can get general information about the reliability of different models from magazines and the Internet. *Consumer Reports* publishes information on repair histories of different models and even computes a "Trouble" index, scoring each model on a scale of 1 to 5. By consulting these information sources, a buyer can better distinguish between lemons and plums. In addition, a buyer can pay a mechanic to inspect a particular car before purchasing it.

The problems associated with asymmetric information occur for some types of consumer services, too. Most consumers can't easily determine the quality of service they will receive from an auto repair shop, a landscaper, or a housing remodeler. How can a high-quality service provider distinguish itself from low-quality providers? For a recent approach to solving this problem, read "A Closer Look: Consumer Satisfaction Scores from ValueStar and eBay."

Sellers Provide Guarantees

Used-car sellers also have an incentive to diminish the lemons problem. If a clever supplier could persuade a skeptical consumer that a particular used car is a plum, not a lemon, the seller could probably get more than $2,500 for the car, say $3,250. Suppliers can identify a particular car as a plum in a sea of lemons by offering one of the following guarantees:

▶ Money-back guarantees. The seller could promise to refund the $3,250 price if the car turned out to be a lemon. Because the car is in fact a plum—a fact known by the seller—the buyer will not ask for a refund, so both the buyer and the seller will be happy with the transaction.
▶ Warranties and repair guarantees. The seller could promise to cover any extraordinary repair costs for one year. Because the car is a plum, there won't be any extraordinary repair costs, so both the buyer and the seller will be happy with the transaction.

Lemons Laws

Many states have laws that require automakers to buy back cars that experience frequent problems in the first year of use. For example, under California's Song–Beverly Consumer Warranty Act, also known as the "Lemons Law," auto dealers are required to

A CLOSER LOOK

Consumer Satisfaction Scores from ValueStar and eBay

If you live in the San Francisco Bay area, you can get information about the performance of firms providing consumer services such as medical and dental care, gardening and landscaping, pet grooming, auto repair, and home improvement. ValueStar uses customer-satisfaction surveys to determine how well a firm does relative to its competitors in providing quality service. To get the right to display a Customer-Rated seal, a firm must prove that it has all the required licenses and insurance and must agree to pay for a survey of its past customers. ValueStar uses consumer surveys to compute a consumer-satisfaction score for each company. Any company receiving a score of at least 85 out of 100 has the right to display a Customer-Rated Gold seal for a one-year period.

Another example of consumer satisfaction scores is evident on eBay, the Internet auction site. On eBay, buyers must rely on sellers to honestly disclose the quality of the goods they are

auctioning and to promptly ship them once a consumer pays. Buyers help other purchasers distinguish "good" from "bad" sellers on eBay by rating them online with "stars," indicating how satisfied they were with their transactions.

repurchase vehicles that have been brought back for repair at least four times for the same problem or have been in the mechanic's shop for at least 30 calendar days in the first year following purchase. A vehicle repurchased under the lemons law must be fixed before it is sold to another customer and must be identified as a lemon with a stamp on the title and a sticker on the car that says "lemons law buyback." One problem with enforcing these laws is that lemons can cross state lines without a paper trail. The interstate commerce in lemons has led to new laws in some states requiring the branding of lemons on vehicle titles to follow the car when it crosses state lines.

TEST Your Understanding

6. Explain why it would not be rational for a lemon owner to offer a buyer a money-back guarantee.
7. Suppose that the minimum supply price of plums decreases. Would you expect the market to become "thinner" or "thicker"?
8. Explain why there are profit opportunities in a thin market.

Evidence of the Lemons Effect

The lemons model makes two predictions about markets with asymmetric information. First, the presence of low-quality goods in a market will at least reduce the number of high-quality goods in the market and may even eliminate them. Second, buyers and sellers will respond to the lemons problem by investing in information and other means of distinguishing between low-quality and high-quality goods. What's the evidence for the lemons model?

The Price of a Week-Old Car

If you buy a new car for $20,000 today and then try to sell it a week later, you probably won't get more than $16,000 for it. Even if you drove it just a couple hundred miles, cleaned it up, and returned it to the dealer with that new-car smell, the car will lose about 20% of its value in the first week. You won't fare any better by putting an advertisement in the newspaper or trying to sell the car on eBay. Why does the typical new car lose so much of its value in the first week?

A potential buyer of a week-old car might believe that a person who returns a car after only one week could have discovered it was a lemon and may be trying to get rid of it. Alternatively, the seller could have simply changed his or her mind about the car. The problem is that buyers don't know why the car is being sold, and as long as there is a chance that the car is a lemon, they won't be willing to pay the full "new" price for it. In general, buyers are willing to pay a lot less for a week-old car, and so the owners of high-quality, week-old cars are less likely to put them on the market. This downward spiral ultimately reduces the price of week-old cars by about 20%.

Used Pickup Trucks

Studies of the market for used pickup trucks have provided mixed results concerning the lemons problem.[2] It appears that for trucks less than 10 years old, those sold on the market are just as reliable, on average, as those that remain with their current owners. This provides support for the second implication of the theory of lemons, that people acquire information and develop effective means to deal with the problem of asymmetric information. By contrast, there does seem to be a lemons problem for trucks at least 10 years old, which represent about one-third of transactions. Compared to old trucks that remain with their current owner, old trucks that are sold have significantly higher repair costs, with a difference in cost of about 45%. Old trucks that are sold have a much higher probability of requiring engine and transmission repairs.

California Kiwifruit

Kiwifruit is subject to imperfect information because buyers cannot determine its sweetness—its quality level—by simple inspection. The sweetness level at the time of consumption is determined by the fruit's "maturity"—its sugar content at the time of harvest. Kiwifruit continues to convert starch into sugar after it is picked, so a harvest-time sugar content of 6.5% leads to a sugar content of about 14% at the time of consumption. Fruit that is picked early has a low sugar content at harvest time and never tastes sweet. There is asymmetric information because producers know the maturity of the fruit, but fruit wholesalers and grocery stores, who buy fruit at the time of harvest, cannot determine whether a piece of fruit will ultimately be sweet or sour.

Before 1987, kiwifruit from California suffered from the "lemons" problem.[3] Maturity levels of the fruit varied across producers. On average, the sugar content at the time of harvest was below the industry standard, established by kiwifruit from New Zealand. Given the large number of "lemons" among California kiwifruit, grocery stores were not willing to pay as much for California fruit. In other words, the presence of low-quality (immature) fruit in the mixed market pulled down the price of California fruit. Mature kiwifruit is more costly to produce than immature fruit, and the low price decreased the production of mature fruit. This is similar to low used-car prices decreasing the number of high-quality used cars on the market. In general, adverse selection led to low prices and a relatively large volume of low-quality kiwifruit from California.

In 1987, California producers implemented a federal marketing order to address the lemon–kiwi problem. The federal order specified a minimum maturity standard (6.5% sugar content at the time of harvest), and as the average quality of California fruit increased, so did the price. Within a few years, the gap between California and New Zealand prices had decreased significantly.

Used Baseball Pitchers

Professional baseball teams compete with each other for players. After six years of play in the major leagues, a player has the option of becoming a free agent and offering his services to the highest bidder. A player is likely to switch teams if the new team offers him a higher salary than his original team. One of the puzzling features of the free-agent market is that pitchers who switch teams are more prone to injuries than pitchers who don't. On average, pitchers who switch teams spend 28 days per season on the disabled list; pitchers who do not switch teams spend only five days per season on the disabled list.[4] This doesn't mean that all the switching pitchers are lemons; many of them are injury-free and are terrific additions to their new teams. But on average, the switching pitchers spend five times longer recovering from injuries.

This puzzling feature of the free-agent market for baseball players is explained by asymmetric information and adverse selection. Because the coaches, physicians, and trainers from the player's original team have interacted with the player on a daily basis for several years, they know from experience whether he is likely to suffer from injuries that prevent him from playing. In contrast, the new team has much less information. Its physicians can examine the pitcher, and the team can check league records to see how long the pitcher has spent on the disabled list, but these measures do not eliminate the asymmetric information. The original team has several years of daily experience with the pitcher and has better information about the pitcher's physical health.

To illustrate the lemons problem for pitchers, consider the incentives for a team to outbid another team for a pitcher. Suppose the market price for pitchers is $1 million

Baseball pitchers who switch teams are more prone to injuries than those who don't switch.

per year, and a pitcher who is currently with the Chicago Cubs is offered this salary by another team. If the Cubs think the pitcher is likely to spend a lot of time next season recovering from injuries, they won't try to outbid the other team for the pitcher: They will let the pitcher switch teams. But if the Cubs think the pitcher will be injury-free and productive, he will be worth more than $1 million to the Cubs, so they will outbid other teams and keep him. In general, an injury-prone pitcher is more likely to switch teams. As in the used-car market, there are many "lemons" on the used-pitcher market. The market for baseball players playing other positions (outfield, infield) does not suffer from the adverse selection, perhaps because the injuries that affect their performance are easier for other teams to detect.

Although you may think it's bizarre to compare baseball pitchers to used cars, people in baseball don't think so. They recognize the similarity between the two markets. Jackie Moore, who managed a free-agent camp where teams looking for players can see free agents in action, sounds like a used-car salesman: "We want to get players off the lot. We want to cut a deal. How many camps can you go into where you can look at a player and take him home with you?"[5]

Uninformed Sellers and Knowledgeable Buyers: Insurance

So far, we have explored the effects of asymmetric information when sellers are more knowledgeable than buyers. The same sort of problems occur when buyers are more knowledgeable than sellers. The best example of superior knowledge on the demand side of the market is insurance. A person who buys an insurance policy knows much more about his or her risks and needs for insurance than the insurance company knows. For example, when you buy an auto insurance policy, you know more than your insurance company about your driving habits and your chances of getting into an accident. We'll see that insurance markets suffer from the adverse-selection problem: Insurance companies must pick from an adverse or undesirable selection of customers.

Health Insurance

To illustrate the information problems in the market for insurance, consider health insurance provided to individual consumers. Suppose there are two types of consumers, low-cost consumers with relatively low medical expenses (an average of $2,000 per year) and high-cost consumers with relatively high medical expenses (an average of $6,000 per year). The amount a consumer is willing to pay for an insurance policy covering all medical expenses increases with the anticipated medical expenses, so high-cost people are willing to pay more for health insurance.

The insurance company cannot distinguish between high-cost and low-cost people, but it still must pick a price for its coverage. To simplify matters, let's assume that there are no administrative costs, so the only cost for the insurance company is the medical bills it pays for its customers. Let's also assume that the insurance company sets the price equal to its average cost per customer, equal to the total medical bills paid by the insurance company divided by the number of customers. These assumptions simplify the math without affecting the basic results.

What is the insurance company's average cost per customer? To determine the average cost in a mixed market, we must answer three questions:

▶ What is the cost of providing medical care to a high-cost person?
▶ What is the cost of providing medical care to a low-cost person?
▶ What fraction of the customers are low-cost people?

Suppose that half the population is high-cost and the other half is low-cost. Let's assume that the insurance company is somewhat naive and initially assumes that the mix of insurance buyers will be the same as the population mix. In other words, the insurance company initially assumes that half its customers will be high-cost and half will be low-cost. In this case, the average cost per customer is $4,000, that is, the average of $2,000 for each low-cost customer and $6,000 for each high-cost customer.

There is asymmetric information in the insurance market because potential buyers know from everyday experience and family histories what type of customer they are, either low-cost or high-cost. For each person, the question is: Given the single market price for all insurance, for low-cost and high-cost people alike, should I buy insurance? The answers to this question are shown in two demand curves, one for each type. In Figure 8.3, the demand curve for the high-cost people is higher than the curve for the low-cost people, reflecting their larger benefits from having medical insurance.

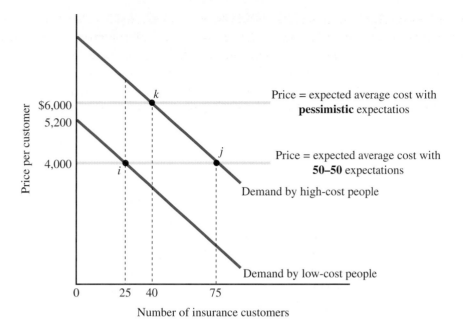

FIGURE 8.3 **All Insurance Customers Are High-Cost People**

If insurance companies assume there will be a 50–50 split between high-cost and low-cost customers, the average cost (and price) is $4,000. At this price, there are 25 low-cost customers (point *i*) and 75 high-cost customers (point *j*). This is not an equilibrium because the expectation of a 50–50 split are not realized, and the insurance company loses money. If insurance companies are pessimistic (assume that all customers will be high-cost), the average cost (and price) is $6,000. At this price, only high-cost people will buy insurance (point *k*), so pessimism is an equilibrium.

Equilibrium with All High-Cost Consumers

Table 8.3 shows two scenarios for our hypothetical insurance market, with numbers consistent with the demand curves shown in Figure 8.3. In the first column, we assume that firms initially assume a 50–50 mix of customers. As we saw earlier, if sellers expect a 50–50 split between the two types, the average cost per customer is $4,000, and that's the price they charge for medical insurance. From the demand curves in Figure 8.3, we know that at this price, 25 low-cost people will buy insurance (point *i*), along with 75 high-cost people (point *j*). In this case, insurance companies are too optimistic and underestimate the fraction of customers with large medical bills. The actual fraction of high-cost customers is 75%, and the actual average cost is $5,000 (equal to 0.25 times $2,000, plus 0.75 times $6,000). The company's average cost of $5,000 exceeds its price of $4,000, so the firm will lose money.

Suppose that after observing the outcome in the first column, insurance companies become very pessimistic. They assume that all their customers will be high-cost people. Under this assumption, the average cost per customer is $6,000, the average cost per high-cost customer, and that's the pessimistic price. As shown in Figure 8.3, this price exceeds the maximum that low-cost people are willing to pay for insurance ($5,200), so none of the low-cost consumers will buy insurance at this price. But a total of 40 high-cost consumers will buy insurance at this price (point *k*). In other words, all the customers will be high-cost people, so the company's pessimism is justified. The

	50–50 Expectations	Equilibrium: Pessimistic Expectations
Supply Side of Market		
Cost of serving a high-cost customer	$6,000	$6,000
Cost of serving a low-cost customer	$2,000	$2,000
Assumed fraction of high-cost customers	50%	100%
Assumed chance of low-cost customers	50%	0%
Expected average cost per customer (price)	$4,000	$6,000
Demand Side of Market		
Number of high-cost customers	75	40
Number of low-cost customers	25	0
Total number of customers	100	40
Actual fraction of high-cost customers	75%	100%
Actual average cost per customer	$5,000	$6,000

price chosen by the insurance company equals the actual average cost of providing service, so this is an equilibrium. This is shown in the second column of Table 8.3.

The domination of the insurance market by high-cost people is another example of the adverse-selection problem. The uninformed side of the market (sellers in this case) must choose from an undesirable or adverse selection of consumers. The asymmetric information in the market generates a downward spiral of price and quantity:

▶ The presence of high-cost consumers in the market pulls up the average cost of service, pulling up the price.
▶ An increase in price decreases the quantity of low-cost consumers who purchase insurance.
▶ The decrease in the quantity of low-cost consumers pulls up the average cost of insurance.

In the extreme case, this downward spiral continues until all insurance customers are high-cost people.

Our example of health insurance indicates that only high-cost people buy insurance. A more realistic outcome is a thin market, with a relatively small number of low-cost people buying insurance. The adverse-selection problem could be less severe, but still will be present as long as insurance companies cannot distinguish perfectly between low-cost and high-cost people.

Responding to Adverse Selection in Insurance: Group Insurance

Insurance companies use group insurance plans to diminish the adverse-selection problem. By enrolling all the employees of an organization in one or two insurance plans, they ensure that all workers, not just high-cost people, join the pool of consumers. In our example, group insurance would generate a 50–50 mix of low-cost and high-cost customers, and the break-even price would be $6,000. In contrast, when a firm sells insurance to individuals, the low-cost people have an incentive to go without insurance, leading to the adverse-selection problem and higher prices.

Most insurance companies use **experience rating** to set their prices for group insurance. They charge different prices to different firms, depending on the past medical bills of the firm's employees. A firm whose employees have low medical bills pays a low price for its employees' health insurance. Experience rating gives firms an incentive to decrease the health costs of their workers. As a result, they have an incentive to invest in safety and health programs for their workers. They also have an incentive to avoid hiring applicants with health problems. Under experience rating, a firm that hires a worker with above-average medical costs will ultimately pay a higher price for its group insurance.

> **Experience rating**
> A situation in which each firm pays a different price for medical insurance, depending on the past medical bills of its employees.

The Uninsured

One implication of asymmetric information in the insurance market is that many low-cost consumers who are not eligible for a group plan will not carry insurance. Given the adverse-selection problem, the price for an individual insurance plan is relatively high, and many consumers go without insurance. This is a contributing factor to the problem of the "uninsured." In 2002, about 44 million people (about 14% of the U.S. population) were not covered by health insurance. About 70% of working-age people have private insurance, and another 10% have some sort of government insurance, leaving 20% without health insurance. In general, the uninsured are the people and their families who do not receive insurance through their employers, are unemployed or between jobs, or are poor but do not qualify for Medicaid. The uninsured obtain care for medical emergencies but typically do not receive routine—and less costly—preventive care.

The problem of uninsured people does not show any signs of improving. A recent proposal for universal coverage from the national government, which would have required each employer to provide health insurance for all its workers, was soundly defeated. Stanford health economist Victor Fuchs has suggested a plan under which everyone would receive a voucher—a coupon from the government they could use toward the purchase of their own health insurance.[6] The difficulty with any voucher plan is that new taxes would be necessary to finance it. Most European countries that provide universal coverage to their citizens finance it with a value-added tax—essentially a national sales tax. Clearly, introducing a new tax or raising existing tax rates to finance a voucher plan would be very controversial.

Other Types of Insurance

The same logic of adverse selection applies to the markets for other types of insurance, including life insurance, home insurance (for theft and property damage), and automobile insurance. Buyers know more than sellers about their risks, so there is adverse selection, with high-risk individuals more likely to buy insurance. Life insurance companies provide group coverage to get a broader base of consumers and also

A CLOSER LOOK

Genetic Testing, Thrill Seekers, and Insurance

You probably know someone who is impulsive and excitable, a thrill seeker who keeps life interesting for those of us who are more relaxed and mellow. Scientists recently identified one of the genes responsible for novelty-seeking behavior and discovered that about 15% of the people in Israel, Europe, and the United States carry the gene.[7] Scientists figure that about half of novelty-seeking behavior among people is linked to their genes, which might make them more inclined to take up skydiving or bungee jumping and engage in other risky behavior.

If you managed a life insurance company, would you like to know whether each customer has the novelty-seeking gene? It would reduce the problem of asymmetric information and allow you to charge different prices for insurance, leading to lower prices for people who are less inclined to take risks. The same is true for other genetic information that reveals an individual's likelihood of developing heart disease or cancer: An insurance company with genetic information could charge different prices, including lower prices for consumers whose genetic makeup makes them less likely to develop health problems.

The development of genetic tests has led to fears that insurance companies will use the results of the tests to engage in genetic discrimination—denying insurance or charging higher prices to people with unfavorable genes. Federal employees are protected by an executive order that forbids genetic discrimination. For the public at large, there are proposals in Congress to outlaw the practice.

try to distinguish between high-risk and low-risk people with physical exams. But because the companies are unable to distinguish between high-risk and low-risk people with sufficient precision, the adverse selection persists. For an example of how insurance companies might use new technology to more precisely identify people with higher risks of death, read "A Closer Look: Genetic Testing, Thrill Seekers, and Insurance."

Moral Hazard

Does insurance affect people's risk-taking behavior? The answer is, yes. Insurance causes people to take greater risks because they know part of the cost of an undesirable outcome will be borne by their insurance companies. Here are some examples of people taking greater risks because they have insurance:

▶ Irma could buy a fire extinguisher for her kitchen. If she had to pay for any property damage caused by a fire, she would definitely buy a fire extinguisher. But because her homeowner's insurance covers property damage from fires, she doesn't buy a fire extinguisher.

▶ Harry decides how carefully to drive his car. If he had to pay for all repairs resulting from a collision out of his own pocket, he would drive very carefully. But since his auto insurance covers some of the repair costs, he drives more recklessly than he otherwise would.

▶ Flo can either fly on a commercial airline or hitch a ride with her pilot friend in a four-seat airplane. Traveling in small airplanes is much riskier. If Flo dies in an airplane crash, her family will lose the income she would otherwise earn. If she didn't have life insurance to offset these income losses, she would be less likely to risk harming her family by flying on the small plane instead of the commercial airline. But because she knows her family will collect $1 million in life insurance, she is willing to take the risk.

The problem of **moral hazard** is that insurance encourages risky behavior. More precisely, moral hazard occurs when an insured party takes an unobserved action (not observed by the insurer) that affects the probability of the event that triggers payment from the insurer. For example, Harry's unobserved action is reckless driving, which increases the probability of a collision, an event that triggers payment from his auto insurance company. Just as collision insurance encourages risky driving, life insurance encourages risky activities such as flying small airplanes, parachuting, and bungee jumping. Similarly, health insurance encourages risky behavior such as smoking, drinking, and unhealthy diets.

For another example of moral hazard, consider insurance provided for bank deposits. When you deposit money in a Savings and Loan (S&L), the money doesn't just sit in a vault. The S&L will invest the money, loaning it out and expecting to make a profit when loans are repaid with interest. Unfortunately, some loans are not repaid, and the S&L could lose money and be unable to return your money. To protect people who put their money in S&Ls and other banks, the Federal Deposit Insurance Corporation (FDIC) insures the first $100,000 of your deposit, so if the S&L goes bankrupt, you'll still get your money back. The federal deposit insurance law was enacted in 1933 in response to the bank failures of the Great Depression.

Moral hazard
Insurance encourages risky behavior.

If he didn't have life insurance, would he still jump?

How does deposit insurance affect you and the people who manage the S&L? If you know you'll get your money back no matter what happens to the S&L, you may deposit your money there without evaluating the S&L's performance and the riskiness of its loans to borrowers and investments in the stock market. The manager of an S&L will also be more likely to make risky investments knowing that if it doesn't pay off and the S&L goes bankrupt, the federal government will reimburse depositors. Recognizing this moral hazard problem, the federal government has historically limited S&Ls to relatively safe investments.

In the 1980s, the federal government loosened some of the investment restrictions on S&Ls, and S&L managers subsequently began investing in volatile securities, including high-risk commercial mortgages and junk bonds. When these risky investments failed, many of the S&Ls went into bankruptcy. The government then bailed out the failed S&Ls, at a total cost to taxpayers of about $200 billion.

Economic Puzzle

Bicycle Theft Insurance

At Wheeler State University, one out of every 10 bicycles was stolen in 2002. When a group of young entrepreneurs discovered that no one on campus had bicycle theft insurance, they decided to go into the insurance business, offering one-year theft insurance for $15 per bike. They sold 100 policies in 2003 and expected 10 of their 100 customers (10% of them) to lose their bicycles to theft. The entrepreneurs figured that their total revenue would more than cover the cost of replacing 10 bicycles, leaving a tidy profit. By the end of 2003, a total of 20 insured bicycles had been stolen, and the students lost a bundle of money on their little enterprise. What happened?

The key to solving this puzzle is the fact that the 10% theft rate occurred in 2002 when *no one* had theft insurance. When the entrepreneurs offered theft insurance the next year, they expected the same theft rate. Because of moral hazard, however, the students who bought theft insurance were less careful in protecting their bikes, perhaps using less secure locks or leaving their bikes on campus overnight. As a result, the theft rate for insured bikes was 20%, not 10%. The entrepreneurs lost money because they did not anticipate that insurance would increase risk-taking. ■

TEST Your Understanding

9. Your favorite baseball team just announced that it signed two pitchers from the free-agent market. What's your reaction?

10. Complete the statement with numbers: Suppose that the average annual malpractice cost is $40,000 for reckless doctors and $2,000 for careful doctors. If half the insured doctors are reckless, the insurance company will earn zero economic profit if the price of insurance is _____. If careful doctors are not willing to pay any more than $5,000 for insurance, the price required for zero economic profit is _____.

11. Many professional athletes purchase insurance against career-ending injuries. Would you expect the insured players to act differently from those who don't have insurance?

Economic Experiment

Rolling for Lemons

In this experiment, students play the role of consumers purchasing used cars. Over half the used cars on the road (57%) are plums, and the remaining cars (43%) are lemons. Each consumer offers a price for a used car and then rolls a pair of dice to find out whether he or she gets a lemon or a plum. In general, rolling a big number is good news: To get a plum, you need to roll a big number. The higher the price you offer, the smaller the number you must roll to get a plum. Here is how the experiment works:

- Each consumer tells the instructor how much he or she is offering for a used car and then rolls the dice.

- The instructor tells the consumer whether the number rolled is large enough to get a plum. If the number is not large enough, the consumer gets a lemon.

- The consumers' scores equal the difference between the maximum amount they are willing to pay for the type of car they got ($1,200 for a plum and $400 for a lemon) and the price they actually paid. For example, if Otto offers $500 and gets a plus, his score is $700. If Carla offers $600 and gets a lemon, her score is −$200.

- The instructor announces the result of each transaction to the class.

- There are three to five buying periods. At the end of the last trading period, each consumer adds up his or her score. ●

Economic Experiment

Bike Insurance

This experiment shows the effect of asymmetric information on the market for bicycle insurance. Consider a city with two types of bike owners; some face a relatively high probability of bike theft, and others face a relatively low probability of bike theft. Bike owners know from experience whether they face a high probability or a low probability of theft, but the insurance company cannot distinguish between the two types of owners. For the city as a whole, 20% of bicycles are stolen every year. Here is how the experiment works:

- The class is divided into small groups. Each group represents an insurance company that must pick a price at which to offer bike theft insurance. The insurance company must pay $100 for each insured bike that is stolen.

- The instructor has a table showing, for each price of bike insurance, how many owners of each type (high probability and low probability) will purchase insurance. Using the numbers supplied by the instructor, each insurance company can compute its total revenue (the price per bike insured times the number of insured bikes), the number of bikes stolen, and the company's total replacement cost.

- The group's score for a trading period equals the company's profit, which is the total revenue less the total replacement cost for stolen bikes.

- The experiment runs for several trading periods, and a group's score equals the sum of its profits over these trading periods. ●

USING THE TOOLS

We've seen what happens when one side of the market—either buyers or sellers—has better information than the other side. In a market for a used good, sellers know more than buyers, and the market will be dominated by low-quality goods. In an insurance market, buyers know more than sellers, and the market will be dominated by high-risk consumers. Here are some opportunities to do your own economic analysis of markets with asymmetric information.

1. Rising Insurance Rates

At a large state university, an insurance company provides group medical coverage for university employees. When the company discovered that some of the younger employees had switched to insurance companies with lower rates, it increased its rates. This is puzzling because you might think the insurance company would drop its rates to prevent other employees from switching to other companies. Indeed, the rate hike caused more employees to switch. Did the insurance company act irrationally?

2. Purchasing a Fleet of Used Cars

You are responsible for buying a fleet of 10 used cars for your employees and must pick either brand B cars or brand C cars. For your purposes, the two brands are identical except for one difference: Based on your market experience with the two brands, you figure that 50% of B cars are lemons and only 20% of C cars are lemons. You are willing to pay $1,000 for a known lemon and $3,000 for a known plum. If the price of B cars is $1,800 and the price of C cars is $2,200, which brand of car should you pick?

3. State Auto Insurance Pool

Consider a state in which automobile drivers are divided equally into two types of drivers: careful and reckless. The average annual auto insurance claim is $400 for a careful driver and $1,200 for a reckless driver. Suppose the state adopts an insurance system in which all drivers are placed in a common pool and allocated to insurance companies randomly. An insurance company cannot refuse coverage to any driver it is assigned, but a driver who is unhappy with the insurance company has the option of being reassigned (randomly) to another insurance company. By law, each insurance company must charge the same price to all its customers. Predict the price of auto insurance under two alternative policy scenarios: (a) mandatory auto insurance ; (b) voluntary auto insurance.

4. Skydiver Question

Several of your friends have offered to take on a tandem skydiving adventure: Strapped together with a single set of parachutes (main and emergency), you jump out of an airplane and then either float to earth or crash. All your skydiving friends are equally skillful, and none of them has the thrill-seeker gene. You can ask each of them one (only one) question. What's your question? Provide the answer you're looking for in a skydiving mate.

SUMMARY

In this chapter, we've seen what happens when one of the assumptions underlying most supply and demand analysis—that people make informed decisions—is violated. If either buyers or sellers don't have reliable information about a particular good or service, the market will suffer from the adverse-selection problem. The uninformed side of the market picks from an adverse selection of goods or customers. Here are the main points of the chapter:

1 The adverse-selection problem occurs when one side of the market cannot distinguish between high-quality and low-quality goods. The presence of low-quality goods pulls down the price that buyers are willing to pay, which decreases the quantity of high-quality goods supplied, which further decreases the average quality and the price. In the extreme case, only low-quality goods are sold.

2 A "thin" market occurs when the sellers of high-quality goods have a relatively low minimum supply price, so some high-quality goods are sold.

3 In a market subject to asymmetric information, buyers have an incentive to invest in information to help make better choices, and sellers have an incentive to provide quality guarantees.

4 Insurance markets suffer from adverse selection because compared to insurance sellers, buyers have better information about the risks they face.

5 The moral hazard problem is that insurance encourages risky behavior because part of the cost of an unfavorable outcome will be paid by an insurance company.

KEY TERMS

adverse-selection problem, 174
asymmetric information, 171

experience rating, 185
mixed market, 171

moral hazard, 187
thin market, 174

PROBLEMS AND DISCUSSION QUESTIONS

1 Use the notion of adverse selection to explain a classic quip from Groucho Marx: "I won't join any club that is willing to accept me as a member."

2 The following table shows some scenarios for different used-car markets. Which markets are in equilibrium? Graph each equilibrium, using Figure 8.1 as a model.

	Scenario A	Scenario B	Scenario C
Assumed chance of getting a lemon	60%	80%	95%
Willingness to pay for a used car	$6,000	$5,000	$4,500
Number of lemons supplied	70	40	90
Number of plums supplied	30	10	10
Total number of used cars supplied	100	50	100

3 You're thinking about buying a used camera at a price of $60. You are willing to pay $20 for a lemon and $100 for a plum. Under what circumstances would it be wise to buy a used camera? Are these circumstances likely to occur? Explain.

4 Suppose that both buyers and sellers of used cars are ignorant: No one can distinguish between lemons and plums. Would you expect the market to be dominated by lemons?

5 Suppose that a new lie detector is 100% accurate. Discuss the implications of the device for the adverse-selection problem in the used-car market.

6 When a person applies for life insurance, the insurance agent asks the applicant about his or her occupation. Why should this matter to the insurance company?

7 Scientists have recently developed new genetic tests that could be used by an insurance company to determine whether a potential customer is likely to

develop certain diseases. Discuss the trade-offs associated with allowing insurance companies to use these tests.

8 On the campus of Bike University, half the bikes are expensive (replacement value = $100) and half are cheap (replacement value = $20). There is a 50% chance that any particular bike—expensive or cheap—will be stolen in the next year. Suppose a firm offers bike theft insurance for $40 per year: The firm will replace any insured bike that is stolen. If the firm sells 20 insurance policies, will it make a profit? Explain.

9 In a given year, there is a 10% chance that a fire in Ira's warehouse will cause $100,000 in property damage. If Ira spent $5,000 on a fire-prevention program, the probability of a fire would drop to zero. If Ira doesn't have fire insurance, will he spend the money on the prevention program? If he has an insurance policy that covers 80% of the property damage from a fire, will he spend the money on the prevention program? At what coverage rate (40%, 50%, 60%, 70%) will Ira be indifferent about spending money on the prevention program?

10 As Kira tries to decide whether or not to do a bungee jump, she asks to make one phone call. If there is a moral hazard problem, whom will she call?

MODEL ANSWERS TO QUESTIONS

Chapter-Opening Questions

1 Buyers recognize that some of the week-old cars are returned because they are troublesome, so they are not willing to pay the full price. The lower price dissuades some owners of trouble-free cars from selling them, so the fraction of troublesome cars increases, further decreasing the price.

2 Like the used-car market, the used-pitcher market has asymmetric information: Compared to a new team, the pitcher's original team has better information on the pitcher's health. The original team will let the other team win the bidding for the pitcher if its "inside information" on the pitcher's health suggests that he is likely to be injured and thus unable to play.

3 California kiwifruit suffered from the adverse-selection problem because sellers knew more than buyers about the eventual sweetness of the fruit. The regulations specified a minimum maturity level, increasing the average quality of fruit (sweetness), increasing the equilibrium price of California kiwifruit.

4 Insurance companies use group insurance plans to diminish the adverse-selection problem.

3 It is easy to determine the size of an apple but not easy to determine the quality of a car.

4 Adverse selection.

5 Yes; 70% of the cars are lemons.

6 The buyer will eventually return the car and get a full refund, perhaps after putting a lot of miles on it or abusing it.

7 Thicker; the lower the minimum supply price, the larger the quantity supplied at each price, so the more plums in the market.

8 There will be a large gap between the amount a buyer is willing to pay for a true plum and the amount a plum owner is willing to accept.

9 You may be skeptical about the new player because free-agent pitchers who switch teams spend a long time on the disabled list. Before reading this chapter, you might have been more optimistic about the pitchers.

10 $21,000 (the average of the two cost figures); $40,000 (the cost for reckless doctors).

11 Insured athletes are likely to spend less effort avoiding injuries, knowing that the insurance company will compensate them for a career-ending injury.

Test Your Understanding

1 Buyers, sellers.

2 $2,500, the average value of the two types of cars.

NOTES

1. George Akerlof, "The Market for 'Lemons': Quality Uncertainty and the Market Mechanism," *Quarterly Journal of Economics*, August 1970, pp. 488–500.

2. Eric Bond, "A Direct Test of the Lemons' Model: The Market for Used Pickup Trucks," *American Economic Review*, September 1982, 72, pp. 836–840; Michael Pratt and George Hoffer, "Test of the Lemons Model: Comment," *American Economic Review*, September 1984, 74, pp. 798–800; Eric Bond, "Test of the Lemons' Model: A Reply," *American Economic Review*, September 1984, 74, pp. 801–804.

3. Christopher Ferguson and Hoy Carman, "Kiwifruit and the 'Lemon' Problem: Do Minimum Quality Standards Work?" Working Paper, 2003.

4. Kenneth Lehn, "Information Asymmetries in Baseball's Free Agent Market," *Economic Inquiry*, vol. 22, January 1984, pp. 37–44.

5. Chris Sheridan, "Free Agents at End of Baseball's Earth," Associated Press, printed in *Corvallis Gazette-Times*, April 15, 1995, p. B1.

6. Victor Fuchs, "Economics, Values, and Health Reform," *American Economic Review*, March 1996, pp. 1–26.

7. "Genetic Discrimination Feared," Associated Press Online, June 26, 2000; Malcolm Ritter, "A Thrill a Minute: Geneticists Find Personality Link," *The Oregonian*, January 2, 1996, p. A1.

The Optimal Level of Pollution and Pollution Taxes

Application: Finding the Optimal Level
    of Sulfur Dioxide Emissions
A Firm's Response to a Pollution Tax
The Market Effects of a Pollution Tax

Traditional Regulation: Uniform Abatement and Command-and-Control Policies

Uniform Abatement with Permits
Command and Control
Market Effects of Pollution Regulations

Marketable Pollution Permits

Voluntary Exchange and Marketable
    Permits
Supply, Demand, and the Price
    of Marketable Permits
Application: Marketable Permits for Sulfur
    Dioxide

Global Warming and Public Policy

The Consequences of Global Warming
The Kyoto Agreement and Developing
    Nations
The Effects of a Carbon Tax
Marketable Permits and Offsets

Ozone Pollution and the Automobile

Using the Tools

Environmental Policy

I n 2001, a group of students from an economics course at Hobart and William Smith Colleges joined an auction for the right to discharge sulfur dioxide into the atmosphere. Sulfur dioxide is an important ingredient in air pollution and acid rain. It causes thousands of premature deaths each year and destroys vegetation, damages buildings, and kills fish. Among the other bidders for the sulfur dioxide permits were energy giants Enron and Ohio Power Company. The students paid $181 for a permit and promised to hold it rather than using it. As a result, there is one less ton of sulfur dioxide in the air.

The auction for sulfur dioxide permits is an example of the economic approach to pollution. In Chapter 6, we introduced the notion of market failure, which happens when production generates external costs such as air or water pollution. The sulfur dioxide discharged by electricity producers imposes an external cost on society, and because producers ignore these costs in their decisions, the market fails to operate efficiently. As we'll see in this chapter, the best response to market failure is not to abandon markets, but instead to use markets to reduce pollution in the most efficient manner. We'll discuss two market-oriented policies, pollution taxes and auctions for pollution permits. The chapter's theme is that often the economic solution to market failure is to create markets where they do not currently exist.

In this chapter, we'll contrast the economic approach to pollution with the traditional regulatory approach, which uses rules and regulations. Here are some of the practical questions we answer:

1 What is the optimal level of sulfur dioxide pollution?
2 How would a tax on the pollution from electricity generation affect the price of electricity and the volume of pollution?
3 Why did Dawn Schrepel, a consultant in Washington D.C., buy 10 tons of carbon dioxide as thank-you gifts for her student interns?
4 If we want drivers to pay for the damages caused by urban smog, what's the appropriate gasoline tax?

The Optimal Level of Pollution and Pollution Taxes

Should we eliminate all pollution? Although a pristine environment with pure water and air sounds appealing, there would be some very unappealing consequences. To reduce air pollution, we could eliminate trucks, but shipping goods by horse-drawn wagon would result in higher freight costs and higher prices for most products—and a different sort of pollution. We could reduce water pollution by shutting down all the paper mills, but reverting to parchment and slate boards would be unwieldy. Given the consequences of eliminating pollution, it is sensible to allow some pollution to occur. The policy question is: What's the optimal level of pollution?

The most convenient way to discuss pollution policies is in terms of pollution abatement, that is, reductions in pollution from some starting level. We can use the marginal principle to determine the optimal level of pollution abatement.

 MARGINAL *Principle*

Increase the level of an activity if its marginal benefit exceeds its marginal cost, but reduce the level if the marginal cost exceeds the marginal benefit. If possible, pick the level at which the marginal benefit equals the marginal cost.

According to this principle, we should cut pollution to the level where the marginal benefit of abatement equals the marginal cost.

The marginal principle focuses our attention on the trade-offs from pollution—its costs and benefits. From society's perspective, there are many benefits from pollution abatement:

▶ Better health. Cleaner water means less sickness from waterborne pollutants, and cleaner air means fewer respiratory problems and thus lower health care costs and fewer sick days taken by workers.
▶ Increased enjoyment of the natural environment. Improving the air quality increases visibility and improves the health of trees. Improving the water quality enhances recreational activities such as swimming, boating, and fishing.
▶ Lower production costs. Some firms are dependent on clean water for survival: Farmers use water for irrigation; some manufacturers use clean water as part of the production process.

On the other hand, pollution abatement is costly because resources—labor, capital, and land—are used in the abatement process. Using the marginal principle, we look for the level of pollution abatement where the marginal benefit equals the marginal cost.

Application: Finding the Optimal Level of Sulfur Dioxide Emissions

Sulfur dioxide (SO_2) emissions contribute to health problems such as upper respiratory illness, bronchitis, coughing episodes, and chest discomfort. SO_2 is a contributing factor—along with nitrogen oxide and other pollutants—in thousands of premature deaths each year. When sulfur dioxide is combined with nitrogen oxides and other chemicals in the atmosphere, the result is acid rain, which damages vegetation, kills aquatic life, and damages buildings.

A recent study estimated the marginal benefits and marginal costs of reducing SO_2 emissions from electricity generation facilities, looking ahead to the year 2010.[1] The study reached a number of conclusions, which are summarized next and outlined in Figure 9.1. The figure shows the marginal-benefit and marginal-cost curves related to this abatement. Notice that along the horizontal axis, abatement increases as we move to the right, while the amount discharged decreases. The sum of abatement and discharges is 9.1 million tons.

The following is a summary of the study's conclusions:

1 For each additional ton of SO_2 discharged into the atmosphere, the costs associated with premature deaths and health problems increases by about $3,500. In other words, the marginal benefit of abating SO_2 is roughly constant at $3,500 per ton.

2 The marginal cost of abatement increases with the amount abated, from about $500 per ton for the first 2 million tons abated to over $6,000 for the last ton abated. The first 2 million tons can be abated at a relatively low cost by switching to coal with a lower sulfur content. The next several million tons can be abated, at a higher cost, by installing scrubbers that remove sulfur from coal smoke. Further abatement requires a switch from coal to natural gas, a more expensive fuel.

3 The study concluded that the efficient level of abatement is 8 million tons per year, leaving 1.1 million tons of SO_2 discharged in 2010.

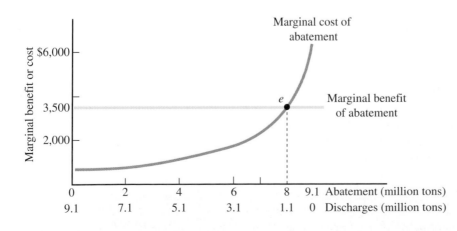

FIGURE 9.1

The Optimum Level of Sulfur Dioxide Emissions in 2010

The optimum level of pollution abatement is where the marginal benefit of abatement equals its marginal cost.

Source: Based on Spencer Banzhaf, Dallas Burtraw, and Karen Palmer, "Efficient Emission Fees in the U.S. Electricity Sector," Resources for the Future Discussion Paper 02-45, October 2002.

The current level of emissions is about 10 million tons per year. Under the provisions of the Clean Air Act passed by the U.S. government in 1990, emissions are scheduled to drop to 1.25 million tons by 2010, just above the optimal level determined by the independent study and shown in Figure 9.1.

A Firm's Response to a Pollution Tax

The economic approach to pollution is to get firms to pay for the waste they generate, just as they pay for labor, capital, and materials. The costs of labor, capital, and materials are the **private costs** of production, the costs borne by the firm producing the product. The **external costs of production** are those production costs imposed on people outside the firm, for example, the costs associated with health problems and premature deaths from sulfur dioxide. The **social cost of production** is the sum of the firm's private cost and the external cost imposed on others. The idea of a **pollution tax** is to "internalize" the externality—make the firm responsible for these external costs. When the tax equals the external cost imposed on others, the externality is said to be internalized. In our example, the tax is equal to the external cost of $3,500 per ton.

A polluting firm will respond to a pollution tax in the same way as it responds to the prices of labor and materials. The firm will use the marginal principle to decide how much waste to generate and how much to abate. Figure 9.2 shows the marginal cost of abating SO_2 for an electricity generator. The marginal cost is $2,200 for the first ton abated (point g), and the marginal cost increases, to $3,500 for the sixth ton abated (point i) and $4,500 for the seventh ton (point j). The marginal cost increases with the amount abated because the firm must use progressively more costly means of cutting emissions. From the firm's perspective, the marginal benefit of abatement is the $3,500 savings in pollution taxes from abating a ton of SO_2 rather than discharging it into the air. The firm satisfies the marginal principle at point i, with 6 tons of abatement because for the first 6 tons, the marginal benefit of abatement (not having to pay the $3,500 tax) is greater than or equal to the marginal cost. The firm stops at 6 tons

Private cost of production

The production cost borne by a firm, which typically includes the costs of labor, capital, and materials.

External cost of production

A cost incurred by people outside the firm.

Social cost of production

Private cost plus external cost.

Pollution tax

A tax or charge equal to the external cost per unit of waste.

FIGURE 9.2

The Firm's Response to a SO₂ Tax

From the perspective of a firm subject to a pollution tax, the marginal benefit of abatement is the $3,500 pollution tax that can be avoided by cutting pollution by 1 ton. The firm satisfies the marginal principle at point i, with 6 tons of abatement, leaving 2 tons of SO_2 discharged into the atmosphere.

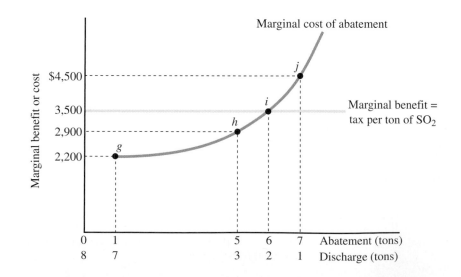

because the marginal cost of abating a seventh ton is $4,500 (shown by point *j*), which exceeds the $3,500 tax. Instead of paying $4,500 to abate one more ton, the firm will instead pay the $3,500 tax.

The Market Effects of a Pollution Tax

Consider the effect of a pollution tax on the market for the product produced by the polluting firms. The tax increases the cost of producing the product because firms pay for abatement and pay pollution taxes on any remaining waste they generate. As we saw in Chapter 7, a tax shifts the supply curve upward by the amount of the tax, decreasing the equilibrium quantity and increasing the equilibrium price. A pollution tax increases the price and decreases the quantity produced.

We can use the results of the study of the electricity market cited earlier to show the effects of pollution taxes. The appropriate pollution taxes for the two major pollutants from electricity generation are as follows:

▶ Sulfur dioxide. Electric power plants are responsible for about two-thirds of SO_2 emissions. As we saw earlier in the chapter, the marginal damage from SO_2 is $3,500 per ton, so that's the appropriate tax.
▶ Nitrogen oxides (NO_x). Power plants are also responsible for about one-quarter of the nation's NO_x emissions, a contributing factor in acid rain and the most important factor in urban smog. The study found that the appropriate tax for NO_x is about $1,100 per ton.

In Figure 9.3, the pollution taxes increase the cost of producing electricity, shifting the supply curve upward. The equilibrium moves from point *i* to point *f*, where the demand curve intersects the new supply curve. According to the electricity study, the pollution taxes would increase the price of electricity from $64.90 to $67.60 per megawatt hour, a 4% increase. The price elasticity of demand for electricity is 0.28, so the 4% increase in price decreases the quantity of electricity demanded by 1.1%, from

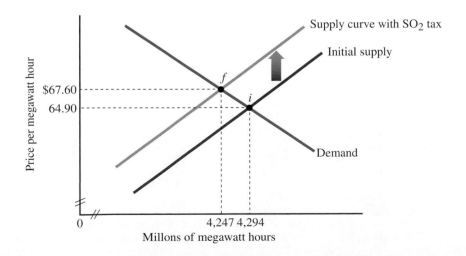

FIGURE 9.3

The Effects of SO₂ and NOₓ Taxes on the Electricity Market
The pollution tax increases the cost of producing electricity, shifting the market supply curve up. The equilibrium moves from point *i* to point *f*. The tax increases the equilibrium price from $64.90 to $67.60 per megawatt hour and decreases the equilibrium quantity.

4,294 to 4,247 megawatt hours. Like other taxes, the pollution tax is shifted forward on to consumers in the form of a higher price, and they respond by consuming less of the polluting good. When consumers face the full cost of producing electricity, they buy less of it.

Figure 9.4 shows the effects of the pollution taxes on the energy sources used to generate electricity, again using the results of the electricity study cited earlier. Producers respond to the taxes by switching to low-sulfur coal, which is more expensive but results in lower SO_2 taxes. The share of power generated with low-sulfur coal increases from 0.43 to 0.53. The taxes increase the cost of using coal relative to the cost of using natural gas and nuclear power, so the share of electricity from these other sources increases while the share of power from coal decreases. These shifts to cleaner energy sources decrease the amount of SO_2 and NO_x emissions per unit of electricity generated.

These pollution taxes decrease the total amount of air pollution for two reasons. First, as shown in Figure 9.3, the increase in the price of electricity decreases the quantity demanded by 1%. Second, as shown in Figure 9.4, the shift to cleaner energy sources means that each unit of electricity generates less pollution. The combined effect of these two changes is a substantial reduction in pollution: SO_2 decreases to 11% of its initial volume, and NO_x decreases to 30% of its initial volume. An added bonus of the pollution tax is that the government could use the revenue from the tax to cut other taxes, for example the income tax.

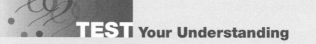

TEST Your Understanding

1. Why is the marginal cost curve for abatement positively sloped?
2. Explain how a pollution tax internalizes the pollution externality.
3. How does a pollution tax cause consumers to help reduce pollution?

FIGURE 9.4

Responses to SO_2 and NO_x Taxes on Electricity Generation
Taxes on SO_2 and NO_x cause electricity generators to switch to low-sulphur coal and to alternative energy sources that generate less SO_2 and NO_x.

Source: Based on Spencer Banzhaf, Dallas Burtraw, and Karen Palmer, "Efficient Emission Fees in the U.S. Electricity Sector," Resources for the Future Discussion Paper 02-45, October 2002.

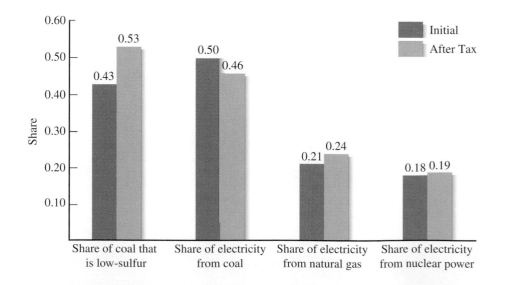

Traditional Regulation: Uniform Abatement and Command-and-Control Policies

Although the economic approach to pollution is to get polluters to pay for the waste they generate, governments often take a different approach. Under a traditional regulation policy, the government tells each firm how much pollution to abate and what abatement techniques to use.

Uniform Abatement with Permits

To illustrate the effects of regulation, consider an area with two electricity generators. Suppose that in the absence of pollution-abatement efforts, each firm would discharge 8 tons of pollution per hour. Suppose the government sets a target abatement level of 10 tons of SO_2 per hour, divided equally between the two firms. As shown in the second row of Table 9.1, if each firm abates 5 tons as the government requires, the firm would still discharge 3 tons of SO_2. Under a **uniform abatement policy**, the government would issue three pollution permits to each firm.

A uniform abatement policy is likely to be inefficient because it does not take advantage of the differences in abatement costs between the two firms. The marginal costs of abatement for the two firms are shown in the last two columns of Table 9.1. To show the inefficiency of the uniform abatement policy, imagine they agree to swap 1 ton. That is, instead of each firm having to abate 5 tons, we'll have the high-cost firm abate 4 tons and the low-cost firm abate 6 tons. The overall cost of abatement would then be as follows:

Uniform abatement policy
A policy under which each polluter is required to reduce pollution by the same amount.

▶ One *less* ton of abatement by the high-cost firm. As shown in the last column, the marginal cost of the fifth ton abated is $4,100, so the high-cost firm would save $4,100 by abating 4 tons instead of 5 tons.
▶ One *more* ton of abatement by the low-cost firm. As shown in the third column, the marginal cost of abating one additional ton—the sixth—is $3,500, so the low-cost firm would bear an additional cost of $3,500.
▶ The swap would generate the same amount of abatement (10 tons total), at a lower overall cost. The high-cost firm would save $4,100 and the low-cost firm incurs a $3,500 cost, so the net savings to the industry would be $600 (equal to $4,100 − $3,500).

TABLE 9.1
Marginal Cost of Abatement for Two Firms

Tons of Pollution Discharged (per hour)	Tons of Pollution Abated (per hour)	Marginal Abatement Cost per Ton	
		Low-Cost Firm	High-Cost Firm
4	4	$2,700	**$3,500**
3	5	2,900	4,100
2	6	**3,500**	5,100
1	7	4,500	6,500

The basic problem with the uniform abatement policy is that it treats firms equally with respect to pollution abatement, even though the firms are unequal in terms of their abatement costs.

In contrast, a pollution tax would exploit the differences in abatement costs. We saw in Figure 9.2 that if the pollution tax is $3,500, the low-cost firm will satisfy the marginal principle by abating 6 units. That's the quantity at which the marginal benefit (the tax savings) equals the marginal abatement cost; it is shown in the third column of Table 9.1. From the fourth column, we see that the tax will cause the high-cost firm to choose 4 units of abatement because that's the quantity at which its marginal cost of abatement equals the $3,500 tax. The tax is superior to the uniform abatement policy because it gets the low-cost firm to do more abating. The low-cost firm abates more but also pays less in pollution taxes.

Command and Control

Command-and-control policy

A policy under which the government commands each firm to produce no more than a certain volume of pollution and specifies the pollution-control technology used.

Traditional regulation policies have another dimension that contribute to higher compliance costs. When the government mandates each firm to produce no more than a certain volume of pollution and requires it be done with a particular abatement technology, this is called a **command-and-control policy**. The problem with this approach is that the mandated abatement technology—the control part of the policy—is unlikely to be the most efficient technology for two reasons.

▶ The regulatory policy specifies a single abatement technology for all firms. Because the producers of a polluting good often use different materials and production techniques, an abatement technology that is efficient for one firm may be inefficient for others.

▶ The regulatory policy decreases the incentives to develop more efficient abatement technologies. The command part of the policy specifies a maximum volume of waste for each firm, so there is no incentive to cut the volume of waste below the maximum allowed. In other words, the benefit of developing new technologies is relatively small because there is no payoff from using them. In contrast, a pollution tax provides the right incentives: If the firm develops a new technology that cuts pollution, it will pay less in pollution taxes.

A command-and-control policy causes firms to use inefficient abatement technologies, so production costs will be higher than they would be under a pollution tax.

Market Effects of Pollution Regulations

How do the market effects of pollution regulation compare to the effects of a pollution tax? Recall that the uniform abatement policy achieves the same reduction in pollution at a higher cost because it doesn't exploit differences in abatement costs across firms. In addition, the "control" part of command and control may lead to relatively costly abatement techniques because there's no incentive to develop better ones. This will cause the supply curve for the polluting good to shift upward by a larger amount than it would with a tax. A larger supply shift causes a larger increase in the equilibrium price and a larger reduction in quantity. The inefficiency of regulations is passed on to consumers, who pay higher prices.

One advantage of the command-and-control policy is its predictability. The policy specifies how much waste each firm can produce, so we can predict the total volume of waste. In contrast, we don't know exactly how firms will respond to the pollution tax—they could pollute a little or a lot, depending on the tax and the cost of abating pollution—so it is difficult to predict the total volume of waste that will be emitted.

We've seen that one problem with traditional environmental policy is that it is inflexible. It doesn't allow firms to use the most efficient abatement methods available. For an example of different abatement strategies, read "A Closer Look: Dear Abby and Environmental Policy."

A CLOSER LOOK

Dear Abby and Environmental Policy

A person with the moniker "Dreading Winter" wrote to advice columnist Abigail Van Buren with a pollution problem.[2] Her neighbors heated their home with a wood-burning stove, and the smell and smoke from the wood fire gave Dreading Winter burning eyes, a stuffy nose, and painful sinuses. She offered the neighbors $500 to stop burning wood, but they declined the offer. The readers of "Dear Abby" offered the following suggestions to Dreading Winter:

▶ Buy the neighbors a catalytic add-on for the wood stove or a wood-chip gasifier for an oil furnace. In either case, there would be much less air pollution from burning wood.

▶ Soak a towel in water, swish it around the room, and watch the smoke disappear.

▶ Leave a saucer of vinegar in each room to eliminate the smoke odor.

▶ Pay your neighbors to hire a chimney sweep to clean their flue.

▶ Seal and caulk your windows to keep the smoke outside (at a cost less than $500).

▶ Use the $500 to purchase an air purifier for your home.

These suggestions demonstrate a fundamental idea behind environmental economics: There is usually more than one way to deal with a pollution problem. The economic question is: What is the most efficient (least costly) way to reduce the problem? In some cases, it may be more efficient to prevent the pollution (switch to an alternative fuel or install a catalytic add-on to the stove) than to clean up the environment after it has been polluted (install an air purifier). In other cases, cleanup will be more efficient than prevention.

Marketable Pollution Permits

In recent years, policymakers have developed a new approach to environmental policy. It involves **marketable pollution permits**, sometimes called "pollution allowances." Here is how a government runs a system of marketable pollution permits:

▶ Pick a target pollution level for a particular area.
▶ Issue just enough permits to meet the pollution target.
▶ Allow firms to buy and sell the permits among themselves.

In the policy world, this is known as a "cap-and-trade" system: The government "caps" the emissions of each firm through its allocation of permits and then allows firms to trade them.

Voluntary Exchange and Marketable Permits

Making pollution permits marketable is sensible because it allows mutually beneficial exchanges between firms with different abatement costs. This is another illustration of the principle of voluntary exchange:

THE *Principle* OF VOLUNTARY EXCHANGE

A voluntary exchange between two people makes both people better off.

Firms will buy and sell pollution permits only when an exchange will make both firms better off. This happens when the firms have different abatement costs.

To illustrate the effects of marketable permits, let's return to the example of electricity generators with different abatement costs, shown in Table 9.1. Suppose the government issues each firm thee pollution permits, allowing it to generate 3 tons of SO_2 per hour. Here is a voluntary exchange that will make both firms better off and decrease abatement costs without changing the total amount of pollution.

▶ If a high-cost firm got a fourth permit, the firm could avoid the fifth ton of abatement and save $4,100 in abatement cost. Therefore, the firm is willing to pay up to $4,100 for another permit.
▶ If a low-cost firm gave up one of its permits, its abatement cost would increase by $3,500, so the firm is willing to accept as little as $3,500 for one of its permits.

The firms could cut a deal by splitting the difference between the willingness to pay ($4,100) and the willingness to accept ($3,500). If they agreed on a price of $3,800, each would get a net benefit of $300. The high-cost firm would pay $3,800 to save $4,100 in abatement cost; the low-cost firm would receive $3,800 but pay only $3,500 in additional abatement cost. Making the permits marketable exploits differences in abatement costs across firms, so we as a society can achieve the same level of abatement at a lower total cost.

The first program of marketable pollution permits, started in 1976 by the U.S. Environmental Protection Agency, allowed limited trading of permits for several air-borne pollutants. Trading was later extended to lead in gasoline (in 1985) and then to the chemicals responsible for the depletion of the ozone layer (in 1988). As we'll see later in the chapter, there are now active markets for permits to discharge sulfur dioxide, carbon dioxide, and nitrogen oxides.

Supply, Demand, and the Price of Marketable Permits

We can use a model of supply and demand to represent the market for pollution permits. Figure 9.5 depicts a trading system introduced in the Los Angeles basin for smog pollutants like NO_x. The supply curve for permits is vertical at the fixed number of permits provided by the government. The demand for permits comes from firms that can use a permit to avoid paying for pollution abatement, and the willingness to pay for a permit equals the savings in abatement costs. In Figure 9.5, the demand curve for permits is negatively sloped, meaning that the larger the number of permits available, the lower the willingness to pay for a permit. This is sensible because with more permits and pollution, the marginal cost of abatement will be relatively low. With a fixed supply of 100 permits in 1994, the equilibrium price, shown by the intersection of the demand curve and the 1994 supply curve, is $7.

Under the LA smog program, the number of NO_x permits decreased each year, and in 2003 reached its goal of cutting NO_x discharges to 30% of the level attained in 1994.[3] In Figure 9.5, the decrease in the number of permits from 100 to 30 shifts the

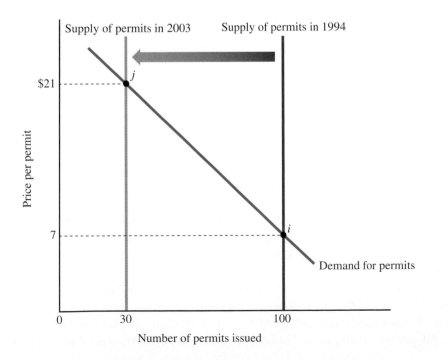

FIGURE 9.5

The Market for Pollution Permits
The equilibrium price of permits is shown by the intersection of the demand curve and the vertical supply curve. The supply curve is vertical because each year the government specifies a fixed number of permits. A decrease in the number of permits shifts the supply curve to the left, increasing the equilibrium price.

supply curve to the left, increasing the equilibrium price of permits from $7 to $21. Polluters in Los Angeles responded to the higher permit prices by abating more. The Los Angeles Department of Water and Power installed abatement equipment—at a cost of $40 million—because abatement was cheaper than buying pollution permits. Libbey Glass Company installed low-pollution burners in its plant, dropping its emissions below the volume allowed by its permits. The company sold its extra permits to other firms, generating income for Libbey. The firms that bought the permits from Libbey were able to continue production using their existing abatement equipment.

Application: Marketable Permits for Sulfur Dioxide

The Clean Air Act of 1990 established a system of marketable pollution permits (also know as allowances) for SO_2. Under the "cap-and-trade" program, in 1990 the government issued permits for SO_2 emissions based on a firm's emission levels 10 years earlier. Each company initially received enough permits to discharge between 50 and 70% of the volume it had discharged a decade earlier, and over time, the number of permits decreased. Firms can also buy or sell the permits. For example, if a permit were priced at $160 (per ton of pollution emitted), a firm with an abatement cost of more than $160 can buy a permit from a firm with an abatement cost of less than $160. A report from the National Acid Precipitation Assessment Program (NAPAP) showed that being able to buy and sell permits lowered the total cost of abatement by 15 to 20%.[4] By 2002, total SO_2 emissions dropped to about half of what they were in 1970.

The permits for SO_2 pollution are now bought and sold on the Chicago Board of Trade.[5] Each year the Environmental Protection Agency issues permits to existing SO_2 sources but withholds some permits for auction. Utilities can also put their permits up for bid on the Chicago Board of Trade. In 2002, a total of 127,388 permits were auctioned at an average price of $167 per ton. Individuals and environmental groups are allowed to buy the permits and, if they wish, reduce pollution by withdrawing them from the market. In 2001, a total of 31 permits went to schools and environmental groups, including the students mentioned in the chapter opener, who paid $181 for a permit.[6]

Why Did the Price of Permits Drop?

In the last year, the price of marketable SO_2 permits in a certain state dropped by 20%. During that time, the state's economy was stable and the number of permits issued by the state didn't change. A recent news article highlighted technological advances in smokestack scrubbers, which remove sulfur from the gases emitted by power plants. Why did the price of pollution permits drop?

The key to solving this puzzle is the innovation in scrubber technology. A pollution permit allows a firm to avoid paying for abatement, and the higher the abatement cost that can be avoided, the larger the amount a firm is willing to pay for a permit. A technological innovation that decreases abatement costs will decrease firms' willingness to pay for a permit, so the price will drop. In graphical terms, a decrease in the benefits of having a permit (savings in abatement cost) shifts the demand curve for permits downward and to the left because buying and using the new equipment will become cheaper relative to buying permits. With a fixed number of permits, the equilibrium price will drop. ∎

TEST Your Understanding

4. Explain why a command-and-control policy shifts the market supply curve by a larger amount.
5. Complete the statement with "low" or "high": Under a system of marketable pollution permits, a firm with _____ abatement costs will buy permits from a firm with _____ abatement costs.
6. Why does a switch to marketable pollution permits decrease total abatement costs?

Global Warming and Public Policy

Here is a simple experiment that explains global warming. On a warm day, park your car in a sunny spot, close the windows, and wait. Solar energy in the form of visual and ultraviolet light will come through the car windows and heat the air in the car. This is the greenhouse effect: If all the windows are closed, there is no way for the heat to escape, so the temperature in the car (or in a greenhouse) will increase.

The windows of the car are like the earth's atmosphere. Solar energy comes through the atmosphere and heats the air near the earth's surface. Certain types of gases in the atmosphere (called greenhouse gases) trap this heat close to the earth's surface and are beneficial. Without these gases, the earth's surface temperature would be far below freezing, so most forms of life would die off. Unfortunately, we are pumping more of these greenhouse gases into the atmosphere, and according to most experts, the result is that the earth's temperature is increasing. Just as rolling up a window in a parked car increases the temperature in the car, increasing the volume of greenhouse gases increases the temperature near the earth's surface.

The volume of carbon dioxide, by far the most important greenhouse gas, has increased by about 25% over the last century. Humans have altered the carbon cycle, the movement of carbon between the earth's atmosphere and the plant material on the earth's surface. When a plant grows, it converts carbon dioxide from the atmosphere into carbon and stores this carbon in its tissue. When we burn oil, coal, and gas (the fossilized remains of old plants), the carbon stored in the plant material combines with oxygen to form carbon dioxide, which is released back into the atmosphere. To put it bluntly, plants suck in carbon dioxide and we blow it back out when we burn plant material. In the last century, we have blown out more carbon than plants have been able to suck in, so the volume of carbon dioxide in the atmosphere has increased. By digging up stored carbon and burning it, we've thrown the carbon cycle out of whack and increased the volume of greenhouse gases in the atmosphere.

The Consequences of Global Warming

Most scientists agree that human activity is a factor in global warming. A recent report from National Academy of Sciences, the nation's most prestigious scientific body, concluded that "greenhouse gases are accumulating in the Earth's atmosphere as a result of

The National Academy of Sciences has concluded that greenhouse gases have raised sea levels.

human activities" and that the "human induced warming and associated sea level changes are expected to continue through the 21st century."[7] The report notes that there is considerable uncertainty about how our ecosystems will respond to a rapid increase in carbon dioxide and temperatures. The practical policy question is: Should we wait to find out the consequences of an increase in atmospheric carbon dioxide, or should we do something now to reduce the accumulation of greenhouse gases?

How would an increase in temperatures affect the earth's environment and the global economy? Most scientists expect total rainfall to increase, with some areas getting more rain and others getting less. The increase in carbon dioxide will make all plants—crops and weeds alike—grow faster. Overall, the net effect on agriculture is likely to be negative because scientists expect less rainfall in areas with fertile soil and more rainfall in areas with less productive soil. An increase in global temperatures would also melt glaciers and the polar ice caps, raising sea levels. As a result, a large amount of land currently used for agriculture or living space could be inundated. Of course, we could build dikes to protect low-lying areas, but such protective measures are very expensive.

The Kyoto Agreement and Developing Nations

The United Nations officially recognized the greenhouse effect in 1995, when its International Panel on Climate Change noted that human activity had a "discernible influence" on global temperatures. In 1997, the Kyoto Conference on global warming produced an agreement under which the largest industrial nations pledged to reduce their carbon dioxide emissions to just below 1990 levels by the year 2008. In 2001, the United States government announced that it would not participate in the Kyoto Agreement. To meet the abatement targets, the participating nations must make large and costly changes in their energy systems.

Developing nations were exempted from the Kyoto deal over the strenuous objections of some industrialized nations. As the economies of developing nations grow over the next few decades, they are likely to rely on coal, which is inexpensive and easy to transport, as a major source of energy. Because coal generates about twice as much carbon dioxide as natural gas, the nations will produce a large volume of carbon dioxide emissions. The exemption of the developing nations is a stumbling block in the effort to control the accumulation of greenhouse gases.

The Effects of a Carbon Tax

One approach to carbon emissions is to impose a tax equal to the marginal external cost of carbon. Because of the uncertainties associated with predicting the effects of carbon emissions on the earth's climate and the economic consequences of climate changes, any estimates of external cost from carbon are highly speculative.

Although we don't know what the appropriate **carbon tax** would be, we do know that a system of fuel taxes based on the carbon content of each fuel would decrease carbon emissions. For example, a carbon tax of $100 per ton would translate into a tax of $0.28 per gallon of gasoline (about 14% of the price), a tax of $12 per barrel of oil (about 50% of the price), and a tax of $70 per ton of coal (over twice the price).[8] The tax on coal would be relatively high because of its higher carbon content. A carbon tax would reduce greenhouse emissions in several ways:

Carbon tax
A tax based on a fuel's carbon content.

▶ The price of gasoline would increase, causing people to drive less and buy more energy-efficient vehicles.
▶ The tax would increase the price of electricity, decreasing the quantity of electricity demanded and the quantity of fossil fuels burned.
▶ The higher price of home heating would cause people to turn down their thermostats and improve the heating efficiency of their homes, perhaps by installing energy-efficient windows or more insulation.
▶ Some electricity producers would switch from coal to natural gas, which has a lower carbon content and thus would have a lower carbon tax. Others would switch to noncarbon energy sources such as the wind, the sun, and geothermal sources.

In 2002, New Zealand announced plans to implement a tax of $12 per ton of carbon, starting in 2007. New Zealand ranks fourth (behind the United States, Australia, and Canada) in per capita carbon emissions. About half of the greenhouse gases come from the methane emitted from the country's 50 million sheep and cattle during digestion.[9] However, New Zealand farmers and ranchers will be exempt from the tax, over the strenuous objection of coal producers, who will pay a 20% tax.

Marketable Permits and Offsets for Carbon?

One alternative to a carbon tax is a system of marketable permits for carbon emissions. Under a cap-and-trade system, each electric utility would be required to either cut its carbon emissions or purchase carbon permits (or allowances) from utilities that cut their emissions more than the mandated amount. This approach has been adopted by

Denmark, which set a goal of reducing greenhouse gases from electricity generators by 20% by 2005.[10] Other countries around the world are developing plans for similar cap-and-trade plans.

A second alternative is to combine marketable permits with **pollution offsets** (also known as reduction credits). When a company pays for a project that reduces greenhouse gas emissions, the project offsets a part of the firm's own emissions. This approach has been adopted by the Chicago Climate Exchange (CCX), which facilitates both trades among polluters and offsets, such as reforestation and renewable energy projects. Participation in CCX is voluntary. When a firm joins CCX, it agrees to reduce its contribution to greenhouse gases by 4% within four years, by (a) cutting its own emissions, (b) paying for extra reductions by other firms, or (c) paying for offset projects such as reforestation. Among the members of CCX are Ford Motor Company, Dupont, Motorola, IBM, American Electric Power, the City of Chicago, and Tufts University. In the first auctions in 2003, the price for CO_2 emissions was about $1 per ton.

The experience of American Electric Power (AEP), the nation's largest electricity producer, illustrates how CCX works.[11] AEP bought 10,000 acres of fallow land and planted walnut trees, which each year will withdraw about 71,000 tons of carbon dioxide from the air and convert it into solid wood. As long as the wood doesn't burn or decompose, AEP can use the trees to offset some of its carbon emissions. The cost of tree farming is $1.25 per ton of carbon absorbed or "sequestered," which is small relative to the alternative—converting the company's generators from coal to natural gas at a cost of about $50 per ton of carbon abated. One problem with the tree-farming approach is that it would require a huge amount of land—about 1 million acres—to meet the utility's obligation to cut its carbon emissions by 4%. It is clear that the utility will be forced to take other measures to reduce its emissions.

In 2003, worldwide trading in carbon dioxide credits totaled 71 million tons, a tiny but growing fraction of the world's 7 billion tons of carbon emissions.[12] The average price for a CO_2 credit was $5 per ton, and most of the credits were issued for projects in Latin America, Asia, and Europe. For another example of reducing atmospheric CO_2, read "A Closer Look: Giving the Gift of CO_2."

Pollution offset

A credit received for supporting a project that either reduces the pollution emissions of another firm or organization or results in the absorption of pollutants; also known as a reduction credit.

A CLOSER LOOK

Giving the Gift of CO_2

Dawn Schrepel, a consultant in Washington D.C., found the perfect thank-you gift for each of her 10 interns: a ton of carbon dioxide. She purchased the CO_2 for $17 per ton through Natsource, an energy brokerage firm in New York City. Ms. Schrepel didn't hand her interns giant tanks of CO_2, but instead gave them a piece of paper stipulating that a 1,200-acre patch of grassland in a natural preserve in Illinois would be maintained in its natural state, meaning that the ton of carbon dioxide embedded in the plant material would stay in the plants, not be released into the atmosphere.[13]

Ozone Pollution and the Automobile

Ozone pollution (more commonly known as smog) is one of our most persistent environmental problems. Smog results from the mixing of several pollutants, including nitrogen oxides, sulfur dioxide, and volatile organic compounds. Although atmospheric ozone is beneficial because it blocks harmful ultraviolet light, ozone is harmful when it comes in contact with living things, as it does at ground level. Smog causes health problems, triggering asthma attacks in the 15 million people in the United States who suffer from asthma and worsening other respiratory problems, leading to premature deaths. Smog also retards plant growth and decreases agricultural productivity. Because of health and other problems created by smog, The Environmental Protection Agency (EPA) has established standards for smog concentrations in urban areas. Nonetheless, on 7,600 different occasions in 1999 ozone pollution levels rose above these healthful levels in 43 U.S. states.

The Breathmobile provides a visible reminder of the health effects of smog in Los Angeles.[14] The mobile asthma clinic, housed in a 34-foot recreational vehicle and staffed by a physician, a nurse, and a respiratory therapist, provides free diagnosis and treatment for asthmatic schoolchildren in low-income neighborhoods of Los Angeles. The clinic identifies and treats children who experience aggravated asthma symptoms on smoggy days.

The automobile is by far the biggest source of the pollutants that lead to smog. We currently use a command-and-control approach to regulate automobile pollution: The Environmental Protection Agency tells automakers what abatement equipment to install in cars. The equipment does not control the total emissions of the car, just the pollution per mile driven. If people buy cleaner cars but then drive more miles, total emissions can actually increase.

An alternative to the current policy is to levy an annual pollution tax on each car.[15] At the end of the year, a car would be tested to determine the volume of pollution per mile driven. The tax per mile would equal the volume of pollution per mile times a tax

The automobile is by far the largest creator of smog, causing respiratory problems for millions of people.

per unit of pollution. At the end of a year, the car owner would pay a pollution tax equal to the tax per mile times the miles driven during the year. For example, if a car generated 2 units of pollution per mile, and the tax per unit of pollution were $0.01, the tax per mile would be $0.02. If the car were driven 10,000 miles each year, the annual pollution tax would be $200. The pollution tax would encourage people to buy cleaner cars, maintain their emissions equipment, drive less, and use alternative modes of transportation. The tax is consistent with the idea that people should pay the full cost of driving their automobiles, including the external costs.

One alternative to a direct pollution tax on automobile travel is a gasoline tax. According to a recent study, the smog-related damages from automobiles average about $0.02 per mile driven, which translates to an average of $0.40 per gallon of gasoline. Burning gasoline contributes to global warming, and if the appropriate carbon tax is $100 per ton of carbon, the associated gasoline tax would be about $0.28 per gallon. Adding the $0.40 tax for smog damage and the $0.28 tax for global warming, the gasoline tax would be $0.68 per gallon. This tax would be added to the current gasoline taxes (a federal tax of $0.18 and state taxes that average about $0.22) because these current taxes pay for highway construction and maintenance. A gasoline tax would be inferior to a real pollution tax because a driver's gasoline tax bill would not depend directly on pollution, so there would be less incentive to drive cleaner cars.

Figure 9.6 shows the market effects of a gasoline tax equal to $0.68 per gallon. The tax shifts the supply curve upward by the amount of the tax, as shown by points *i* and *t*. The new equilibrium is shown by point *f*, with an equilibrium price of $2.00 (up from $1.60) and an equilibrium quantity of 80 million gallons (down from 100 million gallons). The equilibrium price rises by $0.40, which is less than the $0.68 tax. As we saw earlier in the book, a tax is shifted forward to consumers in the form of a price hike ($0.40 in this example) and backward onto input suppliers in the form of lower prices for inputs. The decrease in the quantity of gasoline produced will decrease the demand for crude oil, decreasing its price. In other words, part of the gasoline tax will be borne by people and governments who own crude oil.

FIGURE 9.6

The Market Effects of a Gasoline Tax

A gasoline tax of $0.68 per gallon shifts the supply curve upward by the amount of the tax, and increases the equilibrium price by $0.40. The tax is shifted forward onto consumers, who pay $0.40 more per gallon, and backward onto input suppliers, who receive lower prices for crude oil.

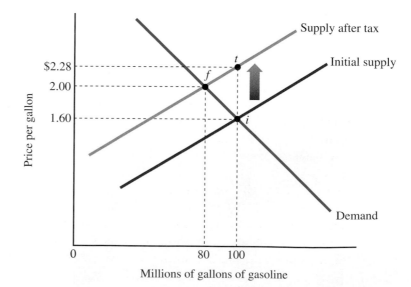

TEST Your Understanding

7. Suppose a carbon tax increases the price of electricity by 10% and the price elasticity of demand for electricity is 0.28. Predict the change in the quantity of electricity demanded.
8. Suppose a gasoline tax increases the price of gasoline by 30%. List the possible responses by consumers that would contribute to a decrease in the quantity of gasoline demanded.
9. If it is sensible to tax people for the CO_2 emitted by their cars, should we subsidize them for growing trees?

Economic Experiment

Pollution Permits

In this pollution-permit experiment, students play the role of paper firms that buy or sell pollution permits. The class is divided into groups of three to five students, with each group representing a firm that produces 1 ton of paper per period. The instructor provides each firm with data about its cost of production. The cost depends on how much waste the firm generates: The smaller the volume of waste, the higher the production cost. Here is an example:

Gallons of waste generated	2	3	4
Production cost per ton	$36	$26	$20

Each firm receives three pollution permits for each of the five trading periods. A firm that does not sell any of its permits to other firms has the right to generate 3 gallons of waste in that period. A firm that sells one of its three permits can generate only 2 gallons of waste, and a firm that buys a permit from another firm can generate 4 gallons of waste.

At the beginning of each of the five trading periods, firms meet in the trading area to buy or sell pollution permits for that day. Each firm can buy or sell one permit per day. Once a transaction has been arranged, the buyer and the seller inform the instructor of the transaction, record the transaction on their report cards, and then leave the trading area. The firm's objective is to maximize profit, and each trading period, we compute the firm's profit with the following equation:

profit = price of paper − production cost + revenue from permit sold − cost of permit purchased

In each period, a firm will either buy or sell a permit, so we compute the firm's profit with just three numbers. For example, using the production cost numbers shown in the table, if the price of paper is $50 per ton and a firm buys a permit for $5, the firm's profit is:

profit = $50 − $20 + 0 − $5 = $30

If another firm sold a permit for $5, the firm's profit would be $16:

profit = $50 − $36 + $5 − 0 = $19

For the fourth and fifth trading periods, several environmental groups have the option of buying pollution permits. Each environmental group is given a fixed sum of money to spend on permits, and its objective is to get as many permits as possible, reducing the total volume of pollution in the process. ●

USING THE TOOLS

This chapter explores the merits of several environmental policies, including a pollution tax, pollution regulations, and marketable pollution permits. Now you can use what you've learned to do your own economic analysis of environmental problems.

1. Market Effects of a Carbon Tax

Consider the market for gasoline. In the initial equilibrium, the price is $2.00 per gallon and the quantity is 100 million gallons. The price elasticity of demand is 1.0, and the price elasticity of supply is 2.0. Suppose the government imposes a carbon tax, and the tax is expected to shift the gasoline supply curve to the left by 24%.
a. Use a supply–demand diagram to show the market effects of the carbon tax.
b. Predict the new equilibrium price and quantity of gasoline.

2. Trading Pollution Permits

Consider two firms whose marginal abatement costs are shown here. Suppose the government issues thee pollution permits to each firm and then allows the firms to buy and sell the permits.

a. Consider the possibility of a single pollution permit changing hands. If the firms split the difference between the willingness to pay for a permit and the willingness to accept, what's the price of a permit?
b. Consider next the possibility that more than one permit will change hands. Once the buying and selling of permits has stopped, how much pollution will each firm generate?

3. The Optimal Level of Pollution and the Pollution Tax

Suppose the marginal benefit of pollution abatement is $29 for the first unit abated and decreases by $1 for each additional unit, to $28 for the second unit, $27 for the third, and so on. The marginal cost of abatement is $2 for the first unit abated and increases by $2 for each additional unit abated, to $4 for the second unit, $6 for the third unit, and so on.
a. What is the optimal level of pollution abatement?
b. Compute the pollution tax that would generate the optimum level of pollution.

Tons of Pollution Discharged (per hour)	Tons of Pollution Abated (per hour)	Marginal Abatement Cost	
		Firm L	Firm H
5	7	$2,200	$3,100
4	8	2,400	3,300
3	9	2,600	3,500
2	10	2,800	3,700
1	11	3,000	3,900
0	12	3,200	4,100

SUMMARY

The theme of this chapter is that the best way to control pollution is to rely on the exchange principle and markets. A pollution tax internalizes the external cost of pollution, causing firms to cut the pollution per unit of output and consumers to buy less of a polluting product. A cap-and-trade system for emissions achieves a pollution target at the lowest possible cost because the firms with the lowest cost do most of the abatement. The use of offsets (pollution-reduction credits) provides another low-cost means of cleaning up the environment. Here are the main points of the chapter:

1 The optimum level of pollution abatement is where the marginal benefit equals the marginal cost.

2 A tax on the emissions of electricity generators would decrease total emissions as firms switch to cleaner fuels and consumers buy less electricity at the higher price.

3 Compared to a pollution tax, traditional pollution regulations lead to higher production costs and higher product prices.

4 The economic approaches to global warming include a carbon tax and a cap-and-trade system of carbon dioxide permits.

5 Urban smog is a continuing problem, in part because the traditional command-and-control policies are less effective than an annual automobile pollution tax.

KEY TERMS

carbon tax, 209
command-and-control policy, 202
external cost of production, 198

marketable pollution permits, 204
pollution offset, 210
pollution tax, 198

private cost of production, 198
social cost of production, 198
uniform abatement policy, 201

PROBLEMS AND DISCUSSION QUESTIONS

1 Use a supply–demand graph to show a situation in which the equilibrium quantity of a polluting good is 20 tons but a pollution tax decreases the equilibrium quantity of the good to zero. Is this situation likely to occur?

2 The following table shows the production cost per ton of paper for different levels of pollution. Suppose the government imposes a pollution tax of $8 per gallon of waste. How much waste will the typical firm abate, and how much will it generate? Illustrate your answer with a completely labeled graph.

Pollution Discharged (gallons)	Pollution Abated (gallons)	Production cost (per ton of paper)
6	0	$20
5	1	22
4	2	26
3	3	32
2	4	40
1	5	50
0	6	62

3 Suppose the government adopts a zero-tolerance pollution policy for the production of paper. In other words, the government requires each paper mill to eliminate all its water pollution. The production costs of the typical firm are shown in the table for Problem 2.
   a. What is the production cost per ton under the zero-tolerance policy?
   b. If the government uses a pollution tax to implement its zero-tolerance policy, what is the smallest tax that would cause the typical firm to voluntarily pick zero pollution?

4 Consider the use of marketable pollution permits for the control of sulfur dioxide emissions from two electric utilities: Old Power and Light (OPL) and Young Power and Light (YPL). The following table shows the production cost for the two utilities with different volumes of sulfur dioxide emissions:

Tons of Sulfur Dioxide Discharged	Production Cost for OPL	Production Cost for YPL
10	$10,000	$10,000
9	12,000	10,500
8	16,000	11,500
7	22,000	11,500

Assume that the government issues 10 marketable pollution permits to OPL and 8 marketable permits to YPL.
   a. Will any permits be traded? Explain.
   b. Suppose the government had issued 9 permits to YPL and 9 permits to OPL. Will any permits be traded? If so, predict the equilibrium price for a permit.

5 One of the objections to a carbon tax is that it would be regressive: Poor people would pay a large fraction of their incomes to cover the tax. How could we overcome this objection?

6 You are the economic consultant to a member of Congress. Someone has just introduced a bill that would impose a $50 carbon tax, which will, of course, affect the market for home heating oil. Would you expect the entire tax to be paid by consumers? Why or why not? Your job is to determine which side of the market—consumers or input suppliers—will pay the larger part of the tax. What additional information do you need?

7 Consider the effects of a decrease in the abatement costs shown in Table 9.1. Suppose each of the cost numbers decreases by $2,000. Predict the price of a pollution permit.

8 Recall the discussion of how the low-cost and high-cost firms in Table 9.1 react to a pollution tax of $3,500. The low-cost firm abates 6 tons, and the high-cost firm abates only 4 tons. Does the fact that one firm is responsible for more abatement strike you as unfair? Why or why not?

9 A state issued some marketable permits for sulfur dioxide emissions to several electricity generators and set up a special marketing office to help firms buy and sell the permits. Most of the permits were given to the utilities with the oldest generating facilities. One year later, none of the permits had been bought or sold. This was puzzling to the state officials and the people in the marketing office. Why didn't the marketable-permit program work? How could the program be changed to encourage trading?

MODEL ANSWERS TO QUESTIONS

Chapter-Opening Questions

1 As shown in Figure 9.1, the optimum level for the year 2010 is 1.1 million tons.
2 The price of electricity would increase by 4%, and the volume of SO_2 would decrease to 11% of its current level, and the volume of NO_x would decrease to 30% of its current level.
3 She bought the CO_2 as a means of offsetting carbon emissions that contribute to global warming.
4 About $0.40 per gallon.

Test Your Understanding

1 The cost of abating the first unit of pollution in relatively low, but the marginal cost increases as a firm uses more sophisticated and costly means to reduce pollution further.

2 A pollution tax transfers an external cost, borne by people outside the firm, to the firm itself.

3 A tax increases the equilibrium price of the polluting good, and consumers buy less of it.

4 The policy increases production costs by a larger amount because it does not exploit differences in abatement costs and may employ relatively inefficient abatement technology.

5 High, low.

6 Low-cost firms sell some of their permits to high-cost firms, and the extra abatement cost incurred by the low-cost firms is less than the abatement cost saved by the high-cost firms.

7 The quantity demanded decreases by 2.8% (= 10% times 0.28).

8 Driving less frequently to the mall or grocery store; ridesharing for work trips; switching to mass transit, walking, or biking; moving closer to work or other frequent destinations; buying a more fuel-efficient car; getting more frequent tune-ups.

9 A tree decreases the volume of carbon dioxide in the atmosphere and diminishes the problem of global warming, so there is an external benefit. A subsidy could internalize the externality, encouraging people to plant and maintain trees.

NOTES

1. Spencer Banzhaf, Dallas Burtraw, and Karen Palmer, "Efficient Emission Fees in the U.S. Electricity Sector," Resources for the Future Discussion Paper 02-45, October 2002.
2. Abigail Van Buren, "Aid for Reader's Winter Woe," Sacramento Bee, February 15, 1984.
3. Gary Polakovic, "Cost of Clean Air Credits Soars in Southland," Los Angeles Times, September 5, 2000, page B.
4. 1990 Integrated Assessment Report (Washington, DC: U.S. National Acid Precipitation Assessment Program, 1991).
5. Environmental Protection Agency, "EPA Announces Results of Acid Rain Reduction Auction," Environmental News, March 28, 2002.
6. HWS helps clear air, Syracuse Herald-American, April 8, 2001.
7. National Academy of Science, Climate Change Science: An Analysis of Some Key Questions (Washington, DC: National Academy Press, 2001).
8. William D. Nordhaus, "Economic Approaches to Global Warming, in Global Warming: Economic Policy," Responses, edited by Rudiger Dornbush and James M. Poterba (Cambridge, MA: MIT Press, 1991).
9. Graeme Peters, "New Zealand Plans Carbon Tax to Meet Kyoto Targets," Reuters News Service October 18, 2002.
10. Sigurd Lauge Pedersen, "The Danish CO2 Emissions Trading System," RECIEL vol. 9, no. 3, 2000, pp. 223–231; "Domestic Emissions Trading: Denmark," National Round Table on the Environment and the Economy (*http://www.nrtee-trnee.ca/EmissionsTrading*).
11. Thomas Kellner, "Got Gas?" Forbes, March 17, 2003, p. 56.
12. "Greenhouse Gas Trading Doubled in 2003—World Bank," Reuters News Service, December 4, 2003.
13. Nina Sovich, "Selling Smoke," Time Inside Business April 2003.
14. South Coast Air Quality Management District, "New Mobile Asthma Clinic to Serve L.A." County Children, May 12, 2000.
15. Edwin S. Mills and Lawrence J. White, "Government Policies Towards Automobile Emissions Control," in Approaches to Air Pollution Control, edited by Anne Frielaender (Cambridge, MA: MIT Press, 1978).

An Overview of Government Spending and Taxes

External Benefits and Inefficiency

Public Goods and External Benefits
Private Goods with External Benefits
Public Goods and the Free-Rider Problem
Overcoming the Free-Rider Problem

Applications: Asteroids and Wildlife

Asteroid Diversion
Preservation of Wolves

Public Choice

Voting and the Median-Voter Rule
Alternative Models of Government:
    Self-Interests and Special Interests
Which Theory or Viewpoint Is Correct?
Using the Tools

Public Goods and Public Choice

ere is the text from a TV newscast in the year 2070:

> Boomer, the 200-meter asteroid on a collision path with the earth, is expected to land at about 10:00 tomorrow morning in the heart of the world's breadbasket, the American Midwest. The energy expected to be released by the impact will exceed the total explosive yield of all the nuclear weapons on the planet. Although Boomer is much smaller than the asteroid that caused the extinction of the dinosaurs about 65 million years ago, it is large enough to cause significant changes in the world's climate. The collision will generate a stratospheric dust cloud that will inhibit photosynthesis and retard plant growth, resulting in lower agricultural yields and higher food prices throughout the world.

> Could this catastrophe have been averted? Yes, according to scientists at the National Aeronautics and Space Administration. In 1996, scientists developed the technology for an asteroid-diversion system: Large optical telescopes would detect an asteroid on a collision course with the earth, and an orbiting gossamer mirror of coated polyester would focus a tight beam of sunlight on the asteroid, vaporizing enough of its surface to change its path. In a U.N. debate over the asteroid-diversion system, everyone agreed that the potential benefits of the system would outweigh the costs, but no one was willing to pay for the system. Why couldn't the nations of the world agree on such an important program, one that would have prevented tomorrow's catastrophe?

n this chapter, we'll see that if a particular good generates external benefits, government intervention can make beneficial transactions happen. For example, the cost of an asteroid-diversion program is so high that no single person would provide such a program. We will never have such a program—even if its benefits exceed its costs—unless we make a collective decision about what sort of diversion program to develop and how to pay for it. The purpose of government is to help make this sort of collective decision. The hypothetical newscast suggests that some sort of multinational arrangement will be necessary to launch an asteroid-diversion program.

This chapter explores the economic challenges associated with providing—and paying for—goods that generate external benefits. We'll also take a look at some alternative theories on government decision-making. Here are some practical questions that we'll answer:

1 What would happen if we eliminated taxes and paid for government programs with voluntary contributions instead?
2 Is it sensible to pay landowners to host endangered wildlife such as wolves and spotted owls?
3 It often seems there is little difference between candidates running for election. Why?

An Overview of Government Spending and Taxes

Although it's convenient to talk about "the" government, there are thousands of governments in the United States, and each citizen deals with at least three different levels of government. Figure 10.1 shows the budget breakdown for the three levels of government. There are more than 80,000 local governments in the United States, including municipalities (city governments), counties, school districts, and special districts responsible for providing services such as water, fire protection, and libraries. Local governments spend most of their money on education (kindergarten through high school), public welfare and health (payments to poor households and support for public hospitals), highways, fire protection, and police and corrections. For states, the biggest spending programs are education (including colleges and universities), public welfare, highways, health and hospitals, and corrections (state courts and prisons). For the federal government, the biggest spending programs are programs for the elderly (Social Security and Medicare), national defense, income security (payments to the poor), and interest on the national debt.

**Percentages of
Government Spending
on Various Programs**

*Source: Statistical Abstract of
the United States, 2002.*

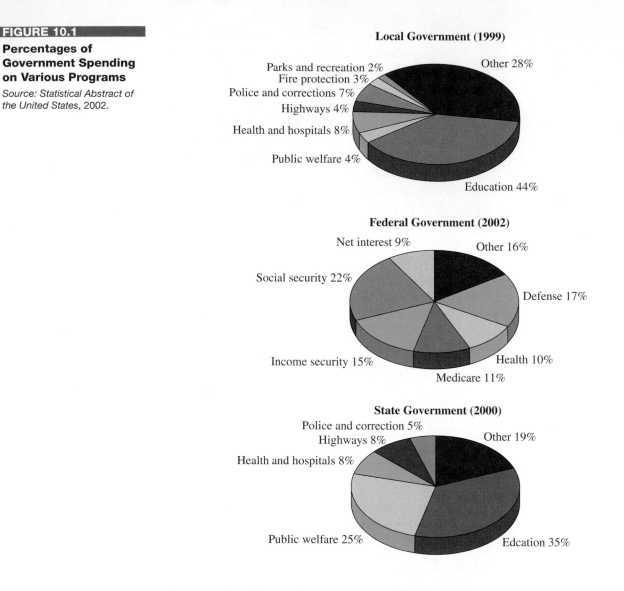

External Benefits and Inefficiency

In Chapter 5, we saw that when there are neither external benefits nor external costs, the market equilibrium is efficient. When a government intervenes in an efficient market, the result is inefficiency. In this chapter, we'll see that a market with external benefits is inefficient, so there is an opportunity for government to promote efficiency.

To illustrate the idea of external benefits and inefficiency, consider a dam built for flood-control purposes. There are 100,000 people in the valley below the dam, and each person gets a $5 benefit from the dam. The total benefit of the dam is $500,000 (equal to 100,000 people times $5 per person), which exceeds the $200,000 total cost of the dam. Because the total benefit exceeds the total cost, the dam should be built. The problem is that no single person will build the dam because the $200,000 cost exceeds the $5 personal benefit. In other words, if we rely on the forces of supply and demand, with each person considering only personal benefits and costs of a dam, it won't be built.

The government can solve this problem by collecting enough taxes to pay for the dam. Suppose the government proposes to collect $2 per person to pay for the dam. The tax raises $200,000 in tax revenue ($2 per person times 100,000 people), which is just high enough to pay the $200,000 cost of the dam. Most people will support this proposal because the $2 tax per person is less than the $5 benefit per person. The government can use its taxing power to provide a good that would otherwise not be provided.

Public Goods and External Benefits

The dam is an example of a **public good**. A public good is available for everyone to utilize, regardless of who pays for it and who doesn't. In contrast, each unit of a **private good** is consumed by a single person or household. For example, only one person can eat a hot dog. If a government hands out free cheese to the poor, is the free cheese a public good or a private good? Although anyone can get in line for the cheese, only one person can actually consume a particular piece of cheese, so the free cheese is a private good that happens to be available free of charge from the government. Similarly, an apartment in a public housing project can be occupied by a single household, so it is a private good provided by the government.

We can be more precise about the difference between public and private goods. Private goods are *rival* in consumption (only one person can consume the good) and *excludable* (a person who does not pay for the good can be prevented from consuming it). Public goods are *nonrival* in consumption: The fact that one person benefits from a good does not prevent another person from benefiting, too. For example, the fact that I benefit from a flood-control dam doesn't reduce your benefit from the dam. Public goods are also *nonexcludable*: It is impractical to exclude people who don't pay. Some examples of public goods are national defense, law enforcement, space exploration, the preservation of endangered species, the protection of the earth's ozone layer, and fireworks shows. If someone refuses to pay for one of these public goods, it would be impractical to prevent that person from consuming or benefiting from the good.

Private Goods with External Benefits

In contrast to a public good, a private good can be utilized by a single person or household. But some private goods generate benefits for people who are not directly consuming the good. For example, suppose if I replace the peeling paint on my house with a fresh coat of paint. I benefit from the new paint because it protects my house from decay and my house will look better, at least to me. Assuming that I've avoided an obnoxious color, my neighbors will also benefit from the improved appearance of the neighborhood.

As another example of a private good with external benefits, consider LoJack, the system used to recover stolen vehicles. A small, silent transmitter hidden in a vehicle allows police to track a stolen car. A thief who steals a LoJack-equipped car won't keep the car for long and is likely to get caught, so LoJack is an effective deterrent to car theft. Car thieves cannot distinguish between cars with and without LoJack, so the system decreases the payoff from car theft in general, decreasing the number of thefts. Therefore, people who install LoJack systems generate benefits for themselves and for other car owners who don't have LoJack.

Public good

A good that is available for everyone to consume, regardless of who pays and who doesn't.

Private good

A good that is consumed by a single person or household.

Another example of a private good with external benefits is education. Most of the benefits of education go to the student because education increases his or her productivity and potential earnings, and presumably makes everyday life easier and more interesting. There are two sorts of external benefits from education:

1 Workplace externalities. In most workplaces, people work in groups and teamwork is important. A well-educated person understands instructions readily and is more likely to suggest ways to improve the production process. As a result, when a well-educated person joins a work team, the productivity of everyone on the team increases. Higher productivity generally leads to higher profits for firms, and members of the team are more likely to earn higher salaries.

2 Civic externalities. Citizens in a democratic society make collective decisions by voting in elections, and each citizen must live with these decisions. A well-educated person is more likely to vote intelligently, so there are external benefits for other citizens.

Because of these external benefits from education, the government uses various policies to encourage people to become educated. Local governments provide free education through high school. States subsidize students at public colleges and universities, providing college education at a fraction of its actual cost. In addition, the federal government provides financial aid to students in both public and private schools.

The government subsidizes other goods that generate external benefits. Subsidies for on-the-job training and education encourage workers and firms to invest in human capital and increase labor productivity. It is sensible for the government to subsidize training and education because some of the benefits are transferred to other firms when workers change employers. Another example is research at universities and other nonprofit organizations. If a research project provides knowledge or technology that leads to the development of new products or the improvement of old ones, the benefits from the project spill over onto consumers and producers. When there are external benefits, the government can encourage people to take actions that benefit other people. By making beneficial transactions happen, the government can increase efficiency.

Public Goods and the Free-Rider Problem

Most public goods are supported by taxes. What would happen if we eliminated taxes and asked people to contribute money to pay for national defense, dams, city streets, and the police? Would people contribute enough money to support these programs at their current levels?

The problem with using voluntary contributions to support public goods is known as the **free-rider problem**. Each person has a financial incentive to try to get the benefits of a public good without paying for it. That is, some people will try to get a "free ride" at the expense of others who do pay. Of course, if everyone tries to get a free ride, there will be no money to support the public good, so it won't be provided. The flip side of the free-rider problem is the chump problem: No one wants to be the chump—the person who gives free rides to other people—so no one contributes any money. The free-rider problem suggests that if taxes were replaced with voluntary contributions, the government would be forced to cut back or eliminate many programs.

Free-rider problem

A problem that occurs when people try to benefit from a public good without paying for it.

Why Build a Three-Faced Clock Tower?

Economic **Puzzle**

Back in the days before inexpensive wristwatches, most people did not carry their own timepieces. Many towns built clock towers to help their citizens keep track of time. The towns paid for the clock towers with voluntary contributions from citizens. One town in the northeastern United States built a four-sided tower but put clock faces on only three sides of the tower. To most people, this seems bizarre. If you build a clock tower, why not put clock faces on all four sides?

The key to solving this puzzle is the free-rider problem. It turns out that one of the town's wealthy citizens refused to contribute money to help build the clock tower. The town officials decided not to put a clock face on the side of the tower facing the wealthy citizen's house. In other words, the citizen tried—unsuccessfully—to get a free ride. The problem is that other citizens on the same side of town also suffered from not seeing the clock. In this case, preventing a free ride by one citizen caused problems for other citizens. ■

Overcoming the Free-Rider Problem

Many organizations, including public radio and television, religious organizations, and charitable organizations, raise money through voluntary contributions. So it appears that some people overcome their inclination to be free riders and contribute voluntarily to organizations that provide public goods. The successful organizations use a number of techniques to encourage people to contribute.

▶ Giving contributors private goods such as coffee mugs, books, musical recordings, and magazine subscriptions. People are more likely to contribute if they get something for it.
▶ Arranging matching contributions. You are more likely to contribute if you know that your $30 contribution will be matched with a contribution from another person.
▶ Appealing to people's sense of civic or moral responsibility.

It's important to note, however, that these organizations are only partly successful in mitigating the free-rider problem. Public radio is one of the success stories, even though the typical public-radio station gets contributions from fewer than a quarter of its listeners.

TEST Your Understanding

1. Explain why the free-rider problem occurs for public goods but not for private goods.
2. Is admission to a nearly empty movie theater a public good or a private good?
3. Is painting your house a public good, a private good, or a private good with external benefits?

Applications: Asteroids and Wildlife

Now that we've discussed some of the economic challenges associated with providing public goods, let's think about two unconventional public goods: The diversion of asteroids and the preservation of wolves.

Asteroid Diversion

How do we apply the concepts of public goods to the issue of protecting the earth from catastrophic collisions with asteroids? On average, the earth is hit by a 200-meter asteroid every 10,000 years, by a 2-kilometer asteroid every million years, and by a 10-kilometer asteroid every 100 million years.[1] As was explained at the beginning of the chapter, we have the technology to divert approaching asteroids.

The diversion of asteroids is a public good in the sense that it is available for everyone's benefit, regardless of who pays and who doesn't. As with any public good, the key to developing an asteroid-diversion program is to collect money to pay for the program. According to NASA scientists, the program would require several new telescopes, which would cost about $50 million to install and about $10 million per year to operate.[2] The cost of the gossamer mirror or the nuclear weapons required to change the path of the asteroid would be $100 million to $200 million. Although it would be sensible to finance the program with contributions from all earthlings, it may be impossible to collect money from everyone. A more likely outcome is that one or more developed countries will finance their own diversion systems.

Preservation of Wolves

We can also apply the concepts of public goods and free riding to the issue of preserving wildlife. There are some trade-offs associated with preserving wolves and other wildlife in Yellowstone Park. To environmentalists, wolves are a part of the natural ecosystem. To ranchers, whose livestock is often eaten by wolves, wolves are pests that should be eliminated or tightly controlled. In other words, there are costs as well as benefits associated with the preservation of wolves, just as there are costs and benefits associated with other public goods such as dams, fireworks, national defense, and space exploration.

One response to the wolf-preservation problem comes from Defenders of Wildlife, an environmental group in Montana. The organization collects money from its members and uses the money to reward landowners who allow wolves to live on their properties. The host landowner receives a payment of $5,000 for each litter of wolf pups reared on the property.[3] In addition, the organization compensates ranchers for livestock killed by wolves. As a result of these programs, ranchers in the Yellowstone area are more likely to support efforts to maintain the wolves as part of Yellowstone Park's ecosystem. The programs treat preservation as a public good, one

Innovative programs that compensate ranchers for livestock lost to wolves help preservation efforts.

that is supported by money contributed by people who benefit from preservation. The organization has collected contributions from thousands of people despite the free-rider problem.

Public Choice

We have discussed the challenges associated with providing and paying for goods that generate external benefits. In this part of the chapter, we look at how governments actually operate, exploring some contrasting views of government that have emerged from a field of study known as **public choice economics**. We'll start with a model of government decisions based on voting and then look at some alternative models.

Public choice economics
A field of economics that explores how governments actually operate.

Voting and the Median-Voter Rule

As citizens in a democracy, we pick people to make public decisions. We vote for people to represent our viewpoints in legislative bodies (city council members, state legislators, and congressional representatives), and we vote for people in executive positions (mayors, governors, and presidents). The basic idea of a democracy is that the government will take actions that are approved by the majority of citizens. If governments are responsive to voters, the voting public ultimately makes all the important decisions, and the actions of the government will reflect their preferences.

One finding of public choice economics is known as the **median-voter rule**. According to the median-voter rule, the choices made by government will reflect the preferences of the median voter, defined as the voter whose preferences lie in the

Median-voter rule
A rule suggesting that the choices made by government will reflect the preferences of the median voter.

middle of the set of all voters' preferences; half the voters want more of something (for example, a larger government budget) and half want less (a smaller government budget). As we'll see, this rule has some interesting implications for decision-making and politics.

To see the logic of this rule, consider a state where there are two candidates for governor—Penny and Buck—and the only issue in the election is how much the state should spend on education. Each citizen will vote for the candidate whose proposed education budget is closest to the citizen's preferred budget. Figure 10.2 shows citizens' preferences for education spending, with different preferred budgets on the horizontal axis and the number of voters on the vertical axis. For example, two citizens have a preferred budget of $1 billion, four have a preferred budget of $2 billion, and so on. The median budget, which splits the rest of the voters into two equal groups (20 voters on either side), is $5 billion.

Suppose the two candidates start out with very different proposed education budgets. Penny proposes a budget of $3 billion, and Buck proposes $7 billion. The 20 citizens with preferred budgets less than or equal to $4 billion will vote for Penny because her proposed budget is closest to their preferred budgets. Buck's supporters include the 20 citizens with preferred budgets greater than or equal to $6 billion. The two candidates will split the 10 voters with a preferred budget of $5 billion (halfway between the two proposed budgets), so each candidate will get a total of 25 votes, resulting in a tie.

Penny could increase her chance of being elected by increasing her proposed budget. Let's say she proposes $4 billion instead of $3 billion. The voters with a preferred budget of $5 billion will switch to Penny because Penny's $4 billion proposal is now closer to their $5 billion preferred budget than Buck's $7 billion. Penny won't lose any of her other votes either, so she will win the election by a vote of 30 (2 + 4 + 6 + 8 + 10) to 20 (8 + 8 + 4). If Buck is smart, he will realize that he could get more votes by moving toward the median budget. For example, if he decreases his proposed budget to $6 billion, the election would result in a tie vote again. Penny

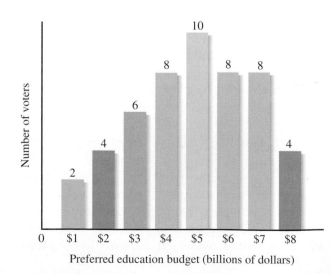

FIGURE 10.2

The Median-Voter Rule

If Penny proposes a $3 billion budget and Buck proposes a $7 billion budget, the election will result in a tie. By moving toward the median budget, Penny can increase her chance of being elected. Both candidates will propose a budget close to the $5 billion preferred budget of the median voter.

and Buck will continue to move their proposed budgets toward the median budget ($5 billion) until they both propose budgets that are very close to the median budget.

There are powerful forces pulling the two candidates toward the preferences of the median voter. As long as Penny proposes a smaller budget than Buck, the people with small preferred budgets will continue to vote for her. The benefit of moving toward the median is that she can take some votes from Buck. Similarly, Buck doesn't have to worry about people with large preferred budgets but can concentrate instead on the battle for voters in the middle. The result is that by election day, the two candidates have adopted virtually the same position: The position of the median voter. Voters trying to choose between two candidates may feel they don't have much choice. In fact, the median-voter rule says that the choices made by government will reflect the preferences of the median voter, regardless of who wins the election.

The logic of the median-voter result also applies to competition among some types of sellers. Read "A Closer Look: Are Politicians Like Ice-Cream Vendors?"

Although we usually think that people make political decisions by voting in elections, it is also possible to "vote with your feet." In 1956, economist Charles M. Tiebout suggested that a household's choice of which community to live in is based in part on the tax and spending policies of different communities. Households express their preferences by moving to communities that offer the best package of services and taxes. A community with inefficient public services will experience a

A CLOSER LOOK — Are Politicians Like Ice-Cream Vendors?

Imagine a one-mile stretch of beach with 120 swimmers and sunbathers distributed evenly along the beach. Suppose each person on the beach will purchase one ice-cream cone. If there are two ice-cream vendors on the beach selling an identical product, where will they locate? The most efficient arrangement would be to divide the beach into two half-mile territories and locate each vendor at the middle of his or her territory. As shown in Panel A of Figure 10.3, Lefty would be at the quarter-mile mark, and Righty would be at the three-quarter-mile mark. If beachgoers patronize the closest vendor, each vendor would sell 60 ice-cream cones. This arrangement will minimize the total travel costs of ice-cream patrons.

Is this an equilibrium arrangement? If Lefty were to move to the right—to the half-mile mark, the median location that splits consumers into two equal halves—he would not lose any of his customers to his left but would capture part of Righty's market. As shown in Panel B of Figure 10.3, Lefty would then be the closest vendor for the people located between the half-mile mark and the five-eighths mark. Therefore, Lefty would sell 75 cones (up from 60) and Righty would sell only 45 cones. To protect her market, Righty would move to the median location too, locating right next to Lefty. By doing so, Righty can recover her 50% share of the market, again serving the consumers on the right half of the beach. At any other location, she would get less than half the market, given Lefty is at the median location. In equilibrium, shown in Panel C of Figure 10.3, both vendors pick the median location and each serves half the market.

The outcome of the ice-cream vendors' game is the same as the politicians' game. Like the politicians, the vendors have an incentive to move to the median location, so there is no real difference between the two vendors.

FIGURE 10.3

Competition on a Beach Leads to a Median Location for Both Sellers

A: If the two sellers start at the one-quarter- and three-quarter-mile marks, each has a territory of one-half mile and sells 60 cones.

B: If Lefty moves to the median location, his territory increases to the 5/8 mile mark, and he sells 75 cones, compared to 45 for Righty.

C: Righty can recover her lost territory by moving to the median location. In equilibrium, both sellers locate at the median location and each has half the market.

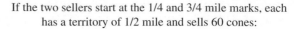

If the two sellers start at the 1/4 and 3/4 mile marks, each has a territory of 1/2 mile and sells 60 cones:

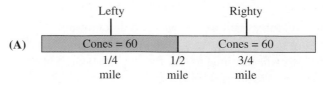

If Lefty moves to the median location, his territory increases to the 5/8 mile mark, and he sells 75 cones, compared to 45 for Righty:

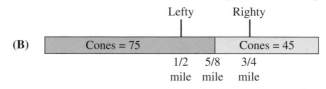

Righty can recover her lost territory by moving to the median location. In equilibrium, both sellers locate at the median location and each has half the market:

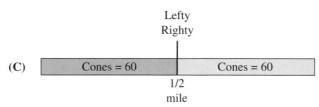

loss in population, perhaps causing the local officials to make the public services more efficient.

It is clear that people vote with their ballots *and* with their feet. In both cases, citizens can express their preferences for public goods, taxes, and public policies. These two sources of citizen power limit the ability of governments to take actions that are inconsistent with the preferences of most voters.

Alternative Models of Government: Self-Interests and Special Interests

Several economists, including Nobel laureate James Buchanan, have suggested a model of government that focuses on the selfish behavior of government officials. According to this view, politicians and bureaucrats pursue their own narrow interests, which, of course, may differ from the public interest. For example, politicians or bureaucrats may gain prestige from starting a new spending program even if the cost of the program exceeds its social benefit. Because voters don't have much information about the costs and benefits of public services, they may not be in a position to evaluate the actions of politicians or bureaucrats and vote accordingly.

The self-interest theory of government explains why voters sometimes approve explicit limits on taxes and government spending. For example, most states have limits on the amount of property taxes that can be raised, and many states also limit total government spending. According to the self-interest theory of government, limitations on taxes and spending are necessary safeguards against politicians and bureaucrats who benefit from larger budgets.

Another model of government is based on the idea that small groups of people manipulate government for their own gain. Suppose the total benefit of a dam is less than its total cost, so the project is inefficient, but a few farmers reap large benefits from the dam, while the costs are spread over a million taxpayers. The farmers have a strong incentive to spend time and money to convince policymakers to build the dam. In contrast, if the tax is only $1 per person, not many taxpayers will make their preferences known to policymakers because the marginal benefit (the $1 tax savings) is less than the marginal cost (the opportunity cost of their time). If politicians listen to people who express their preferences and contribute money to political campaigns, the inefficient project may be approved. This is an example of a special-interest group (farmers) manipulating the government at the expense of a larger group (all taxpayers). In general, when a few people share the benefit from a project and a large number of people share the cost, the government is more likely to approve inefficient projects.

In general, whenever benefits are concentrated on a few citizens but costs are spread out over many citizens, we expect special-interest groups to form. Special-interest organizations often use lobbyists to express their views to government officials and policymakers.

Which Theory or Viewpoint Is Correct?

Which of these theories or viewpoints best describes the actual practices of governments? This is a very difficult question. Economists and political scientists have studied many dimensions of the decision-making processes underlying tax policies and spending policies. There is evidence that people do vote with ballots and with their feet, and that these two forms of voting make a difference. There is also evidence that government officials sometimes pursue their own interests and those of special-interest groups. The field of public choice is a very active area of research involving both economists and political scientists.

TEST Your Understanding

4. In Figure 10.2, suppose that 32 additional citizens appear, and each has a preferred budget of $2 billion. How will the new citizens affect the election?
5. Do you think all citizens have the same opportunity to vote with their feet, picking the communities with the best combination of public services and taxes?
6. Does your ability to vote with your feet vary with the level of government? Compared to the municipal level, is foot voting more or less likely at the state level? What about the national level?

Economic Experiment

Voluntary Contributions

Do people really try to get free rides? Or would most people contribute at least some money to support a public good? Here is a classroom experiment that helps to answer this question.

- The instructor selects 10 students at random and gives each student 10 dimes (or play money).
- Each student can contribute money to support a public good by dropping 1, 2, or 3 dimes into a public-good pot. Each student has the option of keeping all the dimes and not contributing anything. The contributions are anonymous; none of the students knows how much the other students contribute.
- For each dime in the pot, the instructor adds 2 dimes. For example, if the students contribute a total of 40 dimes, the instructor adds 80 dimes, for a total of 120 dimes in the pot. The 2-for-1 match represents the idea that the benefits of public goods exceed the costs. In this case, the benefit–cost ratio is 3 to 1.
- The instructor divides the money in the public-good pot equally among the 10 students. For example, if there are 120 dimes in the pot, each student receives 12 dimes.
- Steps 2 through 4 can be repeated 4 or 5 times.

We can change the experiment to mimic the compulsory tax system. The instructor could require each student to contribute 3 dimes, the maximum amount, each round. Would a switch to a compulsory tax system make the students better off or worse off? ●

USING THE TOOLS

In this chapter, we explained why the government provides public goods. Because of the free-rider problem, we can't rely on voluntary contributions to support public goods and subsidies, so we use taxes to support public programs. Here are some opportunities to do your own economic analysis of public goods and taxes.

1. Stream Preservation

Consider a trout stream that is threatened with destruction by a nearby logging operation. Each of the 10,000 local fishers would be willing to pay $5 to preserve the stream. The owner of the land would incur a cost of $20,000 to change the logging operation to protect the stream.
a. Is the preservation of the stream efficient from the social perspective?
b. If the landowner has the right to log the land any way he wants, will the stream be preserved?
c. Propose a solution to this problem. Describe a transaction that would benefit the fishers and the landowner.
d. Will your proposed solution work?

2. Marginalism and Contributions

Consider the voluntary contributions experiment described at the end of the chapter. Margie, one of the students participating in the free-rider experiment, thinks in marginal terms and asks the following question: "If I contribute one dime, how will that affect my payoff from the experiment?"
a. Answer her question, assuming that her contribution does not affect the contribution of other students.
b. Suppose Margie uses the marginal principle to make all her decisions. Will she contribute the extra dime?

SUMMARY

In this chapter, we've seen that governments can solve the problems caused by external benefits. We've also examined different views on how governments really make decisions. Here are the main points of the chapter:

1 We can use government—with its taxing authority—to make collective decisions about the provision of public goods.

2 A system of voluntary contributions suffers from the free-rider problem: People do not have a financial incentive to contribute to the support of public goods.

3 The choices made by government will reflect the preferences of the median voter, defined as the voter whose preferences lie in the middle of the set of all voters' preferences.

KEY TERMS

free-rider problem, 222
median-voter rule, 225

private good, 221
public choice economics, 225

public good, 221

PROBLEMS AND DISCUSSION QUESTIONS

1 A three-person city is considering a fireworks display. Bertha is willing to pay $100 for the proposed fireworks display, Marian is willing to pay $30, Sam is willing to pay $20. The cost of the fireworks display is $120.
 a. Will any single citizen provide the display on his or her own?
 b. If the cost of the fireworks display is divided equally among the citizens, will a majority vote in favor of the display?
 c. Describe a transaction that would benefit all three citizens.

2 Churches collect substantial sums of money through voluntary contributions. What explains their ability to overcome the free-rider problem at least partially?

3 Consider the voluntary contributions experiment described at the end of the chapter. Suppose the participants make the following agreement: If any single person does not contribute 3 dimes, all the contributions will be returned, and each contributor will receive a refund equal to the amount he or she contributed. How will this agreement affect the outcome of the experiment?

4 The spotted owl is an endangered species that lives in old-growth forests. Logging destroys the habitat of spotted owls. Explain how the lessons from the wolf-preservation program might be applied to the issue of preserving the spotted owl.

5 Each of the 80,000 citizens in a particular county would be willing to pay $0.10 to increase the number of wolf litters by one. Each litter of wolves imposes costs on ranchers (from livestock losses) of $5,000.
 a. Is the provision of an additional litter of wolves efficient from the social perspective?
 b. If ranchers have the right to kill any wolves on their property, will an additional litter be protected?
 c. Propose a solution to this problem. Describe a transaction that would benefit the wolf lovers and the ranchers.

6 Contributions to organizations such as the United Way and the American Cancer Society are tax deductible: For each dollar contributed, a person's tax liability decreases by $0.15 to $0.31. Explain the rationale for this tax policy.

7 Consider the example of the governor's election shown in Figure 10.2. Suppose 18 new people move into the state and each newcomer has a desired education budget of $9 billion.

  a. Will the two candidates change their proposed education budget? If so, how much will each candidate propose?

  b. How would your answer to part (a) change if each newcomer had a desired budget of $15 billion instead of $9 billion?

MODEL ANSWERS TO QUESTIONS

Chapter-Opening Questions

1 A system based on voluntary contributions would suffer from the free-rider problem, with few people contributing money to support the public good.

2 The payments to host landowners treat preservation as a public good supported by money collected from the people who benefit from preservation.

3 A liberal candidate who moves toward the center won't lose the votes of liberal citizens, but will gain some votes from moderate citizens. A conservative candidate who moves toward the center won't lose conservative votes, but will gain moderate votes. Both candidates are likely to adopt the position favored by the median voter.

Test Your Understanding

1 The producer of a private good collects money from each consumer. If you don't pay, you don't get the good. In contrast, it is impossible to prevent people who don't pay from consuming a public good.

2 Although movie admission is nonrival if the theater is nearly empty, it is excludable, so it is a private good.

3 It is a private good with external benefits. Your neighbors benefit from looking at a nicely painted house.

4 The median voter now has a preferred budget of $3 billion: A total of 38 voters have a lower preferred budget ($1 or $2 billion), and a total of 38 voters have a higher preferred budget. Both candidates will propose the median budget ($3 billion).

5 Low-income households cannot afford housing in many neighborhoods, so they have fewer options. Many suburban communities have zoning policies that limit high-density housing, restricting the choices of low-income households. If there is racial discrimination, minority households will have fewer options.

6 At the local level, the typical metropolitan area has many municipalities to choose from, so foot voting is not very costly. At the national level, voting with your feet means renouncing your citizenship and moving far away, so it is more costly.

NOTES

1. Carl Sagan, "A Warning for Us?" *Parade*, June 5, 1994, p. 8; John Boudreau, "Collision Course: Scientists Say There's a Big Asteroid Bang in Our Future," *Washington Post*, April 6, 1994, p. C1.

2. "Mirror Beam Could Deflect Killer Asteroid, Theory Says," *New York Times*, November 9, 1994, p. C6.

3. Terry L. Anderson, "A Carrot to Save the Wolf," *The Margin*, Spring 1992, p. 28.

Part

4

Market Structures and Pricing

Chapter 11

Production Technology and Cost

Chapter 12

Perfect Competition

Chapter 13

Monopoly and Price Discrimination

Chapter 14

Market Entry and Monopolistic Competition

Chapter 15

Oligopoly and Strategic Behavior

Chapter 16

Market Structure and Public Policy

Introduction

Economic Cost Is Opportunity Cost
Short-Run Versus Long-Run Costs

**The Fixed Production Facility:
Short-Run Costs**

Production and Marginal Product
Short-Run Total Cost
Short-Run Average Costs
Short-Run Marginal Cost
The Relationship Between Marginal Cost
 and Average Cost

**Production and Cost
in the Long Run**

Expansion and Replication
Selling Down and Indivisible Inputs
Scaling Down and Labor Specialization
Economies of Scale
Diseconomies of Scale
Actual Long-Run Average-Cost Curves
Short-Run Versus Long-Run Average Cost

**Information Goods
and First-Copy Cost**

Using the Tools

Production Technology and Cost

few years ago the price of a hardback version of Encyclopedia Britannica, the world's leading encyclopedia, was $1,600. Now you can get a CD version of the encyclopedia, along with a dictionary, thesaurus, and world atlas, for only $69.95. Why did the price drop to less than 1/20th of its former value?

An encyclopedia is an information good, and its production involves collecting information—facts, figures, and images—and packaging them for use by consumers. The cost of compiling the information for the first copy of an encyclopedia is huge, but the cost of reproducing the encyclopedia in digital format (CDs) is tiny. The move from hardback encyclopedias to digital ones decreased the cost of production, pulling down the price. In addition, heated competition among rival encyclopedia firms pulled the price down further.

This chapter is about how the cost of producing a particular product varies with the quantity of output produced. As we'll see, the cost of producing a product is determined by production technology—the way a firm combines inputs like capital and labor to produce output. After explaining the link between technology and costs, we'll look at the actual cost curves of several products, including aluminum, hospital services, wind power, and freight services.

In later chapters, we'll use the cost curves discussed in this chapter to explore firms' decisions about whether to enter a market and how much output to produce once they enter. In this chapter, we'll see how to use cost curves to answer the following practical questions:

1 Why is the typical *short-run* average-cost curve shaped like the letter U, while the typical *long-run* average-cost curve is shaped like the letter L?
2 If the short-run average cost of production is the same for two different quantities of output, can it be the same for three different quantities?
3 The cost of producing the first fake killer whale is about three times the cost of producing the second. Why?
4 How does the cost of electricity vary with the size of the wind turbine used to generate it?

Introduction

Why study production costs? The ultimate goal of a firm is to maximize its profit, where profit equals total revenue minus total cost. For most firms, total revenue exceeds total cost by a small margin. For example, the typical convenience store has monthly sales (total revenue) of $76,400, and the cost of sales clerks, utilities, building rent, and merchandise add up to $74,100.[1] The store therefore has $2,300 left over after paying all these costs ($76,400 − $74,100), meaning that the reward for the entrepreneur is just $2,300 per month. Of course, the opportunity cost of the entrepreneur's time is a cost of doing business, too. If this opportunity cost is $2,000 per month, the store's actual profit is only $300 per month. Because this profit margin is so slim, the typical convenience store has a strong incentive to control its costs. If it doesn't, it might actually end up losing money.

In this chapter, we'll look at several ways to measure a firm's cost of production. Given the importance of costs in determining a firm's profit, firms spend a great deal of time and money in computing their costs. They use this information to decide how much to produce and how much to charge for their products. In the chapters following this one, we'll use what we learn about production costs to explore firm's production and pricing decisions.

Economic Cost Is Opportunity Cost

Economic cost

The opportunity cost of production, including both explicit and implicit costs.

Our discussion of the firm's cost is based on the notion of **economic cost**. The computation of economic cost is based on the principle of opportunity cost.

Principle OF OPPORTUNITY COST

The opportunity cost of something is what you sacrifice to get it.

Explicit cost

The firm's actual cash payments for its inputs.

Implicit cost

The opportunity cost of nonpurchased inputs.

A firm's economic cost includes all of its opportunity costs, which can be divided into two types, explicit costs and implicit costs. A firm's **explicit cost** is defined as its actual cash payments for inputs. For example, if a firm spends a total of $3,000 per month on labor, materials, rent, and machinery, its explicit cost is $3,000. This is an opportunity cost because money spent on these inputs cannot be used to buy something else. The firm's **implicit cost** is defined as the opportunity cost of nonpurchased inputs such as the entrepreneur's time or money:

▶ Opportunity cost of the entrepreneur's time. An entrepreneur's economic cost includes the opportunity cost of the time spent running the firm. If an entrepreneur could earn $5,000 per month in another job, the opportunity cost of his or her time is $5,000 per month.

▶ Opportunity cost of the entrepreneur's funds. Many entrepreneurs use their own funds to set up and run their businesses. If an entrepreneur starts a business with money withdrawn from a savings account, the opportunity cost of using these funds is the interest the funds could have earned, for example $1,000 per month.

As shown in Table 11.1, the economic cost for our example is $9,000, including $3,000 in explicit costs and $6,000 in implicit costs.

Short-Run Versus Long-Run Costs

As we saw in Chapter 2, economists distinguish between the short run and the long run in production. The long run is a period long enough that a firm is perfectly flexible in its choice of all inputs, including its production facility. In contrast, when a firm can-

TABLE 11.1

Economic Cost

Explicit cost (purchased inputs)	$3,000
Implicit cost: opportunity cost of entrepreneur's time	5,000
Implicit cost: opportunity cost of funds	1,000
Economic cost	$9,000

not modify its facility, it is operating in the short run. In this chapter, we'll explore both short-run and long-run cost curves. In later chapters, we'll see how firms use these cost curves to make two types of decisions:

▶ A firm with a fixed production facility must decide how much output to produce in that facility. This is a short-run decision because one of the factors of production (the facility) is fixed.

▶ A firm that has decided to enter a market must decide how large a facility to build. This is a long-run decision because none of the factors of production are fixed. The firm starts from scratch and can choose a production facility of any size.

The time required to reach the long run varies across industries. If it takes one day to get a hot-dog cart and start selling hot dogs, the long run for a hot-dog vendor is one day. In contrast, it takes several years to design and build a computer-chip factory, so the long run for a computer-chip producer is several years.

In the last part of the chapter, we'll look at the cost curves for information goods such as music CDs, books, and movie DVDs. The production of these goods requires a substantial expense before any output is produced, but the additional cost to produce the first unit of output is relatively low. For example, producing a movie requires millions of dollars for writers, actors, camera operators, and other crew members, but once the images and sounds are stored in digital format, the cost of burning them onto a DVD is less than a dollar. Similarly, to produce a book, thousands of dollars must be paid to authors, illustrators, and editors. However, once all the words and images are compiled, the cost of printing the book is just a few dollars per unit. As we'll see, the cost curves for information goods are very different from those for other products.

The Fixed Production Facility: Short-Run Costs

Consider first the case of producing with a fixed production facility. Suppose that you have decided to start a small firm to produce plastic paddles for rafts. The production of paddles requires a workshop where workers use molds to form plastic material into paddles. Before we can discuss the cost of production, we need information about the nature of the production process.

Production and Marginal Product

Table 11.2 shows how the quantity of paddles produced varies with the number of workers. A one-worker operation produces one paddle per day, while a two-worker operation produces 5 paddles. The **marginal product of labor** is the change in output from one additional unit of labor. In Table 11.2, the marginal product of the first worker is 1 paddle, compared to a marginal product of 4 paddles for the second worker.

Marginal product of labor
The change in output from one additional unit of labor.

TABLE 11.2

Labor, Output, and
Marginal Product

Labor	Quantity of Output Produced	Marginal Product of Labor
1	1	1
2	5	4
3	8	3
4	10	2
5	11	1
6	11.5	0.50

Why does the marginal product increase as output increases? As we saw earlier in the book, when a firm increases its workforce, individual workers can specialize in particular production tasks. Productivity increases because of the benefits of continuity (less time switching between production tasks) and repetition (each worker becomes more proficient at the assigned task). A two-worker operation produces more than twice as many paddles as a one-person operation because the two workers can specialize, one being responsible for preparing the plastic for the mold and the other responsible for working the mold.

Starting with the third worker, the production process is subject to **diminishing returns**, one of the key principles of economics.

Diminishing returns

As one input increases while the other inputs are held fixed, output increases at a decreasing rate.

 Principle OF DIMINISHING RETURNS

Suppose that output is produced with two or more inputs and we increase one input while holding the other inputs fixed. Beyond some point—called the point of diminishing returns— output will increase at a decreasing rate.

The third worker adds 3 paddles to total output, down from 4 paddles for the second worker. As the firm continues to hire more workers, the marginal product drops to 2 paddles for the fourth worker and 1 paddle for the fifth worker. As we saw earlier in the book, diminishing returns occurs because workers share a production facility, and with a larger workforce, each worker gets a smaller share of the production facility. In the paddle example, the workers share a mold, and as the number of workers increases, they will spend more time waiting to use the mold.

Figure 11.1 provides a graphical representation of this production relationship. The firm's **total product curve** shows the relationship between number of workers (on the horizontal axis) and output (on the vertical axis), *ceteris paribus*. The total-product curve shows the effects of labor specialization as well as diminishing returns. For the first two workers, output increases rapidly because labor specialization increases the marginal product of labor. Starting with the third worker, however, total output increases at a decreasing rate because of diminishing returns.

Total product curve

A curve showing the relationship between the quantity of labor and the quantity of output produced.

FIGURE 11.1

Total Product Curve
The total product curve shows the relationship between the quantity of labor and the quantity of output, given a fixed production facility. For the first 2 workers, output increases at an increasing rate, a result of labor specialization. Hiring additional workers generates diminishing returns, and output then increases at a decreasing rate.

Short-Run Total Cost

We've seen the production relationship between labor and output, so now we're ready to show the relationship between output and production cost. The first step is to specify some numbers for the inputs used in paddle production. Suppose your opportunity cost is $50 per day, and you can hire workers for your workshop at the market wage of $50 per day. Further suppose you can purchase your workshop, including the building and the paddle mold, for $365,000. If the interest rate you could have earned on that money is 10% per year, the opportunity cost of tying up your $365,000 in the workshop is $36,500 per year, or $100 per day.

In the short-run analysis of costs, we divide production costs into two types, fixed cost and variable cost.

▶ **Fixed cost (FC)** is defined as the cost that does not vary with the quantity produced. In our example, the fixed cost is the cost of the workshop, including the cost of the building and the mold. As shown in the third column of Table 11.3, the fixed cost is $100 per day, regardless of how much output is produced.

▶ **Variable cost (VC)** is defined as a cost that varies with the quantity produced. For example, to produce more paddles, you must hire more workers. If the cost per worker is $50 per day, the total variable cost per day is $50 times the number of workers, including you. As shown in the fourth column of Table 11.3, variable cost is $50 for a one-worker operation, $100 for a two-worker operation, and so on.

The firm's **short-run total cost (TC)** equals the sum of fixed and variable costs:

$$TC = FC + VC$$

The total costs for different output levels are shown in the fifth column of Table 11.3.

Figure 11.2 shows the three short-run cost curves. They correspond to columns 3, 4, and 5 in Table 11.1. The horizontal line on the graph shows the fixed cost of $100.

Fixed cost (FC)
Cost that does not depend on the quantity produced.

Variable cost (VC)
Cost that varies as the firm changes its output.

Short-run total cost (TC)
The total cost of production in the short run, when one or more inputs (for example, the production facility) is fixed; equal to fixed cost plus variable cost.

TABLE 11.3 Short-Run Costs

1	2	3	4	5	6	7	8	9
Labor	Output	Fixed Cost (*FC*)	Variable Cost (*VC*)	Total Cost (*TC*)	Average Fixed Cost (*AFC*)	Average Variable Cost (*AVC*)	Average Total Cost (*ATC*)	Marginal Cost (*MC*)
0	0	$100	$0	$100				
1	1	100	$50	150	$100.00	$50.00	$150.00	$50.00
2	5	100	100	200	20.00	20.00	40.00	12.50
3	8	100	150	250	12.50	18.75	31.25	16.67
4	10	100	200	300	10.00	20.00	30.00	25.00
5	11	100	250	350	9.09	22.73	31.82	50.00
6	11.5	100	300	400	8.70	26.09	34.78	100.00

The lower of the two positively sloped curves shows the variable cost. The higher of the two positively sloped curves is total cost, which is the sum of fixed cost and variable cost. The vertical distance between the *TC* curve and the *VC* curve equals the firm's fixed cost. Notice that this distance is the same at any level of output.

Short-Run Average Costs

Average fixed cost (*AFC*)

Fixed cost divided by the quantity produced.

There are three types of average cost. **Average fixed cost (*AFC*)** equals the fixed cost divided by the quantity produced:

$$AFC = \frac{FC}{Q}$$

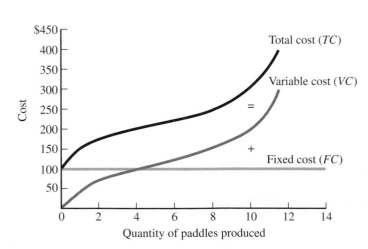

FIGURE 11.2 **Short-Run Costs: Fixed Cost, Variable Cost, and Total Cost**

The short-run total-cost curve shows the relationship between the quantity of output and production costs given a fixed production facility. Short-run total cost equals fixed cost (the cost that does not vary with the quantity produced) plus variable cost (the cost that varies with the quantity produced).

To compute *AFC* for our paddle company, we simply divide the fixed cost by the quantity of paddles produced. In Table 11.2, we divide the number in column 3 by the number in column 2. This gives us the values for *AFC*, which are shown in column 6. Notice that *AFC* decreases from $100 for the first paddle, to $20 for five paddles, and so on. As output increases, the fixed cost is spread over more units, so *AFC* decreases. In Figure 11.3, the *AFC* curve is negatively sloped, reflecting the spreading of a fixed amount over more and more units.

A firm's **average variable cost (*AVC*)** incorporates the costs that vary with the quantity produced. Average variable cost equals the variable cost divided by the quantity produced:

$$AVC = \frac{VC}{Q}$$

To compute *AVC* for our paddle company we simply divide the number in column 4 of Table 11.3 by the number in column 2. That gives us the values for *AVC*, shown in column 7. Notice that for small quantities of output, the *AVC* decreases as the quantity produced increases—from 50 for one paddle, $20 for two paddles, and so on. The declining *AVC* reflects the benefits of labor specialization. Adding workers to a small workforce makes workers more productive on average, so the amount of labor required per unit of output drops, pulling down the average variable cost. By contrast, for large quantities of output, average variable cost increases as output increases, reflecting diminishing returns. Adding workers to a large workforce makes workers less productive on average, pulling up the average variable cost. In Figure 11.3, the *AVC* curve is negatively sloped for small quantities and positively sloped for large quantities.

Average variable cost (*AVC*)

Total variable cost divided by the quantity produced.

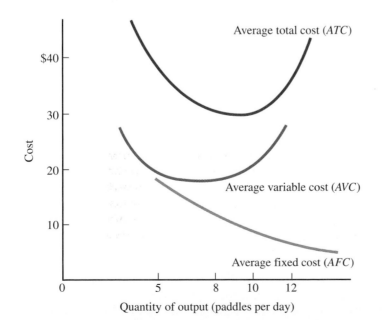

FIGURE 11.3

Short-Run Average Costs

The short-run average-total-cost curve (*ATC*) is U-shaped, a result of spreading fixed cost (which pulls down the average total cost) and diminishing returns (which pulls up the average total cost).

Total cost is the sum of fixed cost and variable cost, so the **average total cost
(*ATC*)**, or what we'll simply call "average cost," is the sum of the average fixed cost and
the average variable cost:

$$ATC = \frac{TC}{Q} = \frac{FC}{Q} + \frac{VC}{Q}$$

For small quantities of output, the *ATC* curve is negatively sloped, a result of two
forces that work together to pull *ATC* down as output increases:

▶ Spreading the fixed cost. For small quantities of output, a one-unit increase in output reduces *AFC* by a large amount because the fixed cost is pretty "thick," being
  spread over just a few units of output. For example, going from one paddle to five
  paddles decreases *AFC* from $100 to $20 per paddle.
▶ Labor specialization. For small quantities of output, *AVC* decreases as output
  increases, a result of labor specialization that increases worker productivity.

These two forces both pull *ATC* downward as output increases, so the curve is negatively sloped for small quantities of output.

What happens once the firm reaches the point at which the benefits of labor specialization are exhausted? As the firm continues to increase output, the average variable
cost increases because of diminishing returns. There is a tug-of-war between two
forces: The spreading of fixed cost continues to pull *ATC* down, while diminishing
returns and rising average variable cost pushes *ATC* up. The outcome of the tug-of-war
depends on the quantity produced, giving the *ATC* curve its U shape.

▶ Intermediate quantities of output (between 3 and 10 paddles). The tug-of-war is won
  by the spreading of fixed cost, because the fixed cost is still relatively "thick" and diminishing returns are not yet very strong. As a result, *ATC* decreases as output increases.
▶ Large quantities of output (11 or more paddles). The tug-of-war is won by diminishing returns and rising average variable cost. In this case, the reductions in *AFC* are
  relatively small because the fixed cost is already spread pretty thinly and diminishing
  returns are severe. As a result, *ATC* increases as output increases.

Short-Run Marginal Cost

The **short-run marginal cost (*MC*)** is the change in short-run total cost per unit
change in output. In other words, it is the increase in total cost associated with a one-
unit increase in output. Mathematically, marginal cost is calculated by dividing the
change in total cost (ΔTC) by the change in output (ΔQ):

$$MC = \frac{\Delta TC}{\Delta Q} = \frac{\text{change in } TC}{\text{change in output}}$$

The marginal cost of the first paddle is the increase in cost associated with hiring
the single worker the firm needs to produce the first paddle, or $50. The ninth column

in Table 11.3 shows the marginal cost for different output levels. When you hire the second worker for $50, output increases to 5 paddles. A $50 increase in total cost increases output by 4 paddles, so the marginal cost is $12.50:

$$MC = \frac{\Delta TC}{\Delta Q} = \frac{\text{change in } TC}{\text{change in output}} = \frac{\$50}{4} = \$12.50$$

In this case, marginal cost decreases as output increases because of labor specialization and rising worker productivity. The first worker produces just 1 paddle, but adding a second worker increases output by 4 paddles. The $50 expense of adding the second worker translates into a $12.50 expense for each of the 4 extra paddles produced. We saw earlier that specialization leads to increasing marginal productivity; now we know that it also leads to decreasing marginal cost. In Figure 11.4, the short-run marginal-cost curve is negatively sloped for the first 5 paddles.

Eventually, the marginal-cost curve is positively sloped. Starting with the fifth paddle, the short-run marginal cost increases as the output increases. When you hire the third worker, output increases from 5 to 8, so the $50 expense translates into a $16.67 expense for each of the three extra paddles produced. Diminishing returns has set in, and marginal cost increases as output increases. The marginal cost increases to $25 for between 8 and 10 paddles ($50/2 paddles), $50 for between 10 and 11 paddles ($50/1 paddle), and so on. In general, decreasing labor productivity causes rising marginal cost.

The Relationship Between Marginal Cost and Average Cost

Figure 11.4 shows the relationship between short-run marginal cost and short-run average total cost. Whenever the marginal cost is less than the average cost (for fewer than 10 paddles), the average cost is falling. In contrast, whenever the marginal cost

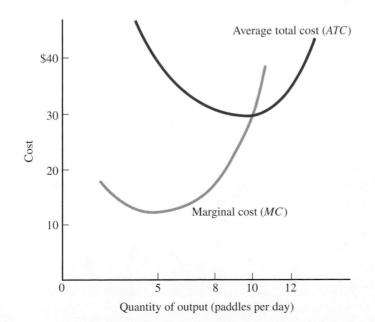

FIGURE 11.4

Short-Run Marginal and Average Cost
The marginal cost curve (*MC*) is negatively sloped for small quantities of output, reflecting the benefits of labor specialization, and positively sloped for large quantities, reflecting diminishing returns. The *MC* curve intersects the average-cost curve (*ATC*) at the minimum point of the average curve. At this point *ATC* is neither falling nor rising.

exceeds the average cost (for more than 10 paddles), the average cost is rising. Finally, when the marginal cost equals the average cost, the average cost is neither rising nor falling. This is where the marginal-cost curve intersects the short-run average total-cost curve at its minimum point.

We can use some simple logic to explain the relationship between average cost and marginal cost. Suppose that you start the semester with a cumulative GPA of 3.0 (a B average) and enroll in a single course that semester—a history course. If you receive a grade of C in history (2.0 for computing your GPA), your GPA will drop below 3.0. Your GPA decreases because the grade in the "marginal" course (the history course) is less than the "average" grade (the starting cumulative GPA), so the marginal grade pulls down your GPA. Suppose that you take an economics class the following semester and get a grade of A (4.0 for computing your GPA). In this case, your GPA will increase because the marginal grade (in economics) is higher than your average (your GPA), so the marginal grade pushes up your GPA. If you were to take a course the following semester and your grade in the course was the same as your GPA, your GPA wouldn't change. To summarize, whenever the marginal grade is less than the average grade, the average will fall; whenever the marginal grade exceeds the average grade, the average will rise; whenever the marginal grade equals the average grade, the average will not change.

Same Average Cost at Two or Three Quantities?

Mr. Large wants to enter the pencil-making business. He gathered some information from two existing pencil manufacturers: Ms. Small and Ms. Medium. The two firms have identical production facilities—identical factories and equipment—but Medium has

more workers. The two firms also pay the same wage to each of their workers and pay the same prices for materials. Although Small produces 1,000 pencils per minute and Medium produces 2,000 per minute, each firm has an average total cost of 10 cents per pencil. The first puzzle is, How can two firms producing different quantities have the same average cost?

We can solve this first puzzle with a quick look at the U-shaped average-cost curve in Figure 11.5. For a small quantity of output (1,000 pencils), the average fixed cost is relatively large (the fixed cost is spread over a small quantity), but the average variable cost is relatively low (diminishing returns are not yet severe). For a medium quantity (2,000 pencils), the average fixed cost is lower, but average variable cost is higher (more severe diminishing returns). Moving from the small quantity to the medium quantity, average fixed cost decreases while average variable cost increases, so it is possible to have the same average cost (10 cents) at the two quantities.

Based on the information about Small and Medium, Large built a production facility identical to the ones used by the other firms. He hired enough workers and bought enough materials to produce 2,500 pencils per minute. Based on the experience of Small and Medium, he expected to produce at the same average cost, 10 cents per pencil. After all, he thought, that's the average cost for 1,000 pencils and 2,000 pencils, so it should also be the average cost for 2,500 pencils. Much to his dismay, his average cost was 14 cents per pencil. The second puzzle is, Why didn't Large have the same average cost as the two other firms?

We can solve this second puzzle with another look at the average total cost curve. In Figure 11.5, Large produces 2,500 pencils at an average cost of 14 cents. With a U-shaped curve, it is possible to have the same average cost with two different quantities, but not three. Moving from 2,000 pencils to 2,500 pencils, diminishing returns become even more severe, pulling up average cost. Although the spreading of fixed costs decreases the average fixed cost, the fixed costs are so "thin" that the advantages of spreading the fixed costs are overwhelmed by diminishing returns and higher average variable cost. ■

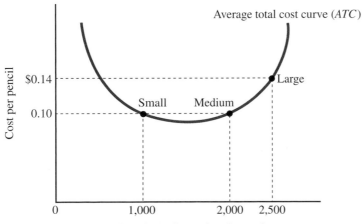

FIGURE 11.5

Different Quantities and the Same Average Cost?

Because the short-run average-total-cost curve is U-shaped, it is possible to have the same short-run average cost at two—but not three—different quantities of output.

Production and Cost in the Long Run

Up to this point, we've been exploring short-run cost curves, which show the cost of producing different quantities of output in a given production facility. We turn next to long-run cost curves, which show production costs in facilities of different sizes. The long run is defined as the period of time over which a firm is perfectly flexible in its choice of all inputs. In the long run, a firm can build a new production facility (factory, store, office, or restaurant) or modify an existing facility.

The key difference between the short run and the long run is that there are no diminishing returns in the long run. Recall that diminishing returns occur because workers share a fixed production facility, so the more workers in the facility, the smaller the share of the facility available for each worker. In the long run, a firm can expand its production facility as its workforce grows, so there are no diminishing returns.

Expansion and Replication

Continuing the example of paddle production, suppose that you have decided to replace your existing workshop with a new one. You have been producing 10 paddles per day at a total cost of $300 per day, or an average cost of $30 per paddle. If you want to produce twice as much output in your new facility, what should you do?

One possibility is simply to double the original operation. You could build two workshops that are identical to the original shop and hire two workforces, each identical to the original workforce. In this case, your total cost will double with your output: Each new shop will produce 10 paddles per day at a cost of $300, so you can produce a total of 20 paddles per day at twice the total cost, $600. A firm's **long-run total cost** is

Long-run total cost (LTC)

The total cost of production in the long run when a firm is perfectly flexible in its choice of all inputs and can choose a production facility of any size.

TABLE 11.4

Long-Run Average Cost

1	2	3	4	5	6
Labor	Output	Labor Cost	Capital Cost	Long-Run Total Cost	Long-Run Average Cost (*LAC*)
3	5	$150	$100	$250	$50
4	10	200	100	300	30
8	20	400	200	600	30
12	30	600	300	900	30

defined as the total cost of production when the firm is perfectly flexible in its choice of all inputs and can choose a production facility of any size. Column 5 in Table 11.4 shows the long-run total cost for different quantities, including 10, 20, and 30 paddles per day. The replication process means the long-run total cost increases proportionately with the quantity produced, from $300 for 10 paddles, to $600 for 20 paddles, to $900 for 30 paddles.

The **long-run average cost of production (*LAC*)** equals the long-run cost divided by the quantity produced. In column 6 of Table 11.4, the long-run average cost is $30 per paddle for 10 or more paddles. Because long-run total cost is proportional to the quantity produced, the long-run *average* cost (*LAC*) doesn't change as output increases. In Figure 11.6, the long-run average-cost curve is horizontal for 10 or more paddles per day.

We've seen that if a firm wants to double its output in the long run, replication is one option. By simply replicating an existing operation, a firm can double its output and its total costs, leaving average cost unchanged. Another possibility is to build a single larger workshop, one that can produce twice as much output at a lower cost than

Long-run average cost of production (*LAC*)

Long-run total cost divided by the quantity of output produced.

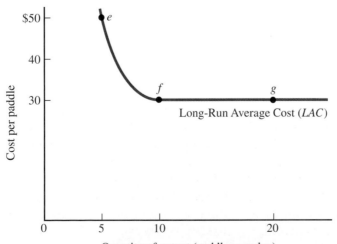

FIGURE 11.6

The Long-Run Average-Cost Curve and Scale Economies
The long-run average-cost curve (*LAC*) is negatively sloped for up to 10 paddles per day, a result of indivisible inputs and the effects of labor specialization. If the firm replicates the operation that produces 10 paddles per day, the long-run average-cost curve will be horizontal beyond 10 paddles per day.

**Long-run marginal cost
(LMC)**

The change in long-run cost
from producing one more unit
of output.

would be possible by simply building two facilities identical to the original. If so, the long-run average cost of producing the larger quantity (for example, 20 paddles) would be less than $30 per paddle.

A firm's **long-run marginal cost (LMC)** is the change in long-run cost resulting from producing one more unit of output. In the long run, the firm is perfectly flexible in choosing its inputs. Therefore, the LMC is the increase in cost when the firm can change its production facility as well as its workforce.

Scaling Down and Indivisible Inputs

What would happen if you decided to scale down your operation, producing only 5 paddles per day instead of 10? Although it's tempting to think that your total costs would be cut in half, that's not necessarily the case. Remember that you use a single mold to produce 10 paddles per day. If you cut your output in half, you would still need the mold, so your capital costs won't be cut in half. If each mold requires a fixed amount of floor space, you would also need the same floor space, so cutting output in half wouldn't decrease the cost of your production facility at all. You would still have a cost of $100 per day for the mold and the workspace. Because cutting output in half doesn't cut capital costs in half, the average cost of 5 paddles will exceed the average cost of 10 paddles.

Indivisible input

An input that cannot be scaled
down to produce a smaller
quantity of output.

The mold is an example of an **indivisible input**, one that cannot be scaled down to produce a smaller quantity of output. When a production process requires the use of indivisible inputs, the average cost of production increases as output decreases, because the cost of the indivisible inputs is spread over a smaller quantity of output.

**The production of many
goods and services involves
inputs, such as this large
ship for ocean cargo service.**

Most production operations use some indivisible inputs, but the costs of these inputs vary. Here are some examples of firms and their indivisible inputs:

► A railroad company providing freight service between two cities must lay a set of tracks between them. The company cannot scale down the tracks by laying a half set of tracks (a single rail).
► A shipping firm uses a large ship to carry TV sets from Japan to the United States.
► A steel producer uses a large blast furnace.
► A hospital uses imaging machines (for X rays, CAT scans, and MRIs).
► A pizzeria uses a pizza oven.

These indivisible inputs cannot be scaled down to produce a smaller quantity of output. For example, it is impractical to produce steel in a toaster oven, just as it is impractical to transport a single TV set across the ocean in a rowboat. For another example of indivisible inputs, read "A Closer Look: Indivisible Inputs and the Cost of Fake Killer Whales."

A CLOSER LOOK
Indivisible Inputs and the Cost of Fake Killer Whales

Sea lions off the Washington coast eat steelhead and other fish, depleting some species threatened with extinction and decreasing the harvest of the commercial fishing industry. Rick Funk, a plastics manufacturer, thinks that a variation on the scarecrow would solve the sea lion problem. Killer whales love to eat sea lions. Funk says that he could build a life-sized fiberglass killer whale, mount it on a rail like a roller coaster, and then send the whale diving through the water to scare off the sea lions. According to Funk, it would cost about $16,000 to make the first whale.[2] Once the mold is made, however, each additional whale would cost an additional $5,000. That means two whales would cost $21,000, three whales would cost $26,000, and so on.

This little story illustrates the effects of indivisible inputs on the firm's cost curves. The mold is an indivisible input, because it cannot be scaled down and still produce whales. If Funk wants to cut his production from two whales per month down to one, he still needs the mold; he cannot simply produce half as many whales with a mold that is half the size. The cost of producing the first whale ($16,000) includes the

How much would it cost to make fake killer whales to scare away sea lions that feast on steelhead and other fish?

cost of the mold, the indivisible input. Once the firm has the mold, the marginal cost for each whale is only $5,000, so the average cost per whale decreases as the number of whales increases.

Scaling Down and Labor Specialization

A second reason for higher average long-run costs in a smaller operation is that labor will be less specialized in the small operation. As we saw earlier in the book, the labor specialization—each worker specializing in an individual production task—makes workers more productive because of continuity (less time switching from one task to another) and repetition (each worker becomes more proficient). Reversing this process, when we reduce the workforce, each worker will become less specialized, performing a wider variety of production tasks. The loss of specialization will decrease labor productivity, so you'll need more than half the original workforce to produce half as much output.

The first row in Table 11.4 shows labor and capital costs in the smaller operation. Suppose that to produce 5 paddles, you'll need 3 workers (including yourself). In this case, your labor cost will be $150. Adding the $100 cost of the indivisible input (the mold and shop space), the total cost of producing 5 paddles per day will be $250, or $50 per paddle. This exceeds the average cost of 10 paddles because in the smaller operation you still need the same amount of capital and your workers are less productive. In Figure 11.6, the average cost of 5 paddles per day exceeds the average cost for larger quantities.

Economies of Scale

Economies of scale

A situation in which an increase in the quantity produced decreases the long-run average cost of production.

A firm experiences **economies of scale** if its long-run average-cost curve is negatively sloped. In Figure 11.6, the paddle producer experiences economies of scale between points *e* and *f*. For example, at point *e*, the long-run average cost of producing 5 paddles per day is $50, compared to $30 for 10 paddles (point *f*) and larger quantities. An increase in output from 5 to 10 paddles decreases the long-run average cost of production because (1) the firm spreads the cost of an indivisible input over a larger quantity and (2) labor specialization increases worker productivity, decreasing average cost. In other words, there are some economies (that is, cost savings) associated with scaling up the firm's operation.

As we will see later in the book, recent technological innovations have decreased the cost of producing electricity from the wind, leading to the development of wind farms. There are scale economies in the production of electricity from wind because although large wind turbines are more costly than small ones, the higher cost is more than offset by greater generating capacity. For the details, read "A Closer Look: Scale Economies in Wind Power."

One way to quantify the extent of scale economies in the production of a particular good is to determine the minimum efficient scale for producing the good. The **minimum efficient scale** is defined as the output at which scale economies are exhausted. In graphical terms, the minimum efficient scale is the quantity at which the long-run average-cost curve becomes horizontal, for example, point *f* in Figure 11.6. If a firm starts out with a quantity of output below the minimum efficient scale, an increase in output will decrease its long-run average cost. Once the minimum efficient scale has been reached, an increase in output no longer decreases the long-run average cost. In Britain, the minimum efficient scale for an

Minimum efficient scale

The output at which the long-run average-cost curve becomes horizontal.

A CLOSER LOOK

Scale Economies in Wind Power

There are scale economies in the production of electricity from wind because the cost of purchasing, installing, and maintaining a wind turbine increases less than proportionately with the generating capacity of the turbine. The table shows the various costs of a small turbine (150 kilowatt capacity) and a large turbine (600 kilowatt capacity), each with an assumed lifetime of 20 years.[3]

Costs of Wind Turbines

	Small Turbine (150 kilowatt)	Large Turbine (600 kilowatt)
Purchase price of turbine	$150,000	$420,000
Installation cost	**$100,000**	$100,000
Operating and maintenance cost	$75,000	$126,000
Total cost	$325,000	$646,000
Electricity generated (kilowatt hours)	5 million	20 million
Average cost (per kilowatt hour)	$0.065	$0.032

The larger turbine has four times the generation capacity (20 million kilowatt hours versus 5 million kilowatt hours), but its purchase price is less than three times as much, its installation cost is the same, and its operating and maintenance costs are less than twice as much. The average cost per kilowatt hour is only $0.032 for the large turbine, compared to $0.065 for the smaller turbine.

oil refinery is 10 million tons of oil per year (about 10% of the British market).[4] In the United States, the minimum efficient scale for automobiles is between 200,000 and 400,000 autos per year.[5] This means that a production facility serving between 3% and 6% of the U.S. market would be large enough to fully exploit the economies of scale in auto production.

Diseconomies of Scale

If a firm's long-run average cost curve is positively sloped, the firm experiences **diseconomies of scale**, meaning that when the firm increases its output, its long-run average cost of production increases. Diseconomies of scale can occur for two reasons:

▶ *Coordination problems.* One of the problems of a large organization is that it requires several layers of management (a bureaucracy) to coordinate the activities of the different parts of the organization. If an increase in the firm's output requires additional layers of management, the long-run average-cost curve may be positively sloped.

▶ *Increasing input costs.* When a firm increases its output, it will demand more of each of its inputs and *may* be forced to pay higher prices for some of these inputs. For example, a construction firm may be forced to pay more for workers to attract more of them. Alternatively, a firm may have to hire workers who are less skilled. An increase in input prices will increase the long-run average cost of production, generating a positively sloped long-run average-cost curve.

The experience of General Motors suggests there are diseconomies of scale in the production of automobiles, largely because of coordination problems.[6] General Motors is one-third bigger than Ford and larger than the two biggest Japanese automakers combined (Toyota and Nissan). Nonetheless, the average cost of a GM automobile is $200 to $2,000 higher than the average cost of automobiles produced by other firms.

Firms recognize the possibility of diseconomies of scale and adopt various strategies to avoid them. An example of a firm that adjusts its operations to do so is 3M. According to Gordon Engdahl, the company's vice president for human resources, "We made a conscious effort to keep our units as small as possible because it keeps them flexible and vital. When one gets too large, we break it apart. We like to say that our success in recent years amounts to multiplication by division."[7]

Actual Long-Run Average-Cost Curves

Figure 11.7 shows the actual long-run average-cost curves for several products: Aluminum production, truck freight, and hospital services.[8] Each long-run average-cost curve is negatively sloped for small quantities of output and relatively flat (almost horizontal) over a large range of output. In addition, each curve has a slight positive slope for large quantities of output. In other words, these curves are L-shaped. Other studies suggest that the long-run cost curves of a wide variety of goods and services have the same shape.

Why is the typical long-run average-cost curve L-shaped? The long-run average-cost curves are negatively sloped for small quantities of output because there are economies of scale resulting from indivisible inputs and labor specialization. They then level off and are horizontal over a wide range of output because once a firm reaches a certain scale, its long-run total cost increases proportionately with its output, reflecting its ability to increase inputs and outputs proportionately. This leads to a constant long-run average total cost (LAC).

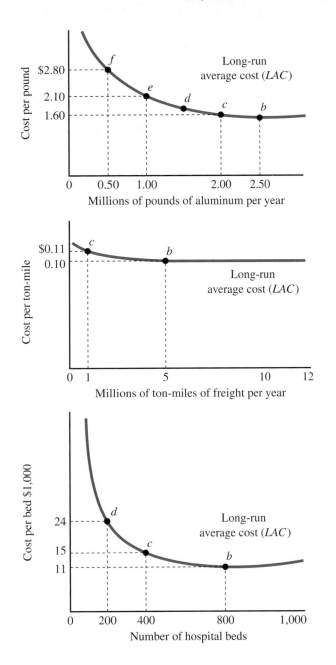

FIGURE 11.7

Actual Long-Run Average-Cost Curves for Three Products: Aluminum, Truck Freight, and Hospital Services

Short-Run Versus Long-Run Average Cost

Why is the firm's short-run average-cost curve U-shaped, while the long-run average-cost curve is L-shaped? For large quantities of output, the short-run curve is positively sloped because of diminishing returns and the resulting increases in the labor cost per unit of output. In the long run, the firm can scale up its operation by building a larger production facility, so the firm does not suffer from diminishing returns. If there are no diseconomies of scale, the long-run average-cost curve will be negatively sloped or horizontal. If the firm experiences some diseconomies of scale, the long-run average-cost curve will eventually be positively sloped, but the short-run average-cost curve will be much steeper.

TEST Your Understanding

5. Draw a line connecting each item on the left with the appropriate item on the right.

   Diseconomies of scale   Negatively sloped long-run average-cost curve

   Economies of scale   Positively sloped long-run average-cost curve

   Indivisible inputs

   Labor specialization

   Coordination problems

6. When you mention that most firms have L-shaped long-run average-cost curves, your new boss says, "You're wrong. Haven't you heard of diminishing returns?" How should you respond?

7. What portion of a long-run average-cost curve is explained by the notion of replication?

Information Goods and First-Copy Cost

We've discussed costs in the short run, when a firm cannot change its production facility, and the long run, when a firm can pick a facility of any size. Consider next the special case of producing an information good such as a music CD, a movie on DVD, or a book. In all three cases, the cost of producing the first copy is very high, but the marginal cost of reproduction is very low.

We'll illustrate the production costs of information goods with a music CD. Suppose that your band, Adam Smith and the Invisible Hands, has decided to produce a music CD. The cost of recording a set of songs is $100,000. This amount includes the band's opportunity cost of time spent in the recording studio and the cost of studio time ($200 per hour). Once the tracks are recorded and put in a digital format, you can have CDs burned at a cost of $1 per CD, regardless of the number burned.

Table 11.5 shows the relationships between the quantity of CDs produced and production cost. In this case, you are using the production facilities of other firms, so the distinction between short run and long run is unimportant. The marginal cost is constant at $1, but the average cost decreases with the quantity produced. For example, the cost of the first CD is a whopping $100,001, but the average cost drops to $11 for the 10,000th CD and

TABLE 11.5 Average Cost of an Information Good

Quantity of CDs	Recording Cost	Burning Cost	Total Cost	Average Cost	Marginal Cost
0	$100,000	0	$100,000		
1	100,000	$1	100,001	$100,001	$1
1,000	100,000	1,000	101,000	101	1
5,000	100,000	5,000	105,000	21	1
10,000	100,000	10,000	110,000	11	1
50,000	100,000	50,000	150,000	3	1

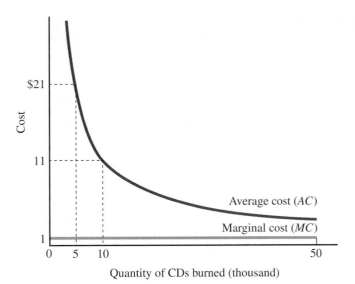

FIGURE 11.8

Average-Cost Curve for an Information Good
For an information good such as a music CD the cost of producing the first copy is very high, but the marginal cost of reproduction is low and constant.

$3 for the 50,000th CD. In Figure 11.8, the average-cost curve is negatively sloped and gets closer and closer to the horizontal marginal-cost curve as the quantity produced increases, reflecting the spreading of the fixed recording cost over a larger number of CDs.

With this production technology, the "first-copy" cost is relatively large because it is costly to generate the digital information to be burned onto CDs. The first-copy cost is the $100,001 required to generate the information and then make the first copy. There are many other examples of products with large first-copy costs, including software, phone books, business directories, maps, and the book you are holding. To produce a book, a publisher must first arrange all the words and images into a coherent manuscript. The cost of producing this information—including the opportunity costs of the authors, editors, photographers, graphic artists, and typesetters—is very large. Once the stream of words and images—on pages or in digital format—is generated, the publisher can reproduce the information, with a relatively low marginal cost for paper, ink, and printing-press time. Most publishers use outside presses to actually print their books, with a constant marginal cost per book produced.

USING THE TOOLS

This chapter has explained the economics behind the firm's short- and long-run cost curves. Here are some opportunities to use those curves as graphical tools in your own economic analysis.

1. Changing Costs

Return to the paddle production example and refer to Table 11.2. Compute the short-run average cost for 10 paddles with the following changes: (a) your opportunity cost of work time triples, from $50 to

$150; (b) the interest rate for invested funds is cut in half, from 10% to 5%; (c) labor productivity doubles (the quantity produced by each workforce doubles).

2. The Cost of Breaking Up an Aluminum Firm

Consider a large aluminum firm that initially produces two million pounds of aluminum per year. Suppose that an antitrust action breaks up the firm into two smaller firms, each of which produces half as much as the original firm. Use the information in Figure 11.7 to predict the effects on the long-run average cost of producing aluminum.

3. Popularity and Information Goods

You are the manager of the band whose CD production costs are shown in Table 11.5. Your objective is to sell as many CDs as you can and break even (the break-even point is where your total revenue just equals your total cost). If you pick a price of $21, you will sell 5,000 CDs. The slope of the demand curve is –$0.002 per CD sold.

a. If you want to maximize sales while breaking even, what price should you choose? Illustrate with a completely labeled graph.

b. Suppose an interview in *Rolling Stone* makes more people aware of your music and the demand curve shifts to the right. If you still want

to break even and maximize sales, will you increase or decrease your price? Illustrate with a completely labeled graph.

4. Deregulation and the Cost of Trucking

Assume that the market for truck freight is initially served by a single regulated firm. If the market is deregulated, several new firms, unconstrained by regulations, will enter the market. At a public hearing on the issue of deregulation, the manager of the regulated firm issued a grim warning to the regulatory authorities: "If you deregulate this market, four or five firms will enter the market, and the unit cost of truck freight will at least triple. There are big economies of scale in trucking services, so a single large firm is much more cost-efficient than several small firms would be. If you want firms in your city to pay three times as much for their truck freight, go ahead and deregulate this market." Use the information in Figure 11.7 to comment on this statement.

SUMMARY

In this chapter, we explored the cost side of a firm, explaining the shapes of the firm's short-run cost curves and long-run cost curves. Here are the main points of the chapter:

1 The positively sloped portion of the short-run marginal-cost curve (*MC*) results from diminishing returns.

2 The short-run average-total-cost curve (*ATC*) is U-shaped because of the conflicting effects of (a) fixed costs being spread over a larger quantity of output and (b) diminishing returns.

3 The long-run average-cost curve (*LAC*) is horizontal over some range of output because replication is an option, so doubling output will no more than double long-run total cost.

4 The long-run average-cost curve (*LAC*) is negatively sloped for small quantities of output because there are indivisible inputs that cannot be scaled down and a smaller operation has limited opportunities for labor specialization.

5 Diseconomies of scale arise if there are problems in coordinating a large operation or higher input costs in a larger organization.

KEY TERMS

average fixed cost (*AFC*), 240
average variable cost (*AVC*), 241
diminishing returns, 238
diseconomies of scale, 252
economic cost, 236

economies of scale, 250
explicit cost, 236
fixed cost (*FC*), 239
implicit cost, 236
indivisible input, 248

long-run average cost of production (*LAC*), 247
long-run marginal cost (*LMC*), 247
long-run total cost (*LTC*), 246
marginal product of labor, 237

minimum efficient scale, 250
short-run average total cost (ATC), 242

short-run marginal cost (MC), 242
short-run total cost (TC), 239

variable cost (VC), 239
total product curve, 238

1 Suppose that the indivisible inputs used in the production of shirts have a cost per day of $400. To produce one shirt per day, the firm must also spend a total of $5 on other inputs (labor, materials, and other capital). For each additional shirt, the firm incurs the same additional cost ($5). Compute the average cost for 40 shirts, 100 shirts, 200 shirts, and 400 shirts. Draw the long-run average-cost curve for 40 to 400 shirts per day.

2 Consider a firm with the following short-run costs:

Quantity	Variable Cost (VC)	Total Cost (TC)
1	30	90
2	50	110
3	90	150
4	140	200
5	200	260

a. What is the firm's fixed cost?
b. Compute short-run marginal cost (MC), short-run average variable cost (AVC), and short-run average total cost (ATC) for the different quantities of output.
c. Draw the three cost curves. Explain the relationship between the MC curve and the ATC curve and the relationship between the AVC curve and the ATC curve.

3 Given the following relationship between labor input and the quantity produced, compute the marginal product of labor for the different input levels. Then draw the total product curve and the marginal-product curve.

Labor	Output
0	0
1	5
2	11
3	15
4	18
5	19

4 Consider a firm that has a fixed cost of $60 per minute. Complete the following table:

Output	FC	VC	TC	MC	AFC	AVC	ATC
1	___	10	___	___	___	___	___
2	___	18	___	___	___	___	___
3	___	30	___	___	___	___	___
4	___	45	___	___	___	___	___
5	___	65	___	___	___	___	___
6	___	90	___	___	___	___	___

5 Consider a firm that has constant marginal returns. That means that the first worker is just as productive as the second, who is just as productive as the third, and so on. The same is true for all the firm's inputs.
a. Draw the firm's short-run marginal cost curve (MC).
b. Explain why this firm's cost curve differs from the short-run marginal-cost curve for paddle production.

6 Beaverduck Bus Company wants to compute the cost of adding a third daily bus between Eugene and Corvallis, Ore. Comment on the following statement of Abby Abacus, the company's accountant: "If we add the third bus, our total cost would increase from $700 to $780. Therefore, the marginal cost of the third bus is $260 ($780 divided by 3)."

7 You want to know the short-run marginal cost of producing a Chevrolet Caprice. Comment on the following statement from an analyst in the production department: "The marginal cost of a Caprice, given our current volume, is $12,500. Of course, the actual marginal cost depends on the number of cars produced. The larger the number produced, the lower the unit cost because we will spread out our design and tooling costs over more cars."

8 Explain the difference between diseconomies of scale and diminishing returns. Based on the cost curves you've seen in this chapter, which is more pervasive?

9 Suppose that one firm generates 30 billion kilo-watthours of electricity, which is about three times the output of a second electricity firm. Which firm will have a higher cost per kilowatthour? Use the information in Figure 11.7 to predict the difference in the average costs of the two firms.

10 As a child, you recorded the costs of your lemonade stand and drew your long-run average-cost curve. Now you work in a computer-chip factory. Would you expect any similarities between the long-run average-cost curve for lemonade and the long-run average-cost curve for the chip factory? Would you expect any differences?

11 A hammer manufacturer has just hired you to advise the firm on its production costs. In your first meeting with production managers, you hear the following statements. Are they true or false? Explain.

a. "If the production process is subject to diminishing returns, the long-run average-cost curve will be positively sloped."

b. "At the current output level, this factory is subject to diminishing returns. Therefore, the firm is operating along the upward-sloping portion of its short-run marginal-cost (*MC*) curve."

c. "At the current output level, this factory is subject to diminishing returns. Therefore, the firm is operating along the upward-sloping portion of its short-run average-total-cost (*ATC*) curve."

d. "The short-run average total cost of producing 250 hammers is less than the short-run average cost of producing 260 hammers. Therefore, the short-run marginal cost of 260 hammers is less than the short-run average cost of 260 hammers."

MODEL ANSWERS TO QUESTIONS

Chapter-Opening Questions

1 The short-run average-cost curve reflects diminishing returns, which pulls up short-run average cost as output increases. There are no diminishing returns in the long run.

2 As explained in the "Economic Puzzle: Same Average Cost at Two or Three Quantities," a U-shaped average cost curve has the same average cost for two quantities.

3 As explained in "A Closer Look: Indivisible Inputs and the Cost of Fake Killer Whales," the cost of the first whale includes the cost of the mold, an indivisible input.

4 As shown in "A Closer Look: Scale Economies in Wind Power," the average cost with a large turbine (600 kilowatts) is about half the average cost with a smaller one (150 kilowatts).

Test Your Understanding

1 The principle of diminishing returns.

2 If the firm is operating in the region of diminishing returns, an increase in output will have two con-flicting effects: Diminishing returns pull up average cost, while spreading the fixed costs pulls it down. If the initial quantity of output is large enough, diminishing returns will be more powerful than spreading the fixed cost, so *ATC* will increase.

3 The marginal cost is less than the average cost, so the marginal cost pulls down the average cost. *ATC* will decrease, at least for small increases in output.

4 Average.

5 Draw lines from "diseconomies of scale" and "coordination problems" to "positively sloped long-run average-cost curve." Draw lines from "economies of scale," "indivisible inputs," and "labor specialization" to "negatively sloped long-run average-cost curve."

6 Diminishing returns occur when we increase output in an existing production facility. The principle of diminishing returns is applicable in the short run, not in the long run. To draw the long-run cost curve, we assume that we can change the size of the production facility.

7 The horizontal portion of the *LAC* curve.

NOTES

1. Emily Lambert and John Turrettine, "Unplugged," *Forbes Magazine*, November 25, 2002, pp. 239–232.

2. Sandi Doughton, "Killer Whale Latest Idea on Sea Lions," *The Oregonian*, January 7, 1995.

3. Danish Wind Turbine Manufacturers Association. Guided Tour of Wind Energy (http://www.windpower.dk).

4. Aubrey Silberson, "Economies of Scale in Theory and Practice," *Economic Journal*, vol. 82, 1972, pp. 369–391.

5. Walter Adams and James W. Brock, "Automobiles," Chapter 4 in *The Structure of the American Economy*, 9th ed., edited by Walter Adams and James W. Brock (Upper Saddle River, NJ: Prentice Hall, 1995).

6. Walter Adams and James W. Brock, "Automobiles," Chapter 4 in *The Structure of the American Economy*, 9th ed., edited by Walter Adams and James W. Brock (Upper Saddle River, NJ: Prentice Hall, 1995).

7. Frederick C. Klein, "At 3M Plants, Workers Have Flexibility, Involvement—And Their Own Radios," *Wall Street Journal*, February 5, 1982, p. 1.

8. Laurits Christensen and William H. Greene, "Economies of Scale in U.S. Electric Power Generation," *Journal of Political Economy*, vol. 84, 1976, pp. 655–676. Reprinted by permission of The University of Chicago Press; Joel P. Clark and Merton C. Flemings, "Advanced Materials and the Economy," *Scientific American,* vol. 255, October 1986, pp. 51–60. Copyright © 1986 by Scientific American, Inc. All rights reserved; Roger Koenker, "Optimal Scale and the Size Distribution of American Trucking Firms," *Journal of Transport Economics and Policy,* January 1977, p. 62; Harold A. Cohen, "Hospital Cost Curves with Emphasis on Measuring Patient Care Output," in *Empirical Studies in Health Economics,* edited by Herbert E. Klarman (Baltimore, MD: Johns Hopkins University Press, 1970); John Johnson, *Statistical Cost Analysis* (New York: McGraw-Hill, 1960).

Preview: Alternative Market Structures

The Firm's Short-Run Output Decision

The Total Approach: Computing Total
    Revenue and Total Cost
The Marginal Approach
Economic Profit and the Break-Even Price

The Firm's Shut-Down Decision

Total Revenue, Variable Cost,
    and the Shut-Down Decision
The Shut-Down Price
Fixed Costs and Sunk Costs
Application: Break-Even and Shut-Down
    Prices for Corn Farmer

Short-Run Supply Curves

The Firm's Short-Run Supply Curve
The Short-Run Market Supply Curve
Market Equilibrium

The Long-Run Supply Curve for an Increasing-Cost Industry

Production Cost and Industry Size
Drawing the Long-Run Market Supply
    Curve
Application: Increasing-Cost Industries—
    Wolfram, Sugar, Rental Housing

Short-Run and Long-Run Effects of Changes in Demand

The Short-Run Response to an Increase
    in Demand
The Long-Run Response to an Increase
    in Demand

Long-Run Supply for a Constant-Cost Industry

Long-Run Supply Curve for a Constant-
    Cost Industry
Application: Hurricane Andrew
    and the Price of Ice
Using the Tools

Perfect Competition

n 1992, Hurricane Andrew struck the
southeastern United States, leaving millions of
people without electricity for several days.
Refrigerators stopped working, and thousands of
people suddenly needed a lot of ice to cool and
preserve their food. The price of a bag of ice immediately
rose from $1 to $5. The same sort of price hikes occurred for
chain saws (for clearing downed trees), bottled water, tarpaper (for
repairing roofs), and plywood. If you had been the governor of Florida in
1992, what would you have done about the price hikes?

T his is the first of four chapters exploring the decisions made by firms in different types of markets. Markets differ in the number of firms that compete against one another for customers. At one extreme is a monopoly, a market with a single seller. In this chapter, we'll look at the other extreme—a perfectly competitive market. In a **perfectly competitive market**, hundreds or even thousands of firms sell a standardized or homogeneous product. Each firm realizes that it cannot affect the market price, so each firm takes the market price as given. A firm has no reason to cut its price to sell more because it can sell as much as it wants at the market price. A firm has no reason to increase its price because it would lose all its customers to one of the other firms selling at the market price.

Perfectly competitive market has two other features. First, on the demand side of the market, there are hundreds or even thousands of buyers, each of whom takes the market price as given. Second, there are no barriers to market entry, so firms can easily enter or exit the market. To summarize, here are the five features of a perfectly competitive market:

▶ There are many sellers (hundreds or even thousands).
▶ There are many buyers (hundreds or even thousands).
▶ The product is standardized or homogeneous.
▶ Firms can freely enter or leave the market.
▶ Both buyers and sellers take the market price as "given."

If you're thinking that the model of perfect competition is not very realistic, you're right. Most firms have some flexibility over their prices. When a firm increases its price slightly, it will certainly sell less, but the quantity sold will probably not drop to zero. Although perfect competition is rare, it's a good starting point for analyzing a firm's decisions because a price-taking firm's decisions are easy to understand. The firm doesn't have to pick a price; it just decides how much to produce, given the market price. Once you understand this simple case, you will be ready to tackle the more complex decisions that must be made when firms choose their own prices. We'll discuss this scenario in later chapters.

In this chapter, we'll see how perfectly competitive firms use information on revenues and costs to decide how much output to produce when the price is a given. We'll see how the law of supply applies to firms in a perfectly competitive market, both in the short run and the long run. Here are some practical questions that we answer:

1 You and some fellow students have a firm that delivers packages by bicycle. If you want to determine whether you are maximizing your profit, what information do you need?

2 If a firm is losing money, when does it make sense to operate at a loss?

Perfectly competitive market

A market with hundreds or thousands of sellers and buyers of a standardized good. Each buyer and seller takes the market price as given. Firms can easily enter or exit the market.

3 If you want to provide phone service in the United States, you must first invest millions of dollars. In Pakistan, you can start providing phone service after an investment of only $310. What explains the difference?

Preview: Alternative Market Structures

Before we delve into perfect competition, it will be useful to see how our discussion of perfect competition fits into the general scheme of the book. After discussing perfect competition in this chapter, we'll look at three other market structures in the next three chapters. The key difference between perfect competition and these other market structures is the assumption of price-taking by perfectly competitive firms.

Let's start by distinguishing between a market demand curve and the demand curve for an individual firm. As we saw earlier in the book, the market demand curve shows the relationship between the price and the quantity that can be sold in the market, assuming that all firms charge the same price. In contrast, the **firm-specific demand curve** shows the relationship between the price charged by a specific firm and the quantity that can be sold by that firm. In a monopoly, a single firm serves the entire market, so the firm-specific demand curve is the same as the market demand curve. There is a single price in the market, and everything is sold by the single firm. As shown in Panel A of Figure 12.1, the monopolist can choose any point on the market demand curve, recognizing that the higher the price, the smaller the quantity it will sell.

As shown in Panel B of Figure 12.1, things are different for a perfectly competitive firm. The firm-specific demand curve is horizontal—perfectly elastic. A perfectly competitive firm can sell as much as it wants at the market price of $12, but if it raises its price even a penny, it will sell nothing.

Most markets lie between the extremes of monopoly and perfect competition. Table 12.1 provides a preview of three alternative market structures.

Firm-specific demand curve

A curve showing the relationship between the price charged by a specific firm and the quantity that can be sold by that firm.

FIGURE 12.1

Monoply Versus Perfect Competition

In Panel A, the demand curve facing a monopolist is the market demand curve. In Panel B, a perfectly competitive firm takes the market price as given, so the firm-specific demand curve is horizontal. The firm can sell all it wants at the market price, but would sell nothing if it charged a higher price.

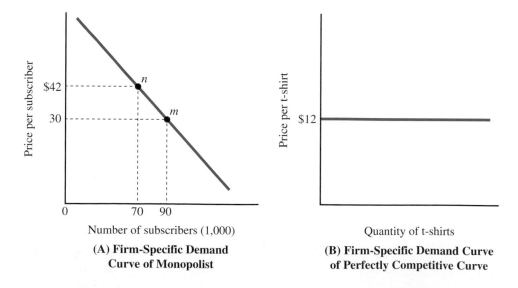

(A) Firm-Specific Demand Curve of Monopolist

(B) Firm-Specific Demand Curve of Perfectly Competitive Curve

TABLE 12.1 Characteristics of Different Types of Markets

	Perfect Competition	Monopolistic Competition	Oligopoly	Monopoly
Number of firms	Very large number (hundreds or more)	Many	Few	One
Type of product	Standardized (homogeneous)	Differentiated	Standardized or differentiated	Unique
Firm-specific demand curve	Price-taker: Demand is perfectly elastic	Demand is price elastic but not perfectly elastic	Demand is less elastic than demand facing monopolistically competitive firm	Firm faces market demand curve
Entry conditions	No barriers	No barriers	Large barriers from economies of scale or government policies	Large barriers from economies of scale or government policies
Examples	Corn, plain T-shirts	Toothbrushes, music stores, groceries	Air travel, automobiles, beverages, cigarettes, long-distance phone services	Local phone service, patented drugs

▶ Chapter 13: Monopoly. A single firm serves the entire market. A monopoly occurs when the barriers to market entry are very large. This can result from very large economies of scale or a government limit on the number of firms. Some examples of goods with large-scale economies are local phone service, cable TV, and electric power transmission. Some examples of monopolies established by government policy are drugs covered by patents and the selling of food and firewood in national parks.

▶ Chapter 14: Monopolistic competition. There are many firms, each selling a slightly different product. Some examples are restaurants, gas stations, and drug stores. There are no barriers to entering the market, so there are many firms.

▶ Chapter 15: Oligopoly. There are just a few firms in the market, which can be a result of the same two barriers to entry we discussed with monopoly: economies of scale and government policies limiting the number of firms in the market. Some product examples are automobiles, airline travel, and breakfast cereals. The large economies of scale in automobile production result from the large start-up costs, with billions of dollars required to build factories and assembly plants. In contrast, a person can start producing corn with a much smaller initial investment.

The Firm's Short-Run Output Decision

We'll start our discussion of perfect competition with an individual firm's decision about how much to produce. The firm's objective is to maximize its **economic profit** which equals its **total revenue** minus its total economic cost. Recall that economic cost includes all the opportunity costs of production, including both explicit costs

Economic profit
Total revenue minus total economic cost.

Total revenue
The money the firm gets by selling its product; equal to the price times the quantity sold.

(cash payments) and implicit costs (the entrepreneur's opportunity costs). In Chapter 11, we saw that the cost of production varied with the quantity produced. In this chapter, we'll see how economic profit varies with the quantity produced and how a firm can pick the quantity that maximizes its economic profit.

It's important to note that economic profit differs from the conventional notion of profit. When accountants compute a firm's cost, they include explicit costs, but ignore implicit costs. Accountants focus on the flow of money into and out of a firm, so they ignore costs that do not involve explicit transactions. **Accounting profit** equals total revenue minus explicit costs. Because accountants ignore implicit costs, accounting profit usually exceeds economic profit.

We will use the market for plain T-shirts to illustrate decision-making in a perfectly competitive market. Some plain T-shirts are sold directly to consumers, and others are sold to firms that imprint words and images on the T-shirts and then sell the finished shirts to consumers. Plain T-shirts are produced in countries around the world, by a large number of producers.

Accounting profit

Total revenue minus explicit costs.

The Total Approach: Computing Total Revenue and Total Cost

One way to decide how much to produce involves computing the total revenue and total cost of different quantities of output. We looked at the cost side of the profit equation in Chapter 11, and the revenue side for a perfectly competitive market is straightforward. A firm's total revenue is the money it gets by selling its product. Total revenue is equal to the price of the product times the quantity sold. For example, if a firm sells 8 T-shirts at $12 per shirt, total revenue is $96. If our T-shirt producer has an economic cost of $63, the firm's profit would be $33 (equal to $96 − $63).

Table 12.2 shows the total revenue and total costs of a hypothetical producer of plain cotton T-shirts. As shown in the second and third columns, there is a fixed cost of $17, and variable cost increases with the amount produced. The fourth column shows total

TABLE 12.2

Deciding How Much to Produce When Price = $12

1 Output: Shirts per Minute	2 Fixed Cost	3 Variable Cost	4 Total Cost	5 Total Revenue	6 Profit	7 Marginal Revenue (Price)	8 Marginal Cost
0	$17	$0	$17	$0	−$17		
1	17	5	22	12	−10	$12	$5
2	17	6	23	24	1	12	1
3	17	9	26	36	10	12	3
4	17	13	30	48	18	12	4
5	17	18	35	60	25	12	5
6	17	25	42	72	30	12	7
7	17	34	51	84	33	12	9
8	**17**	**46**	**63**	**96**	**33**	**12**	**12**
9	17	62	79	108	29	12	16
10	17	83	100	120	20	12	21

cost, the sum of fixed and variable costs. As shown in the fifth column, with a price of $12 per shirt, the firm's total revenue is $12 times the number of shirts produced. The sixth column shows economic profit, defined as total revenue minus total cost.

Figure 12.2 shows one way to choose the quantity of output that maximizes profit. We're looking for the largest profit, the biggest gap between total revenue and total cost. For example, for 5 shirts, the gap is $25 (total revenue equals $60, and total cost equals $35). Moving down the table and across the figure, we see that profit increases to $30 for 6 shirts, and profit is maximized at $33 when the firm produces either 7 or 8 shirts. When profit reaches its highest level with two different quantities (7 and 8 shirts in this example), we assume that the firm produces the larger quantity. When the firm produces 8 shirts, its total revenue is $96 and its total cost is $63, leaving a profit of $33.

The Marginal Approach

The other way to decide how much output to produce involves the marginal principle, the general decision-making rule that is one of the key principles of economics.

MARGINAL *Principle*

Increase the level of an activity if its marginal benefit exceeds its marginal cost, but reduce the level if the marginal cost exceeds the marginal benefit. If possible, pick the level at which the marginal benefit equals the marginal cost.

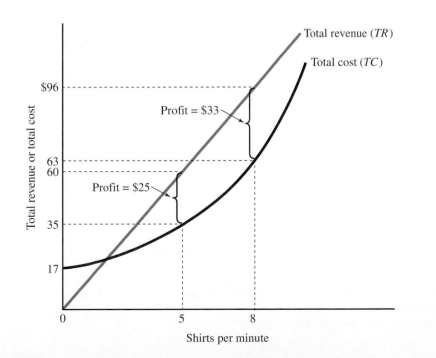

FIGURE 12.2

Using the Total Approach to Choose an Output Level
Economic profit is shown by the vertical distance between the total-revenue curve and the total-cost curve. To maximize profit, the firm chooses the quantity of output that generates the largest vertical difference between the two curves.

Since our firm is in the business to make money, the "benefit" it gets from producing
shirts is revenue. The *marginal* benefit—or **marginal revenue**—of producing shirts
is the change in total revenue that results from selling one more shirt. A perfectly competitive firm takes the market price as given, so the marginal revenue—the change in
total revenue from one more shirt—is simply the price.

$$\text{marginal revenue} = \text{price}$$

The marginal principle tells us that the firm will maximize its profit by choosing
the quantity at which price equals marginal cost:

> To maximize profit, produce the quantity where price = marginal cost

In Figure 12.3, the horizontal line shows the market price for T-shirts, which our shirt
producer takes as given. The price line intersects the marginal-cost curve at 8 shirts per
minute, so that's the quantity that satisfies the marginal principle and maximizes profit.

To see that an output of 8 shirts per minute maximizes the firm's profit, imagine
the firm produced only 5 shirts per minute. Could the firm make more profit by producing more—that is 6 shirts instead of 5?

▶ From the seventh row of numbers in Table 12.2 and point *b* in Figure 12.3, we know
that the marginal cost of the sixth shirt is $7.
▶ The price of shirts is $12, so the marginal revenue is $12.

Because the extra revenue from the sixth shirt (price = $12) exceeds the extra cost
(marginal cost = $7), the production and sale of the sixth shirt increases the firm's total

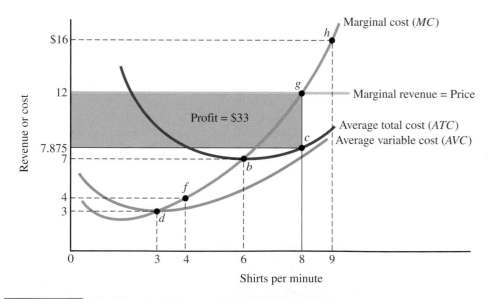

FIGURE 12.3 **The Marginal Approach to Picking an Output Level**
A perfectly competitive firm takes the market price as given, so the marginal benefit, or
marginal revenue, equals the price. Using the marginal principle, the typical firm will maximize
profit at point *g*, where the market price ($12) equals the marginal cost. Economic profit equals
the difference between the price and the average cost ($4.125 = $12 − $7.875) times the
quantity produced (8 shirts per minute), or $33 per minute.

profit by $5 (equal to $12 − $7). Therefore, it is sensible to produce the sixth shirt. The same logic applies, with different numbers for marginal cost, for the seventh shirt. For the eighth shirt, marginal revenue equals marginal cost, so the firm's profit doesn't change. To be consistent with the marginal principle, we'll assume that the firm produces to the point at which marginal revenue equals marginal cost. In this case, the firm produces the eighth shirt.

If the firm produced more than 8 shirts, it would earn less than the maximum profit. Imagine the firm initially produced 9 shirts. From Table 12.2 and the marginal-cost curve in Figure 12.3, we see that the marginal cost of the ninth shirt is $16 (point *h*), which exceeds the marginal revenue (the market price) of $12. The ninth shirt adds more to cost ($16) than it adds to revenue ($12), so producing the shirt decreases the firm's profit by $4. The marginal principle suggests that the firm should choose point *g*, with an output of 8 shirts. As you can see, the output decision is the same whether we use the marginal approach or the total approach.

The advantage of the marginal approach is that it is easier to apply. To use the total approach, a firm needs information on the total revenue and total cost for all possible output levels. In contrast, a firm can apply the marginal principle by simply increasing its output by one unit and computing the marginal revenue (the price) and the marginal cost. Using the marginal principle, the firm should produce more output if the price exceeds the marginal cost, or produce less if the opposite is true. The firm can use the marginal principle to fine-tune its decision until the price equals the marginal cost.

Economic Profit and the Break-Even Price

We've seen that the perfectly competitive firm maximizes its profit by producing the quantity at which its marginal revenue (price) equals its marginal cost. How much profit does the firm earn? The firm's economic profit equals its total revenue minus its total cost. One way to compute a firm's total economic profit is to multiply the average profit per unit produced (the gap between the price and the average cost) by the quantity produced:

$$\text{economic profit} = (\text{price} - \text{average cost}) \cdot \text{quantity produced}$$

In Figure 12.3, the average cost of producing 8 shirts is $7.875 (point *c*), so the economic profit is $33:

$$\text{economic profit} = (\$12 - \$7.875) \cdot 8 = \$33$$

In Figure 12.3, the firm's profit is shown by the area of the shaded rectangle. The area of a rectangle is the height of the rectangle times its width. In Figure 12.3, the height of the profit rectangle is the average profit ($12 − $7.875 = $4.125 per shirt), and the width is the quantity produced (8 shirts), so the profit is $33.

How will a decrease in price affect the firm's output decision and its profit? A decrease in price shifts the marginal-revenue (price) line downward, so it will intersect the marginal-cost curve at a smaller quantity. For example, if the price drops to

$9, the firm will satisfy the marginal principle by producing 7 shirts per minute (where marginal cost = $9, as shown in Table 12.2). If the price drops to $7, profit would be maximized at point *b*, where the marginal cost equals $7. Point *b* is the minimum point of the *ATC* curve, where marginal cost equals average total cost. This is **the break-even price**, defined as the price at which the firm will have zero economic profit. At this price, the average total cost equals the price, so the economic profit per shirt is zero. Remember that zero economic profit means that the firm is making just enough money to cover all its costs, including the opportunity costs of the entrepreneur.

Break-even price

The price at which the economic profit is zero; price equals average total cost.

Fewer Deliveries and More Profit?

Consider a student-run delivery firm that delivers packages by bicycle, charging $13 per package and paying each of its workers $12 per hour. One day, one of the workers was two hours late to work, and the number of packages delivered that day decreased by 1 package. According to a worker enrolled in an economics course, this was actually beneficial to the firm: Less output means more profit. Why?

   The key to solving this puzzle is the marginal principle. The marginal benefit (revenue) of a delivery is the market price of $13. When the worker was late, output dropped by one unit, resulting in $13 less in revenue, but costs dropped by $24 (two hours times $12 per hour). In other words, the marginal cost of a package delivered ($24), exceeds the marginal revenue of delivering it ($13), so the firm will earn more profit if it hires less labor and delivers fewer packages. ■

TEST Your Understanding

1. Explain why a perfectly competitive firm takes prices as given.
2. Complete the statement: A perfectly competitive firm will produce the quantity of output at which _____ equals _____.
3. Suppose the market price of sugar is 22 cents per pound. If a sugar farmer produces 100,000 pounds, the marginal cost of sugar is 30 cents per pound. Is the farmer maximizing profit? If not, should the farmer produce more sugar or less sugar?

The Firm's Shut-Down Decision

Consider next the decisions faced by a firm that is losing money. Suppose the price of shirts drops to $4, which is so low that the firm's total revenue is less than its total cost. In Table 12.3, the marginal principle tells the firm to produce 4 shirts at this price, but the firm's total cost of $30 exceeds its total revenue of $16, so the firm will lose $14 per minute. For an unprofitable firm like this one, the question is, Should the firm continue to operate at a loss, or shut down?

TABLE 12.3

Deciding How Much to Produce When Price = $4

1	2	3	4	5	6	7	8
Output: Shirts per Minute	Fixed Cost	Variable Cost	Total Cost	Total Revenue	Profit	Marginal Revenue (Price)	Marginal Cost
$0	$17	$0	$17	$0	−$17	$4	$0
1	17	5	22	4	−18	4	5
2	17	6	23	8	−15	4	1
3	17	9	26	12	−14	4	3
4	**17**	**13**	**30**	**16**	**−14**	**4**	**4**
5	17	18	35	20	−15	4	5
6	17	25	42	24	−18	4	7

Total Revenue, Variable Cost, and the Shut-Down Decision

The decision to shut down is a short-run decision, a day-to-day decision to temporarily halt production in response to market conditions. Suppose our shirt factory hires workers by the day, so the shut-down decision is made at the beginning of each day. The decision-making rule is:

operate if total revenue > variable cost
shut down if total revenue < variable cost

As we saw in Chapter 11, a firm's variable cost includes all the costs that vary with the quantity produced. In the case of the shirt firm, it would include the costs of workers, raw materials (cotton, thread), and the cost of heating and powering the factory for the day. It does not include the $17 fixed cost of the production facility—for example, the cost of the machines or the factory itself—because these costs are not affected by the decision to operate or shut down.

Although the decision is made at the beginning of each day, we can use the revenue and costs per minute to compare total revenue to variable cost. From Table 12.3, for a quantity of 4 shirts per minute (the best quantity, given a price of $4), the variable cost is $13 per minute, so total revenue ($16) exceeds variable cost ($13). The firm is better off operating the facility because its total revenue of $16 exceeds the cost of operating the facility for each minute of the day. The firm cannot do anything about the $17 fixed cost, but by paying an additional $13 to operate the factory, the firm can get $16 in revenue. The benefit of operating the facility exceeds the variable cost, so it is sensible to produce 4 shirts per minute.

Of course, the firm will not operate the factory at any price. If the price drops to $1, the firm would be better off shutting the factory down for the day. In this case, the quantity that satisfies the marginal principle is 2 shirts per day (see the third row of numbers in Table 12.3, where marginal cost = $1), with a variable cost of $6 per minute. Total revenue in this case would be $2 per minute ($1 per shirt times 2 shirts), which is less than the variable cost, so the firm is better off shutting down. With this low price, the firm's total revenue is not high enough to cover the variable cost associated with operating the facility let alone any of the fixed costs, so it is better to shut down for the day.

The Shut-Down Price

Instead of calculating total revenue and comparing it to variable cost, we can use a shortcut to determine whether it is sensible to continue to operate—look at the price. Total revenue equals the price times the quantity produced, and variable cost equals the average variable cost times the quantity produced. Therefore, total revenue will exceed variable cost if the price exceeds the average variable cost. The firm should continue to operate if price exceeds the average variable cost; otherwise, it should shut down.

operate: price > average variable cost
shut down: price < average variable cost

In Figure 12.3, with a price of $4, the marginal principle is satisfied at point *f*, and this price exceeds the average variable cost of producing 4 shirts. Therefore, it is sensible to continue operating, even at a loss.

The firm's **shut-down price** is the price at which the firm is indifferent between operating and shutting down. To find the shut-down price, we find the minimum point on the *AVC* curve. In Figure 12.3, the minimum *AVC* is $3 at a quantity of 3 shirts per minute, so the shut-down price is $3 (shown by point *d*). The average variable cost never drops below $3, so if the price drops below $3, it would be impossible to generate enough revenue to even cover the firm's variable cost. When the price equals the shut-down price, the firm is generating just enough revenue to cover its variable costs, so it is just as well off either operating or shutting down.

Shut-down price

The price at which the firm is indifferent between operating and shutting down; equal to the minimum average variable cost.

A firm will shut down an unprofitable factory if the total revenue from the factory is less than the variable cost of operating it.

How long will a firm continue to operate at a loss? Let's think about what happens when the firm must decide whether or not to build a new production facility. The firm will build a new facility—and stay in the market—only if the price of shirts exceeds the average total cost of production. In other words, the firm will stay in the market only if the market price is high enough for its total revenue to cover *all* the costs of production, including the cost of the new facility. In other words, the price must be greater than or equal to the firm's break-even price. Although a firm might operate an existing facility at a loss (a short-run decision), it won't replace it if the new facility will be unprofitable too (a long-run decision).

Fixed Costs and Sunk Costs

It's important to note that the decision whether to operate or shut down does not incorporate the fixed costs of the production facility. If we assume that the facility cannot be rented out to some other firm while the shirt firm isn't using it, the fixed cost is a **sunk cost**. A sunk cost is an expenditure that has already been made and cannot be recovered. Once the firm incurs this cost, it cannot be avoided by shutting down the factory. Therefore, the firm should ignore the cost of the facility when deciding whether to operate or shut down.

Sunk cost

A cost a firm has already paid or has agreed to pay some time in the future.

This is just one example of the notion that sunk costs are irrelevant. The marginal principle tells us that what matters is the costs that depend on what we do, not costs that we can do nothing about. Suppose a dairy farmer spills two-thirds of a 300-gallon load of milk on the way to an ice-cream plant. Should the farmer return to the farm, or deliver the remaining 100 gallons? As long as the marginal cost of delivering the milk (the opportunity cost of the farmer's time and the cost of fuel) is less than the amount the farmer will be paid for the remaining 100 gallons, it is sensible to deliver the milk. The spilt milk is a sunk cost that is irrelevant to the delivery decision. The farmer should not cry over spilt milk, but deliver the rest.

Application: Break-Even and Shut-Down Prices for Corn Farmer

To illustrate the notions of break-even and shut-down prices, let's look at these prices for the typical corn farmer. The break-even or zero-profit price is $0.72 per bushel.[1] At this price, the farmer will produce at the minimum point of the average total-cost curve, with the average cost equal to the market price of $0.72. At a higher price, the farmer will make a positive economic profit. For example, if the price is $0.92 per bushel and the farmer produces 50,000 bushels, the economic profit will be $10,000 (equal to the output of 50,000 bushels times the profit margin of $0.20 = $0.92 − $0.72).

The corn farmer's shut-down price is $0.44. At this price, total revenue equals the farmer's variable cost, so the farmer is indifferent about operating as opposed to shutting down. At a price between the shut-down price ($0.44) and the break-even price ($0.72), the farmer will lose money but will continue to operate at a loss because total revenue will exceed the variable cost of growing corn. For example, if the price is $0.50, the farmer will operate at a loss in the short run. However, if the price drops below the shut-down price of $0.44, the farmer will shut down, not bringing any crops to market in a particular year.

In the long run, farmers will exit the corn market if the price is not high enough to cover all the costs of growing corn, including the costs of the production facility. In the long run, the price must be high enough to cover the costs of land, machinery, and vehicles. In other words, farmers will exit the market if the price stays below the break-even price of $0.72. If the price is below this level, the farmer will not raise enough revenue to cover all the costs of growing corn and will exit the market.

TEST Your Understanding

4. Complete the statement with a number: If a lamp producer can sell 40 lamps per day at a price of $20 per lamp, the benefit of operating its production facility is _____ per day.
5. Complete the statement with "operate" or "shut down": Consider a firm with total revenue of $500, total cost of $700, and variable cost of $400. The firm should _____ its production facility.
6. Complete the statement: A firm that is losing money should continue to operate if the market price exceeds _____.

Short-Run Supply Curves

Now that we've explored the output decision of a price-taking firm, we're ready to show how a firm responds to changes in the market price of its product. We'll represent the relationship between price and quantity supplied with two short-run supply curves, one for the individual firm and one for the entire market.

The Firm's Short-Run Supply Curve

Firm's short-run supply curve

A curve showing the relationship between the price of a product and the quantity of output supplied by a firm in the short run.

The **firm's short-run supply curve** shows the relationship between the market price and the quantity supplied by the firm over a period of time during which one input—the production facility—cannot be changed. In the case of shirt producers, the firm's supply curve answers the following question: At a given market price for shirts, how many shirts will the firm produce? We have already used the marginal principle to answer this question for several different prices. At a price of $12, marginal revenue (price) equals marginal cost when the firm produces 8 shirts per minute (shown by point *g* in Figure 12.3). The firm will produce 6 shirts when the price is $7 (point *b*) and 4 shirts when the price is $4 (point *f*).

The firm's short-run supply curve is the part of the firm's short-run marginal-cost curve above the shut-down price. The shut-down price for the shirt firm is $3, so as shown in Figure 12.4, the short-run supply curve is the marginal-cost curve starting at $3. For any price above the shut-down price, the firm will choose the quantity at which price equals marginal cost, so we can read the firm's quantity supplied directly from its

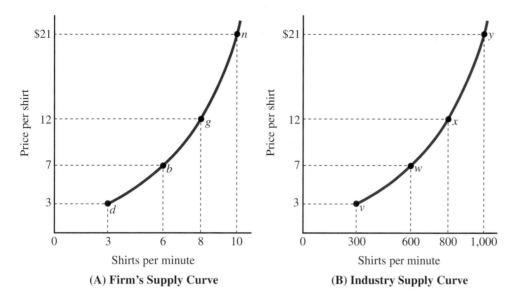

FIGURE 12.4

Short-Run Supply Curves

In Panel A, the firm's short-run supply curve is the part of the marginal-cost curve above the shut-down price. In Panel B, there are 100 firms in the market, so the market supply at a given price is 100 times the quantity supplied by the typical firm. At a price of $7, each firm supplies 6 shirts per minute (point *b*), so the market supply is 600 shirts per minute (point *w*).

(A) Firm's Supply Curve

(B) Industry Supply Curve

marginal-cost curve. If the price is $7, the firm will supply 6 shirts per minute (point *b*). As the price increases, the firm responds by supplying more shirts: 8 shirts at a price of $12 (point *g*) and 10 shirts at a price of $21 (point *n*).

What about prices below the shut-down price? If the price drops below the shut-down price, the firm's total revenue will not be high enough to cover its total variable cost, so the firm will shut down and produce no output. In Panel A of Figure 12.4, the firm's supply curve starts at point *d*, indicating that the quantity supplied is zero for any price less than $3.

The Short-Run Market Supply Curve

The **short-run market supply curve** shows the relationship between the market price and the quantity supplied by all firms in the short run. Panel B of Figure 12.4 shows the short-run market supply curve when there are 100 identical shirt firms. For each price, we get the quantity supplied for the entire market by multiplying the quantity supplied by the typical firm (from the individual supply curve) by 100. At a price of $7, each firm produces 6 shirts (point *b* in Panel A), so the market supply is 600 shirts (point *w* in Panel B). If the price increases to $12, each firm produces 8 shirts (point *g* in Panel A), so the market supply is 800 shirts (point *x* in Panel B).

What happens if firms are not identical but instead have different individual supply curves? To compute the market supply in this case, we would add the quantities supplied by the hundreds of firms in the market. The assumption that firms are identical is harmless: It makes it easier to derive the market supply curve from the supply curve of the typical firm, but it does not change the analysis.

For another example of a competitive market, consider phone service in the developing world. In many parts of the developing world, people cannot afford their own phones and have traditionally relied on pay phones. The recent development of mobile phones has generated a new competitive industry in many developing nations. Read "A Closer Look: Wireless Women."

Short-run market supply curve

A curve showing the relationship between price and the quantity supplied in the short run.

Market Equilibrium

Figure 12.5 shows a perfectly competitive market in equilibrium. For a short-run equilibrium, two conditions are satisfied.

1 At the market level, the quantity of the product supplied equals the quantity demanded. The demand curve intersects the short-run market supply curve at a price of $7 and a quantity of 600 shirts per minute (Panel A).

2 The typical firm in the market maximizes its profit, given the market price. Given the market price of $7, each of the 100 firms maximizes profit by producing 6 shirts per minute (Panel B).

In Figure 12.5, the market has reached a short-run equilibrium because the price of $7 generates a total of 600 shirts per minute, exactly the quantity demanded by consumers at this price.

In the long run, firms can enter or leave an industry, and existing firms can modify their facilities or build new facilities. The market reaches a long-run equilibrium when the two conditions for short-run equilibrium are met, and a third long-run condition holds as well.

3 Each firm in the market earns zero economic profit, so there is no incentive for other firms to enter the market.

In Figure 12.5, at the quantity chosen by the typical firm (6 shirts), the price ($7) equals the average total cost, so each firm makes zero economic profit, with total revenue equal to total cost. In other words, the market price equals the break-even price. When economic profit is zero, the firm's revenue is high enough to cover all its costs—

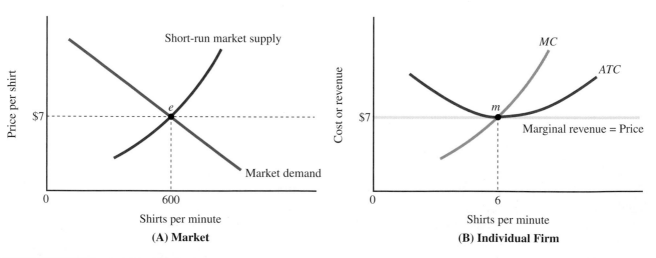

FIGURE 12.5 **Market Equilibrium**

In Panel A, the market demand curve intersects the short-run market supply curve at a price of $7. In Panel B, given the market price, the typical firm satisfies the marginal principle at point *m*, producing 6 shirts per minute. The $7 price equals the average cost at the equilibrium quantity, so economic profit is zero, and no other firms will enter the market.

including the opportunity costs of the entrepreneur—but not high enough to cause additional firms to enter the market. Each firm that is already in the market makes just enough money to stay in business, so there is no incentive for new firms to enter the market, and no incentive for existing firms to leave.

TEST Your Understanding

7. Complete the statement: The firm's short-run supply curve shows the relationship between _____ and _____.

8. Suppose that you want to draw the firm's short-run supply curve. What information do you need?

9. Suppose there are 100 identical firms in a perfectly competitive industry. At a price of $22, the typical firm supplies 50 units of output. What is the market quantity supplied at a price of $22?

A CLOSER LOOK   Wireless Women

In Pakistan, many poor villagers cannot afford their own phones, and phone service is provided by thousands of "wireless women," entrepreneurs who invest $310 in wireless phone equipment (transceiver, battery, charger), a signboard, a calculator, and a stopwatch. Then they sell phone service to their neighbors, charging by the minute and second. On average, their net income is about $2 per day, about three times the average per capita income in Pakistan.[2] The market for phone service has the features of a perfectly competitive market, with easy entry, a standardized good, and a large enough number of suppliers that each takes the market price as given.

The Long-Run Supply Curve
for an Increasing-Cost Industry

**Long-run market supply
curve**

A curve showing the
relationship between the market
price and quantity supplied in
the long run.

Let's look at the **long-run market supply curve**, which shows the relationship
between the market price and the quantity supplied by all firms in the long run, a
period long enough that firms can enter or leave the market. Suppose the typical shirt
firm produces 6 shirts per minute, using a standard set of inputs, including a factory,
some workers, and raw materials (cotton and thread). In a perfectly competitive industry, there are no restrictions on entry, so anyone can use the standard set of inputs to
produce 6 shirts per minute.

Increasing-cost industry

An industry in which the
average cost of production
increases as the total output of
the industry increases; the
long-run supply curve is
positively sloped.

We'll start with the case of an **increasing-cost industry**, defined as an industry
in which the average cost of production increases as the total output of the industry
increases. The average cost increases as the industry grows for two reasons:

▶ *Increasing input price.* As an industry grows, it competes with other industries for
limited amounts of various inputs, and this competition drives up the prices of
these inputs. For example, suppose that the shirt industry competes against other
industries for a limited amount of cotton. To get more cotton to produce more
shirts, firms in the shirt industry must outbid other industries for the limited
amount available, and this drives up the price of cotton.

▶ *Less productive inputs.* A small industry will use only the most productive inputs,
but as the industry grows, firms may be forced to use less productive inputs. For
example, a small shirt industry will use only the most skillful workers, but as the
industry grows, it will hire less skillful workers. As the average skill level of the
industry's workforce decreases, the average cost of production increases: A firm will
require more labor time—and pay more in labor costs—to produce each shirt.
Another example of progressively less productive inputs is the production of agricultural products such as sugar. Because of variation in climate and soil conditions,
it is cheaper to grow sugar in some areas than in others. As the quantity of sugar
produced increases, growers are forced to produce sugar in areas with less favorable
climates and soil conditions, and this results in higher costs.

Production Cost and Industry Size

Table 12.4 shows hypothetical data on the cost of producing shirts. Let's start with the
first row, which shows the firm's production costs in an industry with 100 firms and a
total of 600 shirts produced per day (6 shirts per firm). To compute the total cost for
the typical firm, we add the cost of the firm's production facility (the cost of the shirt
factory), the cost of labor, and the cost of materials. In the first row, the total cost of the
typical firm producing 6 shirts per minute is $42, and the average cost is $7 per shirt
($42 divided by 6 shirts). In the second row, if the number of firms doubles to 200 and
each firm continues to produce 6 shirts per minute, the total output of the industry
will double to 1,200 shirts per minute. For the two reasons listed earlier (higher input
prices and less productive inputs), the total cost per firm increases to $60, so the aver-
age cost per shirt increases to $10. In the last row, when the total output of the industry
increases to 1,800 shirts per minute, the average cost per shirt increases to $13.

TABLE 12.4
Industry Output and
Average Production Cost

Number of Firms	Industry Output	Shirts per Firm	Total Cost for Typical Firm	Average Cost per Shirt
100	600	6	$42	$7
200	1,200	6	60	10
300	1,800	6	78	13

The shirt industry is an example of an increasing-cost industry. In the last column of Table 12.4, the average cost increases from $7 for an industry that produces 600 shirts, to $10 for an industry that produces 1,200 shirts, and so on. The increase in average cost reflects the higher input prices and less productive inputs in a larger industry.

Drawing the Long-Run Market Supply Curve

The long-run supply curve tells us how much output will be produced at each price in the long run, when the number of firms in the market can change. Recall that in the long-run equilibrium, each firm makes zero economic profit, meaning that the price equals the average cost of production:

$$\text{long-run equilibrium: price = average cost}$$

The data in Table 12.4 shows three points on the long-run supply curve. At a price of $7, a total of 100 firms will be in the market, with each producing 6 shirts per hour. This combination (price = $7 and quantity = 600 shirts) is on the long-run supply curve because the price equals the average cost. Each firm makes zero economic profit, so there is no incentive for firms to either enter or exit the market. This is shown by point *e* in Figure 12.6. Suppose the price of shirts increases. At the higher price, shirt making will be more profitable, and firms will enter the market, increasing total output. Firms will continue to enter the market until the economic profit becomes zero again, which happens when the average cost again equals the price. From Table 12.4, we see that entry will continue until the market reaches 200 firms producing 1,200 shirts at an average cost and price of $10. This is shown by point *h* in Figure 12.6. Point *j* shows another point on the long-run supply curve, with a price of $13 and a quantity of 1,800 shirts.

The long-run supply curve in Figure 12.6 is positively sloped, as it will be for any increasing-cost industry. This is another example of the law of supply. An increase in the price of shirts initially makes shirt production profitable, so firms enter the market and produce more shirts. As industry-wide output increases, the greater demand for cotton and labor pulls up input costs, pulling up the average cost of producing shirts. Firms will continue to enter the market until the average cost rises to the point where it equals the price of shirts. The positively sloped supply curve tells us that the market won't produce a larger quantity of shirts unless the price rises to cover the higher average cost associated with the larger industry.

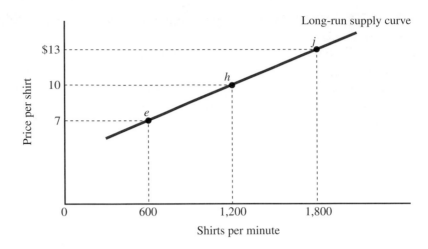

FIGURE 12.6 **Long-Run Market Supply Curve**
The long-run market supply curve shows the relationship between the price and quantity supplied in the long run, when firms can enter or leave the industry. At each point on the supply curve, the market price equals the long-run average cost of production. Because this is an increasing-cost industry, the market supply curve is positively sloped.

Application: Increasing-Cost Industries—Wolfram, Sugar, Rental Housing

For an example of the law of supply with market entry, consider the market for wolfram during World War II. Wolfram is an ore of tungsten, an alloy required to make heat-resistant steel for armor plate and armor-piercing shells. During World War II, the United States and its European allies bought up all the wolfram produced in Spain, thus denying the Axis powers, Germany and Italy, this vital military input. However, the wolfram buying program was very costly to the Allied powers for two reasons:[3]

▶ The Allied powers had to outbid the Axis powers for the wolfram, so the price increased from $1,144 per ton to $20,000 per ton.
▶ Spanish firms responded to the higher prices by supplying more wolfram. Workers poured into the Galatia area in Spain, where they used simple tools to gather wolfram from the widely scattered outcroppings of ore. Because of this market entry, the quantity of wolfram supplied increased tenfold. Because wolfram miners obeyed the law of supply, the Allied powers were forced to buy a huge amount of wolfram, much more than they had expected.

The sugar industry is another example of an increasing-cost industry. If the price of sugar is only 11 cents per pound, sugar production is profitable in areas with relatively low production costs, including the Caribbean, Latin America, Australia, and South Africa.[4] At a price of 11 cents, the world supply of sugar equals the amount produced in these areas. As the price increases, sugar production becomes profitable in areas where production costs are higher, and as these areas enter the world market, the quantity of sugar supplied increases. For example, at a price of 14 cents per pound, sugar production is profitable in the European Community, too. At a price of 24 cents, production is profitable even in the United States.

In many communities, the rental-apartment industry is an increasing-cost industry. Most communities use zoning laws to restrict the amount of land available for apartments. Consequently, when housing firms announce plans to build more apartments, there is fierce competition for the small amount of zoned land available for apartments. As a result, the cost of land for apartments—and the rent that a housing firm must charge to cover its production costs—increases by a large amount.[5]

TEST Your Understanding

10. Complete the statement: The long-run supply curve shows the relationship between _____ (on the horizontal axis) and _____ (on the vertical axis).
11. Use Table 12.4 to compute the average cost in a 400-firm industry, assuming the total cost of the typical firm in such an industry is $96.
12. Circle the three items in the following list that go together: Positively sloped supply curve, horizontal supply curve, increasing-cost industry, increasing average cost of production, constant average cost of production.

Short-Run and Long-Run Effects of Changes in Demand

We can use what we've learned about the short-run and long-run supply curves to get a deeper understanding of perfectly competitive markets. Let's use the two supply curves to explore the short-run and the long-run effects of a change in demand in a perfectly competitive market.

The Short-Run Response to an Increase in Demand

Figure 12.7 shows the short-run effects of an increase in the demand for shirts. Panel A shows what's happening at the market level. Let's start with the initial equilibrium shown by point *i*: The original demand curve intersects the short-run market supply curve at a price of $7 per shirt and a quantity of 600 shirts. When demand increases, the new demand curve intersects the supply curve at a price of $12 and a quantity of 800 shirts (point *s*). In Panel B, an increase in price from $7 to $12 increases the output per firm from 6 shirts to 8 shirts. At this quantity, the $12 price now exceeds the average total cost, so the typical firm makes an economic profit (shown by the shaded rectangle).

This is not a long-run equilibrium, because each firm is making a positive economic profit. Firms will enter the profitable market, and as they compete for

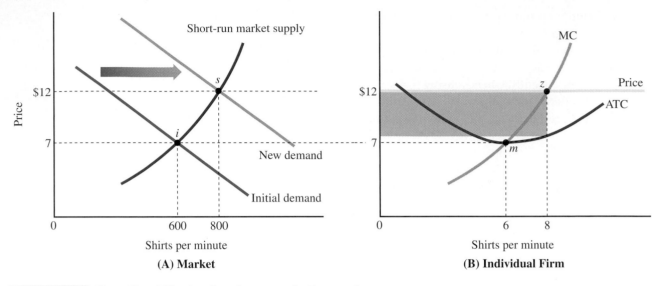

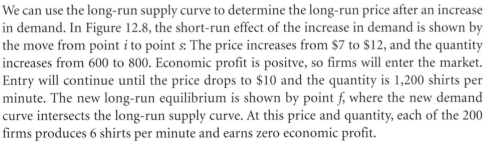

FIGURE 12.7 **Short-Run Effects of an Increase in Demand**

An increase in demand increases the market price to $12, causing the typical firm to produce 8 shirts instead of 6. Price exceeds the average total cost at the 8-shirt quantity, so economic profit is positive. Firms will enter the profitable market.

customers, the price of shirts will decrease. New firms will continue to enter the market until the price drops to the point at which economic profit is zero. The question is, How far does the price drop?

The Long-Run Response to an Increase in Demand

We can use the long-run supply curve to determine the long-run price after an increase in demand. In Figure 12.8, the short-run effect of the increase in demand is shown by the move from point *i* to point *s*: The price increases from $7 to $12, and the quantity increases from 600 to 800. Economic profit is positve, so firms will enter the market. Entry will continue until the price drops to $10 and the quantity is 1,200 shirts per minute. The new long-run equilibrium is shown by point *f*, where the new demand curve intersects the long-run supply curve. At this price and quantity, each of the 200 firms produces 6 shirts per minute and earns zero economic profit.

Figure 12.8 shows how the price of shirts changes over time. An increase in demand causes a large upward jump in the price (from point *i* to point *s*) in the short run, followed by a slide downward to the new long-run equilibrium price (from point *s* to point *f*). In the short run, firms respond to an increase in price by squeezing more output from their existing production facilities. Because of diminishing returns, it is very costly to increase output in the short run, so the price must increase by a large amount to cover these much higher production costs. Consequently, the short-run supply curve is very steep.

The higher price causes new firms to enter the market, and as they enter, the price gradually drops to the point at which each firm makes zero economic profit. The long-run supply curve is relatively flat because firms enter the industry and build new factories, so there are no diminishing returns to pull up costs.

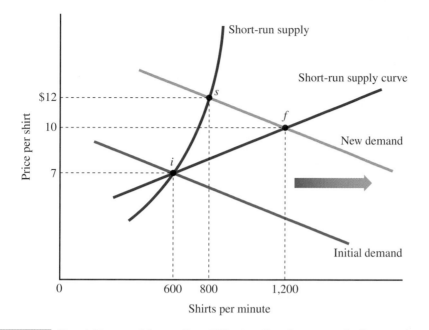

FIGURE 12.8 Short-Run and Long-Run Effects of an Increase in Demand
The short-run supply curve is steeper than the long-run supply curve because production facilities are fixed, and there are diminishing returns in the short run. In the short run, an increase in demand increases the price from $7 (point *i*) to $12 (point *s*). But in the long run, firms can enter the industry and build more plants, so the price eventually drops to $10 (point *f*). The large initial upward jump in price after an increase in demand is followed by a downward slide to the new long-run equilibrium price.

Long-Run Supply for a Constant-Cost Industry

So far we have examined products that are produced by increasing-cost industries, whose average cost increases as the industry expands. We turn next to a **constant-cost industry**. In a constant-cost industry, average cost doesn't change as the industry expands. That is, the prices of inputs such as labor and materials do not change as the total output of the industry increases. This will happen if the industry consumes only a small amount of the input available, meaning that events in the industry—increases or decreases in output—do not affect the price of the input. As a result, the average cost of production for the typical firm doesn't change as the industry grows. In Table 12.3, the shirt industry would be a constant-cost industry if the average cost of shirts were constant at $7, regardless of how many shirts were produced.

Constant-cost industry
An industry in which the average cost of production is constant; the long-run supply curve is horizontal.

Long-Run Supply Curve for a Constant-Cost Industry

As an example of constant-cost industry, consider the production of birthday-cake candles. As the industry grows, it will use more workers and materials (for wicks, wax, and dyes), but because the industry is such a small part of the markets for labor and materials, the prices of these inputs won't change. As a result, the average cost of production won't change as the industry grows.

FIGURE 12.9

Long-Run Supply Curve for a Constant-Cost Industry

In a constant-cost industry, input prices do not change as the industry grows, so the average production cost is constant, and the long-run supply curve is horizontal. For the candle industry, the cost per candle is constant at $0.05, so the supply curve is horizontal at $0.05 per candle.

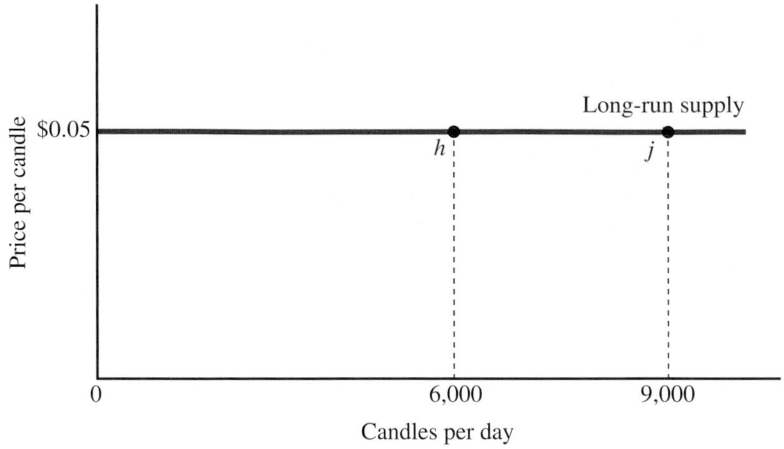

The long-run supply curve for a constant-cost industry is horizontal at the constant average cost of production. If the average cost of birthday-cake candles is $0.05 per candle (including the cost of materials and labor), the long-run supply curve for candles will be horizontal at $0.05, as shown by Figure 12.9. At any lower price, the quantity of candles supplied would be zero because in the long run, no rational firm would provide candles at a price less than the average cost of production. At any higher price, firms would enter the candle industry in droves, and entry would continue until the price dropped to the constant average cost of candles ($0.05).

Application: Hurricane Andrew and the Price of Ice

For an example of the effects of an increase in demand in a constant-cost industry, let's look at the short-run and long-run effects of a hurricane. In 1992, Hurricane Andrew struck the southeastern United States, leaving millions of people without electricity for several days. Figure 12.10 shows the short- and long-run effects of the hurricane on the price of ice, which was used to cool and preserve food in areas without electricity. Before the hurricane, the market was at point *i*, with a price of $1 per bag of ice. The long-run supply curve is horizontal, indicating that the ice industry is a constant-cost industry.

In the short run (a day or two), the number of ice suppliers is fixed. The increase in demand caused by the hurricane moved the market from point *i* to point *s*, and the price rose to $5 per bag of ice. In the long run, firms responded to the higher price by entering the market. Many people trucked ice from distant locations and sold it from trucks parked on streets and highways. As these firms entered the ice market in the days after the hurricane, the price of ice gradually dropped, and the market eventually reached the intersection of the new demand curve and the long-run supply curve (point *f*), with a price equal to the prehurricane price. In the case of the retail ice industry, the long run is just a few days.

This pattern of price changes following the hurricane was observed in other markets. Immediately after the hurricane, $200 chain saws were sold for $900, but the price dropped steadily as new roadside firms entered the market. The same sort of price changes occurred for bottled water, tarpaper, and plywood. The basic pattern was a large upward jump in price followed by a downward slide to the long-run equilibrium price.

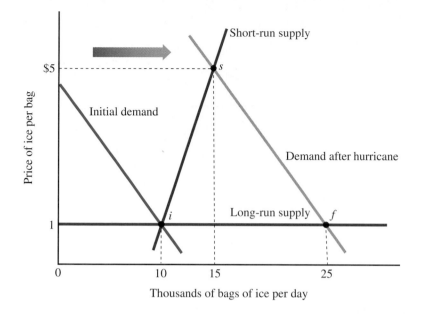

FIGURE 12.10

**Hurricane Andrew
and the Price of Ice**
A hurricane increases the
demand for ice, shifting the
demand curve to the right.
In the short run, the supply
curve is relatively steep, so
the price rises by a large
amount—from $1 to $5. In
the long run, firms enter the
industry, pulling the price
back down. Because ice
production is a constant-
cost industry, the supply
curve is horizontal, and the
large upward jump in price
is followed by a downward
slide back to the original
price.

Public officials are often tempted to pass laws prohibiting what's called price goug-
ing, charging high prices for scarce goods after a natural disaster. One effect of such
laws is to slow the transition from the short run to the long run. The people who set up
roadside stands to sell ice were motivated by the high price. If the price were controlled
at $1 per bag, few people would have incurred the large expenses associated with truck-
ing the ice from distant locations and setting up roadside stores. The result would have
been less ice and more spoiled food. An alternative to a law regulating prices is to leave
prices to the market and help to ease the transition from short run to long run by making it easier for entrepreneurs to enter the market.

Butter Prices

Several years ago, people became concerned about the undesirable health effects of eating
butter. The demand for butter dropped, decreasing its price. Some time later, the price of
butter started rising steadily, although demand hadn't been changing. After several
months of price hikes, the price of butter reached the price observed before demand
decreased. According to a consumer watchdog organization, the rising price of butter was
evidence of a conspiracy on the part of butter producers. Is there some other explanation
for the rising price of butter?

The key to solving this puzzle is the distinction between the short run and the long
run. In Figure 12.11, the short-run effect of a decrease in demand is shown by the move
from point *i* (price = $2.00) to point *s* (price = $1.44). In the short run, not many firms
will leave the market when the price drops, so the decrease in demand will cause a large
price drop. Although many of the remaining firms will lose money, they will stay in the
market if their total revenue covers their total variable cost. In the long run, however,
unprofitable firms will leave the market, causing the price to rise. In Figure 12.11, the new
long-run equilibrium is shown by point *f*, with a price of $2.00. The pattern of a large
price drop followed by a gradual increase in price is a normal pattern for a perfectly competitive market. ■

Economic Puzzle

FIGURE 12.11

The Short-Run and Long-Run Effects of a Decrease in the Demand for Butter

In the short run, a decrease in demand for butter decreases the price from $2.00 (point *i*) to $1.44 (point *s*). In the long run, firms leave the industry, and the price rises, reaching the original price (point *f*). In a constant-cost industry, changes in demand do not affect the long-run price.

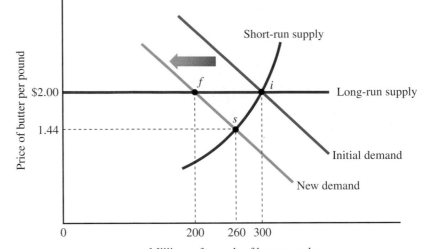

TEST Your Understanding

13. Explain why the short-run supply curve is steeper than the long-run supply curve.
14. Suppose the demand for shirts decreases. Describe the short-run and the long-run effects on the price of shirts.
15. Under what circumstances would an increase in demand for a particular good not affect the price of the good in the long run?

USING THE TOOLS

We've seen how a perfectly competitive firm can use its cost curves to decide how much to produce and whether to continue operating an unprofitable operation. We've also explored the short- and long-run effects of changes in demand. Here are some opportunities to do your own economic analysis.

1. Advice for an Unprofitable Firm

You've been hired as an economic consultant to a price-taking firm that produces baseball caps. The firm already has a factory, so it is operating in the short run. The price of caps is $5, the hourly wage is $12, and each cap requires $1 worth of material. At the current level of output (15 workers and 60 caps), the firm is losing money: Its total cost exceeds its total revenue. The firm has experimented with different workforces and discovered that 14 workers

would produce only 57 caps. Your job is to tell the firm which of these four options to take:

● Option 1: Shut down the unprofitable operation.
● Option 2: Continue to produce 60 caps per hour.
● Option 3: Produce more caps.
● Option 4: Produce fewer caps.

2. Maximizing the Profit Margin

According to the marginal principle, the firm should choose the quantity of output at which price equals marginal cost. A tempting alternative is to maximize the firm's profit margin, defined as the difference between price and short-run average total cost. Use the firm's short-run cost curves to evaluate this approach. Draw the firm's short-run supply curve and compare it to the supply curve of a firm that maximizes its profit.

3. Market Effects of an Increase in Housing Demand

Consider the market for apartments in a small city. In the initial equilibrium, the monthly rent (the price) is $500, and the quantity is 10,000 apartments. Suppose that the population of the city suddenly increases by 24%. The price elasticity of demand for apartments is 1.0. The short-run price elasticity of supply is 0.20, and the long-run price elasticity of supply is 0.50.

a. Depict graphically the short- and long-run effects of the increase in population.
b. By what percentage will the price increase in the short run? (Use the price-change formula from Chapter 5.)
c. By what percentage will the price increase in the long run?

SUMMARY

In this chapter, we explored the decisions made by perfectly competitive firms and the implications of these decisions for the supply side of the market. In the short run, a firm uses the marginal principle to decide how much output to produce. In the long run, a firm will enter a market if the price exceeds the average cost of production. Here are the main points of this chapter:

1 A price-taking firm should produce the quantity of output at which the marginal revenue (the price) equals the marginal cost of production.

2 An unprofitable firm should continue to operate if its total revenue exceeds its total variable cost.

3 The long-run supply curve will be positively sloped if the average cost of production increases as the industry grows.

4 The long-run supply curve is flatter than the short-run supply curve because there are diminishing returns in the short run, but not in the long run.

5 An increase in demand causes a large upward jump in price, followed by a downward slide to the new long-run equilibrium price.

KEY TERMS

accounting profit, 264
break-even price, 268
constant-cost industry, 281
economic profit, 263
firm-specific demand curve, 262

increasing-cost industry, 276
long-run market supply curve, 276
marginal revenue, 266
perfectly competitive market, 261
short-run supply curve, 272

short-run market supply curve, 273
shut-down price, 270
sunk cost, 271
total revenue, 263

PROBLEMS AND DISCUSSION QUESTIONS

1 In the following table, provide the numbers for marginal cost. Then use the data to draw the short-run supply curve for tables.

Tables per Hour	Total Cost	Marginal Cost
3	120	—
4	155	—
5	200	—
6	270	—

2 The following table shows short-run marginal costs for a perfectly competitive firm:

Output	100	200	300	400	500
Marginal cost	$5	$10	$20	$40	$70

    a. Use this information to draw the firm's marginal-cost curve.

    b. Suppose the shut-down price is $10. Draw the firm's short-run supply curve.

    c. Suppose there are 100 identical firms with the same marginal-cost curve. Draw the short-run industry supply curve.

3 Consider the choices facing an unprofitable (and perfectly competitive) firm. The firm currently produces 100 units per day and sells them at a price of $22 each. At the current output quantity, the firm's total cost is $3,000 per day, its variable cost is $2,500 per day, and its marginal cost is $45.

    a. Evaluate the following statement from the firm's accountant: "Given our current production level, our variable cost ($2,500) exceeds our total revenue ($2,200). We should shut down our production facility."

    b. Illustrate your answer with a graph showing short-run cost curves and the revenue curve of a perfectly competitive firm.

4 You've been hired by an unprofitable firm to determine whether it should shut down its unprofitable operation. The firm currently uses 70 workers to produce 300 units of output per day. The daily wage (per worker) is $100, and the price of the firm's output is $30. Although you don't know the firm's fixed cost, you know that it is high enough that the firm's total cost exceeds its total revenue. Should the firm continue to operate at a loss?

5 Consider the following statement from a wheat farmer to his workers: "The price of wheat is very low this year, and the most I can get from the crop is $35,000. If I paid you the same amount as I paid you last year ($30,000), I'd lose money because I also have to worry about the $20,000 I paid three months ago for seed and fertilizer. I'd be crazy to pay a total of $50,000 to harvest a crop I can sell for only $35,000. If you are willing to work for half as much as last year ($15,000), my total cost will be $35,000, so I'll break even. If you don't take a pay cut. I won't harvest the wheat." Is the farmer bluffing, or will the farm workers lose their jobs if they reject the proposed pay cut?

6 Consider a firm that uses the following rule to decide how much output to produce: If the profit margin (price minus short-run average total cost) is positive, the firm will produce more output. Use the firm's short-run cost curves to evaluate this approach. Draw the firm's short-run supply curve and compare it to the short-run supply curve of a profit-maximizing firm.

7 Consider the following data on the relationship between the price of gasoline (in real terms, adjusted for inflation) and the quantity of gasoline sold per day in the city of Ceteris Paribus:

Year	Price	Gallons per Day
1995	1.00	50,000
1996	1.10	53,000

If possible, draw the industry supply curve and compute the price elasticity of supply.

8 Between 1995 and 2005, the number of U.S. households with DVD players increased dramatically. Predict the implications for the price of DVD rentals in the short run and the long run.

9 Suppose each lamp manufacturer produces 10 lamps per hour. In the following table, fill in a number wherever you see a _____.
Then use the data in the table to draw the long-run supply curve for lamps.

Number of Firms	Industry Output	Total Cost for Typical Firm	Average Cost per Lamp
40	_____	$300	$_____
80	_____	$360	$_____
120	_____	$420	$_____

10 Suppose that a new technology decreases the amount of labor time required to produce a particular good. Would you expect all firms eventually to adopt the new technology?

11 Draw a long-run supply curve for haircutting that is consistent with the following statement: "The haircutting industry in our city uses a tiny fraction of the electricity, scissors, and commercial space available on the market. In addition, the industry uses only about 100 of the 50,000 people who could cut hair."

12 Draw a long-run supply curve for pencils and explain why you drew it as you did.

MODEL ANSWERS TO QUESTIONS

Chapter-Opening Questions

1 To use the marginal principle, you need information on marginal cost and marginal revenue (the price). As explained in "Economic Puzzle: Fewer Deliveries and More Profit?" you could use data on labor input and output, along with the wage, to compute the marginal cost.

2 It would be sensible to shut down if your total revenue is less than your variable cost. Otherwise, it would be sensible to continue operating.

3 As explained in "A Closer Look: Wireless Women," individuals can enter the market for phone service by investing $310 in mobile phone equipment. They provide phone service for villagers who lack home phones, charging by the minute or second of usage.

Test Your Understanding

1 The firm is such a tiny part of the market that no matter how much output it produces, it will not affect the market price.

2 Marginal revenue (or price), marginal cost.

3 The farmer is not maximizing profit because the marginal revenue (price) is less than the marginal cost. The farmer should produce less sugar.

4 $800 ($20 per lamp times 40 lamps).

5 Operate.

6 Average variable cost.

7 Price, quantity supplied.

8 You need the short-run marginal-cost curve and the shut-down price. If you have the average variable-cost curve and the marginal-cost curve, you can figure out the shut-down price by finding the price at which the two curves intersect.

9 5,000 units (50 units per firm times 100 firms).

10 Quantity supplied, price.

11 The average cost per shirt is $16 ($96 ÷ 6 shirts).

12 The related terms are positively sloped supply curve, increasing-cost industry, and increasing average cost of production.

13 There are diminishing returns in the short run, so production costs increase rapidly as a firm increases its output.

14 In the short run, the price would drop by a large amount. Then the price would start to rise. If the shirt industry is an increasing-cost industry, the new long-run price would be less than the original price.

15 If the good is produced by a constant-cost industry, one with a horizontal long-run supply curve.

NOTES

1. Walter Adam, *The Structure of the American Economy,* 8th ed. (Upper Saddle River, NJ: Prentice Hall, 1990).
2. TeleCommons Development Group, "Grameen Telecom's Village Phone Programme: A Multi-Media Case Study," (http://www.telecommons.com/villagephone).
3. D. I. Gordon and R. Dangerfield, *The Hidden Weapon* (New York: Harper & Brothers, 1947), pp. 105–116.
4. Frederic L. Hoff and Max Lawrence, "Implications of World Sugar Markets, Policies, and Production Costs for U.S. Sugar,"*Agricultural Economic Research Report* 543 (Washington, DC: U.S. Department of Agriculture, Economic Research Service, November 1985).
5. Frank De Leeuw and Nkanta Ekanem. "The Supply of Rental Housing," *American Economic Review,* vol. 61, 1971, pp. 806–817.

The Monopolist's Output Decision

Total Revenue and Marginal Revenue
The Marginal Principle and the Output
    Decision
Using the Marginal Principle to Pick the
    Profit-Maximizing Quantity and Price

The Social Cost of Monopoly

Deadweight Loss from Monopoly
Application: Ending the Monopoly
    on Internet Registration
Rent Seeking: Using Resources to Get
    Monopoly Power
Monopoly and Public Policy

Patents and Monopoly Power

Incentives for Innovation
Trade-Offs from Patents

Price Discrimination

Application: Senior Discounts
    in Restaurants
Price Discrimination and the Elasticity of
    Demand
Application: Movie Admission
    and Popcorn

Monopoly and Price Discrimination

he Coca-Cola Company recently built a new football scoreboard for a large state university. Now football fans can enjoy the latest in scoreboard graphics as they watch the game. In addition, Coca-Cola gave $2.3 million dollars to remodel the university's student center,[1] providing students with a comfortable place to meet, eat, talk, and relax. What explains this outburst of apparent generosity? Does it have anything to do with the fact that Coca-Cola was recently given the exclusive right to sell beverages on campus—a monopoly? Who is really paying for the scoreboard and the student center?

I n Chapter 12, we explored the decisions made by firms in a perfectly competitive market, a market where there are hundreds or thousands of firms. This chapter deals with the opposite extreme: a **monopoly**, a market served by a single firm. In contrast with a perfectly competitive or price-taking firm, a monopolist controls the price of its product, so we can refer to a monopolist as a "price maker." A monopolist has **market power**, the ability to affect the price of a product. Of course, consumers obey the law of demand, and the higher the price a monopolist charges, the smaller the quantity it will sell.

A monopoly occurs when something prevents more than one firm from entering the market. Among the possible barriers to entry are patents, government licensing, and large economies of scale in production.

▶ A **patent** grants an inventor the exclusive right to sell a new product for some period of time, currently 20 years under international rules.
▶ Under a licensing policy, the government chooses a single firm to sell a particular product. Some examples are licensing for radio and television stations, off-street parking in cities, and vendors in national parks.
▶ A **natural monopoly** occurs when the scale economies in production are so large that only a single large firm can survive. In other words, the market can support only one firm. Some examples are cable TV service, electricity transmission, and water systems. In such a market, a single firm will be profitable, but the entry of a second firm will ensure that both firms lose money.

In this chapter we will discuss "unnatural" monopolies, which result from artificial barriers to entry. Later in the book, we'll explore the reasons for natural monopolies and the public-policy responses to them.

This chapter examines the production and pricing decisions of a monopoly and the implications for society as a whole. As we'll see, monopoly is inefficient from society's perspective because it produces too little output. We'll also discuss the trade-offs with patents, which lead to monopoly and higher prices but also encourage innovation. We'll also explore the issue of price discrimination. Price discrimination (which is perfectly legal although not always popular) occurs when firms charge different prices to different types of consumers. Although we discuss price discrimination by a monopolist, it also happens in markets with more firms (oligopoly and monopolistic competition). Here are some of the practical questions that we consider:

1 What are the trade-offs associated with patents and other policies that grant monopoly power?
2 When the patent on a popular pharmaceutical drug expires, what happens to the price of the drug?
3 Why are hardback books so much more expensive than paperback books?
4 Why do senior citizens typically pay less than everyone else for admission to a movie, but pay the same as everyone else for popcorn?

The Monopolist's Output Decision

Like other firms, a monopolist must decide how much output to produce, given its objective of maximizing profit. We learned about production costs in an earlier chapter, so we start our discussion with the revenue side of the monopolist's profit picture. Then we show how a monopolist picks a price and a quantity.

Total Revenue and Marginal Revenue

A firm's total revenue—the money it gets by selling its product—equals the price times the quantity sold. In this part of the chapter, we'll assume that the firm charges the same price to all of its customers. Table 13.1 shows how to use a demand schedule (in the first two columns) to compute a firm's total revenue (in the third column). At a price of $16, the firm doesn't sell anything, so its total revenue is zero. To sell 1 unit, the firm must cut its price to $14, so its total revenue is $14. To get consumers to buy 2 units instead of just 1, the firm must cut its price to $12. The total revenue associated with selling 2 units is $24. As the price continues to drop and the quantity sold increases, total revenue increases for a while, but then starts falling. To sell 5 units instead of 4, the firm cuts its price from $8 to $6, and total revenue decreases from $32 to $30. The total revenue associated with selling 6 units is even lower ($24). The top panel in Figure 13.1 shows the relationship between quantity sold and total revenue.

The firm's marginal revenue is defined as the change in total revenue that results from selling 1 more unit of output. In Table 13.1, we compute marginal revenue by taking the difference between the total revenue from selling a certain quantity of output (for example, 3 units), and the total revenue from selling 1 fewer unit of output (for example, 2 units). As shown in the fourth row in the table, the total revenue from selling 3 units is $30 and the total revenue from selling 2 units is only $24, so the marginal revenue from selling the third unit is $6. As shown in the table and in the lower panel of Figure 13.1, marginal revenue is positive for the first 4 units sold. Beyond 4 units, selling an additional unit results in lower total revenue, so marginal revenue is negative. For example, the marginal revenue for the fifth unit is −$2, and the marginal revenue for the sixth unit is −$6.

TABLE 13.1			
Demand, Total Revenue, and Marginal Revenue			

Price	Quantity Sold	Total Revenue	Marginal Revenue
$16	0	0	—
$14	1	$14	$14
$12	2	$24	10
$10	3	$30	6
$8	4	$32	2
$6	5	$30	−2
$4	6	$24	−6

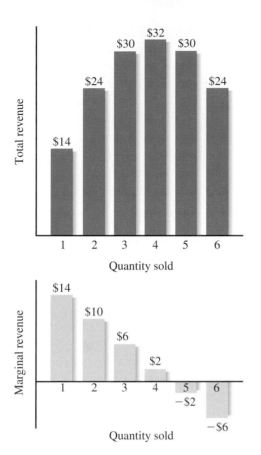

FIGURE 13.1

Total Revenue and Marginal Revenue
As the firm cuts its price to sell more output, its total revenue rises for the first 4 units sold, but then decreases for the fifth and sixth units. Therefore, marginal revenue (the change in total revenue from selling one more unit) is positive for the first 4 units sold and then becomes negative.

Table 13.1 and Figure 13.1 illustrate the trade-offs associated with cutting a price to sell a larger quantity. When the firm cuts its price from $12 to $10, there is good news and bad news:

▶ Good news: The firm collects $10 from the new customer (the third), so revenue increases by $10.
▶ Bad news: The firm cuts the price for all its customers, so it gets less revenue from the customers who would have been willing to pay the higher price ($12). Specifically, the firm collects $2 less from each of the two original customers, so revenue decreases by $4.

The combination of good news and bad news leads to a net increase in total revenue of only $6, resulting from the $10 gained from the new customer minus the $4 lost on the first two customers. In other words, the marginal revenue from the third unit ($6) is less than the price ($10).

We can use a simple formula to compute marginal revenue. The formula quantifies the good news and bad news from selling one more unit.

marginal revenue = new price − (old quantity × slope of demand curve)

The first part of the formula is the good news, the new price ($10 in our example) received for the extra unit sold. The second part of the formula is the bad news from selling one more unit, the revenue lost by cutting the price for the original customers. The revenue loss is equal to the old quantity (2 units in our example) times the slope of the demand curve (the change in price required to sell one more unit of output ($2 in our example):

$$\text{marginal revenue} = \$10 - (2 \text{ units} \times \$2 \text{ per unit}) = \$6$$

Similarly, to sell the fifth unit, the firm would cut the price from $8 to $6, and marginal revenue is actually negative:

$$\text{marginal revenue} = \$6 - (4 \text{ units} \times \$2 \text{ per unit}) = -\$2$$

Notice that for all but the first unit sold, the marginal revenue is less than the price. Marginal revenue equals the price (the good news) minus the revenue lost on previous units sold at a lower price (the bad news). The firm must cut the price to sell more, and the bad news guarantees that the marginal revenue is less than the price. As the quantity sold increases, the revenue loss (bad news) increases as well because the firm must cut the price for more consumers. Therefore, the larger the quantity sold, the larger the gap between price and marginal revenue. The only time marginal revenue equals price is for the first unit sold: There is no bad news because the firm didn't have any customers before cutting the price to sell the first unit.

You may recall from the previous chapter that things are different for a perfectly competitive firm, which can sell as much as it wants at the market price. If a perfectly competitive firm sells one unit at $12, it can sell a second unit at the same price, so its marginal revenue is $12 for the second unit sold, just as it was $12 for the first unit sold. For a perfectly competitive firm, marginal revenue is always equal to the price, no matter how many units the firm sells. A perfectly competitive firm does not cut the price to sell more, so there is no bad news associated with selling more. In contrast, a monopolist must cut the price to sell more, so marginal revenue is less than price.

Figure 13.2 shows the demand curve and marginal-revenue curve for the data shown in Table 13.1. Because the firm must cut its price to sell more output, the marginal-revenue curve lies below the demand curve. For example, the demand curve shows that the firm will sell 3 units at a price of $10 (point *d*), but the marginal revenue for this quantity is only $6 (point *i*). For quantities of 5 units and greater, marginal revenue is negative because when the firm cuts its price to sell 1 additional unit, the bad news dominates the good news: The amount the firm loses on its original customers exceeds the amount it gains on the new one, so total revenue drops.

The Marginal Principle and the Output Decision

We use a simple example to explain how a monopolist can use the marginal principle to decide how much output to produce. Sneezy, who holds a patent on a new drug that cures the common cold, must decide how much of the drug to produce. Sneezy can use the marginal principle to make this decision.

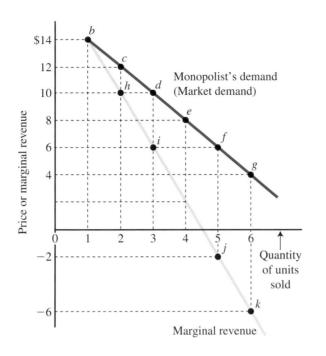

FIGURE 13.2

The Demand Curve and the Marginal-Revenue Curve
Marginal revenue is equal to the price for the first unit sold but is less than the price for all other units sold. To increase the quantity sold, a firm cuts its price and receives less revenue on the units that could have been sold at the higher price. Therefore, beyond the first unit sold, the marginal-revenue curve lies below the demand curve.

MARGINAL *Principle*

Increase the level of an activity if its marginal benefit exceeds its marginal cost, but reduce the level if the marginal cost exceeds the marginal benefit. If possible, pick the level at which the marginal benefit equals the marginal cost.

Sneezy's activity is producing the cold drug, and he will pick the quantity at which the marginal revenue from selling one more unit (the marginal benefit) equals the marginal cost associated with that unit.

The first two columns in Table 13.2 show the relationship between the price of the cold drug and the quantity demanded. We can use these numbers to draw the market demand curve, as shown in Figure 13.3. Because Sneezy is a monopolist—the only

TABLE 13.2

Using the Marginal Principle to Pick a Price and Quantity

Price (per Dose)	Quantity Sold (Doses)	Marginal Revenue	Marginal Cost	Total Revenue	Total Cost	Profit
$18	600	$12	$4.00	$10,800	$5,710	$5,090
$17	700	$10	$4.60	$11,900	$6,140	$5,760
$16	800	$8	$5.30	$12,800	$6,635	$6,165
$15	900	$6	$6.00	$13,500	$7,200	$6,300
$14	1,000	$4	$6.70	$14,000	$7,835	$6,165
$13	1,100	$2	$7.80	$14,300	$8,560	$5,740
$12	1,200	0	$9.00	$14,400	$9,400	$5,000

FIGURE 13.3

The Monopolist Picks a Quantity and a Price
To maximize profit, the monopolist picks point *n*, where marginal revenue equals marginal cost. The monopolist produces 900 doses per hour at a price of $15 (point *m*). The average cost is $8 (point *c*), so the profit per dose is $7 (equal to the $15 price minus the $8 average cost) and the total profit is $6,300 (equal to $7 per dose times 900 doses). The profit is shown by the shaded rectangle.

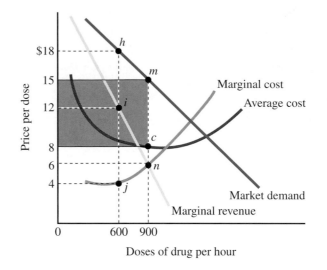

seller of the drug—the market demand curve shows how much he will sell at each price. The demand curve is negatively sloped, consistent with the law of demand. For example, at a price of $18 per dose, the quantity demanded is 600 doses per hour (point *h*), compared to 900 doses at a price of $15 (point *m*).

Like other monopolists, Sneezy must cut his price to sell a larger quantity, so marginal revenue is less than price. This is shown in the third column of Table 13.2 and in Figure 13.3. We can use the marginal-revenue formula explained earlier to compute marginal revenue for different quantities of output. The slope of the demand curve is $0.01 per dose. To simplify the arithmetic, rather than using the "new" price and "old" quantity, we can use a matched pair of price and quantities from the demand curve to get an approximation of marginal revenue. When the change in price is relatively small (for example, $0.01), the difference between the new and old price is small enough to be ignored. For example, at a price of $18, the quantity sold is 600 doses, so marginal revenue is $12:

$$\text{marginal revenue} = \$18 - (600 \text{ doses} \times \$0.01) = \$12$$

Similarly, at a price of $15, the quantity is 900 doses and marginal revenue is $6:

$$\text{marginal revenue} = \$15 - (900 \text{ doses} \times \$0.01) = \$6$$

Using the Marginal Principle to Pick the Profit-Maximizing Quantity and Price

We're ready to show how a monopolist can use the marginal principle to pick a quantity to produce. To maximize his profit, Sneezy should produce the quantity at which the marginal revenue equals marginal cost. By looking at the numbers in Table 13.2, we can see that this happens with a quantity of 900 doses, as shown in the fourth row. In

Figure 13.3, the marginal-revenue curve intersects the marginal-cost curve at point *n* with a quantity of 900 doses, so that's the quantity that maximizes profit. To get consumers to buy this quantity, the price must be $15 (point *m* on the demand curve). The average cost of production is $8 per dose (shown by point *c*), so the profit per dose is $7 ($15 minus $8). Sneezy's profit equals the profit per dose ($7) times the quantity sold (900 doses), or $6,300 per hour.

To show that a quantity of 900 doses maximizes Sneezy's profit, let's see what would happen if he picked some other quantity. Suppose he decided to produce 599 doses per hour at a price just above $18 (just above point *h* on the demand curve). Could he make more profit by cutting his price by enough to sell one more dose? Sneezy should answer two questions:

▶ What is the extra cost associated with producing dose number 600? As shown by point *j* on the marginal-cost curve, the marginal cost of the 600th dose is $4.
▶ What is the extra revenue associated with dose number 600? As shown by point *i* on the marginal-revenue curve, the marginal revenue is $12.

If Sneezy wants to maximize his profit, he should produce the 600th dose because the $12 extra revenue exceeds the $4 extra cost, so his total profit will increase by $8. The same argument applies, with different numbers for marginal revenue and marginal cost, for doses 601, 602, and so on, up to 900 doses. Sneezy should continue to increase the quantity produced as long as the marginal revenue exceeds the marginal cost. The marginal principle is satisfied at point *n*, with a total of 900 doses.

Why should Sneezy stop at 900 doses? Beyond 900 doses, the marginal revenue from an additional dose will be less than the marginal cost associated with producing it. Although Sneezy could cut his price and sell a larger quantity, an additional dose would add less to revenue than it adds to cost, so his total profit would decrease. As shown in the fifth row in Table 13.2, Sneezy could sell 1,000 doses at a price of $14, but the marginal revenue at this quantity is only $4, while the marginal cost at this quantity is $6.70. Producing the 1,000th dose would decrease Sneezy's profit by $2.70. For any quantity exceeding 900 doses, the marginal revenue is less than the marginal cost, so Sneezy should produce exactly 900 doses.

Let's review what we've learned about how a monopolist picks a quantity and how to compute the monopoly profit. The three-step process is as follows.

1 Find the quantity that satisfies the marginal principle, that is, the quantity at which marginal revenue equals marginal cost. In the drug example shown in Figure 13.3, marginal revenue equals marginal cost at point *n*, so the monopolist produces 900 doses.
2 Using the demand curve, find the price associated with the monopolist's chosen quantity. In Figure 13.3, the price associated with 900 doses is $15 (point m).
3 Compute the monopolist's profit. The profit per unit sold equals the price minus the average cost, and the total profit equals the profit per unit times the number of units sold. In Figure 13.3, the profit is shown by the shaded rectangle, with height equal to the profit per unit sold and width equal to the number of units sold.

TEST Your Understanding

1. Why is a monopolist's marginal revenue less than its price?
2. Complete the statement with a number: At a price of $15 per CD, a firm sells 80 CDs per day. If the slope of the demand curve is $0.10 per CD, marginal revenue is _____.
3. You want to determine the quantity of output produced by a monopolist. What information do you need, and how would you use it?
4. At a price of $18 per CD, the marginal revenue of a CD seller is $12. If the marginal cost of CDs is $9, should the firm increase or decrease the quantity produced? Should it increase or decrease its price?

The Social Cost of Monopoly

Why should we as a society be concerned about monopoly? Most people are not surprised to hear that a monopolist uses its market power to charge a relatively high price. If this were the end of the story, a monopolist would simply gain at the expense of consumers. In other words, a monopoly would change how we slice the economic "pie," with a bigger slice for producers and a smaller slice for consumers. As we'll see in this part of the chapter, the social consequences of monopoly go beyond the redistributional effects associated with a different slicing of the pie: A monopoly causes inefficiency and actually reduces the size of the pie, so there is less in total to divide among consumers and producers.

Deadweight Loss from Monopoly

How does a monopoly differ from a perfectly competitive market? To show the difference, let's consider an example of an arthritis drug that could be produced by a monopoly or a perfectly competitive industry. Let's take the long-run perspective—a period of time long enough that a firm is perfectly flexible in its choice of inputs and can enter or leave the market.

Consider the monopoly outcome first. Let's assume that the long-run average cost of producing the arthritis drug is constant at $8 per dose. As we saw in Chapter 11, if average cost is constant, the marginal cost equals average cost. In Panel A of Figure 13.4, the long-run marginal-cost curve is the same as the long-run average-cost curve. Given the demand and marginal-revenue curves in Panel A of Figure 13.4, the monopolist will maximize profit where marginal revenue equals marginal cost (point *n*), producing 200 doses per hour at a price of $18 per dose. The monopolist's profit is $2,000 per hour —a $10 profit per dose ($18 − $8) times 200 doses.

Consider next the market for the arthritis drug under perfect competition. We're assuming that the arthritis drug industry is a constant-cost industry: Input prices do not change as the industry grows, so the long-run market supply curve is horizontal at the long-run average cost of producing the drug ($8 per dose). In Panel B of Figure

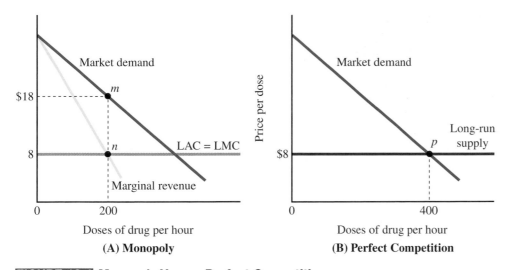

(A) **Monopoly**

(B) **Perfect Competition**

**FIGURE 13.4 Monopoly Versus Perfect Competition:
Its Effect on Quantity and Price**

(A) Monopoly The monopolist picks the quantity at which long-run marginal cost equals
marginal revenue (200 doses per hour, as shown by point *n*). As shown by point *m* on the
demand curve, the price associated with this quantity is $18 per dose.
(B) Perfect Competition The long-run supply curve of a perfectly competitive, constant-cost
industry intersects the demand curve at point *p*. The equilibrium price is $8, and the
equilibrium quantity is 400 doses per hour.

13.4, the horizontal long-run supply curve intersects the demand curve at point *p*, with
an equilibrium price of $8 and an equilibrium quantity of 400 doses per hour.
Compared to a monopoly outcome, the perfectly competitive outcome has a lower
price ($8 instead of $18 per dose) and a larger quantity (400 doses instead of 200).

To examine the social cost of monopoly power, let's imagine that we start with a
perfectly competitive market and then switch to a monopoly. Consumers will be worse
off under monopoly, and we can use the concept of consumer surplus to determine
just how much worse off they will be. As we saw in Chapter 7, consumer surplus is
shown by the area between the demand curve and the horizontal price line. In Figure
13.5, the monopoly price is $18, so the consumer surplus associated with the monop-
oly is shown by triangle *C*. In contrast, the perfectly competitive price is $8, so the con-
sumer surplus with perfect competition is shown by the larger triangle consisting of
triangle *C*, rectangle *R*, and triangle *D*. In other words, a switch from perfect competition to monopoly decreases consumer surplus by the areas *R* and *D*.

▶ *Rectangle R.* The switch to monopoly increases the price by $10 per dose.
 Consumers buy 200 doses from the monopolist and pay $10 extra on each of these
 doses, which results in a loss of $2,000 per hour for consumers.
▶ *Triangle D.* The switch to monopoly decreases the quantity consumed because the
 price increases and consumers obey the law of demand. Consumers lose consumer
 surplus on the doses they would have consumed at the lower price. This loss to consumers is shown by triangle *D* and amounts to $1,000—one-half the base of the tri-
 angle (200 doses) times the height of the triangle ($10). The total loss of consumers
 is the sum of the areas of rectangle *R* and triangle *D*, or $3,000.

FIGURE 13.5

FIGURE 13.5

The Deadweight Loss from a Monopoly
A switch from perfect competition to monopoly increases the price from $8 to $18 and decreases the quantity sold from 400 to 200 doses. Consumer surplus decreases by an amount shown by the areas *R* and *D*, while profit increases by the amount shown by rectangle *R*. The net loss to society is shown by triangle *D* (the deadweight loss of monopoly).

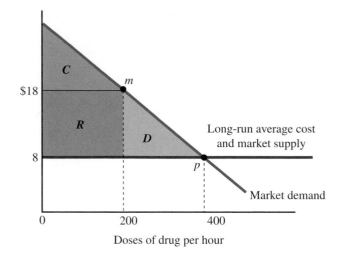

Deadweight loss from monopoly

A measure of the inefficiency from monopoly; with a constant-cost industry, equal to the difference between the consumer-surplus loss from monopoly pricing and the monopoly's profit.

It's clear that consumers lose from monopoly, but what about the monopolist? Under perfect competition, each firm makes zero economic profit. In contrast, the monopolist earns positive economic profit, shown by rectangle *R* in Figure 13.5. The monopolist's profit is $2,000, equal to the quantity produced (200 doses) times the $10 profit per dose (equal to the $18 price minus the $8 average cost). This gain by the monopolist comes at the expense of consumers.

Because only part of the loss experienced by consumers is recovered by the monopolist, there is a net loss from switching to monopoly. Consumers lose rectangle *R* and triangle *D*, but the monopolist gains only rectangle *R*. That leaves triangle *D* as the net loss or **deadweight loss from monopoly**. The word *deadweight* indicates that this loss is not offset by a gain to anyone. In contrast, rectangle *R* is lost by consumers but gained by the monopolist. Consumers lose triangle *D* because in a perfectly competitive market, they would receive some consumer surplus from the 201st through 400th doses, which of course a monopolist would not produce. The lesson is that monopoly is inefficient because, compared to a perfectly competitive market, the monopolist produces less output.

Application: Ending the Monopoly on Internet Registration

For an illustration of the inefficiency of monopoly, we can look at what happens when a government-sanctioned monopoly ends. In February, 1999, the U.S. government announced plans to end the five-year monopoly held by Network Solutions Inc. for registering Internet addresses. Network Solutions had an exclusive government contract to register Web addresses (also known as domain names) ending in .net, .org, .edu, and .com. The company registered almost 2 million names in 1998, collecting $70 for each address and charging an annual renewal fee of $35. The government's plan to introduce competition had some restrictions—an entering firm had to meet strict requirements for security and backup measures and liability insurance. Two new competitors, Register.com and Tucows.com, cut prices to between $10 and $15 per year.[2] In addition, the new firms offered registration periods of up to 10 years (compared to 2 years under the monopoly) and permitted up to 63 characters in each domain name (compared to a limit of 26 characters under the monopoly). Network Solutions, the original monopolist, quickly matched its competitors' lower prices and expanded service options.

Rent Seeking: Using Resources to Get Monopoly Power

Another source of inefficiency from a government-sanctioned monopoly is that firms use resources to acquire monopoly power. Because a monopoly will earn a large profit, firms are willing to spend a great deal of money to persuade the government to erect barriers to entry that grant monopoly power (via licenses, franchises, and tariffs). In Figure 13.5, a firm would be willing to spend up to $2,000 per hour to get a monopoly on the arthritis drug. One way to get monopoly power is to hire lobbyists to persuade legislators and other policymakers to grant monopoly power. This is an example of **rent seeking**.

Rent seeking is inefficient because it uses resources that could be used in other ways. For example, the people employed as lobbyists could instead produce goods and services. In Figure 13.5, if the monopolist spent all its potential profit ($2,000 per hour) on rent-seeking activity, the net loss to society would be areas R and D, not just area D. A classic study of rent seeking by economist Richard Posner found that firms in some industries spent up to 30% of their total revenue to get monopoly power.[3]

At the beginning of this chapter, we saw that Coca-Cola helped a state university to build a new football scoreboard and remodel its student center. Was this an act of generosity? In return for the scoreboard and the remodeled student center, Coca-Cola earned the exclusive right to sell beverages on campus. Like any monopolist, Coca-Cola will use its monopoly power to charge higher prices for beverages, so the cost of

Rent seeking

The process of using governments to obtain economic profit.

Some organizations hire lobbyists to try to persuade legislatures to grant them monopoly power.

the scoreboard and student center actually comes out of the pockets of students. Although Coca-Cola has a monopoly on beverages, some of the profit from the monopoly goes to the university to pay for the scoreboard and the student center.

Monopoly and Public Policy

Given the social costs of monopoly, the government has a number of policies to intervene in markets that are dominated by a single firm or could become a monopoly. We'll examine these policies later in the book. In the case of natural monopoly (a market that can support only a single firm), the government can intervene by regulating the price charged by the natural monopolist. In other markets, the government uses antitrust policies to break up monopolies into smaller companies and prevent corporate mergers that would lead to a monopoly. These policies are designed to promote competition, leading to lower prices and more production.

Patents and Monopoly Power

One source of monopoly power is a government patent that gives a firm the exclusive right to produce a product for 20 years. As we'll see, a patent encourages innovation because the innovators know they will earn monopoly profits on a new product over the period covered by the patent. If the monopoly profits are large enough to offset the substantial research and development costs of a new product, a firm will develop the product and become a monopolist. Granting monopoly power through a patent may be efficient from the social perspective because it may precipitate the development of products that would otherwise not be developed.

Incentives for Innovation

Let's use the arthritis drug to show why a patent encourages innovation. Suppose that Hanna hasn't yet developed the drug, but she believes the potential benefits and costs of developing the drug are as follows:

▶ The economic cost of research and development would be $14 million, including all the opportunity costs of the project.
▶ The estimated annual economic profit from a monopoly would be $2 million (in today's dollars).
▶ Hanna's competitors will need three years to develop and produce their own versions of the drug, so if Hanna isn't protected by a patent, her monopoly will last only three years.

Based on these numbers, Hanna won't develop the drug unless she receives a patent that lasts at least 7 years. That's the length of time she needs to recover her research and development costs of $14 million ($2 million per year times 7 years). If there is no patent and she loses her monopoly in 3 years, she will earn a profit of $6 million, which is less than her research and development costs. On the other hand, with a 20-year patent she will earn $40 million, which is more than enough to recover her costs.

Trade-Offs from Patents

Is the patent for Hanna's drug beneficial from the social perspective? The patent grants monopoly power to Hanna, and she responds by charging a higher price and producing less than the quantity that would be produced in a perfectly competitive market (200 doses per hour instead of 400). From society's perspective, 400 doses would be better than 200 doses, but we don't have that choice. Hanna won't develop the drug unless a patent protects her from competition for at least 7 years. Therefore, society's choice is between 200 doses (the patent and monopoly outcome) and zero doses. Because 200 doses is clearly better than none, the patent is beneficial from society's perspective.

What about a product that would be developed without the protection of a patent? Suppose Marcus could develop a new drug with a research and development project costing $5 million. If Marcus does not have a patent for his new drug, he would earn monopoly profits of $2 million per year for 3 years, a total of $6 million. Because his research and development costs are low relative to the monopoly profit, a 3-year monopoly will generate enough profit to cover his costs, so he will develop the new drug even without a patent. Therefore, if the government issues a 20-year patent, the only effect is to prolong Marcus's monopoly, and that means the patent would be inefficient from society's perspective.

What are the general conclusions about the merits of the patent system? As usual, there are some trade-offs. It is sensible to grant a patent for a product that would otherwise not be developed, but not sensible to grant one for a product that would be developed even without a patent. Unfortunately, no one knows in advance whether a particular product would be developed without a patent, so the government can't be selective in granting patents. Therefore, while the patent system will cause the development of some products that would not occur without patent protection, some patents will merely prolong a firm's monopoly power and generate higher prices.

What happens when a patent expires? New firms will enter the market, and the resulting competition for consumers will decrease prices. The transition from monopoly to competition is not always a smooth one, as you'll see in "A Closer Look: Barriers to Generic Drugs."

TEST Your Understanding

5. True or false: A monopoly is inefficient solely because the monopolist gets a profit at the expense of consumers.
6. Who bears the cost of the scoreboard built by Coca-Cola?
7. How much would you be willing to pay for a monopoly for off-street parking if your average cost is $30 per space per day and you could charge $35 per space per day for 500 spaces?
8. Consider the arthritis example. Will Hanna develop the drug without a patent if she will have a monopoly for five years instead of just three years?

A CLOSER LOOK

Barriers to Generic Drugs

When the patent for a popular pharmaceutical drug expires, other firms introduce generic versions of the drug. The generics are virtually identical to the original branded drug, but they sell at a much lower price. The producers of branded drugs have an incentive to delay the introduction of generic drugs, and sometimes use illegal means to do so.

In 1999, the Federal Trade Commission (FTC) launched a probe of four large pharmaceutical companies to determine whether they unfairly stifled competition from generic producers. The FTC is investigating allegations that the makers of branded drugs made deals with generic suppliers to keep generics off the market. The alleged practices include cash payments and exclusive licenses for new versions of the branded drug.[4]

- ▶ Eli Lilly and Company announced a deal under which Sepracor, Inc. would have the exclusive right to sell a purified version of Prozac (the antidepressant with annual sales of $2.8 billion). In effect, this deal would extend Lilly's monopoly over the drug for another 15 years.
- ▶ Abbott Laboratories was accused of paying $24 million per year to Ivax Corporation and an undisclosed amount to Novartis AG to delay the launch of their generic versions of Hytrin, Abbott's hypertension drug. Similar allegations of payoffs to generic suppliers have been levied against

Hoechst AG in connection with its annual payment of $40 million to Andrx Corporation, which had produced—but not sold—a generic version of Cardizem, Hoechst's heart medication.

Another tactic used by the producers of branded drugs is to claim that generics are not as good as the branded drug. Dupont has asserted that generic versions of its Coumadin (a blood thinner) are not equivalent to Coumadin, and may pose risks to patients.

Price Discrimination

Up to this point in the book, we've assumed that a firm charges the same price to all its consumers. As we'll see in this part of the chapter, a firm may be able to divide consumers into two or more groups and charge a different price to each group, a practice known as **price discrimination**. For example, airlines offer discount tickets to travelers who are flexible in their departure times, and movie theaters have lower prices for senior citizens.

Although price discrimination is widespread, it is not always possible. A firm has an opportunity for price discrimination if three conditions are met:

Price discrimination

The process under which a firm divides consumers into two or more groups and picks a different price for each group.

1 *Market power.* The firm must have some control over its price, facing a negatively sloped demand curve for its product. Although we will discuss price discrimination by a monopolist, any firm that faces a negatively sloped demand curve can charge different prices to different consumers. In fact, the only type of firm that cannot engage in price discrimination is a perfectly competitive price-taking firm. Such a firm faces a horizontal demand curve, taking the market price as given. For all other types of markets (monopoly, oligopoly, monopolistic competition), price discrimination is possible.

2 *Different consumer groups.* Consumers must differ in their willingness to pay for the product or in their responsiveness to changes in price (as measured by the price elasticity of demand). In addition, the firm must be able to identify different groups of consumers, for example, business travelers versus tourists, students versus nonstudents, seniors versus nonseniors.

3 *Resale is not possible.* It must be impractical for one consumer to resell the product to another consumer. Airlines prohibit consumers from buying and reselling tickets. If they allowed consumers to sell discount tickets to each other, you could go into the business as a ticket broker, buying discount airline tickets one month ahead and then selling them to business travelers one week before the travel date. In general, the possibility of resale causes price discrimination to break down.

One approach to price discrimination is to offer a discount (resulting in a lower price) to some types of consumers. The firm identifies a group of customers who are not willing to pay the regular price and then offers a discount to people in that group. Here are some examples of price discrimination with discounts for certain groups of consumers:

▶ Discounts on airline tickets. Airlines offer discount tickets to travelers who spend Saturday night away from home because they are likely to be tourists, not business travelers. The typical tourist is not willing to pay as much for air travel as the typical business traveler. Airlines also offer discount tickets to people who plan weeks ahead, because tourists plan longer ahead than business travelers.

▶ Discount coupons for groceries and restaurant food. The typical coupon-clipper is not willing to pay as much as the typical consumer.

▶ Manufacturers' rebates for appliances. A person who takes the trouble to mail a rebate form to the manufacturer is not willing to pay as much as the typical consumer.

▶ Senior-citizen discounts on airline tickets, restaurant food, drugs, and entertainment.

▶ Student discounts on movies and concerts.

The only legal restriction on price discrimination is that a firm cannot use it to drive rival firms out of business.

The challenge for a firm is to figure out which groups of consumers should get discounts. Firms can experiment with different prices and look for groups of consumers that are most sensitive to price. In September of 2000, Amazon.com started charging different prices for different types of consumers. For example, consumers who used Netscape's browser paid $65 for the *Planet of the Apes* DVD, while the users of Explorer paid $75 for the same DVD.[5] Prices also varied with the consumer's Internet service provider and the number of previous purchases from Amazon. An Amazon spokeswoman said that the company varied prices in a random fashion, as part of ongoing tests to see how consumers respond to price changes. In other words, it appears that Amazon was assessing the willingness to pay of different types of consumers. In principle, Amazon could use the data collected to develop systems of price discrimination, giving discounts to the most price-sensitive consumers. After widespread protests of the Amazon pricing experiments, the company stopped the practice and issued refunds to about 7,000 consumers who paid relatively high prices.

Application: Senior Discounts in Restaurants

Consider a restaurant whose patrons can be divided into two groups, senior citizens and others. In Figure 13.6, the demand curve for senior citizens is lower than the demand curve for other citizens, reflecting the assumption that the typical senior is willing to pay less than the typical nonsenior, perhaps because senior citizens have lower income and more time to shop for low prices.

Under a price-discrimination plan, the restaurant will simply apply the marginal principle twice, once for seniors and a second time for non-seniors. This is sensible because the two groups have different demands for restaurant meals, so the restaurant should treat them differently. Panel A of Figure 13.6 shows how to pick a price for senior citizens. The marginal principle (marginal revenue = marginal cost) is satisfied at point e, with 280 senior meals per day. Therefore, the appropriate price for seniors is $3 (point d on the senior demand curve). In Panel B of Figure 13.6, the marginal principle is satisfied at point c for nonseniors, with 260 meals per day and a price of $6 per meal.

We know that the application of the marginal principle maximizes profit in each segment of the market. Therefore, charging different prices ($3 for seniors, $6 for nonseniors) maximizes the restaurant's total profit. If the restaurant were instead to charge a single price for both groups, say $5, the profit from each group would be lower, so the restaurant's total profit would be lower too.

Price Discrimination and the Elasticity of Demand

We can use the concept of price elasticity of demand to explain why price discrimination increases the restaurant's profit. From Chapter 5, we know that when demand is elastic ($E_d > 1$), there is a negative relationship between price and total revenue: When

FIGURE 13.6

The Marginal Principle and Price Discrimination

To engage in price discrimination, the firm divides potential customers into two groups, and applies the marginal principle twice, once for each group. Using the marginal principle, the profit-maximizing prices are $6 for nonseniors (point *f*), and $3 for seniors (point *d*).

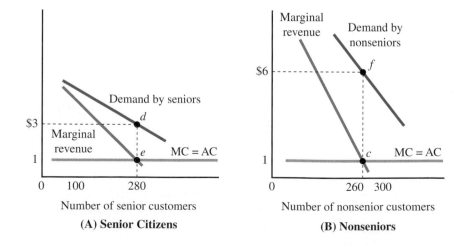

the price decreases, total revenue (price times quantity sold) increases because the percentage increase in quantity demanded exceeds the percentage decrease in price.

Suppose the restaurant initially has a single price of $5 for both seniors and nonseniors. Compared to other consumers, senior citizens have more elastic demand for restaurant meals, in part because they have lower income and more time to shop for low prices. A price cut for senior citizens brings good news and bad news for the restaurant:

▶ Good news: Demand is highly elastic, so total revenue increases by a large amount.
▶ Bad news: More meals are served, so total cost increases.

If the senior demand for meals is highly elastic (E_d is well above 1.0), the good news will dominate the bad news: The increase in revenue will more than offset the increase in cost. Consequently, a price cut will increase the firm's profit.

For nonseniors, the firm will have an incentive to increase the price above the initial common price of $5. Suppose nonseniors have a mildly elastic demand for meals (E_d is just above 1.0). A price hike for nonseniors brings bad news on the revenue side and good news on the cost side.

▶ Bad news: Demand is mildly elastic, so total revenue decreases by a small amount.
▶ Good news: Fewer meals are served, so total cost decreases.

If the demand by nonseniors is mildly elastic, the good news will dominate the bad news: The savings in production costs will exceed the revenue loss. Consequently, the price hike for nonseniors will increase the firm's profit.

The same logic applies to other cases of price discrimination. A firm will charge a higher price to consumers with relatively inelastic demand. For an example of price discrimination based on weather conditions, read "A Closer Look: Interacting with a Soda Vending Machine on a Hot Day."

A CLOSER LOOK   Interacting with a Soda Vending Machine on a Hot Day

On a hot day, are you willing to pay more for an ice-cold can of Coke? If so, you're the type of consumer Coca-Cola Company had in mind when it developed a high-tech vending machine, complete with heat sensors and microchips, that charges a higher price when the weather is hot.[6] According to Douglas Ivester, the head of Coca-Cola, the desire for a cold drink increases when it is hot, so "it is fair that it should be more expensive. The machine will simply make the process more automatic."

The announcement of the new vending machine led to howls of protest from consumers. In response, Coca-Cola Company said that it would not actually use the new machine, but was "exploring innovative technology and communication systems that can actually improve product availability, promotional activity and even offer consumers an interactive experience when they purchase a soft drink from a vending machine." Based on the reaction to the news of the heat-sensing vending machine, you can imagine the "interactive experience" when a hot and thirsty consumer discovers the higher price for a cold drink on a hot day.

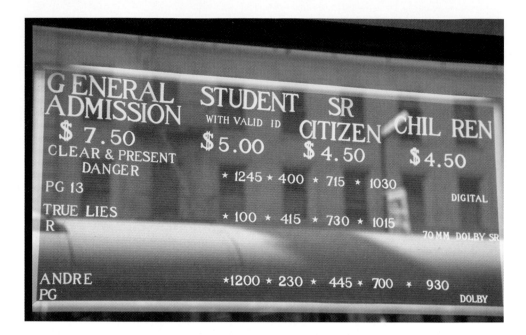

Application: Movie Admission and Popcorn

Recall the chapter-opening question about senior discounts for movies. Why do senior citizens typically pay less to get into movies but pay the same as everyone else for popcorn? A senior discount for movie admission is not an act of generosity by a firm, but part of the firm's pricing strategy designed to increase profit. Senior citizens are typically willing to pay less than other citizens for movies, so a theater divides its consumers into two groups—seniors and others—and offers a discount to seniors. This price discrimination in favor of senior citizens increases the theater's profit. Why don't theaters offer a senior discount for popcorn? Unlike admission to the theater, popcorn can be easily transferred from one customer to another. If senior citizens could buy popcorn at half the regular price, many nonseniors would get seniors to buy popcorn for them, so the theater wouldn't sell as much popcorn at the regular price. Price discrimination for popcorn would not be profitable.

Why Are Hardback Books So Expensive?

Most books are published in two forms—hardback and paperback—the paperback edition being published and available for sale several weeks or months later than the hardback edition. The cost of producing a hardback book is only about 20% higher than the cost of producing the same book as a paperback, but the price of a hardback book is about three times the price of a paperback book. Why?

The key to solving this puzzle is the fact that hardback books are published first, followed by the paperback edition. Booksellers use hardbacks and paperbacks to distinguish between two types of consumers: those who are willing to pay a lot and those who are willing to pay a little. The people who are willing to pay the most are eager to read the book as soon as it comes out, so they pay $18 for a hardback book. The people who are willing to pay less are more patient and are willing to wait a few months for the $6 paperback version. The pricing of hardback and paperback books is another example of price discrimination, with consumers with less elastic demand paying a higher price. ∎

TEST Your Understanding

9. Why is aspirin sold in airports so much more expensive than aspirin sold in grocery stores?

10. Complete the statement with "increase" or "decrease": Suppose a firm starts with a single price and then switches to a price-discrimination scheme. The firm will _____ the price for the group of consumers with the less elastic demand and _____ the group with the more elastic demand.

11. In many lounges and bars, the cover charge for women is less than the charge for men. Why?

Economic Experiment

Price Discrimination

Here is an experiment that shows how a monopolist—a museum—picks different prices for different consumer groups. Some students play the roles of consumers, and others play the roles of museum managers. Here is how the experiment works:

- The instructor picks a small group of students (three to five) to represent the museum. There is a fixed marginal cost of each museum patron (for ticket-takers, guides, cleanup, and other tasks).

- There are 40 consumers (potential museum patrons), and half the consumers are senior citizens with senior-citizen cards. Each consumer receives a number indicating how much he or she is willing to pay for a trip to a museum.

- In each round of the experiment, each museum posts two prices: one for senior citizens and one for nonseniors. Consumers then decide whether to buy a ticket at the relevant posted price.

- A consumer's score in a particular round equals the difference between his or her willingness to pay and the amount actually paid for a museum admission.

- A museum's score equals its profit, equal to its total revenue minus its total cost ($2 times the number of patrons).

- The experiment is run for five rounds. At the end of the experiment, each consumer computes his or her score by adding up the consumer surpluses. The museum's score equals the sum of the profits from the five rounds. ●

1. Textbook Pricing: Publishers versus Authors

Consider the problem of setting a price for a textbook. The marginal cost of production is constant at $20 per book. The publisher knows from experience that the slope of the demand curve is $0.20 per textbook: Starting with a price of $44, a price cut of $0.20 will increase the quantity demanded by 1 textbook. For example, here are some combinations of price and quantity:

Price per textbook	$44	$40	$36	$32	$30
Quantity of textbooks	80	100	120	140	150

a. What price will the publisher choose?
b. Suppose that the author receives a royalty payment equal to 10% of the total sales revenue from the book. If the author could choose a price, what would it be?
c. Why do the publisher and the author disagree about the price for the book?
d. Design an alternative author-compensation scheme under which the author and the publisher would choose the same price.

2. Payoff for Casino Approval

In 1996, developers interested in building an American Indian casino in Creswell, Oregon, placed a curious announcement in the local newspaper. If local voters approved the casino, the developers promised to give citizens $2 million per year. Given an adult population of about 1,600, each adult in Creswell would receive a cash payment of $1,250 per year.

a. Why did the developers propose this deal? Why aren't similar deals proposed for new clothing stores, music stores, or auto repair shops?
b. If the deal goes through and you moved to Creswell, would you expect to get $1,250 per year?

3. Price Discrimination in a Campus Film Series

You manage a campus film series and charge different prices to students and faculty members. The current prices and numbers of tickets sold are as follows:

	Price	Number of Viewers	Slope of Demand Curve
Students	$3	100	$0.01 per ticket
Faculty	$4	50	$0.10 per ticket

The marginal cost of another viewer is zero. Does the current pricing scheme maximize your total revenue? If not, how should you change your prices?

4. Pricing First-Run Movies and Early Apples

If you see a movie when it first comes out, you pay much more than you would if you waited a month or two for the movie to appear at a second-run movie theater. If you buy apples early in the harvest season, you pay more than you would if you waited until the middle of the harvest season. Are both movies and apples subject to price discrimination?

SUMMARY

In this chapter, we've seen some of the subtleties of monopolies and their pricing policies. Compared to a perfectly competitive market, a monopoly means a higher price, a smaller quantity, and resources wasted when firms seek monopoly power. On the positive side, some of the products we use today might never have been invented without the patent system and the monopoly power it grants. Firms with market power often use price discrimination to increase their profits. Here are the main points of the chapter:

1 Compared to a perfectly competitive market, a market served by a monopolist will have a higher price, a smaller quantity of output, and a deadweight loss to society.
2 Some firms spend money and use resources to acquire monopoly power, a process known as rent seeking.
3 Patents protect innovators from competition, leading to higher prices for new products but greater incentives to develop new products.
4 To engage in price discrimination, a firm divides its customers into two or more groups and charges lower prices to groups with more elastic demand.
5 Price discrimination is not an act of generosity; it's an act of profit maximization.

KEY TERMS

deadweight loss from monopoly, 298
market power, 289
monopoly, 289

natural monopoly, 289
patent, 289

price discrimination, 302
rent seeking, 299

PROBLEMS AND DISCUSSION QUESTIONS

1 Consider a restaurant that charges $10 for all you can eat and has 30 customers at this price. The slope of the demand curve is $0.10 per meal, and the marginal cost of providing a meal is $3. What price will satisfy the marginal principle and maximize the restaurant's profit?
2 The National Park Service grants a single firm the right to sell food and other goods in Yosemite National Park. Discuss the trade-offs associated with this policy.
3 Since 1963, many state governments that outlaw commercial lotteries have introduced state lotteries to raise revenue for state and local governments. In 1994, the net revenue from state lotteries was about $10 billion. Would you expect the state lotteries to have higher or lower paybacks (total prize money divided by the total amount of money collected) than commercial games of chance such as horse racing and slot machines? Explain.
4 Consider the Slappers, a hockey team that plays in an arena with 8,000 seats. The only cost associated with staging a hockey game is a fixed cost of $6,000: The team incurs this cost regardless of how many people attend a game. The demand curve for hockey tickets has a slope of $0.001 per ticket ($1 divided by 1,000 tickets): Each $1 increase in price

decreases the number of tickets sold by 1,000. For example, here are some combinations of price and quantity:

Price per ticket	$4	$5	$6	$7
Quantity of tickets	8,000	7,000	6,000	5,000

The owner's objective is to maximize the profit per hockey game (total revenue minus the $6,000 fixed cost).
  a. What price will maximize profit?
  b. If the owner picks the price that maximizes profit, how many seats in the arena will be empty?
  c. Is it rational to leave some seats empty?
5 The government allows professional sports associations (collections of teams) to restrict the number of teams. How do these barriers to entry affect the price of tickets to professional sporting events and the number of tickets sold? If we eliminated these barriers to entry, what would happen to ticket prices and total attendance at sporting events?
6 Consider a monopolist who owns a natural spring that produces water that, according to nearby residents, has a unique taste and healing properties.

The monopolist has a fixed cost of installing plumbing to tap the water but no marginal cost. The demand curve for the spring water is linear. Depict graphically the monopolist's choice of a price and quantity. At the profit-maximizing quantity, what is the price elasticity of demand? If the spring were owned by an efficiency-minded government, what price would it charge?

7 In the board game Monopoly, when a player gets the third deed for a group of properties (for example, the third orange property: St. James, New York, and Tennessee Avenues), the player doubles the rent charged on each property in the group. Similarly, a player who has a single railroad charges a rent of $25, while a player who has all four railroads charges a rent of $200 for each railroad. Are these rules consistent with the analysis of monopoly in this chapter?

8 Adam Smith predicted that a monopolist would charge "the highest price which can be got." Do you agree?

9 Suppose the drug company Bristol-Meyers-Squibb announces that it will increase the price of Taxol, the cancer-fighting drug, by 10%. According to a consumer advocate, "The price hike will increase Bristol's total revenue from Taxol by 10%." Do you agree? What is the advocate assuming about the price elasticity of demand for Taxol? Is this assumption realistic?

10 Comment on the following statement from a member of a city council: "Several of the merchants in our city offer discounts to our senior citizens. These discounts obviously decrease the merchants' profits, so we should decrease the merchants' taxes to offset their losses on senior-citizen discounts."

11 Consider an airline that initially has a single price ($300) for all consumers. At this price, it has 120 business travelers and 80 tourists. The airline's marginal cost is $100. The slope of the business demand curve is −$2 per traveler, and the slope of the tourist demand curve is −$1 per traveler. Does the single-price policy maximize the airline's profit? If not, how should it change its prices?

12 Why are senior-citizen discounts common for services such as admission to museums and other entertainment events but uncommon for consumer goods such as hardware, appliances, and automobiles?

13 An advertisement for an early-bird sale at a fabric store notes that people who buy fabric between 6:00 and 7:00 A.M. receive a 40% discount, and people who shop between 7:00 and 8:00 A.M. receive a 20% discount. What is the rationale for such a pricing scheme?

14 Car companies offer many options on new cars, including automatic transmissions, CD players, leather trim, and heated seats. The markup on these options (the difference between the price consumers pay and the cost incurred by the car company) is higher for leather trim and CD players than it is for automatic transmissions. Why?

MODEL ANSWERS TO QUESTIONS

Chapter-Opening Questions

1 The bad news is that a monopolist charges a higher price. The good news is that monopoly profits encourage innovation.

2 In response to competition from generic equivalents, the producer of the branded drug usually decreases its price, but the price of the branded drug is still higher than the price of generic drugs.

3 Consumers who are eager to read a book are willing to pay more, so they buy the expensive hardback version because it comes out first. People who are willing to pay less wait for the cheaper paperback version a few months later.

4 If seniors are willing to pay less for movies than others, price discrimination will increase the theater's profits. Because popcorn can easily be purchased for someone else, seniors will pay the same price as everyone else.

Test Your Understanding

1 To sell one more unit, the monopolist must cut the price. Marginal revenue equals the price minus the revenue lost from selling goods at a lower price to the original customers.

2 $MR = \$15 - (80 \text{ units} \times \$0.10 \text{ per unit}) = \$7$.

3 You need the marginal-revenue curve and the marginal-cost curve. The monopolist will pick the quantity at which the two curves intersect.

4 Marginal revenue exceeds marginal cost, so the firm should increase the quantity produced. To increase the quantity, the firm must cut its price.

5 False. The inefficiency (the deadweight social loss) results from a smaller quantity.

6 Campus consumers, who pay more for soft drinks because of the Coca-Cola monopoly.

7 The profit per space is $5 ($35 − $30), so the daily profit is $2,500 ($5 per space × 500 spaces). You are willing to pay up to $2,500 per day for the monopoly.

8 If Hanna's monopoly profit lasts five years, she'll earn a total of $10 million, which is still less than the cost of the research and development project ($14 million). She won't develop the drug.

9 People looking for aspirin in airports usually have a headache or expect one. They are willing to pay more than a headache-free grocery shopper: The airport shopper has a less elastic demand. Firms engage in price discrimination, charging a higher price to the group of consumers with the less elastic demand (airport customers).

10 Increase, decrease.

11 If women are willing to pay less than men for admission into a cocktail lounge or bar (they have a more elastic demand), price discrimination may increase the bar's profit. A discounted cover charge works well because the good purchased (admission) cannot be transferred to men.

NOTES

1. Jeannie Donnelly, "OSU Beverages Will Be Provided Exclusively by Coca-Cola," *The Daily Barometer*, May 27, 1994, p. 1.

2. "Tucows.com to Slash Domain Name Registration Rates," *News Bytes News Network*, January 11, 2000; "Network Solutions Offers 10-Year.Com Registrations," *News Bytes News Network*, January 18, 2000; "Register.com Latest to Offer Long Domain Names," *News Bytes News Network*, January 11, 2000.

3. Richard A. Posner, "The Social Costs of Monopoly and Regulation," *Journal of Political Economy*, vol. 83, 1975, pp. 807–827.

4. Ralph T. King, Jr., "FTC Widens Probe into Generic-Drug Barriers," *Wall Street Journal*, March 9, 1999, p. B8.

5. Linda Rosencrance, "Amazon charging different prices on some DVDs," *Computerworld*, September 5, 2000.

6. Rance Crain, "Is Thirst for Alpha Status behind Coke's High-Tech Talk?" *Advertising Age*, vol. 70, November 22, 1999, p. 26.

The Effects of Market Entry

Entry Squeezes Profits from Three Sides
Application: Woofer, Tweeter,
   and the Stereo Business
Entry Effects in the Real World

Monopolistic Competition

When Entry Stops: Long-Run Equilibrium
Trade-Offs Between Average Cost
   and Variety
Application: Location and Consumer
   Travel Costs
Using the Tools

Market Entry and Monopolistic Competition

*T*weeter just inherited a lot of money, enough to start her own car-stereo business. Woofer owns the only store in town selling car stereos, and he prices each stereo at $230. Woofer's average cost per stereo is $200, so he earns a profit of $30 on each one he sells. Should Tweeter use her inheritance to open her own car-stereo store? If she does, will she make a profit of $30 per stereo, just like Woofer?

Like entrepreneurs around the world, Tweeter has a difficult decision to make. Before she decides whether or not to enter the car-stereo market, she must predict how much she would be able to charge for her car stereos and how much it would cost her to supply them. Before she enters the market, there is a $30 gap between price and average cost per stereo, but the price is likely to drop when she enters the market and begins competing with Woofer for customers. In addition, Tweeter may have a higher average cost per stereo than Woofer. If the price she can get for her stereos drops below her average cost, Tweeter will lose money and would be better off using her inheritance some other way.

This chapter is about market entry. We explore a firm's decision to enter a market and examine the consequences of entry on prices and profits. Firms are motivated by economic profit and will enter a market as long as there is economic profit to be made. As we'll see, the entry of firms squeezes profit in three ways: The price decreases; the average cost of production increases; and the quantity sold per firm decreases. Eventually, the entry process stops, and we can count the number of firms serving the market. If entry stops at a single firm, we have a natural monopoly, a topic to be covered in Chapter 16. If there are a few firms, we have oligopoly, to be discussed in the next chapter. If many firms enter the market, we have monopolistic competition, the topic of the later part of this chapter.

Monopolistic competition is a sort of hybrid between monopoly and perfect competition. The label may seem like an oxymoron, similar to "act naturally" and "tight slacks," but it actually conveys the two key features of the market. First, each firm in the market produces a good that is slightly different from the products of other firms, so each firm has a narrowly defined *monopoly*. The products sold by different firms in the market are close substitutes for one another, so there is keen *competition* between firms for consumers. For example, your local grocery store may stock several brands of toothbrushes with different design features. If the price of one brand increases, some loyal customers will continue to buy the brand, but others will switch to different brands that are close substitutes. Some other examples of monopolistic competition are the markets for bread, clothing, restaurant meals, and gasoline. In each case, firms in the market sell products that are close, but not perfect substitutes.

The analysis in this chapter is based on two assumptions. First, we assume there are no barriers to entry: There are no patents or government licensing programs that limit the number of firms. Second, we assume that firms do not act strategically: Each firm acts on its own, taking the actions of other firms as given. This means that firms already in the market do not conspire to fix prices and do not try to prevent other firms from entering the market. In the next chapter, we'll explore several types of strategic behavior in a market with just a few firms, an oligopoly.

The theme of this chapter is that market entry decreases prices and increases the market quantity. Here are some practical questions we answer in the chapter:

1 How did the deregulation of trucking services in the 1980s affect the prices and the profits of trucking firms?
2 If telephone service becomes available on the Internet, what are the implications for traditional providers of phone service?
3 How do restrictions on Internet wine sales affect wine prices?

Monopolistic competition

A market served by many firms selling slightly different products.

The Effects of Market Entry

Consider a market served by a single profitable firm, a monopolist. As we saw earlier in the book, a firm in any market can use the marginal principle to decide how much output to produce.

MARGINAL *Principle*

Increase the level of an activity if its marginal benefit exceeds its marginal cost, but reduce the level of the activity if the marginal cost exceeds the marginal benefit. If possible, pick the level of the activity at which the marginal benefit equals the marginal cost.

Consider a firm whose activity is producing toothbrushes. The marginal benefit of producing toothbrushes is the marginal revenue from selling one more brush. In Figure 14.1, if a single firm produces toothbrushes, the firm-specific demand curve is the same as the market demand curve. A firm that is considering entering the toothbrush market must make a long-run decision about what size and type of production facility to build. Therefore, the long-run cost curves—which show production costs for a firm that hasn't committed to a particular production facility—are relevant for the firm's entry decision. In Figure 14.1, the long-run average cost curve is L-shaped, which, as we saw in Chapter 11, is consistent with empirical studies of production costs. If the average cost decreases as output increases (that is, if the average-cost curve is negatively sloped), the marginal cost must be less than the average cost. In Figure 14.1, the marginal-cost curve lies below the negatively sloped average-cost curve.

As we saw in Chapter 13, the monopolist will maximize profit by picking the quantity at which marginal revenue equals marginal cost. In Figure 14.1, this happens at point *n*, with a quantity of 300 toothbrushes. From the market demand curve, we can see that the price associated with this quantity is $2.00. Given an average cost of

FIGURE 14.1

Profit Maximization by a Single Producer
The single toothbrush producer (a monopolist) picks point *n* (where marginal revenue equals marginal cost), supplying 300 toothbrushes per minute at a price of $2.00 (point *m*) and an average cost of $0.90 (point *c*). Economic profit (shown by the shaded rectangle) is $330.

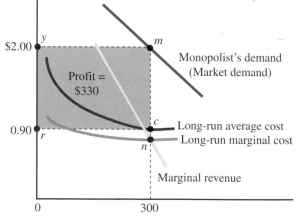

Toothbrushes per minute

$0.90 per toothbrush, the monopolist's profit per unit is $1.10 (equal to $2.00 minus $0.90), so the total profit (shown by the shaded area) is $330. Given the large profits in the toothbrush market, will a second firm enter the market?

Entry Squeezes Profits from Three Sides

Suppose a second firm, producing a nearly identical product, enters the market. When the second firm enters, the firm-specific demand curve for the original firm will shift to the left. At any particular price, some consumers will patronize the new firm, so there will be fewer consumers willing to purchase toothbrushes from the first firm. In other words, the first firm will sell fewer brushes at each price. In Figure 14.2, the firm-specific demand curve for the first firm—the original monopolist—shifts to the left, and profit decreases for three reasons:

1 The market price drops. The marginal principle is satisfied at point x, so the first firm now produces 200 toothbrushes at a price of $1.85 (point e). The competition between the two firms causes the price to drop, from $2.00 to $1.85.
2 The quantity produced by the first firm decreases. The first firm produces only 200 toothbrushes, down from the 300 it produced as a monopolist.
3 The first firm's average cost of production increases. The decrease in the quantity produced causes the firm to move upward along its negatively sloped average-cost curve to a higher average cost per toothbrush (from $0.90 to $1.00).

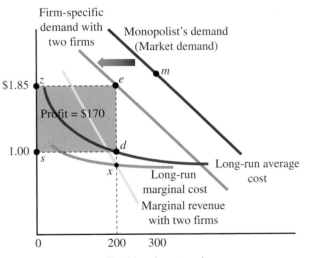

FIGURE 14.2 Entry by Another Firm Decreases Price and Squeezes Profit
The entry of a second toothbrush producer shifts the firm-specific demand curve for the original firm to the left: A smaller quantity is sold at each price. The marginal principle is satisfied at point x, so the firm produces a smaller quantity (200 instead of 300 toothbrushes) at a higher average cost ($1.00 instead of $0.90 per toothbrush) and sells at a lower price ($1.85 instead of $2.00). Economic profit drops to $170.

The combination of a lower price, a higher average cost, and a smaller quantity means that the first firm earns less profit. The profit rectangle (shown by points *y*, *m*, *c*, and *r* in Figure 14.1 and points *z*, *e*, *d*, and *s* in Figure 14.2) shrinks because the top of the rectangle (determined by the price) sinks, the bottom of the rectangle (determined by the average cost) rises, and the right side of the rectangle (determined by the quantity) moves to the left. In our example, the profit drops from $330 to $170.

What about the second firm? If we assume that the second firm has access to the same production technology as the first firm and pays the same prices for its inputs, the cost curves for the second firm will be the same as the cost curves for the first firm. If the product of the second firm is nearly identical to the product as the first firm, the firm-specific demand curve for the second firm will be nearly identical to the firm-specific demand curve for the first firm. As an approximation, we can use Figure 14.2 to represent both firms. Each firm produces 200 toothbrushes at an average cost of $1.00 per toothbrush and sells them at a price of $1.85.

Application: Woofer, Tweeter, and the Stereo Business

For an example of the effects of entry on price, cost, and profit, recall Tweeter's hypothetical entry decision described at the beginning of the chapter. Woofer the monopolist initially sells 10 stereos per day at a price of $230 and an average cost of $200 per stereo. Suppose that if Tweeter enters the market, the price will drop to $225 and her average cost will be $205, so she could earn a profit of $20 per stereo. Although Tweeter's entry squeezes profit from both sides—decreasing the market price and increasing the average cost—there is still some profit to be made, so she will enter the market. Of course, other firms may also enter the market, so Tweeter should not count on making a $20 profit per stereo for very long.

Entry Effects in the Real World

Empirical studies of real markets provide overwhelming evidence that entry decreases market prices and firms' profits.[1] In one study of the retail pricing of tires, a market with only two tire stores had a price of $55 per tire, compared to a price of $53 in a market with three stores, $51 with four stores, and $50 with five stores.[2] In other words, the larger the number of stores, the lower the price of tires.

A recent change in public policy shows what happens when the government eliminates artificial barriers to entry. The Motor Carrier Act of 1980 eliminated the government's entry restrictions on the trucking industry, most of which had been in place since the 1930s. New firms entered the trucking market, and freight prices dropped by about 22%.[3] The market value of a firm's trucking license reflects the profit the firm can earn in the market. As a result of increased competition and lower prices from deregulation, the average value of a trucking license dropped from $579,000 in 1977 to less than $15,000 in 1982.[4]

A CLOSER LOOK

Restricting Entry of On-Line Wine Merchants

As electronic commerce has spread to more and more goods and services, there are some products that face online sales restrictions. For example, many states in the U.S. prohibit the direct shipping of wine from winemakers to consumers. In these states, the only way to buy wine directly from a winemaker is to travel to a winery. Other U.S. states require special licenses for consumers buying wine and for firms shipping it.

The Federal Trade Commission (FTC) recently examined the effects of Virginia' direct-shipping ban on the prices and availability of the most popular wines in that state.[5] In Northern Virginia, wine consumers can buy wine from a wide variety of traditional sellers, including specialty wine shops, beverage megastores, and some grocery stores. Yet despite the widespread competition among traditional retailers, online prices were much lower. For wine with prices of $20 or greater, the online prices were between $4.40 and $7.19 lower. All 83 of the most popular wines were available online, but 15 of them were not available at any local store.

Why does the direct-shipping ban persist? Although some people claim that the ban reduces underage drinking, the FTC report debunks this claim. Teenagers looking for alcohol rarely use credit cards to buy expensive wine by the case. It appears that the shipping bans come from the political pressure exerted

by traditional merchants, who want to stifle competition. According to Jerry Ellig, an FTC economist who interviewed people about the shipping ban, traditional merchants say that that e-commerce is great in every other market, but not in theirs.

TEST Your Understanding

1. Complete the statement: A firm picks the quantity of output at which _____ equals _____.
2. Draw a graph showing the effect of the entry of a second firm on the firm-specific demand curve for the original firm (a monopolist).
3. Complete the statement with "increases" or "decreases": The entry of an additional firm _____ the profit per unit of output because entry _____ the price and _____ the average cost of production.
4. Suppose that when Tweeter enters the car-stereo market, the price drops by $20 and the average cost per unit increases by $15. Is it sensible to enter the market?

Monopolistic Competition

Let's think about how many firms will actually enter a particular market. Under monopolistic competition, many firms enter the market. Here are the characteristics of a market that is subject to monopolistic competition:

1 *Many firms.* Because there are relatively small economies of scale, small firms can produce their products at about the same average cost as large firms. Because even a small firm can cover its costs, the market can support many firms.

2 *A differentiated product.* The firms sell slightly different products. Product differentiation may be in the form of differences in physical characteristics, location, services, and the aura or image associated with the product.

3 *No artificial barriers to entry.* There are no patents or government regulations preventing firms from entering the market.

These characteristics explain the logic behind the label "monopolistic competition." Because of product differentiation, each firm is the sole seller of a narrowly defined good. For example, each firm in the toothbrush market uses a unique design for its toothbrushes, so each is a monopolist for its unique toothbrush. Because the products from different firms are close substitutes, there is keen competition for consumers. When one firm increases its price, many of its consumers will switch to the products of other firms because they are close substitutes. In other words, the demand for the product of a monopolistically competitive firm is very price elastic: An increase in price decreases the quantity demanded by a relatively large amount because consumers can easily switch to another firm selling a similar product.

Product differentiation

A strategy monopolistic firms use to distinguish their products from competitors'.

Let's take a closer look at the notion of **product differentiation**, one of the key features of monopolistic competition. Firms in such a market differentiate their products in several ways:

▶ *Physical characteristics.* A firm can distinguish its products from the products of other firms by offering a different size, color, shape, texture, or taste. For example, toothpastes differ in flavor, color, texture, whitening capability, and alleged ability to fight decay and plaque. Some other examples of goods that are differentiated by their physical characteristics are athletic shoes, dress shirts, appliances, and pens.

▶ *Location.* Some products are differentiated by where they are sold. Some examples are gas stations, music stores, video stores, grocery stores, movie theaters, and ice-cream parlors. In each case, firms sell the same product but at different locations.

▶ *Services.* Some products are distinguished by the services that come with them. For example, some stores provide informative and helpful salespeople, whereas others require consumers to make decisions on their own. Other examples of services that can differentiate products are home delivery (for appliances and pizza) and free technical assistance (for computer hardware and software).

▶ *Aura or image.* Some firms use advertising to make their products stand out from a group of nearly identical products. In this case, product differentiation is a matter of perception rather than reality. Some examples are aspirin, designer jeans, and motor oil.

When Entry Stops: Long-Run Equilibrium

We'll use the toothbrush example to illustrate the features of monopolistic competition. The producers of toothbrushes differentiate their products with respect to color, bristle design, handle size and shape, and durability. We saw earlier that after a second firm enters the toothbrush market, both firms still make a profit. Will a third firm enter this lucrative market? The entry of a third firm will shift the firm-specific demand curve for each firm farther to the left, decreasing the market price, decreasing the quantity produced per firm, and increasing the average cost per toothbrush. If after the third firm enters the market profit is still positive for all three firms, a fourth firm will enter.

Because there are no barriers to entering the toothbrush market, firms will continue to enter the market until each firm makes zero economic profit. Figure 14.3 shows the long-run equilibrium from the perspective of the typical firm in a monopolistically competitive market. As more firms enter the market, the market share of the typical firm decreases, so its firm-specific demand curve shifts to the left to the position shown in Figure 14.3. After the shift, the typical firm satisfies the marginal principle at point *g* by selling 55 brushes per minute at a price of $1.35 (point *h*) and an average cost of $1.35. Since the price equals the typical firm's average cost, the typical firm makes zero economic profit. Each firm's revenue is high enough to cover all its costs—including the opportunity cost of all its inputs—but not enough to cause additional firms to enter the market. In other words, each firm makes just enough money to stay in business.

Trade-Offs Between Average Cost and Variety

We've seen that market entry leads to lower prices and a larger total quantity in the market. At the same time, entry decreases the output per firm and increases the average cost of production. But the higher average cost comes from having more firms in the market, and more firms means more product variety. In a toothbrush market with a dozen firms, consumers can choose from at least a dozen types of differentiated

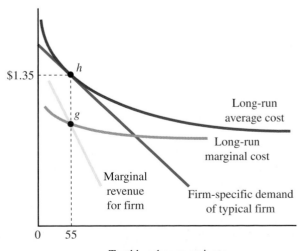

0   55

Toothbrushes per minute

FIGURE 14.3

Long-Run Equilibrium with Monopolistic Competition

In a monopolistically competitive market, new firms will continue to enter the market until economic profit is zero. The typical firm picks the quantity at which its marginal revenue equals its marginal cost (point *g*). Economic profit is zero because the price equals the average cost (shown by point *h*).

toothbrushes. Consumers value variety, and so it is impossible to make a clear-cut case for or against monopolistic competition.

For another example of the trade-offs between average cost and variety, consider restaurant meals. The typical large city has dozens of Italian restaurants, each of which has a slightly different menu and prepares its food in slightly different ways. In this example, the benefit of product differentiation is variety: Consumers can pick from restaurants offering a wide variety of menus and preparation techniques. Although a city with a single Italian restaurant would have a lower average cost of preparing Italian meals—a result of scale economies in producing meals—there would be less variety for restaurant patrons. In addition, a single restaurant would have monopoly power and would charge higher prices.

The same logic applies to articles of clothing such as jeans and shirts, which are differentiated according to their fit, color, design, and durability and the aura associated with the label. There is a trade-off between production cost and variety: If we all wore uniforms, the average cost of producing clothing would be lower, but most people prefer to wear a variety of clothes.

Application: Location and Consumer Travel Costs

Your city probably has several video stores, each of which sells a particular DVD at about the same price. Everything else being equal, you are likely to purchase DVDs from the most convenient store, but if a store across town offers lower prices, you might purchase your DVD there instead. In other words, each video store has a monopoly in its own neighborhood but competes with video stores in the rest of the city.

Figure 14.4 shows the long-run equilibrium in the market for DVDs. Because there are no barriers to entering the market, new video stores will enter the market

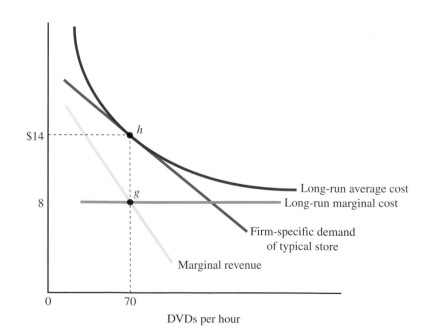

FIGURE 14.4

Long-Run Equilibrium with Spatial Competition: Video Stores

Video stores and other retailers differentiate their products by selling them at different locations. The typical firm chooses the quantity of DVDs at which its marginal revenue equals its marginal cost (point *g*). Economic profit is zero because the price equals average cost (shown by point *h*).

until each store makes zero economic profit. The typical video store satisfies the marginal principle at point *g*, selling 70 DVDs per hour at a price of $14 per DVD (point *h*) and an average cost of $14 per DVD. The price equals the store's average cost, so the typical store makes zero economic profit. Each store's revenue is high enough to cover all its costs—including the opportunity cost of all its inputs—but not enough to cause additional stores to enter the market. In other words, the firm makes just enough money to stay in business.

When firms differentiate their products by offering them at more locations, the benefit of having more firms is that consumers travel shorter distances to get the product. If a large metropolitan area had only one video store, the average cost of production would be lower, but prices would be higher and video consumers would spend much more time traveling to buy DVDs.

Lower Profit per Unit Sold?

Economic Puzzle

Consider a local phone company that initially has 1 million customers, each paying $25 per month. The average production cost per customer is $20 per month, so the firm's profit per customer is $5 (equal to $25 − $20), and its total profit is $5 million per month. Suppose a new firm enters the market, providing phone communication over the Internet. The original phone company decided to hold the line on price, maintaining its original $25 price after the new firm entered the market. The firm's objective was to keep the same $5 profit from each of its customers. Although the company expected to lose customers to the new competitor, it still expected to make the same profit per customer. The reality was different from the firm's expectations: Not only did the company lose customers, its profit per customer dropped. Why?

The key to solving this puzzle is to recognize that entry normally squeezes profit in three dimensions: Lower price, smaller quantity, and higher average cost. If a firm maintains its original price after entry, it can get the same revenue per customer, but if there are scale economies in production, the decrease in the number of customers will increase the average cost per customer. That's because the phone company will have fewer customers to share its fixed costs, so the average cost per customer increases. For example, if the company loses 20% of its customers and its average cost increases to $22, its profit per customer will drop to $3. ∎

TEST Your Understanding

5. Explain the logic behind the label monopolistic competition. What is monopolistic, and what form does the competition take?
6. List the two conditions required for long-run equilibrium in monopolistic competition.
7. Suppose each new firm entering the car-stereo market in Tweeter's town decreases the price by $5 per stereo and increases the average cost per stereo by $5. How many firms will enter the market?

Economic Experiment

Fixed Costs and Entry

Here is an experiment that shows the implications of entry for prices and profits. Students play the role of entrepreneurs who must decide whether to enter the market for lawn cutting. If they decide to enter the market, they must then decide how much to charge for cutting lawns.

- There are eight potential lawn-cutting firms (each represented by one to three students). There are two sorts of costs for firms: a fixed cost per day and a marginal cost of cutting each lawn. Each firm can cut up to two lawns per day.
- There are 16 potential consumers who are willing to pay different amounts to have their lawns cut.
- The experiment has two stages. In the first stage, each potential firm decides whether to enter the market. The entry decision is sequential: The instructor will go down the list of potential firms, one at a time, and give each firm the option of entering the market. The entry decisions are public knowledge. When a firm enters the market, it incurs a fixed cost of $14.
- Each firm in the market posts a price for lawn cutting, and consumers shop around and decide whether to purchase lawn care at the posted prices. Each trading period lasts several minutes, and each firm can change its posted price up to three times each period.
- A consumer's score in a trading period equals the difference between the amount that the consumer is willing to pay for lawn care and the price actually paid.
- A firm's score equals its profit, which is its total revenue minus its total cost (the fixed cost of $14 plus the variable cost, equal to $3 per lawn times the number of lawns cut. ●

USING THE TOOLS

We've used the tools of economics to explore the firm's entry decision, showing that a firm will enter a market if the price will exceed the average cost of production. Here are some opportunities to use these tools to do your own economic analysis of markets.

1. How Many Music Stores?

Consider the city of Discville, where zoning laws allow for only one music store. The city's music store sells CDs at a price of $20 with an average cost of $12. Suppose the city eliminates its restrictions on music stores, allowing additional stores to enter the market. According to an expert in the music market, "Each additional music store will decrease the price of CDs by $2 per CD and increase the average cost of selling CDs by $1 per CD." How many music stores will enter the market?

2. How Many Gas Stations?

Consider a city that initially allowed only one gasoline station to operate. When Jane, a staff member of a local employment agency, heard that the city had decided to relax its restrictions and allow more gasoline stations to operate in the city, she decided to identify some unemployed workers who could apply for the new station manager jobs. She knew that the city's single gas station pumped 20,000 gallons of gasoline per hour and its long-run average-cost curve reaches its minimum point with an output of 5,000 gallons per hour. Therefore, Jane reasoned, the city would soon have a total of four gas stations (20,000 gallons divided by 5,000 gallons per station) and would need three new station managers. You can imagine Jane's surprise when she discovered that there would be five new gas stations instead of three. Why did Jane underestimate the number of new gasoline stations?

3. Opposition to a New Drugstore

The city of Drugville is evaluating a request by a drugstore chain to open a new drugstore in the city. Consider the following statement from a citizen at a public hearing: "The output of the typical drugstore in our city is about 80% of the output at which its long-run average cost is minimized, so the average cost of drugs is higher than the minimum cost. The new drugstore would increase the average cost even further, so all our drugstores—including the new one—would be unprofitable, and consumers would pay higher prices for drugs." Assume that the citizen is correct in stating that the typical drugstore produces at 80% of the output at which average cost is minimized. Do the citizen's conclusions (all stores will be unprofitable and consumers will pay higher prices) follow logically from the facts?

4. Business Licenses

The following table shows how the market price, the quantity per firm, and the average cost of production vary with the number of firms in the market.

Number of Firms	Price	Quantity per Firm	Average Cost
1	$20	38	$ 9
2	$18	35	$10
3	$16	32	$11
4	$14	29	$12
5	$12	26	$13
6	$10	23	$14
7	$ 8	20	$15

A business license allows a firm to operate the business for one day. Each license will be auctioned to the highest bidder. Each firm can buy only one license. The auctioneer will auction up to seven business licenses, and the auction will continue as long as someone bids a positive amount for one of the licenses. How much would you be willing to pay for a license?

SUMMARY

This chapter is about market entry and monopolistic competition. In a monopolistically competitive market, entry continues until each firm in the market makes zero economic profit. Firms can differentiate their products by picking a distinct physical design, level of service, location, or product aura. Here are the main points of the chapter:

1 As firms enter a market, the market price drops and the average cost of production increases because each firm produces less output over which to spread its fixed costs.

2 In a monopolistically competitive market, firms compete for customers by producing differentiated products.

3 In the long-run equilibrium with monopolistic competition, price equals average cost and economic profit is zero.

KEY TERMS

monopolistic competition, 313   product differentiation, 318

1 Consider the city of Discville, where zoning laws limit the number of video arcades to one. The city's only video arcade has a price of $0.50 per game, with an average cost of $0.34 cents per game. Suppose that the city eliminates its restrictions on video arcades, allowing additional firms to enter the market. According to an expert in the arcade market, "Each additional video arcade will decrease the price of games by $0.02 and increase the average cost of providing video games by $0.03." What is the equilibrium number of video arcades?

2 Jean-Luc owns the only wig store in town and sells 30 wigs per week at a price of $70 per wig, with an average cost of $35 per wig. Some experts have reported the following facts on the wig market: (a) The average cost of wig selling increases by $2 for every one-unit decrease in the number of wigs sold. For example, if Jean-Luc sold only 29 wigs per week, his average cost would be $37. (b) The price of wigs decreases by $1 for every one-unit increase in the number of wigs sold; that is, the slope of the market demand curve is $1. Suppose Sinead opens a second wig store in town and sells her wigs at a price of $60 each. If Jean-Luc sells wigs at the same price as Sinead, will the profit per firm be positive or negative?

3 The city of Zoneville currently uses zoning laws to restrict the number of pizzerias. Under a proposed law, the restrictions on pizzerias would be eliminated. Consider the following statement by an expert in the pizza industry: "A pizzeria reaches the horizontal portion of its long-run average-cost curve at an output of about 1,000 pizzas per day. The city's existing pizzeria sells 3,000 pizzas per day. Based on these facts, I predict that if the city eliminates the restrictions on pizzerias, we will soon have three pizzerias (3,000 pizzas divided by 1,000 pizzas per pizzeria)." If we assume that the expert's facts about production costs are correct, is the expert's conclusion (three pizzerias) correct?

4 A prominent feature of Mao's Communist China was the blue uniform worn by all citizens.
   a. Explain the trade-offs associated with the use of uniforms. What were the benefits, and what were the costs?
   b. Suppose people had a choice among 10 types of uniforms rather than being required to wear a single type. Would you expect the benefits of requiring uniforms to decrease by a little or a lot?

5 Consider the "Fixed Costs and Entry" experiment. Suppose the fixed cost per day is $18 per firm and the marginal cost is $4. Each firm can cut up to three lawns per day. The market demand curve is linear, with a vertical intercept of $70 and a slope of −$1 per lawn. Predict the outcome of the experiment, including the equilibrium price, quantity, and number of firms. Explain the reasoning behind your predictions.

6 Under a franchising arrangement, a firm such as McDonald's sells the right to operate retail outlets. Your job is to determine how many franchises McDonald's should sell in Burgerburg.
   a. List the information you need and explain how you would use it.
   b. Provide a numerical example in which McDonald's should sell four franchises.
   c. If you purchase one of the four franchises, would you be better off if McDonald's sold fewer or more franchises? Use your numerical example to defend your answer.

7 Consider a city that issues licenses to pet groomers. Initially, the city does not allow the licenses to be bought and sold. Shortly after an economist joins the city licensing authority, the city decides to allow the licenses to be bought and sold on the open market. Much to the surprise of the licensers, the price of the licenses was zero: No one was willing to pay a positive amount for a pet grooming license.
   a. Explain why the price of grooming licenses was zero.
   b. Illustrate your answer with a supply–demand diagram.

MODEL ANSWERS TO QUESTIONS

Chapter-Opening Questions

1 Because many firms entered the market, prices dropped by about 22% and the profit per license decreased.

2 Market entry reduces a firm's profit by decreasing the price and quantity sold, and increasing the average cost. As explained in "Economic Puzzle: Lower Profit per Unit Sold," if a local phone company doesn't change its price when another firm enters the market, it will still earn less profit per customer because the average cost per customer will increase.

3 Consumers in states with online wine sales pay lower prices and choose from a wider variety of wines.

Test Your Understanding

1 Marginal revenue, marginal cost.

2 The firm-specific's demand curve shifts to the left: At each price, the firm sells a smaller quantity.

3 Decreases, decreases, increases.

4 No. The new price would be $210 per stereo, which would be less than the new average cost of $215 per stereo.

5 Each firm has a monopoly in the sale of its differentiated product, but the firms compete with others that sell similar products.

6 First, each firm picks the profit-maximizing quantity, where $MR = MC$. Second, profit is zero, meaning price = average cost.

7 With four firms in the market, the price is $215 per stereo and the average cost is $215 per stereo, so each firm makes zero economic profit.

NOTES

1. Leonard W. Weiss, ed., *Concentration and Price* (Cambridge, MA: MIT Press, 1989).

2. Timothy F. Bresnahan and Peter C. Reiss, "Entry and Competition in Concentrated Markets," *Journal of Political Economy*, vol. 99, October 1991, pp. 977–1009.

3. Theodore E. Keeler, "Deregulation and Scale Economies in the U.S. Trucking Industry: An Econometric Extension of the Survivor Principle," *Journal of Law and Economics*, vol. 32, October 1989, pp. 229–253.

4. Thomas Gale Moore, "Rail and Truck Reform—The Record So Far," *Regulation*, November/December 1988, pp 57–62.

5. Virgina Postrel, "Laws that Limit Online Shoppers," *New York Times*, July 17, 2003, p. B1; (*www.ftc.gov*).

What Is an Oligopoly?

Cartel Pricing and the Duopolists' Dilemma

Price Fixing and the Game Tree
Predicting the Outcome of the Price-Fixing
    Game
Representing a Game with a Payoff Matrix
The Prisoners' Dilemma

Overcoming the Duopolists' Dilemma

Guaranteed Price Matching
Repeated Pricing Games with Retaliation
    for Underpricing
Application: Different Airline Ticket Prices

Price Fixing and the Law

Alternative Models of Oligopoly Pricing

Price Leadership
The Kinked Demand-Curve Model

**The Insecure Monopolist and Entry
Deterrence**

The Passive Approach: Do Nothing to Deter
    Entry
The Entry Deterrence Approach: Use Limit
    Pricing to Deter Entry
Limit Pricing
When Is the Passive Approach Better?
Applications: Aluminum, Plane Tickets,
    and Campus Bookstores
Entry Deterrence and Contestable Markets

The Advertisers' Dilemma

Game Theory and Nash Equilibrium

Using the Tools

Oligopoly and Strategic Behavior

hen Paul Allen, one of the billionaire founders of Microsoft, announced the June 2000 grand opening of the Experience Music Project museum in Seattle, there was an outbreak of messages on the Internet chat site dedicated to Jimi Hendrix, the rock legend. Four Hendrix fanatics who had been exchanging messages on the chat site for several months decided to travel to Seattle to meet each other and celebrate the opening of the museum. They all flew in for the occasion, and the discussion among the Web pals eventually turned to the cost of their airline tickets. Although each of the four traveled about the same distance to Seattle, they paid very different prices for their airline tickets.

▶ Katrina was puzzled and upset: "Brian lives in a city that is served by a single airline, and so do I. But Brian paid $370 and I paid $400." Why is the price lower in Brian's city?

▶ Jason was puzzled and upset, too: "Melissa lives in a city that is served by two airlines, and so do I. But Melissa paid $350 and I paid $400." Why is the price higher in Jason's city?

In this chapter, we explain these puzzling differences in prices. The monopolist in Brian's city could be charging a low price to discourage other firms from entering the market. The two airlines in Jason's city could have agreed upon a price-fixing scheme under which they do not compete with one another but instead collude and charge the same high price.

T his is the fourth chapter on decision-making by firms. In earlier chapters, we looked at perfect competition (many firms selling a homogeneous product), monopoly (a market with a single firm), and monopolistic competition (a market with dozens of firms). In this chapter, we look at an **oligopoly**, a market with just a few firms. Given the small number of firms in an oligopoly, the actions of any single firm have a big effect on the other firms, so they act strategically. Before a firm takes a particular action, it considers the possible reactions of its rivals. For example, before Southwest Airlines cuts its fares in an attempt to sell more tickets, it will consider the possible reactions by other airlines. If the rivals maintain their old fares, Southwest's fare cut would increase its sales and profit. But if the rivals match the lower fare, it could be a disaster for Southwest.

We will use some simple concepts from game theory to explore the strategic interactions of oligopolists. **Game theory** is a framework to explore the actions and reactions of interdependent decision-makers. The theory can be applied to the game of chess as well as the decisions of oligopolists. A chess player develops a strategy to win the game, anticipating his opponent's reaction to each of his moves. Similarly, an oligopolist develops a strategy to maximize profit, anticipating the reactions of rival firms. We'll use game theory to discuss three business strategies: price fixing (conspiring to keep prices high), entry deterrence (preventing an additional firm from entering the market), and advertising. Here are some of the practical questions we answer:

1 You've probably heard an advertisement that goes like this: "If you buy a stereo from us and find the same stereo for sale somewhere else for a lower price, we'll pay you the difference in price." Does this refund policy lead to higher or lower stereo prices?
2 Suppose two airlines agree to charge the same high price for air travel between two cities. Will this pricing agreement persist?
3 When is it sensible for a monopolist to be passive and let a second firm enter the market?
4 Why might two firms each spend millions of dollars on advertising when both firms would be better off if neither advertised?

What Is an Oligopoly?

In an oligopoly, a few firms have market power—the power to control prices. Economists use **concentration ratios** to measure the degree of concentration in a market. For example, a four-firm concentration ratio is the percentage of total output in a market produced by the four largest firms. In Table 15.1, the four-firm concentration ratio for cigarettes is 99%, indicating that the largest four firms produce 99% of the cigarettes in the United States. According to one rule of thumb, if the four-firm concentration ratio is greater than 40%, the market is considered an oligopoly.

Oligopoly
A market served by a few firms.

Game theory
A framework to explore the actions and reactions of interdependent decision-makers.

Concentration ratio
A measure of the degree of concentration in a market; the four-firm concentration ratio is the percentage of the market output produced by the four largest firms.

TABLE 15.1

Concentration Ratios in Selected Manufacturing Industries

Industry	Four-Firm Concentration Ratio (%)	Eight-Firm Concentration Ratio (%)
Cigarettes	99	Not available
Primary copper smelting	95	Not available
Primary battery manufacturing	90	98
Household laundry equipment	90	Not available
Breweries	90	94
Guided missiles and space vehicles	89	99
Electric lamp bulbs	89	94
Small arms (weapons)	89	94
House slippers	85	96
Military vehicles	85	92
Breakfast cereals	83	94
Household refrigerators and freezers	82	97
Motor vehicles and car bodies	82	92
Photographic and photocopy equipment	81	85
Flavoring syrup	81	88
Soybean processing	80	95
Chocolate manufacturing from cacao beans	80	93

Source: U.S. Bureau of the Census, 1997 Census of Manufacturing, *Concentration Ratios in Manufacturing* (Washington, DC: U.S. Government Printing Office, 2001).

An alternative measure of market concentration is the Herfindahl-Hirschman Index (HHI). It is calculated by squaring the market share of each firm in the market and then summing the resulting numbers. For example, consider a market with two firms, one with a 60% market share and a second with a 40% share. The HHI for the market is 5,200, computed by adding the square of 60 (3,600) to the square of 40 (1,600). In contrast, for a market with ten firms, each with a 10% market share, the HHI is 1,000 (equal to ten times the square of ten). According to the guidelines established by the U.S. Department of Justice in 1992, a market is "unconcentrated" if the HHI is below 1,000 and "highly concentrated" if the HHI is above 1,800. For example, a market with 5 firms, each with a 20% market share, has a HHI of 2,000 (five times the square of 20), and would be considered highly concentrated.

An oligopoly—a market with just a few firms—occurs for three reasons:

1 *Government barriers to entry.* As we saw in Chapter 13, the government may limit the number of firms in a market by issuing patents or controlling the number of business licenses.

2 *Advertising campaigns.* In some markets, a firm cannot enter a market without a substantial investment in an advertising campaign. For example, the breakfast-cereal oligopoly results from the huge advertising campaigns required to get a foothold in the market. As in the case of economies of scale in production, just a few firms will enter the market.

3 *Economies of scale in production.* As we will see in Chapter 16, a natural monopoly occurs when there are relatively large economies of scale in production, so a single firm produces for the entire market. In some cases, scale economies are not large enough to generate a natural monopoly, but are large enough to generate a natural oligopoly, with a few firms serving the entire market.

Cartel Pricing and the Duopolists' Dilemma

One of the virtues of a market economy is that firms compete with one another for customers, and this leads to lower prices. But in some markets, firms cooperate instead of competing with one another. Eighteenth-century economist Adam Smith recognized the possibility that firms would conspire to raise prices: "People of the same trade seldom meet together, even for merriment and diversion, but the conversation ends in a conspiracy against the public, or in some contrivance to raise prices."[1] We'll see that raising prices is not simply a matter of firms getting together and agreeing on higher prices. An agreement to raise prices is likely to break down unless the firms find some way to punish a firm that violates the agreement.

We'll use a market with two firms—a **duopoly**—to explain the key features of an oligopoly. The basic insights from a duopoly apply to oligopolies with more than two firms. Consider a duopoly in the market for air travel between two hypothetical cities. The two airlines can compete for customers on the basis of price, or they can cooperate and conspire to raise prices. To simplify matters—and to keep the numbers manageable—let's assume that the average cost of providing air travel is constant at $300 per passenger. As shown in Figure 15.1, the average cost is constant, which means that marginal cost equals average cost.

Duopoly
A market with two firms.

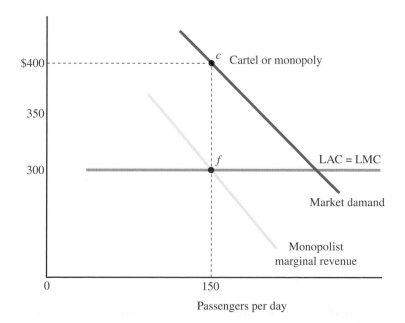

A Cartel Picks the Monopoly Price
Point *c* shows the outcome with a successful price-fixing arrangement (a cartel). The total output is 150 passengers, and the price is $400 per passenger. Each firm serves 75 passengers at an average cost of $300 per passenger and earns a profit of $7,500 per day.

Cartel

A group of firms that collude explicitly, coordinating their pricing decisions.

    A **cartel** is a group of firms that collude explicitly, coordinating their pricing decisions. In our airline example, the two airlines could form a cartel and choose the monopoly price. In Figure 15.1, the firm-specific demand curve for a monopolist is the market demand curve, and the marginal-revenue curve intersects the marginal-cost curve at a quantity of 150 passengers per day (point *f*). If the two airlines act as one, they will pick the monopoly price of $400 and split the monopoly output, each serving 75 passengers per day. The average cost per passenger is $300, so each airline earns a daily profit of $7,500 (a profit of $100 per passenger times 75 passengers). An arrangement under which the two firms act as one, coordinating their pricing decisions, is also known as **price fixing**. As we'll see later in the chapter, cartels and price fixing are illegal under U.S. antitrust laws.

Price fixing

An arrangement in which two firms coordinate their pricing decisions.

    What would happen if the two firms competed against one another? If they do, each firm faces its own demand curve. The firm-specific demand curve is to the left of the market demand curve because consumers are divided between the two firms: At a given price, the number of passengers served by a single firm will be less than the number served by both firms together. Panel A in Figure 15.2 shows the perspective of the individual firm. Given the firm-specific demand curve and marginal-revenue curve, the marginal principle is satisfied at point *m*, where marginal revenue equals marginal cost. This means that each of the two firms in the duopoly serves 100 passengers at a price of $350 (point *n*). Panel B shows the market perspective: The price is $350, and the quantity is 200 passengers (100 passengers for each firm). Given an average cost of $300, each firm earns a profit of $5,000 (the $50 profit per passenger times the 100 passengers it carries). In contrast, when the two firms conspire to fix the price as a cartel instead of competing, each earns more ($7,500). As a cartel, they also carry fewer total passengers: 150 passengers versus 200 when they compete.

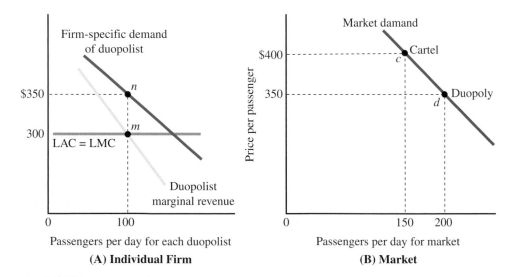

FIGURE 15.2 **Competing Duopolists Pick a Lower Price**

At the individual firm (duopolist) level, marginal revenue equals marginal cost at point *m*, so each firm serves 100 passengers at a price of $350 per passenger (shown by point *n* in Panel A). Given an average cost of $300 per passenger, each duopolist earns a profit of $5,000 (the $50 profit per passenger times 100 passengers). At the market level (Panel B), the duopoly outcome has a quantity of 200 passengers (100 passengers per firm) at a price of $350 per passenger (point *d*).

Price Fixing and the Game Tree

Clearly, each firm would earn more profit under a price-fixing agreement, but will the firms reach such an agreement? We can answer this question with the help of a **game tree**, a graphical tool that provides a visual representation of the consequences of alternative strategies. Each firm must choose a price for airline tickets, either a high price (the cartel price of $400) or a low price (the duopoly price of $350). Each firm can use the game tree to develop a pricing strategy, knowing that the other firm is also choosing a price.

Figure 15.3 shows the game tree for the price-fixing game. Let's call the managers of the airlines Jack and Jill. The game tree has three components:

▶ The squares are decision nodes. For each square, there is a player (Jack or Jill) and a list of the player's options. For example, the game starts at square **X**, where Jill has two options: the high price or the low price.

▶ The arrows show the path of the game from left to right. Jill chooses her price first, so we move from square **X** to one of Jack's decision nodes, either square **Y** or square **Z**. If Jill chooses the high price, we move from square **X** to square **Y**. Once we reach one of Jack's decision nodes, he chooses a price (high or low), and then we move to one of the rectangles. For example, if Jack chooses the high price too, we move from square **Y** to rectangle 1.

▶ The rectangles show the profits for the two firms. When we reach a rectangle, the game is over, and the players receive the profits shown in the rectangle. There is a profit rectangle for each of the four possible outcomes of the price-fixing game.

We've already computed the profits for two profit rectangles. The first rectangle shows what happens when each firm chooses the high price. This is the cartel or price-fixing outcome, with each firm earning $7,500. The fourth rectangle shows what happens when each firm chooses the low price. This is the duopoly outcome, with each firm earning $5,000.

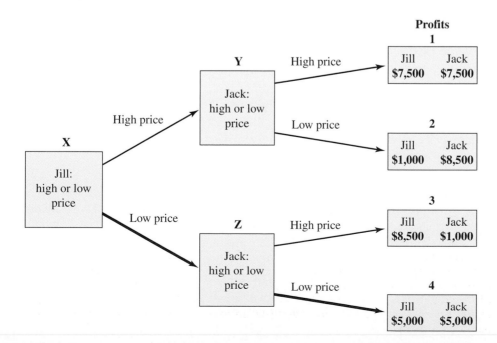

Game tree

A graphical representation of the consequences of different strategies.

FIGURE 15.3

Game Tree for a Price-Fixing Game
The path of the game is square **X** to square **Z** to rectangle 4: Each firm picks the low price and earns a profit of $5,000. The duopolists' dilemma is that each firm would make more profit if both picked the high price, but neither firm will do so, fearing that the other firm would pick the low price.

TABLE 15.2

Duopolists' Profits When They Choose Different Prices

	Jill: Low Price	**Jack: High Price**
Price	$350	$400
Quantity	170	10
Average cost	$300	$300
Profit per passenger	$50	$100
Profit	$8,500	$1,000

What would happen if the two firms chose different prices? If Jill chooses the low price and Jack chooses the high price, Jill will capture a large share of the market and gain at Jack's expense. In the first column of Table 15.2, Jill serves 170 passengers at a price of $350 each and an average cost of $300 per passenger, so her profit is $8,500 (a $50 profit per passenger times 170 passengers). In the second column, Jack serves only 10 passengers at a price of $400 each and the same average cost, so his profit is $1,000 (a $100 profit per passenger times 10 passengers). This is shown by rectangle 3 in Figure 15.3: The path of the game is square **X** to square **Z** to rectangle 3. The other underpricing outcome is shown by rectangle 2. In this case, Jill chooses the high price, and Jack chooses the low price, so Jack gains at Jill's expense. The roles are reversed and so are the numbers in the profit rectangle.

Predicting the Outcome of the Price-Fixing Game

We can predict the outcome of the price-fixing game by a process of elimination. We'll eliminate the rectangles that would require one or both of the firms to act irrationally, leaving us with the rectangle showing the outcome of the game.

▶ If Jill chooses the high price, we'll move along the upper branches of the tree and eventually reach rectangle 1 or 2, depending on what Jack does. Although Jill would like Jack to choose the high price too, this would be irrational for Jack, because he can make more profit by choosing the low price. Therefore, we can eliminate rectangle 1.

▶ If Jill chooses the low price, we'll move along the lower branches of the tree, eventually reaching rectangle 3 or 4, depending on Jack's choice. Jack won't choose the high price because then Jill would gain at his expense. Therefore, we can eliminate rectangle 3.

We've eliminated the two rectangles involving a high price for Jack (1 and 3). This means that the low price is a **dominant strategy** for Jack: Regardless of what Jill does, Jack's best choice is the low price.

There are now two rectangles left (2 and 4), and Jill's action will determine which rectangle we'll reach. Jill knows that Jack will choose the low price regardless of what she does, so she can either choose a high price and allow Jack to gain at her expense (rectangle 2) or choose the low price, too (rectangle 4). It would be irrational for Jill to allow herself to be underpriced, so we can eliminate rectangle 2.

Dominant strategy

An action that is the best choice for a player, no matter what an opponent does.

The remaining rectangle shows the outcome of the game: Each player chooses the low price. The thick arrows show the path of the game, from square **X** to square **Z** to rectangle 4.

Both firms will be unhappy with this outcome because each could earn a higher profit with rectangle 1. To get there, however, each firm must choose the high price. The **duopolists' dilemma** is that although both firms would be better off if they both chose the high price, each firm chooses the low price. There is a big payoff from underpricing the other firm and a big penalty from being underpriced, so both firms will pick the low price. As we'll see later, the firms can avoid this dilemma, but only if they find some way to prevent underpricing. For a description of how vitamin producers succeeded in an international price-fixing scheme, read "A Closer Look: Vitamin, Inc. Gets Busted."

Duopolists' dilemma

A situation in which both firms in a market would be better off if both chose the high price but each chooses the low price.

A CLOSER LOOK — Vitamin, Inc. Gets Busted

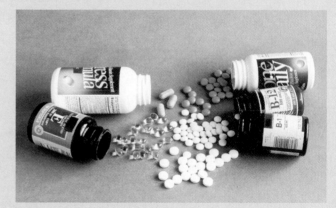

In April 2000, the U.S. Department of Justice announced that four former executives of drug companies pled guilty to conspiring to fix the prices of bulk vitamins worldwide. It was the largest price-fixing case in history. The leading companies involved in the illegal cartel were Hoffman-La Roche (with 60% of the U.S. vitamin market), BASF AG (with 28% market share), and Rhone-Poulenc (with 7% market share). They were joined by other vitamin producers from Japan, Switzerland, and Canada. The announcement brought the number of Swiss and German executives imprisoned for the case to six, with fines for the individual executives and their companies totaling $1 billion.[2]

For almost a decade, these executives conspired to stifle competition around the globe, by fixing prices on vitamins A, B2, B5, C, E, and beta carotene. The executives called their group "Vitamin, Inc." and met regularly in hotel rooms to carve up the market. Market shares for each region were specified down to a half percentage point, and prices for each vitamin were agreed upon down to the penny. For vitamin "premixes" (used for livestock feed and human food such as breakfast cereals), the executives rigged the bidding process for contracts, specifying a price and designating a "winner" for each contract. To help prevent cheating, they had "budget meetings" to check each other's data on sales and market shares. The cartel managed to boost the prices of vitamins, with markups averaging about 20%, or even more at the high-end of the vitamin price range. For example, the price of vitamin A nearly doubled, from about $12 per pound to $20.

LaRoche ultimately paid a fine of $500 million, about half of its annual revenue from its vitamin business in the United States. BASF paid a fine of $225 million. Rhone-Poulenc broke ranks early in the investigation, and by cooperating with Justice investigators, avoided any fines. A group of Japanese companies paid a total of $137 million.

Representing a Game with a Payoff Matrix

Table 15.3 shows an alternative way to represent a price-fixing game. The table is a payoff matrix, which shows the payoffs to the players for different combinations of actions (price choices). The payoff matrix is used to represent a **simultaneous decision-making game**, defined as games in which two players make their choices simultaneously. In contrast, a **sequential decision-making game** is typically represented by game trees like the one in Figure 15.3. So if we change the price-fixing game to make the firms' decisions simultaneous rather than sequential, we can use the payoff matrix.

Each cell of the payoff matrix shows the payoffs to the two players for a particular pair of actions, one for each player. In each cell of the matrix, the payoff to Jill (the name that appears on the left side of the matrix) is listed first, followed by the payoff to Jack (the name above the matrix). If both firms pick the low price, each makes a profit of $5,000. In contrast, if both pick the high price, each earns $7,500. If one firm picks the low price and the other picks the high price, the low-price firm earns $8,500 and the high-price firm earns only $1,000.

We can use the payoff matrix to predict the outcome of the price-fixing game. Jill doesn't know whether Jack will pick the low price or the high price. If he picks the low price, Jill's best response is the low price because she can earn $5,000, compared to $1,000 if she picks the high price. If Jack picks the high price, Jill's best action is still the low price, which earns her $8,500 compared to $7,500 for the high price. In other words, the low price is the dominant strategy for Jill. Knowing this, Jack will pick the low price too. Therefore, the outcome is the same as with the game-tree approach: Both firms will pick the low price.

The Prisoners' Dilemma

The duopolists' dilemma is similar to the classic prisoners' dilemma. Consider two people, Bonnie and Clyde, who have been accused of committing a crime. The police give each person an opportunity to confess to the crime, with Bonnie speaking first and Clyde second. The traditional version of the story involves a simultaneous decision-making game: The two are put in separate rooms, and each makes a choice without the other person knowing what that choice is. The results are the same with simultaneous or sequential decision-making. We'll use the sequential approach—the approach we used with Jack and Jill—to emphasize the similarities to the price-fixing scenario.

The police confront Bonnie and Clyde with the game tree shown in Figure 15.4. If both confess, each gets 5 years in prison (rectangle 4). If neither confesses, the police can convict them on a lesser charge, and each gets 2 years (rectangle 1). If only one confesses

TABLE 15.3

Payoff Matrix for Simultaneous Game

		Jack			
		Low Price		**High Price**	
Jill	**Low Price**	$5,000	$5,000	$8,500	$1,000
	High Price	$1,000	$8,500	$7,500	$7,500

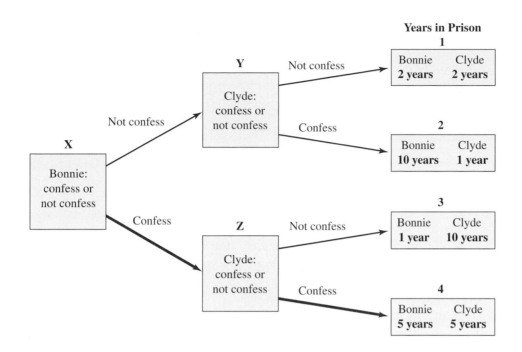

Years in Prison

FIGURE 15.4

Game Tree for a Prisoners' Dilemma
The path of the game is square **X** to square **Z** to rectangle 4: Each person confesses and gets 5 years in prison. The prisoners' dilemma is that each person would be better off if neither confessed, but both actually confess.

and implicates the other, the confessor is rewarded with a 1-year prison sentence and the other gets 10 years. Clyde, who goes second, will confess no matter what Bonnie does:

▶ If she does not confess: He will choose rectangle 2 over rectangle 1, getting 1 year in prison instead of 2.
▶ If she confesses: He will choose rectangle 4 over rectangle 3, getting 5 years in prison instead of 10.

Bonnie can predict Clyde's choices, so she realizes that her choice is between rectangle 2 and rectangle 4, and confessing gives her 5 years instead of 10. Although both criminals would be better off if they both kept quiet, they implicate each other because the police reward them for doing so. There is an incentive for squealing, just as there is an incentive for one duopolist to underprice the other.

TEST Your Understanding

1. Complete the statement with *d* or *c*: Rectangle 1 in Figure 15.3 is associated with point _____ in Figure 15.2, while rectangle 4 is associated with point _____.
2. Use Figure 15.3 to complete the statement: If each firm picks the low price, the path of the game is square _____ to square _____ to rectangle _____, and each firm earns a profit of _____.
3. Suppose Jack promises that if Jill chooses the high price, he will too. If Jack's objective is to maximize his profit, what will he do after Jill chooses the high price? If you were Jill, would you believe Jack's promises to choose the high price? Which price would you choose?

Overcoming the Duopolists' Dilemma

The duopolists' dilemma occurs because the two firms are unable to coordinate their pricing decisions and act as one. Each firm has an incentive to underprice the other firm because the low-price firm will capture a larger share of the market and earn a larger profit. There are two ways to avoid this dilemma: guaranteed price matching and playing the pricing game repeatedly, with a system of retaliation for underpricing.

Guaranteed Price Matching

The duopolists' dilemma occurs because of the possibility of underpricing. There is a big payoff from underpricing the other firm, and a big penalty from being underpriced by the other firm. This concern about underpricing causes both firms to pick the low price. As we'll see, guaranteed price matching eliminates the possibility of underpricing, and makes price fixing possible.

> **Guaranteed price-matching strategy**
>
> A strategy where a firm guarantees it will match a lower price by a competitor; also known as a "meet-the-competition" policy.

To eliminate the incentive for underpricing, one firm can guarantee that it will match its competitor's price. Suppose Jill places the following advertisement in the local newspaper: "If you buy a plane ticket from me and then discover that Jack offers the same trip at a lower price, I will pay you the difference between my price and Jack's price. If I charge you $400 and Jack's price is only $350, I will pay you $50." This pricing strategy is known as **guaranteed price matching**: Jill guarantees that she will match Jack's price. It is also known as a "meet-the-competition" policy. Jill's promise to match Jack's lower price is credible because she announces it in the newspaper.

How will Jack respond to Jill's price-matching scheme? In effect, Jill tentatively chooses the high price but will instantly switch to the low price if Jack picks the low price. After a $50 refund, Jill's price will be $350, the same as Jack's. Jack will respond to Jill's price-matching scheme in one of two ways:

▶ *Choose the high price.* If Jack matches Jill's announced high price, each firm will earn a profit of $7,500 (rectangle 1 in the game tree in Figure 15.3).

▶ *Choose the low price.* If Jack tries to underprice Jill, she will switch to the low price, and each will earn a profit of only $5,000 (rectangle 4 in the game tree).

Jack's decision is easy: A pair of high prices is more profitable than a pair of low prices, so he will choose the high price, just like Jill.

Jill's price-matching scheme eliminates the duopolists' dilemma and makes cartel pricing possible, even without creating a formal cartel. The duopolists' dilemma disappears because underpricing is no longer possible. The motto of the price-matching scheme is "High for one means high for all, and low for one means low for all." It would be irrational for Jack to choose the low price because he knows that Jill would match it. Once the possibility of underpricing has been eliminated, the duopoly will be replaced by an informal cartel, each firm charging the price that would be charged by a monopolist.

To most people, the notion that guaranteed price matching can lead to higher prices is surprising. After all, Jill promises to give refunds if her price exceeds Jack's, so we might expect her to keep her price low to avoid giving out a lot of refunds. In fact, she doesn't have to worry about refunds because she knows that Jack will also choose the high price. In other words, Jill's promise to issue refunds is an empty promise. Although consumers might think Jill's refund policy will protect them from high prices, the policy guarantees that they will pay the high price.

Repeated Pricing Games with Retaliation for Underpricing

Up to this point, we've assumed that the price-fixing game is played only once. Each firm chooses a price and sticks with that price for the lifetime of the firm. What happens when two firms play the price-fixing game repeatedly, setting prices over an extended period of time? We'll see that repetition makes price fixing more likely because firms can punish a firm that cheats on a price-fixing agreement, whether it's formal or informal.

Firms use several strategies to maintain a price-fixing agreement. We explore three, all of which involve punishing a firm that underprices the other firm. Continuing our airline example, suppose Jack and Jill choose their prices at the beginning of each month. Jill chooses the cartel price ($400) for the first month and then waits to see what price Jack chooses. Jill could use one of the following strategies to punish Jack if he underprices her:

1 *A duopoly pricing strategy.* Jill continues to choose the high price until Jack underprices her. Once that happens, she chooses the duopoly price ($350 in our example) for the remaining lifetime of her firm. Jill allows herself to be underpriced only once. Then she abandons the idea of cartel pricing and accepts the duopoly outcome, which is less profitable than the cartel outcome but more profitable than being underpriced by the other firm.

2 *A grim-trigger strategy.* When Jack underprices Jill, she responds by dropping her price to a level at which each firm will make zero economic profit forever. This is called the **grim-trigger strategy** because grim consequences are triggered by Jack's underpricing.

3 *A tit-for-tat strategy.* Starting in the second month. Jill chooses whatever price Jack chose the preceding month. As long as Jack chooses the cartel price, the cartel arrangement will persist, but if Jack underprices Jill, the cartel will break down. In Figure 15.5, Jack underprices Jill in the second month, so Jill chooses the low price for the third month, resulting in the duopoly outcome. To restore the cartel outcome. Jack must eventually choose the high price, allowing Jill to underprice him for one month. This happens in the fourth month. In the fifth month, the cartel is restored. So, although Jack can gain at Jill's expense in the second month, if he wants to restore cartel pricing, he must allow her to gain at his expense during the fourth month. This is called a **tit-for-tat strategy**. You do exactly what your opponent did to you in the last round to encourage them to cooperate rather than compete. Several studies have shown that a tit-for-tat is the most effective strategy to promote cooperation.

Grim-trigger strategy

A strategy where a firm responds to underpricing by choosing a price so low that each firm makes zero economic profit.

Tit-for-tat

A strategy where one firm chooses whatever price the other firm chose in the preceding period.

A Tit-for-Tat Pricing Strategy
Under a tit-for-tat retaliation strategy, the leading firm (Jill, the square) chooses whatever price the other firm (Jack, the circle) chose the preceding month.

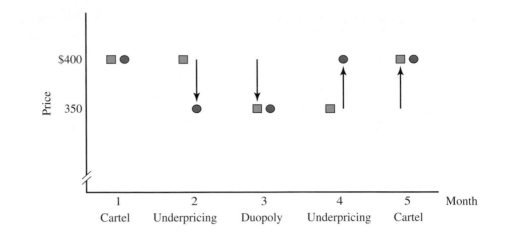

These three pricing schemes promote cartel pricing by penalizing the underpricer. To decide whether to underprice Jill, Jack must weigh the short-term benefit against the long-term cost:

▶ The short-term benefit is the increase in profit in the current period. If Jack underprices Jill, he can increase his profit from $7,500 (Jack's profit if both firms pick the high price) to $8,500 (Jack's profit if he chooses the low price and Jill chooses the high price). Therefore, the short-term benefit of underpricing is $1.000.
▶ The long-term cost is the loss of profit in later periods. Jill will respond to Jack's underpricing by cutting her price, and this decreases Jack's profit. For example, if Jill retaliates with the duopoly price, Jack will lose the opportunity for a monthly profit of $5,000 for the remaining lifetime of his firm.

If the two firms expect to share the market for a long time, the long-term cost of underpricing will exceed the short-term benefit, so underpricing is less likely. The threat of punishment makes it easier to resist the temptation to cheat on the cartel.

Application: Different Airline Ticket Prices

At the beginning of this chapter, we saw that Jason paid more for his plane ticket than Melissa did for hers, even though both live in cities that are served by two airlines. The two airlines in Melissa's city may suffer from the duopolists' dilemma: Although they would prefer the high price ($400), they both choose the low price ($350). In contrast, an airline in Jason's city could use a guaranteed price-matching scheme, promising to refund the difference between its price and the price of the other airline. The price-matching scheme eliminates underpricing, so each airline will choose the high price ($400). Jason pays a higher price because the price-matching scheme allows the airlines in his city to engage in cartel pricing (price fixing).

Price Fixing and the Law

Under the Sherman Antitrust Act of 1890 and subsequent legislation, explicit price fixing is illegal. It is illegal for firms to discuss their pricing strategies or their methods of punishing a firm that underprices other firms. In one of the early price-fixing cases (Addyston Pipe, 1899), six manufacturers of cast-iron pipe met to fix prices in certain geographical areas. Several months after the Supreme Court ruled that their cartel pricing was illegal, the firms merged into a single firm, so instead of acting like a monopolist, which was illegal, they became a monopolist. Here are some other examples of price fixing:

1 *Electric generators (1961).* General Electric and Westinghouse were convicted of fixing prices for electrical generators, resulting in fines of over $2 million and imprisonment or probation for 30 corporate executives.

2 *Soft drinks (1986).* The Coca-Cola Bottling Company of North Carolina paid a fine and issued discount coupons to its customers to settle a case involving a conspiracy to fix the prices of soft drinks.

3 *Infant formula (1993).* The three major U.S. producers of infant formula— Abbott Labs, Mead Johnson, and American Home Products—which together served 95% of the market, paid a total of $200 million to wholesalers and retailers to settle lawsuits claiming that they had conspired to fix prices.

4 *Plastic wrap in Japan (1993) .* A Tokyo court found eight Japanese companies guilty of conspiring to fix the prices of the plastic film used for wrapping food. The companies received fines of $54,000 to $73,000, and 15 executives were given suspended jail sentences of six months to one year.

5 *Airline pricing (1994).* In an antitrust lawsuit filed in 1992, the U.S. Justice Department alleged that the nation's airlines used advanced price listing to fix airline ticket prices. Before an airline increased its price, it could post a "suggested" price on a central computer and see whether the other airlines would increase their prices. By March 1994, eight of the nation's largest airlines (United Airlines, USAir Group, American Airlines, Delta Airlines, Northwest Airlines, Continental Airlines, Trans-World Airlines, and Alaska Air) had agreed to drop this practice. According to Ann Bingaman of the antitrust division of the Justice Department, advance price listing allowed airlines to fix prices at an artificially high level, costing consumers an extra $1.9 billion for airline tickets.[3]

6 *Steel beam pricing in Europe (1994).* The European Union Commission fined 16 steel companies a total of 104 million euros ($116 million) for conspiring to fix the price of steel beams.

7 *Carton board pricing in Europe (1994).* The European Union Commission fined 19 manufacturers of carton board a total of 132 million euros ($165 million) for operating a cartel that fixed prices at secret meetings in luxury Zurich hotels.

8 *Food additives (1996).* An employee of Archer Daniels Midland (ADM), a huge food company that likes to call itself "the supermarket to the world," provided audio and videotapes of ADM executives scheming to fix prices. ADM pleaded guilty to the charges of price fixing and was fined $100 million.

9   *Sugar in the United Kingdom (1998).* Four sugar producers that together controlled 90% of the market (British Sugar, Tate & Lyle, Napier Brown, and James Budgett) conspired to fix prices for industrial and retail markets and were fined a total of 50.2 million euros by the European Commission.

10 *Greek and Italian ferry services (1998).* Seven companies offering ferry service between Greece and Italy met regularly to coordinate prices for passengers and vehicles. The fine from the European Commission was relatively light (9.12 million euros) because the cartel had a "fairly limited impact on the market."

11 *Music distribution (2000).* In exchange for subsidies for advertising, music retailers agreed to adhere to the minimum advertised prices (MAP) specified by the distributors. Any retailer that advertised a CD for less than the MAP would lose all of its "cooperative advertising" funds from the distributor. In May 2000, the Federal Trade Commission reached an agreement with music distributors to end their MAP policy. The FTC estimated that the MAP policy imposed an annual cost of $160 million on U.S. music consumers.[4]

Alternative Models of Oligopoly Pricing

Price leadership

An implicit agreement under which firms in a market choose a price leader, observe that firm's price, and match it.

We will discuss two alternative models of oligopoly pricing. Under the model of **price leadership**, one of the oligopolists plays the role of price leader, setting a price with the expectation that the other firms will match the leader's price. Under the second model, firms in an oligopoly go along when one firm increases its price but don't follow a firm when it cuts its price.

Price Leadership

Because explicit price fixing is illegal, firms often rely on implicit pricing agreements to fix prices at the monopoly level. Under a price leadership arrangement, one firm becomes recognized as the price leader. The other firms in the market observe the price chosen by the leader, and then match it. Such an agreement allows firms to cooperate without actually discussing their pricing strategies.

The problem with an implicit pricing agreement is that it relies on indirect signals that are often garbled and misinterpreted. Suppose that two firms have cooperated for several years, both sticking to the cartel price. When one firm suddenly drops its price, the other firm could interpret the price cut in one of two ways:

▶ *A change in market conditions.* Perhaps the first firm has observed a change in demand or production cost and decides that both firms would benefit from a lower price.
▶ *Underpricing.* Perhaps the first firm is trying to increase its market share and profit at the expense of the second firm.

The first interpretation would probably cause the second firm to match the lower price of the first firm, and price fixing would continue at the lower price. In contrast, the second interpretation could trigger a price war, destroying the price-fixing agreement. Because firms often pull the grim trigger when a more moderate response would be appropriate, implicit pricing agreements are difficult to maintain.

Chapter 15   Oligopoly and Strategic Behavior

341

The Kinked Demand Curve Model

The **kinked demand curve model** of oligopoly gets its name from its assumptions about how firms in an oligopoly respond when one firm changes its price. Figure 15.6 shows the demand curve facing Kirk, one of three firms in the oligopoly. Suppose each of the three firms starts out with a price of $6, and Kirk sells 30 units of output (point *k*).

▶ If Kirk increases his price, the other two firms will not change their prices. Kirk will have a higher price than the other firms, so his quantity will decrease by a large amount (from 30 to 10 units).
▶ If Kirk decreases his price, the other firms will decrease their prices. Kirk will have the same (lower) price as other firms, so his quantity will increase by a small amount (from 30 to 33 units).

These assumptions mean that the demand curve of the typical firm has a kink at the prevailing price: It is relatively flat (price-elastic) for higher prices because other firms won't match a higher price but relatively steep (price-inelastic) for lower prices because other firms will match a lower price. Once a price has been established, it will tend to persist because there is a large penalty for a firm that picks a higher price (a large decrease in the quantity sold) and a small benefit for a firm that picks a lower price (a small increase in the quantity sold).

The model of kinked demand is really a model of pessimism. Each firm assumes the worst about how its fellow oligopolists will respond to a change in price: The other firms will not go along with a higher price, but will match a lower price. Although this model may have some intuitive appeal, there is no evidence that firms really act this way. Starting in 1947, various studies of oligopolies have failed to find compelling evidence to support the kinked demand model of oligopoly.[5]

Kinked demand curve model

A model under which firms in an oligopoly match price reductions by other firms but do not match price increases by other firms.

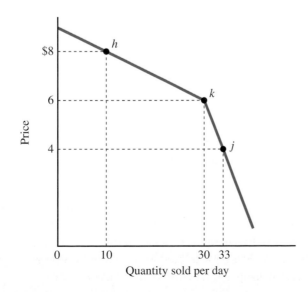

FIGURE 15.6

The Kinked Demand Curve Model
Under the kinked demand model, when one firm increases its price, the other firms don't change their prices, so the quantity sold by the firm will decrease by a large amount. But when one firm decreases its price, the other firms cut their prices too, so the quantity sold by the firm will increase by a small amount.

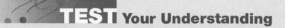

TEST Your Understanding

4. Complete the statement with a number: Suppose Jill adopts a price-matching scheme and Jack offers plane tickets for $350. Under Jill's scheme, she would give each of her customers a refund of _____.

5. Have you ever encountered a guaranteed price-matching scheme? If so, did you think it was good news or bad news for consumers? What do you think now?

6. Which retaliation strategy, the duopoly price or the grim trigger, provides a greater incentive to maintain cartel pricing? Explain.

7. Suppose that Jack and Jill use a tit-for-tat scheme to encourage cartel pricing and Jill chooses the low price for a single month. How long will the two firms deviate from cartel pricing? Explain.

8. Complete the statement with "cost" or "benefit": If two firms expect to be in the market together for a long time, the _____ of underpricing will be large relative to the _____.

The Insecure Monopolist and Entry Deterrence

We've seen what happens when two duopolists try to act as one, fixing the price at the monopoly level. Now let's think about how a monopolist might try to prevent a second firm from entering its market. To explain how a monopolist tries to protect its monopoly, we will use some of the numbers from our airline example, although we will look at a different city with a different cast of characters.

   Suppose that Mona initially has a secure monopoly in the market for air travel between two cities. When there is no threat of entry, Mona uses the marginal principle (marginal revenue = marginal cost) to pick a quantity and a price. In Figure 15.7, we start at point *m*, with a quantity of 150 passengers per day and a price of $400 per passenger. Her profit per passenger is $100 ($400 minus the average cost per passenger of $300), so her daily profit is $15,000. If Mona discovers that Doug, the manager of a second airline, is thinking about entering the market, what will she do? Now that she has an insecure monopoly, she has two options: She can be passive and allow the second airline to enter the market, or she can try to prevent the second airline from entering.

The Passive Approach: Do Nothing to Deter Entry

The passive approach will lead to the duopoly outcome we saw earlier in the chapter. In Figure 15.7, the market will move downward along the demand curve from point *m* to point *d* (the duopoly outcome). In a duopoly, Mona will charge a price of $350 and serves 100 passengers (half the quantity demanded). Her daily profit will be $5,000, equal to the profit per passenger of $50 ($350 – the average cost per passenger of $300) multiplied by 100 passengers.

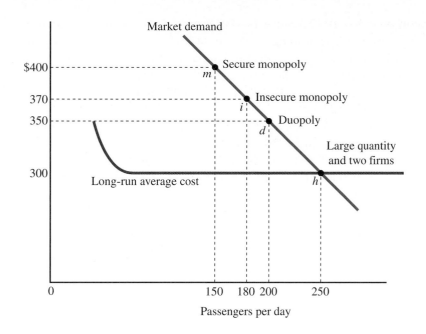

FIGURE 15.7

Deterring Entry with Limit Pricing
Moving downward along the demand curve, point *m* shows the secure monopoly, point *i* shows the insecure monopoly, and point *d* shows the duopoly. Point *h* shows what happens if the insecure monopolist produces a large quantity but a second firm enters anyway.

The Entry Deterrence Approach: Use Limit Pricing to Deter Entry

The second option is to take actions that prevent Doug from entering the market. In thinking about the alternative to the passive approach, Mona must answer two questions:

▶ What must she do to deter entry?
▶ Given what she must do to deter entry, is deterrence more profitable than being passive and sharing the market with a second firm?

To prevent Doug from entering the market, Mona must commit herself to serving a large number of passengers. If she commits to a large passenger load, there won't be enough passengers left for a potential entrant to make a profit. How many passengers must she commit to serve? In Figure 15.7, point *h* shows the point of zero economic profit in the market: If the two firms serve a total of 250 passengers per day, the price ($300) equals average cost, so each firm makes zero economic profit. Suppose that because of economies of scale in providing air travel, the minimum entry quantity is 70 passengers per day: That is, it would be impractical for a firm to serve fewer than 70 passengers. In Figure 15.7, the economies of scale are reflected in a long-run average cost curve is negatively sloped for relatively low levels of output. We can compute the entry-deterring quantity as follows:

entry-deterring quantity = zero economic profit quantity − minimum entry quantity
180 = 250 − 70

If Mona serves 180 passengers and Doug were to enter with the minimum quantity of 70 passengers, the price would drop to average cost, making entry unprofitable.

It's important to note that Mona can't simply announce that she will serve 180 passengers. She must take actions that ensure that 180 passengers—not the secure monopoly quantity of 150 passengers—is her most profitable quantity. In other words, she must commit to 180 passengers. She could commit to the larger passenger load by purchasing a large fleet of airplanes and signing labor contracts that require her to hire a large workforce. The daily cost of serving 180 passengers is $54,000 (the average cost of $300 times 180 passengers), so if she pays this amount up front, her profit-maximizing quantity will be 180 passengers.

Which is more profitable, entry deterrence or the passive duopoly outcome? The deterrence strategy, shown by point *i* in Figure 15.7, generates a price of $370 and a profit per passenger of $70. Total profit is $12,600 (equal to $70 times 180 passengers). This is larger than the $5,000 profit under the passive approach, so deterrence is the best strategy. Figure 15.8 summarizes this example of entry deterrence. Mona makes the first move, choosing either a small quantity (passive approach) or a large one. If she is passive, Doug would enter the market, and they would end up in profit rectangle 1, each earning $5,000. If Mona picks the large quantity, Doug's entry would drive economic profit to zero, so he won't enter. The path is square **X** to square **Z** to rectangle 4.

Limit Pricing

Mona's entry deterrence strategy generates a market price between the price charged by a secure monopolist ($400) and the price charged in a market with two firms ($350). Mona can avoid sharing the market by accepting the lower price associated with an insecure monopoly ($370). The strategy of picking a price that is lower than the normal monopoly price to deter entry is known as **limit pricing**.

For an example of limit pricing, consider the pricing of the Windows operating system by Microsoft Corporation. The Windows operating system runs about 90% of the world's personal computers, so it is natural to think that Microsoft has a monopoly in the market for operating systems. According to economist Richard Schmalensee, an

Limit pricing

A scheme under which a monopolist accepts a price below the normal monopoly price to deter other firms from entering the market.

FIGURE 15.8

Game Tree for Deterring Entry

Mona knows that if she picks the small quantity (the passive approach), Doug will enter, resulting in profit rectangle 1. By picking the large quantity, Mona can ensure that Doug's profit will be zero, so he will not enter, resulting in profit rectangle 4. For Mona, rectangle 4 is better than rectangle 1, so she picks the large quantity and deters entry. The path of the game is square **X** to square **Z** to rectangle 4: Mona earns a profit of $12,600, and Doug gets nothing.

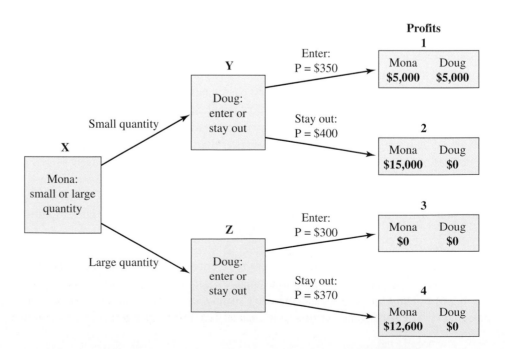

expert on oligopoly and monopoly, Microsoft's profit-maximizing monopoly price is between $900 and $2,000. That's the amount Microsoft would charge if it acted like a secure monopolist.[6] The fact that Microsoft charges only $99 for Windows suggests that Microsoft is an insecure monopolist and picks a low price to discourage entry and preserve its monopoly. If Microsoft charged $2,000 for its operating system, there would be an incentive for other firms to develop alternative operating systems.

Sometimes firms use other means to prevent the entry of other firms into a market. For some examples, read "A Closer Look: Crafty—and Illegal—Entry Deterrence in Europe."

When Is the Passive Approach Better?

Although our example shows that entry deterrence is the best strategy for Mona, it won't be the best strategy for all insecure monopolists. The key variable is the minimum entry quantity. Suppose that the scale economies in air travel were relatively small, so a second firm could enter the market by serving as few as 10 passengers. In this case, if Mona commits to serving only 180 passengers, that won't be enough to deter entry: A firm entering with say, 10, 20, or 30 passengers will still make a profit. If the minimum entry quantity is 10 passengers, the entry-deterring quantity rises to 240 passengers:

$$\text{entry-deterring quantity} = \text{zero economic-profit quantity} - \text{minimum entry quantity}$$
$$240 = 250 - 10$$

The limit price associated with this entry-deterring quantity is $310. Although Mona could deter entry by committing to 240 passengers at a $310 price per ticket, her profit would be only $2,400, compared to $5,000 if she is passive and shares the market with another firm.

The general lesson is that entry deterrence is not sensible when the minimum entry quantity is relatively low. In this case, the quantity required to deter entry is relatively large. As a result, the limit price required to deter entry is close to the average cost of production, and the profit from the insecure monopoly is less than the profit from sharing the market.

A CLOSER LOOK

Crafty—and Illegal—Entry Deterrence in Europe

In recent years, the European Commission has uncovered many examples of entry deterrence that are illegal under the rules of the European Union.[7]

As an example, Van den Bergh Foods, a subsidiary of Unilever, held a dominant position in the market for ice cream in Ireland in 1998. The company provided "free" freezer cabinets to retailers, under the condition that the cabinets were to be used exclusively for the storage of Unilever's products. Irish retailers were reluctant to replace Unilever cabinets, so 40% of retailers offered Unilever products only. The Commission concluded that this practice constituted an abuse of Unilever's dominant position. In 2003, the European Court of First Instance ordered Unilever to share the freezer cabinets with its competitors, including the Mars Company, which had argued that it was unable to sell its ice cream in many retail outlets in Ireland.

Applications: Aluminum, Plane Tickets, and Campus Bookstores

Between 1893 and 1940, the Aluminum Company of America (Alcoa) had a monopoly on aluminum production in the United States.[8] During this period, Alcoa kept other firms out of the market by producing a large quantity and keeping its price low. Although a higher price would have generated more profit in the short run, other firms would have entered the market, so Alcoa's profit would have been lower in the long run.

At the beginning of this chapter, we saw that Katrina paid more for her plane ticket than Brian paid for his, even though they both live in cities that are served by a single airline. If the monopolist in Katrina's city is secure, meaning that there is no threat that another airline will enter the market, the monopolist will charge the normal monopoly price of $400. In Brian's city, an insecure monopolist prevents a second airline from entering the market by committing itself to produce a large quantity and accepting a low price. Brian pays a lower price because he buys his ticket from an insecure monopolist.

We can apply the notion of entry deterrence to your favorite monopoly: your campus bookstore. On most college campuses, the campus bookstore has a monopoly on the sale of textbooks. Other organizations are prohibited, usually by the state government or the college, from selling textbooks on campus. The recent growth of Internet commerce has given students another option: Order textbooks over the Web and have them shipped by mail, UPS, Federal Express, or Airborne Express. Several Web booksellers charge less than the campus bookstore, and the growth of Web book sales threatens the campus bookstore monopoly. If your campus bookstore suddenly feels insecure about its monopoly position, it could cut its prices to prevent Web booksellers from capturing too many of its customers. If it does this, you will pay lower prices even if you don't patronize the Web seller.

Campus bookstores now compete with online booksellers.

Entry Deterrence and Contestable Markets

We've seen that an insecure monopolist may cut its price to prevent other firms from entering the market. The threat of entry moves the market price closer to the price that would occur in a market with two firms. The same logic applies to a monopolized market that could potentially have many firms: The threat of entry will force the monopolist to charge a price that could be close to the one that would occur in a market with many firms. The mere existence of a monopoly does not mean that it will necessarily charge high prices and earn large profits, however. To protect its monopoly, a monopolist may act like a firm in a market with many firms, picking a lower price and earning a smaller profit.

The threat of entry faced by an insecure monopolist like the airline underlies the theory of market contestability. Firms can enter or leave a **contestable market** without incurring large costs. The few firms in a contestable market will be threatened constantly by the entry of new firms, so prices and profits will be low. In the extreme case of perfect contestability, firms can enter and exit a market at zero cost. In this case, the price will be the same as the price that would occur in a perfectly competitive market, one with dozens of firms. Although few markets are perfectly contestable, many markets are contestable to a certain degree, and the threat of entry tends to decrease prices and profits.

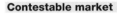

Contestable market

A market in which the costs of entering and leaving are low, so the firms that are already in the market are constantly threatened by the entry of new firms.

Ballpoint Pens from R.I.P.

In 1945, Reynolds International Pen Corporation introduced a revolutionary product: the ballpoint pen. The new type of pen could be produced with a very simple production technology.[9] For three years, Reynolds earned enormous profits on this innovative product. In 1948, Reynolds stopped producing pens, dropping out of the market entirely. What happened?

Economic Puzzle

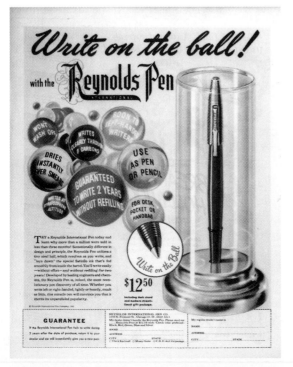

The key to solving this mystery is the fact that Reynolds earned enormous profits for a short time. The simple technology of the ballpoint pen could be easily copied by other producers, so the price required to deter entry was very low. The entry-deterring price was so low that it was better for Reynolds to charge a high price and squeeze out as much profit as possible from a short-lived monopoly. Reynolds sold its pens for $12.50, about 16 times the average production cost ($0.80). By 1948, a total of 100 firms had entered the ballpoint market, and the price had fallen close to the production cost. ■

The Advertisers' Dilemma

We have explored two sorts of strategic behavior of firms in an oligopoly—price fixing and entry deterrence. A third type of strategy concerns advertising. As we'll see, firms in an oligopoly may suffer from an advertisers' dilemma: Although both firms would be better off if neither spent money on advertising, each firm advertises.

Consider the producers of two brands of aspirin. Each firm must decide whether to spend $7 million on an advertising campaign for its product. In Table 15.4, the first two columns of numbers show what happens if neither firm advertises. Each earns $8 million in net revenue (revenue minus production cost) and spends no money on advertising, so the profit is $8 million for each firm. The third and fourth columns of numbers show what happens if each firm spends $7 million on advertising. Net revenue increases from $8 million to $13 million, a benefit of $5 million. This $5 million benefit of advertising is less than the $7 million cost, so the profit earned by each firm falls, from $8 million to $6 million.

What happens if one firm advertises and the other does not? The last two columns of numbers in Table 15.4 show that advertising is profitable for the advertising firm. If Adeline spends $7 million on advertising and Vern spends nothing, Adeline's net revenue increases to $17 million, so her profit increases to $10 million ($17 million − $7 million). Adeline's advertisements cause some of Vern's consumers to switch to Adeline, and Vern's net revenue (and profit) drops to $5 million.

We can use the data in Table 15.4 to construct a game tree for the advertising game. In Figure 15.9, Adeline makes her decision first, followed by Vern.

▶ If neither firm advertises, we go from square **X** to square **Z** to rectangle 4, and the payoff (profit) is $8 million for each firm.
▶ If both firms advertise, we go from square **X** to square **Y** to rectangle 1, and each firm earns a profit of $6 million.
▶ If Adeline advertises and Vern does not, we go from square **X** to square **Y** to rectangle 2, and Adeline earns $10 million, while Vern earns $5 million. If the roles are reversed, we end up in rectangle 3, with Vern, the advertiser, earning $10 million, while Adeline earns $5 million.

To determine the outcome of this advertising game, let's start with Vern's possible actions. If Adeline advertises (we move along the upper branches of the game tree from square **X** to square **Y**), Vern will earn $6 million if he advertises, too (rectangle 1), but only $5 million if he does not advertise (rectangle 2). Therefore, Vern's best response is

	Neither Advertises		Both Advertise		Adeline Advertises	
	Adeline	Vern	Adeline	Vern	Adeline	Vern
Net revenue from sales ($ million)	8	8	13	13	17	5
Cost of advertising ($ million)	0	0	7	7	7	0
Profit ($ million)	8	8	6	6	10	5

TABLE 15.4

Advertising and Profit

to match Adeline's campaign. If Adeline does not advertise (we move along the lower branches from square **X** to square **Z**), Vern will earn $10 million if he advertises but only $8 million if he does not. Therefore, if Adeline does not advertise, Vern's best response is to advertise. To summarize, advertising is Vern's dominant strategy (the best response no matter what Adeline does).

Consider next the options faced by Adeline. She can figure out that advertising is a dominant strategy for Vern. Knowing this, Adeline realizes that the only possible outcomes are shown by rectangles 1 and 3. From her perspective, rectangle 1 ($6 million) is better than rectangle 3 ($5 million), so her best response is to advertise. Both firms advertise, and each earns a profit of $6.

What is the advertisers' dilemma? Both Adeline and Vern would be better off if neither advertised: Each would get a profit of $8 million if neither advertised, compared to $6 million when both advertise. Each firm has an incentive to use advertising to increase its net revenue at the expense of the other. Knowing this, each firm spends

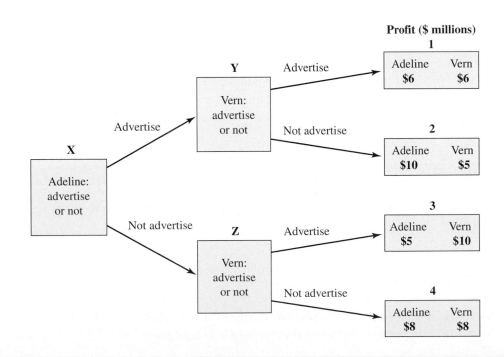

FIGURE 15.9

Game Tree for an Advertisers' Dilemma
Adeline moves first, choosing to advertise or not. Vern's best response is to advertise no matter what Adeline does. Knowing this, Adeline realizes that the only possible outcomes are shown by rectangles 1 and 3. From Adeline's perspective, rectangle 1 ($6 million) is better than rectangle 3 ($5 million), so her best response is to advertise. Both Adeline and Vern advertise, and each earns a profit of $6 million.

$7 million to counter the advertising campaign of the other firm. Stuck in the dilemma, each firm earns $2 million less than it would if neither advertised.

The advertisers' dilemma occurs when advertising causes a relatively small increase in the total sales of the industry but allows a firm that advertises to gain at the expense of firms that don't. In our example, a pair of advertising campaigns costing a total of $14 million increases the industry's net revenue by only $10 million—from $16 million ($8 million each) to $26 million ($13 million each). If the increase in industry net revenue were larger, advertising could benefit both firms. We'll see an example of that type of advertising in the Using the Tools exercise, "Got Milk?"

TEST Your Understanding

9. Complete the statement: Suppose that Mona picks a small quantity of output. In Figure 15.8, the path of the game would be square _____ to square _____ to rectangle _____.

10. In Figure 15.8, Mona would prefer rectangle 2 to rectangle 4. Why can't she get to rectangle 2?

11. Why does a secure monopolist charge a higher price than an insecure monopolist?

Game Theory and Nash Equilibrium

Nash equilibrium

An outcome of a game in which each player is doing the best he or she can, given the action of the other players.

In this chapter, we explore three strategies used by oligopolies to generate profit, including price fixing, entry deterrence, and advertising. We can use game trees to find the equilibrium strategies for oligopolists. For example, in the equilibrium for the advertisers' game, both firms advertise, although it would be better for each firm if neither did. This is a **Nash equilibrium**, named after John Nash, the recipient of the 1994 Nobel Prize in economics. Nash developed his equilibrium concept as a 21-year-old graduate student at Princeton University. His life story, which includes a 25-year bout with schizophrenia and a dramatic recovery, is chronicled in the book *A Beautiful Mind*, later made into a movie starring Russell Crowe as John Nash.[10]

Nash Equilibrium

Each player is doing the best he or she can, given the action of the other player.

In the advertising game, the equilibrium is for both Adeline and Vern to advertise. This is a Nash equilibrium:

▶ If Vern advertises, the best action for Adeline is to advertise.
▶ If Adeline advertises, the best action for Vern is to advertise.

John Nash developed his equilibrium concept as a 21-year-old graduate student at Princeton University.

There are three other possible outcomes in the advertising game, none of which is a Nash equilibrium.

1 *Neither advertises.* This is not a Nash equilibrium because if Vern does not advertise, Adeline' best action is to advertise. Similarly, if Adeline does not advertise, Vern's best action is to advertise.
2 *Only Adeline advertises.* This is not a Nash equilibrium because if Adeline advertises, Vern's best action is to advertise.
3 *Only Vern advertises.* This is not a Nash equilibrium because if Vern advertises, Adeline's best action is to advertise.

In all three cases, at least one of the players has an incentive to change his or her action given what the other player is doing, so we don't have a Nash equilibrium.

We can also apply the notion of Nash equilibrium to the price-fixing game discussed earlier in the chapter. The Nash equilibrium is for both firms to pick the low price.

▶ If Jill picks the low price, the best action for Jack is to pick the low price, too.
▶ If Jack picks the low price, the best action for Jill is to pick the low price, too.

The outcome with both picking the high price is not a Nash equilibrium because if Jill picks the high price, Jack's best action is to pick the low price.

The concept of the Nash equilibrium has been applied to a wide variety of decisions. In addition to strategic decisions for firms, it has been used to analyze the nuclear arms race, terrorism, evolutionary biology, art auctions, environmental policy, and urban development.

Economic Experiment

A Price-Fixing Game

Here is a price-fixing or cartel game for the classroom. You'll have an opportunity to conspire to fix prices in a hypothetical market with five firms. The instructor divides the class into five groups. Each group represents one of five firms that produce a particular good. Each group must develop a pricing strategy for its firm, recognizing that the other groups are choosing prices for their firms at the same time. There are only two choices: a high price (the cartel price) or a low price. The profit of a particular firm depends on the price chosen by the firm and the prices chosen by the four other firms. Here is the profit matrix:

Number of High-Price Firms	Number of Low-Price Firms	Profit for Each High-Price Firm	Profit for Each Low-Price Firm
0	5	—	$ 5
1	4	$2	7
2	3	4	9
3	2	6	11
4	1	8	13
5	0	10	—

From the second row, if one of the five firms chooses the high price, and the other four firms choose the low price, the high-price firm earns a profit of $2, and each low-price firm earns a profit of $7. The game is played for several rounds. In the first three rounds, the firms make their choices without talking to each other in advance. In the fourth and fifth rounds, the firms discuss their strategies, disperse, and then make their choices. The group's score equals the profit earned by the firm. ●

USING THE TOOLS

We've used one of the tools of economics—the game tree—to predict the outcomes of three types of strategic games played by oligopolists: price fixing, entry deterrence, and advertising. Here are some opportunities to use this tool to do your own economic analysis of markets.

1. Advertising and Price Fixing

Consider two sellers of CD players (Cecil and Dee) who suffer from the duopolists' dilemma. Although both Cecil and Dee would be better off if both chose the high price, they both choose the low price. Cecil recently discovered that Dee is planning a big advertising campaign, the purpose of which is to increase her sales at Cecil's expense (without changing her price). Suppose that Cecil has the opportunity to launch his own advertising campaign before Dee starts hers. What sort of advertising campaign should he launch?

2. Entry Deterrence

Your firm sells a popular children's toy. The manager of another firm is thinking about introducing a similar toy. Your average cost of production is constant at $2 per toy. At the current monopoly price of $5 per toy, you sell 120 toys per day. You could prevent the entry of the second firm by increasing your output to 150 toys per day and cutting your price to $4 per toy. If the second firm enters the market, your price would decrease to $3 per toy, and you would sell only 80 toys per day. Should you prevent entry of the second firm?

3. Advertising with Spillover Benefits: Got Milk?

Bessie and George are milk producers, and each must decide whether to spend $7 million on an advertising campaign. If neither advertises, each will earn $10 million in net revenue from sales (net revenue). If both advertise, each will earn $20 million in net revenue and $13 million in profit ($20 million − $7 million for advertising). If only one producer advertises, that firm will earn $16 million in net revenue, and the other firm will earn $15 million in net revenue. Prepare a game tree like Figure 15.9 (assume that Bessie decides first) and predict the outcome of this advertising game. If there is an advertisers' dilemma, how does it differ from the advertisers' dilemma discussed earlier in the chapter? How might the dairy industry solve this dilemma? (*Hint*: Think white mustaches.)

SUMMARY

In this chapter, we've seen that when a few firms share a market, they have an incentive to act strategically. Firms may use cartel pricing or price fixing to avoid competition and keep prices high. If another firm threatens to enter a monopolist's market, the monopolist may cut its price to discourage other firms from entering a market. Here are the main points of the chapter:

1 Each firm in an oligopoly has an incentive to under-price the other firms, so price fixing (also known as cartel pricing) will be unsuccessful unless firms have some way of enforcing a price-fixing agreement.

2 One way to maintain price fixing is a guaranteed price-matching scheme: One firm chooses the high price and promises to match a lower price offered by its competitor.

3 Price fixing is more likely to occur if firms choose prices repeatedly and can punish a firm that chooses a price below the cartel price.

4 To prevent a second firm from entering the market, an insecure monopolist may commit itself to producing a relatively large quantity and accepting a relatively low price.

KEY TERMS

cartel, 330

concentration ratio, 327

contestable market, 347

dominant strategy, 332

duopolists' dilemma, 333

duopoly, 329

game theory, 327

game tree, 331

grim-trigger strategy, 337

guaranteed price-matching
   strategy, 336

kinked demand-curve model, 341

limit pricing, 344

Nash Equilibrium, 350

oligopoly, 327

price fixing, 330

price leadership, 340

sequential decision-making game,
   334

simultaneous decision-making
   game, 334

tit-for-tat, 337

PROBLEMS AND DISCUSSION QUESTIONS

1 Consider two firms, Speedy and Hustle, which provide land transportation from the downtown area to the airport. The practice of guaranteed price matching is illegal. If the two firms act independently (they do not engage in price fixing or any other collusive behavior), each firm will serve 100 passengers per day at a price of $20 per passenger and an average cost of $15 per passenger. Under a price-fixing or cartel arrangement, each firm would serve 75 passengers at a price of $28 and an average cost of $18 per passenger. If one firm charges $20 and the other firm charges $28, the low-price firm will earn a profit of $900, and the high-price firm will earn a profit of $400. Speedy chooses a price first, followed by Hustle. Draw a game tree for the price-fixing game and predict the outcome.

2 Recall the example of the repeated pricing game between Jack and Jill. Suppose that each firm uses the grim-trigger strategy to punish underpricing. Each person expects to go out of business in one month, meaning that each person is about to choose a price for the last time. Which price will each person choose?

3 Many firms have going-out-of-business sales with remarkable bargains. What insights does the material in this chapter provide about such sales?

4 Consider the example of entry deterrence shown in Figure 15.8. Suppose that just one number changes: If Mona chooses a large quantity and Doug stays out, Mona's profit would be $4,500. All the other numbers are the same as those shown in Figure 15.8. Draw a new game tree and predict the outcome: Will Mona choose a large or a small quantity, and will Doug enter or stay out?

5 On Wa-ki-ki beach, there are two hotels, Weird and Bizarre. The practice of guaranteed price matching is illegal. If the two firms act independently (they do not engage in price fixing or any other collusive behavior), each firm will rent 50 rooms per day at a price of $50 per room and an average cost of $45 per room. Under a price-fixing or cartel arrangement, each hotel would rent 30 rooms per day at a price of $60 and an average cost of $48. If one firm charges $50 and the other firm charges $60, the low-price firm will earn a profit of $500, and the

high-price firm will earn a profit of $150. Bizarre picks a price first, followed by Weird.
  a. Suppose each firm must pick a price and maintain its chosen price for the remaining lifetime of the firm. Draw a game tree and predict the outcome.
  b. Suppose the two firms can change their prices daily, and expect to be in business for three more days. Weird announces that he will start with the high price and maintain the price as long as Bizarre does too. If Bizarre undercuts Weird, however, Weird will pick the low price for the remainder of the game. Predict the outcome of the game.

6 Consider the market for air travel between Madison and Chicago. The long-run average cost is constant at $200 per passenger, and the demand curve is linear, with a slope of −$1 per passenger. A secure monopolist would charge a price of $280 and serve 70 passengers per day. The other possible prices are $260 for an insecure monopolist, $250 for the duopoly outcome, and $180 for the case in which one firm picks a large quantity and a low price but a second firm enters anyway.
  a. Use these numbers to draw two figures, one like Figure 15.7 and a second like Figure 15.8. Provide a complete set of numbers, and briefly explain how you got them. Label any curves you draw, and identify the relevant points on your graph.
  b. Use your second figure to predict the outcome of the entry deterrence game. What is the price of air travel?

7 In the state of Turnover, the typical car-stereo seller stays in business for one year. In the state of Longtime, the typical car-stereo seller stays in business for five years. Which state is likely to have higher prices for car stereos?

8 Consider the Jack and Jill repeated-price game described in the text. Suppose Jill uses the duopoly-pricing strategy, and the two firms expect to be in business for three periods.
  a. In the current period, what are Jack's costs and benefits of underpricing?
  b. Will Jack underprice in the final period? If Jill can predict Jack's behavior in the last period, what will she do? What are the implications for the second period?

9 Consider two automobile companies that are considering advertising campaigns. If neither firm advertises, each will earn net revenue of $5 million. If each spends $10 million on advertising, each firm's net revenue will be $12 million. If one advertises and the other does not, the firm that advertises will earn $17 million in net revenue, while the firm that does not will earn $1 million. Draw a game tree and predict the outcome. From the industry perspective, do the benefits of advertising exceed the costs?

MODEL ANSWERS TO QUESTIONS

Chapter-Opening Questions

1 It is likely to lead to higher prices because it eliminates the possibility of underpricing. The promise to issue refunds is an empty promise.

2 The price-fixing arrangement is more likely to persist if the airlines pick prices repeatedly over time, giving the airlines the opportunity to punish anyone who cheats on the agreement.

3 Entry deterrence is not sensible when the minimum entry quantity is relatively low and thus the limit price is relatively low.

4 The firms suffer from the advertisers' dilemma. There is a big payoff from being the only advertiser and a big penalty from not advertising if the other advertises, so both advertise.

Test Your Understanding

1 *c, d.*

2 X, Z, 4, $5,000.

3 He will choose the low price and gain at Jill's expense. Jack's promise is not credible because once Jill chooses the high price, he will earn more profit by choosing the low price. Jill should ignore the incredible promise and choose the low price.

4 $50 ($400 − $350).

5 They are common in appliance and electronics stores and in hardware stores. Many grocery stores honor the coupons of other stores. Although these schemes appear to be good news for consumers, they actually facilitate price fixing and lead to higher prices.

6 The grim-trigger strategy leads to zero economic profit, while the duopoly price leaves each firm with a positive profit. The costs of underpricing are higher with the grim trigger, so there is a greater incentive to charge the cartel price.

7 Two months. In the first month, Jill underprices Jack. In the second month, Jill chooses the high price but is underpriced by Jack, who is punishing her for underpricing him in the first month. In the third month, they both choose the high price.

8 Cost, benefit.

9 X, Y, 1.

10 If she chooses a small quantity, Doug will enter.

11 To prevent the entry of a second firm, an insecure monopolist commits itself to produce a large quantity of output and accepts a low price. A secure monopolist doesn't have to worry about other firms entering the market.

NOTES

1. Adam Smith, *The Wealth of Nations* (New York: Modern Library, 1994).
2. David Barboza, "Tearing Down the Facade of 'Vitamins Inc.'" *New York Times*, October 10, 1999, Section 3, p. 1; Department of Justice, "Four Foreign Executives Of Leading European Vitamin Firms Agree to Plead Guilty to Participating in International Vitamin Cartel," Press Release, April 6, 2000.
3. Sharon Walsh, "Six Airlines to Halt Advance Price Listing," *New York Times News Service*, printed in *The Oregonian*, March 18, 1994, p. B1.
4. Federal Trade Commission, "Record Companies Settle FTC Charges of Restraining Competition in CD Music Market," Press Release, May 10, 2000.
5. George Stigler, "The Kinked Oligopoly Demand Curve and Rigid Prices," *Journal of Political Economy*, vol. 55, 1947, pp. 432–449.
6. "Big Friendly Giant," *The Economist*, January 30, 1999, p. 72.
7. European Commission, *Report on Competition Policy 1998*, pp. 35–39.
8. Leonard W. Weiss, *Economics and American Industry* (New York: Wiley, 1963), pp. 189–204.
9. Thomas Whiteside, "Where Are They Now?" *New Yorker*, February 17, 1951, pp. 39–58.
10. Sylvia Nassar, *A Beautiful Mind* (New York: Simon & Schuster, 1998).

Natural Monopoly

Picking an Output Level
Will a Second Firm Enter?
Price Controls for a Natural Monopoly

Antitrust Policy

Breaking Up Monopolies
Blocking Mergers
Application: Merger Remedies for Xidex
    and Wonder Bread
Regulating Business Practices: Price
    Fixing, Tying, and Cooperative
    Agreements
Application: The Microsoft Case
A Brief History of U.S. Antitrust Policy

**Deregulation of Airlines
and Telecommunications**

Deregulation of Airlines
Deregulation of Telecommunications
    Services

Deregulation of Electricity

Electricity Deregulation in California
Electricity Deregulation in Other U.S.
    States
Using the Tools

Market Structure and Public Policy

In 1997, a U.S. court blocked the proposed merger of Staples and Office Depot, the nation's two largest office-supply retailers. The judge in the case observed that the merger would eliminate Office Depot as a competitor and allow Staples to increase its prices by 13%. Where did the judge get that number?

When you buy groceries, hardware, or office supplies, a scanner at the checkout stand reads bar-code information, recording the price you pay and the quantity you purchase. The scanner system helps retailers keep track of their stock and allows them to instantly change prices without putting new price tags on their products. The scanner data can also be used to observe pricing patterns from firms like Staples. Economists with the Federal Trade Commission (FTC) found an interesting pattern: The prices charged by Staples were lower in cities where Office Depot also had a store. The competition generated by Office Depot led to prices that were, on average, 13% lower.[1]

This chapter looks at various public policies dealing with markets that are dominated by a small number of firms. We'll start with the case of natural monopoly, which occurs when the scale economies in production are so large that only a single large firm can survive. In this case, the government can intervene by regulating the price charged by the natural monopolist. Then we'll look at markets in which the government can affect the number of firms in the market, using various policies to promote competition. The government uses antitrust policies to break up monopolies into several smaller companies, prevent corporate mergers that would reduce competition, and regulate business practices that tend to reduce competition. Sometimes prior government regulations actually end up inhibiting competition, so the government later "de-regulates" an industry to promote more competition. In the last part of the chapter, we'll look at recent deregulation of three markets: air travel, telecommunications, and electricity. In these three markets, the government reversed a long history of regulation, deregulating the industries to promote competition. Here are some practical policy questions that we answer:

1 Two firms, XM Satellite Radio and Sirius Satellite Radio, each spent about $2 billion on satellites and ground stations to provide dozens of radio channels with fewer commercials (and pledge drives) than broadcast radio. Will both firms survive?
2 Why did the government prevent the proposed merger between Heinz and Beech-Nut, the second and third largest firms in the market for baby food?
3 How did the deregulation of air travel affect the price of air travel?

Natural Monopoly

In an earlier chapter, we considered monopolies that resulted from artificial barriers to entry such as patents and government licenses. In this chapter, we'll look at natural monopolies, which occur when the economies of scale for producing a product are so large that only a single firm can survive. Some examples are water systems, electricity transmission, and cable TV service. It is natural for a city to have a single supplier of water service because a second supplier would install a second set of water pipes when a single set of pipes would suffice. Similarly, it is sensible to have a single set of transmission lines for electricity and a single set of cables for TV service.

Picking an Output Level

Figure 16.1 shows the long-run average-cost curve for cable TV service in a particular city. The curve is negatively sloped and steep, reflecting the large economies of scale that occur because of the cost of building and maintaining the system of cables that deliver TV service to individual subscribers. The system of cables strung along power lines is an indivisible input in the sense that it is the same whether the cable firm has 70

FIGURE 16.1

A Natural Monopoly Uses the Marginal Principle to Pick Quantity and Price
Because of the indivisible input of cable service (the cable system), the long-run average-cost curve is negatively sloped. The monopolist chooses point *n* (where marginal revenue equals marginal cost), serving 70,000 subscribers at a price of $27 per unit (point *m*) and an average cost of $21 (point *c*). The profit per subscriber is $6 ($27 – $21).

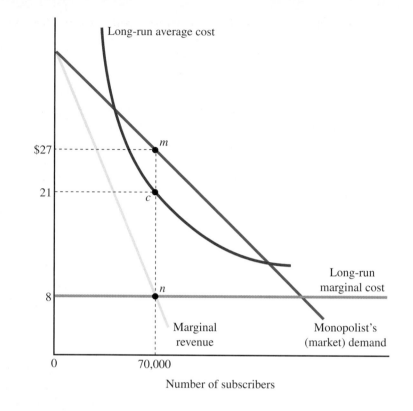

subscribers in the city or 70,000. As the number of subscribers increases, the average cost of cable service decreases because the cost of the indivisible cable system is spread over more people.

What about the long-run marginal cost—the cost to add one subscriber—once the system is built? For each additional subscriber, a cable company incurs the cost of hooking the house into the system and the administrative cost associated with billing the subscriber. To simplify matters, we'll assume that each additional subscriber increases cost by $8 per month, so the marginal-cost curve is horizontal at $8 per subscriber.

Figure 16.1 shows how to use the cost curves and revenue curves to pick the output level that maximizes profit. If a single firm—a monopolist—provides cable service, the monopolist's firm-specific demand curve is the same as the market demand curve: To determine how many subscribers the monopolist will have at a particular price, we look at the market demand curve. The demand curve is negatively sloped, and the marginal-revenue curve lies below the demand curve. The marginal principle is satisfied at point *n*, with 70,000 subscribers. The price associated with this quantity is $27 per subscriber (shown by point *m*) and the average cost is $21 per unit (shown by point *c*), so the profit per subscriber is $6. The price exceeds the average cost, so the cable company will earn a profit.

Will a Second Firm Enter?

If there are no artificial barriers to entry, a second firm could enter the cable TV market. What would happen if a second firm entered the market? In Figure 16.2, the entry of a second firm would shift the firm-specific demand curve of the first firm—the former monopolist—to the left, from D_1 to D_2: At each price, the first firm will have fewer subscribers because it now shares the market with another firm. For example, at a price of $27, there are 70,000 subscribers, or 35,000 for each firm (point t). In general, the larger the number of firms, the lower the firm-specific demand curve for the typical firm.

Will a second firm enter the market? Notice that the demand curve of the typical firm in a two-firm market lies entirely below the long-run average-cost curve, so there is no quantity at which the price exceeds the average cost of production. No matter what price the typical firm charges, it will lose money. The firm's demand curve lies below the average-cost curve because the average-cost curve is steep, reflecting the large economies of scale for cable service. A second firm—with half the market—would have a very high average cost and wouldn't be able to charge a price high enough to cover the cost of building the system in the first place. Therefore, the second firm will not enter the market, so there will be a single firm, a natural monopoly. For an example of a potential new natural monopoly, read "A Closer Look: Will Satellite Radio Be a Natural Monopoly?"

Price Controls for a Natural Monopoly

When a natural monopoly is inevitable, the government often sets a maximum price for the monopolist. There are many examples of natural monopolies that are subject to maximum prices. Local governments regulate utilities and firms that provide water,

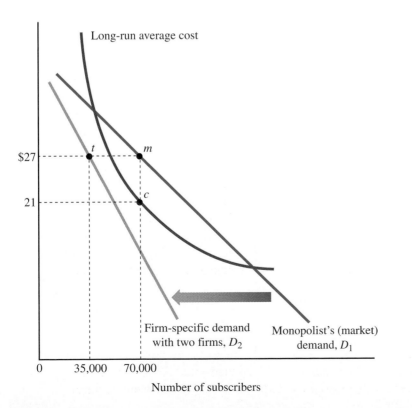

FIGURE 16.2

Will A Second Cable Firm Enter the Market?
The entry of a second cable firm would shift the firm-specific demand curve of the typical firm to the left. After entry, the firm's demand curve lies entirely below the long-run average cost curve. No matter what price the typical firm charges, it will lose money. Therefore, a second firm will not enter the market.

electricity, cable service, and local telephone service. Many state governments use public utility commissions (PUCs) to regulate the electric power industry.

We can use the cable TV market to explain the effects of government regulation on a natural monopoly. Suppose the government sets a maximum price for cable service and forces the cable company to serve all consumers who are willing to pay the maximum price. In other words, the government—not the firm—picks a point on the market demand curve. Under an **average-cost pricing policy**, the government picks the price at which the market demand curve intersects the monopolist's long-run average-cost curve. In Figure 16.3, the average-cost curve intersects the demand curve at point *r*, with a price of $12 per subscriber. This is much lower than the price the firm would choose to maximize its profit ($27). Notice that under the pricing policy, the monopolist has many more subscribers (120,000 versus 70,000), a result of the much lower price ($12 versus $27). The purpose of the average-cost pricing policy is to get the lowest feasible price. The cable company would lose money at any price less than $12, so a lower price isn't feasible.

How will this regulatory policy affect the monopolist's production costs? Under average-cost pricing, a change in the monopolist's production cost will have little effect on its profit because the government will soon adjust the regulated price to keep the price equal to the average cost. The government will increase the regulated price when the monopolist's cost increases, and decrease the price when its cost decreases. Because the monopolist has no incentive to cut costs and faces no penalty for higher costs, its costs are likely to creep upward. As average cost increases, the regulated price will too.

Average-cost pricing policy

A regulatory policy under which the government picks the point on the demand curve at which price equals average cost.

FIGURE 16.3

Regulators Use Average-Cost Pricing to Pick a Monopoly's Quantity and Price
Under an average-cost pricing policy, the government chooses the price at which the demand curve intersects the long-run average-cost curve, point *r* ($12 per subscriber). Compared to the outcome with an unregulated monopoly, the policy leads to a lower price ($12 versus $27) and a larger quantity (150,000 versus 70,000).

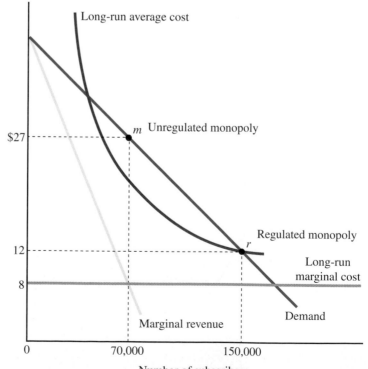

A Decrease in Demand Decreases the Price?

When the population of Fleeburg decreased, the demand for all sorts of goods—including housing and cable TV service—decreased. The decrease in the demand for housing decreased the price of housing, consistent with the laws of supply and demand. By contrast, the price of cable TV service, a regulated natural monopoly in Fleeburg, increased. The higher price for cable service seems to defy the laws of supply and demand. What explains the puzzling increase in price?

The key to solving this mystery is that cable TV is a regulated natural monopoly, with a price equal to the average cost of providing cable service. A decrease in the number of subscribers will cause the cable company to move upward along its negatively sloped average-cost curve to a higher average cost and a higher regulated price. In graphical terms, the demand curve for cable service shifts to the left, so it intersects the negatively sloped average-cost curve at a higher average cost. Intuitively, there are fewer subscribers to share the large fixed cost of the cable system, so each subscriber must pay more. ■

A CLOSER LOOK — Will Satellite Radio Become a Natural Monopoly?

The biggest development in radio since the emergence of the FM band is satellite radio. Two firms—Sirius Satellite Radio and XM Satellite Radio—provide dozens of national radio channels that can be accessed by special radio receivers for cars and homes.[2] The quality of the reception is on par with compact discs and is the same throughout the continental United States. Both firms provide dozens of channels, including music channels with rock and roll, punk, pop, country/western, R&B, and classical music. The information channels include the Bloomberg News Radio, CNBC, C-SPAN, BBC WorldService, NPR Talk, and Public Radio International.

The advantage of satellite radio is that most stations are free of annoying commercials that clutter most broadcast radio stations. The music channels on the Sirius system are commercial-free, and the information channels air just a few minutes of commercials every hour. About half the XM channels are commercial-free, and the others have no more than 6 minutes of commercials every hour (compared to 20 minutes at the typical broadcast radio station). The monthly charge for Sirius is $13. XM radio costs less—$10 per month—reflecting the larger number of commercials on that network.

How many satellite radio systems can the market support? The cost of setting up the system—with satellites and ground stations—is $2 billion, and the break-even point for each firm is about 3 million subscribers. In June 2003, XM radio had 500,000 subscribers, and Sirius had 68,000. The firms expect to reach break-even levels by 2005 or 2006. If their projection of a total market of 50 million subscribers is accurate, each firm could be profitable. Alternatively, if there are fewer than 6 million total subscribers (3 million for each firm), one or both of the firms will fail.

Antitrust Policy

The purpose of antitrust policy is to promote competition among firms. Antitrust policy is used to break up existing monopolies and to prevent existing firms from becoming monopolies. We'll explore three types of antitrust policies.

Breaking Up Monopolies

One form of antitrust policy is to break up a monopoly into several smaller firms. A **trust** is an arrangement under which the owners of several companies transfer their decision-making powers to a small group of trustees, who then make decisions for all the participating firms. Firms in a trust act as a single firm, so an industry that appears to have many firms may in fact be a virtual monopoly.

Trust

An arrangement under which the owners of several companies transfer their decision-making powers to a small group of trustees, who then make decisions for all the firms.

In 1911, the Supreme Court found that Rockefeller had used "unnatural methods" to maintain his monopoly power and drive his rivals out of business.

The label "antitrust" comes from the names of the early conglomerates that were broken up. The classic example is John D. Rockefeller's Standard Oil Trust, which was formed in 1882 when the owners of 40 oil companies empowered nine trustees to make the decisions for all 40 companies. The trust controlled over 90% of the market for refined petroleum products, and the trustees ran it like a monopoly. In 1911, the government ordered its breakup. The Supreme Court found that Rockefeller had used "unnatural methods" to maintain his monopoly power and drive his rivals out of business. In addition to forming the trust, he coerced railroads to give him special rates for shipping, and he spied on his competitors. The government broke up Standard Oil into 34 separate companies, including the corporate ancestors of Exxon, Mobil, Chevron, and Amoco.

After the American Tobacco Company bought 30 of its competitors, it controlled 95% of the U.S. cigarette market. The Supreme Court found that American Tobacco maintained its monopoly power by driving rivals out of business and agreeing to exclusive contracts with wholesalers that prevented them from purchasing cigarettes from other companies. The court-ordered breakup in 1911 led to several new companies, including several of today's big cigarette companies: Reynolds, Liggett and Meyers, and P. Lorillard.

In 1982, the government broke up American Telephone and Telegraph (AT&T) into seven regional phone companies. AT&T had used its legal monopoly in local telephone service to prevent competition in the markets for long-distance service and communications equipment. After an eight-year legal battle, AT&T agreed to form seven Regional Bell Operating Companies, transforming "Ma Bell" into seven "Baby Bells." The new AT&T was allowed to compete in the market for long-distance service, where it faced competition from newcomers MCI and Sprint. AT&T was also allowed to operate in the market for communications equipment, where it faced competition from newcomers Mitel and Northern Telecom.

Blocking Mergers

A **merger** occurs when two firms combine their operations. A second type of antitrust policy is to block corporate mergers that would reduce competition and lead to higher prices. We saw in Chapter 14 that as the number of firms in a market increases, competition among firms drives down prices. Because a merger decreases the number of firms in a market, it is likely to lead to higher prices. In 1994, Microsoft tried to purchase Intuit, the maker of Quicken, a personal-finance software package that was a substitute for a similar Microsoft product. The merger would have reduced competition in the personal-finance software market, so the government blocked it.

Of course, the government does not oppose all corporate mergers. One possible benefit from a merger is that the new firm could combine production, marketing, and administrative operations, producing products at a lower average cost. Consumers might reap the rewards in the form of lower prices. In 1997, the Justice Department and the Federal Trade Commission released new guidelines for proposed mergers. The new guidelines allow companies involved in a proposed merger to present evidence that the merger would reduce costs and lead to lower prices, better products, or better service. If the evidence for greater efficiency is convincing, the government might allow

Merger

A process in which two or more firms combine their operations.

a merger that reduces the number of firms in a market. FTC Chairman Robert Pitofsky assessed the effects of the new guidelines as follows[3]:

> There may be some deals that go through which otherwise would not have. But it won't change the result in a large number of cases [rather it will have] the greatest impact in a transaction where the potential anticompetitive problem is modest and efficiencies that would be created are great.

The new guidelines will bring the U.S. antitrust rules closer in line with those of Europe and Canada and could help U.S. companies compete in those markets.

In recent years, the analysis of proposed mergers has shifted from counting the number of firms in a market to predicting how a particular merger would affect price effects. The data generated by retail checkout scanners provides an enormous amount of information about prices and quantities sold. Using this data, economists can determine how one firm's pricing policies affect the sales of that firm and its competitors. Economists can use this information to predict whether a merger would lead to higher prices.

As we saw in the chapter opener, the FTC used pricing data to support its decision to block a proposed merger between Staples and Office Depot. The data showed that prices charged by Staples were lower in cities where Office Depot also had stores. Figure 16.4 shows Staples' revenue and cost curves for one specific product: file folders. Panel A shows what happens when Staples faces no competition from an Office Depot, and Panel B shows what happens when it does. The firm-specific demand curve of Staples is lower in the city where it faces competition with Office Depot because the two firms share the market. Using the marginal principle, Staples picks the quantity and price where its marginal revenue equals its marginal cost. The profit-maximizing price is $14 in a city without an Office Depot and $12 in a city with one.

The FTC used this logic to convince the court that the proposed merger of Staples and Office Depot would lead to higher prices. The judge in the case observed that, "direct evidence shows that by eliminating Staples' most significant, and in

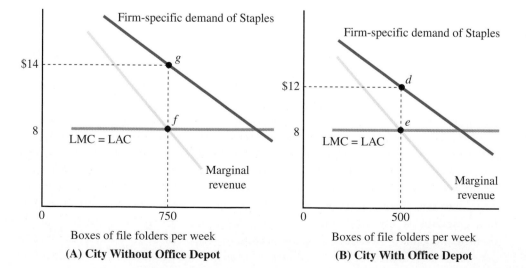

FIGURE 16.4

Pricing by Staples in Cities With and Without Competition

Using the marginal principle, Staples picks the quantity at which its marginal revenue equals its marginal cost. In a city without a competing firm, Staples picks the monopoly price of $14. In a city where Staples competes with Office Depot, the demand facing Staples is relatively low, so the profit-maximizing price is only $12.

(A) City Without Office Depot

(B) City With Office Depot

Boxes of file folders per week

many markets, only, rival, the merger would allow Staples to increase prices or otherwise maintain prices at an anticompetitive level." Evidence from the companies' pricing data showed that the merger would have allowed Staples to increase its prices by about 13%. According to an FTC study, blocking the merger saved consumers an estimated $1.1 billion over five years. For another example of blocking a merger to promote competition and lower prices, read, "A Closer Look: Is Triopoly Better than Duopoly?"

Application: Merger Remedies for Xidex and Wonder Bread

In some cases, the government allows a merger to happen but imposes restrictions on the new company. In 1981, the Federal Trade Commission brought an antitrust suit against Xidex Corporation for its earlier acquisition of two rivals in the microfilm market.[5] By acquiring Scott Graphics, Inc. in 1976 and Kalvar Corporation in 1979, Xidex increased its market share of the U.S. microfilm market from 46% to 71%. As a result, the price of microfilm increased: The price of one type of microfilm (diazo) increased by 11%, and the price of a second type (vesicular) increased by 23%. These price hikes were large enough that Xidex recovered the cost of acquiring its two rivals ($4.2 million for Scott Graphics and $6 million for Kalvar) in less than two years. To settle the antitrust lawsuit, Xidex agreed to license its microfilm technology—at bargain prices—to other firms. The idea was that if other firms have access to the microfilm technology, the competition between Xidex and the competing firms would decrease the price of microfilm.

A CLOSER LOOK   Is Triopoly Better than Duopoly?

In 2001, H.J. Heinz Company announced plans to buy Milnot Holding Company's Beechnut for $185 million. The merger would combine the nation's second- and third-largest sellers of baby food, with a combined market share of 28%. The combined company would still be less than half the size of the market leader, Gerber, with its 70% market share. The Federal Trade Commission successfully blocked the merger, based on two observations:

▶ Most retailers stock only two brands of baby food, Gerber and either Heinz or Beech-Nut. The two smaller companies compete vigorously for shelf space, with discounts, coupons, and other programs that lead to lower prices for consumers. After the merger, the Heinz brand would disappear, leaving Beech-Nut as a secure second brand on the shelves next to Gerber. The elimination of competition for second place would lead to higher prices.

▶ The smaller the number of firms in an oligopoly, the easier it is to coordinate pricing. The FTC argued that "significant market concentration makes it easier for firms in the market to collude, expressly or tacitly, and thereby force price above or farther above the competitive level." In other words, in a market with two firms instead of three, it would be easier for the baby-food manufacturers to fix prices.[4]

In 1995, Interstate Bakeries (the nation's third-largest wholesale baker) tried to buy Continental Baking (the maker of Wonder Bread). Based on grocery store scanner data, the government concluded that Wonder Bread is a close substitute for Interstate's bread: The demand for Wonder Bread increases when the price of Interstate's bread increases, and vice versa.[6] The scanner data showed that when Interstate increased its price, many consumers switched to Wonder Bread, so their bread money went to Continental instead of Interstate. The substitutability of the two brands discouraged Interstate from increasing its prices.

Table 16.1 shows an example of a merger leading to higher prices and smaller quantities. Let's assume that the average cost per loaf of bread is $1.50, and this doesn't change with a merger. The situation before the merger is shown in columns 1 and 3: For each brand, the price per loaf of bread is $2.00, the quantity is 100 loaves, and the profit is $50 (the profit $0.50 per loaf times 100 loaves).

How would a merger affect the incentives to raise prices? After a merger, a single company would earn the profits from both brands (Wonder and Interstate) and pick both prices. Suppose the new company increased the price of Interstate bread to $2.20 but kept the price of Wonder Bread at $2.00. The price hike would bring bad news and good news for the new company:

▶ Bad news: Less profit on Interstate Bread. As shown in columns 3 and 4, the price hike decreases the quantity of Interstate bread from 100 to 70 loaves. Although the profit per loaf increases to $0.70 (the new price of $2.20 minus the average cost of $1.50), only 70 loaves are sold, so the profit from the brand drops to $49, down from $50. The bad news is the $1 loss of profit on Interstate Bread.

▶ Good news: More profit on Wonder Bread. As shown in columns 1 and 2, the increase in the price of Interstate Bread increases the quantity of Wonder Bread sold from 100 to 110 loaves. The profit per loaf is still $0.50 per bread, so the profit on Wonder Bread increases to $55, up from $50. The good news is the extra $5 of profit on Wonder Bread.

In this case, the good news ($5 more profit from Wonder) exceeds the bad news ($1 less profit from Interstate), so the price hike increases the total profit of the merged com-

TABLE 16.1 A Merger Increases Prices

	Wonder Brand		Interstate Brand		Total	
	Before Merger	After Merger	Before Merger	After Merger	Before Merger	After Merger
Average cost	$1.50	$1.50	$1.50	$1.50		
Price	$2.00	$2.00	$2.00	$2.20		
Quantity	100	110	100	70	200	180
Profit	$50	$55	$50	$49	$100	$104
Column	1	2	3	4	5	6

pany. This is shown in columns 5 and 6. Although the total quantity drops, total profit increases by $4. A merger means that this good news stays within the larger firm, encouraging that firm to increase prices.

The lesson from this example is that a merger of two firms selling close substitutes may lead to higher prices. That's what the Department of Justice concluded in the case of Interstate Bakeries and Continental Bakery. The government allowed the merger between the two companies but forced Interstate to sell some of its brands and bakeries. For example, Interstate sold the rights to sell its Weber brand bread to Four-S Baking Company. The idea was to ensure that other companies would be able to compete with the new merged company.

Check the Yellow Pages?

On Katrina's first day on the job as an economist with the Federal Trade Commission, she was put on a team examining a proposed merger between the country's second- and fourth-largest hardware store chains. Her job was to predict whether a merger would increase hardware prices. Her boss handed her some disks with checkout scanner data from the second-largest chain. Each disk contained scanner data from one small town, listing the prices and quantities of hammers, wrenches, nuts, bolts, rakes, glue, drills, and hundreds of other hardware products. Her boss also gave her the telephone Yellow Pages for each small town. What can she do with the disks and the Yellow Pages?

The key to solving this puzzle is to recognize the similarity to the case of Staples and Office Depot. A merger of the country's second- and fourth-largest hardware chains could reduce competition and lead to higher prices. If the scanner data showed that prices are lower in some towns, Katrina could look in the Yellow Pages to see which towns have hardware stores from both chains and which don't. If the towns that are served by both chains have lower prices, the proposed merger would probably decrease competition and increase prices. ■

Regulating Business Practices: Price Fixing, Tying, and Cooperative Agreements

The third type of antitrust policy involves the regulation of business practices. The government may intervene when a specific business practice increases market concentration in an already concentrated market. Among the practices that are subject to scrutiny are price fixing (discussed in Chapter 15) and **tie-in sales** (forcing a buyer of one product to purchase a second product). The FTC recently charged a pharmaceutical company with tying the sale of clozapine, an antipsychotic drug, to a blood testing and monitoring system. Another illegal business practice is a cooperative agreement to limit advertising. The FTC recently charged a group of auto dealers with restricting comparative and discount advertising.

The Robinson–Patman Act prohibits selling products at "unreasonably low prices" with the intent of reducing competition, a practice known as **predatory pricing**. A firm engages in predatory pricing when it sells a product at a price below its production costs, forcing its rivals to do the same or leave the market. Once the predator's

Tie-in-sales
A business practice under which a consumer of one product is required to purchase another product.

Predatory pricing
A pricing scheme under which a firm decreases its price to drive a rival out of business and increases the price when the other firm disappears.

rivals drop out of the market, the firm then charges a monopoly price, well above its production cost. This will be a profitable strategy if the firm can charge the monopoly price for a long enough period to offset the losses it experienced while driving its rivals out of business.

But is predatory pricing really practical? Consider a market with two firms, one of which is determined to have the market to itself. By cutting its price below its cost, the firm can drive its competitor out of business, losing perhaps $10 million in the process. If it increases its price next year, there may be nothing to prevent a new firm from entering the market. If so, it would have to cut its price below its cost again to drive the new firm out. The problem with predatory pricing is that it never ends; the firm must repeatedly lose money to drive out an endless series of competitors.

Application: The Microsoft Case

In recent years, the most widely reported antitrust actions have involved Microsoft Corporation, the software giant. Microsoft receives royalties from computer makers that install the Microsoft operating software on their computers. The curious—and illegal—feature of the original arrangement was that Microsoft received a royalty for every computer made by the firm, even if the firm installed other operating systems on some of its computers. This scheme discouraged computer makers from using software from Microsoft's rivals, and the courts declared the practice illegal in 1994.

The case of *United States v. Microsoft Corporation* demonstrated that Microsoft stifled competition in the software industry. Under an initial ruling, the remedy was to break up the corporation into two companies, one producing the Windows operating system and a second producing application software. On appeal, this remedy was rejected, and instead Microsoft was directed to release more technical information about how its operating system works and to refrain from retaliating against computer-makers that install software from other companies.

A Brief History of U.S. Antitrust Policy

Table 16.2 provides a brief summary of the history of antitrust policy. The first legislation was the Sherman Antitrust Act of 1890, which made it illegal to monopolize a market or to engage in practices that result in a restraint of trade. Because the act did not specify which practices were illegal, it led to conflicting court rulings.

Many of the ambiguities of the Sherman Act were resolved by the Clayton Act of 1914. The Clayton Act outlawed specific practices that discourage competition, including tying contracts (requiring a consumer who buys one product to buy a second product) and price discrimination that reduces competition (discussed in Chapter 13). The act also outlawed mergers resulting from the purchase of a competitor's stock when such a merger would substantially reduce competition.

More recent legislation clarified and extended antitrust laws. The Robinson–Patman Act of 1936 prohibited predatory pricing. The Celler–Kefauver Act of 1950

TABLE 16.2	

1890 Sherman Act: Made it illegal to monopolize a market or to engage in practices that result in a restraint of trade.

1914 Clayton Act: Outlawed specific practices that discourage competition, including tying contracts, price discrimination for the purpose of reducing competition, and stock-purchase mergers that would substantially reduce competition.

1914 Federal Trade Commission Act: Established to enforce antitrust laws.

1936 Robinson-Patman Act: Prohibited selling products at "unreasonably low prices" with the intent of reducing competition.

1950 Celler-Kefauver Act: Outlawed asset-purchase mergers that would substantially reduce competition.

1980 Hart-Scott-Rodino Act: Extended antitrust legislation to proprietorships and partnerships.

closed a loophole in the Clayton Act by prohibiting one firm from purchasing another firm's physical assets (like buildings and equipment) when the acquisition would reduce competition substantially. The Hart–Scott–Rodino Act of 1980 extended antitrust legislation to proprietorships and partnerships. Before this act, antitrust legislation applied only to corporations.

Two government organizations, the Antitrust Division of the Department of Justice and the Federal Trade Commission, are responsible for initiating actions against individuals or firms that may be violating antitrust laws. The courts have the power to impose penalties on the executives found to be in violation of the laws, including fines and prison sentences. In some cases, the government seeks no penalties but directs the firm to discontinue illegal practices and take other measures to promote competition.

TEST Your Understanding

4. List three types of antitrust policies.
5. Why was the federal government concerned about the merger of Interstate Bakeries and Continental Baking?
6. What are the essential provisions of the new guidelines for corporate mergers?

Deregulation of Airlines and Telecommunications

Up to this point in the chapter, we have discussed government policies that address the problems that result from market concentration. When a monopoly is inevitable, the government can regulate a natural monopoly to prevent excessive prices. When the merger of two firms would increase concentration, the government can prevent the merger and thereby promote competition. In this part of the chapter, we shift the emphasis and look at situations in which government regulations inhibit competition rather than promote it. When a regulation inhibits competition, reversing the course—deregulation—can promote it. We explore the recent deregulation of two markets: air travel and telecommunications. The Airline Deregulation Act of 1978 eliminated entry restrictions and price controls in the market for air travel. The Telecommunications Act of 1996 eliminated most price controls for cable television and established a framework for entry into the markets for cable television service, local telephone service, and Internet service.

Deregulation of Airlines

Consider first the deregulation of airline service.[7] Before 1978, the Civil Aeronautics Board (CAB) regulated interstate air travel by limiting entry into the market and controlling prices. About 90% of the markets were monopolized, and studies indicated that prices were 30% to 50% higher than they would have been in a more competitive environment. The Airline Deregulation Act of 1978 eliminated most of the entry restrictions and price controls, and the CAB eventually disappeared.

Deregulation led to lower prices, which fell by about 28%, on average. By 1998, deregulation had generated $24 billion in savings for passengers. Several factors contributed to the lower prices: competition from incumbent carriers (18% of the savings), competition from Southwest Airlines (31%), competition from other entrants (10%), and improvements in carriers' operating efficiencies (41%). Although prices fell on most routes, about a quarter of routes actually experienced price increases. In general, prices were lower on long routes and higher on short routes. This is not surprising, because the CAB had a policy of setting long-haul fares above average cost and short-haul fares below average cost.

A continuing problem is that many airports are dominated by just one or two airlines. In 1998, there were 12 hub airports where the two largest carriers had at least 85% of the market. At these airports, fares were 23% higher than at other airports with more competition, including low-cost carriers like Southwest Airlines.

Deregulation of Telecommunication Services

Consider next the deregulation of telecommunication services.[8] The Telecommunications Act of 1996 established new rules for firms involved in the transmission of video, voice, and data in order to promote competition in those markets. Several provisions of the act affect the Regional Bell Operating Companies (the Baby Bells) that were formed as a result of the breakup of AT&T in 1982. Here are the most important provisions of the act:

▶ *Local telephone service.* The act opened local telephone service to competition. New firms will now compete with the Baby Bells for local-service customers. In addition, cable TV firms might eventually provide telephone service over their cables.

▶ *Cable TV service.* Price controls for cable TV services were eliminated, and telephone companies will now be allowed to enter the market for cable TV services.

▶ *Long-distance service.* Once there is sufficient competition for local telephone service, the Baby Bells will be allowed to enter the long-distance market.

The challenge in deregulating local telephone service is to develop a set of rules giving competitors access to the copper wires leading into residences. That access is currently controlled by the Baby Bells. After a slow start, there has been some progress in opening up local telephone service to competition, with most of the progress in large cities. As competition spreads, we can expect lower prices for local service, just as we saw with the deregulation of long-distance service in 1984.

Deregulation of Electricity

Consider next the deregulation of electricity. The electricity industry has been regulated as a natural monopoly since its early days. There are three stages of producing electricity: generation in power plants, transmission along high-voltage lines, and distribution to final users along low-voltage lines. The transmission stage is subject to economies of scale because a city can be served by one set of transmission lines from power plants. There are substantial fixed costs associated with laying the transmission lines, so it is sensible to lay one set of lines and regulate the single firm as a natural monopolist. The same economies of scale occur when it comes to the distribution of power to individual users.

Until recently, there were also substantial economics of scale in electricity generation. The minimum efficient scale for power plants was large relative to the size of the markets they served, meaning that a single firm could supply the market more efficiently than several small firms. Under traditional electricity regulation, public and private utilities were responsible for all three phases of electricity production: They generated electricity in their own power plants and then used their own transmission and distribution systems to deliver electricity to consumers. State and local governments granted each utility a monopoly over a particular geographical area and set the price of electricity at a level so the utility earned a reasonable or "fair" accounting profit, including a fair return on capital investment. This is the average-cost pricing we discussed earlier in the chapter. Because utilities were responsible for all three stages of production, there was just one price to control—the retail price charged to consumers.

In the 1990s, there was growing pressure to deregulate the electricity market. Technological innovations reduced the economies of scale in electricity generation, so generation was no longer a true natural monopoly. For example, the minimum efficient scale for combined cycle gas turbine technology (CCGT) is about one-fifth the scale of a traditional power plant. Instead of a single power source for a city, there could be many generators, with competition among alternative producers leading to lower prices. A second factor in the pressure for deregulation was the substantial variation in electricity prices across states. For example, the price was 10 cents per kilowatt hour (kWh) in some northeastern states (Massachusetts, Connecticut, and New York),

6 cents in some central states (Indiana and Wisconsin), and 5 cents in northwestern states (Oregon and Washington). In California, the price was 9.5 cents per kWh. Consumers in high-price states called for deregulation to allow electricity to be transmitted across state lines.

Electricity Deregulation in California

The state of California reformed its electricity regulation program in 1998. Although the plan is often labeled "California's Deregulation Plan," the label is inaccurate because although some regulations were eliminated, others remained in force. In an attempt to foster competition at the generation level, the state's utilities sold off their generating facilities to the highest bidders. The wholesale price of electricity (paid by utilities and other energy retailers to generators) was allowed to fluctuate with market forces. In contrast, the retail price was subject to strict controls: It was rolled back by 10% and was to be maintained at this level for several years.

Two years after the reform program was implemented, the California electricity market was in disarray. Because of growing demand and a delay in getting new generation facilities up and running, utilities did not have enough power to meet demand and were forced to implement rolling blackouts—cutting off the power supply for an hour in alternating areas. The wholesale price for electricity soared above $200 per megawatt hour (MWh) while the retail price remained at about $60 per MWh. Electric utilities lost money on each kilowatt they sold, totaling billions of dollars. By 2001, the retailer/utilities had lost $12 billion, and in early 2001 one of the state's largest utilities, Pacific Gas and Electric, filed for bankruptcy.

The higher wholesale price was caused by a combination of higher fuel costs for generators, a drought that decreased supply from hydroelectric generators in the

Electricity deregulation in California caused rolling power outages. Wholesale prices for electricity were allowed to fluctuate, but retail prices were not.

Pacific Northwest, and price manipulation by generating companies. The objective of the reform plan had been to promote competition in the generating market, but after the utilities sold their power plants to the highest bidders, just a few companies controlled most of the power generated in the state. As we saw earlier in the book, firms in oligopolies have the power to charge a price higher than the competitive price, and there is evidence that's what happened in California. One study suggests that the market price was almost twice the competitive price and that generating companies used a strategy of withholding supply (taking plants off line to create an artificial shortage) to manipulate prices.[9]

The California energy crisis is an example of the "perfect storm" explanation of disasters. Although no one factor that contributed to the problem—an increase in demand for electricity, stagnant supply, rising fuel costs, retail price controls, price manipulation, or the drought in the Pacific Northwest—by itself would have caused major problems, their convergence in 2001 led to an electricity crisis.

Electricity Deregulation in Other U.S. States

In the mid-1990s, Pennsylvania and New York restructured their electricity markets, with both moving toward deregulation. Consumers in both states can now choose from several electricity retailers. Some retailers also generate their own power, whereas others buy power from generating companies and transmit it to business and residential users. Consumers can get on the Internet and type in their zip codes to get a list of alternative suppliers. By April 2001, almost 800,000 Pennsylvanians had selected alternative electricity suppliers.

The early experience with electricity deregulation in the two states is mixed. Prices are lower in Pennsylvania but much higher in New York. Under the New York plan, utilities sold off their generating plants to the highest bidders. The plants were sold to a small number of firms, and the purchase prices were much higher than expected, reflecting the expectations that in the deregulated market with a small number of firms, each could charge a high price. Over a one-year period, the average bill from Con Ed, a generating company in New York, increased by about 38% as a result of higher fuel costs and perhaps some exercise of market power by Con Ed.

It is too early to determine the long-term effects on electricity deregulation. The energy debacle in California has provided some important lessons for policymakers in other states. Many other states are at earlier stages of the deregulation process and may modify their plans to avoid some of the problems generated by the perfect storm in California.

TEST Your Understanding

7. Did the deregulation of the airline industry lead to low prices in all cities?
8. Under what conditions will the Baby Bells be allowed to provide long-distance service?
9. List the factors that contributed to the California energy crisis.

USING THE TOOLS

In this chapter, we've explored some policy issues concerning firms in concentrated industries. We've looked at different government antitrust policies and examined the effects of deregulation on competition and prices. Here are some opportunities to do your own economic analysis.

1. Environmental Costs for Regulated Monopoly

The Bonneville Power Administration (BPA) is a regulated monopoly in the Northwest that uses dozens of hydroelectric dams to generate electricity. Unfortunately, the BPA's dams block the paths of migrating fish, contributing to the decline of several species. Suppose that BPA spends $100 million to make its hydroelectric dams less hazardous for migrating fish. Who will bear the cost of this program?

2. Cost Savings from a Merger

Consider the following statement from a firm that has proposed a merger between two companies: "The two companies could save about $50 million per year by combining our production, marketing, and administrative operations. In other words, we could realize substantial economies of scale. Therefore, the government should allow the merger." In light of the new guidelines concerning mergers, how would you react to this statement?

3. Willingness to Pay for New Airport Gates

Your city is considering an airport expansion project that would increase the number of airport gates and allow additional airlines to serve your city. According to a recent report, the additional competition made possible by the new gates would decrease the average airline fare from $220 to $200 and increase the number of passengers from 400 to 600 per day. The city would borrow money to finance the project, and the daily payment required to pay off the loan (over 20 years) would be $8,100. Is the project worthwhile from a social perspective?

SUMMARY

In this chapter, we've explored public policies for markets with a few dominant firms. In the case of natural monopoly, the government can regulate prices. In other industries, the government uses antitrust policies to affect the number of firms in the market, encouraging competition that leads to lower prices. Here are the main points of the chapter:

1 A natural monopoly occurs when there are large-scale economies in production, so the market can support only one firm.

2 Under an average-cost pricing policy, the regulated price for a natural monopoly is equal to the average cost of production.

3 The government uses antitrust policy to break up some dominant firms, prevent some corporate mergers, and regulate business practices that reduce competition.

4 The modern approach to merger policy uses price data to predict the effects of a merger.

5 In most circumstances, predatory pricing is unprofitable because the monopoly power is costly to acquire and hard to maintain.

6 The deregulation of the airline industry led to more competition and lower prices on average, but higher prices in some markets.

KEY TERMS

average-cost pricing policy, 360   predatory pricing, 367   trust, 362
merger, 363   tie-in sales, 367

PROBLEMS AND DISCUSSION QUESTIONS

1 Consider a regulated natural monopoly with an initial price (equal to average cost) of $3 per unit. Suppose the demand for the monopolist's product increases. What will happen to the price? How does this differ from the effects of an increase in demand for a product produced in a perfectly competitive market?

2 Consider a natural monopolist. Here are some data on its prices and quantities:

Price per unit	$20	$19	$18	$17	$16
Quantity (units)	100	120	140	160	180
Marginal revenue	—	—	—	—	—

   a. Complete the table: For each quantity, use the formula for marginal revenue (from Chapter 13) to compute the marginal revenue.

   b. Draw the monopolist's demand curve and the monopolist's marginal-revenue curve.

   c. Suppose that the monopolist's long-run marginal cost is $9. How much output should the monopolist produce?

3 Consider a market that is initially served by two firms, each of which charges a price of $10 and sells 100 units of the good. The long-run average cost of production is constant at $9 per unit. Suppose a merger would increase the price to $14 and reduce the total quantity sold from 200 to 150. Compute the consumer loss associated with the merger. How does it compare to the increase in profit? What is the net loss from the merger?

4 Consider an allegation that a firm is engaging in predatory pricing. Why might you be skeptical about such a claim?

5 A construction project at your city's airport is nearing completion, and your job is to decide how to use the 10 new gates of the airport. The city is currently served by Gotcha Airlines, which has offered the city $20 million to help cover the cost of the airport construction project. In return, the new gates would be designated for the exclusive use of Gotcha. What trade-offs are associated with accepting Gotcha's offer?

6 As the recently appointed head of the Federal Communications Commission, your job is to develop a set of rules for the use of the cables laid by cable television companies. You must decide whether Internet Service Providers (ISPs) should be able to access the cable company's lines, and, if so, at what price.

MODEL ANSWERS TO QUESTIONS

Chapter-Opening Questions

1 For each firm, the break-even output is about three million subscribers. In 2003, neither firm had reached this level, but both expect to do so by 2005 or 2006.

2 The two firms compete vigorously for shelf space alongside the market leader, Gerber, so eliminating one brand would lead to less competition and higher prices.

3 Deregulation decreased prices on average, but increased concentration in some cities led to higher fares in those cities.

Test Your Understanding

1 Marginal revenue, marginal cost.

2 The firm's demand curve shifts to the left: At each price, the firm sells a smaller quantity.

3 Below.

4 Breaking up monopolies, blocking mergers, and regulating business practices (price fixing, tying, and price discrimination).

5 Scanner data showed that the white breads produced by the two firms were close substitutes. An unregulated merger would have reduced competition and led to higher prices.

6 Companies that are involved in a proposed merger can present evidence that the merger would reduce costs and lead to lower prices, better products, or better service for consumers. If the evidence for this is convincing, the government might allow a merger that reduces the number of firms in a market.

7 No. On average, prices decreased, but travelers to and from some cities that are served by only one or two airlines pay higher prices.

8 Sufficient competition in the market for local telephone service.

9 An increase in demand for electricity, stagnant supply, rising fuel costs, retail price controls, price manipulation, and drought in the Pacific Northwest.

NOTES

1. "The Economics of Antitrust: The Trustbuster's New Tools," *The Economist*, May 2, 1998, pp. 62–64.; *Federal Trade Commission v. Staples, Inc.*, 970 F. Supp. 1066 (D.D.C. 1997, Hogan, J); U.S. Federal Trade Commission, *Promoting Competition, Protecting Consumers: A Plain English Guide to Antitrust Laws* (*http://www.ftc.gov/bc/compguide/index.htm*).

2. Associated Press Wire News, "Satellite Radio Takes Off in U.S.," June 1, 2003.

3. John R. Wilke, "New Antitrust Rules May Ease Path to Mergers," *Wall Street Journal*, April 9, 1997, pp. A3–A4.

4. *Wall Street Journal*, "Baby-Food Makers Heinz, Beech-Nut Call Off Merger Following Court Ruling," April 27, 2001; United State District Court for the District of Columbia, "*Federal Trade Commission v. H. J. Heinz Company*: Memorandum in Support of Plaintiff's Motion for Preliminary Injunction," July 24, 2000.

5. David M. Barton and Roger Sherman, "The Price and Profit Effects of Horizontal Merger: A Case Study," *Journal of Industrial Economics*, vol. 33, December 1984, pp. 165–177.

6. "The Economics of Antitrust: The Trustbuster's New Tools," *The Economist*, May 2, 1998, pp. 62–64.

7. William G. Shepherd and James W. Brock, "Airlines," Chapter 10 in *The Structure of American Industry*, edited by Walter Adams and James W. Brock (Upper Saddle River, NJ: Prentice Hall, 1995); Clifford Winston, "U.S. Industry Adjustment to Economic Deregulation," *Journal of Economic Perspectives*," vol. 12, no. 3, Summer 1998, pp. 89–110; Paul MacAvoy, *Industry Regulation and the Performance of the American Economy* (New York: W. W. Norton, 1992); Alfred E. Kahn, "Airline Deregulation—A Mixed Bag But a Clear Success Nonetheless," *Transportation Law Journal*, vol. 16, 1988, pp. 229–252; Steven A. Morrison, "Airline Service: The Evolution of Competition Since Deregulation," Chapter 6 in *Industry Studies*, 3rd ed., edited by Larry Duetsch (New York: Sharpe, 2002).

8. Susan McMaster, "Telecommunications: Competition and Network Access," Chapter 14 in *Industry Studies*, 3rd ed., edited by Larry Duetsch (New York: Sharpe, 2002).

9. Paul Joskow and Edward Kahn, "A Quantitative Analysis of Pricing Behavior in California's Wholesale Electricity Market During Summer 2000," NBER Working Paper 8157, March 2001.

Part 5

The Labor Market and Income Distribution

Chapter 17

The Labor Market and the Distribution of Income

Chapter 18

Beyond Perfect Competition: Unions, Monopsony, and Imperfect Information

The Demand for Labor

Labor Demand by an Individual Firm
    in the Short Run
Market Demand for Labor in the Short Run
What About Labor Demand in the Long
    Run?
Short-Run versus Long-Run Demand

The Supply of Labor

The Individual Labor-Supply Decisions:
    How Many Hours to Work?
The Market Supply Curve for Labor

Labor Market Equilibrium

Changes in Demand and Supply for Labor
The Market Effects of the Minimum Wage
    Laws
The Trade-Offs from Immigration

**Explaining Differences in Wages
and Income**

Why Do Wages Differ Across
    Occupations?
The Gender Pay Gap
Racial Discrimination
Why Do College Graduates Earn Higher
    Wages?

The Distribution of Income

Income Distribution Facts
Recent Changes in the Distribution
    of Income
Changes in the Top End of Income
    Distribution: 1920–1998
Using the Tools

The Labor Market and the Distribution of Income

$\mathcal{R}$ecent reports on the earnings of college graduates have made the jobs of college recruiters easier:[1]

▶ In 1972, the typical college graduate earned 43% more than a high-school graduate.

▶ In 2000, the typical college graduate earned 94% more than a high-school graduate.

These facts raise two questions: First, why do college graduates earn so much more than high-school graduates? Second, why did the earnings gap almost double during the last three decades?

U
p to this point in the book, we have discussed the markets for final goods and services. In this chapter, we switch to the market for one of the factors of production, labor. Labor costs are responsible for about three-fourths of production costs, and for most people, labor income is by far the most important source of income. We'll use a model of supply and demand to see how wages are determined and why wages differ between college graduates and high-school graduates, men and women, and people in different occupations. Here are some of the practical questions we answer:

1 If the wage increases, will an individual work more hours or fewer hours?
2 If a worker switches from a relatively safe factory job to a job in a steel mill, by how much will his or her wage increase?
3 Why do women, on average, earn only about 75% as much as men?
4 Why has the distribution of income become more unequal in the last 30 years?

The Demand for Labor

We can use supply and demand curves to show how wages are determined and show how changes in the labor market affect wages and employment. We'll start with the demand side of the labor market, looking first at how an individual firm can use the key principles of economics to decide how many workers to hire.

The demand for labor and other productive inputs is different from the demand for consumer products such as stereos, books, haircuts, and pizza. Firms use workers to produce the products demanded by consumers, and so economists say that labor demand is a "derived demand." That is, it is determined by or derived from the demand for the products produced by workers. As we'll see in this chapter, the demand for labor is determined by the demand for consumer products and the price of those products.

Labor Demand by an Individual Firm in the Short Run

Consider a perfectly competitive firm that produces rubber balls. Because this firm is perfectly competitive, it takes the price of its output and the prices of its inputs as given. Because it hires a tiny fraction of the workers in the labor market, it takes the market wage as given and can hire as many workers as it wants at that wage. In addition, the firm produces a tiny fraction of the rubber balls sold in the market, so it takes the price of its output as given. Let's say the price of rubber balls is $0.50.

Consider the firm's hiring decision in the short run, defined as the period during which at least one input—for example, its factory—cannot be changed. We can use two of the key principles of economics to explain the firm's hiring decision. Recall the marginal principle:

MARGINAL *Principle*

Increase the level of an activity if its marginal benefit exceeds its marginal cost, but reduce the level if the marginal cost exceeds the marginal benefit. If possible, pick the level at which the marginal benefit equals the marginal cost.

The firm will pick the quantity of labor at which the marginal benefit of labor equals the marginal cost of labor. It can hire as many workers as it wants at the market wage, so the marginal cost of labor equals the hourly wage. If the wage is $8 per hour, the extra cost associated with one more hour of labor—the marginal cost—is $8, regardless of how many workers the firm hires.

What is the marginal benefit of labor? The firm hires labor to produce balls, so the marginal benefit equals the monetary value of the balls produced with an additional hour of labor. Table 17.1 shows how to compute the marginal benefit associated with different quantities of labor. The first two columns show the relationship between the number of workers and the quantity of balls produced. Recall the principle of diminishing returns:

Principle OF DIMINISHING RETURNS

Suppose that output is produced with two or more inputs and we increase one input while holding the other inputs fixed. Beyond some point—called the point of diminishing returns—output will increase at a decreasing rate.

TABLE 17.1 Using the Marginal Principle to Make a Labor Decision

Number of Workers	Balls per Hour	Marginal Product of Labor	Price per Ball	Marginal Revenue Product of Labor (*MRP*)	Marginal Cost when Wage = $8
1	26	26	$0.50	$13	$8
2	50	24	0.50	$12	$8
3	72	22	0.50	$11	$8
4	92	20	0.50	$10	$8
5	**108**	**16**	**0.50**	**$ 8**	**$8**
6	120	12	0.50	$ 6	$8
7	128	8	0.50	$ 4	$8
8	130	2	0.50	$ 1	$8

To simplify matters, we'll assume diminishing returns start to occur with the second worker, but as we saw earlier in the book, the **marginal product of labor**, the change in output from one additional unit of labor, typically rises for the first few workers and then eventually decreases. As shown in the third column of Table 17.1, marginal product of labor decreases as the number of workers increases, from 26 for the first worker, to 24 for the second worker, and so on.

The marginal benefit of labor equals the **marginal-revenue product of labor (MRP)**, defined as the extra revenue generated by one additional worker. To compute the *MRP*, we multiply the marginal product of labor by the price of output ($0.50 per ball in this example):

$$MRP = \text{marginal product} \times \text{price of output}$$

Figure 17.1 shows the marginal-revenue product curve. Because the marginal product drops as the number of workers increases, the *MRP* curve is negatively sloped, falling from $11 for the third worker (point *n*) to $8 for the fifth worker (point *m*), and so on.

A firm can use its *MRP* curve to decide how much labor to hire at a particular wage. In Figure 17.1, the marginal-cost curve is horizontal at the market wage ($8). The perfectly competitive firm takes the wage as given, so the marginal-cost curve is also the labor-supply curve faced by the firm. The marginal principle is satisfied at point *m*, where the marginal cost equals the marginal-revenue product. The firm will hire 5 workers because for the first 5 workers, the marginal benefit (the *MRP*) is greater than or equal to the marginal cost (the $8 wage). It would not be sensible to hire another worker because the additional revenue from the sixth worker ($6) would be less than the $8 additional cost of that worker. If the wage increases to $11, the firm will satisfy the marginal principle at point *n*, hiring only 3 workers.

The *MRP* curve is also the firm's **short-run demand curve for labor**, which shows the relationship between the wage and the quantity of labor demanded in the

Marginal product of labor
The change in output from one additional unit of labor

Marginal-revenue product of labor (MRP)
The extra revenue generated from one more unit of labor; *MRP* is equal to the price of output times the marginal product of labor.

Short-run demand curve for labor
A curve showing the relationship between the wage and the quantity of labor demanded over the short run, the period when the firm cannot change its production facility.

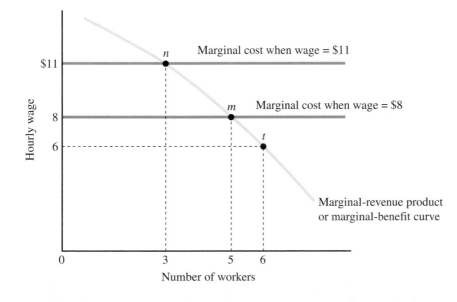

FIGURE 17.1

The Marginal Principle and the Firm's Demand for Labor
Using the marginal principle, the firm picks the quantity of workers at which the marginal benefit (the marginal revenue product of labor) equals the marginal cost (the wage). The firm's short-run demand curve for labor is the marginal revenue product curve.

short run, the period when the firm cannot change its production facility. The demand curve answers the following question: At each wage, how many hours of labor does the firm want to hire? We've already used the *MRP* curve to answer this question for two different wages ($11 and $8), and we can do the same for any other wage. Because the *MRP* curve is a marginal-benefit curve, and the firm uses the marginal principle to decide how much labor to hire, the *MRP* curve is the same as the firm's demand curve for labor. If you pick a wage, the *MRP* curve tells you exactly how much labor the firm will demand at that wage.

What sort of changes would cause the demand curve to shift? To draw the labor-demand curve, we fix the price of the output and the productivity of workers. Therefore, an increase in the price of the output will increase the *MRP* of workers, shifting the entire demand curve for labor to the right: At each wage, the firm will hire more workers. This is shown in Figure 17.2. An increase in the price of balls shifts the labor-demand curve to the right. At a wage of $8, the firm hires 7 workers instead of 5. Similarly, if workers become more productive, the increase in the marginal product of labor will increase the *MRP* and shift the demand curve to the right. Conversely, a decrease in price or labor productivity would shift the demand curve to the left.

Market Demand for Labor in the Short Run

To draw the short-run market demand curve for labor, we add the labor demands of all the firms that use a particular type of labor. In the simplest case, all firms are identical, and we simply multiply the number of firms by the quantity of labor demanded by the typical firm. If there were 100 firms and each hired 5 workers at a wage of $8, the market demand for labor would be 500 workers. Similarly, if the typical firm hired 3 workers at a wage of $11, the market demand would be 300 workers.

FIGURE 17.2

An Increase in the Price of Output Shifts the Labor-Demand Curve

An increase in the price of the good produced by workers increases the marginal revenue product at each quantity of workers, shifting the demand curve to the right. At each wage, the firm will demand more workers. For example, at a wage of $8, the demand for labor increases from 5 workers (point *m*) to 7 workers (point *z*).

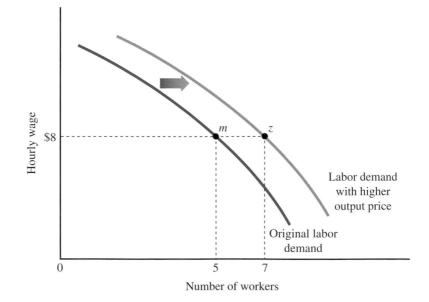

What About Labor Demand in the Long Run?

Recall that in the long run, firms can enter or leave the market and firms already in the market can change all of their inputs, including their production facilities. The **long-run demand curve for labor** shows the relationship between the wage and the quantity of labor demanded over the long run when the number of firms in the market can change and firms in the market can modify their production facilities.

Although there are no diminishing returns in the long run, the market demand curve is still negatively sloped. As the wage increases, the quantity of labor demanded decreases for two reasons:

▶ *The* **output effect**. An increase in the wage will increase the cost of producing balls, and firms will pass on at least part of the higher labor cost to their consumers: Prices will increase. According to the law of demand, firms will sell fewer balls at the higher price, so they will need less of all inputs, including labor.
▶ *The* **input-substitution effect**. An increase in the wage will cause the firm to substitute other inputs for labor. At a wage of $4, it may not be sensible to use much machinery in the ball factory, but at a wage of $20, it may be sensible to mechanize the factory, using more machinery and fewer workers.

The output effect reinforces the input-substitution effect, so the market demand curve is negatively sloped.

The notion of input substitution applies to other labor markets as well. For the most graphic examples of factor substitution, we can travel from a developed country such as the United States, Canada, France, Germany, or Japan to a less-developed country in South America, Africa, or Asia. Wages are much lower in the less-developed countries, so production tends to be more labor-intensive. In other words, labor is less costly relative to machinery and equipment, so labor is substituted for these other inputs. Here are some examples:

▶ Mining. U.S. firms use huge earth-moving equipment to mine for minerals, while many firms in less-developed countries use thousands of workers, digging by hand.
▶ Furniture. Firms in developed countries manufacture furniture with sophisticated machinery and equipment, while many firms in less-developed countries make furniture by hand.
▶ Accounting. Accountants in developed countries use computers and sophisticated software programs, while some accountants in less-developed countries use simple calculators and ledger paper.

Short-Run versus Long-Run Demand

How does the short-run demand curve for labor compare to the long-run demand curve? There is less flexibility in the short run because firms cannot enter or leave the market and they cannot modify their production facilities. As a result, the demand for labor is less elastic in the short run. That means the short-run demand curve is steeper than the long-run demand curve. You may recall that we used the same logic to explain

Long-run demand curve for labor
A curve showing the relationship between the wage and the quantity of labor demanded over the long run, when the number of firms in the market can change and firms can modify their production facilities.

Output effect
The change in the quantity of labor demanded resulting from a change in the quantity of output produced.

Input-substitution effect
The change in the quantity of labor demanded resulting from an increase in the price of labor relative to the price of other inputs.

why the short-run supply curve for a product (plain cotton T-shirts) was steeper than the long-run supply curve for the product.

TEST Your Understanding

1. The owner of a professional basketball team is considering hiring a new player for $3 million per year. Under what circumstances would it be sensible to hire the player?
2. Complete the statement with "increase" or "decrease": According to the output effect, a decrease in the wage will _____ production costs, so the price of output will _____. The quantity of output produced will _____, so the demand for labor will _____.
3. Explain the input-substitution effect associated with a decrease in the wage.

The Supply of Labor

The labor-supply curve answers the following question: How many hours of labor will be supplied at each wage? When we speak of a labor market, we are referring to the market for a specific occupation in a specific geographical area. Consider the supply for nurses in the city of Florence. The supply question is, How many hours of nursing services will be supplied at each wage? To answer that question, we must think about how many nurses are in the city and how many hours each nurse works.

The Individual Labor-Supply Decision: How Many Hours to Work?

Let's start with an individual's decision about how many hours to work. The decision to work is a decision to sacrifice some leisure time for money: Each hour of work reduces leisure time by one hour. Therefore, the demand for leisure is the flip side of the supply of labor. The price of leisure time is the income sacrificed for each hour of leisure, that is, the hourly wage.

We know from Chapter 4 that an increase in the price of a good has two effects: A substitution effect and an income effect. An increase in the wage—the price of leisure—has two effects on the demand for leisure: The **substitution effect** and the **income effect**.

Consider first the substitution effect. The worker faces a trade-off between leisure time and consumer goods such as music, books, food, and entertainment. For each hour of leisure time Leah takes, she loses one hour of work time, and her income drops by an amount equal to the wage. Therefore, she has less money to spend on consumer goods. For example, if the wage is $8 per hour, each hour of leisure decreases the amount of income available to spend on consumer goods by $8. When the wage increases to, say, $10, Leah will sacrifice more income—and consumer goods—for each hour of leisure she takes. Given the larger sacrifice of consumer goods per hour of leisure time, she will demand less leisure. That means that she will work more hours

Substitution effect for leisure demand
The change in leisure time resulting from a change in the wage (the price of leisure) relative to the price of other goods.

Income effect for leisure demand
The change in leisure time resulting from a change in real income caused by a change in the wage.

and earn more money for consumer goods. In other words, as the wage increases, she will substitute income—and the consumer goods it buys—for leisure time.

Consider next the income effect of an increase in the wage. For most people, leisure is a normal good in the sense that the demand for leisure increases as real income increases. An increase in the wage increases Leah's real income in the sense that she can afford more of all goods, including leisure time. Suppose Leah has a total of 100 hours per week to divide between leisure and work. At a wage of $10, she works 36 hours and has 64 hours of leisure. She also earns $360 ($10 per hour times 36 hours of work) and spends that amount on consumer goods. If her wage increases to $15, her real income increases because she can have more consumer goods and more leisure time. For example, if she worked only 30 hours, she could buy $450 worth of consumer goods ($15 per hour × 30 hours) and have 70 hours of leisure (100 hours per week − 30 hours of work). The increase in real income causes Leah to consume more of all normal goods, including leisure time. The increase in real income causes her to demand more leisure and supply less labor.

As you can see, in the labor market the income and substitution effects of an increase in wages have opposite results: The substitution effect decreases the desired leisure time, while the income effect increases the desired leisure time. Therefore, we can't predict whether an increase in the wage will cause Leah to demand more leisure time (supply less labor) or less leisure (supply more labor).

A simple example will show why we can't predict a worker's response to an increase in the wage. Suppose each nurse initially works 36 hours per week at an hourly wage of $10 and the wage increases to $12. Here are three reasonable responses to the higher wage:

1 Lester works fewer hours. If Lester works 30 hours instead of 36 hours, he gets 6 hours of extra leisure time and still earns the same income per week ($360 = 30 hours × $12 per hour).

2 Sam works the same number of hours. If Sam continues to work 36 hours per week, he gets an additional $72 of income ($2 per hour × 36 hours) and the same amount of leisure time.

3 Maureen works more hours. If Maureen works 43 hours instead of 36 hours, she sacrifices 7 hours of leisure time but earns a total of $516, compared to only $360 at a wage of $10 per hour.

Empirical studies of the labor market confirm that each of these responses is reasonable. When the wage increases, some people work more, others work less, and others work about the same amount.[2] In most labor markets, the average number of hours per worker doesn't change very much as the wage changes because the increases in work hours from people like Maureen are nearly offset by decreases in work hours from people like Lester.

The Market Supply Curve for Labor

Now that we know how individual workers respond to changes in wages, we're ready to consider the supply side of the labor market. The **market supply curve for labor** shows the relationship between the wage and the quantity of labor

Market supply curve for labor
A curve showing the relationship between the wage and the quantity of labor supplied.

FIGURE 17.3

Supply, Demand, and Labor Market Equilibrium

At the market equilibrium (point *e*, with wage = $15 per hour and quantity = 16,000 hours), the quantity supplied equals the quantity demanded, so there is neither excess demand for labor nor excess supply of labor.

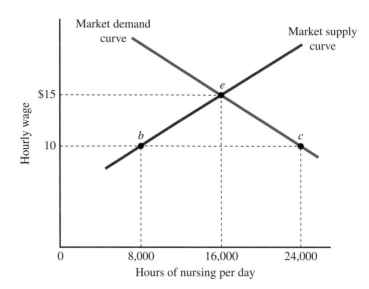

supplied. In Figure 17.3, the market supply curve for labor is positively sloped, consistent with the law of supply: The higher the wage (the price of labor), the larger the quantity of labor supplied. An increase in the wage affects the quantity of nursing supplied in three ways:

1 Hours worked per employee. When the wage increases, some nurses will work more hours, while others will work fewer hours, and others will work the same number of hours. We don't know for certain whether the average number of work hours will increase, decrease, or stay the same, but the change in the average number of hours worked is likely to be relatively small.

2 Occupational choice. An increase in the nursing wage will cause some workers to switch from other occupations to nursing and motivate more new workers to pick nursing over other occupations.

3 Migration. Some nurses in other cities will move to Florence to earn the higher wages offered there.

The second and third effects reinforce one another, so an increase in the wage causes movement upward along the market supply curve. If the wage of Florence nurses increases from $10 to $15 per hour, the quantity of nurses supplied increases from 8,000 hours per day (point *b*) to 16,000 hours per day (point *e*). Although individual workers may not work more hours as the wage increases, the supply curve is positively sloped because an increase in the wage changes workers' occupational choices and causes migration.

Another decision relevant for labor supply is whether a person will be in the workforce at all. Some people choose alternative pursuits, including education, leisure, and raising families. For a discussion of workers' retirement decisions and the impact of early retirement on European societies, read, "A Closer Look: The Economics of Not Working."

A CLOSER LOOK

The Economics of Not Working

In the last 30 years, the amount of time spent in retirement has increased dramatically.[3] People are retiring at earlier ages and living longer. In Britain, only about a quarter of people aged 60–64 work, down from about three-quarters 30 years ago. Over the same period, the life expectancy at age 60 increased from 15 years to 20 years. In the European Union, only 39% of people aged 55–64 are working, compared to about three-fourths of people aged 25–54.

This is great news for older folks, but it is causing a strain on systems that support retirees. If current trends continue, the share of national income spent by developed countries to support their retirees will increase from about 15% to 22%, and people in the workforce will pay higher taxes. One simple solution would be to increase the retirement age, matching longer life spans with more time in the workforce. Compared to 30 years ago, the typical person today works 5 fewer years because of earlier retirement but earns 10 more years of retirement income (5 years from earlier retirement and 5 years from a longer life span). The Prime Minister of France suggests

that to prevent a growing financial burden, the French must (a) extend working life by 6 years, (b) raise contributions to retirement accounts by half, or (c) reduce benefits by a third. Another solution would be to encourage workers to save for their own retirement years, which would eventually reduce the tax burden on the general public.

Response to a Wage Cut?

Economic Puzzle

Elise is the absentee owner of a sweater factory that employs 50 workers. After hearing that changes in wages cause nearly offsetting changes in the number of hours that people work—leaving total hours unchanged—she decides to cut wages in her sweater factory by 10%. She expected that the total hours worked and total output would remain about the same. Much to her surprise, the total output of her factory dropped by 90%. What happened?

The key to solving this puzzle is that workers respond to a wage cut in two ways. First, they can work more or fewer hours, and we know that, on average, they will work about the same number of hours. Second, they can quit and go to work for another firm. In a labor market with many potential employers, a firm that cuts its wage below the market wage will lose most if not all of its workers. ■

Labor Market Equilibrium

We're ready to put supply and demand together to think about equilibrium in the labor market. A market equilibrium is a situation in which there is no pressure to change the price of a good or service. Figure 17.3 shows the equilibrium in the market for nurses. The supply curve intersects the demand curve at point *e*, so the equilibrium wage is $15 per hour and the equilibrium quantity is 16,000 hours of nursing per day. At this wage, there is neither an excess demand for labor nor an excess supply of labor, so the market has reached an equilibrium.

Changes in Demand and Supply for Labor

How would a change in the demand for nurses affect the equilibrium wage of nurses? We know from Chapter 4 that a change in demand causes the equilibrium price and the equilibrium quantity to move in the same direction: An increase in demand increases the equilibrium price and quantity, whereas a decrease in demand decreases the equilibrium price and quantity. For example, suppose that the demand for medical care increases. Nurses help provide medical care, so an increase in the quantity of medical care demanded will shift the demand curve for nurses to the right: At each wage, firms will demand more hours of nursing services. As shown in Figure 17.4, an increase in demand increases the equilibrium wage and the equilibrium quantity of nursing services.

How would a change in supply of nurses affect the equilibrium wage of nurses? We know from Chapter 4 that a change in supply causes price and quantity to move in opposite directions: An increase in supply decreases the equilibrium price but increases the equilibrium quantity, whereas a decrease in supply increases the equilibrium price but decreases the equilibrium quantity. Suppose a new television program makes nursing look like an attractive occupation, causing a large number of youngsters to become nurses rather than accountants, lawyers, or doctors. The supply curve for nurses will shift to the right: At each wage, more nursing hours will be supplied. The equilibrium wage will decrease, and the equilibrium quantity will increase.

FIGURE 17.4

The Market Effects of an Increase in Demand for Labor

An increase in the demand for nursing services shifts the demand curve to the right, moving the equilibrium from point *e* to point *f*. The equilibrium wage increases from $15 to $17 per hour, and the equilibrium quantity increases from 16,000 hours to 19,000 hours.

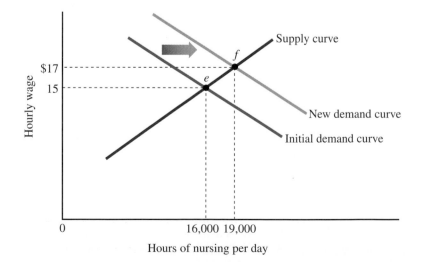

The Market Effects of the Minimum Wage Laws

We can use the model of the labor market to show how various public policies like the federally mandated minimum wage affect total employment. In 2001, the federal minimum wage was $5.15 per hour. Figure 17.5 shows the effects of a minimum wage on the market for restaurant workers. The market equilibrium is shown by point *e*: The supply of restaurant workers equals demand at a wage of $4.70 and a quantity of 50,000 worker hours per day. Suppose a minimum wage is established at $5.15 per hour. At this wage, the quantity of labor demanded is only 49,000 hours (point *d* on the demand curve). In other words, the minimum wage decreases the quantity of labor used by restaurants by 1,000 hours per day.

What are the trade-offs associated with the minimum wage? From the perspectives of restaurant workers and restaurant diners, there is good news and bad news:

▶ Good news for some restaurant workers. Some workers keep their jobs and receive a higher wage ($5.15 per hour instead of $4.70 per hour).
▶ Bad news for some restaurant workers. Some workers lose their jobs. If the typical workday for restaurant workers is five hours, the loss of 1,000 hours of restaurant work per day translates into a loss of 200 jobs.
▶ Bad news for diners. The increase in the wage increases the cost of producing restaurant meals, increasing the price of meals.

There are winners and losers from the minimum wage: Workers who keep their jobs gain at the expense of other workers and at the expense of diners. A recent study suggests that a 10% increase in the minimum wage decreases the number of minimum-wage jobs by about 1%.[4]

In recent years, there has been growing concern in the United States about poor working conditions and low wages for foreign workers who produce products for U.S. consumers. For a discussion of this issue, read "A Closer Look: Foreign Sweatshops and Industry Codes of Conduct."

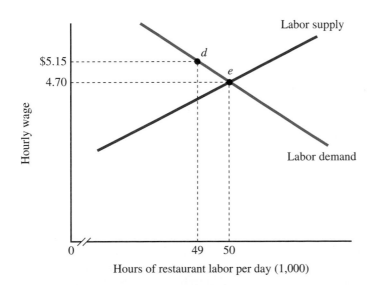

Hours of restaurant labor per day (1,000)

FIGURE 17.5

The Market Effects of a Minimum Wage

The market equilibrium is shown by point e. The wage is $4.70 per hour, and the quantity of labor is 50,000 labor hours per day. A minimum wage of $5.15 per hour decreases the quantity of labor demanded to 49,000 hours per day. Although some workers receive a higher wage, others lose their jobs or work fewer hours.

A CLOSER LOOK

Foreign Sweatshops and Industry Codes of Conduct

Several widely publicized reports have documented poor working conditions and low wages in foreign factories that produce shoes, clothing, and toys for U.S. corporations.[6] In 1996, a report revealed that part of Wal-Mart's Kathie Lee Collection was produced in Honduras by people working 20 hours per day for $0.31 per hour. Similar reports suggested that goods sold by Nike, Disney, and Mattel were produced in overseas sweatshops. Some human-rights activists have organized protests to publicize what they consider unethical business practices and have organized consumer boycotts.

The corporations have responded to the uproar by monitoring the firms that produce their goods and establishing codes of conduct for foreign suppliers. The Council on Economic Priorities, an interest group in New York, inspects workplaces and awards the "Social Accountability 8000" to businesses that meet its criteria for wages and working conditions. The Apparel Industry Partnership, a group that includes social activists and apparel firms, is developing a code of conduct for apparel producers. The group was pleased to see the results of a survey suggesting that three-fourths of America's shoppers would be willing to pay higher prices for clothes and shoes bearing a "No Sweat" label. Some companies have hired accounting firms such as PriceWaterhouseCoopers to audit their foreign suppliers. On campus, the United Students Against Sweatshops is developing a code of conduct for companies that produce products bearing university logos. The efforts to monitor the labor practices of foreign suppliers raise several questions:

▶ The improvement of working conditions and higher wages will increase the cost of producing the products. By how much will prices increase?

Corporations with overseas production facilities responded to the uproar over sweatshops by monitoring the foreign firms that produce the goods for the corporations and establishing codes of conduct for foreign suppliers.

▶ How much are consumers really willing to pay for "No Sweat" products?
▶ How many customers will firms selling "No Sweat" products lose to firms that don't meet the codes of conduct?
▶ How many apparel workers will lose their jobs?

The Trade-offs from Immigration

Since about 1850, international migration has played an important role in labor markets. In the first wave of immigration, from 1850 to 1913, over one million people migrated to the Americas each year. Most of the immigrants were from European countries. After several decades of war and economic depressions, massive immigration resumed in 1945. This time, most of the immigrants were from less-developed countries.

Immigration creates winners and losers within the economy. The increase in the supply of labor decreases wages for the native workers who have the same skill level as the immigrants. Because the average U.S. immigrant has less education and earns less income than the average native, immigrants compete with low-skill natives, decreasing their wages. On the benefit side, the decrease in the wages of low-skill labor decreases production costs and product prices, so consumers benefit. In general, we expect low-skill workers to lose as a result of immigration because the lower wages will dominate the benefits of lower consumer prices. In contrast, we expect high-skill workers to benefit from lower prices.

In 1994, economist George Borjas found that the net effect of immigration to the United States was positive, consistent with the idea that exchange increases efficiency and the size of the overall economic pie.[5] Immigration decreases the wages of low-skilled natives by $133 billion, but it generates benefits for consumers and firms totaling $140 billion. The net gain to the economy is $7 billion per year, about one tenth of 1% of total income. Immigration also changes how the economic pie is sliced, with high-skill workers gaining at the expense of low-skill workers. These conflicting effects lead to spirited debates over immigration policy.

TEST Your Understanding

4. Your objective is to earn exactly $120 per week. If your wage decreases from $6 to $4 per hour, how will you respond?
5. Each worker in a certain occupation works exactly 40 hours per week, regardless of the wage. Does this mean that the market supply curve for the occupation is vertical (a fixed quantity, regardless of the wages)?
6. Complete the following: A decrease in the supply of nurses will _____ the equilibrium wage and _____ the equilibrium quantity of nursing services.

Explaining Differences in Wages and Income

Now that we know how the equilibrium wage for a particular occupation is determined, we're ready to explain why wages vary from one job to another. Let's think about why some occupations pay more than others, why women earn less than men, and why college graduates earn more than high-school graduates.

Why Do Wages Differ Across Occupations?

There is substantial variation in wages across occupations. Most professional athletes earn more than medical doctors, who earn more than college professors, who earn more than janitors. We'll see that the wage for a particular occupation will be high if the supply of workers in that occupation is small relative to the demand for those workers.

This is shown in Figure 17.6, where the supply curve intersects the demand curve at a high wage. The supply of workers in a particular occupation could be small for four reasons:

1   *Few people with the required skills.* To play professional baseball, people must be able to hit balls thrown at them at about 90 miles per hour. The few people who have this skill are paid a lot of money because baseball owners compete with one another for skillful players, bidding up the wage. The same logic applies to other professional athletes, musicians, and actors. The few people who have the skills required for these occupations are paid high wages.

2   *High training costs.* The skills required for some occupations can only be acquired through education and training. For example, the skills that are required of a medical doctor can only be acquired in medical school, and legal skills can only be acquired in law school. If it is costly to acquire these skills, a relatively small number of people will become skilled, and they will receive high wages. The higher wage compensates workers for their training costs.

3   *Undesirable job features.* Some occupations are dangerous, and only a relatively small number of people are willing to work under these conditions. The workers with the greatest risk of losing their lives on the job are lumberjacks, boilermakers, taxicab drivers, and mine workers. The workers who choose dangerous occupations receive high wages, so they are compensated for the danger associated with their jobs. Each year, one in 10,000 steelworkers is killed on the job. To compensate for the higher risk of getting killed on the job, steelworkers receive a wage premium of 3.7%, or about $700 more per year than they would in another occupation, given their skills and education.[7] The same logic applies to other undesirable job features. For example, wages are higher for jobs that are stressful or dirty or that force people to work at odd hours.

4   *Artificial barriers to entry.* As we'll see in the next chapter, government and professional licensing boards restrict the number of people in certain occupations, and labor unions restrict their membership. These supply restrictions increase wages.

FIGURE 17.6

The Equilibrium Wage when Labor Supply Is Low Relative to Demand

If supply is low relative to demand—because few people have the skills, training costs are high, or the job is undesirable—the equilibrium wage will be high.

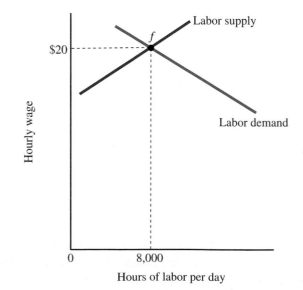

The Gender Pay Gap

Why do women, on average, earn less than men? In the United States, the typical woman earns about 75% as much as the typical man. The gender gap is smaller in European nations but much larger in Japan. An important factor in the gender gap is the concentration of women in occupations that have low wages. Given the distribution of men and women in different occupations, about half of female workers would have to change occupations to achieve equal gender representation in all occupations.[8]

A recent study explored several factors that contribute to the gender pay gap.[9] The study observed a gap of about 20% among workers aged 26–34. The study identified four factors that contribute to the gender gap.

▶ *Difference in worker skills and productivity.* More productive workers receive higher wages. On average, women have less education and work experience, so they receive lower wages. The study concluded that lower productivity is the most important factor in the gender gap.

▶ *Differences in occupational preferences.* Wages vary across occupations: Clerical and service occupations receive lower wages than craft and professional occupations. Compared to men, women express stronger preferences for low-wage occupations such as clerical and service occupations, and weaker preferences for some high-wage occupations such as craft and operator occupations. In contrast, women have slightly stronger preferences for high-wage professional and technical occupations. On balance, the general orientation of women toward low-wage occupations contributes to the gender gap.

▶ *Occupational discrimination.* Given the variation in wages across occupations, if employers have a bias against hiring women for high-paying occupations, women will receive lower wages. The study shows that on average, women are less successful than men in attaining their desired occupations, and this occupational discrimination by employers explains between 7% and 25% of the gender gap.

▶ *Wage discrimination.* If employers pay women less than their equally productive male counterparts, women's wages will be lower. The results of the study on this issue are mixed, with some evidence that wage discrimination is a significant factor in the gender pay gap.

The general conclusion of the study is that differences in productivity and occupational status are the most important factors in the gender pay gap. The relatively large number of women in low-paying occupations results both from the occupational preferences of women and employer discrimination that inhibits occupational attainment for women.

Racial Discrimination

What about differences in earnings by race? In 1995, African American males who worked full time earned 73% as much as their white counterparts earned, while African American females earned 86% as much as their white counterparts. Hispanic males earned 62% as much as white males, while Hispanic females earned 73% as much as white females.[10] For both males and females, part of the earnings gap is caused by differences in productivity: On average, whites have more education and work experience, so they are paid higher wages. Part of the wage gap is caused by racial discrimination. Some African American and Hispanic workers are paid lower wages for similar jobs, and others are denied opportunities to work in some high-paying jobs.

How much of the earnings gap is caused by discrimination? A recent study suggests that racial discrimination decreases the wages of African American men by about 13%.[11] Another study[12] shows that these earnings differences have decreased over the last few decades and that the differences are now small enough that "most of the disparity in earnings between blacks and whites in the labor market of the 1990s is due to the differences in skills they bring to the market, and not to discrimination within the labor market." The differences in skills brought to the labor market are caused by a number of factors, including past discrimination that has inhibited the acquisition of job skills and differences in educational opportunities. For example, in urban areas, about one-third of African American high-school students have above-

A CLOSER LOOK   Racial Discrimination in Hiring

Imagine that two recent high-school graduates apply for low-skill jobs advertised in the newspaper. The jobs include waiting tables, dishwashing, and working in warehouses. One man is white and admits to serving 18 months in prison for selling cocaine. The other applicant is an African American man without a criminal record. Which applicant has a greater chance of being called back for a second interview? In a carefully designed experiment with college students posing as job applicants, the white applicant with a criminal record was called back 17% of the time, while the crime-free African American applicant was called back only 14% of the time. In other words, the disadvantage of being African American is roughly equivalent to the disadvantage of spending 18 months in prison.[13]

This experiment in Milwaukee revealed substantial racial discrimination in hiring for low-skill jobs. According to Devah Pager, the researcher who conducted the experiment,

In these low-wage, entry-level markets, race remains a huge barrier. Affirmative-action pressures aren't operating here. Employers don't spend a lot of time screening applicants. They want a quick signal whether the applicant seems suitable. Stereotypes among young black men remain so prevalent and so strong that race continues to serve as a major signal of characteristics of which employers are wary.

In another experiment, economists responded in writing to help-wanted ads in Chicago and in Boston, using hypothetical names that were likely to be identified by employers as either white or African American. Applicants named Greg Kelly or Emily Walsh were 50% more likely to be called for interviews than those named Jamal Jackson or Lakisha Washington. Having a white-sounding name on an application was equivalent to about eight additional years of work experience. The researchers experimented with different resumes for both types of applicants. Adding work experience and computer skills increased the likelihood of interviews by 30% for white-sounding applicants but only 9% for those whose names suggested an African American background.

average scores on reading and math exams, compared to about two-thirds of white students.

Some recent experiments have demonstrated that for participants in the market for low-skill jobs, race matters. Specifically, job applicants who are African American are treated less favorably than whites. For a discussion of two experiments, read "A Closer Look: Racial Discrimination in Hiring."

Why Do College Graduates Earn Higher Wages?

In 1999, the typical college graduate earned 80% more than the typical high-school graduate. There are two explanations for the college premium.

The first explanation is based on supply and demand analysis. A college education provides the skills necessary to enter certain occupations, so a college graduate has more job options than a high-school graduate. Both high-school grads and college grads can fill jobs that require only a high-school education, so the supply of workers for these low-skill jobs is plentiful, and the equilibrium wage for these jobs is low. In contrast, there is a smaller supply of workers for jobs that require a college education, so the wages in these high-skill jobs are higher than the wages for low-skill jobs. This is the **learning effect** of a college education: College students learn the skills required for certain occupations, increasing their human capital.

The second explanation of the college premium requires a different perspective on college and its role in the labor market. Suppose certain skills are required for a particular job, but an employer cannot determine whether a prospective employee has these skills. For example, most managerial jobs require the employee to manage time efficiently, but it is impossible for an employer to determine whether a prospective employee is a good manager of time. Suppose that these skills are also required to complete a college degree. For example, to get passing grades in all your classes, you must be able to use your time efficiently. When you get your college degree, firms will conclude that you have some of the skills they require, so they may hire you instead of an equally skilled high-school graduate. This is the **signaling effect** of a college education: People who complete college provide a signal to employers about their skills. This second explanation suggests that colleges simply provide a testing ground where students can reveal their skills to potential employers.

Over the last three decades, this wage gap, or "college premium," has almost doubled. The most important factor in doubling the college premium is technological change. Changes in technology have increased the demand for college graduates relative to the demand for other workers. In all sectors of the economy, firms are switching to sophisticated machinery and equipment that require highly skilled workers. Consequently, the share of jobs that require a college education has increased steadily, increasing the demand for college graduates. Of course, the supply of college graduates has increased too, but not by as much as demand. Because the increase in demand is large relative to the increase in supply, the wages of college graduates have increased. Another factor in the growing college premium is the pace of technological change. Workers with more education can more easily learn new skills and new jobs, so firms are willing to pay more for college graduates.

Learning effect
The increase in a person's wage resulting from the learning of skills required for certain occupations.

Signaling effect
The increase in a person's wage resulting from the signal of productivity provided by completing college.

TEST Your Understanding

7. Complete the statement with "demand" or "supply": The wage for a particular occupation will be low if _____ is small relative to _____.
8. The wages of police officers vary from city to city. What could explain the wage differences?
9. In some countries, it is customary to tip restaurant waiters. What are the implications for the wages paid to waiters?

The Distribution of Income

In 2001, the median household income in the United States was $42,228, but this simple average tells only part of the income story. Some households earn much more income, and others earn much less. In this part of the chapter, we'll discuss the extent of income inequality in the United States and explore some of the reasons why the households with the highest income are receiving a larger and larger share of total income.

Income Distribution Facts

Table 17.2 shows the distribution of income without considering the effects of taxes or noncash transfers such as food stamps, public housing, or medical care. To compute the numbers in the table, we take four steps.

1 Rank the nation's households according to income: The household with the highest income is at the top of the list, and the household with the lowest income is at the bottom of the list.
2 Divide the households into five groups, or "quintiles": The lowest fifth includes the poorest 20% of households (the lowest 20% of the list), the second fifth is the next poorest 20%, and so on. The second column of the table shows the income ranges for each of the five groups: The lowest fifth includes households with income up to $17,970, the second fifth includes households with income between $17,971 and $33,314, and so on.

TABLE 17.2

Shares of Income Earned by Different U.S. Groups, 2001

Income Group	Income Range	Percent of Total Income
Lowest fifth	0 to $17,970	3.5%
Second fifth	$17,971 to $33,314	8.7
Middle fifth	$33,315 to $53,000	14.6
Fourth fifth	$53,001 to $83,500	23.0
Highest fifth	$83,501 and greater	50.1

Source: *Money Income in the United States: 2001*, Table A-2.

3 Compute each group's income by adding up the income received by all the households in the group.

4 Compute each group's percentage of total income (the number in the third column of the table) by dividing the group's income by the nation's total income.

What explains the differences in the incomes of U.S. households? There are five key factors:

1 Differences in labor skills and effort. Some people have better labor skills than others, so they earn higher wages. Labor skills are determined by innate ability and education. In addition, some people work longer hours or at more demanding jobs, so they earn more income.

2 Inheritances. Some people inherit large sums of money and earn income by investing this money.

3 Luck and misfortune. Some people are luckier than others in investing their money, starting a business, or picking an occupation. Among the unlucky people are those who develop health problems that make it difficult to earn income.

4 Discrimination. Some people are paid lower wages or have limited opportunities for education and work because of their race or gender.

5 Redistribution programs. The government uses various redistribution programs like welfare and Social Security to give money to individual households. These cash transfers are included in the computations of income in Table 17.2.

How does government policy affect the distribution of income? In the absence of government cash transfers, the share of the lowest quintile would be 0.90 %, while the share of the highest quintile would be 55.6 %. Adding cash transfers increases the share of the lowest quintile to 3.5%. Adding in taxes (higher for the rich) and the value of noncash transfers (higher for the poor) increases the share of the lowest quintile to 4.7%, while the share of the highest quintile drops to 46.5%. In other words, government transfer and tax policies reduce income inequality.

Recent Changes in the Distribution of Income

Table 17.3 shows the changes in the distribution of income between 1970 and 2001. The share of the top fifth rose from 43.3% to 50.1%, while the share of every other group dropped. By historical standards, these changes in the distribution of income were very rapid. What caused these changes in the distribution in income?

It appears that the most important reason for growing inequality is what labor economists call an increase in the demand for skill.[14] In the labor market, the demand for highly skilled (highly educated) workers has increased relative to the demand for less-skilled (less-educated) workers. As a result, the wage gap between the two groups has widened. As we saw at the beginning of the chapter, in the last three decades, the college premium has increased significantly. At the same time, the premium for advanced degrees increased. Finally, the dropout penalty (the wage gap between high-school graduates and dropouts) has nearly doubled.

TABLE 17.3

Changes in U.S. Income Shares, 1970–2001

Year	Lowest Fifth	Second Fifth	Third Fifth	Fourth Fifth	Highest Fifth
2001	3.5	8.7	14.6	23.0	50.1
2000	3.6	8.9	14.8	23.0	49.8
1995	3.7	9.1	15.2	23.3	48.7
1990	3.9	9.6	15.9	24.0	46.6
1985	4.0	9.7	16.3	24.6	45.3
1980	4.3	10.3	16.9	24.9	43.7
1975	4.4	10.5	17.1	24.8	43.2
1970	4.1	10.8	17.4	24.5	43.3

Why did the demand for skill increase over the last three decades? There are two main reasons.

▶ *Technological change.* Advances in technology have simultaneously decreased the demand for less-educated workers and increased the demand for college graduates and people with advanced degrees. While the new technology has made it possible to replace many low-skilled workers with "smart" machines and computers, it has increased the demand for workers who have the education and skills required to produce the new technology and use it.

▶ *Increased international trade.* An increase in international trade means more exports and imports. Trade allows developed countries like the United States to easily export goods produced with high-skilled labor and import goods produced with low-skilled labor. As a result, the expansion of international trade in the last three decades has increased the demand for high-skilled workers and decreased the demand for low-skilled workers in the United States.

Economists have not yet reached a consensus on the relative importance of these two factors.

Changes in the Top End of Income Distribution: 1920–1998

Figure 17.7 shows the trends in the income shares of the several groups at the top of the income distribution. The upper line shows the share for the top decile (top 10%) of income earners. The income share was just over 40% in 1917 and just under 45% at the start of World War II. The share plunged during the war and leveled out in the postwar period at about 33%. The share started increasing in 1970, rising from 32% to 42% by 1998. The middle line shows the income share for the top 5% of earners. It follows a similar pattern, with lower shares after the war, a long period of relative stability, and then increases starting in 1970. The lower line, showing the income share for the top 1% of the distribution, shows a similar pattern.

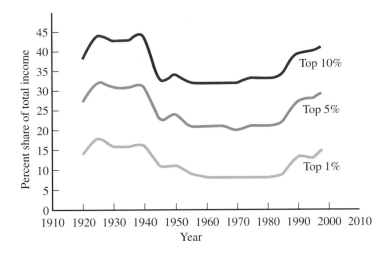

FIGURE 17.7

Top Income Distribution Shares, 1920–1998

Source: Thomas Piketty and Emmanuel Saez, "Income Inequality in the United States, 1913–1998," Working Paper 8467, National Bureau of Economic Research, 2001.

What caused these patterns? Recent studies of the trends for the top decile generated the following observations:[15]

1 During World War II, the income share of the top decile decreased because government wage controls compressed wages. In addition, the government increased tax rates on invested money (stock dividends, interest earnings, and entrepreneurial income) to support the war effort, and these rates remained relatively high until the 1980s. The higher tax rates decreased the return that could be earned on investments and slowed the rate at which fortunes were amassed.

2 The stability of the income share in the period 1945–1970 is puzzling because one would expect wages to rebound after wage controls ended following World War II. During this time period, there *was* a postwar rebound in top-decile wages in France and other countries, just not in the United States.

3 Between 1920 and 1998, the share of income from wages increased at the expense of income from investments. For the top decile, the share of income from wages rose from 58% to 84%. For the top 1%, the wage share rose from 42% to 70%.

4 The increase in the income shares since 1970 has been caused by rapid increases in the compensation of the highest-wage workers—the executives of large corporations and other organizations. Most of the action in the top decile is in the top 1% of earners, and most of the action at the top is in rising wages, not increases in investment income. After adjusting for inflation, the salaries of top executives increased by about 6% per year in the 1990s, much more rapidly than average salaries.

5 The chief executives in the United States are paid much more than their counterparts in other developed nations. For example, U.S. executives receive 3 to 4 times more than their counterparts in Britain, Germany, and France. In the United States, the average pay for a chief executive is 24 times the pay of the average production worker. In Germany, the average executive is paid only 8 times as much as the average production worker.

6 The U.S. experience in the last 30 years contrasts sharply with that of France, where the income share of the top decile actually decreased between 1970 and 1998, from 33% to 32%.

USING THE TOOLS

We've seen how to use supply and demand curves to explain differences in wages and to predict the effects of changes in the labor market on the equilibrium wage and employment. Here are some opportunities to do your own economic analysis.

1. Market Effects of Immigration

In the initial equilibrium, the wage for farm workers is $5 per hour. The elasticity of supply of farm workers is 2.0, and the elasticity of demand for farm workers is 1.0. Suppose that immigration increases the supply of farm workers by 12%: The supply curve shifts to the right by 12%.
a. Predict the effect of immigration on the wage paid to farm workers: By how much will the wage increase or decrease?
b. How will immigration affect the cost of producing food and the equilibrium price of food?

2. Demand for Newskids

Consider the market for newspaper delivery kids in Kidsville. Each newskid receives a piece rate of $2 per subscriber per month and has a fixed territory that initially has 100 subscribers. The price elasticity of demand for subscriptions is 2.0. Suppose the new city council of Kidsville passes a law that establishes a minimum piece rate of $3 per subscriber per month. As a result, the publisher increases the monthly price of a subscription by 20%. How will the new law affect the monthly income of the typical newskid?

SUMMARY

We've seen how wages are determined in perfectly competitive labor markets and why wages differ from one occupation to another. We've also looked at the distribution of income in the United States and explored possible reasons for growing inequality. Here are the main points of the chapter:

1 The wage in a particular occupation will be relatively high if supply is small relative to demand. This will occur if (a) few people have the skills required for the occupation, (b) training costs are high, or (c) the job is dangerous or stressful.

2 College graduates earn more than high-school graduates because a college education provides new skills and allows people to reveal their skills to employers.

3 There are trade-offs with a minimum wage: Some workers earn higher income, but others lose their jobs.

4 The wealthiest 20% of families in the United States earn about half of total income, while the wealthiest 10% earn 42% of total income. At the other end of the income distribution, the poorest 20% earn only 3.5% of total income.

KEY TERMS

income effect for leisure
   demand, 384
input-substitution effect, 383
learning effect, 395
long-run demand curve
   for labor, 383

marginal product of labor, 381
marginal-revenue product of labor
   (*MRP*), 381
market supply curve
   for labor, 385
output effect, 383

short-run demand curve
   for labor, 381
signaling effect, 395
substitution effect for leisure
   demand, 384

PROBLEMS AND DISCUSSION QUESTIONS

1 You are an economic consultant to a city that just imposed a payroll tax of $1 per hour of work. This payroll tax is paid by workers through a payroll deduction: For each hour of work, the employer deducts $1 and sends the money to the city government. The initial wage (before the tax) is $10, and total employment is 20,000 hours per day. Use a graph to show the effect of the tax on the equilibrium wage and employment.

2 We discussed the response of Lester, Sam, and Maureen to an increase in the wage. Which person's response is closest to your own? If your wage increased, would you work more hours, fewer hours, or about the same number of hours?

3 Critically appraise the following statement from Mr. Chuckles: "The law of supply says that an increase in price increases the quantity supplied. A decrease in the income tax rate will increase the worker's net wage, so each worker will work more hours. As a result, the revenue from the income tax will increase."

4 Consider two markets for carpenters: the city of Portland and the United States. Draw two supply curves for carpenters: one for the city of Portland and one for the United States. In which market would you expect a more elastic supply of carpenters?

5 The advocates of higher salaries for teachers point out that most teachers have college degrees and that teaching children is an important job.

a. Why aren't teachers' salaries higher, given the importance of the job and the education required?

b. Suppose a new law requires that teachers are paid the same hourly wage as college graduates who work in business. Predict the effects of this law on the market for teachers.

6 Comment on the following: "There is no substitute for an airline pilot: Someone has to fly the plane. Therefore, an increase in the wage of airline pilots will not change the number of pilots used by the airlines."

7 Suppose a new government program improves worker safety in coal mines. Use a graph to predict the effect of the program on the equilibrium wage for coal workers.

8 Under some occupational licensing laws, licensed members of an occupation write licensing exams. An example is the bar exam for licensing lawyers. How might this practice limit entry into an occupation?

9 One response to the gap in wages between men and women is a policy called comparable worth, under which the government specifies a minimum wage for some occupations, typically the occupations with a disproportionate number of women. Evaluate the merits of such a policy. What are the trade-offs?

MODEL ANSWERS TO QUESTIONS

Chapter-Opening Questions

1 When the wage increases, some people work more, others work less, and others work about the same amount.

2 As we saw in the section on wages for different occupations, the worker's income would increase by about 3.7%.

3 The gender gap results from differences in productivity and occupational status.

4 Two of the factors contributing to greater inequality are (a) technological change that increases the demand for high-skilled labor and decreases the demand for low-skilled labor, and (b) increased international trade, which decreases the demand for low-skilled labor.

Test Your Understanding

1 If the marginal-revenue product of the new player exceeds $3 million. For example, if the player increased the revenue from ticket sales by $4 million, it would be sensible to hire the player.

2 Decrease, decrease, increase, increase.

3 As the wage decreases, labor will become less expensive relative to other inputs, so the firm will substitute labor for other inputs.

4 You will work 30 hours per week instead of 20 hours.

5 No. An increase in the wage will increase the number of workers because of changes in occupational choices and migration.

6 Increase, decrease.

7 Demand, supply.

8 Wages are higher in cities where police officers face a greater chance of being killed on the job.

9 Waiters in tipping countries will have lower wages than waiters in nontipping countries.

NOTES

1. W. Michael Fox and Beverly J. Fox, "What's Happening to Americans' Income?" The *Southwest Economy, Federal Reserve Bank of Dallas,* Issue 2, 1995, pp. 3–6; *U.S. Bureau of the Census, Statistical Abstract of the United States 2002,* Table 654 (Washington, DC: U.S. Government Printing Office, 2002).

2. Mark Killingsworth, *Labor Supply* (New York: Cambridge University Press, 1983).

3. "Early Retirement? Don't Even Think about It," *The Economist,* March 23, 2002, p. 53; "French Pensions: Work Now, Enjoy Later," *The Economist,* February 8, 2003, p 54.

4. Victor R. Fuchs, Alan B. Krueger, and James M. Poterba, "Why Do Economists Disagree About Policy? The Role of Beliefs about Parameters and Values," *Journal of Economic Literature,* vol. 36, no. 3, 1998, pp. 1387–426.

5. George Borjas, "The New Economics of Immigration," *Atlantic Monthly,* November 1996, pp. 73–78; George Borjas, "The Economics of Immigration," *Journal of Economic Literature,* vol. 32, 1994, pp. 1667–717.

6. "Stamping Out the Sweatshops: Dress Code," *The Economist,* April 19, 1997; "Sweatshop Wars," *The Economist,* February 27, 1999.

7. Craig Olson, "An Analysis of Wage Differentials Received by Workers on Dangerous Jobs," *Journal of Human Resources,* vol. 16, Spring 1981, pp. 167–185.

8. Suzanne Bianchi and Daphne Spain, "Women, Work, and Family in America," *Population Bulletin,* vol. 51, no. 3, 1998, pp. 2–48.

9. Eric J. Solberg, "Occupational Assignment, Hiring Discrimination, and the Gender Pay Gap," *Atlantic Economic Journal* 32 (2004), pp. 11–27.

10. U.S. Department of Labor, *Employment and Earnings* (Washington, DC: U.S. Government Printing Office, 1996).

11. William Darity and Patrick Mason, "Evidence on Discrimination in Employment: Codes of Color, Codes of Gender," *Journal of Economic Perspectives,* vol. 12, no. 2, 1998, pp. 63–90.

12. James Heckman, "Detecting Discrimination," *Journal of Economic Perspectives*, vol. 12, no. 2, 1998, pp. 101–116.

13. David Wessel, "Racial Discrimination Is Still at Work in U.S.," *Wall Street Journal*, September 4, 2003, p. A2.

14. Finis Welch, "In Defense of Inequality," *American Economic Review*, vol. 89, no. 2 (1999), pp. 1–17.

15. Thomas Piketty and Emmanuel Saez, "Income Inequality in the United States, 1913–1998," Working Paper 8467, National Bureau of Economic Research, 2001; Alan Krueger, "Attempting to Explain Income Inequality," *New York Times*, April 4, 2002, page C2.

Labor Unions

A Brief History of Labor Unions
   in the United States
Labor Unions and Wages
Effects of Unions on Worker Productivity
   and Turnover

Monopsony Power

Picking a Workforce and a Wage
Monopsony versus Perfect Competition
Monopsony and a Minimum Wage
Monopsony and the Real World

**Imperfect Information
and Efficiency Wages**

Using the Tools

Beyond Perfect Competition: Unions, Monopsony, and Imperfect Information

In the early days of the automobile industry, the prevailing wage for autoworkers was $3 per day. Assembly-line jobs were repetitive and tedious, and the turnover rate of workers was very high. When Henry Ford decided to increase the daily wage for his workers from $3 to $5, most observers were baffled. They figured that Ford's labor costs would be almost twice as high as those of his rivals, so he would lose a lot of money and quickly go out of business. The wage hike appeared to be a great act of generosity but very bad business. You can imagine their surprise when Ford's profit doubled from $30 million to $60 million. How was this possible? How can higher wages lead to higher profits?

This chapter continues our discussion of labor markets, exploring three topics that take us beyond the simple model of perfect competition discussed in the previous chapter. One of the assumptions of perfect competition in the labor market is that each worker acts independently of other workers, taking the market wage as given. We start the chapter with a discussion of labor unions, which enable workers to act collectively, controlling the supply of labor and negotiating wages. A second assumption for perfect competition is that each firm takes the wage as given, meaning that it can hire an unlimited number of workers at the prevailing market wage. In the second part of the chapter, we see what happens when a single firm dominates the demand for labor, giving it the opportunity to determine the market wage. A third assumption of perfect competition is perfect information: Each firm knows the productivity level of each worker. In the third part of this chapter, we see what happens when firms cannot distinguish between workers with different productivities. We'll use the notion of imperfect information in the labor market to explain Henry Ford's puzzling wage hike.

Moving beyond the model of perfect competition provides some important insights into real labor markets. Here are some of the practical questions that we address:

1 How do unions affect wages and worker productivity?
2 If a city has a single hospital, how would that affect the wages and total employment of nurses?
3 Could a minimum wage actually increase total employment?

Labor Unions

A **labor union** is an organized group of workers that can influence wages. Acting as a group, union members have some control over the wages and fringe benefits they receive. There are two types of labor unions:

▶ A **craft union** includes workers from a particular occupation, such as plumbers, bakers, or electricians.
▶ An **industrial union** includes all types of workers from a single industry, such as steelworkers or autoworkers.

There are also umbrella organizations that include many individual unions. The largest of these "unions of unions" is the AFL-CIO (the American Federation of Labor–Congress of Industrial Organizations). Unions use **collective bargaining** to negotiate contracts covering wages, fringe benefits, job security and working conditions.

Labor union

An organized group of workers. Unions try to increase job security, improve working conditions, and increase wages and fringe benefits for their members.

Craft union

A labor organization that includes workers from a particular occupation, for example, plumbers, bakers, or electricians.

Industrial union

A labor organization that includes all types of workers from a single industry, for example, steelworkers or autoworkers.

Collective bargaining

Negotiations between a union and a firm over wages, working conditions, and job security.

A Brief History of Labor Unions in the United States

As shown in Panel A of Figure 18.1, about one-sixth of all workers in the United States belong to a union, down from about one-third of workers 40 years ago. Among private-sector workers, the unionization rate is 8.5% whereas 37.5% of public-sector workers belong to unions. As shown in Panel B, unionization rates are higher in most other industrial countries. For a description of the working conditions that led to the formation of the first unions, read "A Closer Look: Working Conditions and Unions."

Let's take a brief look at the history of labor organizations in the United States. In the nineteenth century, there were all sorts of craft unions, and the main umbrella organizations were the Knights of Labor (founded in 1869) and the AFL (founded in 1881). The CIO (formed in 1931) was a collection of industrial unions that represented semiskilled workers in mass production, including workers in the automobile, rubber, and steel industries. The CIO merged with the AFL in 1955. In the last 30 years, the fraction of the workforce in unions has decreased, but the number of government workers in unions and employee associations has more than doubled.

Labor unions have been empowered by the states and the federal government. The most important labor legislation gave workers the right to form unions, but limited their power:

▶ The Wagner Act (1935) guaranteed workers the right to join unions and required each firm to bargain with a union formed by a majority of its workers. The National Labor Relations Board (NLRB) was established to enforce the provisions of the Wagner Act.

▶ The Taft–Hartley Act (1947) gave government the power to stop strikes that "imperiled the national health or safety" and allowed states to pass **right-to-work laws**. These laws, which are currently in force in 21 states, outlaw union shops, defined as workplaces where union membership is required as a condition of employment.

▶ The Landrum–Griffin Act (1959) was a response to allegations of corruption and misconduct by union officials. This act guaranteed union members the right to fair elections, made it easier for them to monitor union finances, and made the theft of union funds a federal offense.

Labor Unions and Wages

There is evidence that unions raise the wages of union workers. For the U.S., the consensus is that union workers earn about 15% more than nonunion workers doing the same work.[1] Most other industrialized countries have a smaller union "markup." The markup is about 10% in the United Kingdom, about 12% in Canada, and about 5% in both Japan and Germany. The markup is relatively small for unionized firms that operate in a competitive product market, but larger for firms with little competition in the product market. In other words, unions have their largest effects on the wages paid by monopolists and oligopolists. The higher wages decrease the profits of these firms, so union workers gain at the expense of the owners of the firms.

Unions try to increase the wages of their members in three ways. First, unions organize workers and negotiate a higher wage. Suppose workers in a particular industry form an industrial union and agree on a union wage that exceeds the equilibrium wage. Like a minimum wage imposed by a government, a wage negotiated by a union

Right-to-work laws

Laws that prohibit union shops, where union membership is required as a condition of employment

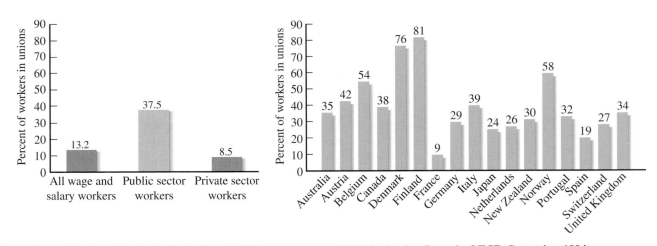

(A) Unionization Rates in the United States, 2002

(B) Unionization Rates in OECD Countries, 1994

FIGURE 18.1 **Unionization Rates in the United States and OECD Countries**

Sources: U.S. Bureau of Labor Statistics; OECD Statistics

means that some workers will earn higher wages but other workers who are willing to work will not have the opportunity to do so. To deal with this problem, the union can reduce the number of workers by restricting membership or can share the smaller number of jobs among union members.

Another way to increase the union wage is to promote the products produced by union workers. You've probably seen advertisements encouraging people to buy products with the "union label." As we learned in Chapter 17, the demand for labor is a

A CLOSER LOOK

Working Conditions and Unions

Labor unions arose in the late 1800s and early 1900s largely in response to awful working conditions in factories. In garment factories, iron plants, and textile mills, laborers worked 14-7—about 14 hours per day, seven days a week. The long workweek was not new to those who had worked on farms, but the working conditions were. Men, women, and children as young as age 5 operated clattering machinery so dangerous that many workers lost their sight, hearing, and limbs. For the early union organizers, the key demands were higher wages, shorter hours, and safer work environments. One reason for the decline of unions since the 1940s is the passage of legislation that limits work hours and improved the safety of workplaces.

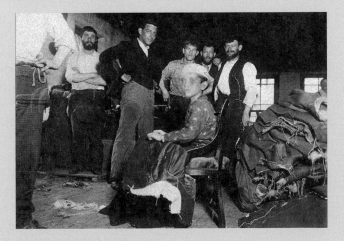

derived demand, so an increase in the demand for a final good will increase the demand for labor used to produce that good, increasing the equilibrium wage. This approach can be used together with a negotiated union wage to prevent an excess supply of labor at the union wage.

A third approach—which may or may not increase wages—is to impose work rules that increase the amount of labor required to produce a given quantity of output. This is called **featherbedding**. One example of featherbedding is requiring a minimum crew size, which forces a firm to hire more workers than it needs to perform a particular task. For example, the typical unionized airline hires three workers to guide an airplane into the gate, whereas nonunion airlines use only two workers. In the past, railroad unions forced railroads to use firemen (whose job was to shovel coal) on diesel-powered engines, which don't use coal.

Featherbedding

Work rules that increase the amount of labor required to produce a given quantity of output.

Featherbedding may or may not increase the demand for labor. Although it forces the firm to use more labor per unit of output, it also decreases the quantity of output. A firm that is forced to hire workers it doesn't need will have higher production costs, resulting in higher prices for its products. Consumers respond to higher prices by purchasing less output, so although the firm may use more labor per unit of output, it sells less output. If output falls by a large amount, the quantity of labor demanded by the firm will actually decrease, decreasing the wage and total employment.

A different approach to managing union employment comes from Volkswagen A.G., Europe's largest automaker. In 1993, Volkswagen got its labor unions to switch to a four-day, 28-hour workweek, down from a five-day, 36-hour workweek. If workers hadn't accepted the shorter workweek and lower pay, Volkswagen would have eliminated 30,000 of its 100,000 jobs in Germany. In other words, the switch to the shorter workweek preserved 30,000 union jobs in the automobile industry.[2] Some analysts suggest that shorter workweeks for union workers will become more common as European unions grapple with lower demand for their workers.

Effects of Unions on Worker Productivity and Turnover

We've seen that unions lead to higher wages, meaning that unions increase production costs. What are the possible benefits of unions? First, unions may increase worker productivity by facilitating communication between workers and managers. The evidence on worker productivity is mixed. Some studies show higher productivity in unionized firms, and others show lower productivity. Union workers are more productive when the union facilitates smooth relations between labor and management.

A second possible benefit of unions is lower turnover among workers. If a worker is unhappy with a job, one option is to quit. From the firm's perspective, this is costly because the firm loses an experienced worker and must train a new one. A dissatisfied worker who belongs to a union has a second option: The worker can use the union as an intermediary to discuss job issues with managers. This sort of communication can solve problems before they become so severe that the worker quits. There is evidence that firms whose workers are in unions have lower turnover rates, in part because they facilitate communication between workers and managers.[3] These lower turnover rates lead to lower training costs and a more experienced workforce. The savings for unionized firms is equivalent to a 1 to 2% reduction in costs.

Monopsony Power

In the previous chapter, we assumed that each employer is such a small part of the labor market that the employer takes the market wage as given. In graphical terms, the labor-supply curve faced by the firm is horizontal at the market wage. In contrast, some labor markets have a single employer, so the lack of competition for workers gives the firm some control over wages. Of course, the lower the wage, the smaller the quantity of labor supplied. For example, if your city has a single hospital, there will be a single employer of surgical nurses. This is the case of **monopsony**: There is a single buyer of a particular input. The classic example of a pure monopsony is a company town, where most or all the workers are employed by a single firm.

Monopsony
A market in which there is a single buyer of an input.

Picking a Workforce and a Wage

A monopsonist faces a positively sloped market supply curve of labor. If the monopsonist hires more workers, it must pay a higher wage to attract them away from other activities. In Figure 18.2, the firm can hire 7 workers at a wage of $10 (point *c*) and 8 workers at a wage of $12 (point *d*). The firm's **marginal labor cost** (also known as marginal factor cost) is defined as the increase in total labor cost from one more unit of labor. When the firm decides to hire 8 workers instead of 7, its total labor cost increases from $70 per hour ($10 per worker per hour times 7 workers) to $96 per hour ($12 per worker per hour times 8 workers), an increase of $26. Therefore, the firm's marginal labor cost for the eighth worker is $26 (shown by point *e* in Figure 18.2).

Marginal labor cost
The increase in total labor cost resulting from one more unit of labor.

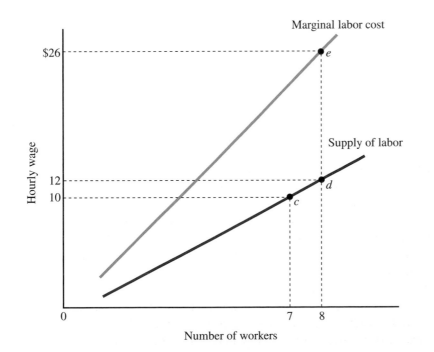

FIGURE 18.2

The Supply of Labor and Marginal Labor Cost for a Monopsonist
To hire more workers, the monopsonist must pay a higher wage, so the marginal labor cost exceeds the wage. To hire the eighth worker, the firm increases the wage from $10 to $12. The marginal labor cost for the eighth worker is $26, equal to $12 paid to the eighth worker plus $14 extra money paid to the 7 original workers, each of whom receives $2 more per hour.

As shown in Figure 18.2, the marginal labor cost exceeds the hourly wage. The reason is that when the firm increases the wage to hire one more worker, it must increase the wage for all of its workers. To hire the eighth worker, the firm pays $12 to the new worker, but it also pays an extra $2 for each of the 7 workers who were willing to work at the $10 wage. We compute the marginal labor cost as follows:

marginal labor cost = wage paid to new worker
+ (change in wage × quantity of original workers)
$26 = $12 + ($2 × 7)

In this case, the marginal labor cost is $26, including $12 for the new worker and $14 for the original workers.

Figure 18.3 shows the hiring decision of the monopsonist. The firm can use the marginal principle to determine how many workers to hire.

MARGINAL *Principle*

Increase the level of an activity if its marginal benefit exceeds its marginal cost, but reduce the level if the marginal cost exceeds the marginal benefit. If possible, pick the level at which the marginal benefit equals the marginal cost.

The firm chooses the quantity of labor at which the marginal benefit of labor equals the marginal cost. As we saw in the previous chapter, the marginal benefit of labor equals the marginal-revenue product of labor—that is, the increase in revenue generated by an

FIGURE 18.3

The Hiring Decision of a Monopsonist
The monopsonist chooses point *m*, where the marginal benefit of labor (the marginal-revenue product) equals the marginal labor cost, hiring 40 workers. The labor-supply curve indicates that to hire 40 workers, the monopsonist must pay a wage of $4 (point *w*).

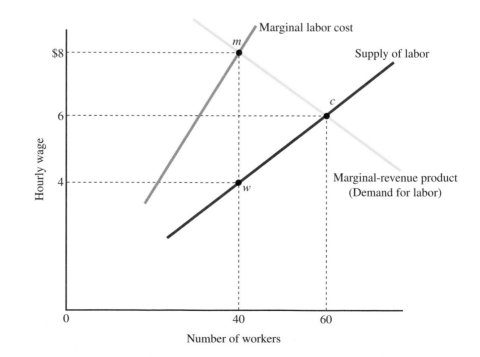

additional worker. The marginal-revenue product curve is also the demand curve for labor. In Figure 18.3, the marginal-labor cost curve intersects the marginal-revenue product curve at point *m*, so the monopsonist hires 40 workers. As shown by the labor-supply curve, to hire 40 workers, the firm must pay a wage of $4 (shown by point *w*).

Why does the monopsonist stop at 40 workers when it could hire an additional worker for just over $4, and that worker would have a marginal-revenue product of just under $8? To hire one more worker, the monopsonist must increase the wage to $4.10. The marginal-labor cost of the 41st worker incorporates the higher wages that must be paid to the first 40 workers:

$$\text{marginal labor cost} = \text{wage paid to new worker}$$
$$+ (\text{change in wage} \times \text{quantity of original workers})$$
$$\$8.10 = \$4.10 + (\$0.10 \times 40)$$

Because a higher wage must be paid to the 40 original workers, the marginal-labor cost ($8.10) exceeds the marginal-revenue product (less than $8.00), so the firm stops at 40 workers.

Monopsony versus Perfect Competition

How does the monopsony outcome compare to the perfectly competitive outcome? Any firm that hires workers—either a monopsonist or perfect competitor—will continue to hire more workers until the marginal cost equals the marginal benefit (the marginal revenue product). For a perfectly competitive firm, the marginal cost is simply the wage. For a monopsonist, the marginal cost is the marginal labor cost, which exceeds the wage because the monopsonist must increase its wage to hire more workers. The monopsonist will hire fewer workers because its higher marginal cost equals the marginal benefit at a smaller quantity of labor. Compared to a collection of perfectly competitive firms, each of which takes the price as given, a monopsonist will hire fewer workers. In Figure 18.3, the perfectly competitive equilibrium is shown by the intersection of the demand curve (marginal-revenue product curve) and the supply curve. The equilibrium wage is $6 and the equilibrium quantity is 60 workers.

You may have noticed the similarity between a monopsonist and a monopolist. A monopolist (a single seller) uses its market power to increase the price of output; a monopsonist (a single buyer) uses its market power to decrease the wage. The monopolist produces an artificially small quantity of output; the monopsonist hires an artificially small quantity of a particular input, such as labor. Table 18.1 summarizes the key features of a monopolist and a monopsonist.

What is the role of a labor union in a labor market with a single buyer? Monopsony leads to an artificially low wage, and a union may lead to an artificially high wage. A market with both a union and a monopsonist will have a wage somewhere between the two extremes, depending on the bargaining power of the two sides. In such a market, the market powers on the two sides of the market counteract each other, leading to a wage between the artificially low monopsony wage and the articially high union wage.

TABLE 18.1

Monopoly versus Monopsony

Monopoly	Monopsony
Single seller of output	Single buyer of input
High price of output	Low price of input
Small quantity of output	Small quantity of input

Monopsony and a Minimum Wage

In the previous chapter, we showed that a minimum wage decreases the quantity of labor demanded below the equilibrium level. In this case, there is a trade-off between higher wages and total employment. How does this analysis change when a monopsonist has market power on the demand side of the market?

Figure 18.4 shows the effects of a minimum wage of $7. This wage exceeds the monopsony wage of $4 as well as the perfectly competitive wage of $6. The minimum wage rules out wages below $7, so the supply curve facing the firm is horizontal up to 70 workers. The first through the 70th workers are willing to work at the minimum wage, so to get an additional worker (say the 41st), the firm doesn't have to pay any more than it did for the first 40 workers. The marginal labor cost is the minimum wage of $7, the same amount for the first worker, the 10th worker, and so on, up to 70 workers. If the firm wants to hire more than 70 workers, it must pay a wage higher

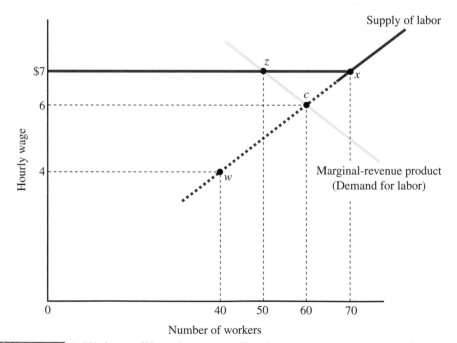

FIGURE 18.4 **A Minimum Wage Increases Employment by a Monopsonist**

With a minimum wage, the labor-supply curve is horizontal at the minimum wage ($7) up to the point where the minimum-wage line intersects the original supply curve. Beyond that point, the supply curve is the same as the original curve. As long as the supply curve is horizontal, the marginal labor cost for the monopsonist equals the minimum wage. The monopsonist chooses point z, where the marginal benefit of labor (the marginal-revenue product) equals the marginal labor cost. The minimum wage increases the quantity of labor from 40 workers to 50.

than the minimum. The wage that would be required is shown by the market supply curve beyond point *x*. But for fewer than 70 workers, the supply curve facing the firm is horizontal, so the marginal labor cost is constant at the minimum wage of $7.

To maximize its profit, the firm will pick the quantity of labor at which the marginal benefit equals the marginal cost. At point *z*, the marginal labor cost (shown by the horizontal portion of the new supply curve) equals the marginal benefit (shown by the marginal-revenue product curve), so the monopsonist will hire 50 workers, up from 40 workers before the minimum wage. In other words, the minimum wage increases the quantity of labor demanded.

How does this analysis compare to the analysis of the minimum wage in the previous chapter? You may recall that in a perfectly competitive market, the minimum wage decreases the quantity of labor. In Figure 18.4, competitive outcome is shown by point *c*, with 60 workers. So a minimum wage of $7 generates less than the competitive quantity but more than the monopsony quantity (40 workers). Starting from the monopsony outcome, a minimum wage of $7 moves the market closer to the perfectly competitive outcome. In fact, if the minimum wage were set at $6 (the competitive level), the market would reach the competitive quantity of 60 workers. The minimum wage essentially makes the monopsonist into a price-taking firm. With a minimum-wage law in place, the monopsonist acts like a perfectly competitive firm, taking the minimum wage as given. That's why the minimum wage increases the quantity of labor demanded by the monopsonist.

Monopsony and the Real World

Although a pure monopsony like a company town is rare, the insights from the monopsony model are relevant for actual labor markets. The essential feature of the model is that if an individual firm wants to hire additional workers, it must increase its wage to attract more workers. In other words, the firm faces a positively sloped supply curve for workers, not a horizontal curve. We saw that a positively sloped supply curve generates a marginal labor cost curve above the supply curve, and the profit-maximizing quantity of labor is less than the perfectly competitive quantity (where the supply curve intersects the demand curve).

A firm could face a positively sloped labor-supply curve for several reasons. British economist Joan Robinson (1903–1983), a leader in the modeling of imperfect competition, listed the reasons:[4]

> There may be a certain number of workers in the immediate neighbourhood and to attract those from farther afield it may be necessary to pay a wage equal to what they can earn near home plus their fares to and fro; or there could be workers attached to the firm by preference or custom and to attract others it may be necessary to pay a higher wage. Or ignorance may prevent workers from moving from one to another in response to differences in the wages offered by the different firms.

In other words, there are frictions in the labor market that require a firm to pay a higher wage to get more workers, meaning the supply curve is positively sloped. With a positively sloped supply curve, the marginal labor cost exceeds the wage, and the firm will hire fewer workers than would be hired in a perfectly competitive market. For some evidence of labor frictions, read "A Closer Look: Pubs and the Labor-Supply Curve."

A CLOSER LOOK

Pubs and the Labor-Supply Curve

In his book, *Monopsony in Motion: Imperfect Competition in Labor Markets*, labor economist Alan Manning provides some unconventional evidence of positively sloped labor-supply curves.[5] He notes that "people go to the pub to celebrate when they get a job, rather than greeting the news with a shrug of the shoulders. . . . " In other words, a new job is a big deal.

If a pub celebration seems like the obvious response to a new job, consider what happens when each firm faces a horizontal supply curve for labor, with a single market wage. A firm has no incentive to pay a higher wage because it can hire as many workers as it wants at the market wage. And if the firm paid a lower wage, all of its workers would instantly switch to other firms paying the market wage. In this perfectly competitive environment, a worker won't celebrate a new job because the new job pays the same as any other job.

Suppose instead that the supply curve facing a firm is positively sloped. To hire more workers, the firm must pay a higher wage. For most workers, the market wage will be greater than the opportunity cost, meaning that they are willing to work for less than they ultimately get. In other words, each worker gets a producer surplus. People celebrate a new job because they switch jobs to get a bigger producer surplus.

Manning also notes that people also "go to the pub to drown their sorrows when they lose their jobs." This wouldn't be sensible with a horizontal supply curve because someone who loses a job could instantly get another one at the same wage. But with a positively sloped supply curve, losing a job means losing a producer surplus.

TEST Your Understanding

1. Suppose a union's objective is to maximize total employment in a particular occupation, but it cannot affect the demand for labor. Employers are perfectly competitive, taking the market wage as given. What should the union do?
2. Complete the statement with "high" or "low": A monopolist sells its output at a relatively _____ price, while a monopsonist buys its inputs at a relatively _____ price.
3. Fill the blanks: A monopsonist hires workers to the quantity at which _____ equals _____.

Imperfect Information and Efficiency Wages

Up to this point, our discussion of labor markets has been based on the assumption of perfect information. Each employer knows the productivity level of each worker and only hires a worker if the marginal benefit (the marginal-revenue product) exceeds the marginal cost. In some markets, workers differ in their skill levels and the amount of effort they exert on the job. At the time of hiring, employers cannot always distinguish between skillful and unskillful workers or between hard workers and lazy workers. In other words, there is asymmetric information in the labor market. What happens when there is asymmetric information?

We know from our discussion of the market for used cars in Chapter 8 that asymmetric information causes high-quality and low-quality goods to be sold in a mixed market at a single price. Suppose there are two types of workers:

▶ Low-skill workers, whose marginal revenue product = $100 per day
▶ High-skill workers, whose marginal revenue product = $200 per day

The employer cannot distinguish between these two types of workers before hiring them, and offers a single wage to all, realizing that it will probably hire some workers of each type.

What is the appropriate wage in this case? Suppose the opportunity cost of high-skill workers is $130 and a firm offers a wage of $110. Because the wage is less than the opportunity cost of high-skill workers, only low-skill workers will apply for jobs. The firm will lose money because the $110 wage exceeds the $100 marginal-revenue product of the low-skill workers. To get some high-skill workers, the employer must pick a wage that exceeds the $130 opportunity cost of high-skill workers. If the firm increases its wage, it will attract more high-skill workers and the average productivity of its workforce will increase. Depending on the responses of the two types of workers to the higher wage, a firm could make more profit by offering a higher wage. This is known as **paying efficiency wages**: The firm pays a higher wage to increase the average productivity of its workforce.

Another reason for paying relatively high wages is to encourage employees to work hard. Firms realize that their employees can vary their work efforts, from working hard to hardly working (shirking). To encourage their employees to work hard, employers fire workers who are caught shirking. The penalty associated with being fired will be much greater if the firm pays a wage above the worker's opportunity cost. For example, suppose a worker could earn $80 per day in another job. If the firm pays its workers $100 per day, a worker who is fired—and then immediately gets a job with another firm—would take a pay cut of $20 per day. This is another example of paying efficiency wages: By increasing the wage, the firm increases the work effort of its employees and increases the average productivity of its workforce.

Another reason for paying efficiency wages is to reduce turnover in the workforce. If one firm pays a higher wage than its competitors, that discourages workers from switching employers. The firm paying the higher wage will have lower turnover and thus incur smaller costs in hiring and training workers.

Paying efficiency wages
The practice of a firm paying a higher wage to increase the average productivity of its workforce.

Higher Wages at Ford Motor Company

Recall the chapter opener about Henry Ford's puzzling wage hike. Ford increased the daily wage for his workers from $3 to $5, and his profit doubled from $30 million to $60 million. Why did higher wages lead to more profit?

The key to solving this puzzle is the concept of efficiency wages. When Ford raised the wage, the average productivity of Ford workers increased by about 50%, a result of several changes in the workforce:[6]

- The pool of job applicants improved, so Ford could choose better workers.
- Fewer workers were fired for shirking.
- Fewer workers quit voluntarily.
- The rate of absenteeism was cut in half.

In the words of Henry Ford, "There was no charity in any way involved. . . . The payment of five dollars a day for an eight-hour day was one of the finest cost cutting moves we ever made." ■

Economic **Puzzle**

TEST Your Understanding

4. Explain how an increase in the wage can increase the average productivity of a firm's workforce.
5. Why is the marginal labor cost always greater than the wage?

USING THE TOOLS

We've seen the effects of market power on both sides of the labor market and the effects of asymmetric information on wages. Here are some opportunities to do your own economic analysis.

1. Effects of a Nurses Union

Suppose that the nurses in the city of Florence form a union and that to work as a nurse you must belong to the union. The nurses do not allow new members to join the union, so the supply of nurses decreases by 3% per year as older union members retire. Before the union was formed, the equilibrium wage was $15 and the equilibrium quantity was 16,000 hours per day.
a. Depict graphically the effect of the union on the nursing market.
b. If the price elasticity of demand for nursing is 1.5, by what percentage would the wage of nurses increase each year?

2. Effects of a Higher Minimum Wage

Using Figure 18.3 as a starting point, suppose the minimum wage is set at $9. Depict graphically the

effects of the minimum wage on total employment. Predict the new quantity of labor. Does the quantity of labor increase or decrease?

3. Equilibrium with Efficiency Wages

Consider a labor market with asymmetric information: Each worker knows his or her marginal-revenue product, but firms cannot distinguish between low-skill and high-skill workers. Each low-skill worker has an opportunity cost of $80 and a marginal revenue product of $100, and each high-skill worker has an opportunity cost of $130 and a marginal-revenue product of $200. The workforce is divided equally between the two types of workers. Your job is to predict the equilibrium wage in the market given that each firm takes the price as given and earns zero economic profit. Try the following wages: (a) $90, (b) $100, (c) $140, (d) $150, (e) $170.

SUMMARY

In this chapter, we extended our discussion of labor markets beyond the simple world of perfectly competitive markets, with each side of the labor market taking the market wage as given. Unions achieve market power on the supply side of the market, and a monopsonist achieves market power on the demand side of the market. When there is imperfect information, with workers

knowing more about their productivity than employers, this asymmetric information provides an incentive for firms to increase wages in order to attract better workers. Here are the main points of the chapter:

1 There are trade-offs with union wage: Some workers earn higher wages, but others lose their jobs.

2 A monopsonist hires fewer workers than a perfectly competitive firm and pays a lower wage

3 In a monopsonistic market, a minimum wage may increase total employment.

4 A firm that pays efficiency wages may increase the average productivity of its workers and increase its profit.

KEY TERMS

collective bargaining, 405
craft union, 405
featherbedding, 408

industrial union, 405
labor union, 405
marginal labor cost, 409

monopsony, 409
paying efficiency wages, 415
right-to-work laws, 406

PROBLEMS AND DISCUSSION QUESTIONS

1 Suppose a union's objective is to maximize the total income of nurses (total money spent by firms on nurses). At the current wage, the price elasticity of demand for nurses is 1.5. Should the union increase or decrease the union wage? Explain.

2 Suppose that featherbedding increases the labor time per unit of output from 5 hours to 6 and increases the firm's production cost and its price by 15%. The firm initially produces and sells 100 units of output. If the price elasticity of demand for the firm's product is 2.0, how will featherbedding affect the firm's total demand for labor?

3 Consider the following data on the number of workers, wages, marginal labor cost, and marginal-revenue product. The first three rows show the supply side of the market, and the last two rows show the demand side.

a. How many workers will a monopsonist hire?
b. Pick a minimum wage that would generate the perfectly competitive outcome.

4 Suppose that half of the workers have low productivity, with marginal-revenue product of $50 and an opportunity cost of $60, and the other half have high productivity, with marginal-revenue product of $100 and an opportunity cost of $80.

a. If the firm offers a wage equal to the average productivity of workers, will the firm be profitable?
b. If the firm pays a wage of $90, will it be profitable?

Wage	$5	$6	$7	$8	$9	$10	$11
Quantity of workers supplied	1	2	3	4	5	6	7
Marginal labor cost	$5	$7	$9	$11	$13	$15	$17
Quantity of workers demanded	1	2	3	4	5	6	7
Marginal-revenue product	$20	$18	$16	$14	$12	$10	$8

MODEL ANSWERS TO QUESTIONS

Chapter-Opening Questions

1 Unions increase wages and may increase productivity by facilitating communication between workers and managers.
2 A monopsonist pays lower wages and hires fewer workers.
3 In a labor market with a monopsonist, a minimum wage may increase total employment.

Test Your Understanding

1 Set the wage at the competitive level. Total employment is maximized at the intersection of supply and demand, so the union should do nothing. It should let the market reach equilibrium on its own.
2 High, low.
3 Marginal-revenue product, marginal labor cost.
4 The firm will attract better applicants, and workers are less likely to shirk.
5 To attract one more worker, the firm must increase the wage. The marginal labor cost equals the wage paid to the new worker plus the extra income that must be paid to the original workers who were working at the old wage.

NOTES

1. Toke Aidt and Zafiris Tzannatos, *Unions and Collective Bargaining: Economic Effects in a Global Environment* (Washington DC: World Bank, 2002).
2. Ferdinand Protzman, "VW Plan for 4-Day Workweek Is Adopted," *New York Times*, November 26, 1993, p. D11; Tyler Marshall, "VW, Unions, OK 20% Reduction in Work Week," *Los Angeles Times*, November 26, 1993, p. A1: "Worldwire," *Wall Street Journal*, July 8, 1994, p. A5.
3. Richard B. Freeman and James Medoff, *What Do Unions Do?* (New York: Basic Books, 1985).
4. Joan Robinson, *The Economics of Imperfect Competition* (London: Macmillan,1933), p. 296.
5. Alan Manning, *Monopsony in Motion: Imperfect Competition in Labor* Markets (Princeton NJ: Princeton University Press, 2003).
6. J. R. Lee, "So-Called Profit Sharing System in the Ford Plant," *Annals of the American Academy of Political and Social Science*, May 1915, pp. 297–310; David Halberstam, *The Reckoning* (New York: William Morrow, 1986), pp. 91–92; Daniel M. G. Graff and Lawrence H. Summers, "Did Henry Ford Pay Efficiency Wages?" *Journal of Labor Economics*, vol. 5, 1987, pp. 557–586.

Part

6

The International Economy

Chapter 19
International Trade and Public Policy

Benefits from Specialization and Trade

Production Possibilities Curve
Comparative Advantage and the Terms
   of Trade
The Consumption Possibilities Curve
The Employment Effects of Free Trade

Protectionist Policies

Import Ban
Quotas and Voluntary Export Restraints
Tariffs
Responses to Protectionist Policies

Rationales for Protectionist Policies

To Shield Workers from Foreign Competition
To Nurture Infant Industries
To Help Domestic Firms Establish
   Monopolies in World Markets

A Brief History of International Tariff and Trade Agreements

Recent Policy Debates and Trade Agreements

Are Foreign Producers Dumping Their
   Products?
Do Trade Laws Inhibit Environmental
   Protection?
Does Trade Cause Inequality?
Why Do People Protest Against Free
   Trade?
Using the Tools

International Trade and Public Policy

t a 2004 press conference, the chairman of the Council of Economic Advisers, Gregory Mankiw, was asked about the fact that many U.S. companies are "outsourcing" jobs—that is, sending jobs Americans used to do to workers abroad to perform. Mankiw responded by saying, "Outsourcing is a growing phenomenon, but it's something we should realize is probably a plus for the economy in the long run." His comments immediately set off a political firestorm. Even the Speaker of the House said of Mankiw: "His theory fails a basic test of real economics."

Does it? As economists have pointed out, outsourcing jobs is part and parcel of specialization, comparative advantage, and free trade. When *New York Times* columnist Thomas Friedman was visiting India to report on the growth of firms there providing services to U.S. companies, he noted that while some skilled tasks like computer programming and cartoon animation were outsourced to India, other tasks formerly done in India were actually being outsourced to the United States. For example, when one animation company wanted to produce an animated epic about the Indian god Krishna, they "outsourced" the script to an Emmy Award-winning writer in the United States. Sometimes the process of trade takes unexpected twists.

Source: Thomas L. Friedman, "What Goes Around . . . ," *New York Times*, February 26, 2004.

As the world economy grows, our policies toward international trade become ever more important. Many people view trade as a "zero-sum game." They believe that if one country gains from international trade, another must lose. Based on this belief, they advocate restricting trade with other countries. Indeed, the United States does restrict trade to protect American jobs in many sectors, like those in the apparel and steel industries. One lesson from this chapter is that free trade could, in principle, make everyone better off. The challenge for policymakers is to develop a set of principles that accomplish this goal—or come as close as possible to accomplishing it.

In this chapter, we discuss the benefits of international trade and the effects of policies that restrict it. Here are some of the practical questions that we will answer:

1 What are the trade-offs associated with free trade? Who wins? Who loses?
2 Why is a tariff (a tax on an imported good) superior to an import quota?
3 Why might the export price of a product be less than its domestic price?
4 Do trade laws inhibit environmental protection?
5 Does trade increase income inequality?

Benefits from Specialization and Trade

What if you lived in a nation that could produce everything it consumed and didn't depend on any other country for its economic livelihood? If you were put in charge of your nation, would you pursue such a policy of national self-sufficiency? Although self-sufficiency might sound appealing, it would actually be better for your country to specialize in the production of some products and then trade some of them to other countries. You saw in Chapter 3 that specialization and exchange can make both parties better off. In this chapter, we use a simple example to explain the benefits of specialization and international trade between two nations.

Let's say there are two nations; each produces computer chips and shirts, and each nation consumes computer chips and shirts. Table 19.1 shows the daily output of the two goods for the two nations, Shirtland and Chipland. In a single day, Shirtland can produce a maximum of either 108 shirts or 36 computer chips, while Chipland can produce a maximum of either 120 shirts or 120 computer chips. The last two rows of the table show the opportunity costs of the two goods. Recall the principle of opportunity cost

Principle OF OPPORTUNITY COST

The opportunity cost of something is what you sacrifice to get it.

TABLE 19.1
Output and Opportunity Cost

	Shirtland	Chipland
Shirts produced per day	108	120
Chips produced per day	36	120
Opportunity cost of shirts	1/3 chip	1 chip
Opportunity cost of chips	3 shirts	1 shirt

In Chipland, there is a one-for-one trade-off of shirts and chips: The opportunity cost of one shirt is one chip, and the opportunity cost of one chip is one shirt. In Shirtland, people can produce three times as many shirts as chips in a given amount of time: The opportunity cost of one chip is three shirts; conversely, the opportunity cost of one shirt is one-third of a chip.

Production Possibilities Curve

Production possibilities curve

A curve showing the combinations of two goods that can be produced by an economy, assuming that all resources are fully employed.

Let's start by seeing what happens if each of these nations is self-sufficient. Each nation can use its resources (labor, land, buildings, machinery, equipment) to produce its own shirts and its own chips. The **production possibilities curve** shows all the feasible combinations of the two goods, assuming that the nation's resources are fully employed. This curve, which we discussed in an earlier chapter, provides a sort of menu of production options. To keep things simple, we assume that the curve is a straight line, indicating a constant trade-off between the two goods. As shown by Shirtland's production possibilities curve in Figure 19.1, the following combinations of chips and shirts are possible:

1 *All shirts and no chips:* point *r*. If Shirtland uses all its resources to produce shirts, it will produce 108 shirts per day.
2 *All chips and no shirts:* point *t*. If Shirtland uses all its resources to produce chips, it will produce 36 chips per day.
3 *Equal division of resources:* point *h*. Shirtland could divide its resources between shirts and chips to produce daily 54 shirts and 18 chips.

All the other points on the line connecting points *r* and *t* are also feasible. One option is point *s*, with 28 chips and 24 shirts. The steepness of the curve's slope—3.0—shows the opportunity cost of computer chips: one chip per three shirts. Figure 19.1 also shows the production possibilities curve for Chipland. Chipland can produce daily 120 shirts and no chips (point *b*), 120 chips and no shirts (point *d*), or any combination of chips and shirts between these two points. In Chipland, the trade-off is one shirt per computer chip: The opportunity cost of a chip is one shirt, so the slope of the production possibilities curve is 1.0.

Each nation could decide to be self-sufficient, picking a point on its production possibilities curve and producing everything it wants to consume. For example, Shirtland could pick point *s*, producing daily 28 chips and 24 shirts, and Chipland

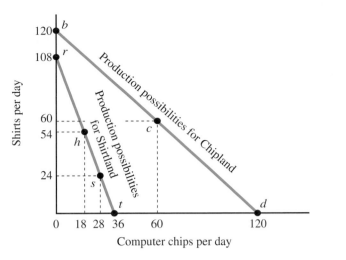

FIGURE 19.1
**Production Possibilities
Curve**
The production possibilities
curve shows the
combinations of two goods
that can be produced with a
nation's resources. For
Chipland, there is a one-for-
one trade-off between the
two goods. For Shirtland,
the trade-off is three shirts
for every computer chip. In
the absence of trade,
Shirtland can pick point *s*
(28 chips and 24 shirts), and
Chipland can pick point *c*
(60 chips and 60 shirts).

Shirtland Possibilites

Point	Shirts	Chips
r	108	0
h	54	18
s	24	28
t	0	36

Chipland Possibilities

Point	Shirts	Chips
b	120	0
c	60	60
d	0	120

could pick point *c*, producing daily 60 chips and 60 shirts. In the language of international trade, this is a case of **autarky**, or self-sufficiency (in Greek, *aut* means "self" and
arke means "to suffice").

Autarky

A situation in which each
country is self-sufficient, so
there is no trade.

Comparative Advantage and the Terms of Trade

Would the two nations be better off if each nation specialized in the production of one
good and traded with the other nation? To decide which nation should produce a particular good, we need to look at each good and figure out which nation has the lower
opportunity cost of producing it. As you saw in Chapter 3, the nation with the lower
opportunity cost has a **comparative advantage** in producing that good. As we
emphasized in Chapter 3, it is comparative advantage that matters for trade—not
absolute advantage, the ability of a nation to produce a particular good at a lower
absolute cost than that of another nation. Let's see how it works.

Comparative advantage

The ability of one person or
nation to produce a good at an
opportunity cost that is lower
than the opportunity cost of
another person or nation.

Absolute advantage

The ability of one person or
nation to produce a good at a
lower absolute cost than
another person or nation.

1   *Chips produced in Chipland.* The opportunity cost of one chip is one shirt
in Chipland, and the opportunity cost of one chip is three shirts in Shirtland.
Chipland has a comparative advantage in the production of chips. Because
Chipland sacrifices fewer shirts to produce one chip, Chipland should produce
chips.

2 *Shirts produced in Shirtland.* The opportunity cost of one shirt is one chip in Chipland, and the opportunity cost of one shirt is 1/3 of a chip in Shirtland. When it comes to producing shirts, Shirtland has a comparative advantage because it sacrifices fewer chips to produce one shirt. Shirtland should therefore produce shirts.

Trade will make it possible for people in each specialized nation to consume both goods. At what rate will the two nations exchange shirts and chips? To determine the **terms of trade**, let's look at how much Shirtland is willing to pay to get one chip and how much Chipland is willing to accept to give up one chip.

Terms of trade

The rate at which two goods will be exchanged.

1 To get one chip, Shirtland is willing to pay up to three shirts. That's how many shirts it would sacrifice if it produced its own chip. For example, if the nations agree to exchange two shirts per chip, Shirtland could rearrange its production, producing one less chip but three more shirts. After exchanging two of the newly produced shirts for one chip, Shirtland will have the same number of chips but one additional shirt.
2 To give up one chip, Chipland is willing to accept any amount greater than one shirt. For example, if the nations agree to exchange two shirts per chip, Chipland could rearrange its production, producing one more chip and one less shirt. After it exchanges the newly produced chip for two shirts, Chipland will have the same number of chips but one additional shirt.

There's an opportunity for mutually beneficial trade to take place between the two countries because the willingness to pay—three shirts by Shirtland—exceeds the willingness to accept—one shirt by Chipland. It's possible for Shirtland and Chipland to split the difference between the willingness to pay and the willingness to accept, exchanging two shirts per chip. This will actually make both countries better off in terms of the total amount of goods they can consume. We'll see why next.

The Consumption Possibilities Curve

A nation that decides to specialize and trade is no longer limited to the options shown by its own production possibilities curve. The **consumption possibilities curve** shows the combinations of two goods (computer chips and shirts in our example) that a nation can consume when it specializes in one good and trades with another nation.

Figure 19.2 shows the consumption possibilities curve for our two nations, assuming that they exchange two shirts per chip.

Consumption possibilities curve

A curve showing the combinations of two goods that can be consumed when a nation specializes in a particular good and trades with another nation.

▶ In Panel A, Chipland specializes in chip production, the good for which it has a comparative advantage. It produces 120 chips and no shirts (point *d*). Given the terms of trade, Chipland can exchange 40 of its 120 chips for 80 shirts, leading to point *x*. At point *x*, Chipland can consume 80 chips and 80 shirts.
▶ In Panel B, Shirtland specializes in shirts production. It produces 108 shirts and no chips (point *r*). Given the terms of trade, it can exchange 80 shirts of its 108 shirts for 40 chips, leading to point *y* on its consumption possibilities curve. Shirtland can consume 28 shirts and 40 ships.

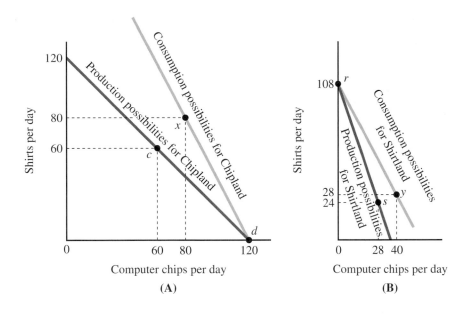

(A)   (B)

FIGURE 19.2

Consumption Possibilities Curve
The consumption possibilities curve shows the combinations of computer chips and shirts that can be consumed if each country specializes and trades. In Panel A, Chipland produces 120 chips and trades 40 of these chips to Shirtland for 80 shirts. In Panel B, Shirtland produces 108 shirts and trades 80 of these shirts to Chipland for 40 chips. The trade allows each nation to consume more.

How do the outcomes with specialization and trade compare to the autarky outcomes? Chipland moves from point *c* (autarky) to point *x*, so trade increases the consumption of each good by 20 units. Shirtland moves from point *s* to point *y*, so this nation consumes 12 additional chips and 4 additional shirts.

In Figure 19.2, each consumption possibilities curve lies above the nation's production possibilities curves, meaning that each nation has more options about how much to consume under specialization and trade. In most cases, a nation picks a point on the consumption possibilities curve that provides more of each good. Of course, this is a very simple example. In the actual world market, there are many countries producing and trading many goods. The marketplace determines what the terms of those trades will be depending upon supply, demand, and pricing.

The Employment Effects of Free Trade

You've now seen that trade allows each nation to consume more of each good. But we haven't yet discussed the effects of trade on employment. Under free trade, each nation will begin to specialize in a single good, causing considerable changes in the country's employment in different industries. In Chipland, the chip industry doubles in size—output increases from 60 to 120 chips per day—while the shirt industry disappears. Workers and other resources will leave the shirt industry and move to the chip industry. In Shirtland, the flow is in the opposite direction: Workers and other resources move from the chip industry to the shirt industry.

Is free trade good for everyone? Switching from self-sufficiency to specialization and trade increases consumption in both nations, so on average, people in each nation benefit from free trade. But some people in both nations will be harmed by free trade. In Chipland, for example, people in the shirt industry will lose their jobs when the shirt industry disappears. Some workers can easily move into the expanding computer-chip industry; for these workers, free trade is likely to be beneficial. However, other shirt workers will be unable to make the move to the chip industry; they will be forced to accept lower-paying jobs or face unemployment. Free trade is likely to make these displaced workers worse off.

There is a saying, "Where you stand on an issue depends on where you sit." In our example, a worker sitting at a sewing machine in Chipland is likely to oppose free trade because that worker is likely to lose a job. A worker sitting at a workstation in a computer-chip fabrication facility is likely to support free trade because the resulting increase in computer-chip exports will generate more employment opportunities in that industry.

TEST Your Understanding

1. Use Figure 19.1 to complete the following statements with numbers: If Chipland starts at point *c* and decides to produce 10 more chips, it will produce _____ shirts. If Shirtland produces only 10 chips, it will produce _____ shirts.
2. In Nation H, the opportunity cost of tables is five chairs, while in Nation B, the opportunity cost of tables is only one chair. Which country should produce tables, and which should produce chairs?
3. Nations H and B split the difference between the willingness to pay for tables and the willingness to accept. What are the terms of trade?
4. List the two bits of information you need to draw the consumption possibilities curve for a particular nation.
5. In Figure 19.2, suppose the nations agree to exchange one shirt for each chip. Will the consumption possibilities curve for Chipland still be above its production possibilities curve?

Protectionist Policies

Now that you know the basic rationale for specialization and trade, we can explore the effects of public policies that restrict it. All the restrictions we explore limit the gains from specialization and trade. We will consider four common import-restriction policies: an outright ban on imports, an import quota, voluntary export restraints, and a tariff.

Import Ban

To show how an import ban affects the market, let's start with an unrestricted market—no import ban. Figure 19.3 shows the market for shirts in Chipland, a nation with a comparative advantage in producing computer chips, not shirts. The domestic supply curve shows the quantity of shirts supplied by firms in Chipland. Looking at point *m*, we see that Chipland firms will not supply any shirts unless the price is at least

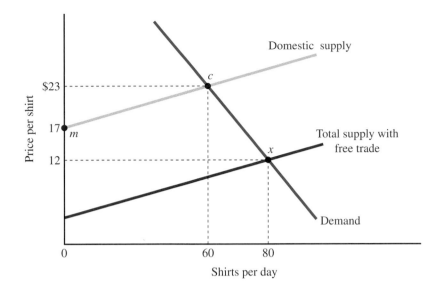

FIGURE 19.3

Effects of an Import Ban

In the free-trade equilibrium, demand intersects the total supply curve at point *x*, with a price of $12 and a quantity of 80 shirts. If shirt imports are banned, the equilibrium is shown by the intersection of the demand curve and the domestic supply curve (point *c*). The price increases to $23.

$17 per shirt. The total supply curve for shirts, which shows the quantity supplied by both domestic firms and foreign firms (in Shirtland), lies to the right of the domestic supply curve. At each price, the total supply of shirts exceeds the domestic supply because foreign firms supply shirts too. Point *x* shows the free-trade equilibrium: The demand curve from domestic residents intersects the total supply curve at a price of $12 per shirt and a quantity of 80 shirts. Because this price is below the minimum price for domestic firms, domestic firms produce no shirts, and all the shirts in Chipland are imported from Shirtland.

What will happen if Chipland bans imported shirts? Foreign suppliers will disappear from the shirt market, so the total supply of shirts will be the domestic supply. In Figure 19.3, point *c* shows the equilibrium when Chipland bans imported shirts: The domestic demand curve intersects the domestic supply curve at a price of $23 per shirt and a quantity of 60 shirts. In other words, the decrease in supply resulting from the import ban increases the price consumers have to pay for shirts and decreases the quantity available for them to buy.

Quotas and Voluntary Export Restraints

An alternative to an import ban is an import quota—a limit on the amount of a good that can be imported. An import quota is a restrictive policy that falls between free trade and an outright ban: Imports are cut but not eliminated. For example, if a quota were put on shirts, the price consumers would have to pay would fall somewhere between the price they would pay with free trade ($12 per shirt, as in our example) and the price they would pay if imported shirts were banned ($23 per shirt). Where exactly the price would fall would depend on how high or low the quotas are.

Import quotas are illegal under international trading rules. To get around these rules, an exporting country will sometimes agree to a **voluntary export restraint (VER)**. A VER is similar to an import ban. When an exporting nation adopts a VER, it

Voluntary export restraint (VER)

A scheme under which an exporting country voluntarily decreases its exports.

Import quota

A limit on the amount of a good that can be imported.

cuts its exports to avoid having to face even more restrictive trade policies importing countries might be tempted to impose on them. Although VERs are legal under world trading rules, they violate the spirit of international free-trade agreements. In any case, quotas and VERs have the same effect. Like a quota, a VER increases the price of the restricted good, making it more feasible for domestic firms to participate in the market.

Figure 19.4 shows the effect of an **import quota** or VER. Starting from the free-trade equilibrium at point *x*, an import quota will shift the total supply curve to the left: At each price there will be a smaller quantity of shirts supplied because foreign suppliers aren't allowed to supply as many. The total supply curve when there is an import quota or VER will lie between the domestic supply curve and the total supply curve under free trade. The equilibrium under an import quota or VER occurs at point *q*, where the demand curve intersects the total supply curve under an import limitation. The $20 price per shirt with the import quota exceeds the $17 minimum price of domestic firms, so domestic firms supply 22 shirts (point *e*). Under a free-trade policy, they would have supplied no shirts.

A quota or a VER produces winners and losers. The winners include foreign and domestic shirt producers. In our example, foreign firms can sell shirts at a price of $20 instead of $12 each, and the price is high enough for domestic firms to participate in the market. This generates benefits for the firms and their workers. The losers are consumers, who pay a higher price for shirts. In some cases, the government issues **import licenses** to some citizens, who can then buy shirts from foreign firms at a low price, such as $12, and sell the shirts at the higher domestic price, $20. Since import licenses provide profits to the holder, they are often awarded to politically powerful firms or individuals; moreover, since they are so valuable, there is the risk that government officials may be paid bribes for the licenses.

We know that consumers pay higher prices for goods that are subject to protectionist policies, but how much more? Here is one example. In the United States, voluntary export restraints on Japanese automobiles in 1984 increased the price of a Japanese car by about $1,300 and the price of a domestic car by about $660.[1]

Import licenses

Rights, issued by a government, to import goods.

FIGURE 19.4

Market Effects of a Quota, a VER, or a Tariff

An import quota shifts the supply curve to the left. The market moves upward along the demand curve to point *q*, which is between point *x* (free trade) and *c* (an import ban). We can reach the same point with a tariff that shifts the total supply curve to the same position.

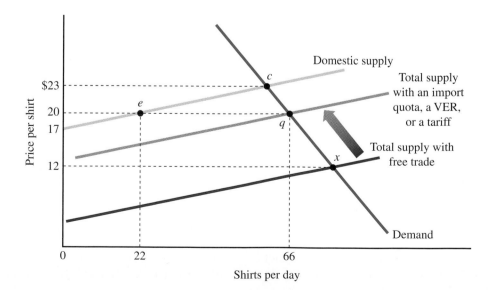

Tariffs

An alternative to a quota or a VER is an import **tariff**, which is a tax on an imported good. Tariffs have the same effect as quotas and VERs. We know from our earlier discussions that a tax shifts the supply curve to the left and increases the equilibrium price. In Figure 19.4, suppose the tariff shifts the total supply curve with free trade so that it intersects the domestic demand curve at point *q*. In other words, we reach the same point we reached with the quota: Consumers pay the same $20 price per shirt, and domestic firms produce the same quantity: 22 shirts.

There is one fundamental difference between a quota and a tariff. An import quota allows importers to buy shirts from foreign suppliers at a low price—say, $12 per shirt—and sell them for $20 each, the artificially high price. In other words, importers make money from the quota. Under a tariff, the government gets the money, collecting $8 per shirt from foreign suppliers. Citizens in Chipland will prefer the tariff to the quota because the government can use the revenue from the tariff to cut other taxes or expand public programs.

In the real world, tariffs can have major effects. One trade expert estimated that cutting industrial tariffs by 50% would increase the output of the world's economy by $270 billion per year. Similar easing of restrictions on agricultural products would cut the world's food bill by $100 billion.[2]

Responses to Protectionist Policies

A restriction on imports is likely to lead to further restrictions on trade. For example, if Chipland bans shirt imports, the shirt industry in Shirtland might retaliate by banning computer chips from Chipland. A trade war of this sort could escalate to the point where the two nations return to self-sufficiency. If this happens, the two countries

Tariff
A tax on an imported good.

At times countries will try to restrict imports through tariffs, quotas, or voluntary export restraints. Automobile imports have been subject to voluntary export restraints.

would be forced to scale back their consumption. We can see that by looking back at Figure 19.2: Chipland will move from point *x* to point *c*, and Shirtland will move from point *y* to point *s*. This sort of retaliatory response is common. Because it is, we know that protecting one industry in a nation is likely to harm that nation's other exports. Chipland's shirt industry, if protected from imports, may grow, but it will be at the expense of its computer-chip industry.

There are many examples of import restrictions that have led to retaliatory policies and substantially lessened trade. The most famous was the Smoot–Hawley tariff of 1930. When the United States increased its average tariff on imports to 59%, its trading partners retaliated with higher tariffs on U.S. products. The resulting trade war reduced international trade and deepened the worldwide depression of the 1930s.

The threat of retaliatory policies may persuade a nation to loosen its protectionist policies. For example, in 1995, the United States announced that it would impose 100% tariffs on Japanese luxury cars if Japan didn't ease its restrictions on imported auto parts. Just hours before the tariffs were to take effect, the two nations reached an agreement that was expected to increase the sales of U.S. auto parts to Japanese firms. In 2002, President Bush imposed tariffs on steel. However, when faced with the threat of retaliatory policies in Europe, he ended the sanctions in 2003.

Import restrictions also create an incentive to smuggle goods. The restrictions create a gap between the cost of purchasing the restricted goods abroad and the price goods can be sold for in the protected economy, so there is a profit to be made.

TEST Your Understanding

6. Complete the following statement: If a country bans the importation of a particular good, the market equilibrium is shown by the intersection of the _____ curve and the _____ curve.
7. Complete the statement with "above" or "below." The equilibrium price under an import quota is _____ the price that occurs with an import ban and _____ the price that occurs with free trade.
8. From the perspective of consumers, which is better, a tariff or a quota?
9. In Figure 19.4, what fraction of the shirt market is supplied by domestic firms under a quota system?

Rationales for Protectionist Policies

Why would a government impose protectionist policies like an import ban, quota, VER, or tariff? There are three possible reasons:

1 To shield workers from foreign competition
2 To nurture infant industries until they mature
3 To help domestic firms establish monopolies in world markets

To Shield Workers from Foreign Competition

One of the most basic arguments for protectionism is that it shields workers in industries that would be hurt by trade. Suppose that relative to the United States, nations in the Far East have a comparative advantage in producing textiles. If the United States were to reduce existing tariffs on textiles, domestic manufacturers could not compete. They would have to close their factories and lay off workers. In an ideal world, the laid-off workers would take new jobs in other sectors of the economy. In practice, this is difficult. Many workers don't immediately have the skills to go to work in other sectors, and obtaining these skills takes time. Moreover, the textile industry is heavily concentrated in the southeastern part of the United States. Politicians from that region will try to keep tariffs in place to prevent the temporary unemployment and changes in employment patterns in their areas—they have an incentive to protect their own constituents, even though it may cause major economic losses for the economy. The result of this protection will be less-efficient production, higher prices, and lower consumption for the United States. How much does it cost to protect a job? "A Closer Look: The Cost of Protecting Jobs" presents some recent evidence.

To Nurture Infant Industries

During World War II, the United States built hundreds of boats, called Liberty ships, for the Navy. As more and more of these ships were built, each required fewer hours to complete because workers acquired knowledge during the production process and got better at it. Engineers and economists call this phenomenon **learning by doing**. To

Learning by doing
Knowledge gained during production that increases productivity.

A CLOSER LOOK — The Cost of Protecting Jobs

The Federal Reserve Bank of Dallas recently examined the cost the United States paid to protect jobs in 20 different industries. Below are the top five industries in terms of costs per job saved:

Protected Industry	Jobs Saved	Annual Cost per Job Saved
Benzenoid chemicals	216	$1,376,436
Luggage	226	1,285,078
Softwood lumber	605	1,044,271
Sugar	2,261	826,104
Polyethylene resins	298	812,928

The annual costs of saving a job in these industries is staggering—in three of these cases it is over a million dollars a year! In other industries, the costs per job may be a bit lower, but the total cost to the economy is much higher because the number of jobs saved is much greater. In textiles and apparels, the annual cost per job is "only" $199,241, but the total cost of protecting this industry is $33.6 billion a year.

Source: Federal Reserve Bank of Dallas, *Annual Report 2002*, p. 19.

A CLOSER LOOK

Protection for Candle Makers

In response to the spread of protectionism, the French economist Frédéric Bastiat (1801–1851) wrote the following fictitious petition, in which French candle makers asked for protection from "unfair" competition:

We are suffering from the intolerable competition of a foreign rival, placed, it would seem, in a condition so far superior to ours for the production of light, that he absolutely inundates our national market at a price fabulously reduced. The moment he shows himself, our trade leaves us—all of our customers apply to him; and a branch of native industry, having countless ramifications, is all at once rendered completely stagnant. This rival . . . is none other than the sun.

What we pray for is, that it may please you to pass a law ordering the shutting up of all windows, sky-lights, dormer win-

dows, curtains, blinds, bull's eyes; in a word all openings, holes, chinks, clefts, and fissures, by or through which the light of the sun has been in use to enter houses, to the prejudice of the meritorious manufactures with which we . . . have accommodated our country—a country which, in gratitude, ought not to abandon us now.

Does it not argue to the greatest inconsistency to check as you do the importation of coal, iron, cheese, and goods of foreign manufacture, merely because . . . their price approaches zero, while at the same time you freely admit, and without limitation, the light of the sun, whose price is during the whole day at zero?

Source: Frédéric Bastiat, *Economics Sophisms* (Edinburgh: Oliver & Boyd, 1873), pp. 49–53.

learn a new game, such as Ping-Pong, you learn by doing. At first, you may find it difficult to play, but your skills improve as you go along.

Tariffs and other protectionist policies are often defended on the grounds that they protect new or **infant industries** that are in the early stages of learning by doing. A tariff shields a young industry from the competition of its more mature rivals. After the infant industry "grows up," the tariff can eventually be eliminated because the industry is able to compete. In practice, infant industries rarely become competitive with their foreign rivals. During the 1950s and 1960s, many Latin American countries used tariffs and other policies to protect their young manufacturing industries from foreign competition. Unfortunately, the domestic industries never became as efficient as foreign suppliers, and the Latin American countries that tried this policy suffered. Another problem with protecting an infant industry is that once an industry is given tariff protection, it is difficult to take it away. For an interesting discussion of the merits of protecting an industry from "unfair" competition, read "A Closer Look: Protection for Candle Makers."

Infant industries

Industries that are at an early stage of development.

To Help Domestic Firms Establish Monopolies in World Markets

If the production of a particular good requires extremely large economies of scale, the world market will support only a few, or perhaps just one, firm. In this case, a nation might be tempted to adopt policies to ensure a company within its borders will end up being the world monopolist. Suppose the commercial aircraft industry can support only one large firm; if two firms enter the industry, both will lose money. A nation could agree to provide financial support to a domestic firm to guarantee that the firm will make a profit. With such a guarantee, the domestic firm will enter the industry. Knowing this, a foreign firm will be reluctant to enter, so the domestic firm will capture the monopoly profit. The country the successful firm is located in will benefit from higher production and more jobs for its citizens.

One famous example of this is the case of Airbus, an airplane manufacturing consortium in Europe. Several European countries provided large subsidies for the firms producing the Airbus brand of planes. These subsidies allowed the firms associated with Airbus to underprice some of their rivals in the United States, and at least one U.S. manufacturer of commercial airplanes was forced out of business.

What could go wrong with these monopoly-creation policies? If both nations subsidize their domestic firms, both firms will enter the market and lose money. The taxpayers in both countries will then have to pay for the subsidies. And there is the possibility a nation may pick the wrong industry to subsidize. Together, the British and French subsidized an airplane known as the Concorde, which flew at supersonic speeds, rapidly shuttling passengers between Europe and the United States. Although the Concorde captured the market, the market was not worth capturing. The venture lost money because the Concorde was very costly to develop and fly and few people were willing to pay a large premium for supersonic travel. The Concorde stopped flying in 2003.

TEST Your Understanding

10. Comment on the following statement: If we eliminated our textile tariffs, the dislocated workers could easily switch to other jobs.
11. Explain the infant-industry argument.
12. List the two problems associated with subsidizing an industry in the hope of establishing a worldwide monopoly.

A Brief History of International Tariff and Trade Agreements

Since 1980, the average U.S. tariff has been about 5% of the value of imported goods, a rate that is close to the average tariffs in Japan and most European nations but very low by historical standards. As we noted earlier, when the Smoot–Hawley tariffs were implemented in the 1930s, the average U.S. tariff was a whopping 59% of a product's price. Tariffs are lower today because several international agreements subsequently reduced them.

The first major trade agreement following World War II was the **General Agreement on Tariffs and Trade (GATT)**. This agreement was initiated in 1947 by the United States and 23 other nations and now has over 146 member nations. There

General Agreement on Tariffs and Trade (GATT)

An international agreement that has lowered trade barriers between the United States and other nations.

have been nine rounds of GATT negotiations over tariffs and trade regulations, resulting in progressively lower tariffs for the member nations. The last completed set of negotiations, the Uruguay round (1994), decreased tariffs by about one-third of the previous level. In 1995, the **World Trade Organization (WTO)** was formed to enforce GATT and other international trade agreements. Under GATT's "most favored nation" provision, a country that reduces tariffs for one nation must do so for all members of GATT. This provision helps reduce tariffs throughout the world.

A new round of trade negotiations began in Doha, Qatar in 2001. In these negotiations, the member countries set an ambitious agenda, including cutting the protections for agricultural and service products. The Qatar round focused on giving a large share of the benefits gained from trade liberalization to developing countries, who felt that they did not gain as much in the previous round compared to the developed countries.

In addition to the large group of nations involved in the WTO, other nations have formed trade associations to lower trade barriers and promote international trade. Here are some of the most well-known agreements:

▶ The North American Free Trade Agreement (NAFTA) took effect in 1994 and will be implemented over a 15-year period. The agreement will eventually eliminate all tariffs and other trade barriers between Canada, Mexico, and the United States.
▶ The European Union (EU) was designed to remove all trade barriers within Europe and create a single market. Initially, the EU consisted of just six countries: Belgium, Germany, France, Italy, Luxembourg, and the Netherlands. Denmark, Ireland, and the United Kingdom joined in 1973; Greece in 1981; Spain and Portugal in 1986; and Austria, Finland, and Sweden in 1995. In 2004, the biggest ever enlargement took place with 10 new countries joining the EU.
▶ The leaders of 18 Asian nations have formed an organization called Asian Pacific Economic Cooperation (APEC). In 1994, APEC signed a nonbinding agreement to reduce trade barriers among these nations.

Some economists are concerned that these regional trade agreements may stand in the way of broader international trade agreements under GATT. Although regional agreements may lead to reduced tariffs for neighboring, or member, countries, they do little to promote efficiency across the globe. For example, a Belgian firm may find it easier to sell goods into France than a firm from South America that has a lower cost of production.

Recent Policy Debates and Trade Agreements

We're now ready to discuss three recent policy debates concerning international trade:

1 Are foreign producers dumping their products?
2 Do trade laws inhibit environmental protection?
3 Does trade cause income inequality?

Are Foreign Producers Dumping Their Products?

Although tariff rates have been reduced in recent years, a number of controversies surrounding free trade remain. One of these controversies relates to **dumping**. A firm is dumping when the price it charges in a foreign market is either lower than the price it charges in its home market or lower than its production cost. Dumping is illegal under international trade agreements; hundreds of cases of alleged dumping are presented to WTO authorities each year. Here are some recent cases in which the WTO concluded that dumping had occurred: Hong Kong VCRs sold in Europe; Chinese bicycles sold in the United States; Asian TV sets sold in Europe; steel from Brazil, India, Japan, and Spain sold in the United States; U.S. beef sold in Mexico; and Chinese computer disks sold in Japan and the United States. Under the current provisions of the WTO, a nation can impose antidumping duties on products that are being dumped within its borders.

Why would a firm dump—charge a low price in the foreign market? The first reason is price discrimination. **Price discrimination** occurs when a firm charges a different price to different customers buying the same product. If a firm has a monopoly in its home market but faces strong competition in a foreign market, it will naturally charge a higher price in the home market. What the firm is doing is using its monopoly power to charge higher prices to consumers at home and charge lower prices to consumers abroad where it faces competition. This strategy maximizes its profits.

To illustrate how international price discrimination works, let's look at the case of Korean VCRs.[3] In the 1980s there were only three firms, all Korean, selling VCRs in Korea, but there were dozens of firms selling VCRs in Europe. The lack of competition in Korea generated very high prices for Korean consumers: They paid much more than European consumers paid for identical Korean VCRs and VCRs produced by firms in other countries. Essentially, Korean firms used their market power to discriminate against consumers in their own country. When international trade authorities concluded these companies were, indeed, dumping VCRs in Europe, the Korean firms responded by cutting prices in their home market. However, they didn't increase their prices in Europe— much to the delight of European consumers and the dismay of European producers, who had sought relief from the dumping in the first place.

This brings up a second reason for dumping: **predatory pricing**—cutting prices in an attempt to drive rival firms out of business. The predatory firm sets its price below its production cost. The price is low enough that both the predator and its prey (a firm in the foreign market) lose money. After the prey goes out of business, the predator increases its price to earn a monopoly profit.

Although the rationale for antidumping laws is to prevent predatory pricing, it is difficult to determine whether low prices are the result of this or price discrimination. Many economists are skeptical about how frequently predatory pricing actually occurs versus price discrimination; they suspect that many nations use their antidumping laws as protectionist policies in disguise. Because WTO rules limit tariffs and quotas, some nations may be tempted to substitute antidumping duties for these protectionist policies.

Until the 1990s, antidumping cases were brought almost exclusively by Australia, New Zealand, Europe, Canada, and the United States. However, starting in the 1990s,

Dumping

A situation in which the price a firm charges in a foreign market is lower than either the price it charges in its home market or the production cost.

Price discrimination

The process under which a firm divides consumers into two or more groups and picks a different price for each group.

Predatory pricing

A pricing scheme under which a firm decreases its price to drive a rival out of business, and increases the price when the other firm disappears.

the number of antidumping cases alleged by developing countries began to rise. Today, approximately half of the cases are brought by developing countries. Professor Thomas Prusa of Rutgers University has studied antidumping and found that it is a potent weapon for protecting domestic industries. If an antidumping case is settled and a tariff is imposed as a result, imports typically fall by 50% to 70% during the first three years of the protection period. Even if a country loses a claim, imports still fall by 15% to 20%.[4]

Do Trade Laws Inhibit Environmental Protection?

In recent trade negotiations, a new player—environmental groups—appeared on the scene. Starting in the early 1990s, environmentalists began to question whether policies that liberalized trade could harm the environment. They were concerned whether increased trade would lead to world-wide environmental degradation. An important issue that attracted their attention was the killing of dolphins by tuna fishers.

Anyone who catches tuna with a large net will also catch the dolphins that swim with the tuna, and most of the dolphins will die. In 1972, the United States outlawed the use of tuna nets by U.S. ships. However, ships from other nations, including Mexico, were still catching tuna with nets and selling that tuna in the United States. The United States responded with a boycott of Mexican tuna caught with nets. The Mexican government complained to an international trade authority that the tuna boycott was an unfair trade barrier. The trade authority agreed with Mexico and forced the United States to remove the boycott.

Under current WTO rules, a country can adopt any environmental standard it chooses, as long as it does not discriminate against foreign producers. For example, the United States can limit the exhaust emissions of all cars that operate in the United States. As long as emissions rules apply equally to all cars, domestic and imports, the rules are legal according to the WTO. An international panel upheld U.S. fuel efficiency rules for automobiles on this principle.

The tuna boycott was a violation of WTO rules because killing dolphins does not harm the U.S. environment directly. For the same reason, the United States cannot ban imported goods produced by factories that generate air or water pollution in other countries. It is easy to understand why WTO rules do not allow countries to restrict trade on the basis of the methods that are used to produce goods and services. Countries differ in the value they place on the environment. For example, a poor nation may be willing to tolerate more pollution if it means attaining a higher standard of living for its citizens.

If trade restrictions cannot be used to protect the dolphins and deal with other global environmental problems, what else can we do? International agreements have been used for a variety of different environmental goals, from limiting the harvest of whales to reducing the chemicals that deplete the ozone layer. These agreements are difficult to reach, however, so some nations will be tempted to use trade restrictions to pursue environmental goals. If they do, they will encounter resistance because WTO rules mean that a nation can pursue its environmental goals only within its own borders.

The ban by the European Union of hormone-treated beef is one example of how environmental and health concerns can affect international trade.

Trade disputes about environmental issues are part of a larger phenomenon that occurs when trade issues and national regulations collide. At one time, most trade disputes were simply matters of protecting domestic industries from foreign competition. Agriculture, textile, and steel industries around the world frequently benefited from various forms of protection. But in recent years, a new breed of trade disputes has erupted revolving around social problems and the role of government regulation should play in solving them.

The European Union, for example, has banned imports of hormone-treated beef. The United States and Canada successfully challenged this ban with the WTO. They argued that there was no scientific evidence that concluded hormone-treated beef adversely affected human health. The European Union refused to rescind the ban and, as a consequence, the United States and Canada were permitted to impose tariffs on a wide range of European products that affected many of its industries.

The European Union's ban on hormone-treated beef was intended to protect European farmers from imports, but it also reflected the nervousness of Europeans about technology. After all, Europe banned all hormone-treated beef, not just imported beef. Shouldn't a country have a right to pursue this policy, even if it is not based on the best science of the day? Although the costs of the policy are straightforward in terms of higher beef prices, the benefits, in terms of potential safety and peace of mind, are much more difficult to assess. Similar issues will arise as genetically modified crops become more commonplace. As a world trading community, we will have to decide at what point we allow national policy concerns to override principles of free trade.

Does Trade Cause Inequality?

Inequality in wages has been growing in the United States since 1973. The wages of skilled workers have risen faster than the wages of unskilled workers. World trade has also boomed since 1973. Could there be a connection between the two?

Trade theory suggests a link between increased trade and increased wage inequality. Here is how they might be linked. Suppose the United States produces two types of goods: one using skilled labor (say, airplanes) and one using unskilled labor (say, textiles). The United States is likely to have a comparative advantage in products that use skilled labor, and developing countries are likely to have a comparative advantage in products that use unskilled labor. An increase in world trade will increase both exports and imports. An increase in U.S. exports means we'll need to produce more goods requiring skilled labor, so the domestic demand for skilled labor will increase and so will the wages of these workers. At the same time, an increase in U.S. imports means that we'll be buying more goods produced by unskilled laborers abroad, so the demand for unskilled workers here will decrease, and these people's wages will fall. As a result, the gap between the wages of the two types of workers in the United States will increase.

Economists have tried to determine how much trade has contributed to growing wage inequality in the United States. As usual, there are other factors that make such a determination difficult. It is difficult, for example, to distinguish between the effects of trade and the effects of technical progress. Technical change, such as the rapid introduction and use of computers, will also tend to increase the demand for skilled workers and decrease the demand for unskilled workers. Economists have noted, however, that the exports of goods using skilled labor and the imports of goods using unskilled labor have both increased, just as the theory predicts. Nonetheless, at least some of the increased wage inequality is caused by international trade.

One response to this undesirable side effect of trade is to use trade restrictions to protect industries that use unskilled workers. Another approach is to make the transition to an economy with more skilled than unskilled jobs less traumatic. In the long run, of course, workers will move to industries that require skilled labor, and they will eventually earn higher wages. However, in the short run the government could facilitate the transition by providing assistance for their education and training.

Why Do People Protest Against Free Trade?

We have seen that there are important policy issues surrounding trade. Under current international trade rules, a country cannot dictate the terms under which another country actually produces the goods and services that it sells—even if it harms the environment. It is also possible that free trade can contribute to inequality within the United States. But do these reasons explain the passion we sometimes see in protests against free trade, such as the riots in 1999 in Seattle at a WTO meeting or the protestors dressed in death masks gathering at world trade meetings?

Possibly, but it is more likely that the protestors are driven by something more basic. As we have seen in this chapter, trade and specialization provide important

In recent years, the World Trade Organization has generated considerable political controversy in the United States and abroad.

opportunities to raise living standards throughout the globe. But they also mean that individuals and nations surrender some of their independence and sovereignty. By not producing precisely what we consume, we become dependent on others to trade. By cooperating with other nations, we need to develop agreed-upon rules that, at times, limit our own actions.

The protestors may simply not understand the principles of trade, but they also may be subconsciously reacting against a perceived loss in independence and control. But in today's world, "no man is an island." Nations have become increasingly dependent on one another. Multinational corporations are the ultimate symbol of this interdependence, producing and distributing goods on a global scale. As symbols, companies like McDonald's or Nike can come under attack by the protestors. The benefits of trade, however, are so vast that countries will need to find ways to address issues of sovereignty and control while retaining an open and prosperous trading system.

TEST Your Understanding

13. What is dumping?
14. What restrictions do WTO rules place on a nation's environmental policies?
15. Consider a nation having a comparative advantage in the production of goods using unskilled labor. What types of workers will benefit from increased trade, and what types of workers will lose?

Economic Experiment

Protectionist Policies

Recall the market equilibrium experiment from Chapter 4. We can modify the experiment to show the effects of protectionist policies on equilibrium prices and quantities. On the supply side of the market, there are domestic apple producers and foreign apple producers; the domestic producers have higher unit costs. After several trading periods without any government intervention, you can change the rules as follows:

a. Apple imports are banned: Foreign producers cannot participate in the market.
b. There is a tariff (a tax on imports) of $5 per bushel. ●

USING THE TOOLS

In this chapter, we've discussed the trade-offs associated with protectionist policies and have used supply and demand curves to show the market effects of protectionist policies. Here are some opportunities to do your own economic analysis.

1. Incentives for Smuggling

If a country bans imports, smugglers may try to penetrate its markets. Suppose Chipland bans shirt imports, causing some importers to bribe customs officials, who "look the other way" as smugglers bring shirts into the country. Your job is to combat shirt smuggling. Use the information in Figure 19.3 in this chapter to answer the following questions:

a. Suppose importers can sell their shirts on the world market at a price of $12 per shirt. How much is an importer willing to pay to get customs officials to look the other way?
b. What sort of change in trade policy would make your job easier?

2. Trade in Genetically Modified Crops

Suppose the residents of a country become fearful of using genetically modified crops in their food supply. Consider the following two possible scenarios:

a. Aware of consumer sentiment, the largest supermarket chains in the country vow they will not purchase food products that use genetically modified crops.
b. The government, aware of voter sentiment during an election year, bans the import of the food products that use genetically modified crops.
   In both cases, no genetically modified crops enter the country. Do either of these cases run afoul of WTO policies?

3. Ban on Shoe Imports

Consider a country that initially consumes 100 pairs of shoes per hour, all of which are imported. The price of shoes is $40 per pair before the ban. Depict graphically the market effects of the ban.

4. Tariffs on Steel Imports

When the United States placed a tariff on steel imports in 2002, foreign producers naturally complained. But there were also complaints from U.S. firms operating in other industries. Why would other types of firms strongly object to the tariffs on U.S. steel imports?

SUMMARY

In this chapter, we discussed the benefits of specialization and trade, and we explored the trade-offs associated with protectionist policies. There is a basic conflict between consumers, who prefer free trade because free trade decreases prices, and workers in the protected industries, who want to keep their jobs. Here are the main points of the chapter:

1 If one country has a comparative advantage vis-à-vis another country in producing a particular good (a lower opportunity cost), specialization and trade will benefit both countries.

2 An import ban or an import quota increases prices, protecting domestic industries, but domestic consumers pay the price.

3 Because the victims of protectionist policies often retaliate, the protection of a domestic industry can harm an exporting industry.

4 A tariff (tax on imports) generates revenue for the government, whereas an import quota—a limit on imports—generates revenue for foreigners or importers.

5 In principle, the laws against dumping are designed to prevent predatory pricing. In practice, predatory pricing laws are often used to shield domestic industries from competition and allegations of it are hard to prove.

6 Under WTO rules, each country may pursue its environmental goals only within its own borders.

7 International trade has contributed to the widening gap between the wages of low-skilled and high-skilled labor.

KEY TERMS

absolute advantage, 423
autarky, 423
comparative advantage, 423
consumption possibilities curve, 424
dumping, 435
General Agreement on Tariffs and Trade (GATT), 433

import licenses, 428
import quota, 428
infant industries, 432
learning by doing, 431
predatory pricing, 435
price discrimination, 435
production possibilities curve, 422

tariff, 429
terms of trade, 424
voluntary export restraint (VER), 427
World Trade Organization (WTO), 434

PROBLEMS AND DISCUSSION QUESTIONS

1 In one minute, Country B can produce either 1,000 TVs and no computers or 500 computers and no TVs. Similarly, in one minute, Country C can produce either 2,400 TVs or 600 computers.
   a. Compute the opportunity costs of TVs and computers for each country. Which country has a comparative advantage in producing TVs? In producing computers?
   b. Draw the production possibilities curves for the two countries.

2 In Country U, the opportunity cost of a computer is 10 pairs of shoes. In Country C, the opportunity cost of a computer is 100 pairs of shoes.

a. Suppose the two countries split the difference between the willingness to pay for computers and the willingness to accept computers. Compute the terms of trade, that is, the rate at which the two countries will exchange computers and shoes.

b. Suppose the two countries exchange one computer for the number of shoes dictated by the terms of trade you computed in part (a). Compute the net benefit from trade for each country.

3 In Figure 19.2, suppose the two countries trade 35 computer chips for 70 shirts. For each country, compute the amounts of chips and shirts consumed.

4 Consider two countries, Tableland and Chairland, each capable of producing tables and chairs. Chairland can produce the following combinations of chairs and tables:
- ▶ All chairs and no tables: 36 chairs per day
- ▶ All tables and no chairs: 18 tables per day

Tableland can produce the following combinations of chairs and tables:
- ▶ All chairs and no tables: 40 chairs per day
- ▶ All tables and no chairs: 40 tables per day

In each country, there is a fixed trade-off of tables for chairs.
  a. Draw the two production possibilities curves, with chairs on the vertical axis and tables on the horizontal axis.
  b. Suppose that each country is initially self-sufficient and divides its resources equally between the two goods. How much does each country produce and consume?
  c. Which country has a comparative advantage in producing tables? Which has a comparative advantage in producing chairs?
  d. If the two countries split the difference between the buyer's willingness to pay for chairs and the seller's willingness to accept, in terms of chairs per table, what are the terms of trade?
  e. Draw the consumption possibilities curves.
  f. Suppose each country specializes in the good for which it has a comparative advantage, and they exchange 14 tables for some quantity of chairs. Compute the consumption bundles—bundles mean the consumption of tables and chairs—for each country.

5 A common approach to restrict automobile imports is to use voluntary export restraints. Evaluate the wisdom of this approach and propose an alternative policy.

6 Evaluate this comment: "If a country bans imports, smuggling is inevitable. We should welcome smuggling because it improves consumer welfare."

7 The European Union is committed to eliminating most of the trade barriers among its member nations. What types of people will benefit? Which types will lose?

8 What is the cost to consumers for each sugar industry job protected by import restrictions? In your opinion, is protecting these jobs worthwhile at this cost? If not, how much should we as a society be willing to pay for each job that is protected?

9 Suppose the president of a nation proposes it switch from a system of import quotas to a system of tariffs, with the idea that the switch will not affect the quantity of goods imported. Who will be in favor of the switch? Who will oppose it? Would you expect the proponents and the opponents to have the same political influence on the president?

10 Suppose residents of one nation are very fearful of biotechnology and they pass a law prohibiting the sale of all genetically altered foods in their country. Another nation, which produces these foods, claims that this law is an unfair trade barrier. In your view, should the first nation be allowed to prevent these imports, even if there is no scientific basis for its claim?

11 Web Exercise. Go to the Website for the World Trade Organization (*http://www.wto.org*) and explore some of the ongoing trade disputes. Pick one or two of these disputes and find additional background information, such as newspaper stories, on the Web. Use this information to understand the nature of the controversy.

12 Web Exercise. Go to the Website for the U.S. Trade Representative (*http://www.ustr.gov*), which is an office within the executive branch of the government. From the Website, what are some of the key trade issues for the U.S. government today?

MODEL ANSWERS TO QUESTIONS

Chapter-Opening Questions

1 The winners are the domestic nation's consumers, who pay lower prices, and the domestic nation's workers in export industries. The losers are people in the domestic nation who lose their jobs as imports replace domestically produced goods.

2 A tariff generates revenue for the government; a quota generates profits for importers.

3 First, if a firm has a monopoly in its home market but faces strong competition in a foreign market, the firm will naturally charge a higher price in the home market (it will price discriminate). Second, a firm may be engaging in predatory pricing—the practice of cutting prices in an attempt to drive rivals out of business.

4 Under current WTO rules, a country cannot adopt any environmental standard that discriminates against foreign producers. For example, the United States cannot impose an import ban on goods that are produced in polluting factories in other nations. This rule means that global environmental issues must be resolved with international agreements, not trade restrictions.

5 Although trade increases income inequality, it is unclear just how much of the recent increase in inequality can be attributed to the expansion of trade.

Test Your Understanding

1 50, 78 (108 − 30).

2 Nation B should produce tables, and Nation H should produce chairs.

3 Three chairs per table: Nation H is willing to pay five chairs, and Nation B is willing to accept one chair.

4 We need to know the maximum output of the good for which the nation has a comparative advantage and the terms of trade.

5 No. The consumption curve will be the same as the production curve.

6 Demand, domestic supply.

7 Below, above.

8 If a quota and a tariff led to the same price for a good, consumers would be indifferent between them. However, as citizens, they should prefer the tariff since the revenue generated goes to the government, which can use it to fund public programs or reduce taxes.

9 Domestic firms supply 22 units, which is one-third of the total equilibrium quantity supplied by the market (66).

10 This is false. Some workers do not have the skills to immediately go to work in other sectors, and it takes time to obtain new skills.

11 It takes some time for a new industry to learn by doing, so it may be sensible to protect a young industry when it is vulnerable to competition from foreign firms. However, in practice this does not work very well.

12 If two nations subsidize firms in the same industry, each nation could lose money. In addition, a nation might pick the wrong industry to subsidize.

13 A foreign firm is dumping when it sells a product in another country at a price below the price it charges in its own market or below its cost. It is difficult to determine whether dumping is occurring, and many countries used dumping laws under the guise of protectionism.

14 A nation's environmental laws must not discriminate against imported goods. The laws must apply equally to imports and domestic goods.

15 The wage of unskilled labor will increase; the wage of skilled labor will decrease.

NOTES

1. *A Review of Recent Developments in the U.S. Automobile Industry Including an Assessment of the Japanese Voluntary Restraint Agreements* (Washington, DC: U.S. International Trade Commission, February 1985).

2. Gary C. Hufbauer, "The Benefits of Open Markets and the Costs of Trade Protection and Economic Sanction," ACCF Center for Policy Research, http://www.accf.org/Hufbauer1297.htm

3. Taeho Bark, "The Korean Consumer Electronics Industry: Reaction to Antidumping Actions," Chapter 7 in *Antidumping: How It Works and Who Gets Hurt*, edited by J. Michael Finger (Ann Arbor, MI: University of Michigan Press, 1993).

4. Virgina Postrel, "Curb Demonstrates Faults of Courting Special Interests," *New York Times*, June 14, 2001, p. C1.

Glossary

Absolute advantage The ability of one person or nation to produce a good at a lower absolute cost than another person or nation.

Accounting profit Total revenue minus explicit costs.

Adverse-selection problem A situation in which the uninformed side of the market must choose from an undesirable or adverse selection of goods.

Asymmetric information A situation in which one side of the market—either buyers or sellers—has better information about the product than the other.

Autarky A situation in which each country is self-sufficient, so there is no trade.

Average fixed cost (AFC) Fixed cost divided by the quantity produced.

Average variable cost (AVC) Total variable cost divided by the quantity produced.

Average-cost pricing policy A regulatory policy under which the government picks the point on the demand curve at which price equals average cost.

Break-even price The price at which the economic profit is zero; price equals average total cost.

Budget line The line connecting all the combinations of two goods that exhaust a consumer's budget.

Budget set A set of points that includes all the combinations of goods that a consumer can afford, given the consumer's income and the prices of the goods.

Carbon tax A tax based on a fuel's carbon content.

Cartel A group of firms that collude explicitly, coordinating their pricing decisions.

Centrally planned economy An economy in which a government bureaucracy decides how much of each good to produce, how to produce the goods, and who gets them.

Ceteris paribus The Latin expression meaning other variables being held fixed.

Change in demand A change in the amount of a good demanded resulting from a change in something other than the price of the good; represented graphically by a shift of the demand curve.

Change in quantity demanded A change in the quantity consumers are willing to buy when the price changes; represented graphically by movement along the demand curve.

Change in quantity supplied A change in the quantity firms are willing to sell when the price changes; represented graphically by movement along the supply curve.

Change in supply A change in the amount of a good supplied resulting from a change in something other than the price of the good; represented graphically by a shift of the supply curve.

Collective bargaining Negotiations between a union and a firm over wages, working conditions, and job security.

Command-and-control policy A policy under which the government commands each firm to produce no more than a certain volume of pollution and specifies the pollution-control technology used.

Comparative advantage The ability of one person or nation to produce a good at a lower opportunity cost than another person or nation.

Complements Two goods related in such a way that a decrease in the price of one good increases the demand for the other good.

Concentration ratio A measure of the degree of concentration in a market; the four-firm concentration ratio is the percentage of the market output produced by the four largest firms.

Constant-cost industry An industry in which the average cost of production is constant; the long-run supply curve is horizontal.

Consumer surplus The difference between a consumer's willingness to pay for a product and the price that he or she pays for the product.

Consumption possibilities curve A curve showing the combinations of two goods that can be consumed when a nation specializes in the production of one good and trades with another nation.

Contestable market A market in which the costs of entering and leaving are low, so the firms that are already in the market are constantly threatened by the entry of new firms.

Craft union A labor organization that includes workers from a particular occupation, for example, plumbers, bakers, or electricians.

Cross elasticity of demand A measure of the responsiveness of the quantity demanded to changes in the price of a related good; computed by dividing the percentage change in the quantity demanded of one good (X) by the percentage change in the price of another good (Y).

Deadweight loss from monopoly A measure of the inefficiency from monopoly; with a constant-cost industry, equal to the difference between the consumer-surplus loss from monopoly pricing and the monopoly's profit.

Deadweight loss from taxation The difference between the total burden of a tax and the amount of revenue collected by the government.

Deadweight loss The decrease in the total surplus of the market.

Demand schedule A table of numbers that shows the relationship between price and quantity demanded, ceteris paribus.

Diminishing returns As one input increases while the other inputs are held fixed, output increases at a decreasing rate.

Diseconomies of scale A situation in which an increase in the quantity produced increases the long-run average cost of production.

Dominant strategy An action that is the best choice for a player, no matter what an opponent does.

Dumping A situation in which the price a firm charges in a foreign market is lower than either the price it charges in its home market or the production cost.

Duopolists' dilemma A situation in which both firms in a market would be better off if both chose the high price but each chooses the low price.

Duopoly A market with two firms.

Economic cost The opportunity cost of production, including both explicit and implicit costs.

Economic profit Total revenue minus total economic cost.

Economics The study of choice when there is scarcity, that is, a situation in which resources are limited and can be used in different ways.

Economies of scale A situation in which an increase in the quantity produced decreases the long-run average cost of production.

Elastic demand The price elasticity of demand is greater than 1.

Equimarginal rule Pick the combination of two things that equalizes the marginal benefit per dollar spent.

Excess burden of a tax Another name for deadweight loss.

Excess demand A situation in which, at the prevailing price, consumers are willing to buy more than producers are willing to sell.

Excess supply A situation in which, at the prevailing price, producers are willing to sell more than consumers are willing to buy.

Experience rating A situation in which each firm pays a different price for medical insurance, depending on the past medical bills of its employees.

Explicit cost The firm's actual cash payments for its inputs.

External cost of production A cost incurred by people outside the firm.

Factors of production The inputs used to produce goods and services.

Featherbedding Work rules that increase the amount of labor required to produce a given quantity of output.

Firm's short-run supply curve A curve showing the relationship between the price of a product and the quantity of output supplied by a firm in the short run.

Firm-specific demand curve A curve showing the relationship between the price charged by a specific firm and the quantity that can be sold by that firm.

Fixed cost (FC) Cost that does not depend on the quantity produced.

Free-rider problem A problem that occurs when people try to benefit from a public good without paying for it.

Game theory A framework to explore the actions and reactions of interdependent decision-makers.

Game tree A graphical representation of the consequences of different strategies.

General Agreement on Tariffs and Trade (GATT) An international agreement that has lowered trade barriers between the United States and other nations.

Grim-trigger strategy A strategy where a firm responds to underpricing by choosing a price so low that each firm makes zero economic profit.

Guaranteed price-matching strategy A strategy where a firm guarantees it will match a lower price by a competitor; also known as a "meet-the-competition" policy.

Implicit cost The opportunity cost of nonpurchased inputs.

Import licenses Rights, issued by a government, to import goods.

Import quota A limit on the amount of a good that can be imported.

Income effect The change in consumption resulting from a change in purchasing power caused by a price change.

Income effect for leisure demand The change in leisure time resulting from a change in real income caused by a change in the wage.

Income elasticity of demand A measure of the responsiveness of the quantity demanded to changes in consumer income; computed by dividing the percentage change in the quantity demanded by the percentage change in income.

Increasing-cost industry An industry in which the average cost of production increases as the total output of the industry increases; the long-run supply curve is positively sloped.

Indifference curve A curve showing the different combinations of two goods that generate the same level of utility or satisfaction.

Indifference map A set of indifference curves, each with a different utility level.

Individual demand curve A curve that shows the relationship between price and quantity demanded by an individual consumer, *ceteris paribus.*

Individual supply curve A curve showing the relationship between price and quantity supplied by a single firm, *ceteris paribus.*

Indivisible input An input that cannot be scaled down to produce a smaller quantity of output.

Industrial union A labor organization that includes all types of workers from a single industry, for example, steelworkers or autoworkers.

Inelastic demand The price elasticity of demand is less than 1.

Infant industries Industries that are at an early stage of development.

Inferior good A good for which an increase in income decreases demand.

Input-substitution effect The change in the quantity of labor demanded resulting from an increase in the price of labor relative to the price of other inputs.

Kinked demand curve model A model under which firms in an oligopoly match price reductions by other firms but do not match price increases by other firms.

Labor force The employed plus the unemployed.

Labor union An organized group of workers. Unions try to increase job security, improve working conditions, and increase wages and fringe benefits for their members.

Law of demand The higher the price, the smaller the quantity demanded, ceteris paribus.

Learning by doing Knowledge gained during production that increases productivity.

Learning effect The increase in a person's wage resulting from the learning of skills required for certain occupations.

Limit pricing A scheme under which a monopolist accepts a price below the normal monopoly price to deter other firms from entering the market.

Long-run average cost of production (LAC) Long-run total cost divided by the quantity of output produced.

Long-run demand curve for labor A curve showing the relationship between the wage and the quantity of labor demanded over the long run, when the number of firms in the market can change and firms can modify their production facilities.

Long-run marginal cost (LMC) The change in long-run cost from producing one more unit of output.

Long-run market supply curve A curve showing the relationship between the market price and quantity supplied in the long run.

Long-run total cost (LTC) The total cost of production in the long run when a firm is perfectly flexible in its choice of all inputs and can choose a production facility of any size.

Macroeconomics The study of the nation's economy as a whole.

Marginal benefit The extra benefit resulting from a small increase in some activity.

Marginal change A small, one-unit change in value.

Marginal cost The additional cost resulting from a small increase in some activity.

Marginal labor cost The increase in total labor cost resulting from one more unit of labor.

Marginal product of labor The change in output from one additional unit of labor.

Marginal rate of substitution (MRS) The rate at which a consumer is willing to trade or substitute one good for another.

Marginal revenue The change in total revenue that results from selling one more unit of output.

Marginal-revenue product of labor (MRP) The extra revenue generated from one more unit of labor; MRP is equal to the price of output times the marginal product of labor.

Market An arrangement that allows people to exchange things.

Market demand curve A curve showing the relationship between price and quantity demanded, *ceteris paribus.*

Market economy An economy in which people exchange things, trading what they have for what they want.

Market equilibrium A situation in which the quantity of a product demanded equals the quantity supplied, so there is no pressure to change the price.

Market failure A situation in which a market fails to be efficient because of external benefits, external costs, imperfect information, or imperfect competition.

Market power The ability to affect the price of a product

Market supply curve A curve showing the relationship between price and quantity supplied, *ceteris paribus.*

Market supply curve for labor A curve showing the relationship between the wage and the quantity of labor supplied.

Marketable pollution permits A system under which the government picks a target pollution level for a particular area, issues just enough pollution permits to meet the pollution target, and allows firms to buy and sell the permits; also known as a cap-and-trade system.

Median-voter rule A rule suggesting that the choices made by government will reflect the preferences of the median voter.

Merger A process in which two or more firms combine their operations.

Microeconomics The study of the choices made by households, firms, and government and of how these choices affect the markets for goods and services.

Midpoint method A method of computing a percentage change by dividing the change in the variable by the average value of the variable, or the midpoint between the old value and the new one.

Minimum efficient scale The output at which the long-run average-cost curve becomes horizontal.

Mixed market A market in which products of different qualities are sold for the same price.

Monopolistic competition A market served by many firms selling slightly different products.

Monopoly A market in which a single firm serves the entire market.

Monopsony A market in which there is a single buyer of an input.

Moral hazard Insurance encourages risky behavior.

Nash equilibrium An outcome of a game in which each player is doing the best he or she can, given the action of the other players.

Natural monopoly A market in which the economies of scale are so large that only a single large firm can survive.

Negative relationship A relationship in which an increase in the value of one variable decreases the value of another variable.

Nominal value The face value of an amount of money.

Normal good A good for which an increase in income increases demand.

Normative economics Analysis that answers the question "What ought to be?"

Oligopoly A market served by a few firms.

Opportunity cost What you sacrifice to get something.

Output effect The change in the quantity of labor demanded resulting from a change in the quantity of output produced.

Patent The exclusive right to sell a particular good for some period of time.

Paying efficiency wages The practice of a firm paying a higher wage to increase the average productivity of its workforce.

Perfectly competitive market A market with a very large number of firms, each of which produces the same standardized product in amounts so small that no individual firm can affect the market price.

Perfectly competitive market A market with hundreds or thousands of sellers and buyers of a standardized good. Each buyer and seller takes the market price as given. Firms can easily enter or exit the market.

Perfectly elastic demand The price elasticity of demand is infinite.

Perfectly elastic supply The price elasticity of supply is infinite.

Perfectly inelastic demand The price elasticity of demand equals 0.

Perfectly inelastic supply The price elasticity of supply equals 0.

Pollution offset A credit received for supporting a project that either reduces the pollution emissions of another firm or organization or results in the absorption of pollutants; also known as a reduction credit.

Pollution tax A tax or charge equal to the external cost per unit of waste.

Positive economics Analysis that answers the questions, "What is?" or "What will be?"

Positive relationship A relationship in which an increase in the value of one variable increases the value of another variable.

Predatory pricing A pricing scheme under which a firm decreases its price to drive a rival out of business and increases the price when the other firm disappears.

Price discrimination The process under which a firm divides consumers into two or more groups and picks a different price for each group.

Price elasticity of demand A measure of the responsiveness of the quantity demanded to changes in price; computed by dividing the percentage change in quantity demanded by the percentage change in price.

Price elasticity of supply A measure of the responsiveness of the quantity supplied to changes in price; computed by dividing the percentage change in quantity supplied by the percentage change in price.

Price fixing An arrangement in which two firms coordinate their pricing decisions.

Price leadership An implicit agreement under which firms in a market choose a price leader, observe that firm's price, and match it.

Price ratio The ratio of the price of one good to the price of a second good; the market trade-off.

Price-change formula A formula that shows the percentage change in equilibrium price resulting from a change in demand or supply, given values for the price elasticity of supply and the price elasticity of demand.

Private cost of production The production cost borne by a firm, which typically includes the costs of labor, capital, and materials.

Private good A good that is consumed by a single person or household.

Producer surplus The difference between the price a producer receives for a product and the producer's willingness to accept for the product.

Product differentiation A strategy monopolistic firms use to distinguish their products from competitors'.

Production possibilities curve A curve that shows the possible combinations of products that an economy can produce, given that its productive resources are fully employed and efficiently used.

Public choice economics A field of economics that explores how governments actually operate.

Public good A good that is available for everyone to consume, regardless of who pays and who doesn't.

Quantity demanded The amount of a product consumers are willing to buy.

Quantity supplied The amount of a product firms are willing to sell.

Real value The value of an amount of money in terms of what it can buy.

Rent seeking The process of using governments to obtain economic profit.

Right-to-work laws Laws that prohibit union shops, where union membership is required as a condition of employment

Scarcity A situation in which resources are limited in quantity and can be used in different ways.

Sequential decision-making game A game in which one player makes a choice before the other.

Short-run average total cost (ATC) Short-run total cost divided by the quantity of output; equal to AFC plus AVC.

Short-run demand curve for labor A curve showing the relationship between the wage and the quantity of labor demanded over the short run, the period when the firm cannot change its production facility.

Short-run marginal cost (MC) The change in short-run total cost resulting from producing one more unit of the good.

Short-run market supply curve A curve showing the relationship between price and the quantity supplied in the short run.

Short-run total cost (TC) The total cost of production in the short run, when one or more inputs (for example, the production facility) is fixed; equal to fixed cost plus variable cost.

Shut-down price The price at which the firm is indifferent between operating and shutting down; equal to the minimum average variable cost.

Signaling effect The increase in a person's wage resulting from the signal of productivity provided by completing college.

Simultaneous decision-making game A game in which each player makes a choice without the other person knowing what that choice is.

Slope of a curve The change in the variable on the vertical axis resulting from a one-unit increase in the variable on the horizontal axis.

Social cost of production Private cost plus external cost.

Substitutes Two goods that are related in such a way that an increase in the price of one good increases the demand for the other good.

Substitution effect for leisure demand The change in leisure time resulting from a change in the wage (the price of leisure) relative to the price of other goods.

Substitution effect The change in consumption resulting from a change in the price of one good relative to the price of another good.

Sunk cost A cost a firm has already paid or has agreed to pay some time in the future.

Supply schedule A table of numbers that shows the relationship between price and quantity supplied, *ceteris paribus*.

Tariff A tax on an imported good.

Terms of trade The rate at which two goods will be exchanged.

Thin market A market in which some high-quality goods are sold but fewer than would be sold in a market with perfect information.

Tie-in-sales A business practice under which a consumer of one product is required to purchase another product.

Tit-for-tat A strategy where one firm chooses whatever price the other firm chose in the preceding period.

Total product curve A curve showing the relationship between the quantity of labor and the quantity of output produced.

Total revenue The money the firm gets by selling its product; equal to the price times the quantity sold.

Total surplus The sum of consumer surplus and producer surplus.

Trust An arrangement under which the owners of several companies transfer their decision-making powers to a small group of trustees, who then make decisions for all the firms.

Uniform abatement policy A policy under which each polluter is required to reduce pollution by the same amount.

Unitary elastic The price elasticity of demand equals 1.

Utility The satisfaction experienced from consuming a product.

Utility-maximizing rule Pick the affordable combination that makes the marginal rate of substitution equal to the price ratio.

Variable A measure of something that can take on different values.

Variable cost (VC) Cost that varies as the firm changes its output.

Voluntary export restraint (VER) A scheme under which an exporting country voluntarily decreases its exports.

Willingness to accept The minimum amount a producer is willing to accept as payment for a product; equal to the marginal cost of production.

Willingness to pay The maximum amount a consumer is willing to pay for a product.

World Trade Organization (WTO) An organization that oversees GATT and other international trade agreements.

Answers to Odd-Numbered Problems and Discussion Questions

Chapter 1

1. Truman's sign indicated that the ultimate responsibility for making decisions rested with him: He could not "pass the buck" onto someone else. An economist who provided advice on the trade-offs from a particular policy would help Truman make his decision.
3. What is the extra cost from one more advertisement? How much extra revenue would the firm earn by running one more advertisement?

APPENDIX TO CHAPTER 1
1. a. See Figure S.1.
    b. The slope is $5.
    c. The monthly bill will increase by $15.
3. 10%, −2%, 6%.
5. The number of burglaries will decrease by 4.

Chapter 2

1. a. The opportunity cost of the loan to the friend is the interest the person could have earned if the $100 were in a bank account instead.
    b. The opportunity cost of the logs is the amount of money the firm could get by selling the logs on the log market today.
    c. The opportunity cost of the land is the value of land in its next-best alternative, for example, a classroom building, a library, or a student center.
3. The economic cost is $285,000, the sum of $50,000 for the opportunity cost of Jack's time, $10,000 for the opportunity cost of the building, $75,000 for workers, and $150,000 for supplies.
5. You could compute the marginal cost of a unit and then compute the marginal benefits (in terms of lives saved or medical expenses avoided) for different quantities of units. To satisfy the marginal principle, the city should buy another unit as long as the marginal benefit exceeds the marginal cost.
7. No. Eventually, we expect output to increase at a decreasing rate (diminishing returns) as more and more workers share the machine.

Chapter 3

1. As shown in the following table, both can be made better off from specialization and exchange.

	Abe		Bea		Total	
	Paintings per week	Pizzas per week	Paintings per week	Pizzas per week	Paintings per week	Pizzas per week
Abe and Bea are self-sufficient.	6	24	2	5	8	29
Abe and Bea specialize.	0	36	12	0	12	36
After specializing, Abe and Bea exchange 1 pizza per painting.	0 + 6 = **6** (Abe gets 6 paintings)	36 − 6 = **30** (Abe gives up 6 pizzas)	12 − 6 = **6** (Bea gives up 6 paintings)	0 + 6 = **6** (Bea gets 6 pizzas)	12	36
Gain from specialization and exchange.	0	6	4	1	4	7

3. a. The total score is maximized by having Lucy in the graduate course (score = 60) and Buster in the undergraduate course (score = 24).
    b. Lucy has an absolute advantage in both courses and a comparative advantage in the graduate course: She is three times as productive in the graduate course, but only twice as productive in the undergraduate course.

Chapter 4

1. a. w, $150,200 per day.
    b. demand, increase.
    c. supply, decrease.
3. a. The cost of producing computers will decrease, so the production of computers will be more profitable and firms will supply more of them. The supply curve will shift to the right, decreasing the equilibrium price.
    b. The tax increases the production cost, shifting the supply curve to the left and increasing the equilibrium price.
5. Education at private and at public schools are substitutes, so the tuition hike will shift the demand for private education to the right, increasing the equilibrium price and quantity.

FIGURE S.1 Relationship Between Hours of Tennis and the Monthly Tennis Club Bill

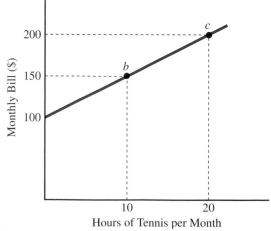

Hours of Tennis per Month

7. If price and quantity both increase, we know from Table 4.5 that demand has increased. We shift the demand curve to the right, increasing the price and quantity.

9. The supply curve for shirts shifts to the left, increasing the equilibrium price and decreasing the equilibrium quantity.

Chapter 5

1. The price elasticity is 1.30 = the percentage change in quantity (13%) divided by the percentage change in price (10%). Demand is elastic.

3. Each brand has many substitute goods (all the other brands), so the demand for a specific brand will be more elastic than the demand for running shoes in general.

5. Inelastic: An increase in price increases total revenue, whereas a decrease in price decreases total revenue.

7. Use the elasticity formula: The 10% increase in the price of beer will decrease the quantity of beer consumed by 13%, decreasing the highway death rate by the same percentage. Therefore, the number of highway deaths will decrease by 13 (13% of 100).

9. a. The predicted change in quantity is 20% = 4 (the elasticity) times the 5% price change. The quantity sold drops from 100 million gallons to 80 million gallons, so the tax will generate $8 million.

   b. The national elasticity is larger, so the analysts would understate the reduction in quantity demanded and thus overestimate the revenue generated by the tax. Specifically, they will predict a quantity of 95 million gallons instead of 80 million gallons and revenue of $9.5 million instead of $8 million. Because it is relatively easy to buy gasoline in a nearby city, the demand for gasoline will be relatively elastic at the city level

Chapter 6

1. a. The MRS (5 rides for one video game) exceeds the price ratio (2 riders per video game).

   b. At point *d* (3 rides and 24 video games), the MRS equals the price ratio.

3. The MRS is less than the price ratio, so you should consume fewer CDs and more movies. For the graph, place CDs on the horizontal axis and movies on the vertical axis. The slope of the budget line is 3 movies per CD. At the initial point, the slope of the indifference curve is 1 movie per CD. The indifference curve is flatter than the budget line, so you should move up the budget line to a higher indifference curve (fewer CDs and more movies).

5. a. Suppose he achieves the same utility level in weeks one and two. If he consumes fewer CDs and more arcade games in week two, he will be further up his indifference curve, with a higher MRS.

   b. He will be better off because balanced consumption is preferred to extremes. Draw a line between the two points on his indifference curve. The midpoint is the average consumption, and it will lie on a higher (more northeasterly) indifference curve.

7. Applying the equimarginal rule, utility is the miles driven on a tank of fuel, and marginal utility is the miles per gallon of fuel (mpg). The rule suggests that to maximize utility, a driver should equate the mpg of gasohol divided by the price of gasohol to the mpg of gasoline divided by the price of gasoline. If the consumer picks one fuel or the other, she or he should pick the fuel that has the higher mpg divided by price. For example, suppose the price of gasohol is $1 per gallon and the price of gasoline is $1.25. If gasohol has a mpg of 18 and gasoline has a mpg of 25, gasoline is a better buy: It provides 20 miles per dollar, compared to 18 miles per dollar for gasohol. Although gasoline is more expensive, its higher mpg more than offsets the higher price per gallon. The rule suggested in the quote is misguided because it doesn't take into account differences in mpg.

Chapter 7

1. We assume that buyers and sellers have enough information to make informed choices and that there are no external benefits and no external costs. The assumption of informed choices is likely to be violated in the case of used cars: Buyers don't know the quality of the car. The assumption of no external benefits is likely to be violated for national defense, space exploration, public radio, and education. The assumption of no external costs is likely to be violated for goods that generate pollution such as paper, transportation (auto and bus), and electricity.

3. a. $A + B + C$
   b. $D + E + F$
   c. $A + B + C + D + E + F$
   d. $A + B + D$
   e. F
   f. $A + B + D + F$
   g. A
   h. $B + D + F$
   i. $A + B + D + F$

5. The supply of clothing to an individual city is much more elastic than the supply of housing, so price controls would decrease the quantity of clothing supplied by a larger amount. In addition, everyone would have to wait in line to get clothing. In contrast, people who occupy rent-controlled apartments don't have to find a new apartment every week, so they avoid most of the queuing and search costs and provide political support for rent control.

7. In the market equilibrium, there are 100 taxis and the price of taxi service is $3, which is just high enough to cover the cost of providing taxi service. If the government issues more than 100 medallions, no one will use the extra medallions, and the medallion policy will have no effect on the market: The price of taxi service will be $3, and the price of a medallion will be zero.

9. For parts (a) and (b), as in the case of taxi medallions, the quantity restrictions will increase the equilibrium price and decrease the equilibrium quantity. For part (c), the import restrictions shift the market supply curve to the left, increas-

ing the equilibrium price and decreasing the equilibrium quantity.

11. a. No. Part of the tax will be shifted backward onto input suppliers, including laborers who work in auto factories and dealerships.

   b. The price elasticity of demand for automobiles and the responsiveness of input suppliers to changes in input prices.

13. The tax increases the equilibrium price to $56 and decreases the equilibrium quantity to 80 rooms. Consumers pay $6 more per room, and suppliers receive a net price of $46 = $56 − $10 tax.

15. The quantity of grooming services hasn't changed, so the demand for services must have decreased, pulling down the price of pet services and thus decreasing the profits of license holders.

Chapter 8

1. Suppose Groucho wants to join a social club to associate with people who are richer than he is, and he assumes that other people join clubs for the same reasons. A club will invite him to join only if he would increase the average income of the club. In other words, Groucho will be invited to join only groups in which most people are poorer than he is, clubs with an adverse selection of people. The same reasoning applies if Groucho wants to associate with people who are wittier than he is and he assumes that other people feel the same way. A club that asks him to join will have an average wit level that is less than his, so he will be forced to interact with dimwits.

3. Suppose you're willing to pay the average value of the two types of cameras ($60) for a 50% chance of getting a plum. If you expect a greater than 50% chance of getting a plum, it will be wise to buy a used camera. Given the adverse-selection problem, your chance of getting a plum is likely to be less than 50%.

5. The detector eliminates the imperfect information problem, so the two types of used cars will be sold in separate markets, with one price for lemons ($2,000 in our example) and another price for plums ($4,000). There is no adverse selection because each buyer knows exactly what type of car he or she will get.

7. Like the lie detector, the genetic tests eliminate the adverse-selection problem, this time for insurance companies. The insurance companies will charge higher prices to those who are likely to contract the diseases and lower prices to those who are not. This may strike many people as unfair.

9. If Ira doesn't have fire insurance, he will spend money on the prevention program because the benefit is the avoidance of an expected loss of $10,000 (a 10% chance of losing $100,000), which exceeds the $5,000 cost. If he has an insurance policy covering 80% of the loss, the benefit is the avoidance of an expected loss of $2,000 (a 10% chance of losing $80,000). The benefit is less than the $5,000 cost, so he won't spend money on the program. Ira will be indifferent with a coverage rate of 50%. In this case, the benefit is the avoidance

FIGURE S.2 **Pollution Tax Makes the Equilibrium Quantity of a Polluting Good Zero**

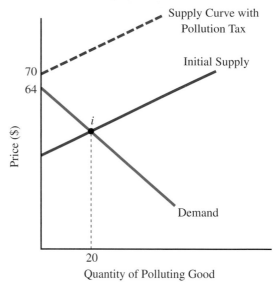

of an expected loss of $5,000 (a 10% chance of losing $50,000), which is equal to the cost.

Chapter 9

1. See Figure S.2. The demand curve intersects the supply curve at 20 units per day. The pollution tax shifts the supply curve upward and to the left by such a large amount that the supply curve lies entirely above the demand curve. For this to occur, the spillover cost from the pollutant must be very high, the cost of abatement must be very high, and the demand for goods must be relatively low.

3. a. The production cost per ton with zero pollution is $62.

   b. The marginal cost associated with going from 1 gallon to 0 gallons is $12. For firms to make this choice, the marginal benefit of abatement (the tax savings) must be at least $12.

5. We could adjust other taxes to mitigate any undesirable effects on the poor. For example, we could decrease the sales tax rate or adjust the income tax rates.

7. The high-cost firm would save $6,100 by getting a fourth permit, and the low-cost firm would bear an additional abatement cost of $5,500 by giving up one of its permits. Splitting the difference, the market price would be $5,800.

9. If the oldest firms have the highest cost-abatement technology, they will hold on to their permits rather than selling them. Trading could be encouraged by giving some permits to newer firms, ones with low-cost abatement technology. Those firms will sell some of the permits if the selling price of permits exceeds the extra abatement cost they incur.

Chapter 10

1. a. No. The cost of $120 exceeds the willingness to pay of each citizen, so no one will provide the display.

b. No. With a cost of $40 per citizen, the cost exceeds the willingness to pay of two of three citizens (Marian and Sam).

c. The total cost ($120) is three-fourths the total willingness to pay ($160 = $100 + $30 + $20). If each citizen paid three-fourths of his or her willingness to pay, the display could be provided and each would be better off.

3. The free-rider problem disappears because if any person does not contribute, the public good won't be provided. This money-back guarantee makes it more likely that everyone will contribute and get 30¢ at the end of the experiment.

5. a. The benefit is $8,000 (80,000 citizens times $0.10 per person), which exceeds the cost of $5,000. Since the benefit exceeds the cost, the provision of the additional litter is socially efficient.

b. No. The benefit to the rancher ($0.10) is less than the cost ($5,000).

c. The citizens could contribute to a wolf-preservation fund to provide the rancher with enough money to offset the cost of a litter of wolves. For example, if each citizen contributed $0.07 (70% of his or her benefit), they could raise a total of $5,600. By paying this amount to the landowner who hosts the wolf litter, the rancher would be better off by $600, and each of the citizens would be better off by $0.03.

7. a. The median voter now has a desired budget of $6 billion, so each candidate will propose a budget very close to $6 billion.

b. The answer will not change because the median voter is still the person with the $6 billion budget.

Chapter 11

1. The average cost is $15 for 40 shirts, $9 for 100 shirts, $7 for 200 shirts, and $6 for 400 shirts.

3.
Labor	Output	Marginal Product
0	0	
1	5	5
2	11	6
3	15	4
4	18	3
5	19	1

5. There are no diminishing returns, so marginal cost is constant.

7. The $12,500 figure includes some of the fixed cost of production (design and tooling costs), so it is an average, not a marginal cost.

9. As shown in Figure 11.7, the average cost for the large generator is $4.60 (point *b*), compared to an average cost of $5.00 for the small generator (point *c*).

11. a. False. The principle of diminishing returns is applicable to the short-run cost curves, not the long-run curves.

b. True. Diminishing returns imply increasing short-run marginal cost.

c. False. Diminishing returns imply increasing short-run marginal cost but do not imply increasing short-run average cost. If the output is small enough, the spreading of fixed costs will generate a negatively sloped short-run average-cost curve even if there are diminishing returns.

d. False. The first sentence implies that the short-run average-cost curve is positively sloped. This means that the short-run marginal cost exceeds the short-run average cost.

Chapter 12

1.
Tables per hour	Total cost	Marginal cost
3	120	—
4	155	35
5	200	45
6	270	70

3. At the current output level, the firm is violating the marginal principle, so it is not doing the best it can. Marginal revenue (the price of $22) is less than the marginal cost ($45); to maximize profit, the firm should produce less output. It is possible that with lower output, total revenue could exceed total cost, and the firm would be profitable. Alternatively, total revenue could be less than total cost, but total revenue could exceed variable cost, so it would be sensible to continue operating.

5. The manager is bluffing. His total revenue ($35,000) exceeds the variable cost ($30,000 for the farm workers). The $20,000 paid for seed and fertilizer was incurred months ago, and it is a sunk cost that will be ignored in the decision about whether to harvest the crop. Because his total revenue exceeds his variable cost, the farmer will harvest the crop even if the workers don't accept a wage cut.

7. We cannot draw a supply curve or complete the price elasticity of supply because we cannot be certain that the other variables that affect the supply of gasoline (the price of inputs, technology) did not change over this period.

9.
Number of firms	Industry output	Total cost for typical firm	Average cost per lamp
40	400	$300	$30
80	800	$360	$36
120	1,200	$420	$42

We have 3 points on the long-run supply curve: At a price of $30, the quantity is 400 lamps; at a price of $36, the quantity is 800 lamps; at a price of $42, the quantity is 1,200 lamps.

11. Because the industry uses such tiny amounts of the relevant inputs, the prices of these inputs won't change as the industry grows. Therefore, the average cost per haircut does not depend on the quantity of haircuts. The long-run supply curve is horizontal, for example, at a constant cost of $10 per haircut.

Chapter 13

1. To maximize profit, the restaurant will pick the quantity at which marginal revenue equals marginal cost. Using the marginal-revenue formula, we can compute the marginal revenue at each price and quantity:

Price	$10	$9	$8	$7
Quantity	30	40	50	60
Marginal revenue	$7	$5	$3	$1

Marginal revenue equals marginal cost at a price of $8 and a quantity of 50 meals.

3. On average, the payback per dollar spent on these lottery games is about 50¢. In other words, for every $100 spent by players, the state pays $50 in prizes. The commercial gambling games have much higher paybacks: The payback per dollar is 81¢ for horse racing and 89¢ for slot machines. The lottery games have lower paybacks because each state has a monopoly on lottery games: The state outlaws commercial lotteries. If the state allowed other organizations to offer lottery games, the competition between commercial and state lottery games would increase the payback from lottery games.

5. The artificial barrier to entry will generate higher prices and a smaller quantity demanded. If we eliminated the barriers, there would be more teams, and ticket prices would fall, increasing total attendance.

7. Monopoly power increases prices in the game of Monopoly, consistent with the conclusions in this chapter. In monopoly, prices increase with monopoly power despite the fact that the quantity provided on the market does not decrease. In contrast, in the normal analysis of monopoly, price increases because the quantity drops, and the market moves up the market demand curve.

9. The consumer advocate is assuming that the demand for the drug is perfectly inelastic, so an increase in price does not have any effect on the quantity demanded. This is unrealistic and is inconsistent with the law of demand.

11. The marginal revenue for business travelers is $MR = \$300 - 2.0 ¥ 120 = \$60$, which is less than the marginal cost, so the airline should increase the price for business travelers. The marginal revenue for tourists is $MR = \$300 - 1.0 \times 80 = \$220$, which is greater than the marginal cost, so the airline should decrease the price for tourists.

13. This price-discrimination scheme is based on the notion that bargain hunters are early birds. The large discounts for early fabric purchases attract consumers who would otherwise not buy fabric at the regular price.

Chapter 14

1. The following table shows price and average cost for different numbers of arcades. Price exceeds average cost for the first four arcades, so the equilibrium number of arcades is 4.

Number of arcades	1	2	3	4	5
Price	$0.50	$0.48	$0.46	$0.44	$0.42
Average cost	$0.34	$0.37	$0.40	$0.43	$0.46

3. There are two logical errors in the expert's statement. First, the entry of firms will decrease the market price, and the market will move downward along the market demand curve. Therefore, the total quantity of pizzas demanded will exceed 3,000 (the quantity associated with the monopoly price). Second, as shown in all the examples in this chapter, we expect the typical firm to operate along the negatively sloped portion of its average-cost curve, not the horizontal portion. In other words, we expect each firm to produce fewer than 1,000 pizzas per day. These two observations suggest that there will be more than three pizzerias. For example, if the decrease in price increases the quantity demanded to 4,000 and each store produces only 800 pizzas per day, there will be five pizzerias (4,000 divided by 800).

5. A firm that cuts three lawns will have a total cost of $30 ($18 in fixed cost + $12 in variable cost (3 lawns times $4 per lawn), or an average cost of $10 per lawn. In equilibrium, the price will be equal to average cost, which happens with a quantity of 60 lawns. Dividing the 60 lawns cut by 3 lawns per firm, there will be 20 firms in equilibrium.

7. The city must have issued a sufficiently large number of licenses that entry continued to the point where economic profit reached zero. In graphical terms, the demand curve facing the typical firm is tangent to the negatively sloped average-cost curve: Average cost equals price, so economic profit is zero and no one is willing to pay anything for a license.

Chapter 15

1. See Figure S.3. The profit per firm under the duopoly outcome is $500 (a profit of $5 per passenger times 100 passengers). The profit per firm under the cartel is $750 (a profit of

FIGURE S.3 Game Tree for Airporter Price-Fixing Game

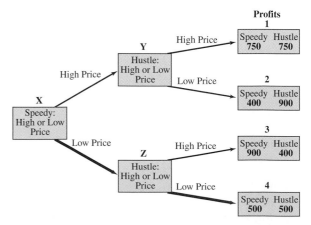

$10 per passenger times 75 passengers). Each firm will pick the low price. The path of the game is X to Z to rectangle 4.

3. One reason for low prices at these sales is that there is no punishment for underpricing the other firm. Any prior arrangement for cartel pricing would evaporate when one firm knows that it will soon go out of business.

5. If both firms pick the high price, each will get a profit of $360. If both pick the low price, each will get a profit of $250. For each firm, picking the low price is the dominant strategy. If firms pick prices each day, Bizarre weighs the benefit of undercutting ($140 on the day of undercutting) against the cost (the difference between the high-price profit, $360, and the low-price profit, $250, times the number of days remaining after the undercutting). On the first day, the cost is $220, which exceeds the benefit of $140. Assuming that Bizarre is not savvy enough to think about the end game (the last day), she will not undercut Weird.

7. The longer the time both firms will be in the market, the greater the opportunity for punishing a firm that undercuts, so the more likely price fixing will work. Longtime is more likely to have price fixing that keeps prices high.

9.

	Neither Advertises		Both Advertise		Only A Advertises	
	A	B	A	B	A	B
Net revenue from sales ($ million)	5	5	12	12	17	1
Cost of advertising ($ million)	0	0	10	10	10	0
Profit ($ million)	5	5	2	2	7	1

The outcome is that although both would be better off if neither advertises, both will advertise—the advertisers' dilemma. From the industry perspective, the benefit of a pair of advertising campaigns is $14 million, compared to a cost of $20 million.

Chapter 16

1. An increase in demand shifts the demand curve to the right, and the new demand curve will intersect the negatively sloped long-run average-cost curve at a larger quantity and a lower average cost (price). The exploitation of scale economies will cause the regulated price to drop. In contrast, in a competitive market, an increase in demand increases the equilibrium price if the supply curve is positively sloped.

3. Consumer surplus decreases by $700. For the 150 that are units sold at the higher price, consumers lose an amount equal to the change in price ($4) times the quantity consumed (150), or $600. In addition, the price hike reduces the quantity consumed, and the loss of consumer surplus for the

151st through the 200th units is equal to the change in price ($4) times the change in quantity (50 units) times 1/2, or an additional $100. The total profit of the firms increases from $200 ($1 per unit times 200 units sold) to $750 ($5 per unit times 150 units). The increase in profit ($550) is less than the loss of consumer surplus ($700), so the net loss for society is $150.

5. Giving the gates to Gotcha will allow the airline to maintain its monopoly power and continue to charge higher prices than would occur if there was competition.

Chapter 17

1. The payroll tax shifts the supply curve to the left: At every price, a smaller quantity is supplied. The leftward shift of the supply curve increases the equilibrium wage to a wage above $10.

3. Some people will work fewer hours, so they will pay less in taxes: They pay a lower rate on fewer hours. Other people will work the same number of hours and pay less in taxes too: They pay a lower rate on the same number of hours. Even a person who works more hours could pay less in taxes: If the increase in hours is small relative to the decrease in the hourly tax rate, the tax bill (hours times the tax rate) will actually decrease. The only people who will pay more in taxes are the workers who increase their hours by an amount that is large relative to the decrease in the hourly rate.

5. a. The supply of teachers is large relative to demand, so wages are relatively low. This could result from the psychological rewards from teaching, the work hours, or the free summer time.
   b. This is effectively a minimum wage for teachers, and it has the same effect as a minimum wage for any occupation: The increase in the wage will decrease the quantity demanded, so some teachers will lose their jobs.

7. Let's assume that the program is paid for by government, not coal companies. The program will increase the supply of coal workers, shifting the supply curve to the right. The equilibrium wage will decrease.

9. Like a minimum wage, a comparable-worth policy that increases wages in some occupations will decrease the quantity of labor demanded, so fewer workers will be hired. In addition, higher wages lead to higher production costs and output prices, so consumers will be harmed. An alternative policy is to break down the barriers that have discouraged women from choosing certain occupations.

Chapter 18

1. The demand is elastic, so a decrease in price will generate a large change in quantity demanded, and total income (wage times number of workers) will increase. To maximize total income, the union should cut wages.

3. a. For the first 4 workers, the marginal revenue product (MRP) exceeds the marginal labor cost (MLC), so the firm should hire 4 workers.

b. The competitive outcome is the quantity at which the wage equals the MRP. This happens with wage = $10 and a quantity of 6 workers. A minimum wage of $10 would generate this outcome.

Chapter 19

1. a. In Country B, the opportunity cost of 1 computer is 2 TVs, and the opportunity cost of 1 TV is 1/2 of a computer. In Country C, the opportunity cost of 1 computer is 4 TVs, and the opportunity cost of 1 TV is 1/4 of a computer. Country B has the comparative advantage of producing computers, and Country C the comparative advantage of producing TVs.
   b. The production possibility curves are straight lines for both countries, the slope being the opportunity costs and the intercepts being the maximum level of production of each good.

3. Chipland produces 120 chips and exchanges them for 70 shirts, ending up with 85 chips and 70 shirts. Shirtland produces 108 shirts and exchanges 70 of them for 35 chips, ending up with 35 chips and 35 shirts.

5. If the VERs were replaced with a tariff, the government would collect revenue. Under VERs, the importers earn large profits.

7. Consumers will benefit because prices will decrease. As each nation shifts its production to the goods for which it has a comparative advantage, workers in expanding industries will benefit, while workers in other industries will lose. The challenge for policymakers is to facilitate this transition.

9. Taxpayers will favor the shift because they will earn revenue. The firms importing goods will lobby against this because they will lose the profits they earn from the quotas. Firms may be more effective in lobbying than taxpayers because the losses are concentrated among a few firms, but the benefits are spread widely across taxpayers.

Index

A

Abbott Laboratories, 302, 339
Absolute advantage, 423
Absolute advantage, comparative
    advantage and, 48
Accounting profit, 264
Accounting rules, 52
Acid rain, 197
Actual long-run average-cost curves,
    252–253
Addyston Pipe, 339
Adverse-selection problem, 174
    responding to, in insurance, 184–185
Advertisers' dilemma, 348–350
Advertising
    campaign, 328
    cooperative, 340
Airborne Express, 346
Airline Deregulation Act (1978), 370
Airlines
    deregulation of, 370
    ticket prices of, 338, 339
Air pollution, reducing, 194
Alaska Air, 339
Alcoa, 346
Allen, Paul, 326
Alternative market structures, 262–263
Aluminum production, 346
Amazon, 303
American Airlines, 339
American Electric Power (AEP), 210
American Federation of Labor (AFL),
    406
American Federation of Labor-Congress
    of Industrial Organizations (AFL-
    CIO), 405
American Home Products, 339
American Tobacco Company, 363
Amoco, 363
Antidumping laws, rationale for, 435–436
Antitrust policies, 6, 362–369
    airline deregulation and, 370
    blocking mergers, 363–364
    in breaking up monopolies, 300, 362–363
    cartels, price fixing and, 330
    electrical deregulation and, 371–373
    history of United States, 368–369
    purpose of, 362
    regulation of business practices and,
        367–368
    telecommunications service
        deregulation and, 370–371

Apartment prices, population growth
    and, 82–83
Apple Computer, 120
Archer Daniels Midland (ADM), 339
Artificial barriers to entry, 289, 392
Asia-Pacific Economic Cooperation
    (APEC), 434
Assembly-line jobs, 404
Assumptions, 8–9
Asteroid-diversion program, 218–219,
    224
Asymmetric information, 171, 182
    effects of, 181–182
AT&T, 363
    breakup of, 370–371
Autarky, 423, 425
Automobiles
    insurance for, 185
    ozone pollution and, 211–212
Average cost
    relationship between marginal cost
        and, 243–244
    short-run versus long-run, 253
Average-cost pricing policy, 360
Average fixed cost (AFC), 240–241
Average total cost (ATC), 242
Average variable cost (AVC), 241

B

Barriers to entry
    artificial, 289, 392
    government, 328
BASF AG, 333
Bastiat, Frédéric, 432
BBC WorldService, 361
BeechNut, 357, 365
Benefits
    external, 146–147, 220–223
    marginal, 32, 197
Bicycle theft insurance, 188
Bingaman, Ann, 339
Bloomberg News Radio, 361
Borjas, George, 391
Break-even prices, 268
    for corn farmer, 271–272
    economic profit and, 267–268
Breathmobile, 211
British Sugar, 340
Buchanan, James, 228
Buchholz, Todd, 50
Budget line, 122, 123, 132
Budget set, 122

Bush, George W., 429
Business decisions, informed, 15
Business practices, regulating, 367–368
Butter prices, 283
Buyers
    investment in information, 177
    uninformed, 172

C

California, electricity deregulation in,
    372–373
Canada, antitrust rules in, 364
Cap- and-trade system, 209–210
Carbon, marketable permits and offsets
    for, 209–210
Carbon dioxide, 207
Carbon tax, 209
    effects of, 209
    market effects of, 214
Carlyle, Thomas, 15
Cartels, 330
    duopolists' dilemma and pricing by,
        329–333
Celler-Kefauver Act (1950), 368–369
Centrally planned economy, 52
Ceteris paribus, 9–10, 20, 62, 66, 95, 128,
    238
Chaloupka, Frank, 98n
Change, marginal, 10
Change in demand
    change in quantity demanded versus,
        71–72
    market effects of, 71–75
    price effects of, 112–114
Change in quantity demanded, 63
    change in demand versus, 71–72
    predicting, 103
Change in quantity supplied, 66
    change in supply versus, 76–77
    predicting, 111
Change in supply
    market effects of, 76–80
    price effects of, 114–115
Chevron, 363
Chicago, city of, 210
Chicago Climate Exchange (CCX), 210
Choices, 5–6
Chow, Gregory, 98n
Cigarette tax, 160
Civic externalities, 222
Civil Aeronautics Board (CAB), 370
Clayton Act (1914), 368

Clean Air Act (1990), 198
CNBC, 361
Coca-Cola, 288, 299–300, 305, 339
Collectibles, 29–30
Collective bargaining, 405
College
    cost of, 30–31
    education received at, 103–104
    wages earned by graduates of, 395
Command-and-control policy, 202, 211
Comparative advantage, 423
    absolute advantage versus, 48
    exchange and, 45–50
    international trade and, 49–50
    terms of trade and, 423–424
Competition, imperfect, 147
Complementary good, 74
Complements, 74
Concentration ratios, 327–328
Congress of Industrial Organizations
    (CIO), 406
Constant-cost industry, 296
    long-run supply curve for, 281–282
Consumer choice, reasons for studying,
    121
Consumer choice theory
    applications of, 129–134
    steps in, 121
Consumer constraints, 122–123
    preferences and, 121–125
Consumer preferences, 123–125
    consumer constraints and, 121–125
Consumer satisfaction, 178
Consumer surplus, demand curve and, 140
Consumption expenditures, 427
Consumption possibilities, production
    and, 47–48
Consumption possibilities curve,
    424–425
Contestable markets, entry deterrence
    and, 347
Continental Airlines, 339
Continental Baking, 366
Continuity, productivity and, 49
Contracts, 51
Cooperative advertising, 340
Cost curves for information goods, 237
Costs
    economic, 236
    explicit, 236
    fixed, 239
    implicit, 236
    labor, 379
    marginal, 32
    short-run average, 240–242

short-run total, 239–240
short-run versus long-run, 236–237
variable, 239
Council on Economic Priorities, 390
Craft unions, 405, 406
Cross elasticity of demand, 109–110
C-SPAN, 361

D

Deadweight loss, 149–150, 162
    from monopoly, 296–298
    tax burden and, 161–162
Decision-making game
    sequential, 334
    simultaneous, 334
Decisions, personal and managerial, 13
Defenders of Wildlife, 224
Delta Airlines, 339
Demand
    cross elasticity of, 109–110
    decreases in, 74–75
    derived, 379
    elastic, 96
    elasticity of price discrimination and,
        304–305
    excess, 69–70
    income elasticity of, 109
    increases in, 72–74
    inelastic, 96
    long-run response to increase, 280
    in making predictions, 103–110
    market effects of changes in, 71–75
    perfectly elastic, 96–97
    perfectly inelastic, 96
    price elasticity of, 95–102
    short-run response to increase, 279–280
    unitary elastic, 96
Demand curve, 61–65, 293
    consumer surplus and, 140
    drawing, 127–128
    elasticity along linear, 101–102
    individual, 62–63
    market, 64–65
Demand for labor, 379–384
    by individual firm in short run,
        379–382
    in long run, 383
    market, in short run, 382
    short-run versus long-run, 383–384
Demand schedule, 62
Deregulation
    of airlines, 370
    of electricity, 371–373
    of telecommunication services,
        370–371

Derived demand, 379
Developing countries
    exemptions from Kyoto agreement, 209
    pricing medical care in, 104
Diminishing returns, 37, 238
Direct-shipping ban, 317
Discount, 303
Discrimination
    occupational, 393
    price, 302–307, 435
    wage, 393
Diseconomies of scale, 252
Domestic firms, establishment of
        monopolies by, in world markets,
        432–433
Dominant strategy, 332
Drug prices, decrease in, 86
Dumping, 435–436
Duopolists' dilemma, 333
    overcoming, 336–338
Duopoly, 329
Duping, 210
DuPont, 302
DVD elasticity, 107–108

E

EBay, 178
Economic analysis, modern problems
        and, 6–8
Economic cost, 236
Economic fluctuations, 14–15
Economic growth, 7
Economic profit, 263
    break-even price and, 267–268
Economics
    defined, 2, 3
    growth of, 14
    normative, 5
    of not working, 387
    positive, 4
Economic uncertainty, government in
        reducing, 56
Economic way of thinking, 8–12
Economies of scale, 250–251
    in production, 329
Economists, agreement among, 6
Economy
    decisions in modern, 5–6
    market, 51
Education
    college, 30–31, 103–104, 395
    as example of private good with
        external benefits, 222
Efficiency, 2
    invisible hand and, 145

Efficiency wages, 415
    imperfect information and, 414–416
Elastic demand, 96
Elasticity
    along linear demand curve, 101–102
Elasticity of demand, price
        discrimination and, 304–305
Electricity
    deregulation of, 371–373
Eli Lilly, 302
Ellig, Jerry, 317
Ellwood, David, 98n
Employment
    free trade and, 425–426
Entrepreneurs, 53
Entry deterrence
    contestable markets and, 347
    in Europe, 345
    insecure monopolist and, 342–348
Environmental economics, 203
Environmental policy, 194–214
    command-and-control, 202
    global warming and public, 207–210
    marketable pollution permits,
        204–206
    market effect of pollution regulations,
        202–203
    optimal level of pollution and
        pollution taxes, 195–200
    ozone pollution and automobile,
        211–212
    uniform abatement with permits,
        201–202
Environmental protection, impact of
        trade laws on, 436–437
Equilibrium
    with all high-cost consumers,
        183–184
    with all low-quality goods, 172–174
    labor market, 387–391
Equimarginal rule, 133–134
Europe, antitrust rules in, 364
European Commission, 345
European Union (EU), 434
    environment and, 437
European Union Commission, 339
Excess burden of tax, 162
Excess demand, 69–70
Excess supply, 70–71
Exchange
    comparative advantage and, 45–50
    division of labor and, 48–49
Expansion, 246–247
Experience rating, 185
Explicit cost, 236

External benefits, 146–147
    inefficiency and, 220–223
    private goods with, 221–222
    public goods and, 221
External costs, 147
    of production, 198
Externalities
    civic, 222
    internalizing, 198
    workplace, 222
Exxon, 363

F

Factors of production, 28
Farmer, break-even and shut-down prices
        for corn, 271–272
Featherbedding, 408
Federal budget deficit, 6
Federal Deposit Insurance Corporation
        (FDIC), 187
Federal Express, 346
Federal Trade Commission (FTC), 369
    direct-shipping ban and, 317
    merger policy of, 363
    probe of pharmaceutical companies,
        302
Firms
    entrance of second, 358–359
    labor demand by individual, in short
        run, 379–382
    response to pollution tax by,
        198–199
    short-run output decision of,
        263–268
    shut-down decision of, 268–272
Firm-specific demand curve, 262
First-copy cost, information goods and,
        254–255
Fixed costs, 239
Fixed production facility, short-run costs
        for, 237–245
Food additives, 339
Ford Motor, 210, 415
Foreign competition, shielding workers
        from, 430
Foreign sweatshops, industry codes of
        conduct and, 390
Formulas to compute values, 23–24
Free-rider problem, 222
    overcoming, 223
    public goods and, 222
Free trade
    employment effects of, 425–426
    protests on, 438–439
Friedman, Thomas, 420

G

Game theory, 327
Nash equilibrium and, 350–351
Game tree
    for advertisers' dilemma, 349
    for deterring entry, 344
    price fixing and, 331–332
    prisoners' dilemma and, 334–335
Gasoline tax as alternative to direct
        pollution tax, 212
GDP. *See* Gross domestic product (GDP)
Gender pay gap, 393
General Agreement on Tariffs and Trade
        (GATT), 433–434
General Electric Corporation (GE), 339
Generic drugs, barriers to, 302
Genetic testing, 186
Gerber, 365
Global warming
    consequences of, 207–208
    public policy and, 207–210
Goods
    complementary, 74
    inferior, 73, 109
    normal, 73, 109
Government
    alternative models of, 228–229
    barriers to entry by, 328
    enforcement of rules of exchange, 56
    intervention in markets, 146–147
    in reducing economic uncertainty, 56
    role of, in market economy, 55–57
    spending by, and taxes, 219–220
Graphs
    computing slope, 19–20
    defined, 17
    drawing, 18–19
    in showing relationships, 17–23
Greenhouse gases, 207–208
Grim-trigger strategy, 337
Group insurance, 184–185
Guaranteed price matching, 336–337
Guarantees, provision of, by sellers, 177

H

Hardback books, costs of, 306–307
Hart-Scott-Rodino Act (1980), 369
Hayek, Friedrich, 51
Health insurance, 182
Heinz, H. J., Company, 357, 365
Hendrix, Jimi, 326
Herfindahl-Hirschman Index (HHI), 328
Highway deaths, 103–104
Hoechst AG, 302

Hoffman-La Roche, 333
Home insurance, 185
Horizontal axis, 18
Houthakker, H. F., 98*n*
Human organs, market for used, 156
Hurricane Andrew, price of ice and, 282–283

I

IBM, 210
Ice, price of, Hurricane Andrew and, 282–283
Immigration, trade-offs from, 390–391
Imperfect competition, 147, 413
Imperfect information, 147, 171
    efficiency wages and, 414–416
Implicit cost, 236
Imports
    bans on, 426–427
    quotas on, 428
    restrictions on, 6, 151–156
Import licenses, 428
Import taxes, 6
Incentives, 10–11, 12
    for innovation, 300–301
Income
    changes in top end of distribution, 398–400
    distribution of, 396–400
    recent changes in distribution of, 397–398
Income effect, 63–64, 384
Income elasticity of demand, 109
Increasing-cost industry, 276
    long-run supply curve for, 276–279
Indifference curves, 123–125
Indifference map, 125
Individual demand curve, 62–63
Individual labor-supply decision, 384–385
Individual supply curve, 66
    slope of, 67
Indivisible inputs, 248–249
    scaling down and, 248
Industrial union, 405
Industries, nurturing infant, 431–432
Industry codes of conduct, foreign sweatshops and, 390
Inelastic demand, 96
Inferior goods, 73, 109
Inflation, 131–132
Information
    asymmetric, 171, 181–182
    buyers investment in, 177
    imperfect, 147, 171
    and efficiency wages, 414–416

Information goods
    cost curves for, 237
    first-copy cost and, 254–255
Innovation
    incentives for, 300–301
    productivity and, 49
Input-substitution effect, 383
Insurance, 52, 181–186
    adverse-selection problem and, 184–185
    automobile, 185
    bicycle theft, 188
    group, 184–185
    health, 182
    home, 185
    life, 185
    types of, 185–186
International Panel on Climate Change, 208
International tariff and trade agreements, 433–434
Internet registration, ending monopoly on, 298–299
Interstate Bakeries, 366
Intuit, 363
Invisible hand, 5–6, 52–53
    efficiency and, 145
Ivax Corporation, 302
Ivester, Douglas, 305

J

James Budgett, 340
Japan, economic problems of, 8
Jobs, costs of protecting, 431
Justice, U.S. Department of, 363
    Antitrust Division of, 369

K

Kalvar Corporation, 365
Kathie Lee Collection, 390
Keynes, John Maynard, 8
Kinked demand curve model, 341
Knights of Labor, 406
Knowledgeable sellers, 172
Koppel, Ted, 86
Kyoto Conference global warming, 208–210

L

Labor, division of, and exchange, 48–49
Labor costs, 379
    marginal, 409
Labor demand
    in long run, 383
    in short run, 382

Labor market
    college graduates in, 395
    differences in wages and income in, 391–396
    income distribution and, 396–400
Labor market equilibrium, 387–391
    changes in demand and supply for labor, 388
    effects of minimum wage laws, 389
    gender pay gap, 393
    racial discrimination and, 393–395
    response to wage cut, 387
    trade-offs from immigration, 390–391
Labor specialization, scaling down and, 250
Labor-supply curve, pubs and, 414
Labor unions, 405–408
    collective bargaining and, 405
    history of, in United States, 406
    monopsony and, 411
    type of, 405
    wages and, 406–408
Landrum-Griffin Act (1959), 406
Law of demand, 63, 95, 96
Law of supply, 66, 95
Laws
    lemons, 177–178
    minimum wage, 389
    price fixing and, 339–340
    right-to-work, 406
    zoning, 279
Learning by doing, 431–432
Learning effect, 395
Leisure demand
    income effect for, 384, 385
    substitution effect for, 384–385
Lemons laws, 177–178
Lemons problem, 171–176
    evidence of, 179–181
    responding to, 176–178
Levy, David, 15
Licensing, 151–156, 289
    market efficiency and, 153
    winners and losers from, 154
Life insurance, 185
Liggett and Meyers, 363
Limit pricing, 343–345
LoJack, 221
Long-run
    labor demand in, 383
    production and cost in, 246–253
Long-run average cost of production, 247
Long-run effects of changes in demand, 279–280

Long-run equilibrium, monopolistic competition and, 319
Long-run marginal cost, 247, 358
Long-run market supply curve, drawing, 277
Long-run response, to increase in demand, 280
Long-run supply curve
    for constant-cost industry, 281–284
    for increasing-cost industry, 276–279
Long-run total cost, 246–247
Lorillard, P., 363
Luxury taxes, 160–161

M

Macroeconomics, 14–15
Mankiw, Gregory, 420
Manning, Alan, 414
Marginal approach, marginal benefit equaling marginal cost, 265–267
Marginal-benefits, 32
    marginal-cost curves and, 197
Marginal change, 10
Marginal cost, 32
    long-run, 358
    relationship between average cost and, 243–244
Marginal labor cost, 409
Marginal principle, 32–35
    individual supply curves and, 67
    labor demand and, 380
    marginal benefits exceeding marginal cost, 196
    marginal benefits versus marginal costs, 32
    market entry and, 314
    monopsony and, 410
    output decision and, 292–294
    in picking profit-maximizing quantity and price, 294–295
    slope of individual supply curve, 67
Marginal product
    of labor, 237–238, 381
    production and, 237–238
Marginal rate of substitution (MRS), 124
Marginal-revenue, 266, 290–292
Marginal-revenue curve, 293
Marginal-revenue product of labor (MRP), 381
Marketable pollution permits, 204–206
    offsets for carbon, 209–210
    price of, 206
    for sulphur dioxide, 206
    supply, demand, and price of, 205–206
    voluntary exchange and, 204–205

Market demand curve, 64–65
Market demand for labor in short run, 382
Market economy, 51
    role of government in, 55–57
Market effects
    of changes in demand, 71–75
    of changes in supply, 76–80
    of minimum wage laws, 389
    of pollution regulations, 202–203
    of pollution tax, 199–200
    of simultaneous changes in demand and supply, 80–81
Market efficiency, licensing and, 153
Market entry, 313–321
    effects of, 314–316
    profit and, 315–316
    in real world, 316
    of wine merchants, 317
Market equilibrium, 69–71, 85, 87–88, 220, 274–275
    efficiency and, 142–145
Market failure, 54, 147, 194
Market power, 289, 302–303
Market price, 151
Markets, 13, 36, 51–55
    government intervention in, 146–147
    mixed, 171
    shortcoming of, 54–55
    thin, 174–175
    virtues of, 52–53
Market supply curve, 68
    for labor, 385–386
Mars Company, 345
Marshall, Alfred, 9–10
Maximization of utility, 125–129
Maximum prices, setting, 148
McDonald's, 439
MCI, 363
Mead Johnson, 339
Medallion sale, shortfall from, 154
Median-voter rule, 225–228
Medical care, 103–104
    pricing of, in developing countries, 104
Mergers, 363
    blocking, 363–364
Microeconomics, 12–14
    defined, 12
Microsoft Corporation, 326, 344–345, 363, 368
Microsoft Corporation, *U.S.* v., 368
Midpoint method, 100–101
Military spending, 29–30
Milnot Holding Company, 365
Minimum advertised prices (MAP), 340
Minimum efficient scale, 250–251
Minimum prices, setting, 150–151

Minimum wage, 5–6
    market effects of, 389
    monopsony and, 412–413
Mitel, 363
Mixed market, 171
Mobil, 363
Model, using, to predict changes in price and quantity, 82–84
Modern consumer theory, old utility theory versus, 130
Modern problems, economic analysis and, 6–8
Money-back guarantees, 177
Monopolies, 263, 289
    breaking up, 362–363
    deadweight loss from, 296–298
    ending, on Internet registration, 298–299
    natural, 289, 300, 357
    public policy and, 300
    social cost of, 296–300
    unnatural, 289
Monopolist
    insecure, and entry deterrence, 342–348
    output decision of, 290–295
Monopolistic competition, 263, 318–321
    defined, 313
    long-run equilibrium and, 319
    trade-offs between average cost and variety, 319–320
Monopoly
    establishment of, by domestic firms, in world markets, 432–433
Monopoly power
    patents and, 300–301
    using resources to get, 299–300
Monopsony, 409–414
    defined, 409
    labor unions and, 411
    minimum wage and, 412–413
    perfect competition versus, 411
    real world and, 413
Moral hazard, 186–188
Motor Carrier Act (1980), 316
Motorola, 210
Movie admission and popcorn, 306
Multinational corporations, 439
Music piracy, 129–131

N

Napier Brown, 340
Nash, John, 350
Nash equilibrium, 350
    game theory and, 350–351
National Acid Precipitation Assessment Program (NAPAP), 206

National Labor Relations Board (NLRB), 406

Natural monopoly, 289, 300, 357–361
    defined, 357
    entrance of second firm, 358–359
    picking output level in, 357–358
    price controls for, 359–360
    satellite radio as, 361

Negative relationship, 18–19, 21–23

Network Solutions Inc., 298

Nevin, John R., 98n

Nike, 439

Nominal value, 38

Nonlinear relationships, 21–23

Normal good, 73, 109

Normative economics, 5

North American Free Trade Agreement (NAFTA), 434

Northern Telecom, 363

Northwest Airlines, 339

NPR Talk, 361

O

Occupational discrimination, 393

Occupations, differences in wages across, 391–392

Office Depot, 367
    merger between Staples and, 356, 364–365

Oligopoly, 263, 327–351
    advertisers' dilemma and, 348–350
    alternative models of pricing, 340–341
    cartel pricing and duopolists' dilemma, 329–333
    defined, 327–329
    game theory and, 327, 350–351
    insecure monopolist and entry deterrence and, 342–348
    kinked demand curve model of, 341
    Nash equilibrium and, 350–351
    overcoming duopolists' dilemma, 336–337
    payoff matrix and, 334
    price fixing and, 330–333
    prisoners' dilemma and, 334–335

Online music stores, 129–131

Opportunity cost, 27–31, 236
    defined, 27
    principle of, 236
    production possibilities curve and, 28–29
    specialization and, 45, 421–422

Output decision
    marginal principle and, 292–294
    monopolist's, 290–295

Output effect, 383

Output level, picking, in natural monopoly, 357–358

Outsourcing, 420

Ozone pollution and automobile, 211–212

P

Patents, 52, 289
    monopoly power and, 300–301
    trade-offs from, 301

Payoff matrix, 334

Per capita income, 7, 8

Percentage changes, computing, 23–24

Perfect competition, 260–284
    alternative market structures, 262–263
    assumptions of, 405
    firm's short-run output decision, 263–268
    firm's shut-down decision, 268–272
    long-run supply curve for increasing-cost industry, 276–279
    long-run supply for constant-cost industry, 281–284
    marginal revenue for firm in, 292
    market in, 61, 97, 261
    monopsony versus, 411
    short-run and long-run effects of changes in demand, 279–280
    short-run supply curves, 272–275

Perfectly elastic demand, 96–97

Perfectly elastic supply, 111–112

Perfectly inelastic demand, 96

Perfectly inelastic supply, 111–112

Pitofsky, Robert, 364

Polinski, Mitchell, 98n

Pollution
    market effects of regulations, 202–203
    optimal level of, 195–200

Pollution abatement, 194–195
    benefits from, 196
    marginal benefit of, 198–199
    marginal cost of, 197–198

Pollution allowance, 204

Pollution offsets, 210

Pollution permits, 6, 213
    trading, 214

Pollution taxes, 198
    firm's response to, 198–199
    market effects of, 199–200
    optimal level of pollution and, 195–200, 214

Population growth, apartment prices and, 82–83

Positive economics, 4

Positive relationship, 18

Poultry consumption, increases in, 85–86

Poverty in Africa, 7

Predatory pricing, 367–368, 435

Predictions, using price elasticity of demand in making, 103–110

Price
    controlling, 148–151
    explaining changes in, 84–86
    predatory, 435
    predicting changes in, using supply and demand elasticities, 112–115
    using model to predict changes in, 82–84

Price-change formula, 113, 115

Price controls for natural monopoly, 359–360

Price discrimination, 289, 302–307, 435
    elasticity of demand and, 304–305

Price effects
    of change in demand, 112–114
    of change in supply, 114–115

Price elasticity of demand, 95–103
    computing, 99–101
    defined, 95
    factors determining, 98–99
    international comparisons of, 99

Price elasticity of supply, 110–112

Price-fixing, 330
    game tree and, 331–332
    law and, 339–340
    predicting outcome of, 332–333

Price leadership, 340

Price matching, guaranteed, 336–337

Price ratio, 123

Pricing
    alternative models of oligopoly, 340–341
    average, 360
    limit, 343–345
    predatory, 367–368

Pricing games, repeated, with retaliation for underpricing, 337–338

Principle of diminishing returns, labor demand and, 380

Prisoners' dilemma, 334–335

Private costs, 198

Private goods, 221
    with external benefits, 221–222

Producer surplus, supply curve and, 141–142

Product accounts, 420, 423

Product differentiation, 318

Production
    consumption possibilities and, 47–48
    cost in long run and, 246–253

economies of scale in, 329
   marginal product and, 237–238
Production costs, reasons for studying, 235
Production possibilities curve, 422–423
   opportunity cost and, 28–29
   scarcity and, 28
   shifting, 30
Production possibilities frontier, 29
Product safety and apples, 83
Profit
   accounting, 264
   economic, 263, 267–268
   market entry and, 315–316
Profit-maximizing quantity and price, using marginal principle to pick, 294–295
Property crime, 106–107
Prosperity, 2
Protectionist policies, 426–430
   rationales for, 430–433
   responses to, 429–430
Prusa, thomas, 436
Public choice, 225–229
Public choice economics, 225
Public goods, 221
   asteroid diversion as, 224
   external benefits and, 221
   free-rider problem and, 222
   wolf preservation of, 224–225
Public policies
   evaluating, 13–14
   monopoly and, 300
Public Radio International, 361
Public utility commissions (PUCs), 360
Pubs, labor-supply curve and, 414

Q

Qatar round, 434
Quantity
   controlling, 151–156
   explaining changes in, 84–86
   using model to predict changes in, 82–84
Quantity demanded, 62, 70
Quantity supplied, 65, 70
Quicken, 363
Quotas, 427–428, 428
   differences between tariffs and, 429

R

Racial discrimination, labor market equilibrium and, 393–395
Real value, 38
Reduction credits, 210

Regional Bell Operating Companies, 370–371
Register.com, 298
Relationships
   negative, 18–19, 21–23
   nonlinear, 21–23
   positive, 18
   using graphs to show, 17–23
Rental-apartment industry, 279
Rent control, 148–150
Rent seeking, 299–300
Repetition, productivity and, 49
Replication, 246–247
Restaurants, senior discounts in, 304
Revenue
   marginal, 290–292
   total, 290–292
Reynolds International Pen Corporation, 347–348, 363
Rhone-Poulenc, 333
Right-to-work laws, 406
Robinson, Joan, 413
Robinson-Patman Act (1936), 367–368
Rockefeller, John D., 363
Rogers, Will, 111
Rules of exchange, government enforcement of, 56

S

Satellite radio as natural monopoly, 361
Savings and Loan (S&L), 187
Scaling down
   indivisible inputs and, 248
   labor specialization and, 250
Scarcity, 3
   production possibilities curve and, 28
Scarf, Herbert, 98n
Schmalensee, Richard, 344–345
Scott Graphics, 365
Scrubber technology, 206
Second firm, entrance of, 358–359
Self-interest theory of government, 228–229
Sellers
   knowledgeable, 172
   provision of guarantees by, 177
Senior discounts in restaurants, 304
Sequential decision-making game, 334
Sherman Antitrust Act (1890), 368–369
Short run
   labor demand by individual firm in, 379–382
   market demand for labor in, 382
Short-run average costs, 240–242

Short-run costs for fixed production facility, 237–245
Short-run demand curve for labor, 381–382
Short-run effects of changes in demand, 279–280
Short-run marginal cost, 242–243
Short-run market supply curve, 273
Short-run output decision, 263–268
Short-run response to increase in demand, 279–280
Short-run supply curves, 272–275
Short-run total cost, 239–240
Shoven, John, 98n
Shut-down decision, 268–272
Shut-down prices, 270–271
   for corn farmer, 271–272
Signaling effect, 395
Simultaneous decision-making game, 334
Sirius Satellite Radio, 357, 361
Slope, formula for, 24
Slope of a curve, 19–20
   moving along curve versus shifting the curve, 20–21
Smith, Adam, 10, 36, 48–49, 53
   invisible hand and, 52–53, 145
   possibility of firms conspiring to raise prices, 329
Smog, 211
Smooth-Hawley tariff (1930), 429, 433
Social Accountability 8000, 390
Social costs
   of monopoly, 296–300
   of production, 198
Solar energy, 207
Soviet economy, 145
Special interest theory of government, 229
Specialization
   benefits from, 421–422
   gains from trade and, 45–47
Sprint, 363
Standard Oil Trust, 363
Staples, merger of Office Depot and, 356, 364–365
Steel beam pricing in Europe, 339
Substitutes, 74
Substitution effect, 63, 384–385
Sugar industry, 278–279
Sulfur dioxide emissions, finding optimal level of, 197–198
Sulfur dioxide permits, 206
   auction for, 194, 195
Sunk cost, 271

Supply
  decreases in, 79–80
  excess, 70–71
  increases in, 77–78
  price elasticity of, 110–112
Supply and demand, 61
  for marketable permits, 205–206
Supply curve, 65–69
  individual, 66
  market, 68
  producer surplus and, 141–142
Supply of labor, 384–387
  market supply curve for, 385–386
Supply schedule, 66
Surplus, total, 142

T

Taft-Hartley Act (1947), 406
Tangency condition, 125–126
Tariffs, 429
  differences between quotas and, 429
Tate & Lyle, 340
Tax credit for children, 163
Taxes
  deadweight loss and burden of, 161–162
  luxury, 160–161
  payment of, 157–162
  unit, 158
Taxi medallions, 152–153
Tax shifting, 157–160
Taylor, Lester B., 98n
Technological innovation and computers, 83–84
Telecommunications Act (1996), 370
Telecommunication services, deregulation of, 370–371
Terms of trade, comparative advantages and, 423–424
"Thinking at the margin," 10
Thin market, 174–175, 177
Tie-in sales, 367
Tit-for-tat strategy, 337–338
Total cost, computing, 264–265
Total product curve, 238
Total revenue, 263, 290–292
  computing, 264–265
  predicting changes in, 104–106
Total surplus, 142, 143–145
Trade
  benefits from, 421–422
  comparative advantage and, 49–50
  employment effects of free, 425–426
  policy debates over trade agreements and, 434–439

protectionist policies, 426–430
specialization and gains from, 45–47
terms of, and comparative advantage, 423–424
wage inequality and, 438
Trade agreements, policy debates and, 434–439
Trade deficits, 6
Trade-offs, 3
  between average cost and variety, 319–320
  from immigration, 390–391
  from patents, 301
Traffic congestion, 6–7
Transit deficits, 106–107
Trans-World Airlines, 339
Trust, 362–363
Tucows.com, 298
Tufts University, 210
Turnover, effect of unions on, 408
Tweeter, 312, 316

U

Underpricing, 340
  repeated pricing games with retaliation for, 337–338
Unemployment, 15
Uniform abatement policy, 201–202
Unilever, 345
Uninformed buyers, 172
Uninsured, 185
Unions
  effects of, on worker productivity and turnover, 408
  working conditions and, 407
Unitary elastic demand, 96
United Airlines, 339
U.S. trade deficit, 6
United Students Against Sweatshops, 390
Unit tax, 158
Unnatural monopolies, 289
UPS, 346
USAir Group, 339
Utility, 123
  maximizing, 125–129
Utility-maximizing rule, 128
MRS = price ratio, 126–127
Utility theory, modern consumer theory versus, 130

V

Values
  formulas to compute missing, 24
  using formulas to compute, 23–24
ValuStar, 178

Van den Bergh Foods, 345
Variable cost, 239
Variables, 9–10
  change in one of, 21
Vertical axis, 18
Volkswagen, 408
Voluntary exchange, 35–36, 139–140
  marketable permits and, 204–205
  specialization and, 47
Voluntary export restraints, 427–428

W

Wage discrimination, 393
Wages
  of college graduates, 395
  differences in, across occupations, 391–392
  efficiency, and imperfect information, 414–416
  gender pay gap and, 393
  inequality in, and trade, 438
  labor unions and, 406–408
  racial discrimination and, 393–395
  response to cuts in, 387
Wagner Act (1935), 406
WalMart, 390
Warranties, 177
Weather, coffee and, 84
Westinghouse, 339
Willingness to accept, 141
Willingness to pay, 140
Wind power, increasing supply of, 79
Wine merchants, restricting entry of on-line, 317
Wolfram, 278
Wolves, preservation of, 224–225
Worker productivity, effect of unions on, 408
Working conditions, unions and, 407
Workplace externalities, 222
World Trade Organization (WTO), 434
  environment and, 436
  protests at meetings of, 438–439

X

Xidex Corporation, 365
XM Satellite Radio, 357, 361

Y

Y axis, 18

Z

Zero-sum game, 421
Zoning laws, 279

ECONOMICS

Principles of Economics:

Ayers/Collinge, *Economics: Explore & Apply Enhanced Edition*

Case/Fair, *Principles of Economics 7e*

O'Sullivan/Sheffrin, *Economics: Principles and Tools 4e*

Macroeconomics:

Ayers/Collinge, *Macroeconomics: Explore & Apply, Enhanced Edition*

Blanchard, *Macroeconomics 3e*

Case/Fair, *Principles of Macroeconomics 7e*

Colander/Gamber, *Macroeconomics*

Froyen, *Macroeconomics: Theories and Policies 8e*

O'Sullivan/Sheffrin, *Macroeconomics: Principles and Tools 4e*

Survey of Economics:

Collinge/Ayers, *Economics by Design: Survey and Issues 3e*

Farnham, *Economics for Managers*

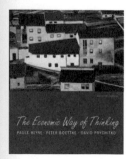

Heyne/Boettke/ Prychitko, *The Economic Way of Thinking 11e*

O'Sullivan/Sheffrin, *Survey of Economics: Principles and Tools 2e*

Microeconomics:

Ayers/Collinge, *Microeconomics: Explore & Apply, Enhanced Edition*

Case/Fair, *Principles of Microeconomics 7e*

Eaton/Eaton/Allen, *Microeconomics 5e*

Mathis/Koscianski, *Microeconomic Theory: An Integrated Approach*

O'Sullivan/Sheffrin, *Microeconomics: Principles and Tools 4e*

Pindyck/Rubinfeld, *Microeconomics 6e*

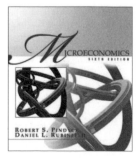

Managerial Economics:

Keat/Young, *Managerial Economics 4e*

Milgrom/Roberts, *Economics, Organization, and Management*

Petersen/Lewis, *Managerial Economics 5e*

Other Titles:

Adams/Brock, *The Structure of American Industry 11e*

Blau/Ferber/Winkler, *The Economics of Women, Men, and Work 4e*

Boardman/Greenberg/Vining/Weimer, *Cost Benefit Analysis: Concepts and Practice 2e*

Bogart, *The Economics of Cities and Suburbs*

Cole/Grossman, *Principles of Law and Economics*

DiPasquale/Wheaton, *Urban Economics and Real Estate Markets*

Folland/Goodman/Stano, *Economics of Health and Health Care 3e*

Fort, *Sports Economics*

Greene, *Econometric Analysis 5e*

Heilbroner/Milberg, *The Making of Economic Society 11e*

Hess, *Using Mathematics in Economic Analysis*

Lynn, *Economic Development: Theory and Practice for a Divided World*

Reynolds/Masters/Moser, *Labor Economics and Labor Relations 11e*

Roberts, *The Choice: A Fable of Free Trade and Protectionism Revised Edition*

Schiller, *The Economics of Poverty and Discrimination 9e*

Weidenbaum, *Business and Government in the Global Marketplace 7e*

For more information on these titles and the rest of Prentice Hall's best-selling Economics list, please visit www.prenhall.com/economics